The Collected Writings of Walt Whitman

WALT WHITMAN

Prose Works 1892

VOLUME II

COLLECT AND OTHER PROSE

Edited by Floyd Stovall

NEW YORK UNIVERSITY PRESS 1964

The frontispiece is the photograph, 1888, used by Whitman as the title page of *Complete Poems & Prose*. From the Feinberg Collection.

LIBRARY OF CONGRESS CATALOG CARD NUMBER: 60–15980

MANUFACTURED IN THE UNITED STATES OF AMERICA

The Collected Writings of Walt Whitman

GRATEFUL ACKNOWLEDGMENT IS MADE TO

Mr. Charles E. Feinberg,

WHOSE ASSISTANCE MADE POSSIBLE THE ILLUSTRATIONS IN THIS VOLUME AND WHO ALSO MADE AVAILABLE TO THE PUBLISHER THE RESOURCES OF THE FEINBERG COLLECTION.

Preface

In *The Collected Writings of Walt Whitman*, the two volumes of *Prose Works 1892*, of which this is the second, contain all the prose of Whitman's 1892 edition of *Complete Prose Works* except "Pieces in Early Youth," which he had added as an appendix to *Specimen Days & Collect* in 1882. These pieces are consolidated with other early work in a volume entitled *The Early Poems and the Fiction*, edited for *Collected Writings* by Thomas L. Brasher. All of *Collect and Other Prose*, except the few items mentioned below, is reprinted without change other than to correct obvious errors from the honored text, the *Complete Prose Works* of 1892. "Collect," which with "Specimen Days" completed the contents of *Specimen Days & Collect*, consists chiefly of *Democratic Vistas*, the early prefaces, the essays, and miscellaneous notes that had been previously published at least once. The other prose of the present volume was drawn, except as noted below, from *November Boughs* (1888) and *Good-Bye My Fancy* (1891), each of them itself a collection.

With the approval of the General Editors and the Advisory Editorial Board, I have incorporated in this volume seven pieces which Whitman omitted from *Complete Prose Works*. The longest and most important of these, "A Backward Glance O'er Travel'd Roads," which Whitman probably omitted because he had just printed it as a concluding statement in his final edition of *Leaves of Grass*, properly belongs in this edition of his prose works along with the prefaces of 1855, 1872, and 1876. "Preface Note to 2d Annex," which Whitman omitted in 1892 perhaps because he had inserted it in his last edition of *Leaves of Grass* in its original position at the head of the poems from *Good-Bye My Fancy*, and the three items not reprinted by Whitman—"Note at Beginning" and "Note at End," from *Complete Poems & Prose* (1888), and the prefatory note to the 1889 edition of *Leaves of Grass*—are included in this edition on the ground that they belong with the other prefaces. The last two pieces, "The Old Man Himself" and "Walt Whitman's Last," both published in *Lippincott's Magazine* during Whitman's lifetime, are included because of their intrinsic interest and their close relationship to other late prose.

For additional information on the manuscript and printed sources of

Collect and Other Prose, the reader is referred to the Preface to *Specimen Days*, the first volume of this edition of *Prose Works 1892*. It is a pleasure to reaffirm the acknowledgments and thanks there expressed to individuals and institutions that have in various ways assisted me in this work, in particular to Charles E. Feinberg, whose kindness and generosity were unfailing, and to Gay Wilson Allen, whose wise planning, in consultation with the Advisory Editorial Board, fitted these volumes into the total pattern of the *Collected Writings*. Special thanks are due to Sculley Bradley, whose patient and skillful editorial advice and assistance in preparing my manuscript for the press are here gratefully acknowledged.

FLOYD STOVALL

CONTENTS

Note on the Textual Variants

All textual notes comparing the present text of "Collect" with Whitman's autograph manuscript, or with a printed clipping which he included as manuscript, have reference, unless a different source is specified, to the printer's copy of *Specimen Days & Collect*, now in the Feinberg Collection. The same holds true of the printer's copy of *Good-Bye My Fancy*, and of *November Boughs* except those parts of which the printer's copy no longer is extant or has been otherwise unavailable. The symbol "MS," when used without qualification, always refers to the printer's copy of one of these volumes, as identified by the source of the passage concerned. There is no printer's copy or manuscript for *Complete Prose Works*, which was printed in 1892 from the plates of *Specimen Days & Collect*, *November Boughs*, and *Good-Bye My Fancy*. The symbols used for the titles of books and periodicals are listed under "Abbreviations."

In this text the lines of each titled section are numbered in a separate sequence. Whitman's footnotes are treated as part of the text, but for convenience of reference their lines are numbered separately; *e.g.*, 1*n*, 2*n*, etc. Always, unless the requirements of printing make it impossible, variant readings appear on the lower part of the page which, in this edition, contains the passages to which they pertain. The initial number in each textual note corresponds with that of the annotated line of the text. Where verbal change is concerned the first entry after this number is the key word or phrase from the line of text annotated; the variant readings follow in reverse chronological order, each reading separated from that preceding by a terminal bracket. Elisions within the key phrase are indicated by the mark of ellipsis (. . .) in all cases except "Preface, 1855," where, to avoid confusion with Whitman's use of a series of two or more periods without a corresponding omission, three asterisks (***) are substituted. If two or more early versions of a long passage show only minor differences, the later version will be quoted at length and the variants of earlier versions inserted at the appropriate places in brackets. If the reading in an earlier text is identical with the key word or phrase, it is not mentioned in the note. Autograph MS variants originating before the initial publication of a passage are noted only when they contribute to the meaning of the passage collated or have special significance for the study of Whitman's life or his literary method.

Whitman's use of the series of periods, or leaders, for punctuation is inconsistent, but because it has been argued that he meant to convey some particular subtlety of thought or phrasing by the number of periods employed, each instance of this kind of punctuation is recorded without change. The following variants appearing in texts earlier than *CPW* are not recorded unless they occur in a context annotated for other reasons: the change of initial capitals to lower case letters in common nouns; variations between figures and words to indicate numbers; the shift from "etc." to "&c." or from "ed" to " 'd" in nonsyllabic endings; the change in the position of the comma before or after quotation marks and marks of parenthesis; and minor changes in punctuation, such as the omission of the comma before "and" in a series and the use of a comma in place of a dash or a colon in place of a semicolon, where they do not affect the meaning of the sentence.

Differences between a corrected printer's copy and the published texts usually represent subsequent revisions made by Whitman on some MS or proof sheet which has not always been available. Interpolated comments by the present editor in the textual notes, followed where necessary by the identifying abbreviation "ED.," are enclosed in brackets.

In *Democratic Vistas* Whitman allowed extra spacing between paragraphs at irregular intervals. As the manuscript reveals, he once introduced subtopics in many of these places, but changed his mind before printing *SDC*. In this edition these extra spaces are not shown, but the places at which they would have occurred are found immediately preceding the following lines: 18, 99, 218, 282, 346, 429, 460, 538, 621, 656, 665, 715, 734, 791, 821, 831, 875, 894, 926, 952, 992, 1038, 1081, 1119, 1147, 1211, 1238, 1249, 1276, 1315, 1404, 1460, 1472, 1538, 1592, 1626, 1657, 1740, 1812, 1843, 1855, 1904, 1946.

Passages from earlier publications omitted in *CPW*, if they are relatively short or closely connected with the context, appear in the textual notes below the text; all others are printed in Appendix A. The contents of Appendix A are listed by the titles of the books and periodical from which they are drawn. These titles are arranged in the order of first publication. Cross references are provided to assist the reader in locating related passages in the textual notes and in Appendix A.

ABBREVIATIONS

BOOKS

CPP	*Complete Poems & Prose* (1888)
CPW	*Complete Prose Works* (1892)
DV	*Democratic Vistas* (1871)
DVOP	*Democratic Vistas and Other Papers* (London, 1888)
GBF	*Good-Bye My Fancy* (1891)
LG	*Leaves of Grass*
MDW	*Memoranda During the War* (1875)
NB	*November Boughs* (1888)
RAL	*Reminiscences of Abraham Lincoln*, edited by A. T. Rice (1886)
SDA	*Specimen Days in America* (London, 1887)
SDC	*Specimen Days & Collect* (1882)
SDC Glasgow	*Specimen Days & Collect* (Glasgow, 1883)
TR	*Two Rivulets* (1876)
UPP	*Uncollected Poetry and Prose of Walt Whitman* (2 vols.), edited by Emory Holloway (1921)

MAGAZINES

BLW	*Boston Literary World*
BM	*Baldwin's Monthly*
CEN	*The Century Magazine*
CR	*The Critic*
ER	*The Engineering Record*
GAL	*The Galaxy*
LIP	*Lippincott's Magazine*
LPM	*Frank Leslie's Popular Monthly*
NAR	*The North American Review*
P-L	*Poet-Lore*
SB	University of Virginia *Studies in Bibliography*

NEWSPAPERS

LE	The London (England) *Examiner*
NOP	The New Orleans *Picayune*
NYDG	The New York *Daily Graphic*
NYMJ	The New York *Morning Journal*

NYS The New York *Sun*
NYT The New York *Times*
NYTR The New York *Tribune*
NYWG The New York *Weekly Graphic*
PP The Philadelphia *Press*

Walt Whitman, Prose Works 1892

VOLUME II, COLLECT AND OTHER PROSE

One or Two Index Items.

THOUGH the ensuing COLLECT and preceding SPECIMEN DAYS are both largely from memoranda already existing, the hurried peremptory needs of copy for the printers, already referr'd to—(the musicians' story of a composer up in a garret rushing the middle body and last of his score together, while the fiddlers are playing the first parts down in the concert-room)—of this haste, while quite willing to get the consequent stimulus of life and motion, I am sure there must have resulted sundry technical errors. If any are too glaring they will be corrected in a future edition.

A special word about "PIECES IN EARLY YOUTH," at the end. On jaunts over Long Island, as boy and young fellow, nearly half a century ago, I heard of, or came across in my own experience, characters, true occurrences, incidents, which I tried my 'prentice hand at recording—(I was then quite an "abolitionist" and advocate of the "temperance" and "anti-capital-punishment" causes)—and publish'd during occasional visits to New York city. A majority of the sketches appear'd first in the "Democratic Review," others in the "Columbian Magazine," or the "American Review," of that period. My serious wish were to have all those crude and boyish pieces quietly dropp'd in oblivion—but to avoid the annoyance of their surreptitious issue, (as lately announced, from outsiders,) I have, with some qualms, tack'd them on here. *A Dough-Face Song* came out first in the "Evening Post"—*Blood-Money*, and *Wounded in the House of Friends*, in the "Tribune."

Poetry To-Day in America, &c., first appear'd (under the name of "*The Poetry of the Future*,") in "The North American Review" for February, 1881. *A Memorandum at a Venture*, in same periodical, some time afterward.

Several of the convalescent out-door scenes and literary items, preceding, originally appear'd in the fortnightly "Critic," of New York.

One or Two Index Items.

This prefatory note to "Collect" was printed from two autograph MS pages, each made up of several strips of gray paper pasted together, written in black ink and much revised. Though other matters are mentioned in the note, it was evidently written at the last minute before printing to justify the inclusion of "Pieces in Early Youth," which are omitted from the present edition of "Collect."

14. the "Democratic Review,"] MS before revision: the old "Democratic Review"—

14–15. the "American Review," of that period.] MS before revision: the "American Review."

Collect.

Democratic Vistas.

As the greatest lessons of Nature through the universe are perhaps the lessons of variety and freedom, the same present the greatest lessons also in New World politics and progress. If a man were ask'd, for instance, the distinctive points contrasting modern European and American political and other life with the old Asiatic cultus, as lingering-

Collect.

Under this general title Whitman included the entire contents of SDC after page 200; to the first 200 pages he gave the general title "Specimen Days." In the following notes, all references to the details of printing from manuscript or clippings pertain to the printer's copy from which SDC was printed, now in the Feinberg Collection. From the plates of SDC 1882, with very minor revisions, "Collect," like "Specimen Days," was reprinted in SDC Glasgow 1883, in CPP 1888, and in CPW 1892. "Democratic Vistas" and the miscellaneous pieces under the general title "Notes Left Over" were included, together with the letter to Dr. I. Fitzgerald Lee and some new material from periodical publications, in DVOP, published in London in 1888.

Democratic Vistas.

Printed in SDC from clipped or unbound pages of TR, which in turn had been printed from the plates of DV. In 100 copies of TR (Wells and Goldsmith, *Concise Bibliography*, p. 21), DV was printed from the unrevised plates of DV 1871 (or, possibly, made up of unbound sheets left over). These copies have the words "Centennial Edition" in gilt on the backstrip. (The present editor has seen six or eight copies so marked and has had reliable reports from persons who have seen others.) All copies stamped "Centennial Edition," so far as is known, differ in the text of DV from copies of the regular edition, printed from revised plates, in the following respects: On page 60 (DV line 1626) the revision of the DV text is inserted in ink, not printed; and on page 81, in the sixth paragraph of "General Notes" (see line 34 of the section of SDC subtitled "British Literature"), the word "Cervantes" has no apostrophe after the final "s" as it does in the regular edition of TR. Since the printer's copy for SDC 1882 has in type the change on page 60 but not the change on page 81, it seems likely that Whitman used clipped or unbound pages of the regular edition of TR for the main part of DV and clipped or unbound pages of either DV 1871 or the Centennial Edition for "General Notes," or, in any case, for that part of them transferred to "Notes Left Over" under the section subtitle "British Literature," *q.v.*

The text of DV 1871 was based, in part, on Whitman's essay "Democracy," published in GAL, IV, 919–933 (December, 1867), and on his essay "Personalism," published in GAL, V, 540–547 (May, 1868). He had projected a third essay which was not then published and perhaps not finished. All or part of this essay was incorporated with the two earlier essays in DV 1871. DV was reprinted in TR, SDC, SDC

bequeath'd yet in China and Turkey, he might find the amount of them in John Stuart Mill's profound essay on Liberty in the future, where he demands two main constituents, or sub-strata, for a truly grand nationality—1st, a large variety of character—and 2d, full play for human nature to expand itself in numberless and even conflicting directions—(seems to be for general humanity much like the influences that make up, in their limitless field, that perennial health-action of the air we call the weather—an infinite number of currents and forces, and contributions, and temperatures, and cross purposes, whose ceaseless play of counterpart upon counterpart brings constant restoration and vitality.) With this thought—and not for itself alone, but all it necessitates, and draws after it—let me begin my speculations.

America, filling the present with greatest deeds and problems, cheerfully accepting the past, including feudalism, (as, indeed, the present is but the legitimate birth of the past, including feudalism,) counts, as I reckon, for her justification and success, (for who, as yet, dare claim success?) almost entirely on the future. Nor is that hope unwarranted. To-day, ahead, though dimly yet, we see, in vistas, a copious, sane, gigantic offspring. For our New World I consider far less important for what it has done, or what it is, than for results to come. Sole among nationalities, these States have assumed the task to put in forms of lasting power and practicality, on areas of amplitude rivaling the operations of the physical kosmos, the moral political speculations of ages, long, long deferr'd, the democratic republican principle, and the theory of development and perfection by voluntary standards, and self-reliance. Who else, indeed, except the United States, in history, so far, have accepted in unwitting faith, and, as we now see, stand, act upon, and go security for, these things?

But preluding no longer, let me strike the key-note of the following strain. First premising that, though the passages of it have been written at widely different times, (it is, in fact, a collection of memoranda, perhaps for future designers, comprehenders,) and though it may be open to the

Glasgow, *DVOP* (London, 1888), and *CPP* (1888) before the edition of 1892. All these texts are collated in the following notes. The main text of *DV* 1871 consists of pages 3–78, the "General Notes" of pages 79–84. The text based on the essay "Democracy" includes lines 368–893 and the text based on the essay "Personalism" includes lines 894–1275. In *SDC* 1882 and later texts "General Notes" was omitted from *DV*. Most of it was used in "Notes Left Over," *q.v.*

At intervals in the MS Whitman inserted, sometimes in black ink and sometimes in red ink, directions to the printer for spacing between paragraphs. He also inserted at intervals subtitles in red ink between paragraphs, all of which are lined out in black ink. These cancelled subtitles are listed in Appendix IV, 1.

charge of one part contradicting another—for there are opposite sides to the great question of democracy, as to every great question—I feel the parts harmoniously blended in my own realization and convictions, and present them to be read only in such oneness, each page and each claim and assertion modified and temper'd by the others. Bear in mind, too, that they are not the result of studying up in political economy, but of the ordinary sense, observing, wandering among men, these States, these stirring years of war and peace. I will not gloss over the appaling dangers of universal suffrage in the United States. In fact, it is to admit and face these dangers I am writing. To him or her within whose thought rages the battle, advancing, retreating, between democracy's convictions, aspirations, and the people's crudeness, vice, caprices, I mainly write this essay. I shall use the words America and democracy as convertible terms. Not an ordinary one is the issue. The United States are destined either to surmount the gorgeous history of feudalism, or else prove the most tremendous failure of time. Not the least doubtful am I on any prospects of their material success. The triumphant future of their business, geographic and productive departments, on larger scales and in more varieties than ever, is certain. In those respects the republic must soon (if she does not already) outstrip all examples hitherto afforded, and dominate the world.*

* "From a territorial area of less than nine hundred thousand square miles, the Union has expanded into over four millions and a half—fifteen times larger than that of Great Britain and France combined—with a shore-line, including Alaska, equal to the entire circumference of the earth, and with a domain within these lines far wider than that of the Romans in their proudest days of conquest and renown. With a river, lake, and coastwise commerce estimated at over two thousand millions of dollars per year; with a railway traffic of four to six thousand millions per year, and the annual domestic exchanges of the country running up to nearly ten thousand millions per year; with over two thousand millions of dollars invested in manufacturing, mechanical, and mining industry; with over five hundred millions of acres of land in actual occupancy, valued, with their appurtenances, at over seven thousand millions of dollars, and producing annually crops valued at over three thousand millions

1–17. Printed in *SDC* from two pages of autograph *MS*. Not in *TR* and *DV*.
24. After "offspring." *TR* and *DV* begin a new paragraph.
28. moral political] *TR* and *DV:* moral and political
30. self-reliance] *TR* and *DV:* self-suppliance
34. But . . . of the] *TR* and *DV:* But let me strike at once the key-note of my purpose in the
35. though the passages] *TR* and *DV:* though passages
41–42. page . . . modified] *TR* and *DV:* page modified
45. appaling] *TR* and *DV:* appalling
49. this essay.] *TR* and *DV:* this book.
After "this book." *TR* and *DV* begin a new paragraph.

Admitting all this, with the priceless value of our political institutions, general suffrage, (and fully acknowledging the latest, widest opening of the doors,) I say that, far deeper than these, what finally and only is to make of our western world a nationality superior to any hitherto known, and outtopping the past, must be vigorous, yet unsuspected Literatures, perfect personalities and sociologies, original, transcendental, and expressing (what, in highest sense, are not yet express'd at all,) democracy and the modern. With these, and out of these, I promulge new races of Teachers, and of perfect Women, indispensable to endow the birth-stock of a New World. For feudalism, caste, the ecclesiastic traditions, though palpably retreating from political institutions, still hold essentially, by their spirit, even in this country, entire possession of the more important

of dollars; with a realm which, if the density of Belgium's population were possible, would be vast enough to include all the present inhabitants of the world; and with equal rights guaranteed to even the poorest and humblest of our forty millions of people—we can, with a manly pride akin to that which distinguish'd the palmiest days of Rome, claim," &c., &c., &c.—*Vice-President Colfax's Speech, July 4, 1870.*

LATER—*London "Times," (Weekly,) June 23, '82.*

"The wonderful wealth-producing power of the United States defies and sets at naught the grave drawbacks of a mischievous protective tariff, and has already obliterated, almost wholly, the traces of the greatest of modern civil wars. What is especially remarkable in the present development of American energy and success is its wide and equable distribution. North and south, east and west, on the shores of the Atlantic and the Pacific, along the chain of the great lakes, in the valley of the Mississippi, and on the coasts of the gulf of Mexico, the creation of wealth and the increase of population are signally exhibited. It is quite true, as has been shown by the recent apportionment of population in the House of Representatives, that some sections of the Union have advanced, relatively to the rest, in an extraordinary and unexpected degree. But this does not imply that the States which have gain'd no additional representatives or have actually lost some have been stationary or have receded. The fact is that the present tide of prosperity has risen so high that it has overflow'd all barriers, and has fill'd up the back-waters, and establish'd something like an approach to uniform success."

20*n*–36*n*. This note, printed from a newspaper clipping, appears for the first time in *SDC*.

59. fully acknowledging] *TR* and *DV:* cheerfully acknowledging [Change made in the proof]

61. hitherto known] [*SDC* and all later texts, including 1892, have "hither known," but since both *TR* and *DV* have "hitherto known" and since there is no change indicated on the clipping, "hither" must have been a typographical error and is therefore corrected in the present text.—ED.]

fields, indeed the very subsoil, of education, and of social standards and literature.

I say that democracy can never prove itself beyond cavil, until it founds and luxuriantly grows its own forms of art, poems, schools, theology, displacing all that exists, or that has been produced anywhere in the past, under opposite influences. It is curious to me that while so many voices, pens, minds, in the press, lecture-rooms, in our Congress, &c., are discussing intellectual topics, pecuniary dangers, legislative problems, the suffrage, tariff and labor questions, and the various business and benevolent needs of America, with propositions, remedies, often worth deep attention, there is one need, a hiatus the profoundest, that no eye seems to perceive, no voice to state. Our fundamental want to-day in the United States, with closest, amplest reference to present conditions, and to the future, is of a class, and the clear idea of a class, of native authors, literatuses, far different, far higher in grade than any yet known, sacerdotal, modern, fit to cope with our occasions, lands, permeating the whole mass of American mentality, taste, belief, breathing into it a new breath of life, giving it decision, affecting politics far more than the popular superficial suffrage, with results inside and underneath the elections of Presidents or Congresses—radiating, begetting appropriate teachers, schools, manners, and, as its grandest result, accomplishing, (what neither the schools nor the churches and their clergy have hitherto accomplish'd, and without which this nation will no more stand, permanently, soundly, than a house will stand without a substratum,) a religious and moral character beneath the political and productive and intellectual bases of the States. For know you not, dear, earnest reader, that the people of our land may all read and write, and may all possess the right to vote—and yet the main things may be entirely lacking?—(and this to suggest them.)

View'd, to-day, from a point of view sufficiently over-arching, the problem of humanity all over the civilized world is social and religious, and is to be finally met and treated by literature. The priest departs, the divine literatus comes. Never was anything more wanted than, to-day, and here in the States, the poet of the modern is wanted, or the great literatus of the modern. At all times, perhaps, the central point in any

73. art] *TR* and *DV:* arts
75. After "influences." *TR* and *DV* begin a new paragraph.
80. hiatus the] *TR* and *DV:* hiatus, and the
89–90. teachers, . . . as] *TR* and *DV:* teachers and schools, manners, costumes, and, as
96. all read] *TR* and *DV:* all know how to read
98. to suggest] *TR* and *DV:* to supply or suggest

nation, and that whence it is itself really sway'd the most, and whence it sways others, is its national literature, especially its archetypal poems. Above all previous lands, a great original literature is surely to become the justification and reliance, (in some respects the sole reliance,) of American democracy.

Few are aware how the great literature penetrates all, gives hue to all, shapes aggregates and individuals, and, after subtle ways, with irresistible power, constructs, sustains, demolishes at will. Why tower, in reminiscence, above all the nations of the earth, two special lands, petty in themselves, yet inexpressibly gigantic, beautiful, columnar? Immortal Judah lives, and Greece immortal lives, in a couple of poems.

Nearer than this. It is not generally realized, but it is true, as the genius of Greece, and all the sociology, personality, politics and religion of those wonderful states, resided in their literature or esthetics, that what was afterwards the main support of European chivalry, the feudal, ecclesiastical, dynastic world over there—forming its osseous structure, holding it together for hundreds, thousands of years, preserving its flesh and bloom, giving it form, decision, rounding it out, and so saturating it in the conscious and unconscious blood, breed, belief, and intuitions of men, that it still prevails powerful to this day, in defiance of the mighty changes of time—was its literature, permeating to the very marrow, especially that major part, its enchanting songs, ballads, and poems.*

To the ostent of the senses and eyes, I know, the influences which stamp the world's history are wars, uprisings or downfalls of dynasties, changeful movements of trade, important inventions, navigation, military or civil governments, advent of powerful personalities, conquerors, &c. These of course play their part; yet, it may be, a single new thought, imagination, abstract principle, even literary style, fit for the time, put in shape by some great literatus, and projected among mankind, may duly cause changes, growths, removals, greater than the longest and bloodiest war, or the most stupendous merely political, dynastic, or commercial overturn.

In short, as, though it may not be realized, it is strictly true, that a few

* See, for hereditaments, specimens, Walter Scott's Border Minstrelsy, Percy's collection, Ellis's early English Metrical Romances, the European continental poems of Walter of Aquitania, and the Nibelungen, of pagan stock, but monkish-feudal redaction; the history of the Troubadours, by Fauriel; even the far-back cumbrous old Hindu epics, as indicating the Asian eggs out of which European chivalry was hatch'd; Ticknor's chapters on the

41*n*. the far-back] *TR* and *DV:* the far, far back

124. powerful] *TR* and *DV:* powerfully

first-class poets, philosophs, and authors, have substantially settled and given status to the entire religion, education, law, sociology, &c., of the hitherto civilized world, by tinging and often creating the atmospheres out of which they have arisen, such also must stamp, and more than ever stamp, the interior and real democratic construction of this American continent, to-day, and days to come. Remember also this fact of difference, that, while through the antique and through the medivæal ages, highest thoughts and ideas realized themselves, and their expression made its way by other arts, as much as, or even more than by, technical literature, (not open to the mass of persons, or even to the majority of eminent persons,) such literature in our day and for current purposes, is not only more eligible than all the other arts put together, but has become the only general means of morally influencing the world. Painting, sculpture, and the dramatic theatre, it would seem, no longer play an indispensable or even important part in the workings and mediumship of intellect, utility, or even high esthetics. Architecture remains, doubtless with capacities, and a real future. Then music, the combiner, nothing more spiritual, nothing more sensuous, a god, yet completely human, advances, prevails, holds highest place; supplying in certain wants and quarters what nothing else could supply. Yet in the civilization of to-day it is undeniable that, over all the arts, literature dominates, serves beyond all—shapes the character of church and school—or, at any rate, is capable of doing so. Including the literature of science, its scope is indeed unparallel'd.

Before proceeding further, it were perhaps well to discriminate on certain points. Literature tills its crops in many fields, and some may flourish, while others lag. What I say in these Vistas has its main bearing on imaginative literature, especially poetry, the stock of all. In the department of science, and the specialty of journalism, there appear, in these States, promises, perhaps fulfilments, of highest earnestness, reality, and life. These, of course, are modern. But in the region of imaginative, spinal and essential attributes, something equivalent to creation is, for our age and lands, imperatively demanded. For not only is it not enough that the

Cid, and on the Spanish poems and poets of Calderon's time. Then always, and, of course, as the superbest poetic culmination-expression of feudalism, the Shaksperean dramas, in the attitudes, dialogue, characters, &c., of the princes, lords and gentlemen, the pervading atmosphere, the implied and express'd standard of manners, the high port and proud stomach, the regal embroidery of style, &c.

132. imagination, abstract principle] *TR* and *DV:* imagination, principle
143. After "to come." *TR* and *DV* begin a new paragraph.
168–169. is . . . imperatively] *TR* and *DV:* is imperatively

new blood, new frame of democracy shall be vivified and held together merely by political means, superficial suffrage, legislation, &c., but it is clear to me that, unless it goes deeper, gets at least as firm and as warm a hold in men's hearts, emotions and belief, as, in their days, feudalism or ecclesiasticism, and inaugurates its own perennial sources, welling from the centre forever, its strength will be defective, its growth doubtful, and its main charm wanting. I suggest, therefore, the possibility, should some two or three really original American poets, (perhaps artists or lecturers,) arise, mounting the horizon like planets, stars of the first magnitude, that, from their eminence, fusing contributions, races, far localities, &c., together, they would give more compaction and more moral identity, (the quality to-day most needed,) to these States, than all its Constitutions, legislative and judicial ties, and all its hitherto political, warlike, or materialistic experiences. As, for instance, there could hardly happen anything that would more serve the States, with all their variety of origins, their diverse climes, cities, standards, &c., than possessing an aggregate of heroes, characters, exploits, sufferings, prosperity or misfortune, glory or disgrace, common to all, typical of all—no less, but even greater would it be to possess the aggregation of a cluster of mighty poets, artists, teachers, fit for us, national expressers, comprehending and effusing for the men and women of the States, what is universal, native, common to all, inland and seaboard, northern and southern. The historians say of ancient Greece, with her ever-jealous autonomies, cities, and states, that the only positive unity she ever own'd or receiv'd, was the sad unity of a common subjection, at the last, to foreign conquerors. Subjection, aggregation of that sort, is impossible to America; but the fear of conflicting and irreconcilable interiors, and the lack of a common skeleton, knitting all close, continually haunts me. Or, if it does not, nothing is plainer than the need, a long period to come, of a fusion of the States into the only reliable identity, the moral and artistic one. For, I say, the true nationality of the States, the genuine union, when we come to a mortal crisis, is, and is to be, after all, neither the written law, nor, (as is generally supposed,) either self-interest, or common pecuniary or material objects—but the fervid and tremendous IDEA, melting everything else with resistless heat, and solving all lesser and definite distinctions in vast, indefinite, spiritual, emotional power.

It may be claim'd, (and I admit the weight of the claim,) that common and general worldly prosperity, and a populace well-to-do, and with all

176. After "charm wanting." *TR* and *DV* begin a new paragraph.
216. on these] *TR* and *DV:* on those

life's material comforts, is the main thing, and is enough. It may be argued that our republic is, in performance, really enacting to-day the grandest arts, poems, &c., by beating up the wilderness into fertile farms, and in her railroads, ships, machinery, &c. And it may be ask'd, Are these not better, indeed, for America, than any utterances even of greatest rhapsode, artist, or literatus?

I too hail those achievements with pride and joy: then answer that the soul of man will not with such only—nay, not with such at all—be finally satisfied; but needs what, (standing on these and on all things, as the feet stand on the ground,) is address'd to the loftiest, to itself alone.

Out of such considerations, such truths, arises for treatment in these Vistas the important question of character, of an American stock-personality, with literatures and arts for outlets and return-expressions, and, of course, to correspond, within outlines common to all. To these, the main affair, the thinkers of the United States, in general so acute, have either given feeblest attention, or have remain'd, and remain, in a state of somnolence.

For my part, I would alarm and caution even the political and business reader, and to the utmost extent, against the prevailing delusion that the establishment of free political institutions, and plentiful intellectual smartness, with general good order, physical plenty, industry, &c., (desirable and precious advantages as they all are,) do, of themselves, determine and yield to our experiment of democracy the fruitage of success. With such advantages at present fully, or almost fully, possess'd—the Union just issued, victorious, from the struggle with the only foes it need ever fear, (namely, those within itself, the interior ones,) and with unprecedented materialistic advancement—society, in these States, is canker'd, crude, superstitious, and rotten. Political, or law-made society is, and private, or voluntary society, is also. In any vigor, the element of the moral conscience, the most important, the verteber to State or man, seems to me either entirely lacking, or seriously enfeebled or ungrown.

I say we had best look our times and lands searchingly in the face, like a physician diagnosing some deep disease. Never was there, perhaps, more hollowness at heart than at present, and here in the United States. Genuine belief seems to have left us. The underlying principles of the States are not honestly believ'd in, (for all this hectic glow, and these melodramatic screamings,) nor is humanity itself believ'd in. What penetrating eye does not everywhere see through the mask? The spectacle is

237. verteber] *TR* and *DV:* vertebrae
239. our times] *TR* and *DV:* our time

appaling. We live in an atmosphere of hypocrisy throughout. The men believe not in the women, nor the women in the men. A scornful superciliousness rules in literature. The aim of all the *littérateurs* is to find something to make fun of. A lot of churches, sects, &c., the most dismal phantasms I know, usurp the name of religion. Conversation is a mass of badinage. From deceit in the spirit, the mother of all false deeds, the offspring is already incalculable. An acute and candid person, in the revenue department in Washington, who is led by the course of his employment to regularly visit the cities, north, south and west, to investigate frauds, has talk'd much with me about his discoveries. The depravity of the business classes of our country is not less than has been supposed, but infinitely greater. The official services of America, national, state, and municipal, in all their branches and departments, except the judiciary, are saturated in corruption, bribery, falsehood, mal-administration; and the judiciary is tainted. The great cities reek with respectable as much as non-respectable robbery and scoundrelism. In fashionable life, flippancy, tepid amours, weak infidelism, small aims, or no aims at all, only to kill time. In business, (this all-devouring modern word, business,) the one sole object is, by any means, pecuniary gain. The magician's serpent in the fable ate up all the other serpents; and money-making is our magician's serpent, remaining to-day sole master of the field. The best class we show, is but a mob of fashionably dress'd speculators and vulgarians. True, indeed, behind this fantastic farce, enacted on the visible stage of society, solid things and stupendous labors are to be discover'd, existing crudely and going on in the background, to advance and tell themselves in time. Yet the truths are none the less terrible. I say that our New World democracy, however great a success in uplifting the masses out of their sloughs, in materialistic development, products, and in a certain highly-deceptive superficial popular intellectuality, is, so far, an almost complete failure in its social aspects, and in really grand religious, moral, literary, and esthetic results. In vain do we march with unprecedented strides to empire so colossal, outvying the antique, beyond Alexander's, beyond the proudest sway of Rome. In vain have we annex'd Texas, California, Alaska, and reach north for Canada and south for Cuba. It is as if we were somehow being endow'd with a vast and more and more thoroughly-appointed body, and then left with little or no soul.

246. appaling] *TR* and *DV:* appalling
255. me about] *TR* and *DV:* me (1869–70) about
257. The official] *TR* and *DV:* The whole of the official
258–259. are saturated] *TR* and *DV:* are steeped, saturated
275. aspects, and] *TR* and *DV:* aspects, in any superb general personal character, and

Let me illustrate further, as I write, with current observations, localities, &c. The subject is important, and will bear repetition. After an absence, I am now again (September, 1870) in New York city and Brooklyn, on a few weeks' vacation. The splendor, picturesqueness, and oceanic amplitude and rush of these great cities, the unsurpass'd situation, rivers and bay, sparkling sea-tides, costly and lofty new buildings, façades of marble and iron, of original grandeur and elegance of design, with the masses of gay color, the preponderance of white and blue, the flags flying, the endless ships, the tumultuous streets, Broadway, the heavy, low, musical roar, hardly ever intermitted, even at night; the jobbers' houses, the rich shops, the wharves, the great Central Park, and the Brooklyn Park of hills, (as I wander among them this beautiful fall weather, musing, watching, absorbing)—the assemblages of the citizens in their groups, conversations, trades, evening amusements, or along the by-quarters—these, I say, and the like of these, completely satisfy my senses of power, fulness, motion, &c., and give me, through such senses and appetites, and through my esthetic conscience, a continued exaltation and absolute fulfilment. Always and more and more, as I cross the East and North rivers, the ferries, or with the pilots in their pilot-houses, or pass an hour in Wall street, or the gold exchange, I realize, (if we must admit such partialisms,) that not Nature alone is great in her fields of freedom and the open air, in her storms, the shows of night and day, the mountains, forests, seas—but in the artificial, the work of man too is equally great—in this profusion of teeming humanity—in these ingenuities, streets, goods, houses, ships—these hurrying, feverish, electric crowds of men, their complicated business genius, (not least among the geniuses,) and all this mighty, many-threaded wealth and industry concentrated here.

But sternly discarding, shutting our eyes to the glow and grandeur of the general superficial effect, coming down to what is of the only real importance, Personalities, and examining minutely, we question, we ask, Are there, indeed, *men* here worthy the name? Are there athletes? Are there perfect women, to match the generous material luxuriance? Is there a pervading atmosphere of beautiful manners? Are there crops of fine youths, and majestic old persons? Are there arts worthy freedom and a rich people? Is there a great moral and religious civilization—the only justification of a great material one? Confess that to severe eyes, using the

278. vain have we annex'd] *TR* and *DV:* vain do we annex
284. now again (September, 1870)] *TR* and *DV:* now (September, 1870)
287. buildings, façades] *TR* and *DV:* buildings, the façades
306. these . . . crowds] *TR* and *DV:* these seething, hurrying, feverish crowds
310. general superficial effect] *TR* and *DV:* general effect

moral microscope upon humanity, a sort of dry and flat Sahara appears, these cities, crowded with petty grotesques, malformations, phantoms, playing meaningless antics. Confess that everywhere, in shop, street, church, theatre, barroom, official chair, are pervading flippancy and vulgarity, low cunning, infidelity—everywhere the youth puny, impudent, foppish, prematurely ripe—everywhere an abnormal libidinousness, unhealthy forms, male, female, painted, padded, dyed, chignon'd, muddy complexions, bad blood, the capacity for good motherhood deceasing or deceas'd, shallow notions of beauty, with a range of manners, or rather lack of manners, (considering the advantages enjoy'd,) probably the meanest to be seen in the world.*

Of all this, and these lamentable conditions, to breathe into them the breath recuperative of sane and heroic life, I say a new founded literature, not merely to copy and reflect existing surfaces, or pander to what is called taste—not only to amuse, pass away time, celebrate the beautiful, the refined, the past, or exhibit technical, rhythmic, or grammatical dexterity—but a literature underlying life, religious, consistent with science, handling the elements and forces with competent power, teaching and training men—and, as perhaps the most precious of its results, achieving the entire redemption of woman out of these incredible holds and webs of silliness, millinery, and every kind of dyspeptic depletion—and thus insuring to the States a strong and sweet Female Race, a race of perfect Mothers—is what is needed.

And now, in the full conception of these facts and points, and all that they infer, pro and con—with yet unshaken faith in the elements of the

* Of these rapidly-sketch'd hiatuses, the two which seem to me most serious are, for one, the condition, absence, or perhaps the singular abeyance, of moral conscientious fibre all through American society; and, for another, the appaling depletion of women in their powers of sane athletic maternity, their crowning attribute, and ever making the woman, in loftiest spheres, superior to the man.

I have sometimes thought, indeed, that the sole avenue and means of a reconstructed sociology depended, primarily, on a new birth, elevation, expansion, invigoration of woman, affording, for races to come, (as the conditions that antedate birth are indispensable,) a perfect motherhood. Great, great, indeed, far greater than they know, is the sphere of women. But doubtless

49*n*. rapidly-sketch'd hiatuses] *TR* and *DV:* rapidly-sketched portraitures, hiatuses

317. After "material one?" *TR* and *DV* begin a new paragraph.
317. that to] *TR* and *DV:* that rather to

American masses, the composites, of both sexes, and even consider'd as individuals—and ever recognizing in them the broadest bases of the best literary and esthetic appreciation—I proceed with my speculations, Vistas.

First, let us see what we can make out of a brief, general, sentimental consideration of political democracy, and whence it has arisen, with regard to some of its current features, as an aggregate, and as the basic structure of our future literature and authorship. We shall, it is true, quickly and continually find the origin-idea of the singleness of man, individualism, asserting itself, and cropping forth, even from the opposite ideas. But the mass, or lump character, for imperative reasons, is to be ever carefully weigh'd, borne in mind, and provided for. Only from it, and from its proper regulation and potency, comes the other, comes the chance of individualism. The two are contradictory, but our task is to reconcile them.*

The political history of the past may be summ'd up as having grown out of what underlies the words, order, safety, caste, and especially out of the need of some prompt deciding authority, and of cohesion at all cost. Leaping time, we come to the period within the memory of people now living, when, as from some lair where they had slumber'd long, accumulating wrath, sprang up and are yet active, (1790, and on even to the present, 1870,) those noisy eructations, destructive iconoclasms, a fierce sense of wrongs, amid which moves the form, well known in modern history, in the old world, stain'd with much blood, and mark'd by savage reactionary clamors and demands. These bear, mostly, as on one inclosing point of need.

For after the rest is said—after the many time-honor'd and really true

the question of such new sociology all goes together, includes many varied and complex influences and premises, and the man as well as the woman, and the woman as well as the man.

* The question hinted here is one which time only can answer. Must not the virtue of modern Individualism, continually enlarging, usurping all, seriously affect, perhaps keep down entirely, in America, the like of the ancient virtue of Patriotism, the fervid and absorbing love of general country? I have no doubt myself that the two will merge, and will mutually profit and brace each other, and that from them a greater product, a third, will arise. But I feel that at present they and their oppositions form a serious problem and paradox in the United States.

49*n*. to me most] *DVOP:* to be most
52*n*. appaling] *TR* and *DV:* appalling

368–893. This part of *DV* is collated with the *GAL* essay "Democracy" as well as with the other texts.
368. For . . . many] *GAL:* After the rest is said—after many

things for subordination, experience, rights of property, &c., have been listen'd to and acquiesced in—after the valuable and well-settled statement of our duties and relations in society is thoroughly conn'd over and exhausted—it remains to bring forward and modify everything else with the idea of that Something a man is, (last precious consolation of the drudging poor,) standing apart from all else, divine in his own right, and a woman in hers, sole and untouchable by any canons of authority, or any rule derived from precedent, state-safety, the acts of legislatures, or even from what is called religion, modesty, or art. The radiation of this truth is the key of the most significant doings of our immediately preceding three centuries, and has been the political genesis and life of America. Advancing visibly, it still more advances invisibly. Underneath the fluctuations of the expressions of society, as well as the movements of the politics of the leading nations of the world, we see steadily pressing ahead and strengthening itself, even in the midst of immense tendencies toward aggregation, this image of completeness in separatism, of individual personal dignity, of a single person, either male or female, characterized in the main, not from extrinsic acquirements or position, but in the pride of himself or herself alone; and, as an eventual conclusion and summing up, (or else the entire scheme of things is aimless, a cheat, a crash,) the simple idea that the last, best dependence is to be upon humanity itself, and its own inherent, normal, full-grown qualities, without any superstitious support whatever. This idea of perfect individualism it is indeed that deepest tinges and gives character to the idea of the aggregate. For it is mainly or altogether to serve independent separatism that we favor a strong generalization, consolidation. As it is to give the best vitality and freedom to the rights of the States, (every bit as important as the right of nationality, the union,) that we insist on the identity of the Union at all hazards.

The purpose of democracy—supplanting old belief in the necessary absoluteness of establish'd dynastic rulership, temporal, ecclesiastical, and scholastic, as furnishing the only security against chaos, crime, and ig-

71*n*–80*n*. This footnote does not appear in *GAL*.

373–374. No marks of parenthesis in *GAL*.
375–377. canons . . . modesty] *GAL:* canons religion, politics, or what is called modesty
377. After "or art." *TR*, *DV*, and *GAL* begin a new paragraph.
377–378. truth is the key] *GAL:* truth, practically a modern one, is the history and key
382. nations . . . we] *GAL:* nations, we
388. No marks of parenthesis in *GAL*.
388–389. simple idea] *GAL:* simple, but tremendous and revolutionary idea
391. After "support whatever." *GAL* begins a new paragraph with the sentence beginning "The purpose". The three sentences of lines 391–396 are not in *GAL*.

norance—is, through many transmigrations, and amid endless ridicules, arguments, and ostensible failures, to illustrate, at all hazards, this doctrine or theory that man, properly train'd in sanest, highest freedom, may and must become a law, and series of laws, unto himself, surrounding and providing for, not only his own personal control, but all his relations to other individuals, and to the State; and that, while other theories, as in the past histories of nations, have proved wise enough, and indispensable perhaps for their conditions, *this*, as matters now stand in our civilized world, is the only scheme worth working from, as warranting results like those of Nature's laws, reliable, when once establish'd, to carry on themselves.

The argument of the matter is extensive, and, we admit, by no means all on one side. What we shall offer will be far, far from sufficient. But while leaving unsaid much that should properly even prepare the way for the treatment of this many-sided question of political liberty, equality, or republicanism—leaving the whole history and consideration of the feudal plan and its products, embodying humanity, its politics and civilization, through the retrospect of past time, (which plan and products, indeed, make up all of the past, and a large part of the present)—leaving unanswer'd, at least by any specific and local answer, many a well-wrought argument and instance, and many a conscientious declamatory cry and warning—as, very lately, from an eminent and venerable person abroad*—things, problems, full of doubt, dread, suspense, (not new to

* "SHOOTING NIAGARA."—I was at first roused to much anger and abuse by this essay from Mr. Carlyle, so insulting to the theory of America—but happening to think afterwards how I had more than once been in the like mood, during which his essay was evidently cast, and seen persons and things in the same light, (indeed some might say there are signs of the same feeling in these Vistas)—I have since read it again, not only as a study, expressing as it does certain judgments from the highest feudal point of view, but have read it with respect as coming from an earnest soul, and as contributing certain

76*n*. in these Vistas] *TR* and *DV:* in this book

401–402. doctrine or theory that] *GAL:* doctrine of the sovereignty and sacredness of the individual, co-equal with the balance-doctrine that
402–403. train'd in . . . may] *GAL:* trained, may
410. After "on themselves." *GAL* has the following sentence paragraph, omitted in *DV* and later texts: "With such for outset, and a silent, momentary prayer that we may be enabled to tell what is worth the faith within us, we follow on."
411–415. For these lines, through the word "republicanism—" *GAL* has, to begin the paragraph, the following: "Leaving unsaid much that should properly prepare the way for the treatment of this many-sided matter of Democracy—"
418. large part] *TR*, *DV*, and *GAL:* major part
418–419. —leaving] *TR* and *DV:*—Leaving

me, but old occupiers of many an anxious hour in city's din, or night's silence,) we still may give a page or so, whose drift is opportune. Time alone can finally answer these things. But as a substitute in passing, let us, even if fragmentarily, throw forth a short direct or indirect suggestion of the premises of that other plan, in the new spirit, under the new forms, started here in our America.

As to the political section of Democracy, which introduces and breaks ground for further and vaster sections, few probably are the minds, even in these republican States, that fully comprehend the aptness of that phrase, "THE GOVERNMENT OF THE PEOPLE, BY THE PEOPLE, FOR THE PEOPLE," which we inherit from the lips of Abraham Lincoln; a formula whose verbal shape is homely wit, but whose scope includes both the totality and all minutiæ of the lesson.

The People! Like our huge earth itself, which, to ordinary scansion, is full of vulgar contradictions and offence, man, viewed in the lump, displeases, and is a constant puzzle and affront to the merely educated classes. The rare, cosmical, artist-mind, lit with the Infinite, alone confronts his manifold and oceanic qualities—but taste, intelligence and culture, (so-called,) have been against the masses, and remain so. There is plenty of glamour about the most damnable crimes and hoggish meannesses, special and general, of the feudal and dynastic world over there, with its *personnel* of lords and queens and courts, so well-dress'd and so handsome. But the People are ungrammatical, untidy, and their sins gaunt and ill-bred.

Literature, strictly consider'd, has never recognized the People, and, whatever may be said, does not to-day. Speaking generally, the tendencies of literature, as hitherto pursued, have been to make mostly critical and querulous men. It seems as if, so far, there were some natural repugnance between a literary and professional life, and the rude rank spirit of the democracies. There is, in later literature, a treatment of benevolence, a charity business, rife enough it is true; but I know nothing more rare, even in this country, than a fit scientific estimate and reverent appreciation of

sharp-cutting metallic grains, which, if not gold or silver, may be good hard, honest iron.

424. page] *GAL:* paragraph
426. forth a short] *GAL:* forth a thought or two—a short
427. premises of that] *GAL:* premises of the theory of that
443–444. world over there, with] *GAL:* world, with
447. literature, . . . has] *GAL:* literature has
449. as . . . been to] *GAL:* as pursued, are to
451. rude rank spirit] *GAL:* rude spirit

the People—of their measureless wealth of latent power and capacity, their vast, artistic contrasts of lights and shades—with, in America, their entire reliability in emergencies, and a certain breadth of historic grandeur, of peace or war, far surpassing all the vaunted samples of book-heroes, or any *haut ton* coteries, in all the records of the world.

The movements of the late secession war, and their results, to any sense that studies well and comprehends them, show that popular democracy, whatever its faults and dangers, practically justifies itself beyond the proudest claims and wildest hopes of its enthusiasts. Probably no future age can know, but I well know, how the gist of this fiercest and most resolute of the world's war-like contentions resided exclusively in the unnamed, unknown rank and file; and how the brunt of its labor of death was, to all essential purposes, volunteer'd. The People, of their own choice, fighting, dying for their own idea, insolently attack'd by the secession-slave-power, and its very existence imperil'd. Descending to detail, entering any of the armies, and mixing with the private soldiers, we see and have seen august spectacles. We have seen the alacrity with which the American born populace, the peaceablest and most good-natured race in the world, and the most personally independent and intelligent, and the least fitted to submit to the irksomeness and exasperation of regimental discipline, sprang, at the first tap of the drum, to arms—not for gain, nor even glory, nor to repel invasion—but for an emblem, a mere abstraction—for the life, *the safety of the flag*. We have seen the unequal'd docility and obedience of these soldiers. We have seen them tried long and long by hopelessness, mismanagement, and by defeat; have seen the incredible slaughter toward or through which the armies, (as at first Fredericksburg, and afterward at the Wilderness,) still unhesitatingly obey'd orders to advance. We have seen them in trench, or crouching behind breastwork, or tramping in deep mud, or amid pouring rain or thick-falling snow, or under forced marches in hottest summer (as on the road to get to Gettysburg)—vast suffocating swarms, divisions, corps, with every single man so grimed and black with sweat and dust, his own mother would not have known him—his clothes all dirty, stain'd and torn, with sour, accumulated sweat for perfume—many a comrade, per-

453. enough . . . but] *GAL:* enough; but
456. shades—with, in] *GAL:* shades—and in
458–459. war, . . . in all] *GAL:* war, surpassing all the vaunted samples of the personality of book-heroes, in all
460. late secession war] *GAL:* late war
461–462. democracy, . . . practically] *GAL:* democracy practically
464. know, but I well] *GAL:* know, as we well
483–484. rain or thick-falling snow] *GAL:* rain or snow

haps a brother, sun-struck, staggering out, dying, by the roadside, of exhaustion—yet the great bulk bearing steadily on, cheery enough, hollow-bellied from hunger, but sinewy with unconquerable resolution.

We have seen this race proved by wholesale by drearier, yet more fearful tests—the wound, the amputation, the shatter'd face or limb, the slow hot fever, long impatient anchorage in bed, and all the forms of maiming, operation and disease. Alas! America have we seen, though only in her early youth, already to hospital brought. There have we watch'd these soldiers, many of them only boys in years—mark'd their decorum, their religious nature and fortitude, and their sweet affection. Wholesale, truly. For at the front, and through the camps, in countless tents, stood the regimental, brigade and division hospitals; while everywhere amid the land, in or near cities, rose clusters of huge, white-wash'd, crowded, one-story wooden barracks; and there ruled agony with bitter scourge, yet seldom brought a cry; and there stalk'd death by day and night along the narrow aisles between the rows of cots, or by the blankets on the ground, and touch'd lightly many a poor sufferer, often with blessed, welcome touch.

I know not whether I shall be understood, but I realize that it is finally from what I learn'd personally mixing in such scenes that I am now penning these pages. One night in the gloomiest period of the war, in the Patent office hospital in Washington city, as I stood by the bedside of a Pennsylvania soldier, who lay, conscious of quick approaching death, yet perfectly calm, and with noble, spiritual manner, the veteran surgeon, turning aside, said to me, that though he had witness'd many, many deaths of soldiers, and had been a worker at Bull Run, Antietam, Fredericksburg, &c., he had not seen yet the first case of man or boy that met the approach of dissolution with cowardly qualms or terror. My own observation fully bears out the remark.

What have we here, if not, towering above all talk and argument, the plentifully-supplied, last-needed proof of democracy, in its personalities?

502. barracks; and there] *TR*, *DV*, and *GAL:* barracks, (Washington City alone, with its suburbs, at [*GAL:* alone, at] one period, containing in her Army hospitals of this kind, 50,000 wounded and sick men)—and there

508–509. learn'd . . . these pages.] *GAL:* learned in such scenes that I am now penning this article.

510. hospital . . . as] *GAL:* Hospital, as

512–513. surgeon, turning] *GAL:* surgeon, Dr. Stone (Horatio Stone, the sculptor), turning

520–522. These two sentences, not in *GAL*, were inserted in *DV* and appear in all later texts. *GAL* begins a new paragraph with "Grand, common stock!"

528–529. Meantime, general . . . has] *GAL:* Meantime, Humanity (for we will

Curiously enough, too, the proof on this point comes, I should say, every bit as much from the south, as from the north. Although I have spoken only of the latter, yet I deliberately include all. Grand, common stock! to me the accomplish'd and convincing growth, prophetic of the future; proof undeniable to sharpest sense, of perfect beauty, tenderness and pluck, that never feudal lord, nor Greek, nor Roman breed, yet rival'd. Let no tongue ever speak in disparagement of the American races, north or south, to one who has been through the war in the great army hospitals.

Meantime, general humanity, (for to that we return, as, for our purposes, what it really is, to bear in mind,) has always, in every department, been full of perverse maleficence, and is so yet. In downcast hours the soul thinks it always will be—but soon recovers from such sickly moods. I myself see clearly enough the crude, defective streaks in all the strata of the common people; the specimens and vast collections of the ignorant, the credulous, the unfit and uncouth, the incapable, and the very low and poor. The eminent person just mention'd sneeringly asks whether we expect to elevate and improve a nation's politics by absorbing such morbid collections and qualities therein. The point is a formidable one, and there will doubtless always be numbers of solid and reflective citizens who will never get over it. Our answer is general, and is involved in the scope and letter of this essay. We believe the ulterior object of political and all other government, (having, of course, provided for the police, the safety of life, property, and for the basic statute and common law, and their administration, always first in order,) to be among the rest, not merely to rule, to repress disorder, &c., but to develop, to open up to cultivation, to encourage the possibilities of all beneficent and manly outcroppage, and of that aspiration for independence, and the pride and self-respect latent in all characters. (Or, if there be exceptions, we cannot, fixing our eyes on them alone, make theirs the rule for all.)

I say the mission of government, henceforth, in civilized lands, is not repression alone, and not authority alone, not even of law, nor by that

not shirk anything) has

532. I myself . . . the crude] *TR*, *DV*, and *GAL:* I, as Democrat, see clearly enough, (as already illustrated,) the crude

535. The eminent . . . sneeringly] *GAL:* The eminent person, in his conscientious cry just mentioned, sneeringly

536. improve a nation's politics] *GAL:* improve politics

538–539. solid and reflective citizens] *GAL:* solid citizens

540. this essay] *GAL:* this article

540. the ulterior object] *GAL:* the object

542–543. and for . . . always] *GAL:* and the basic common and civil law, always

549. I say the] *GAL:* The

549–550. not . . . authority] *GAL:* not authority

favorite standard of the eminent writer, the rule of the best men, the born heroes and captains of the race, (as if such ever, or one time out of a hundred, get into the big places, elective or dynastic)—but higher than the highest arbitrary rule, to train communities through all their grades, beginning with individuals and ending there again, to rule themselves. What Christ appear'd for in the moral-spiritual field for human-kind, namely, that in respect to the absolute soul, there is in the possession of such by each single individual, something so transcendent, so incapable of gradations, (like life,) that, to that extent, it places all beings on a common level, utterly regardless of the distinctions of intellect, virtue, station, or any height or lowliness whatever—is tallied in like manner, in this other field, by democracy's rule that men, the nation, as a common aggregate of living identities, affording in each a separate and complete subject for freedom, worldly thrift and happiness, and for a fair chance for growth, and for protection in citizenship, &c., must, to the political extent of the suffrage or vote, if no further, be placed, in each and in the whole, on one broad, primary, universal, common platform.

The purpose is not altogether direct; perhaps it is more indirect. For it is not that democracy is of exhaustive account, in itself. Perhaps, indeed, it is, (like Nature,) of no account in itself. It is that, as we see, it is the best, perhaps only, fit and full means, formulater, general caller-forth, trainer, for the million, not for grand material personalities only, but for immortal souls. To be a voter with the rest is not so much; and this, like every institute, will have its imperfections. But to become an enfranchised man, and now, impediments removed, to stand and start without humiliation, and equal with the rest; to commence, or have the road clear'd to commence, the grand experiment of development, whose end, (perhaps requiring several generations,) may be the forming of a full-grown man or woman—that *is* something. To ballast the State is also secured, and in our times is to be secured, in no other way.

We do not, (at any rate I do not,) put it either on the ground that the People, the masses, even the best of them, are, in their latent or exhibited qualities, essentially sensible and good—nor on the ground of their rights; but that good or bad, rights or no rights, the democratic formula is the

555. After "rule themselves." *DV* and *GAL* begin a new paragraph.

569–573. These three sentences, not in *GAL*, were inserted in *DV* and retained in all later texts.

575. now, impediments removed, to] *GAL:* now to

577–578. The marks of parenthesis not in *GAL*.

578–579. full-grown man or woman—that] *GAL:* full-grown manly or womanly Personality—that

only safe and preservative one for coming times. We endow the masses with the suffrage for their own sake, no doubt; then, perhaps still more, from another point of view, for community's sake. Leaving the rest to the sentimentalists, we present freedom as sufficient in its scientific aspect, cold as ice, reasoning, deductive, clear and passionless as crystal.

Democracy too is law, and of the strictest, amplest kind. Many suppose, (and often in its own ranks the error,) that it means a throwing aside of law, and running riot. But, briefly, it is the superior law, not alone that of physical force, the body, which, adding to, it supersedes with that of the spirit. Law is the unshakable order of the universe forever; and the law over all, and law of laws, is the law of successions; that of the superior law, in time, gradually supplanting and overwhelming the inferior one. (While, for myself, I would cheerfully agree—first covenanting that the formative tendencies shall be administer'd in favor, or at least not against it, and that this reservation be closely construed—that until the individual or community show due signs, or be so minor and fractional as not to endanger the State, the condition of authoritative tutelage may continue, and self-government must abide its time.) Nor is the esthetic point, always an important one, without fascination for highest aiming souls. The common ambition strains for elevations, to become some privileged exclusive. The master sees greatness and health in being part of the mass; nothing will do as well as common ground. Would you have in yourself the divine, vast, general law? Then merge yourself in it.

And, topping democracy, this most alluring record, that it alone can bind, and ever seeks to bind, all nations, all men, of however various and distant lands, into a brotherhood, a family. It is the old, yet ever-modern dream of earth, out of her eldest and her youngest, her fond philosophers and poets. Not that half only, individualism, which isolates. There is another half, which is adhesiveness or love, that fuses, ties and aggregates, making the races comrades, and fraternizing all. Both are to be vitalized by religion, (sole worthiest elevator of man or State,) breathing into the proud, material tissues, the breath of life. For I say at the core of democracy, finally, is the religious element. All the religions, old and new, are there. Nor may the scheme step forth, clothed in resplendent beauty

581. either on] *GAL:* either so much on
586. then, perhaps still] *GAL:* then, still
588. aspect] *TR*, *DV*, and *GAL:* aspects
589. reasoning, deductive, clear] *GAL:* reasoning, clear
602. After "abide its time.)" *TR*, *DV*, and *GAL* begin a new paragraph.
605. mass; nothing] *TR*, *DV*, and *GAL:* mass. Nothing
612. only, individualism] *GAL:* only, this Individualism
616. For I say] *GAL:* I say

and command, till these, bearing the best, the latest fruit, the spiritual, shall fully appear.

A portion of our pages we might indite with reference toward Europe, especially the British part of it, more than our own land, perhaps not absolutely needed for the home reader. But the whole question hangs together, and fastens and links all peoples. The liberalist of to-day has this advantage over antique or medieval times, that his doctrine seeks not only to individualize but to universalize. The great word Solidarity has arisen. Of all dangers to a nation, as things exist in our day, there can be no greater one than having certain portions of the people set off from the rest by a line drawn—they not privileged as others, but degraded, humiliated, made of no account. Much quackery teems, of course, even on democracy's side, yet does not really affect the orbic quality of the matter. To work in, if we may so term it, and justify God, his divine aggregate, the People, (or, the veritable horn'd and sharp-tail'd Devil, *his* aggregate, if there be who convulsively insist upon it)—this, I say, is what democracy is for; and this is what our America means, and is doing—may I not say, has done? If not, she means nothing more, and does nothing more, than any other land. And as, by virtue of its kosmical, antiseptic power, Nature's stomach is fully strong enough not only to digest the morbific matter always presented, not to be turn'd aside, and perhaps, indeed, intuitively gravitating thither—but even to change such contributions into nutriment for highest use and life—so American democracy's. That is the lesson we, these days, send over to European lands by every western breeze.

And, truly, whatever may be said in the way of abstract argument, for or against the theory of a wider democratizing of institutions in any

621. A portion . . . indite] *GAL:* Portions of our pages we feel to indite

621–622. Europe, . . . more] *GAL:* Europe more

625–626. only to individualize but to universalize] *TR*, *DV*, and *GAL:* only to universalize, but to individualize

626. The great] *TR* and *DV:* Then the great

626. After "Solidarity has arisen." *GAL* has three paragraphs that were omitted in *DV* and later texts. See Appendix II, *1*.

626. After "Solidarity has arisen." *TR* and *DV* begin a new paragraph, the first sentence of which is the same as in *SDC* except that it begins, "I say of all dangers". The corresponding sentence in *GAL* is as follows: "The curse and canker of Nations politically has been, or, at any rate, will be, as things have come to exist in our day—the having of certain portions of the people set off from the rest by a line drawn—they not privileged as others, but degraded, humiliated, made of no account."

630. account. Much] *GAL:* account. We repeat it, the question is, finally, one of Science—the science of the present and the future. Much

630–631. course, . . . yet] *GAL:* course, yet

633–634. horn'd . . . this] *GAL:* horned and fluke-tailed Devil, *his* aggregate, since you so convulsively insist upon it, O, eminence!)—this

civilized country, much trouble might well be saved to all European lands by recognizing this palpable fact, (for a palpable fact it is,) that some form of such democratizing is about the only resource now left. *That*, or chronic dissatisfaction continued, mutterings which grow annually louder and louder, till, in due course, and pretty swiftly in most cases, the inevitable crisis, crash, dynastic ruin. Anything worthy to be call'd statesmanship in the Old World, I should say, among the advanced students, adepts, or men of any brains, does not debate to-day whether to hold on, attempting to lean back and monarchize, or to look forward and democratize—but *how*, and in what degree and part, most prudently to democratize.

The eager and often inconsiderate appeals of reformers and revolutionists are indispensable, to counterbalance the inertness and fossilism making so large a part of human institutions. The latter will always take care of themselves—the danger being that they rapidly tend to ossify us. The former is to be treated with indulgence, and even with respect. As circulation to air, so is agitation and a plentiful degree of speculative license to political and moral sanity. Indirectly, but surely, goodness, virtue, law, (of the very best,) follow freedom. These, to democracy, are what the keel is to the ship, or saltness to the ocean.

The true gravitation-hold of liberalism in the United States will be a more universal ownership of property, general homesteads, general comfort—a vast, intertwining reticulation of wealth. As the human frame, or, indeed, any object in this manifold universe, is best kept together by the simple miracle of its own cohesion, and the necessity, exercise and profit thereof, so a great and varied nationality, occupying millions of square miles, were firmest held and knit by the principle of the safety and endurance of the aggregate of its middling property owners. So that, from

646. all European] *GAL:* those European

655. After "to democratize." *TR*, *DV*, and *GAL* continue the paragraph with the following three sentences: "The difficulties of the transfer may be fearful; perhaps none here in our America can truly know them. I, for one, fully acknowledge them, and sympathize deeply. But there is Time, and must be Faith; and Opportunities, though gradual and slow, will everywhere abroad be born."

After "be born." *GAL* has another sentence to complete the paragraph, as follows: "And beaming like a star, to any and to all, whatever else may for a while be quenched, shines not the eternal signal in the West?"

After this paragraph, *TR*, *DV*, and *GAL* have a paragraph, deleted in *SDC* and later texts. See Appendix II, 2.

659–660. themselves— . . . The] *GAL:* themselves. The

665. The true . . . will] *GAL:* The gravitation-hold of Liberalism will

667. After "of wealth." *GAL* has the following sentence, deleted in *DV:* "No community furnished throughout with homes, and substantial, however moderate, incomes, commits suicide, or 'shoots Niagara'."

669. necessity, exercise and] *GAL:* necessity and

672. After "owners." *TR*, *DV*, and *GAL* begin a new paragraph.

another point of view, ungracious as it may sound, and a paradox after what we have been saying, democracy looks with suspicious, ill-satisfied eye upon the very poor, the ignorant, and on those out of business. She asks for men and women with occupations, well-off, owners of houses and acres, and with cash in the bank—and with some cravings for literature, too; and must have them, and hastens to make them. Luckily, the seed is already well-sown, and has taken ineradicable root.*

Huge and mighty are our days, our republican lands—and most in their rapid shiftings, their changes, all in the interest of the cause. As I write this particular passage, (November, 1868,) the din of disputation rages around me. Acrid the temper of the parties, vital the pending questions. Congress convenes; the President sends his message; reconstruction is still in abeyance; the nomination and the contest for the twenty-first Presidentiad draw close, with loudest threat and bustle. Of these, and all the like of these, the eventuations I know not; but well I know that behind them, and whatever their eventuations, the vital things remain safe and certain, and all the needed work goes on. Time, with soon or later superciliousness, disposes of Presidents, Congressmen, party platforms, and such. Anon, it clears the stage of each and any mortal shred that thinks itself so potent to its day; and at and after which, (with precious, golden exceptions once or twice in a century,) all that relates to sir potency is flung to moulder in a burial-vault, and no one bothers himself the least bit about it afterward. But the People ever remain, tendencies continue, and all the idiocratic transfers in unbroken chain go on.

In a few years the dominion-heart of America will be far inland, toward the West. Our future national capital may not be where the

* For fear of mistake, I may as well distinctly specify, as cheerfully included in the model and standard of these Vistas, a practical, stirring, worldly, money-making, even materialistic character. It is undeniable that our farms, stores, offices, dry-goods, coal and groceries, enginery, cash-accounts, trades, earnings, markets, &c., should be attended to in earnest, and actively pursued, just as if they had a real and permanent existence. I perceive clearly

81*n*–92*n*. This footnote, not in *GAL*, was inserted in *DV*.
81*n*. distinctly specify, as] *TR* and *DV:* distinctly announce, as
88*n*. are parts] *TR* and *DV:* are vital parts

675. poor, . . . She] *GAL:* poor, and on the ignorant. She
676. women . . . well-off] *GAL:* women well-off
681–682. As . . . the] *TR* and *DV:* As I write this passage, (November, 1868,) the] *GAL:* As I write the
685. nomination] *TR*, *DV*, and *GAL:* nominations
688. the vital] *TR*, *DV*, and *GAL:* the really vital
695. People ever remain] *TR*, *DV*, and *GAL:* People ever remains

present one is. It is possible, nay likely, that in less than fifty years, it will migrate a thousand or two miles, will be re-founded, and every thing belonging to it made on a different plan, original, far more superb. The main social, political, spine-character of the States will probably run along the Ohio, Missouri and Mississippi rivers, and west and north of them, including Canada. Those regions, with the group of powerful brothers toward the Pacific, (destined to the mastership of that sea and its countless paradises of islands,) will compact and settle the traits of America, with all the old retain'd, but more expanded, grafted on newer, hardier, purely native stock. A giant growth, composite from the rest, getting their contribution, absorbing it, to make it more illustrious. From the north, intellect, the sun of things, also the idea of unswayable justice, anchor amid the last, the wildest tempests. From the south the living soul, the animus of good and bad, haughtily admitting no demonstration but its own. While from the west itself comes solid personality, with blood and brawn, and the deep quality of all-accepting fusion.

Political democracy, as it exists and practically works in America, with all its threatening evils, supplies a training-school for making first-class men. It is life's gymnasium, not of good only, but of all. We try often, though we fall back often. A brave delight, fit for freedom's athletes, fills these arenas, and fully satisfies, out of the action in them, irrespective of success. Whatever we do not attain, we at any rate attain the experiences of the fight, the hardening of the strong campaign, and throb with currents of attempt at least. Time is ample. Let the victors come after us. Not for nothing does evil play its part among us. Judging from the main portions of the history of the world, so far, justice is always in jeopardy,

that the extreme business energy, and this almost maniacal appetite for wealth prevalent in the United States, are parts of amelioration and progress, indispensably needed to prepare the very results I demand. My theory includes riches, and the getting of riches, and the amplest products, power, activity, inventions, movements, &c. Upon them, as upon substrata, I raise the edifice design'd in these Vistas.

88*n*–89*n*. progress, indispensably] *TR* and *DV:* progress, and perhaps indispensably

91*n*. Upon them, as] *TR* and *DV:* Upon these, as

696. After "go on." *TR*, *DV*, and *GAL* continue in the same paragraph.

698. may not] *GAL:* will not

699. It is . . . that in] *GAL:* I should say that certainly, in

715–716. America, . . . supplies] *GAL:* America supplies

716–717. making first-class men] *TR*, *DV*, and *GAL:* making grand young men

723. among us. Judging] *DV:* among men. Judging] *GAL:* among men. *Vive*

723–731. These three sentences, not in *GAL*, were inserted in *DV*.

peace walks amid hourly pitfalls, and of slavery, misery, meanness, the craft of tyrants and the credulity of the populace, in some of their protean forms, no voice can at any time say, They are not. The clouds break a little, and the sun shines out—but soon and certain the lowering darkness falls again, as if to last forever. Yet is there an immortal courage and prophecy in every sane soul that cannot, must not, under any circumstances, capitulate. *Vive*, the attack—the perennial assault! *Vive*, the unpopular cause—the spirit that audaciously aims—the never-abandon'd efforts, pursued the same amid opposing proofs and precedents.

Once, before the war, (Alas! I dare not say how many times the mood has come!) I, too, was fill'd with doubt and gloom. A foreigner, an acute and good man, had impressively said to me, that day—putting in form, indeed, my own observations: "I have travel'd much in the United States, and watch'd their politicians, and listen'd to the speeches of the candidates, and read the journals, and gone into the public houses, and heard the unguarded talk of men. And I have found your vaunted America honeycomb'd from top to toe with infidelism, even to itself and its own programme. I have mark'd the brazen hell-faces of secession and slavery gazing defiantly from all the windows and doorways. I have everywhere found, primarily, thieves and scalliwags arranging the nominations to offices, and sometimes filling the offices themselves. I have found the north just as full of bad stuff as the south. Of the holders of public office in the Nation or the States or their municipalities, I have found that not one in a hundred has been chosen by any spontaneous selection of the outsiders, the people, but all have been nominated and put through by little or large caucuses of the politicians, and have got in by corrupt rings and electioneering, not capacity or desert. I have noticed how the millions of sturdy farmers and mechanics are thus the helpless supple-jacks of comparatively few politicians. And I have noticed more and more, the alarming spectacle of parties usurping the government, and openly and shamelessly wielding it for party purposes."

732. aims—the never-] *GAL:* aims—the courage that dies not—the never-

734–735. The sentence in parentheses, not in *GAL*, was inserted in *DV*.

735. foreigner] *GAL:* traveller

737–755. The quotation marks, not in *TR*, *DV*, and *GAL*, were inserted in the proof sheets of *SDC* since they do not appear in the revised printer's copy.

747. or the States] *TR*, *DV*, and *GAL:* or in the States

750–751. by corrupt . . . desert] *GAL:* by electioneering, not desert

751–753. The words "millions of . . . few politicians." resemble the following passage of "The Eighteenth Presidency!" (text of Edward F. Grier's edition, 1956, p. 21): "millions of farmers and mechanics of These States the helpless supple-jacks of a comparatively few politicians." (See also notes to "Rulers Strictly Out of

Sad, serious, deep truths. Yet are there other, still deeper, amply confronting, dominating truths. Over those politicians and great and little rings, and over all their insolence and wiles, and over the powerfulest parties, looms a power, too sluggish maybe, but ever holding decisions and decrees in hand, ready, with stern process, to execute them as soon as plainly needed—and at times, indeed, summarily crushing to atoms the mightiest parties, even in the hour of their pride.

In saner hours far different are the amounts of these things from what, at first sight, they appear. Though it is no doubt important who is elected governor, mayor, or legislator, (and full of dismay when incompetent or vile ones get elected, as they sometimes do,) there are other, quieter contingencies, infinitely more important. Shams, &c., will always be the show, like ocean's scum; enough, if waters deep and clear make up the rest. Enough, that while the piled embroider'd shoddy gaud and fraud spreads to the superficial eye, the hidden warp and weft are genuine, and will wear forever. Enough, in short, that the race, the land which could raise such as the late rebellion, could also put it down.

The average man of a land at last only is important. He, in these States, remains immortal owner and boss, deriving good uses, somehow, out of any sort of servant in office, even the basest; (certain universal requisites, and their settled regularity and protection, being first secured,) a nation like ours, in a sort of geological formation state, trying continually new experiments, choosing new delegations, is not served by the best men only, but sometimes more by those that provoke it—by the combats they arouse. Thus national rage, fury, discussion, &c., better than content. Thus, also, the warning signals, invaluable for after times.

What is more dramatic than the spectacle we have seen repeated, and doubtless long shall see—the popular judgment taking the successful candidates on trial in the offices—standing off, as it were, and observing them and their doings for a while, and always giving, finally, the fit, exactly due reward? I think, after all, the sublimest part of political

the Masses.")

757–758. politicians . . . and over] *GAL:* politicians, and over

763. In saner hours far] *GAL:* Far

765. elected governor] *TR*, *DV*, and *GAL:* elected President or Governor

765–766. The words in parentheses, not in *GAL*, were inserted in *DV*.

775. basest; (certain] *TR*, *DV*, and *GAL:* basest; because (certain

777. ours, . . . formation] *GAL:* ours, in the formation

780. &c., better than] *GAL:* &c., sublimer than

786. After "due reward?" *TR* and *DV* begin a new paragraph.

786–792. These lines, including the short paragraph in *TR* and *DV* (lines 786–790) and the first sentence in the paragraph beginning "Then still" (lines 791 792), do not appear in *GAL*, which begins the next paragraph with "When I pass".

history, and its culmination, is currently issuing from the American people. I know nothing grander, better exercise, better digestion, more positive proof of the past, the triumphant result of faith in human kind, than a well-contested American national election.

Then still the thought returns, (like the thread-passage in overtures,) giving the key and echo to these pages. When I pass to and fro, different latitudes, different seasons, beholding the crowds of the great cities, New York, Boston, Philadelphia, Cincinnati, Chicago, St. Louis, San Francisco, New Orleans, Baltimore—when I mix with these interminable swarms of alert, turbulent, good-natured, independent citizens, mechanics, clerks, young persons—at the idea of this mass of men, so fresh and free, so loving and so proud, a singular awe falls upon me. I feel, with dejection and amazement, that among our geniuses and talented writers or speakers, few or none have yet really spoken to this people, created a single image-making work for them, or absorb'd the central spirit and the idiosyncrasies which are theirs—and which, thus, in highest ranges, so far remain entirely uncelebrated, unexpress'd.

Dominion strong is the body's; dominion stronger is the mind's. What has fill'd, and fills to-day our intellect, our fancy, furnishing the standards therein, is yet foreign. The great poems, Shakspere included, are poisonous to the idea of the pride and dignity of the common people, the life-blood of democracy. The models of our literature, as we get it from other lands, ultramarine, have had their birth in courts, and bask'd and grown in castle sunshine; all smells of princes' favors. Of workers of a certain sort, we have, indeed, plenty, contributing after their kind; many elegant, many learn'd, all complacent. But touch'd by the national test, or tried by the standards of democratic personality, they wither to ashes. I say I have not seen a single writer, artist, lecturer, or what not, that has confronted the voiceless but ever erect and active, pervading, underlying will and typic aspiration of the land, in a spirit kindred to itself. Do you call those genteel little creatures American poets? Do you term that perpetual,

93*n*–98*n*. This footnote, not in *GAL*, was inserted in *DV*.

801. people, . . . or absorb'd] *TR* and *DV:* people, or created a single image-making work that could be called for them—or absorbed] *GAL:* people, or absorbed

806. Shakspere] *TR*, *DV*, and *GAL:* Shakespeare

810–811. princes' favors. Of workers of a certain sort, we have, indeed, plenty] *GAL:* princes' favors. For esthetic Europe is yet exclusively feudal.

The literature of These States, a new projection, when it comes, must be the born outcrop, through all rich and luxuriant forms, but stern and exclusive, of the sole Idea of The States, belonging here alone. Of course, of workers of a certain sort, we have already plenty

812–813. test, . . . they] *GAL:* test, they

814. seen a single] *GAL:* seen one single

pistareen, paste-pot work, American art, American drama, taste, verse? I think I hear, echoed as from some mountain-top afar in the west, the scornful laugh of the Genius of these States.

Democracy, in silence, biding its time, ponders its own ideals, not of literature and art only—not of men only, but of women. The idea of the women of America, (extricated from this daze, this fossil and unhealthy air which hangs about the word *lady*,) develop'd, raised to become the robust equals, workers, and, it may be, even practical and political deciders with the men—greater than man, we may admit, through their divine maternity, always their towering, emblematical attribute—but great, at any rate, as man, in all departments; or, rather, capable of being so, soon as they realize it, and can bring themselves to give up toys and fictions, and launch forth, as men do, amid real, independent, stormy life.

Then, as towards our thought's finalè, (and, in that, overarching the true scholar's lesson,) we have to say there can be no complete or epical presentation of democracy in the aggregate, or anything like it, at this day, because its doctrines will only be effectually incarnated in any one branch, when, in all, their spirit is at the root and centre. Far, far, indeed, stretch, in distance, our Vistas! How much is still to be disentangled, freed! How long it takes to make this American world see that it is, in itself, the final authority and reliance!

Did you, too, O friend, suppose democracy was only for elections, for politics, and for a party name? I say democracy is only of use there that it may pass on and come to its flower and fruits in manners, in the highest forms of interaction between men, and their beliefs—in religion, literature, colleges, and schools—democracy in all public and private life, and in the army and navy.* I have intimated that, as a paramount scheme, it has yet

* The whole present system of the officering and personnel of the army and navy of these States, and the spirit and letter of their trebly-aristocratic rules and regulations, is a monstrous exotic, a nuisance and revolt, and belong here

93*n*. personnel] *TR* and *DV*: *personnel*

818. paste-pot] *GAL:* pasteboard
818. American drama] *GAL:* American opera, drama
821–822. ideals, not . . . only—not of men] *GAL:* ideals, not of men
824. *lady*] *TR*, *DV*, and *GAL:* Lady
825. workers, and, . . . even] *GAL:* and even
831. towards our thought's finalè,] *TR* and *DV:* toward our thought's finale,] *GAL:* toward finale
833. democracy . . . or] *GAL:* democracy, or
835–836. This sentence, beginning "Far, far," is not in *GAL*.
837. this American world] *TR*, *DV*, and *GAL:* this world
839. too, O friend, suppose] *GAL:* too, suppose

few or no full realizers and believers. I do not see, either, that it owes any serious thanks to noted propagandists or champions, or has been essentially help'd, though often harm'd, by them. It has been and is carried on by all the moral forces, and by trade, finance, machinery, intercommunications, and, in fact, by all the developments of history, and can no more be stopp'd than the tides, or the earth in its orbit. Doubtless, also, it resides, crude and latent, well down in the hearts of the fair average of the American-born people, mainly in the agricultural regions. But it is not yet, there or anywhere, the fully-receiv'd, the fervid, the absolute faith.

I submit, therefore, that the fruition of democracy, on aught like a grand scale, resides altogether in the future. As, under any profound and comprehensive view of the gorgeous-composite feudal world, we see in it, through the long ages and cycles of ages, the results of a deep, integral, human and divine principle, or fountain, from which issued laws, ecclesia, manners, institutes, costumes, personalities, poems, (hitherto unequall'd,) faithfully partaking of their source, and indeed only arising either to betoken it, or to furnish parts of that varied-flowing display, whose centre was one and absolute—so, long ages hence, shall the due historian or critic make at least an equal retrospect, an equal history for the democratic principle. It too must be adorn'd, credited with its results—then, when it, with imperial power, through amplest time, has dominated mankind—has been the source and test of all the moral, esthetic, social, political, and religious expressions and institutes of the civilized world—has begotten them in spirit and in form, and has carried them to its own unprecedented heights—has had, (it is possible,) monastics and ascetics, more numerous, more devout than the monks and priests of all previous creeds—has sway'd the ages with a breadth and rectitude tallying Nature's own—has fashion'd, systematized, and triumphantly finish'd and carried out, in its own interest, and with unparallel'd success, a new earth and a new man.

just as much as orders of nobility, or the Pope's council of cardinals. I say if the present theory of our army and navy is sensible and true, then the rest of America is an unmitigated fraud.

848–849. intercommunications, . . . and can] *GAL:* intercommunications, etc., and can

868. and has carried] *TR*, *DV*, and *GAL:* and carried

869. had, (it is possible,) monastics] *GAL:* had monastics

879. surrounding war and revolution] *GAL:* surrounding revolution

884. not ours] *TR*, *DV*, and *GAL:* nor ours

893. The article "Democracy" in *GAL* ends with the sentence and paragraph ending "abandon'd the faith." and is followed by the author's name, "Walt Whitman."

894–1275. This part of the essay is collated with the *GAL* essay "Personalism" as

Thus we presume to write, as it were, upon things that exist not, and travel by maps yet unmade, and a blank. But the throes of birth are upon us; and we have something of this advantage in seasons of strong formations, doubts, suspense—for then the afflatus of such themes haply may fall upon us, more or less; and then, hot from surrounding war and revolution, our speech, though without polish'd coherence, and a failure by the standard called criticism, comes forth, real at least as the lightnings.

And may-be we, these days, have, too, our own reward—(for there are yet some, in all lands, worthy to be so encouraged.) Though not for us the joy of entering at the last the conquer'd city—not ours the chance ever to see with our own eyes the peerless power and splendid *eclat* of the democratic principle, arriv'd at meridian, filling the world with effulgence and majesty far beyond those of past history's kings, or all dynastic sway—there is yet, to whoever is eligible among us, the prophetic vision, the joy of being toss'd in the brave turmoil of these times—the promulgation and the path, obedient, lowly reverent to the voice, the gesture of the god, or holy ghost, which others see not, hear not—with the proud consciousness that amid whatever clouds, seductions, or heart-wearying postponements, we have never deserted, never despair'd, never abandon'd the faith.

So much contributed, to be conn'd well, to help prepare and brace our edifice, our plann'd Idea—we still proceed to give it in another of its aspects—perhaps the main, the high façade of all. For to democracy, the leveler, the unyielding principle of the average, is surely join'd another principle, equally unyielding, closely tracking the first, indispensable to it, opposite, (as the sexes are opposite,) and whose existence, confronting and ever modifying the other, often clashing, paradoxical, yet neither of highest avail without the other, plainly supplies to these grand cosmic politics of ours, and to the launch'd forth mortal dangers of republicanism, to-day or any day, the counterpart and offset whereby Nature restrains the deadly original relentlessness of all her first-class laws. This second principle is individuality, the pride and centripetal isolation of a human being in himself—identity—personalism. Whatever the name, its acceptance and thorough infusion through the organizations of political com-

well as with the other texts.

894–897. For these lines through "principle of the" GAL has the following beginning of the article "Personalism": "To Democracy, the leveller, the unyielding first principle of the"

897. average, is surely] *DVOP:* average, surely

899. existence, confronting] *GAL:* existence, coequal, confronting

900. clashing, paradoxical] *GAL:* clashing, even defiant, paradoxical

902–903. republicanism, . . . counterpart] *GAL:* Republicanism, the analogic counterpart

monalty now shooting Aurora-like about the world, are of utmost importance, as the principle itself is needed for very life's sake. It forms, in a sort, or is to form, the compensating balance-wheel of the successful working machinery of aggregate America.

And, if we think of it, what does civilization itself rest upon—and what object has it, with its religions, arts, schools, &c., but rich, luxuriant, varied personalism? To that, all bends; and it is because toward such result democracy alone, on anything like Nature's scale, breaks up the limitless fallows of humankind, and plants the seed, and gives fair play, that its claims now precede the rest. The literature, songs, esthetics, &c., of a country are of importance principally because they furnish the materials and suggestions of personality for the women and men of that country, and enforce them in a thousand effective ways.* As the top-most claim of a strong consolidating of the nationality of these States, is, that only by such powerful compaction can the separate States secure that full and free swing within their spheres, which is becoming to them, each after its kind, so will individuality, with unimpeded branchings, flourish best under imperial republican forms.

Assuming Democracy to be at present in its embryo condition, and that the only large and satisfactory justification of it resides in the future, mainly through the copious production of perfect characters among

* After the rest is satiated, all interest culminates in the field of persons, and never flags there. Accordingly in this field have the great poets and literatuses signally toil'd. They too, in all ages, all lands, have been creators, fashioning, making types of men and women, as Adam and Eve are made in the divine fable. Behold, shaped, bred by orientalism, feudalism, through their long growth and culmination, and breeding back in return—(when shall we have an equal series, typical of democracy?)—behold, commencing in primal Asia, (apparently formulated, in what beginning we know, in the gods of the mythologies, and coming down thence,) a few samples out of the countless product, bequeath'd to the moderns, bequeath'd to America as studies. For the men, Yudishtura, Rama, Arjuna, Solomon, most of the Old and New Testament characters; Achilles, Ulysses, Theseus, Prometheus, Her-

99*n*–122*n*. This footnote, not in *GAL*, was inserted in *DV*.
104*n*. return—(when] *TR* and *DV:* return, (When

917. After "precede the rest." *TR*, *DV*, and *GAL* begin a new paragraph.
920. After "effective ways." *TR*, *DV*, and *GAL* begin a new paragraph.
926–927. condition, and that] *GAL:* condition, [see article in Galaxy, December, 1867,] and that
929–930. people, . . . it is] *GAL:* people, it is
932. I continue the] *GAL:* I attempt the

the people, and through the advent of a sane and pervading religiousness, it is with regard to the atmosphere and spaciousness fit for such characters, and of certain nutriment and cartoon-draftings proper for them, and indicating them for New World purposes, that I continue the present statement—an exploration, as of new ground, wherein, like other primitive surveyors, I must do the best I can, leaving it to those who come after me to do much better. (The service, in fact, if any, must be to break a sort of first path or track, no matter how rude and ungeometrical.)

We have frequently printed the word Democracy. Yet I cannot too often repeat that it is a word the real gist of which still sleeps, quite unawaken'd, notwithstanding the resonance and the many angry tempests out of which its syllables have come, from pen or tongue. It is a great word, whose history, I suppose, remains unwritten, because that history has yet to be enacted. It is, in some sort, younger brother of another great and often-used word, Nature, whose history also waits unwritten. As I perceive, the tendencies of our day, in the States, (and I entirely respect them,) are toward those vast and sweeping movements, influences, moral and physical, of humanity, now and always current over the planet, on the scale of the impulses of the elements. Then it is also good to reduce the whole matter to the consideration of a single self, a man, a woman, on permanent grounds. Even for the treatment of the universal, in politics,

cules, Æneas, Plutarch's heroes; the Merlin of Celtic bards; the Cid, Arthur and his knights, Siegfried and Hagen in the Nibelungen; Roland and Oliver; Roustam in the Shah-Nemah; and so on to Milton's Satan, Cervantes' Don Quixote, Shakspere's Hamlet, Richard II., Lear, Marc Antony, &c., and the modern Faust. These, I say, are models, combined, adjusted to other standards than America's, but of priceless value to her and hers.

Among women, the goddesses of the Egyptian, Indian and Greek mythologies, certain Bible characters, especially the Holy Mother; Cleopatra, Penelope; the portraits of Brunhelde and Chriemhilde in the Nibelungen; Oriana, Una, &c.; the modern Consuelo, Walter Scott's Jeanie and Effie Deans, &c., &c. (Yet woman portray'd or outlin'd at her best, or as perfect human mother, does not hitherto, it seems to me, fully appear in literature.)

105*n*. democracy?)—behold] *TR* and *DV:* Democracy?)—Behold
111*n*. Aeneas, Plutarch's] *TR* and *DV:* Aeneas, St. John, Plutarch's
114*n*. Shakspere's] *TR* and *DV:* Shakespeare's

935–936. No marks of parenthesis in *TR*, *DV*, and *GAL*.
938. word . . . which] *GAL:* word which
941. history, . . . remains] *GAL:* history remains
943. After "waits unwritten." *TR* and *DV* begin a new paragraph. *GAL* has the following sentence as a separate paragraph: "But I must get me to my theme." *GAL* then begins a new paragraph beginning as follows: "Much is said, and opportunely said, with reference to aggregate-tendencies, masses, those vast" etc.

metaphysics, or anything, sooner or later we come down to one single, solitary soul.

There is, in sanest hours, a consciousness, a thought that rises, independent, lifted out from all else, calm, like the stars, shining eternal. This is the thought of identity—yours for you, whoever you are, as mine for me. Miracle of miracles, beyond statement, most spiritual and vaguest of earth's dreams, yet hardest basic fact, and only entrance to all facts. In such devout hours, in the midst of the significant wonders of heaven and earth, (significant only because of the Me in the centre,) creeds, conventions, fall away and become of no account before this simple idea. Under the luminousness of real vision, it alone takes possession, takes value. Like the shadowy dwarf in the fable, once liberated and look'd upon, it expands over the whole earth, and spreads to the roof of heaven.

The quality of BEING, in the object's self, according to its own central idea and purpose, and of growing therefrom and thereto—not criticism by other standards, and adjustments thereto—is the lesson of Nature. True, the full man wisely gathers, culls, absorbs; but if, engaged disproportionately in that, he slights or overlays the precious idiocrasy and special nativity and intention that he is, the man's self, the main thing, is a failure, however wide his general cultivation. Thus, in our times, refinement and delicatesse are not only attended to sufficiently, but threaten to eat us up, like a cancer. Already, the democratic genius watches, ill-pleased, these tendencies. Provision for a little healthy rudeness, savage virtue, justification of what one has in one's self, whatever it is, is demanded. Negative qualities, even deficiencies, would be a relief. Singleness and normal simplicity and separation, amid this more and more complex, more and more artificialized state of society—how pensively we yearn for them! how we would welcome their return!

In some such direction, then—at any rate enough to preserve the balance—we feel called upon to throw what weight we can, not for absolute reasons, but current ones. To prune, gather, trim, conform, and ever cram and stuff, and be genteel and proper, is the pressure of our days.

958–959. conventions, fall] *GAL:* conventions, venerable authorities, fall
973–974. virtue, . . . is demanded.] *GAL:* virtue, sanity, equipoise, is demanded.
975. simplicity . . . amid] *GAL:* simplicity, amid
981. stuff . . . pressure] *DV:* stuff, is the pressure] *GAL:* stuff, is the prevailing and enormous pressure
984. a half-starved and] *GAL:* a rude and
985–986. conventional, over-corpulent societies] *GAL:* conventional societies
986–987. rotten . . . literature] *GAL:* rotten with literature
987. After "and Art." *TR*, *DV*, and *GAL* begin a new paragraph.
991. women, . . . ahead] *GAL:* women, ahead

While aware that much can be said even in behalf of all this, we perceive that we have not now to consider the question of what is demanded to serve a half-starved and barbarous nation, or set of nations, but what is most applicable, most pertinent, for numerous congeries of conventional, over-corpulent societies, already becoming stifled and rotten with flatulent, infidelistic literature, and polite conformity and art. In addition to establish'd sciences, we suggest a science as it were of healthy average personalism, on original-universal grounds, the object of which should be to raise up and supply through the States a copious race of superb American men and women, cheerful, religious, ahead of any yet known.

America has yet morally and artistically originated nothing. She seems singularly unaware that the models of persons, books, manners, &c., appropriate for former conditions and for European lands, are but exiles and exotics here. No current of her life, as shown on the surfaces of what is authoritatively called her society, accepts or runs into social or esthetic democracy; but all the currents set squarely against it. Never, in the Old World, was thoroughly upholster'd exterior appearance and show, mental and other, built entirely on the idea of caste, and on the sufficiency of mere outside acquisition—never were glibness, verbal intellect, more the test, the emulation—more loftily elevated as head and sample—than they are on the surface of our republican States this day. The writers of a time hint the mottoes of its gods. The word of the modern, say these voices, is the word Culture.

We find ourselves abruptly in close quarters with the enemy. This word Culture, or what it has come to represent, involves, by contrast, our whole theme, and has been, indeed, the spur, urging us to engagement. Certain questions arise. As now taught, accepted and carried out, are not the processes of culture rapidly creating a class of supercilious infidels, who believe in nothing? Shall a man lose himself in countless masses of adjustments, and be so shaped with reference to this, that, and the other, that the simply good and healthy and brave parts of him are reduced and clipp'd away, like the bordering of box in a garden? You can cultivate

992. America . . . originated] *DV* and *GAL:* America, leaving out her politics, has yet morally originated

993–994. models . . . appropriate] *GAL:* models appropriate

996–997. into social . . . but] *TR* and *DV:* into moral, social or esthetic Democracy; but] *GAL:* into the just-mentioned theory; but

997. currents set] *GAL:* currents there set

999. caste, and on the] *GAL:* caste—never was the

1003–1004. voices, is] *GAL:* voices, (and among them the noblest voice in America), is

1006. Culture, or what] *GAL:* Culture, and what

1008. After "questions arise." *DV* and *GAL* begin a new paragraph.

corn and roses and orchards—but who shall cultivate the mountain peaks, the ocean, and the tumbling gorgeousness of the clouds? Lastly—is the readily-given reply that culture only seeks to help, systematize, and put in attitude, the elements of fertility and power, a conclusive reply?

I do not so much object to the name, or word, but I should certainly insist, for the purposes of these States, on a radical change of category, in the distribution of precedence. I should demand a programme of culture, drawn out, not for a single class alone, or for the parlors or lecture-rooms, but with an eye to practical life, the west, the working-men, the facts of farms and jack-planes and engineers, and of the broad range of the women also of the middle and working strata, and with reference to the perfect equality of women, and of a grand and powerful motherhood. I should demand of this programme or theory a scope generous enough to include the widest human area. It must have for its spinal meaning the formation of a typical personality of character, eligible to the uses of the high average of men—and *not* restricted by conditions ineligible to the masses. The best culture will always be that of the manly and courageous instincts, and loving perceptions, and of self-respect—aiming to form, over this continent, an idiocrasy of universalism, which, true child of America, will bring joy to its mother, returning to her in her own spirit, recruiting myriads of offspring, able, natural, perceptive, tolerant, devout believers in her, America, and with some definite instinct why and for what she has arisen, most vast, most formidable of historic births, and is, now and here, with wonderful step, journeying through Time.

The problem, as it seems to me, presented to the New World, is, under permanent law and order, and after preserving cohesion, (ensemble-Individuality,) at all hazards, to vitalize man's free play of special Personalism, recognizing in it something that calls ever more to be consider'd, fed, and adopted as the substratum for the best that belongs to us, (government indeed is for it,) including the new esthetics of our future.

To formulate beyond this present vagueness—to help line and put before us the species, or a specimen of the species, of the democratic ethnology of the future, is a work toward which the genius of our land, with peculiar encouragement, invites her well-wishers. Already certain

1014. cultivate the mountain] *TR*, *DV*, and *GAL:* cultivate the primaeval forests, the mountain
1019. insist, . . . on] *GAL:* insist on
1024. strata, and] GAL: strata of the States, and
1030. After "the masses." *TR*, *DV*, and *GAL* begin a new paragraph.
1034. of offspring, able] *TR*, *DV*, and *GAL:* of men, able
1034–1035. devout believers] *TR*, *DV*, and *GAL:* devout, real men, alive and full, believers
1051–1053. The statement in parentheses, not in *GAL*, was inserted in *DV*.

limnings, more or less grotesque, more or less fading and watery, have appear'd. We too, (repressing doubts and qualms,) will try our hand.

Attempting, then, however crudely, a basic model or portrait of personality for general use for the manliness of the States, (and doubtless that is most useful which is most simple and comprehensive for all, and toned low enough,) we should prepare the canvas well beforehand. Parentage must consider itself in advance. (Will the time hasten when fatherhood and motherhood shall become a science—and the noblest science?) To our model, a clear-blooded, strong-fibred physique, is indispensable; the questions of food, drink, air, exercise, assimilation, digestion, can never be intermitted. Out of these we descry a well-begotten selfhood—in youth, fresh, ardent, emotional, aspiring, full of adventure; at maturity, brave, perceptive, under control, neither too talkative nor too reticent, neither flippant nor sombre; of the bodily figure, the movements easy, the complexion showing the best blood, somewhat flush'd, breast expanded, an erect attitude, a voice whose sound outvies music, eyes of calm and steady gaze, yet capable also of flashing—and a general presence that holds its own in the company of the highest. (For it is native personality, and that alone, that endows a man to stand before presidents or generals, or in any distinguish'd collection, with *aplomb*—and *not* culture, or any knowledge or intellect whatever.)

With regard to the mental-educational part of our model, enlargement of intellect, stores of cephalic knowledge, &c., the concentration thitherward of all the customs of our age, especially in America, is so overweening, and provides so fully for that part, that, important necessary as it is, it really needs nothing from us here—except, indeed, a phrase of warning and restraint. Manners, costumes, too, though important, we need not dwell upon here. Like beauty, grace of motion, &c., they are results. Causes, original things, being attended to, the right manners unerringly follow. Much is said, among artists, of "the grand style," as if it were a thing by itself. When a man, artist or whoever, has health, pride, acuteness, noble aspirations, he has the motive-elements of the grandest style. The rest is but manipulation, (yet that is no small matter.)

Leaving still unspecified several sterling parts of any model fit for the

1065–1068. The marks of parenthesis, not in *GAL*, were inserted in *DV*.
1068. After "whatever" *GAL* ends the sentence and paragraph with the following words: "as claimed of late by the leading American teacher of that theory."
1074. After "and restraint." *TR*, *DV*, and *GAL* begin a new paragraph.
1074. Manners, costumes, too,] *GAL:* Manners, too,
1077. The quotation marks were inserted in *SDC*.
1079. aspirations, he] *GAL:* aspirations and emotions, he
1080. After "small matter.)" *GAL* continues with four additional lines in this paragraph and a paragraph in parentheses. See Appendix, III, 1.

future personality of America, I must not fail, again and ever, to pronounce myself on one, probably the least attended to in modern times—a hiatus, indeed, threatening its gloomiest consequences after us. I mean the simple, unsophisticated Conscience, the primary moral element. If I were asked to specify in what quarter lie the grounds of darkest dread, respecting the America of our hopes, I should have to point to this particular. I should demand the invariable application to individuality, this day and any day, of that old, ever-true plumb-rule of persons, eras, nations. Our triumphant modern civilizee, with his all-schooling and his wondrous appliances, will still show himself but an amputation while this deficiency remains. Beyond, (assuming a more hopeful tone,) the vertebration of the manly and womanly personalism of our western world, can only be, and is, indeed, to be, (I hope,) its all penetrating Religiousness.

The ripeness of Religion is doubtless to be looked for in this field of individuality, and is a result that no organization or church can ever achieve. As history is poorly retain'd by what the technists call history, and is not given out from their pages, except the learner has in himself the sense of the well-wrapt, never yet written, perhaps impossible to be written, history—so Religion, although casually arrested, and, after a fashion, preserv'd in the churches and creeds, does not depend at all upon them, but is a part of the identified soul, which, when greatest, knows not bibles in the old way, but in new ways—the identified soul, which can really confront Religion when it extricates itself entirely from the churches, and not before.

Personalism fuses this, and favors it. I should say, indeed, that only in the perfect uncontamination and solitariness of individuality may the spirituality of religion positively come forth at all. Only here, and on such terms, the meditation, the devout ecstasy, the soaring flight. Only here,

1082. fail, again and ever, to] *GAL:* fail to
1085. element. If I] *GAL:* element. The subtle antiseptic called health is not more requisite to the bodily physiology, than Conscience is to the moral and mental physiology. It emanates the first and last splendor of character, and gives what all the beauty and genius of the world cannot make up for. If I
1090. Our . . . civilizee] *GAL:* Our current triumphant Civilizee
1092. After "deficiency remains." *DV* and *GAL* begin a new paragraph.
1092. Beyond, (assuming] *GAL:* Beyond (continuing, but assuming
1092–1095. This sentence, in the clipping, is covered with a strip of blue paper on which Whitman has written in black ink: "(four lines taken to go in proof)". Apparently he first omitted the lines and then restored them.
1094. is, indeed, to be] *GAL:* is to be
1095. After "Religiousness." *TR*, *DV*, and *GAL* add the following sentence to end the paragraph: "The architecture of Individuality will ever prove various, with countless different combinations; but here they rise as into common pinnacles, some

communion with the mysteries, the eternal problems, whence? whither? Alone, and identity, and the mood—and the soul emerges, and all statements, churches, sermons, melt away like vapors. Alone, and silent thought and awe, and aspiration—and then the interior consciousness, like a hitherto unseen inscription, in magic ink, beams out its wondrous lines to the sense. Bibles may convey, and priests expound, but it is exclusively for the noiseless operation of one's isolated Self, to enter the pure ether of veneration, reach the divine levels, and commune with the unutterable.

To practically enter into politics is an important part of American personalism. To every young man, north and south, earnestly studying these things, I should here, as an offset to what I have said in former pages, now also say, that may-be to views of very largest scope, after all, perhaps the political, (perhaps the literary and sociological,) America goes best about its development its own way—sometimes, to temporary sight, appaling enough. It is the fashion among dillettants and fops (perhaps I myself am not guiltless,) to decry the whole formulation of the active politics of America, as beyond redemption, and to be carefully kept away from. See you that you do not fall into this error. America, it may be, is doing very well upon the whole, notwithstanding these antics of the parties and their leaders, these half-brain'd nominees, the many ignorant ballots, and many elected failures and blatherers. It is the dillettants, and all who shirk their duty, who are not doing well. As for you, I advise you to enter more strongly yet into politics. I advise every young man to do so. Always inform yourself; always do the best you can; always vote. Disengage yourself from parties. They have been useful, and to some extent remain so; but the floating, uncommitted electors, farmers, clerks, mechanics, the masters of parties—watching aloof, inclining victory this side or that side—such are the ones most needed, present and future. For America, if eligible at all to downfall and ruin, is eligible within her-

higher, some less high, only all pointing upward."

1096–1097. The ripeness . . . result that] *TR* and *DV:* Indeed, the ripeness . . . result that] *GAL:* The final work of Religion is a work that

1098–1099. history, and] *GAL:* history (those bald fables in the libraries), and

1101. history—so] *GAL:* history; so

1112. identity] *GAL:* identily

1121–1124. I should . . . America goes best about] *GAL:* I should say, Understand that America goes about

1124–1125. temporary sight, appaling] *TR* and *DV:* temporary sight, appalling] *GAL:* temporary views, appalling

1125–1126. fops (perhaps I myself am not guiltless,) to decry] *TR*, *DV*, and *GAL:* fops to decry

1126. formulation of] *TR*, *DV*, and *GAL:* formulation and *personnel* of

1128. America, it may be, is] *GAL:* America is

1130. nominees, the] *TR*, *DV*, and *GAL:* nominees, and the

self, not without; for I see clearly that the combined foreign world could not beat her down. But these savage, wolfish parties alarm me. Owning no law but their own will, more and more combative, less and less tolerant of the idea of ensemble and of equal brotherhood, the perfect equality of the States, the ever-over-arching American ideas, it behooves you to convey yourself implicitly to no party, nor submit blindly to their dictators, but steadily hold yourself judge and master over all of them.

So much, (hastily toss'd together, and leaving far more unsaid,) for an ideal, or intimations of an ideal, toward American manhood. But the other sex, in our land, requires at least a basis of suggestion.

I have seen a young American woman, one of a large family of daughters, who, some years since, migrated from her meagre country home to one of the northern cities, to gain her own support. She soon became an expert seamstress, but finding the employment too confining for health and comfort, she went boldly to work for others, to house-keep, cook, clean, &c. After trying several places, she fell upon one where she was suited. She has told me that she finds nothing degrading in her position; it is not inconsistent with personal dignity, self-respect, and the respect of others. She confers benefits and receives them. She has good health; her presence itself is healthy and bracing; her character is unstain'd; she has made herself understood, and preserves her independence, and has been able to help her parents, and educate and get places for her sisters; and her course of life is not without opportunities for mental improvement, and of much quiet, uncosting happiness and love.

I have seen another woman who, from taste and necessity conjoin'd, has gone into practical affairs, carries on a mechanical business, partly works at it herself, dashes out more and more into real hardy life, is not abash'd by the coarseness of the contact, knows how to be firm and silent at the same time, holds her own with unvarying coolness and decorum, and will compare, any day, with superior carpenters, farmers, and even boatmen and drivers. For all that, she has not lost the charm of the womanly nature, but preserves and bears it fully, though through such rugged presentation.

Then there is the wife of a mechanic, mother of two children, a woman of merely passable English education, but of fine wit, with all her sex's grace and intuitions, who exhibits, indeed, such a noble female

1143–1144. brotherhood, . . . the ever-overarching] *GAL:* brotherhood, the ever-overarching
1145. party, . . . but] *GAL:* party, but
1149. land, . . . suggestion.] *GAL:* land, equally requires suggestion.
1153–1154. for health] *TR*, *DV*, and *GAL:* for her health
1178. house-tending—she] *TR*, *DV*, and *GAL:* house-tending, she
1187. My . . . described] *TR*, *DV*, and *GAL:* My mother has described

personality, that I am fain to record it here. Never abnegating her own proper independence, but always genially preserving it, and what belongs to it—cooking, washing, child-nursing, house-tending—she beams sunshine out of all these duties, and makes them illustrious. Physiologically sweet and sound, loving work, practical, she yet knows that there are intervals, however few, devoted to recreation, music, leisure, hospitality —and affords such intervals. Whatever she does, and wherever she is, that charm, that indescribable perfume of genuine womanhood attends her, goes with her, exhales from her, which belongs of right to all the sex, and is, or ought to be, the invariable atmosphere and common aureola of old as well as young.

My dear mother once described to me a resplendent person, down on Long Island, whom she knew in early days. She was known by the name of the Peacemaker. She was well toward eighty years old, of happy and sunny temperament, had always lived on a farm, and was very neighborly, sensible and discreet, an invariable and welcom'd favorite, especially with young married women. She had numerous children and grandchildren. She was uneducated, but possess'd a native dignity. She had come to be a tacitly agreed upon domestic regulator, judge, settler of difficulties, shepherdess, and reconciler in the land. She was a sight to draw near and look upon, with her large figure, her profuse snow-white hair, (uncoif'd by any head-dress or cap,) dark eyes, clear complexion, sweet breath, and peculiar personal magnetism.

The foregoing portraits, I admit, are frightfully out of line from these imported models of womanly personality—the stock feminine characters of the current novelists, or of the foreign court poems, (Ophelias, Enids, princesses, or ladies of one thing or another,) which fill the envying dreams of so many poor girls, and are accepted by our men, too, as supreme ideals of feminine excellence to be sought after. But I present mine just for a change.

Then there are mutterings, (we will not now stop to heed them here, but they must be heeded,) of something more revolutionary. The day is coming when the deep questions of woman's entrance amid the arenas of practical life, politics, the suffrage, &c., will not only be argued all around us, but may be put to decision, and real experiment.

Of course, in these States, for both man and woman, we must entirely

1188. knew in] *TR*, *DV*, and *GAL:* knew years ago, in
1196–1197. hair, . . . dark] *TR*, *DV*, and *GAL:* hair, dark
1201–1202. poems, . . . princesses] *GAL:* poems (Enids, Guiniveres, Princesses
1203. our men] *TR*, *DV*, and *GAL:* our young men
1208. woman's entrance] *GAL:* woman's full entrance
1209. politics, . . . will] *TR* and *DV:* politics, trades, &c., will] *GAL:* politics, trades, teaching, etc., will

recast the types of highest personality from what the oriental, feudal, ecclesiastical worlds bequeath us, and which yet possess the imaginative and esthetic fields of the United States, pictorial and melodramatic, not without use as studies, but making sad work, and forming a strange anachronism upon the scenes and exigencies around us. Of course, the old undying elements remain. The task is, to successfully adjust them to new combinations, our own days. Nor is this so incredible. I can conceive a community, to-day and here, in which, on a sufficient scale, the perfect personalities, without noise meet; say in some pleasant western settlement or town, where a couple of hundred best men and women, of ordinary worldly status, have by luck been drawn together, with nothing extra of genius or wealth, but virtuous, chaste, industrious, cheerful, resolute, friendly and devout. I can conceive such a community organized in running order, powers judiciously delegated—farming, building, trade, courts, mails, schools, elections, all attended to; and then the rest of life, the main thing, freely branching and blossoming in each individual, and bearing golden fruit. I can see there, in every young and old man, after his kind, and in every woman after hers, a true personality, develop'd, exercised proportionately in body, mind, and spirit. I can imagine this case as one not necessarily rare or difficult, but in buoyant accordance with the municipal and general requirements of our times. And I can realize in it the culmination of something better than any stereotyped *eclat* of history or poems. Perhaps, unsung, undramatized, unput in essays or biographies—perhaps even some such community already exists, in Ohio, Illinois, Missouri, or somewhere, practically fulfilling itself, and thus outvying, in cheapest vulgar life, all that has been hitherto shown in best ideal pictures.

In short, and to sum up, America, betaking herself to formative action, (as it is about time for more solid achievement, and less windy promise,) must, for her purposes, cease to recognize a theory of character grown of feudal aristocracies, or form'd by merely literary standards, or from any ultramarine, full-dress formulas of culture, polish, caste, &c., and must sternly promulgate her own new standard, yet old enough, and accepting

1212–1213. the oriental . . . possess the] *TR* and *DV:* the Oriental, . . . fully possess the] *GAL:* the Feudal world bequeaths us, and which yet fully possesses the
1216. After "around us." *TR*, *DV*, and *GAL* begin a new paragraph.
1225. delegated—farming] *TR*, *DV*, and *GAL:* delegated, farming
1236–1237. all that . . . pictures.] *GAL:* all the rich pages of old-world Plutarch and Shakespeare, or our own Emerson.
1240–1241. character . . . form'd] *GAL:* character formed
1250. And now, for] *GAL:* And before we close, for
1251. with, even] *GAL:* with, Mentality, Education, and even
1252. venerable shade!] *GAL:* venerable shades!

the old, the perennial elements, and combining them into groups, unities, appropriate to the modern, the democratic, the west, and to the practical occasions and needs of our own cities, and of the agricultural regions. Ever the most precious in the common. Ever the fresh breeze of field, or hill, or lake, is more than any palpitation of fans, though of ivory, and redolent with perfume; and the air is more than the costliest perfumes.

And now, for fear of mistake, we may not intermit to beg our absolution from all that genuinely is, or goes along with, even Culture. Pardon us, venerable shade! if we have seem'd to speak lightly of your office. The whole civilization of the earth, we know, is yours, with all the glory and the light thereof. It is, indeed, in your own spirit, and seeking to tally the loftiest teachings of it, that we aim these poor utterances. For you, too, mighty minister! know that there is something greater than you, namely, the fresh, eternal qualities of Being. From them, and by them, as you, at your best, we too evoke the last, the needed help, to vitalize our country and our days. Thus we pronounce not so much against the principle of culture; we only supervise it, and promulge along with it, as deep, perhaps a deeper, principle. As we have shown the New World including in itself the all-leveling aggregate of democracy, we show it also including the all-varied, all-permitting, all-free theorem of individuality, and erecting therefor a lofty and hitherto unoccupied framework or platform, broad enough for all, eligible to every farmer and mechanic—to the female equally with the male—a towering selfhood, not physically perfect only—not satisfied with the mere mind's and learning's stores, but religious, possessing the idea of the infinite, (rudder and compass sure amid this troublous voyage, o'er darkest, wildest wave, through stormiest wind, of man's or nation's progress)—realizing, above the rest, that known humanity, in deepest sense, is fair adhesion to itself, for purposes beyond—and that, finally, the personality of mortal life is most important with reference to the immortal, the unknown, the spiritual, the only permanently real, which as the ocean waits for and receives the rivers, waits for us each and all.

1254–1255. spirit, . . . tally the] *GAL:* spirit, and tallying the
1256. mighty minister!] *GAL:* mighty ministers!
1258. we too evoke] *TR*, *DV*, and *GAL:* we, too, after our fashion, when art and conventions fail, evoke
1259. After "our days." *TR*, *DV*, and *GAL* begin a new paragraph.
1259. Thus we] *GAL:* Thus, after all, we
1260. promulge . . . as] *DVOP:* promulgate . . . with it, as] *GAL:* promulge as
1262. itself the all-leveling] *GAL:* itself, and indeed, founded upon, the all-levelling
1264. platform, broad] *GAL:* platform of Personalism, broad
1272. finally, the personality] *GAL:* finally, the theme, great as it is, of the personality

Much is there, yet, demanding line and outline in our Vistas, not only on these topics, but others quite unwritten. Indeed, we could talk the matter, and expand it, through lifetime. But it is necessary to return to our original premises. In view of them, we have again pointedly to confess that all the objective grandeurs of the world, for highest purposes, yield themselves up, and depend on mentality alone. Here, and here only, all balances, all rests. For the mind, which alone builds the permanent edifice, haughtily builds it to itself. By it, with what follows it, are convey'd to mortal sense the culminations of the materialistic, the known, and a prophecy of the unknown. To take expression, to incarnate, to endow a literature with grand and archetypal models—to fill with pride and love the utmost capacity, and to achieve spiritual meanings, and suggest the future—these, and these only, satisfy the soul. We must not say one word against real materials; but the wise know that they do not become real till touched by emotions, the mind. Did we call the latter imponderable? Ah, let us rather proclaim that the slightest song-tune, the countless ephemera of passions arous'd by orators and tale-tellers, are more dense, more weighty than the engines there in the great factories, or the granite blocks in their foundations.

Approaching thus the momentous spaces, and considering with reference to a new and greater personalism, the needs and possibilities of American imaginative literature, through the medium-light of what we have already broach'd, it will at once be appreciated that a vast gulf of difference separates the present accepted condition of these spaces, inclusive of what is floating in them, from any condition adjusted to, or fit for, the world, the America, there sought to be indicated, and the copious races of complete men and women, along these Vistas crudely outlined. It is, in some sort, no less a difference than lies between that long-continued nebular state and vagueness of the astronomical worlds, compared with the subsequent state, the definitely-form'd worlds themselves, duly compacted, clustering in systems, hung up there, chandeliers of the universe, beholding and mutually lit by each other's lights, serving for ground of all substantial foothold, all vulgar uses—yet serving still more as an undying chain and echelon of spiritual proofs and shows. A boundless field to fill! A new creation, with needed orbic works launch'd forth, to revolve in free and lawful circuits—to move, self-poised, through the ether, and shine like heaven's own suns! With such, and nothing less, we suggest that

1276–2007. These lines, completing the work, were first printed in *DV* from original MSS. The printer's copy of *DV* is not available and may not have survived; a fragmentary early draft of this portion of *DV* is in the Feinberg Collection, but is not here collated.

New World literature, fit to rise upon, cohere, and signalize in time, these States.

What, however, do we more definitely mean by New World literature? Are we not doing well enough here already? Are not the United States this day busily using, working, more printer's type, more presses, than any other country? uttering and absorbing more publications than any other? Do not our publishers fatten quicker and deeper? (helping themselves, under shelter of a delusive and sneaking law, or rather absence of law, to most of their forage, poetical, pictorial, historical, romantic, even comic, without money and without price—and fiercely resisting the timidest proposal to pay for it.) Many will come under this delusion—but my purpose is to dispel it. I say that a nation may hold and circulate rivers and oceans of very readable print, journals, magazines, novels, library-books, "poetry," &c.—such as the States to-day possess and circulate—of unquestionable aid and value—hundreds of new volumes annually composed and brought out here, respectable enough, indeed unsurpass'd in smartness and erudition—with further hundreds, or rather millions, (as by free forage or theft aforemention'd,) also thrown into the market—and yet, all the while, the said nation, land, strictly speaking, may possess no literature at all.

Repeating our inquiry, what, then, do we mean by real literature? especially the democratic literature of the future? Hard questions to meet. The clues are inferential, and turn us to the past. At best, we can only offer suggestions, comparisons, circuits.

It must still be reiterated, as, for the purpose of these memoranda, the deep lesson of history and time, that all else in the contributions of a nation or age, through its politics, materials, heroic personalities, military eclat, &c., remains crude, and defers, in any close and thorough-going estimate, until vitalized by national, original archetypes in literature. They only put the nation in form, finally tell anything—prove, complete anything—perpetuate anything. Without doubt, some of the richest and most powerful and populous communities of the antique world, and some of the grandest personalities and events, have, to after and present times, left themselves entirely unbequeath'd. Doubtless, greater than any that have come down to us, were among those lands, heroisms, persons, that have not come down to us at all, even by name, date, or location. Others have arrived safely, as from voyages over wide, century-stretching seas. The

1302. women, along] *TR* and *DV:* women, down along
1302. After "crudely outlined." *TR* and *DV* begin a new paragraph.
1323. After "pay for it.)" *TR* and *DV* begin a new paragraph.
1330–1331. market—and] *TR* and *DV:* market,—And
1334. especially . . . literature] *TR* and *DV:* especially, the American literature

little ships, the miracles that have buoy'd them, and by incredible chances safely convey'd them, (or the best of them, their meaning and essence,) over long wastes, darkness, lethargy, ignorance, &c., have been a few inscriptions—a few immortal compositions, small in size, yet compassing what measureless values of reminiscence, contemporary portraitures, manners, idioms and beliefs, with deepest inference, hint and thought, to tie and touch forever the old, new body, and the old, new soul! These! and still these! bearing the freight so dear—dearer than pride—dearer than love. All the best experience of humanity, folded, saved, freighted to us here. Some of these tiny ships we call Old and New Testament, Homer, Eschylus, Plato, Juvenal, &c. Precious minims! I think, if we were forced to choose, rather than have you, and the likes of you, and what belongs to, and has grown of you, blotted out and gone, we could better afford, appaling as that would be, to lose all actual ships, this day fasten'd by wharf, or floating on wave, and see them, with all their cargoes, scuttled and sent to the bottom.

Gather'd by geniuses of city, race or age, and put by them in highest of art's forms, namely, the literary form, the peculiar combinations and the outshows of that city, age, or race, its particular modes of the universal attributes and passions, its faiths, heroes, lovers and gods, wars, traditions, struggles, crimes, emotions, joys, (or the subtle spirit of these,) having been pass'd on to us to illumine our own selfhood, and its experiences—what they supply, indispensable and highest, if taken away, nothing else in all the world's boundless storehouses could make up to us, or ever again return.

For us, along the great highways of time, those monuments stand—those forms of majesty and beauty. For us those beacons burn through all the nights. Unknown Egyptians, graving hieroglyphs; Hindus, with hymn and apothegm and endless epic; Hebrew prophet, with spirituality, as in flashes of lightning, conscience like red-hot iron, plaintive songs and screams of vengeance for tyrannies and enslavement; Christ, with bent head, brooding love and peace, like a dove; Greek, creating eternal shapes of physical and esthetic proportion; Roman, lord of satire, the sword, and the codex;—of the figures, some far off and veil'd, others nearer and visible; Dante, stalking with lean form, nothing but fibre, not a grain of superfluous flesh; Angelo, and the great painters, architects, musicians;

1360. if we were forced] *TR* and *DV:* if we were forced] *SDC* and later texts: if were forced] [The omission of the pronoun "we" in *SDC* was obviously a typographical error; hence the earlier reading is restored.—ED.]
1362–1363. appaling] *TR* and *DV:* appalling

rich Shakspere, luxuriant as the sun, artist and singer of feudalism in its sunset, with all the gorgeous colors, owner thereof, and using them at will; and so to such as German Kant and Hegel, where they, though near us, leaping over the ages, sit again, impassive, imperturbable, like the Egyptian gods. Of these, and the like of these, is it too much, indeed, to return to our favorite figure, and view them as orbs and systems of orbs, moving in free paths in the spaces of that other heaven, the kosmic intellect, the soul?

Ye powerful and resplendent ones! ye were, in your atmospheres, grown not for America, but rather for her foes, the feudal and the old—while our genius is democratic and modern. Yet could ye, indeed, but breathe your breath of life into our New World's nostrils—not to enslave us, as now, but, for our needs, to breed a spirit like your own—perhaps, (dare we to say it?) to dominate, even destroy, what you yourselves have left! On your plane, and no less, but even higher and wider, must we mete and measure for to-day and here. I demand races of orbic bards, with unconditional uncompromising sway. Come forth, sweet democratic despots of the west!

By points like these we, in reflection, token what we mean by any land's or people's genuine literature. And thus compared and tested, judging amid the influence of loftiest products only, what do our current copious fields of print, covering in manifold forms, the United States, better, for an analogy, present, than, as in certain regions of the sea, those spreading, undulating masses of squid, through which the whale swimming, with head half out, feeds?

Not but that doubtless our current so-called literature, (like an endless supply of small coin,) performs a certain service, and may-be, too, the service needed for the time, (the preparation-service, as children learn to spell.) Everybody reads, and truly nearly everybody writes, either books, or for the magazines or journals. The matter has magnitude, too, after a sort. But is it really advancing? or, has it advanced for a long while? There is something impressive about the huge editions of the dailies and weeklies, the mountain-stacks of white paper piled in the press-vaults, and the proud, crashing, ten-cylinder presses, which I can stand and watch any time by the half hour. Then, (though the States in the field of imagination present not a single first-class work, not a single great lite-

1386. Shakspere] *TR* and *DV:* Shakespeare
1400–1401. wider, . . . to-day] *TR* and *DV:* wider, will I mete and measure for our wants to-day
1404. points like] *TR* and *V:* points and specimens like
1416. The sentence beginning "But is", not in *TR* and *DV*, is inserted in MS for *SDC*.

ratus,) the main objects, to amuse, to titillate, to pass away time, to circulate the news, and rumors of news, to rhyme and read rhyme, are yet attain'd, and on a scale of infinity. To-day, in books, in the rivalry of writers, especially novelists, success, (so-call'd,) is for him or her who strikes the mean flat average, the sensational appetite for stimulus, incident, persiflage, &c., and depicts, to the common calibre, sensual, exterior life. To such, or the luckiest of them, as we see, the audiences are limitless and profitable; but they cease presently. While this day, or any day, to workmen portraying interior or spiritual life, the audiences were limited, and often laggard—but they last forever.

Compared with the past, our modern science soars, and our journals serve—but ideal and even ordinary romantic literature, does not, I think, substantially advance. Behold the prolific brood of the contemporary novel, magazine-tale, theatre-play, &c. The same endless thread of tangled and superlative love-story, inherited, apparently from the Amadises and Palmerins of the 13th, 14th, and 15th centuries over there in Europe. The costumes and associations brought down to date, the seasoning hotter and more varied, the dragons and ogres left out—but the *thing*, I should say, has not advanced—is just as sensational, just as strain'd—remains about the same, nor more, nor less.

What is the reason our time, our lands, that we see no fresh local courage, sanity, of our own—the Mississippi, stalwart Western men, real mental and physical facts, Southerners, &c., in the body of our literature? especially the poetic part of it. But always, instead, a parcel of dandies and ennuyees, dapper little gentlemen from abroad, who flood us with their thin sentiment of parlors, parasols, piano-songs, tinkling rhymes, the five-hundredth importation—or whimpering and crying about something, chasing one aborted conceit after another, and forever occupied in dyspeptic amours with dyspeptic women. While, current and novel, the grandest events and revolutions, and stormiest passions of history, are crossing to-day with unparallel'd rapidity and magnificence over the stages of our own and all the continents, offering new materials, opening new vistas, with largest needs, inviting the daring launching forth of conceptions in literature, inspired by them, soaring in highest regions, serving art in its highest, (which is only the other name for serving God, and serving humanity,) where is the man of letters, where is the book, with any

1426–1427. incident, persiflage, &c.] *TR* and *DV:* incident, &c.
1433. serve—but] *TR* and *DV:* serve; but
1438. associations brought] *TR* and *DV:* associations are brought
1439. seasoning hotter] *TR* and *DV:* seasoning is hotter
1439. ogres left] *TR* and *DV:* ogres are left

nobler aim than to follow in the old track, repeat what has been said before—and, as its utmost triumph, sell well, and be erudite or elegant?

Mark the roads, the processes, through which these States have arrived, standing easy, henceforth ever-equal, ever-compact, in their range to-day. European adventures? the most antique? Asiatic or African? old history—miracles—romances? Rather, our own unquestion'd facts. They hasten, incredible, blazing bright as fire. From the deeds and days of Columbus down to the present, and including the present—and especially the late Secession war—when I con them, I feel, every leaf, like stopping to see if I have not made a mistake, and fall'n on the splendid figments of some dream. But it is no dream. We stand, live, move, in the huge flow of our age's materialism—in its spirituality. We have had founded for us the most positive of lands. The founders have pass'd to other spheres—but what are these terrible duties they have left us?

Their politics the United States have, in my opinion, with all their faults, already substantially establish'd, for good, on their own native, sound, long-vista'd principles, never to be overturn'd, offering a sure basis for all the rest. With that, their future religious forms, sociology, literature, teachers, schools, costumes, &c., are of course to make a compact whole, uniform, on tallying principles. For how can we remain, divided, contradicting ourselves, this way?* I say we can only attain harmony and stability by consulting ensemble and the ethic purports, and faithfully building upon them. For the New World, indeed, after two grand stages of preparation-strata, I perceive that now a third stage, being ready for, (and without which the other two were useless,) with unmistakable signs appears. The First stage was the planning and putting on record the political foundation rights of immense masses of people—indeed all people—in the organization of republican National, State, and

* Note, to-day, an instructive, curious spectacle and conflict. Science, (twin, in its fields, of Democracy in its)—Science, testing absolutely all thoughts, all works, has already burst well upon the world—a sun, mounting, most illuminating, most glorious—surely never again to set. But against it, deeply entrench'd, holding possession, yet remains, (not only through the churches and schools, but by imaginative literature, and unregenerate poetry,) the fossil theology of the mythic-materialistic, superstitious, untaught and credulous, fable-loving, primitive ages of humanity.

1450. After "dyspeptic women." *TR* and *DV* begin a new paragraph.
1461. easy, henceforth ever-equal] *TR* and *DV:* easy, ever-equal
1467. on] *TR* and *DV:* upon
1468. After "some dream." *TR* and *DV* begin a new paragraph.
1470. spheres—but] *TR* and *DV:* spheres—But
1480. After "upon them." *TR* and *DV* begin a new paragraph.

municipal governments, all constructed with reference to each, and each to all. This is the American programme, not for classes, but for universal man, and is embodied in the compacts of the Declaration of Independence, and, as it began and has now grown, with its amendments, the Federal Constitution—and in the State governments, with all their interiors, and with general suffrage; those having the sense not only of what is in themselves, but that their certain several things started, planted, hundreds of others in the same direction duly arise and follow. The Second stage relates to material prosperity, wealth, produce, labor-saving machines, iron, cotton, local, State and continental railways, intercommunication and trade with all lands, steamships, mining, general employment, organization of great cities, cheap appliances for comfort, numberless technical schools, books, newspapers, a currency for money circulation, &c. The Third stage, rising out of the previous ones, to make them and all illustrious, I, now, for one, promulge, announcing a native expression-spirit, getting into form, adult, and through mentality, for these States, self-contain'd, different from others, more expansive, more rich and free, to be evidenced by original authors and poets to come, by American personalities, plenty of them, male and female, traversing the States, none excepted—and by native superber tableaux and growths of language, songs, operas, orations, lectures, architecture—and by a sublime and serious Religious Democracy sternly taking command, dissolving the old, sloughing off surfaces, and from its own interior and vital principles, reconstructing, democratizing society.

For America, type of progress, and of essential faith in man, above all his errors and wickedness—few suspect how deep, how deep it really strikes. The world evidently supposes, and we have evidently supposed so too, that the States are merely to achieve the equal franchise, an elective government—to inaugurate the respectability of labor, and become a nation of practical operatives, law-abiding, orderly and well off. Yes, those are indeed parts of the task of America; but they not only do not exhaust the progressive conception, but rather arise, teeming with it, as the mediums of deeper, higher progress. Daughter of a physical revolution—mother of the true revolutions, which are of the interior life, and of the arts. For so long as the spirit is not changed, any change of appearance is of no avail.

The old men, I remember as a boy, were always talking of American independence. What is independence? Freedom from all laws or bonds except those of one's own being, control'd by the universal ones. To lands,

1509. reconstructing, democratizing society.] *TR* and *DV:* reconstructing Society.

to man, to woman, what is there at last to each, but the inherent soul, nativity, idiocrasy, free, highest-poised, soaring its own flight, following out itself?

At present, these States, in their theology and social standards, (of greater importance than their political institutions,) are entirely held possession of by foreign lands. We see the sons and daughters of the New World, ignorant of its genius, not yet inaugurating the native, the universal, and the near, still importing the distant, the partial, and the dead. We see London, Paris, Italy—not original, superb, as where they belong—but second-hand here, where they do not belong. We see the shreds of Hebrews, Romans, Greeks; but where, on her own soil, do we see, in any faithful, highest, proud expression, America herself? I sometimes question whether she has a corner in her own house.

Not but that in one sense, and a very grand one, good theology, good art, or good literature, has certain features shared in common. The combination fraternizes, ties the races—is, in many particulars, under laws applicable indifferently to all, irrespective of climate or date, and, from whatever source, appeals to emotions, pride, love, spirituality, common to humankind. Nevertheless, they touch a man closest, (perhaps only actually touch him,) even in these, in their expression through autochthonic lights and shades, flavors, fondnesses, aversions, specific incidents, illustrations, out of his own nationality, geography, surroundings, antecedents, &c. The spirit and the form are one, and depend far more on association, identity and place, than is supposed. Subtly interwoven with the materiality and personality of a land, a race—Teuton, Turk, Californian, or what not—there is always something—I can hardly tell what it is—history but describes the results of it—it is the same as the untellable look of some human faces. Nature, too, in her stolid forms, is full of it—but to most it is there a secret. This something is rooted in the invisible roots, the profoundest meanings of that place, race, or nationality; and to absorb and again effuse it, uttering words and products as from its midst, and carrying it into highest regions, is the work, or a main part of the work, of any country's true author, poet, historian, lecturer, and perhaps even priest and philosoph. Here, and here only, are the foundations for our really valuable and permanent verse, drama, &c.

But at present, (judged by any higher scale than that which finds the chief ends of existence to be to feverishly make money during one-half of it, and by some "amusement," or perhaps foreign travel, flippantly kill time, the other half,) and consider'd with reference to purposes of patriotism, health, a noble personality, religion, and the democratic adjustments, all these swarms of poems, literary magazines, dramatic plays, resultant so far from American intellect, and the formation of our best ideas, are useless and a mockery. They strengthen and nourish no one, express nothing characteristic, give decision and purpose to no one, and suffice only the lowest level of vacant minds.

Of what is called the drama, or dramatic presentation in the United States, as now put forth at the theatres, I should say it deserves to be treated with the same gravity, and on a par with the questions of ornamental confectionery at public dinners, or the arrangement of curtains and hangings in a ball-room—nor more, nor less. Of the other, I will not insult the reader's intelligence, (once really entering into the atmosphere of these Vistas,) by supposing it necessary to show, in detail, why the copious dribble, either of our little or well-known rhymesters, does not fulfil, in any respect, the needs and august occasions of this land. America demands a poetry that is bold, modern, and all-surrounding and kosmical, as she is herself. It must in no respect ignore science or the modern, but inspire itself with science and the modern. It must bend its vision toward the future, more than the past. Like America, it must extricate itself from even the greatest models of the past, and, while courteous to them, must have entire faith in itself, and the products of its own democratic spirit only. Like her, it must place in the van, and hold up at all hazards, the banner of the divine pride of man in himself, (the radical foundation of the new religion.) Long enough have the People been listening to poems in which common humanity, deferential, bends low, humiliated, acknowledging superiors. But America listens to no such poems. Erect, inflated, and fully self-esteeming be the chant; and then America will listen with pleased ears.

Nor may the genuine gold, the gems, when brought to light at last, be probably usher'd forth from any of the quarters currently counted on. To-day, doubtless, the infant genius of American poetic expression, (eluding those highly-refined imported and gilt-edged themes, and sentimental and butterfly flights, pleasant to orthodox publishers—causing tender spasms in the coteries, and warranted not to chafe the sensitive cuticle of the most exquisitely artificial gossamer delicacy,) lies sleeping far away, happily unrecognized and uninjur'd by the coteries, the art-writers, the talkers and critics of the saloons, or the lecturers in the colleges—lies sleeping, aside, unrecking itself, in some western idiom, or

1570. Of what] *TR* and *DV:* Of the question, indeed, of what
1574. After "nor less." *TR* and *DV* begin a new paragraph.
1584. and the products] *TR* and *DV:* and products
1584. own democratic spirit] *TR* and *DV:* own original spirit
1596. to orthodox publishers] *TR* and *DV:* to New York, Boston, and Philadelphia publishers

native Michigan or Tennessee repartee, or stump-speech—or in Kentucky or Georgia, or the Carolinas—or in some slang or local song or allusion of the Manhattan, Boston, Philadelphia or Baltimore mechanic—or up in the Maine woods—or off in the hut of the California miner, or crossing the Rocky mountains, or along the Pacific railroad—or on the breasts of the young farmers of the northwest, or Canada, or boatmen of the lakes. Rude and coarse nursing-beds, these; but only from such beginnings and stocks, indigenous here, may haply arrive, be grafted, and sprout, in time, flowers of genuine American aroma, and fruits truly and fully our own.

I say it were a standing disgrace to these States—I say it were a disgrace to any nation, distinguish'd above others by the variety and vastness of its territories, its materials, its inventive activity, and the splendid practicality of its people, not to rise and soar above others also in its original styles in literature and art, and its own supply of intellectual and esthetic masterpieces, archetypal, and consistent with itself. I know not a land except ours that has not, to some extent, however small, made its title clear. The Scotch have their born ballads, subtly expressing their past and present, and expressing character. The Irish have theirs. England, Italy, France, Spain, theirs. What has America? With exhaustless mines of the richest ore of epic, lyric, tale, tune, picture, &c., in the Four Years' War; with, indeed, I sometimes think, the richest masses of material ever afforded a nation, more variegated, and on a larger scale—the first sign of proportionate, native, imaginative Soul, and first-class works to match, is, (I cannot too often repeat,) so far wanting.

Long ere the second centennial arrives, there will be some forty to fifty great States, among them Canada and Cuba. When the present century closes, our population will be sixty or seventy millions. The Pacific will be ours, and the Atlantic mainly ours. There will be daily electric communication with every part of the globe. What an age! What a land! Where, elsewhere, one so great? The individuality of one nation must then, as always, lead the world. Can there be any doubt who the leader ought to be? Bear in mind, though, that nothing less than the mightiest original non-subordinated SOUL has ever really, gloriously led, or ever can lead. (This Soul—its other name, in these Vistas, is LITERATURE.)

In fond fancy leaping those hundred years ahead, let us survey America's works, poems, philosophies, fulfilling prophecies, and giving

1626. Long ere the second centennial arrives] *TR* (regular edition): Long ere the Second Centennial arrives] *TR* (Centennial Edition) and *DV:* When the hundredth year of this Union arrives

1627–1628. Cuba. When the present century closes, our population] *TR* (both regular and Centennial) and *DV:* Cuba. The population] [Change made in MS for *SDC*]

form and decision to best ideals. Much that is now undream'd of, we might then perhaps see establish'd, luxuriantly cropping forth, richness, vigor of letters and of artistic expression, in whose products character will be a main requirement, and not merely erudition or elegance.

Intense and loving comradeship, the personal and passionate attachment of man to man—which, hard to define, underlies the lessons and ideals of the profound saviours of every land and age, and which seems to promise, when thoroughly develop'd, cultivated and recognized in manners and literature, the most substantial hope and safety of the future of these States, will then be fully express'd.*

A strong-fibred joyousness and faith, and the sense of health *al fresco*, may well enter into the preparation of future noble American authorship. Part of the test of a great literatus shall be the absence in him of the idea of the covert, the lurid, the maleficent, the devil, the grim estimates inherited from the Puritans, hell, natural depravity, and the like. The great literatus will be known, among the rest, by his cheerful simplicity, his adherence to natural standards, his limitless faith in God, his reverence, and by the absence in him of doubt, ennui, burlesque, persiflage, or any strain'd and temporary fashion.

Nor must I fail, again and yet again, to clinch, reiterate more plainly still, (O that indeed such survey as we fancy, may show in time this part completed also!) the lofty aim, surely the proudest and the purest, in whose service the future literatus, of whatever field, may gladly labor. As we have intimated, offsetting the material civilization of our race, our nationality, its wealth, territories, factories, population, products, trade,

* It is to the development, identification, and general prevalence of that fervid comradeship, (the adhesive love, at least rivaling the amative love hitherto possessing imaginative literature, if not going beyond it,) that I look for the counterbalance and offset of our materialistic and vulgar American democracy, and for the spiritualization thereof. Many will say it is a dream, and will not follow my inferences: but I confidently expect a time when there will be seen, running like a half-hid warp through all the myriad audible and visible worldly interests of America, threads of manly friendship, fond and loving, pure and sweet, strong and life-long, carried to degrees hitherto un-

1651. covert, the lurid] *TR* and *DV:* covert, the artificial, the lurid
1662. population, products] *TR* and *DV:* population, luxuries, products
1665. literature. The] *TR* and *DV:* literature. And still within this wheel, revolves another wheel. The
1666. of civilization, rising] *TR* and *DV:* of modern civilization, giving finish and hue, and rising
1669. Justice. Even] *TR* and *DV:* Justice. I say there is nothing
1671–1672. enchants forever] *TR* and *DV:* enchants me forever
1680. After "thing of all." and before "Its analogy", *TR* and *DV* begin a new para-

and military and naval strength, and breathing breath of life into all these, and more, must be its moral civilization—the formulation, expression, and aidancy whereof, is the very highest height of literature. The climax of this loftiest range of civilization, rising above all the gorgeous shows and results of wealth, intellect, power, and art, as such—above even theology and religious fervor—is to be its development, from the eternal bases, and the fit expression, of absolute Conscience, moral soundness, Justice. Even in religious fervor there is a touch of animal heat. But moral conscientiousness, crystalline, without flaw, not Godlike only, entirely human, awes and enchants forever. Great is emotional love, even in the order of the rational universe. But, if we must make gradations, I am clear there is something greater. Power, love, veneration, products, genius, esthetics, tried by subtlest comparisons, analyses, and in serenest moods, somewhere fail, somehow become vain. Then noiseless, with flowing steps, the lord, the sun, the last ideal comes. By the names right, justice, truth, we suggest, but do not describe it. To the world of men it remains a dream, an idea as they call it. But no dream is it to the wise—but the proudest, almost only solid lasting thing of all. Its analogy in the material universe is what holds together this world, and every object upon it, and carries its dynamics on forever sure and safe. Its lack, and the persistent shirking of it, as in life, sociology, literature, politics, business, and even sermonizing, these times, or any times, still leaves the abysm, the mortal flaw and smutch, mocking civilization to-day, with all its unquestion'd triumphs, and all the civilization so far known.*

Present literature, while magnificently fulfilling certain popular de-

known—not only giving tone to individual character, and making it unprecedently emotional, muscular, heroic, and refined, but having the deepest relations to general politics. I say democracy infers such loving comradeship, as its most inevitable twin or counterpart, without which it will be incomplete, in vain, and incapable of perpetuating itself.

* I am reminded as I write that out of this very conscience, or idea of conscience, of intense moral right, and in its name and strain'd construction, the

graph with the following sentence, omitted in *SDC* and later texts: "I say, again and forever, the triumph of America's democratic formules is to be the inauguration, growth, acceptance, and unmistakable supremacy among individuals, cities, States, and the Nation, of moral Conscience."

1686. After "so far known." *TR* and *DV* have the following sentence, omitted in *SDC*, to end the paragraph: "Such is the thought I would especially bequeath to any earnest persons, students of these Vistas, and following after me."

1689. morbid. It needs tally] *TR* and *DV:* morbid. It needs retain the knowledge, and fulfil the demands, but needs to purge itself; or rather needs to be born again, become unsophisticated, and become sane. It needs tally

mands, with plenteous knowledge and verbal smartness, is profoundly sophisticated, insane, and its very joy is morbid. It needs tally and express Nature, and the spirit of Nature, and to know and obey the standards. I say the question of Nature, largely consider'd, involves the questions of the esthetic, the emotional, and the religious—and involves happiness. A fitly born and bred race, growing up in right conditions of out-door as much as in-door harmony, activity and development, would probably, from and in those conditions, find it enough merely *to live*—and would, in their relations to the sky, air, water, trees, &c., and to the countless common shows, and in the fact of life itself, discover and achieve happiness—with Being suffused night and day by wholesome extasy, surpassing all the pleasures that wealth, amusement, and even gratified intellect, erudition, or the sense of art, can give.

In the prophetic literature of these States (the reader of my speculations will miss their principal stress unless he allows well for the point that a new Literature, perhaps a new Metaphysics, certainly a new Poetry, are to be, in my opinion, the only sure and worthy supports and expressions of the American Democracy,) Nature, true Nature, and the true idea of Nature, long absent, must, above all, become fully restored, enlarged, and must furnish the pervading atmosphere to poems, and the test of all high literary and esthetic compositions. I do not mean the

worst fanaticisms, wars, persecutions, murders, &c., have yet, in all lands, in the past, been broach'd, and have come to their devilish fruition. Much is to be said—but I may say here, and in response, that side by side with the unflagging stimulation of the elements of religion and conscience must henceforth move with equal sway, science, absolute reason, and the general proportionate development of the whole man. These scientific facts, deductions, are divine too—precious counted parts of moral civilization, and, with physical health, indispensable to it, to prevent fanaticism. For abstract religion, I perceive, is easily led astray, ever credulous, and is capable of devouring, remorseless, like fire and flame. Conscience, too, isolated from all else, and from the emotional nature, may but attain the beauty and purity of glacial, snowy ice. We want, for these States, for the general character, a cheerful, religious fervor, endued with the ever-present modifications of the human emotions, friendship, benevolence, with a fair field for scientific inquiry, the right of individual judgment, and always the cooling influences of material Nature.

147*n.*–148*n.* lands, in the past, been] *TR* and *DV:* lands, been
159*n.* endued] *TR* and *DV:* enhued
161*n.* After "material Nature." *TR* and *DV* have the following sentence, omitted

1701–1705. The statement in parentheses does not appear in *TR* and *DV*. It was inserted in black ink on a white strip pasted in MS for *SDC*.
1709. hedges, poseys] *TR* and *DV:* hedges, butterflies, poseys

smooth walks, trimm'd hedges, poseys and nightingales of the English poets, but the whole orb, with its geologic history, the kosmos, carrying fire and snow, that rolls through the illimitable areas, light as a feather, though weighing billions of tons. Furthermore, as by what we now partially call Nature is intended, at most, only what is entertainable by the physical conscience, the sense of matter, and of good animal health—on these it must be distinctly accumulated, incorporated, that man, comprehending these, has, in towering superaddition, the moral and spiritual consciences, indicating his destination beyond the ostensible, the mortal.

To the heights of such estimate of Nature indeed ascending, we proceed to make observations for our Vistas, breathing rarest air. What is I believe called Idealism seems to me to suggest, (guarding against extravagance, and ever modified even by its opposite,) the course of inquiry and desert of favor for our New World metaphysics, their foundation of and in literature, giving hue to all.*

The elevating and etherealizing ideas of the unknown and of unreality must be brought forward with authority, as they are the legitimate heirs of the known, and of reality, and at least as great as their parents. Fearless of scoffing, and of the ostent, let us take our stand, our ground, and never desert it, to confront the growing excess and arrogance of realism. To the cry, now victorious—the cry of sense, science, flesh, incomes, farms, mer-

* The culmination and fruit of literary artistic expression, and its final fields of pleasure for the human soul, are in metaphysics, including the mysteries of the spiritual world, the soul itself, and the question of the immortal continuation of our identity. In all ages, the mind of man has brought up here —and always will. Here, at least, of whatever race or era, we stand on common ground. Applause, too, is unanimous, antique or modern. Those authors who work well in this field—though their reward, instead of a handsome percentage, or royalty, may be but simply the laurel-crown of the victors in the great Olympic games—will be dearest to humanity, and their works, however esthetically defective, will be treasur'd forever. The altitude of literature and poetry has always been religion—and always will be. The Indian Vedas, the Naçkas of Zoroaster, the Talmud of the Jews, the Old Testament, the Gospel of Christ and his disciples, Plato's works, the Koran of Mohammed, the Edda of Snorro, and so on toward our own day, to Swedenborg, and to the invaluable contributions of Leibnitz, Kant and Hegel—these, with such poems only

in *SDC*, to end the footnote: "We want not again either the religious fervor of the Spanish Inquisition, nor the morality of the New England Puritans."

173*n*. Testament, the] *TR* and *DV:* Testament also, the

1714. conscience, the sense] *TR* and *DV:* conscience, the lessons of the esthetic, the sense

1720. Idealism seems] *DVOP:* Idealism seem

chandise, logic, intellect, demonstrations, solid perpetuities, buildings of brick and iron, or even the facts of the shows of trees, earth, rocks, &c., fear not, my brethren, my sisters, to sound out with equally determin'd voice, that conviction brooding within the recesses of every envision'd soul—illusions! apparitions! figments all! True, we must not condemn the show, neither absolutely deny it, for the indispensability of its meanings; but how clearly we see that, migrate in soul to what we can already conceive of superior and spiritual points of view, and, palpable as it seems under present relations, it all and several might, nay certainly would, fall apart and vanish.

I hail with joy the oceanic, variegated, intense practical energy, the

in which, (while singing well of persons and events, of the passions of man, and the shows of the material universe,) the religious tone, the consciousness of mystery, the recognition of the future, of the unknown, of Deity over and under all, and of the divine purpose, are never absent, but indirectly give tone to all—exhibit literature's real heights and elevations, towering up like the great mountains of the earth.

Standing on this ground—the last, the highest, only permanent ground—and sternly criticising, from it, all works, either of the literary, or any art, we have peremptorily to dismiss every pretensive production, however fine its esthetic or intellectual points, which violates or ignores, or even does not celebrate, the central divine idea of All, suffusing universe, of eternal trains of purpose, in the development, by however slow degrees, of the physical, moral, and spiritual kosmos. I say he has studied, meditated to no profit, whatever may be his mere erudition, who has not absorb'd this simple consciousness and faith. It is not entirely new—but it is for Democracy to elaborate it, and look to build upon and expand from it, with uncompromising reliance. Above the doors of teaching the inscription is to appear, Though little or nothing can be absolutely known, perceiv'd, except from a point of view which is evanescent, yet we know at least one permanency, that Time and Space, in the will of God, furnish successive chains, completions of material births and beginnings, solve all discrepancies, fears and doubts, and eventually fulfil happiness—and that the prophecy of those births, namely spiritual results, throws the true arch over all teaching, all science. The local considerations of sin, disease, deformity, ignorance, death, &c., and their measurement by the superficial mind, and ordinary legislation and theology, are to be met by science, boldly accepting, promulging this faith, and planting the seeds of superber laws—of the explication of the physical universe through the spiritual—and clearing the way for a religion, sweet and unimpugnable alike to little child or great savan.

191*n*. for Democracy] *TR* and *DV:* for America

1735. neither] *CPW* and *SDC:* nether] *TR* and *DV:* neither [an obvious error; here corrected.—*ED*.]

demand for facts, even the business materialism of the current age, our States. But wo to the age or land in which these things, movements, stopping at themselves, do not tend to ideas. As fuel to flame, and flame to the heavens, so must wealth, science, materialism—even this democracy of which we make so much—unerringly feed the highest mind, the soul. Infinitude the flight: fathomless the mystery. Man, so diminutive, dilates beyond the sensible universe, competes with, outcopes space and time, meditating even one great idea. Thus, and thus only, does a human being, his spirit, ascend above, and justify, objective Nature, which, probably nothing in itself, is incredibly and divinely serviceable, indispensable, real, here. And as the purport of objective Nature is doubtless folded, hidden, somewhere here—as somewhere here is what this globe and its manifold forms, and the light of day, and night's darkness, and life itself, with all its experiences, are for—it is here the great literature, especially verse, must get its inspiration and throbbing blood. Then may we attain to a poetry worthy the immortal soul of man, and which, while absorbing materials, and, in their own sense, the shows of Nature, will, above all, have, both directly and indirectly, a freeing, fluidizing, expanding, religious character, exulting with science, fructifying the moral elements, and stimulating aspirations, and meditations on the unknown.

The process, so far, is indirect and peculiar, and though it may be suggested, cannot be defined. Observing, rapport, and with intuition, the shows and forms presented by Nature, the sensuous luxuriance, the beautiful in living men and women, the actual play of passions, in history and life—and, above all, from those developments either in Nature or human personality in which power, (dearest of all to the sense of the artist,) transacts itself—out of these, and seizing what is in them, the poet, the esthetic worker in any field, by the divine magic of his genius, projects them, their analogies, by curious removes, indirections, in literature and art. (No useless attempt to repeat the material creation, by daguerreotyping the exact likeness by mortal mental means.) This is the image-making faculty, coping with material creation, and rivaling, almost triumphing over it. This alone, when all the other parts of a specimen of literature or art are ready and waiting, can breathe into it the breath of life, and endow it with identity.

"The true question to ask," says the librarian of Congress in a paper read before the Social Science Convention at New York, October, 1869,

200*n*.–201*n*. by the superficial] *TR* and *DV:* by superficial

1744–1745. materialism—even . . . much—unerringly] *TR* and *DV:* materialism, unerringly

"The true question to ask respecting a book, is, *has it help'd any human soul?*" This is the hint, statement, not only of the great literatus, his book, but of every great artist. It may be that all works of art are to be first tried by their art qualities, their image-forming talent, and their dramatic, pictorial, plot-constructing, euphonious and other talents. Then, whenever claiming to be first-class works, they are to be strictly and sternly tried by their foundation in, and radiation, in the highest sense, and always indirectly, of the ethic principles, and eligibility to free, arouse, dilate.

As, within the purposes of the Kosmos, and vivifying all meteorology, and all the congeries of the mineral, vegetable and animal worlds—all the physical growth and development of man, and all the history of the race in politics, religions, wars, &c., there is a moral purpose, a visible or invisible intention, certainly underlying all—its results and proof needing to be patiently waited for—needing intuition, faith, idiosyncrasy, to its realization, which many, and especially the intellectual, do not have—so in the product, or congeries of the product, of the greatest literatus. This is the last, profoundest measure and test of a first-class literary or esthetic achievement, and when understood and put in force must fain, I say, lead to works, books, nobler than any hitherto known. Lo! Nature, (the only complete, actual poem,) existing calmly in the divine scheme, containing all, content, careless of the criticisms of a day, or these endless and wordy chatterers. And lo! to the consciousness of the soul, the permanent identity, the thought, the something, before which the magnitude even of democracy, art, literature, &c., dwindles, becomes partial, measurable—something that fully satisfies, (which those do not.) That something is the All, and the idea of All, with the accompanying idea of eternity, and of itself, the soul, buoyant, indestructible, sailing space forever, visiting every region, as a ship the sea. And again lo! the pulsations in all matter, all spirit, throbbing forever—the eternal beats, eternal systole and diastole of life in things—wherefrom I feel and know that death is not the ending, as was thought, but rather the real beginning—and that nothing ever is or can be lost, nor ever die, nor soul, nor matter.

In the future of these States must arise poets immenser far, and make great poems of death. The poems of life are great, but there must be the poems of the purports of life, not only in itself, but beyond itself. I have

1780. After "great artist." *TR* and *DV* begin a new paragraph.
1790. race in politics] *DVOP:* race of politics
1797. than any] *DVOP:* then any

eulogized Homer, the sacred bards of Jewry, Eschylus, Juvenal, Shakspere, &c., and acknowledged their inestimable value. But, (with perhaps the exception, in some, not all respects, of the second-mention'd,) I say there must, for future and democratic purposes, appear poets, (dare I to say so?) of higher class even than any of those—poets not only possess'd of the religious fire and abandon of Isaiah, luxuriant in the epic talent of Homer, or for proud characters as in Shakspere, but consistent with the Hegelian formulas, and consistent with modern science. America needs, and the world needs, a class of bards who will, now and ever, so link and tally the rational physical being of man, with the ensembles of time and space, and with this vast and multiform show, Nature, surrounding him, ever tantalizing him, equally a part, and yet not a part of him, as to essentially harmonize, satisfy, and put at rest. Faith, very old, now scared away by science, must be restored, brought back by the same power that caused her departure—restored with new sway, deeper, wider, higher than ever. Surely, this universal ennui, this coward fear, this shuddering at death, these low, degrading views, are not always to rule the spirit pervading future society, as it has the past, and does the present. What the Roman Lucretius sought most nobly, yet all too blindly, negatively to do for his age and its successors, must be done positively by some great coming literatus, especially poet, who, while remaining fully poet, will absorb whatever science indicates, with spiritualism, and out of them, and out of his own genius, will compose the great poem of death. Then will man indeed confront Nature, and confront time and space, both with science, and *con amore*, and take his right place, prepared for life, master of fortune and misfortune. And then that which was long wanted will be supplied, and the ship that had it not before in all her voyages, will have an anchor.

There are still other standards, suggestions, for products of high literatuses. That which really balances and conserves the social and political world is not so much legislation, police, treaties, and dread of punishment, as the latent eternal intuitional sense, in humanity, of fairness, manliness, decorum, &c. Indeed, this perennial regulation, control, and oversight, by self-suppliance, is *sine qua non* to democracy; and a highest widest aim of democratic literature may well be to bring forth, cultivate, brace, and strengthen this sense, in individuals and society. A strong mastership of the general inferior self by the superior self, is to be aided,

1812. In the future . . . arise] *TR* and *DV:* I say in the future of These States must therefore arise
1815–1816. Shakspere] *TR* and *DV:* Shakespeare
1847. this perennial] *TR* and *DV:* the perennial

secured, indirectly, but surely, by the literatus, in his works, shaping, for individual or aggregate democracy, a great passionate body, in and along with which goes a great masterful spirit.

And still, providing for contingencies, I fain confront the fact, the need of powerful native philosophs and orators and bards, these States, as rallying points to come, in times of danger, and to fend off ruin and defection. For history is long, long, long. Shift and turn the combinations of the statement as we may, the problem of the future of America is in certain respects as dark as it is vast. Pride, competition, segregation, vicious wilfulness, and license beyond example, brood already upon us. Unwieldy and immense, who shall hold in behemoth? who bridle leviathan? Flaunt it as we choose, athwart and over the roads of our progress loom huge uncertainty, and dreadful, threatening gloom. It is useless to deny it: Democracy grows rankly up the thickest, noxious, deadliest plants and fruits of all—brings worse and worse invaders—needs newer, larger, stronger, keener compensations and compellers.

Our lands, embracing so much, (embracing indeed the whole, rejecting none,) hold in their breast that flame also, capable of consuming themselves, consuming us all. Short as the span of our national life has been, already have death and downfall crowded close upon us—and will again crowd close, no doubt, even if warded off. Ages to come may never know, but I know, how narrowly during the late secession war—and more than once, and more than twice or thrice—our Nationality, (wherein bound up, as in a ship in a storm, depended, and yet depend, all our best life, all hope, all value,) just grazed, just by a hair escaped destruction. Alas! to think of them! the agony and bloody sweat of certain of those hours! those cruel, sharp, suspended crises!

Even to-day, amid these whirls, incredible flippancy, and blind fury of parties, infidelity, entire lack of first-class captains and leaders, added to the plentiful meanness and vulgarity of the ostensible masses—that problem, the labor question, beginning to open like a yawning gulf, rapidly widening every year—what prospect have we? We sail a dangerous sea of seething currents, cross and under-currents, vortices—all so dark, untried—and whither shall we turn? It seems as if the Almighty had spread before this nation charts of imperial destinies, dazzling as the sun, yet with many a deep intestine difficulty, and human aggregate of

1885. After "shall we turn?" TR and DV begin a new paragraph. TR and DV also have at this point a long footnote, which is deleted in SDC. See Appendix IV, 3.
1887. with many] *TR* and *DV:* with lines of blood, and many
1892. history, a history] *TR* and *DV:* history, the history
1895–1896. the cost. Thought] *TR* and *DV:* the cost. Behold, the anguish of suspense, existence itself wavering in the balance, uncertain whether to rise or fall; already, close behind you or around you, thick winrows of corpses on battlefields, countless

cankerous imperfection,—saying, lo! the roads, the only plans of development, long and varied with all terrible balks and ebullitions. You said in your soul, I will be empire of empires, overshadowing all else, past and present, putting the history of old-world dynasties, conquests behind me, as of no account—making a new history, a history of democracy, making old history a dwarf—I alone inaugurating largeness, culminating time. If these, O lands of America, are indeed the prizes, the determinations of your soul, be it so. But behold the cost, and already specimens of the cost. Thought you greatness was to ripen for you like a pear? If you would have greatness, know that you must conquer it through ages, centuries—must pay for it with a proportionate price. For you too, as for all lands, the struggle, the traitor, the wily person in office, scrofulous wealth, the surfeit of prosperity, the demonism of greed, the hell of passion, the decay of faith, the long postponement, the fossil-like lethargy, the ceaseless need of revolutions, prophets, thunderstorms, deaths, births, new projections and invigorations of ideas and men.

Yet I have dream'd, merged in that hidden-tangled problem of our fate, whose long unraveling stretches mysteriously through time—dream'd out, portray'd, hinted already—a little or a larger band—a band of brave and true, unprecedented yet—arm'd and equipt at every point—the members separated, it may be, by different dates and States, or south, or north, or east, or west—Pacific, Atlantic, Southern, Canadian—a year, a century here, and other centuries there—but always one, compact in soul, conscience-conserving, God-inculcating, inspired achievers, not only in literature, the greatest art, but achievers in all art—a new, undying order, dynasty, from age to age transmitted—a band, a class, at least as fit to cope with current years, our dangers, needs, as those who, for their times, so long, so well, in armor or in cowl, upheld and made illustrious, that far-back feudal, priestly world. To offset chivalry, indeed, those vanish'd countless knights, old altars, abbeys, priests, ages and strings of ages, a knightlier and more sacred cause to-day demands, and shall supply, in a New World, to larger, grander work, more than the counterpart and tally of them.

Arrived now, definitely, at an apex for these Vistas, I confess that the promulgation and belief in such a class or institution—a new and greater literatus order—its possibility, (nay certainty,) underlies these entire

maimed and sick in hospitals, treachery among Generals, folly in the Executive and Legislative departments, schemers, thieves everywhere—cant, credulity, make-believe everywhere. Thought

1909. Pacific . . . a year] *TR* and *DV:* Pacific or Atlantic—a year

1915–1916. illustrious, that far-back feudal] *TR* and *DV:* illustrious, the Feudal

1917. knights, . . . priests] *TR* and *DV:* knights, and the old altars, abbeys, all their priests

speculations—and that the rest, the other parts, as superstructures, are all founded upon it. It really seems to me the condition, not only of our future national and democratic development, but of our perpetuation. In the highly artificial and materialistic bases of modern civilization, with the corresponding arrangements and methods of living, the force-infusion of intellect alone, the depraving influences of riches just as much as poverty, the absence of all high ideals in character—with the long series of tendencies, shapings, which few are strong enough to resist, and which now seem, with steam-engine speed, to be everywhere turning out the generations of humanity like uniform iron castings—all of which, as compared with the feudal ages, we can yet do nothing better than accept, make the best of, and even welcome, upon the whole, for their oceanic practical grandeur, and their restless wholesale kneading of the masses—I say of all this tremendous and dominant play of solely materialistic bearings upon current life in the United States, with the results as already seen, accumulating, and reaching far into the future, that they must either be confronted and met by at least an equally subtle and tremendous force-infusion for purposes of spiritualization, for the pure conscience, for genuine esthetics, and for absolute and primal manliness and womanliness—or else our modern civilization, with all its improvements, is in vain, and we are on the road to a destiny, a status, equivalent, in its real world, to that of the fabled damned.

Prospecting thus the coming unsped days, and that new order in them—marking the endless train of exercise, development, unwind, in nation as in man, which life is for—we see, fore-indicated, amid these prospects and hopes, new law-forces of spoken and written language—not merely the pedagogue-forms, correct, regular, familiar with precedents, made for matters of outside propriety, fine words, thoughts definitely told out—but a language fann'd by the breath of Nature, which leaps overhead, cares mostly for impetus and effects, and for what it plants and invigorates to grow—tallies life and character, and seldomer tells a thing than suggests or necessitates it. In fact, a new theory of literary composition for imaginative works of the very first class, and especially for highest poems, is the sole course open to these States. Books are to be call'd for, and supplied, on the assumption that the process of reading is not a half-

1926. national . . . development] TR and DV: national development

1944. in its real] TR and DV: in this real

1945. Between "fabled damned." and "Prospecting thus", TR and DV have a paragraph omitted in SDC. See Appendix IV, 4.

1948. Between the words "life is for—" and the words "we see, fore-indicated," the remaining lines of that paragraph in TR and DV, and the three following paragraphs, are omitted in SDC. The words "We see, fore-indicated," are the first words of a new paragraph in TR and DV. For these omitted passages see Appendix IV, 5.

sleep, but, in highest sense, an exercise, a gymnast's struggle; that the reader is to do something for himself, must be on the alert, must himself or herself construct indeed the poem, argument, history, metaphysical essay—the text furnishing the hints, the clue, the start or frame-work. Not the book needs so much to be the complete thing, but the reader of the book does. That were to make a nation of supple and athletic minds, well-train'd, intuitive, used to depend on themselves, and not on a few coteries of writers.

Investigating here, we see, not that it is a little thing we have, in having the bequeath'd libraries, countless shelves of volumes, records, &c.; yet how serious the danger, depending entirely on them, of the bloodless vein, the nerveless arm, the false application, at second or third hand. We see that the real interest of this people of ours in the theology, history, poetry, politics, and personal models of the past, (the British islands, for instance, and indeed all the past,) is not necessarily to mould ourselves or our literature upon them, but to attain fuller, more definite comparisons, warnings, and the insight to ourselves, our own present, and our own far grander, different, future history, religion, social customs, &c. We see that almost everything that has been written, sung, or stated, of old, with reference to humanity under the feudal and oriental institutes, religions, and for other lands, needs to be re-written, re-sung, re-stated, in terms consistent with the institution of these States, and to come in range and obedient uniformity with them.

We see, as in the universes of the material kosmos, after meteorological, vegetable, and animal cycles, man at last arises, born through them, to prove them, concentrate them, to turn upon them with wonder and love—to command them, adorn them, and carry them upward into superior realms—so, out of the series of the preceding social and political universes, now arise these States. We see that while many were supposing things established and completed, really the grandest things always remain; and discover that the work of the New World is not ended, but only fairly begun.

We see our land, America, her literature, esthetics, &c., as, substantially, the getting in form, or effusement and statement, of deepest basic elements and loftiest final meanings, of history and man—and the

1957. After "these States." *TR* and *DV* begin a new paragraph.

1970–1971. hand. We see] *TR* and *DV:* hand. After all, we see Life, not bred, (at least in its more modern and essential parts,) in those great old Libraries, nor America nor Democracy favored nor applauded there. We see that

1976. After "customs, &c." *TR* and *DV* begin a new paragraph.

1987. these States. We see that] *TR* and *DV:* These States—their main purport being not in the newness and importance of their politics or inventions, but in new, grander, more advanced Religions, Literatures, and Arts.

We see that

portrayal, (under the eternal laws and conditions of beauty,) of our own physiognomy, the subjective tie and expression of the objective, as from our own combination, continuation, and points of view—and the deposit and record of the national mentality, character, appeals, heroism, wars, and even liberties—where these, and all, culminate in native literary and artistic formulation, to be perpetuated; and not having which native, first-class formulation, she will flounder about, and her other, however imposing, eminent greatness, prove merely a passing gleam; but truly having which, she will understand herself, live nobly, nobly contribute, emanate, and, swinging, poised safely on herself, illumin'd and illuming, become a full-form'd world, and divine Mother not only of material but spiritual worlds, in ceaseless succession through time—the main thing being the average, the bodily, the concrete, the democratic, the popular, on which all the superstructures of the future are to permanently rest.

Origins of Attempted Secession.

Not the whole matter, but some side facts worth conning to-day and any day.

I consider the war of attempted secession, 1860–65, not as a struggle of two distinct and separate peoples, but a conflict (often happening,

1998–1999. native . . . formulation] TR and DV: native formulation
2005. through time—] TR and DV: through Time
2005–2007. These lines, beginning with "the main thing" are inserted in ink; in TR and DV the paragraph ends with "through Time." For the final paragraph in TR and DV, preceding "General Notes," omitted in SDC, see Appendix IV, 6.

[The following portions of DV "General Notes" were reprinted in SDC under the same subtitles, *q.v.*: all of "Society" (DV, pp. 79–80), all of "British Literature" (DV, pp. 80–82) except that part of the second paragraph following "wo. . . .", and all of "General Suffrage, Elections, &c." The second paragraph of "The Late War" (DV, pp. 82–83) was reprinted in SDC as lines 133–152 of "Origins of Attempted Secession" (*q.v.*). For the remaining portions of "General Notes" see Appendix IV, 7–9.]

Origins of Attempted Secession.

Printed in SDC from clippings of the TR text of MDW "Notes," pp. 63–66, and DV "General Notes," pp. 82–83, all pasted to six sheets of gray paper, with connecting passages written between the clippings in black ink. Revisions are in red and black. That part drawn from MDW "Notes" was reprinted, with little change, in "Walt Whitman and the Civil War," LE, March 18, 1876, with the following headnote: "The following is part of a forthcoming work, in which the writer endeavours to take an impartial view of the immediate causes and underlying tendencies of the great Secession contest in 1861–65." The "forthcoming work" was presumably TR. Brief passages had appeared in the First and Second Papers of " 'Tis But Ten Years Since," NYWG, in 1874. Other passages are in "The Eighteenth Presidency!" which Whitman prepared for publication in 1856 but never published;

and very fierce) between the passions and paradoxes of one and the same identity—perhaps the only terms on which that identity could really become fused, homogeneous and lasting. The origin and conditions out of which it arose, are full of lessons, full of warnings yet to the Republic—and always will be. The underlying and principal of those origins are yet singularly ignored. The Northern States were really just as responsible for that war, (in its precedents, foundations, instigations,) as the South. Let me try to give my view. From the age of 21 to 40, (1840–'60,) I was interested in the political movements of the land, not so much as a participant, but as an observer, and a regular voter at the elections. I think I was conversant with the springs of action, and their workings, not only in New York city and Brooklyn, but understood them in the whole country, as I had made leisurely tours through all the middle States, and partially through the western and southern, and down to New Orleans, in which city I resided for some time. (I was there at the close of the Mexican war—saw and talk'd with General Taylor, and the other generals and officers, who were fêted and detain'd several days on their return victorious from that expedition.)

Of course many and very contradictory things, specialties, developments, constitutional views, &c., went to make up the origin of the war—but the most significant general fact can be best indicated and stated as follows: For twenty-five years previous to the outbreak, the controling

the text used in this collation is that of Edward F. Grier (Lawrence, Kansas, 1956). "Origins of Attempted Secession" was omitted in *DVOP*.

1–5. Printed, through "conditions" in line 5, from the autograph MS.

6–132. These lines printed from clippings of *MDW* "Notes," pp. 63–65. In the first clipping the following lines at the beginning of the paragraph were cut away: "*The War, though with two sides, really* ONE IDENTITY *(as struggles, furious conflicts of Nature, for final harmony.)—The Soil it bred and ripen'd from—the North as Responsible for it as the South.*—Of the war of Attempted Secession—the greatest National event of the first Century of the United States, and one among the great events of all Centuries—the main points of its origin, and the *conditions*". The *Examiner* article begins: "Of the War" etc.

7. those origins are] *LE* and *MDW:* those points are

8–9. This sentence may be compared with the following sentence, the last in the twelfth paragraph of the First Paper of "Ten Years," *NYWG:* "A powerful faction, ruling the North, was art and part with the Slaveocracy, and stood then and stands to-day, just as responsible for the Rebellion." (Cf. also notes to "Death of Abraham Lincoln," lines 40–43.)

9. *LE* omits the marks of parenthesis.

10. After "give my view." *LE* and *MDW* begin a new paragraph.

12. observer, and a] *LE* and *MDW:* observer, though a

17. the close of] *LE* and *MDW:* the conclusion of

19. fêted] *LE: fêted*] *MDW:* feted

21–22. specialties, developments, constitutional] *LE* and *MDW:* specialties, prejudices, Constitutional

23. but the most] *LE* and *MDW:* but perhaps the most

"Democratic" nominating conventions of our Republic—starting from their primaries in wards or districts, and so expanding to counties, powerful cities, States, and to the great Presidential nominating conventions—were getting to represent and be composed of more and more putrid and dangerous materials. Let me give a schedule, or list, of one of these representative conventions for a long time before, and inclusive of, that which nominated Buchanan. (Remember they had come to be the fountains and tissues of the American body politic, forming, as it were, the whole blood, legislation, office-holding, &c.) One of these conventions, from 1840 to '60, exhibited a spectacle such as could never be seen except in our own age and in these States. The members who composed it were, seven-eighths of them, the meanest kind of bawling and blowing office-holders, office-seekers, pimps, malignants, conspirators, murderers, fancy-men, custom-house clerks, contractors, kept-editors, spaniels well-train'd to carry and fetch, jobbers, infidels, disunionists, terrorists, mail-riflers, slave-catchers, pushers of slavery, creatures of the President, creatures of would-be Presidents, spies, bribers, compromisers, lobbyers, sponges, ruin'd sports, expell'd gamblers, policy-backers, monte-dealers, duellists, carriers of conceal'd weapons, deaf men, pimpled men, scarr'd inside with vile disease, gaudy outside with gold chains made from the people's money and harlots' money twisted together; crawling, serpentine men, the lousy combings and born freedom-sellers of the earth. And whence came they? From back-yards and bar-rooms; from out of the custom-houses, marshals' offices, post-offices, and gambling-hells; from the President's house, the jail, the station-house; from unnamed by-places, where devilish disunion was hatch'd at midnight; from political hearses, and from the coffins inside, and from the shrouds inside of the coffins; from the tumors

25. conventions . . . starting] *LE* and *MDW:* conventions—starting
27. great . . . conventions] *LE* and *MDW:* great President-Naming Conventions
36. of them, . . . office-holders] *LE* and *MDW:* of them, office-holders
36–46. These lines, beginning with "Office-holders," are also found in "The Eighteenth Presidency!" (pp. 28–29), which (abbreviated "18th Pres.") is included in the collation.
37. office-seekers, pimps, malignants] 18th Pres.: office-seekers, robbers, pimps, exclusives, malignants
37–38. fancy-men, custom-house] 18th Pres.: fancy-men, post-masters, custom-house
41. spies, bribers] *LE* and *MDW:* spies, blowers, electioneerers, bawlers, bribers] 18th Pres.: spies, blowers, electioneerers, body-snatchers, bawlers, bribers
41. compromisers, lobbyers] 18th Pres.: compromisers, runaways, lobbyers
42. duellists] *MDW* and 18th Pres.: duelists
43. weapons, deaf men] 18th Pres.: weapons, blind men, deaf men
44. vile disease] 18th Pres.: vile disorder
45. harlots' money] *LE*, *MDW*, and 18th Pres.: harlot's money
47–53. The sentence beginning "From back-yards" is also found in "The Eight-

and abscesses of the land; from the skeletons and skulls in the vaults of the federal alms-houses; and from the running sores of the great cities. Such, I say, form'd, or absolutely control'd the forming of, the entire personnel, the atmosphere, nutriment and chyle, of our municipal, State, and National politics—substantially permeating, handling, deciding, and wielding everything—legislation, nominations, elections, "public sentiment," &c.—while the great masses of the people, farmers, mechanics, and traders, were helpless in their gripe. These conditions were mostly prevalent in the north and west, and especially in New York and Philadelphia cities; and the southern leaders, (bad enough, but of a far higher order,) struck hands and affiliated with, and used them. Is it strange that a thunder-storm follow'd such morbid and stifling cloud-strata?

I say then, that what, as just outlined, heralded, and made the ground ready for secession revolt, ought to be held up, through all the future, as the most instructive lesson in American political history—the most significant warning and beacon-light to coming generations. I say that the sixteenth, seventeenth and eighteenth terms of the American Presidency have shown that the villainy and shallowness of rulers (back'd by the machinery of great parties) are just as eligible to these States as to any foreign despotism, kingdom, or empire—there is not a bit of difference. History is to record those three Presidentiads, and especially the administrations of Fillmore and Buchanan, as so far our topmost warning and shame. Never were publicly display'd more deform'd, mediocre, snivelling, unreliable, false-hearted men. Never were these States so insulted, and attempted to be betray'd. All the main purposes for which the government was establish'd were openly denied. The perfect equality of slavery with freedom was flauntingly preach'd in the north—nay, the

eenth Presidency!" (p. 28), but in the paragraph preceding the one in which it occurs in *SDC*.

47. From back-yards and bar-rooms; from] 18th Pres.: From lawyers' offices, secret lodges, back-yards, bed-houses, and bar-rooms; from out of

50. disunion was hatch'd] 18th Pres.: disunion is hatched

53–54. cities. Such . . . entire] *LE* and *MDW:* cities. . . . . . .Such, I say, form'd the entire

62. them. Is] *LE* and *MDW:* them. . . . . . .Is

63. stifling cloud-strata?] *LE* and *MDW:* stifling strata?

67. generations. I] *LE* and *MDW:* generations. I

67–81. These lines are also found in "The Eighteenth Presidency!" (pp. 23–24).

67–74. These lines may be compared also with paragraph 12 of the First Paper of "Ten Years," *NYWG* (1874) and with lines 35–40, second paragraph of "Death of Abraham Lincoln" and the textual notes to that section, *q.v.*

68. sixteenth, . . . terms] 18th Pres.: sixteenth and seventeenth terms

69–70. of rulers . . . are] 18th Pres.: of great rulers are

72–73. record those . . . as] 18th Pres.: record these two Presidencies as

77. were openly] 18th Pres.: are openly

78. was flauntingly] 18th Pres.: is flauntingly

superiority of slavery. The slave trade was proposed to be renew'd. Everywhere frowns and misunderstandings—everywhere exasperations and humiliations. (The slavery contest is settled—and the war is long over—yet do not those putrid conditions, too many of them, still exist? still result in diseases, fevers, wounds—not of war and army hospitals—but the wounds and diseases of peace?)

Out of those generic influences, mainly in New York, Pennsylvania, Ohio, &c., arose the attempt at disunion. To philosophical examination, the malignant fever of that war shows its embryonic sources, and the original nourishment of its life and growth, in the north. I say secession, below the surface, originated and was brought to maturity in the free States. I allude to the score of years preceding 1860. My deliberate opinion is now, that if at the opening of the contest the abstract duality-question of *slavery and quiet* could have been submitted to a direct popular vote, as against their opposite, they would have triumphantly carried the day in a majority of the northern States—in the large cities, leading off with New York and Philadelphia, by tremendous majorities. The events of '61 amazed everybody north and south, and burst all prophecies and calculations like bubbles. But even then, and during the whole war, the stern fact remains that (not only did the north put it down, but) *the secession cause had numerically just as many sympathizers in the free as in the rebel States.*

As to slavery, abstractly and practically, (its idea, and the determination to establish and expand it, especially in the new territories, the future America,) it is too common, I repeat, to identify it exclusively with the south. In fact down to the opening of the war, the whole country had about an equal hand in it. The north had at least been just as guilty, if not more guilty; and the east and west had. The former Presidents and

79. was proposed] 18th Pres.: is proposed
81. humiliations. (The] *LE* and *MDW:* humiliations...... (The
81–84. This parenthetical sentence is omitted in *LE.*
81. is long over] *MDW:* is over
87. of that war] *LE* and *MDW:* of this war
90–95. This sentence, not previously printed, was first written in pencil on white paper, crossed out in red ink, and rewritten, with revisions, in black ink between clippings on the gray paper.
103. I repeat, to] *LE* and *MDW:* I say, to
109–113. These lines, not previously printed, were inserted in black ink on the gray base sheet between two clippings.
114. north. As] *LE* and *MDW:* North...... As
121–122. attempt . . . have] *LE* and *MDW:* attempt would of course have
126. result] *LE* and *MDW:* results
127. After "themselves.)" *LE* and *MDW* begin a new paragraph.
127–132. This sentence was also used in paragraph 23 near the end of the Second

Congresses had been guilty—the governors and legislatures of every northern State had been guilty, and the mayors of New York and other northern cities had all been guilty—their hands were all stain'd. And as the conflict took decided shape, it is hard to tell which class, the leading southern or northern disunionists, was more stunn'd and disappointed at the non-action of the free-state secession element, so largely existing and counted on by those leaders, both sections.

So much for that point, and for the north. As to the inception and direct instigation of the war, in the south itself, I shall not attempt interiors or complications. Behind all, the idea that it was from a resolute and arrogant determination on the part of the extreme slaveholders, the Calhounites, to carry the states rights' portion of the constitutional compact to its farthest verge, and nationalize slavery, or else disrupt the Union, and found a new empire, with slavery for its corner-stone, was and is undoubtedly the true theory. (If successful, this attempt might—I am not sure, but it might—have destroy'd not only our American republic, in anything like first-class proportions, in itself and its prestige, but for ages at least, the cause of Liberty and Equality everywhere—and would have been the greatest triumph of reaction, and the severest blow to political and every other freedom, possible to conceive. Its worst result would have inured to the southern States themselves.) That our national democratic experiment, principle, and machinery, could triumphantly sustain such a shock, and that the Constitution could weather it, like a ship a storm, and come out of it as sound and whole as before, is by far the most signal proof yet of the stability of that experiment, Democracy, and of those principles, and that Constitution.

Of the war itself, we know in the ostent what has been done. The numbers of the dead and wounded can be told or approximated, the debt

Paper of "Ten Years," *NYWG*.

127–128. our national democratic experiment] *LE* and *MDW:* our National-Democratic experiment] *NYWG:* our Republican experiment

128. machinery, could] *NYWG:* machinery, (to anticipate again, as we see it clearly enough now,) could

129. the Constitution] *NYWG:* the National Constitution

131–132. experiment, Democracy, and] *NYWG:* experiment and

132. The next sentence, the last on this clipping, which has been deleted in the MS, is as follows: "But the case is not fully stated at that." *NYWG* is the same except that there the sentence ends "that alone." The remaining portions of this paragraph in *LE*, *MDW*, and *NYWG* are used in lines 167 ff.

133–152. These lines were printed from two clippings of the "General Notes" of *DV* as reprinted in *TR*, pp. 82–83, the second paragraph under the subhead "The Late War." For the first paragraph under that subhead, omitted in *SDC*, see Appendix IV, 8.

133. Of the war itself] *TR* and *DV:* Of the Secession War itself

posted and put on record, the material events narrated, &c. Meantime, elections go on, laws are pass'd, political parties struggle, issue their platforms, &c., just the same as before. But immensest results, not only in politics, but in literature, poems, and sociology, are doubtless waiting yet unform'd in the future. How long they will wait I cannot tell. The pageant of history's retrospect shows us, ages since, all Europe marching on the crusades, those arm'd uprisings of the people, stirr'd by a mere idea, to grandest attempt—and, when once baffled in it, returning, at intervals, twice, thrice, and again. An unsurpass'd series of revolutionary events, influences. Yet it took over two hundred years for the seeds of the crusades to germinate, before beginning even to sprout. Two hundred years they lay, sleeping, not dead, but dormant in the ground. Then, out of them, unerringly, arts, travel, navigation, politics, literature, freedom, the spirit of adventure, inquiry, all arose, grew, and steadily sped on to what we see at present. Far back there, that huge agitation-struggle of the crusades stands, as undoubtedly the embryo, the start, of the high preëminence of experiment, civilization and enterprise which the European nations have since sustain'd, and of which these States are the heirs.

Another illustration—(history is full of them, although the war itself, the victory of the Union, and the relations of our equal States, present features of which there are no precedents in the past.) The conquest of England eight centuries ago, by the Franco-Normans—the obliteration of the old, (in many respects so needing obliteration)—the Domesday Book, and the repartition of the land—the old impedimenta removed, even by blood and ruthless violence, and a new, progressive genesis establish'd, new seeds sown—time has proved plain enough that, bitter as they were, all these were the most salutary series of revolutions that could possibly have happen'd. Out of them, and by them mainly, have come, out of Albic, Roman and Saxon England—and without them could not have come—not only the England of the 500 years down to the present,

135–136. Meantime, elections] *TR* and *DV:* Meantime, the war being over, elections

137. results, not only] *TR* and *DV:* results of the War—not only

141. those arm'd] *TR* and *DV:* those wondrous armed

147–148. freedom, the spirit] *TR* and *DV:* freedom, inventions, the spirit

153–155. This first sentence in the paragraph is inserted in ink between clippings.

155–166. These lines were printed without change except in capitalization from a clipping of *MDW* "Notes," p. 66, where they first appeared.

167–183. These lines were printed from a clipping of the last part of a paragraph in *MDW* "Notes," p. 65; they also appear in paragraph 9 of the *LE* article.

167–174. These lines first appeared in paragraph 23 of the Second Paper of "Ten Years," *NYWG*.

167. of that war] *LE, MDW,* and *NYWG:* of the Secession War

170–171. Nation . . . moral] *NYWG:* Nation, a moral

and of the present—but these States. Nor, except for that terrible dislocation and over-turn, would these States, as they are, exist to-day.

It is certain to me that the United States, by virtue of that war and its results, and through that and them only, are now ready to enter, and must certainly enter, upon their genuine career in history, as no more torn and divided in their spinal requisites, but a great homogeneous Nation—free states all—a moral and political unity in variety, such as Nature shows in her grandest physical works, and as much greater than any mere work of Nature, as the moral and political, the work of man, his mind, his soul, are, in their loftiest sense, greater than the merely physical. Out of that war not only has the nationalty of the States escaped from being strangled, but more than any of the rest, and, in my opinion, more than the north itself, the vital heart and breath of the south have escaped as from the pressure of a general nightmare, and are henceforth to enter on a life, development, and active freedom, whose realities are certain in the future, notwithstanding all the southern vexations of the hour—a development which could not possibly have been achiev'd on any less terms, or by any other means than that grim lesson, or something equivalent to it. And I predict that the south is yet to outstrip the north.

174–175. physical. Out] *LE* and *MDW:* physical . . . . . . Out

174–175. In the Second Paper of "Ten Years," paragraph 23 ends with "physical."

175–183. These lines, beginning "Out of", first appeared in the ninth paragraph of the First Paper of "Ten Years," *NYWG.*

175. Out of] *NYWG:* But is it not already dawning upon us that out of

175. the States] *NYWG:* the United States

178. are henceforth to] *LE*, *MDW*, and *NYWG:* are now to

180. southern vexations of] *LE*, *MDW*, and *NYWG:* Southern vexations and humiliations of

180–181. hour—a development which could] *NYWG:* hour; and could

182. that grim lesson, or] *LE*, *MDW*, and *NYWG:* that War, or

183. After this line, *MDW* continues under the same heading with four paragraphs (page 65) that were omitted in *SDC.* The first three of these concluded the *LE* article. For all four paragraphs see *Prose 1892*, I, Appendix XI, 7–9.

Preface, 1855,
to first issue of "Leaves of Grass."

Brooklyn, N. Y.

America does not repel the past, or what the past has produced under its forms, or amid other politics, or the idea of castes, or the old religions—accepts the lesson with calmness—is not impatient because the slough still sticks to opinions and manners and literature, while the life which served its requirements has passed into the new life of the new forms—perceives that the corpse is slowly borne from the eating and sleeping rooms of the house—perceives that it waits a little while in the door—that it was fittest for its days—that its action has descended to the stalwart and well-shaped heir who approaches—and that he shall be fittest for his days.

The Americans of all nations at any time upon the earth, have probably the fullest poetical nature. The United States themselves are essentially the greatest poem. In the history of the earth hitherto, the largest and most stirring appear tame and orderly to their ampler largeness and

Preface, 1855, to first issue of "Leaves of Grass."

Printed in SDC from the clipped pages of the pamphlet published by Trübner (London, 1881), entitled "*Leaves of Grass.* By Walt Whitman. Preface to the Original Edition, 1855." This preface was also reprinted, with punctuation normalized, in the selected *Poems by Walt Whitman*, edited by W. M. Rossetti (London, 1868). These texts are designated in the notes by the respective dates of publication: 1881, 1868, and 1855. In the collation of these texts all changes in punctuation are noted, including the varying number of leaders, or periods in series, in 1855 (all normalized to three in 1881). To avoid confusion, in this section three asterisks are substituted for three periods to indicate ellipses. Revisions on the MS are in pencil except for a few in black ink. This preface was omitted in DVOP. A significant number of passages were transposed from the 1855 Preface to several poems between 1856 and 1871. (See the Variorum Edition of *Leaves of Grass* in this series of *Collected Writings.*)

1. past, * * * has] 1881 and 1868: past, or what it has] 1855: past or what it has

2. forms, * * * castes, or] 1881: forms or amid other politics, or the idea of castes, or] 1855: forms or amid other politics or the idea of castes or

3–4. religions— * * * slough] 1881: religions . . . accepts the lesson with calmness . . . is not so impatient as has been supposed that the slough] 1868: religions; accepts the lesson with calmness; is not so impatient as has been supposed that the slough] 1855: religions . . . . accepts the lesson with calmness . . . is not so impatient as has been supposed that the slough

4. literature, while] 1881, 1868, and 1855: literature while

5–6. forms—perceives] 1881 and 1855: forms . . . perceives] 1868: forms; perceives

7. house—perceives] 1881 and 1855: house . . . perceives] 1868: house; perceives

7–8. door—that * * * days—that] 1881 and 1855: door . . . that * * * days . . . that] 1868: door, that it was fittest for its days, that

9. well-shaped heir who approaches—and] 1881: well shaped heir who approaches . . . and] 1868: well-shaped heir who approaches, and] 1855: wellshaped

stir. Here at last is something in the doings of man that corresponds with the broadcast doings of the day and night. Here is action untied from strings, necessarily blind to particulars and details, magnificently moving in masses. Here is the hospitality which for ever indicates heroes. Here the performance, disdaining the trivial, unapproach'd in the tremendous audacity of its crowds and groupings, and the push of its perspective, spreads with crampless and flowing breadth, and showers its prolific and splendid extravagance. One sees it must indeed own the riches of the summer and winter, and need never be bankrupt while corn grows from the ground, or the orchards drop apples, or the bays contain fish, or men beget children upon women.

Other states indicate themselves in their deputies—but the genius of the United States is not best or most in its executives or legislatures, nor in its ambassadors or authors, or colleges or churches or parlors, nor even in its newspapers or inventors—but always most in the common people, south, north, west, east, in all its States, through all its mighty amplitude. The largeness of the nation, however, were monstrous without a

heir who approaches . . . and

10. earth, have] 1855: earth have

11. nature] 1868: Nature

12. hitherto, the] 1881, 1868, and 1855: hitherto the

15. night. Here is action] 1881, 1868, and 1855: night. Here is not merely a nation, but [1868 and 1855: nation but] a teeming nation of nations. Here is action

16. strings, * * * magnificently] 1855: strings necessarily blind to particulars and details magnificently

17. in masses] 1881, 1868, and 1855: in vast masses

17. for ever] 1855: forever

17–18. heroes. Here the performance] 1881, 1868, and 1855: heroes . . . Here [1868: heroes. Here; 1855: heroes. . . . Here] are the roughs and beards and space and ruggedness and nonchalance that the soul loves. Here the performance

18. performance, disdaining the trivial, unapproach'd] 1855: performance disdaining the trivial unapproached

19. groupings, and] 1881, 1868, and 1855: groupings and

19–20. perspective, spreads] 1855: perspective spreads

20. breadth, and] 1855: breadth and

23. ground, or] 1881 and 1855: ground or

23. apples, or] 1881 and 1855: apples or

23. fish, or] 1881 and 1855: fish or

25. deputies—but] 1881: deputies . . . but] 1868: deputies: but] 1855: deputies . . . . but

27. authors, or] 1868 and 1855: authors or

27. parlors,] 1868: parlours,

28. inventors—but] 1881 and 1855: inventors . . . but] 1868: inventors, but

28–30. people, * * * however, were] 1881, 1868, and 1855: people. Their manners, speech, dress, [1855: manners speech dress] friendships—[1868: friendships,—] the freshness and candour [1855: candor] of their physiognomy—the picturesque looseness of their carriage . . . their [1868: carriage—their] deathless attachment to freedom—their aversion to anything indecorous, or soft, or [1868 and 1855: indecorous or soft or] mean—the practical acknowledgment of the citizens

corresponding largeness and generosity of the spirit of the citizen. Not swarming states, nor streets and steamships, nor prosperous business, nor farms, nor capital, nor learning, may suffice for the ideal of man—nor suffice the poet. No reminiscences may suffice either. A live nation can always cut a deep mark, and can have the best authority the cheapest—namely, from its own soul. This is the sum of the profitable uses of individuals or states, and of present action and grandeur, and of the subjects of poets. (As if it were necessary to trot back generation after generation to the eastern records! As if the beauty and sacredness of the demonstrable must fall behind that of the mythical! As if men do not make their mark out of any times! As if the opening of the western continent by discovery, and what has transpired in North and South America, were less than the small theatre of the antique, or the aimless sleep-walking of the middle ages!) The pride of the United States leaves the wealth and finesse of the cities, and all returns of commerce and agriculture, and all the magnitude of geography or shows of exterior victory, to

of one state by the citizens of all other states—the fierceness of their roused resentment—their curiosity and welcome of novelty—their self-esteem and wonderful sympathy—their susceptibility to a slight—the air they have of persons who never knew how it felt to stand in the presence of superiors—the fluency of their speech—their delight in music, the sure symptom of manly tenderness and native elegance of soul—their [1855: soul . . . their] good temper and open handedness [1868: open-handedness; 1855: openhandedness]—the terrible significance of their elections—the [1868: elections, the] President's taking off his hat to them, not [1868 and 1855: them not] they to him—these, too, are [1868 and 1855: these too are] unrhymed poetry. It awaits the gigantic and generous treatment worthy of it.

The largeness of nature, or the nation, were [1868 and 1855: nature or the nation were]

31–33. Not swarming * * * learning, may] 1881 and 1868: Not nature nor [1868: nature, nor] swarming states, nor streets and steamships, nor prosperous business nor [1868: business, nor] farms, nor [1868: farms nor] capital nor learning, may] 1855: Not nature nor swarming states nor streets and steamships nor prosperous business nor farms nor capital nor learning may

33. man—nor] 1881 and 1855: man . . . nor] 1868: man, nor

35. mark, and] 1855: mark and

35–36. cheapest—namely, from] 1881: cheapest . . . namely, from] 1868: cheapest—namely from] 1855: cheapest . . . namely from

37. states, and] 1855: states and

37. grandeur, and] 1855: grandeur and

38. poets. (As if] 1881, 1868, and 1855: poets.—As if

42. discovery, and] 1855: discovery and

42–43. America, were] 1855: America were

43. antique, or] 1881 and 1855: antique or

43–44. sleep-walking] 1855: sleepwalking

44. ages!) The] 1881, 1868, and 1855: ages! The

45. cities, and] 1855: cities and

45–46. agriculture, and] 1855: agriculture and

46. victory, to] 1855: victory to

47. enjoy * * * full-sized man] 1881, 1868, and 1855: enjoy the breed of full sized [1868: full-sized; 1855: fullsized] men, or one full sized [1868: full-sized;

enjoy the sight and realization of full-sized men, or one full-sized man unconquerable and simple.

The American poets are to enclose old and new, for America is the race of races. The expression of the American poet is to be transcendent and new. It is to be indirect, and not direct or descriptive or epic. Its quality goes through these to much more. Let the age and wars of other nations be chanted, and their eras and characters be illustrated, and that finish the verse. Not so the great psalm of the republic. Here the theme is creative, and has vista. Whatever stagnates in the flat of custom or obedience or legislation, the great poet never stagnates. Obedience does not master him, he masters it. High up out of reach he stands, turning a concentrated light—he turns the pivot with his finger—he baffles the swiftest runners as he stands, and easily overtakes and envelopes them. The time straying toward infidelity and confections and persiflage he withholds by steady faith. Faith is the antiseptic of the soul—it pervades the common people and preserves them—they never give up believing and

1855: fullsized] man

50. After "race of races." *SDC* deletes a long section of the text of 1881, including the last four lines of page 5, all of page 6, and all except the last four lines of page 7. For the deleted part, with variants in 1868 and 1855 shown in brackets, see Appendix I, *1*.

50. The expression] 1881, 1868, and 1855: For such the expression

51. indirect, and] 1881 and 1855: indirect and

53. chanted, and] 1881 and 1855: chanted and

53. illustrated, and] 1881 and 1855: illustrated and

55. creative, and] 1855: creative and

55. After "has vista." *SDC* deletes a long passage of the text of 1881, including all of page 8 except the first three lines and the last three lines. For the deleted part, with variants in the 1868 and 1855 texts shown in brackets, see Appendix I, *2*.

56. legislation, the great poet never] 1881 and 1868: legislation, he never] 1855: legislation he never

57. stands, turning] 1855: stands turning

58. light—he] 1881 and 1855: light . . . he] 1868: light; he

58. finger—he] 1881 and 1855: finger . . . he] 1868: finger; he

59. stands, and] 1881 and 1855: stands and

61. steady faith. Faith is] 1881: steady faith . . . he [1868: faith; he] spreads out his dishes . . . he [1868: dishes; he] offers the sweet firm-fibred [1855: firmfibred] meat that grows men and women. His brain is the ultimate brain. He is no arguer . . . he [1868: arguer, he] is judgment. He judges not as the judge judges, but [1855: judges but] as the sun falling around a helpless thing. As he sees the farthest he [1868: farthest, he] has the most faith. His thoughts are the hymns of the praise of things. In the talk on the soul and eternity and God, off [1855: God off] of his equal plane, he [1855: plane he] is silent. He sees eternity less like a play with a prologue and denouement . . . he [1868: denouement: he; 1855: denouement . . . . he] sees eternity in men and women . . . he [1868: women,—he] does not see men or women [1868 and 1855: men and women] as dreams or dots. Faith is

61. antiseptic] 1881: anti-septic

61. soul—it] 1881 and 1855: soul . . . it] 1868: soul,—it

62. them—they] 1881 and 1855: them . . . they] 1868: them: they

expecting and trusting. There is that indescribable freshness and unconsciousness about an illiterate person, that humbles and mocks the power of the noblest expressive genius. The poet sees for a certainty how one not a great artist may be just as sacred and perfect as the greatest artist.

The power to destroy or remould is freely used by the greatest poet, but seldom the power of attack. What is past is past. If he does not expose superior models, and prove himself by every step he takes, he is not what is wanted. The presence of the great poet conquers—not parleying, or struggling, or any prepared attempts. Now he has passed that way, see after him! There is not left any vestige of despair, or misanthropy, or cunning, or exclusiveness, or the ignominy of a nativity or color, or delusion of hell or the necessity of hell—and no man thenceforward shall be degraded for ignorance or weakness or sin. The greatest poet hardly knows pettiness or triviality. If he breathes into anything that was before thought small, it dilates with the grandeur and life of the universe. He is a seer—he is individual—he is complete in himself—the others are as good as he, only he sees it, and they do not. He is not one of the chorus—he does not stop for any regulation—he is the president of regulation. What the eyesight does to the rest, he does to the rest. Who knows the curious mystery of the eyesight? The other senses corroborate themselves, but

64. person, that] 1881, 1868, and 1855: person that

67–68. artist.

The power] [1881, 1868, and 1855 continue in the same paragraph.] 1881: artist. . . . The power] 1868: artist. The power] 1855: artist. . . . . . The power

68–69. by the greatest poet, but] 1881 and 1868: by him, but] 1855: by him but

70. models, and] 1881 and 1855: models and

70. takes, he] 1855: takes he

71–72. great poet conquers—not parleying, or struggling, or] 1881: greatest poet conquers . . . not parleying, or struggling, or] 1868: greatest poet conquers; not parleying or struggling or] 1855: greatest poet conquers . . . not parleying or struggling or

72–73. way, see] 1855: way see

73. him! There] 1868 and 1855: him! there

73–74. despair, * * * color, or] 1881: despair, or misanthropy, or cunning, or exclusiveness, or the ignominy of a nativity or colour or] 1868 and 1855: despair or misanthropy or cunning or exclusiveness, or [1855: exclusiveness or] the ignominy of a nativity or colour, or [1855: color or]

75. hell—and] 1881: hell . . . and] 1868: hell; and] 1855: hell . . . . . and

76. After "or sin." 1881, 1868, and 1855 begin a new paragraph.

77. anything] 1868 and 1855: any thing

78. small, it] 1855: small it

79–80. seer—he * * * sees it, and] 1881 and 1855: seer . . . he is individual . . . he is complete in himself . . . the others are as good as he, only he sees it and] 1868: seer—he is individual—he is complete in himself: the others are as good as he; only he sees it, and

80. chorus—he] 1881 and 1855: chorus . . . he

this is removed from any proof but its own, and foreruns the identities of the spiritual world. A single glance of it mocks all the investigations of man, and all the instruments and books of the earth, and all reasoning. What is marvellous? what is unlikely? what is impossible or baseless or vague—after you have once just open'd the space of a peach-pit, and given audience to far and near, and to the sunset, and had all things enter with electric swiftness, softly and duly, without confusion or jostling or jam?

The land and sea, the animals, fishes and birds, the sky of heaven and the orbs, the forests, mountains and rivers, are not small themes—but folks expect of the poet to indicate more than the beauty and dignity which always attach to dumb real objects—they expect him to indicate the path between reality and their souls. Men and women perceive the beauty well enough—probably as well as he. The passionate tenacity of hunters, woodmen, early risers, cultivators of gardens and orchards and fields, the love of healthy women for the manly form, seafaring persons, drivers of horses, the passion for light and the open air, all is an old varied sign of the unfailing perception of beauty, and of a residence of the poetic in out-door people. They can never be assisted by poets to perceive—some may, but they never can. The poetic quality is not marshal'd in rhyme or uniformity, or abstract addresses to things, nor in melancholy complaints or good precepts, but is the life of these and much else, and is in the soul.

81. regulation—he] 1881: regulation . . . he] 1868: regulation—he] 1855: regulations . . . he
82. rest, he] 1868 and 1855: rest he
84. own, and] 1855: own and
86. man, and] 1881 and 1855: man and
86. earth, and] 1881 and 1855: earth and
88. vague—after] 1881, 1868, and 1855: vague? after
88. peach-pit, and] 1881: peach-pit and] 1868: peachpit, and] 1855: peachpit and
89. near, and to the sunset, and] 1881, 1868, and 1855: near and to the sunset, and [1855: sunset and]
90. swiftness, * * * or jam?] 1881 and 1868: swiftness, softly and duly, without confusion, or jostling, or [1868: confusion or jostling or] jam.] 1855: swiftness softly and duly without confusion or jostling or jam.
91. animals, fishes and] 1868: animals, fishes, and] 1855: animals fishes and
92. forests, mountains and] 1868: forests, mountains, and] 1855: forests mountains and
92. themes—but] 1881 and 1855: themes . . . but] 1868: themes: but
94. objects—they] 1881: objects . . . they] 1868: objects,—they] 1855: objects . . . . they
96. enough—probably] 1881: enough . . . probably] 1855: enough . . probably
100. beauty, and] 1855: beauty and
100–101. poetic in out-door] 1868: poetic, in outdoor] 1855: poetic in outdoor
101–102. perceive—some may, but] 1881: perceive . . . some may, but] 1868: perceive: some may, but] 1855: perceive . . . some may but
103. uniformity, or] 1881 and 1855: uniformity or
103. things, nor] 1855: things nor
104. else, and] 1855: else and

The profit of rhyme is that it drops seeds of a sweeter and more luxuriant rhyme, and of uniformity that it conveys itself into its own roots in the ground out of sight. The rhyme and uniformity of perfect poems show the free growth of metrical laws, and bud from them as unerringly and loosely as lilacs and roses on a bush, and take shapes as compact as the shapes of chestnuts and oranges, and melons and pears, and shed the perfume impalpable to form. The fluency and ornaments of the finest poems or music or orations or recitations, are not independent but dependent. All beauty comes from beautiful blood and a beautiful brain. If the greatnesses are in conjunction in a man or woman, it is enough—the fact will prevail through the universe; but the gaggery and gilt of a million years will not prevail. Who troubles himself about his ornaments or fluency is lost. This is what you shall do: Love the earth and sun and the animals, despise riches, give alms to every one that asks, stand up for the stupid and crazy, devote your income and labor to others, hate tyrants, argue not concerning God, have patience and indulgence toward the people, take off your hat to nothing known or unknown, or to any man or number of men—go freely with powerful uneducated persons, and with the young, and with the mothers of families—re-examine all you have been told in school or church or in any book, and dismiss whatever insults your own soul; and your very flesh shall be a great poem, and have the richest

106. rhyme, and of uniformity that] 1868: rhyme; and, of uniformity, that
108. laws, and] 1855: laws and
109. lilacs and roses] 1868 and 1855: lilacs or roses
110. chestnuts * * * melons and] 1881: chestnuts, and oranges, and melons, and] 1868 and 1855: chestnuts and oranges and melons and
112. recitations, are] 1868 and 1855: recitations are
112. independent but] 1868: independent, but
114. woman, it is enough—the] 1881: woman, it is enough . . . the] 1855: woman it is enough . . . . the
115. universe; but] 1881: universe . . . but] 1868: universe: but] 1855: universe . . . . but
117. do: Love * * * sun] 1881: do: Love the earth and the sun] 1868 and 1855: do: love [1855: Love] the earth and sun
119. and crazy] 1881: and the crazy
119. labor] 1881 and 1868: labour
120. toward] 1868: towards
121. unknown, or] 1881, 1868, and 1855: unknown or
122. men—go] 1881, 1868, and 1855: men, go
122–123. persons * * * and] 1881, 1868, and 1855: persons and with the young and
123. families—re-examine] 1881, 1868, and 1855: families, read these leaves in the open air every season of every year of your life, re-examine
124. book, and dismiss] 1881, 1868, and 1855: book, dismiss
125. soul; and] 1855: soul, and

fluency, not only in its words, but in the silent lines of its lips and face, and between the lashes of your eyes, and in every motion and joint of your body. The poet shall not spend his time in unneeded work. He shall know that the ground is already plough'd and manured; others may not know it, but he shall. He shall go directly to the creation. His trust shall master the trust of everything he touches—and shall master all attachment.

The known universe has one complete lover, and that is the greatest poet. He consumes an eternal passion, and is indifferent which chance happens, and which possible contingency of fortune or misfortune, and persuades daily and hourly his delicious pay. What baulks or breaks others is fuel for his burning progress to contact and amorous joy. Other proportions of the reception of pleasure dwindle to nothing to his proportions. All expected from heaven or from the highest, he is rapport with in the sight of the daybreak, or the scenes of the winter woods, or the presence of children playing, or with his arm round the neck of a man or woman. His love above all love has leisure and expanse—he leaves room ahead of himself. He is no irresolute or suspicious lover—he is sure—he scorns intervals. His experience and the showers and thrills are not for nothing. Nothing can jar him—suffering and darkness cannot—death and fear cannot. To him complaint and jealousy and envy are corpses buried and

125–126. poem, * * * not] 1881 and 1855: poem and have the richest fluency not

126–127. face, and] 1881 and 1855: face and

127. eyes, and] 1881 and 1855: eyes and

128. body. The] 1881: body . . . The] 1855: body. . . . . The

129–130. is already * * * it, but] 1881 and 1868: is always ready ploughed and manured . . . others [1868: manured: others] may not know it, but] 1855: is always ready ploughed and manured . . . . others may not know it but

131. touches—and] 1881: touches . . . and] 1868: touches, and] 1855: touches . . . . and

133. lover, and] 1855: lover and

134. passion, and] 1881 and 1855: passion and

134–135. happens, and] 1881 and 1855: happens and

135. misfortune, and] 1855: misfortune and

136. baulks] 1868 and 1855: balks

139. highest, he] 1881, 1868, and 1855: highest he

140. daybreak, or the scenes] 1881: daybreak or the scene] 1868: daybreak, or a scene] 1855: daybreak or a scene

140–141. woods, * * * playing, or] 1881 and 1855: woods or the presence of children playing or

142. love above all love has] 1868: love, above all love, has

142. expanse—he] 1881: expanse . . . he] 1855: expanse . . . . he

143. lover—he is sure—he] 1881 and 1855: lover . . . he is sure . . . he

145. him—suffering] 1881: him . . . suffering] 1868: him: suffering] 1855: him . . . . suffering

rotten in the earth—he saw them buried. The sea is not surer of the shore, or the shore of the sea, than he is the fruition of his love, and of all perfection and beauty.

The fruition of beauty is no chance of miss or hit—it is as inevitable as life—it is exact and plumb as gravitation. From the eyesight proceeds another eyesight, and from the hearing proceeds another hearing, and from the voice proceeds another voice, eternally curious of the harmony of things with man. These understand the law of perfection in masses and floods—that it is profuse and impartial—that there is not a minute of the light or dark, nor an acre of the earth and sea, without it—nor any direction of the sky, nor any trade or employment, nor any turn of events. This is the reason that about the proper expression of beauty there is precision and balance. One part does not need to be thrust above another. The best singer is not the one who has the most lithe and powerful organ. The pleasure of poems is not in them that take the handsomest measure and sound.

Without effort, and without exposing in the least how it is done, the greatest poet brings the spirit of any or all events and passions and scenes and persons, some more and some less, to bear on your individual character as you hear or read. To do this well is to compete with the laws that pursue and follow Time. What is the purpose must surely be there,

147. earth—he] 1881: earth . . . he] 1855: earth . . . . he

147–148. shore, * * * than] 1855: shore or the shore of the sea than

148. love, and] 1881 and 1855: love and

150. of miss or hit—it] 1881: of miss or hit . . . it] 1868: of hit or miss—it] 1855: of hit or miss . . . it

151. life—it] 1881: life . . . it] 1855: life . . . . it

152. eyesight, and] 1881 and 1855: eyesight and

152. hearing, and] 1881 and 1855: hearing and

153. voice, eternally] 1881 and 1855: voice eternally

154. man. These] 1881, 1868, and 1855: man. To these respond perfections not [1868: perfections, not] only in the committees that were supposed to stand for the rest, but [1855: rest but] in the rest themselves, just [1868 and 1855: themselves just] the same. These

155. floods—that it is] 1881, 1868, and 1855: floods . . . that [1868: floods—that] its finish is to each for itself and onward from itself . . . that [1868: itself—that] it is

155. impartial—that] 1881 and 1855: impartial . . . that

156. dark, nor] 1881 and 1855: dark nor

156. earth and sea, without] 1868: earth or sea, without] 1855: earth or sea without

157. sky, nor * * * nor] 1881 and 1855: sky nor any trade or employment nor

159. balance. One] 1881 and 1855: balance . . . one] 1868: balance,—one

160–161. organ. The] 1881 and 1855: organ . . . the] 1868: organ: the

161–162. measure and sound] 1881, 1868, and 1855: measure and similes and

and the clue of it must be there—and the faintest indication is the indication of the best, and then becomes the clearest indication. Past and present and future are not disjoin'd but join'd. The greatest poet forms the consistence of what is to be, from what has been and is. He drags the dead out of their coffins and stands them again on their feet. He says to the past, Rise and walk before me that I may realize you. He learns the lesson—he places himself where the future becomes present. The greatest poet does not only dazzle his rays over character and scenes and passions—he finally ascends, and finishes all—he exhibits the pinnacles that no man can tell what they are for, or what is beyond—he glows a moment on the extremest verge. He is most wonderful in his last half-hidden smile or frown; by that flash of the moment of parting the one that sees it shall be encouraged or terrified afterward for many years. The greatest poet does not moralize or make applications of morals—he knows the soul. The soul has that measureless pride which consists in never acknowledging any lessons or deductions but its own. But it has sympathy as measureless as its pride, and the one balances the other, and neither can stretch too far while it stretches in company with the other. The inmost secrets of art sleep with the twain. The greatest poet has lain close betwixt both, and they are vital in his style and thoughts.

The art of art, the glory of expression and the sunshine of the light

sound
163. effort, and] 1855: effort and
163. done, the] 1855: done the
165. persons, some] 1855: persons some
165. less, to] 1855: less to
166. character as] 1868: character, as
167. Time] 1881, 1868, and 1855: time
167–168. there, and] 1881 and 1855: there and
168. there—and] 1881: there . . . and] 1868: there; and] 1855: there . . . . and
169. best, and] 1855: best and
171. be, from] 1881, 1868, and 1855: be from
172. coffins and] 1868: coffins, and
172. feet. He] 1881: feet . . . he] 1868: feet: he] 1855: feet . . . . he
173. lesson—he] 1881: lesson . . . he] 1855: lesson . . . . he
175–176. passions— * * * all—he] 1881 and 1855: passions . . . he finally ascends, and [1855: ascends and] finishes all . . . he] 1868: passions,—he finally ascends and finishes all: he
177. for, or what is beyond—he] 1881: for or what is beyond . . . he] 1868: for or what is beyond—he] 1855: for or what is beyond . . . . he
178. frown; by] 1881 and 1855: frown . . . by] 1868: frown: by
180. afterward] 1855: afterwards
181. morals—he] 1881 and 1855: morals . . . he] 1868: morals,—he
182–183. lessons or deductions but] 1881, 1868, and 1855: lessons but
184. pride, and * * * other, and] 1855: pride and * * * other and
186. both, and] 1855: both and

of letters, is simplicity. Nothing is better than simplicity—nothing can make up for excess, or for the lack of definiteness. To carry on the heave of impulse and pierce intellectual depths and give all subjects their articulations, are powers neither common nor very uncommon. But to speak in literature with the perfect rectitude and insouciance of the movements of animals, and the unimpeachableness of the sentiment of trees in the woods and grass by the roadside, is the flawless triumph of art. If you have look'd on him who has achiev'd it you have look'd on one of the masters of the artists of all nations and times. You shall not contemplate the flight of the gray gull over the bay, or the mettlesome action of the blood horse, or the tall leaning of sunflowers on their stalk, or the appearance of the sun journeying through heaven, or the appearance of the moon afterward, with any more satisfaction than you shall contemplate him. The great poet has less a mark'd style, and is more the channel of thoughts and things without increase or diminution, and is the free channel of himself. He swears to his art, I will not be meddlesome, I will not have in my writing any elegance, or effect, or originality, to hang in the way between me and the rest like curtains. I will have nothing hang in the way, not the richest curtains. What I tell I tell for precisely what it is. Let who may exalt or startle or fascinate or soothe, I will have purposes as health or heat or snow has, and be as regardless of observation. What I experience or portray shall go from my composition without a shred of

189. letters, is] 1855: letters is
189. simplicity—nothing] 1881: simplicity . . . nothing] 1868: simplicity,—nothing] 1855: simplicity . . . . nothing
190. excess, or] 1881, 1868, and 1855: excess or
190. After "definiteness." 1881 begins a new paragraph.
191. impulse and] 1868: impulse, and
191. depths and] 1868: depths, and
191–192. articulations, are] 1855: articulations are
194. animals, and] 1855: animals and
195. roadside, is] 1855: roadside is
196. it you] 1868: it, you
198. gray gull] 1868: grey-gull] 1855: graygull
198. bay, or] 1881 and 1855: bay or
199. horse, or] 1881 and 1855: horse or
199. stalk, or] 1881 and 1855: stalk or
200. heaven, or] 1881 and 1855: heaven or
201. afterward, with] 1855: afterward with
202. great] 1881, 1868, 1855: greatest
202. style, and] 1881 and 1855: style and
203. diminution, and] 1881: diminution and
204. art, I] 1881: art—I] 1868: art,—I
205. elegance, * * * to] 1868 and 1855: elegance or effect or originality to
208. soothe, I] 1868: sooth, I] 1855: sooth I

my composition. You shall stand by my side and look in the mirror with me.

The old red blood and stainless gentility of great poets will be proved by their unconstraint. A heroic person walks at his ease through and out of that custom or precedent or authority that suits him not. Of the traits of the brotherhood of first-class writers, savans, musicians, inventors and artists, nothing is finer than silent defiance advancing from new free forms. In the need of poems, philosophy, politics, mechanism, science, behavior, the craft of art, an appropriate native grand opera, shipcraft, or any craft, he is greatest for ever and ever who contributes the greatest original practical example. The cleanest expression is that which finds no sphere worthy of itself, and makes one.

The messages of great poems to each man and woman are, Come to us on equal terms, only then can you understand us. We are no better than you, what we inclose you inclose, what we enjoy you may enjoy. Did you suppose there could be only one Supreme? We affirm there can be unnumber'd Supremes, and that one does not countervail another any more than one eyesight countervails another—and that men can be good or grand only of the consciousness of their supremacy within them. What do you think is the grandeur of storms and dismemberments, and the deadliest battles and wrecks, and the wildest fury of the elements, and the power of the sea, and the motion of nature, and the throes of human

209. has, and] 1855: has and
211. side and] 1868: side, and
216–217. of first-class * * * nothing] 1881 and 1868: of writers, savans, musicians, inventors and [1868: inventors, and] artists, nothing] 1855: of writers savans musicians inventors and artists nothing
218–219. poems, * * * behavior, the] 1881 and 1868: poems, * * * behaviour, the] 1855: poems philosophy politics mechanism science behaviour, the
219. grand opera] 1855: grand-opera
219–220. shipcraft, or] 1881 and 1868: shipcraft or
220. for ever and ever] 1881: for ever and for ever] 1868 and 1855: forever and forever
222. itself, and] 1855: itself and
223. poems] 1868 and 1855: poets
223. are, Come] 1868: are,—Come
224. terms, only] 1855: terms, Only
225. you, what * * * inclose, what] 1881: you, what we enclose you enclose, what] 1868: you; what we enclose you enclose, what] 1855: you, What we enclose you enclose, What
227. Supremes, and] 1881: Supremes and
228. another—and] 1881: another . . . and] 1855: another . . and
230. dismemberments, and] 1881 and 1855: dismemberments and
231. wrecks, and] 1881 and 1855: wrecks and
231–233. elements, * * * desires, and] 1881 and 1855: elements and the power of the sea and the motion of nature and the throes of human desires and

desires, and dignity and hate and love? It is that something in the soul which says, Rage on, whirl on, I tread master here and everywhere—Master of the spasms of the sky and of the shatter of the sea, Master of nature and passion and death, and of all terror and all pain.

The American bards shall be mark'd for generosity and affection, and for encouraging competitors. They shall be Kosmos, without monopoly or secrecy, glad to pass anything to any one—hungry for equals night and day. They shall not be careful of riches and privilege—they shall be riches and privilege—they shall perceive who the most affluent man is. The most affluent man is he that confronts all the shows he sees by equivalents out of the stronger wealth of himself. The American bard shall delineate no class of persons, nor one or two out of the strata of interests, nor love most nor truth most, nor the soul most, nor the body most—and not be for the Eastern states more than the Western, or the Northern states more than the Southern.

Exact science and its practical movements are no checks on the greatest poet, but always his encouragement and support. The outset and remembrance are there—there the arms that lifted him first, and braced him best—there he returns after all his goings and comings. The sailor

234. says, Rage on, whirl] 1868: says,—Rage on, whirl] 1855: says, Rage on, Whirl

234–235. everywhere—Master] 1868: everywhere; master] 1855: everywhere, Master

235. Master] 1868: master

236. and] 1855: And

237. affection, and] 1868 and 1855: affection and

238–239. competitors. They * * * any one—hungry] 1881: competitors ... They shall be Kosmos ... without monopoly or secrecy ... glad to pass any thing to any one ... hungry] 1868: competitors: they shall be kosmos—without monopoly or secrecy—glad to pass any thing to any one—hungry] 1855: competitors .. They shall be kosmos .. without monopoly or secresy .. glad to pass any thing to any one .. hungry

240. privilege—they shall be riches and privilege—they] 1881 and 1855: privilege ... they [1855: privilege .... they] shall be riches and privilege ... they [1855: privilege .... they] 1868: privilege,—they shall be riches and privilege: they

244. persons, nor] 1881 and 1855: persons nor

244–245. interests, * * * most, nor] 1881 and 1855: interests nor love most nor truth most nor

245–247. soul most, * * * Southern] 1881, 1868, and 1855: soul most nor the body most ... and [1868: most; and; 1855: most .... and] not be for the eastern states more than the western or [1868: western, or] the northern states more than the southern

249. poet, but] 1855: poet but

250. there—there] 1881: there ... there] 1855: there .. there

250–251. first, and braced him best—there] 1881, 1868, and 1855: first and brace him best ... there [1868: best—there; 1855: best .... there]

252. traveler—the] 1881: traveller ... the] 1868: traveller, the] 1855: trav-

and traveler—the anatomist, chemist, astronomer, geologist, phrenologist, spiritualist, mathematician, historian, and lexicographer, are not poets, but they are the lawgivers of poets, and their construction underlies the structure of every perfect poem. No matter what rises or is utter'd, they sent the seed of the conception of it—of them and by them stand the visible proofs of souls. If there shall be love and content between the father and the son, and if the greatness of the son is the exuding of the greatness of the father, there shall be love between the poet and the man of demonstrable science. In the beauty of poems are henceforth the tuft and final applause of science.

Great is the faith of the flush of knowledge, and of the investigation of the depths of qualities and things. Cleaving and circling here swells the soul of the poet, yet is president of itself always. The depths are fathomless, and therefore calm. The innocence and nakedness are resumed —they are neither modest nor immodest. The whole theory of the supernatural, and all that was twined with it or educed out of it, departs as a dream. What has ever happen'd—what happens, and whatever may or shall happen, the vital laws inclose all. They are sufficient for any case and for all cases—none to be hurried or retarded—any special miracle of af-

eler . . the

252–253. anatomist, * * * historian, and lexicographer, are] 1881: anatomist * * * historian and lexicographer, are] 1855: anatomist chemist astronomer geologist phrenologist spiritualist mathematician historian and lexicographer are

253–254. poets, but] 1868: poets; but

254. poets, and] 1855: poets and

255. utter'd, they] 1855: uttered they

256. of it—of them] 1881 and 1855: of it . . . of them] 1868: of it: of them

257. souls. If there] 1881 and 1855: souls . . . always [1855: souls . . . . . always] of their father-stuff [1855: fatherstuff] must be begotten the sinewy races of bards. If there

258. son, and] 1855: son and

259. father, there] 1855: father there

260. are henceforth the] 1881, 1868, and 1855: are the

262. knowledge, and] 1881 and 1855: knowledge and

263. here swells] 1881: here, swells

264. poet, yet] 1868: poet: yet] 1855: poet yet

265. fathomless, and] 1881, 1868, and 1855: fathomless and

265–266. resumed—they] 1881 and 1855: resumed . . . they

266–267. the supernatural, and] 1881, 1868, and 1855: the special and supernatural and [1868: supernatural, and]

267. it, departs] 1855: it departs

268. After "as a dream." 1881 begins a new paragraph.

268. happen'd—what happens, and] 1881 and 1868: happened . . . what [1868: happened, what] happens, and] 1855: happened . . . . what happens and

269. inclose all. They] 1881: enclose all . . . they] 1868: enclose all: they] 1855: enclose all . . . they

270. cases—none] 1881 and 1855: cases . . . none

270. retarded—any special miracle] 1881: retarded . . . any miracle] 1868: retarded—any miracle] 1855: retarded . . . . any miracle

fairs or persons inadmissible in the vast clear scheme where every motion and every spear of grass, and the frames and spirits of men and women and all that concerns them, are unspeakably perfect miracles, all referring to all, and each distinct and in its place. It is also not consistent with the reality of the soul to admit that there is anything in the known universe more divine than men and women.

Men and women, and the earth and all upon it, are to be taken as they are, and the investigation of their past and present and future shall be unintermitted, and shall be done with perfect candor. Upon this basis philosophy speculates, ever looking towards the poet, ever regarding the eternal tendencies of all toward happiness, never inconsistent with what is clear to the senses and to the soul. For the eternal tendencies of all toward happiness make the only point of sane philosophy. Whatever comprehends less than that—whatever is less than the laws of light and of astronomical motion—or less than the laws that follow the thief, the liar, the glutton and the drunkard, through this life and doubtless afterward —or less than vast stretches of time, or the slow formation of density, or the patient upheaving of strata—is of no account. Whatever would put God in a poem or system of philosophy as contending against some being or influence, is also of no account. Sanity and ensemble characterize the great master—spoilt in one principle, all is spoilt. The great master has

271–272. motion and] 1868: motion, and
272. grass, and] 1881 and 1855: grass and
272–273. women and] 1868: women, and
273. them, are] 1855: them are
273–274. miracles, * * * and] 1855: miracles all referring to all and
277. women, * * * are to] 1881 and 1868: women, and the earth, and [1868: earth and] all upon it, are simply to] 1855: women and the earth and all upon it are simply to
279. unintermitted, and] 1855: unintermitted and
279. candor] 1881 and 1868: candour
280. speculates, ever] 1855: speculates ever
280. towards] 1868 and 1855: toward
281. happiness, never] 1855: happiness never
284. that—whatever] 1881 and 1855: that . . . whatever
285. motion—or] 1881 and 1855: motion . . . or
285–286. thief, the liar, the] 1855: thief the liar the
286. glutton * * * life and] 1881 and 1855: glutton and the drunkard through this life and] 1868: glutton, and the drunkard, through this life, and
286–287. afterward—or] 1881: afterward . . . or] 1855: afterward . . . . . . or
287. time, or] 1881 and 1855: time or
287–288. density, or] 1881 and 1855: density or
290. influence, is] 1881, 1868, and 1855: influence is
291. master— * * * all] 1881 and 1855: master . . . spoilt in one principle all] 1868: master:—spoilt in one principle, all
293. mass—he] 1881: mass . . . he] 1855: mass . . . . he
294. great, for] 1855: great for

nothing to do with miracles. He sees health for himself in being one of the mass—he sees the hiatus in singular eminence. To the perfect shape comes common ground. To be under the general law is great, for that is to correspond with it. The master knows that he is unspeakably great, and that all are unspeakably great—that nothing, for instance, is greater than to conceive children, and bring them up well—that to *be* is just as great as to perceive or tell.

In the make of the great masters the idea of political liberty is indispensable. Liberty takes the adherence of heroes wherever man and woman exist—but never takes any adherence or welcome from the rest more than from poets. They are the voice and exposition of liberty. They out of ages are worthy the grand idea—to them it is confided, and they must sustain it. Nothing has precedence of it, and nothing can warp or degrade it.

As the attributes of the poets of the kosmos concentre in the real body, and in the pleasure of things, they possess the superiority of genuineness over all fiction and romance. As they emit themselves, facts are shower'd over with light—the daylight is lit with more volatile light—the deep between the setting and rising sun goes deeper many fold. Each precise object or condition or combination or process exhibits a beauty—the multiplication table its—old age its—the carpenter's trade its—the grand opera

295. great, and] 1881 and 1855: great and

296. great— * * * is] 1881: great . . . that nothing, for instance, is] 1868 and 1855: great—that [1855: great . . . . that] nothing for instance is

297. children, * * * to *be*] 1881 and 1855: children and bring them up well . . . that to be] 1868: children, and bring them up well—that to be

300–301. man and woman exist—but] 1881: man and woman exist . . . but] 1868: men and women exist; but] 1855: men and women exist . . . . but

303. idea—to them it is confided, and] 1881 and 1855: idea . . . to [1855: idea . . . . to] them it is confided and] 1868: idea,—to them it is confided, and

304. it, and] 1881 and 1855: it and

305. After "degrade it." SDC deletes the rest of the paragraph in 1881, including all of page 19 except the first three lines and all of page 20 except the last six. For the deleted part, with variants in 1868 and 1855 shown in brackets, see Appendix I, 3.

306. kosmos] 1881: Kosmos

306–307. real body, and in] 1881, 1868, and 1855: real body and soul and in

307. things, they] 1855: things they

308. themselves, facts] 1855: themselves facts

309. light—the] 1881: light . . . the] 1855: light . . . . the

309. light—the] 1881: light . . . also the] 1868: light—also the] 1855: light . . . . also the

310. many fold] 1868: many-fold

311. beauty—the] 1881: beauty . . . the] 1868: beauty: the] 1855: beauty . . . . the

312–313. grand * * * New York] 1881: grand opera its—the huge hulled clean-shaped New York] 1868: grand opera its: the huge-hulled clean-shaped New York] 1855: grand-opera its . . . . the hugehulled cleanshaped New-York

its—the huge-hull'd clean-shap'd New York clipper at sea under steam or full sail gleams with unmatch'd beauty—the American circles and large harmonies of government gleam with theirs—and the commonest definite intentions and actions with theirs. The poets of the kosmos advance through all interpositions and coverings and turmoils and strategems to first principles. They are of use—they dissolve poverty from its need, and riches from its conceit. You large proprietor, they say, shall not realize or perceive more than any one else. The owner of the library is not he who holds a legal title to it, having bought and paid for it. Any one and every one is owner of the library, (indeed he or she alone is owner,) who can read the same through all the varieties of tongues and subjects and styles, and in whom they enter with ease, and make supple and powerful and rich and large.

These American States, strong and healthy and accomplish'd, shall receive no pleasure from violations of natural models, and must not permit them. In paintings or mouldings or carvings in mineral or wood, or in the illustrations of books or newspapers, or in the patterns of woven stuffs, or anything to beautify rooms or furniture or costumes, or to put upon cornices or monuments, or on the prows or sterns of ships, or to put anywhere before the human eye indoors or out, that which distorts honest shapes, or which creates unearthly beings or places or contingencies, is a nuisance and revolt. Of the human form especially, it is so great it must

314. beauty—the] 1881: beauty . . . the] 1855: beauty . . . . the
315. theirs—and] 1881: theirs . . . and] 1868: theirs, and] 1855: theirs . . . . and
316. kosmos] 1881: Kosmos
318. use—they] 1881: use . . . they] 1855: use . . . . they
318. need, and] 1881 and 1855: need and
319. proprietor, they say, shall] 1855: proprietor they say shall
321. it, having] 1881: it having
322. library, (indeed he or she alone is owner,) who] 1881, 1868, and 1855: library who
324. ease, and make] 1881, 1868, and 1855: ease, and take residence and force toward paternity and maternity, and make
325–326. and large.
These American States, strong] 1881: and large. . . . These American states, strong] 1868: and large. These American states, strong] 1855: and large. . . . . These American states [After "large," 1881, 1868, and 1855 continue in the same paragraph.]
326. accomplish'd, shall] 1855: accomplished shall
327. models, and] 1855: models and
329. books or newspapers] 1881: books and newspapers
329. newspapers, or in the patterns] 1881, 1868, and 1855: newspapers, or in any comic or tragic prints, or in the patterns
329–330. stuffs, or anything] 1881: stuffs or anything] 1855: stuffs or any thing
331. monuments, or] 1881, 1868, and 1855: monuments or
333. shapes, or] 1881 and 1855: shapes or
333. contingencies, is] 1855: contingencies is
334. especially, it] 1855: especially it

never be made ridiculous. Of ornaments to a work nothing outre can be allow'd—but those ornaments can be allow'd that conform to the perfect facts of the open air, and that flow out of the nature of the work, and come irrepressibly from it, and are necessary to the completion of the work. Most works are most beautiful without ornament. Exaggerations will be revenged in human physiology. Clean and vigorous children are jetted and conceiv'd only in those communities where the models of natural forms are public every day. Great genius and the people of these States must never be demean'd to romances. As soon as histories are properly told, no more need of romances.

The great poets are to be known by the absence in them of tricks, and by the justification of perfect personal candor. All faults may be forgiven of him who has perfect candor. Henceforth let no man of us lie, for we have seen that openness wins the inner and outer world, and that there is no single exception, and that never since our earth gather'd itself in a mass have deceit or subterfuge or prevarication attracted its smallest particle or the faintest tinge of a shade—and that through the enveloping wealth and rank of a state, or the whole republic of states, a sneak or sly person shall be discover'd and despised—and that the soul has never once been fool'd and never can be fool'd—and thrift without the loving nod of the soul is only a fœtid puff—and there never grew up in any of the continents of the globe, nor upon any planet or satellite, nor in that condition

335–336. work nothing outre can be allow'd—but] 1881 and 1855: work nothing outre can be allowed . . . but [1855: allowed . . but] 1868: work, nothing outré can be allowed; but

337. air, and] 1855: air and

337. work, and] 1881 and 1855: work and

338. from it, and are necessary] 1881 and 1855: from it and [1855: and are] necessary

339. ornament. Exaggerations] 1881: ornament . . . Exaggerations] 1855: ornament. . . Exaggerations

340–341. are jetted and conceived] 1868: are conceived

342. day. Great] 1881: day . . . Great] 1855: day. . . . . Great

342. States] 1881, 1868, and 1855: states

344. told, no] 1881 and 1855: told there is no] 1868: told, there is no

345. are to] 1881, 1868, and 1855: are also to

345. tricks, and] 1881 and 1855: tricks and

346. candor. All] 1881, 1868, and 1855: candor. [1868: candour.] These [1868 and 1855: Then] folks echo a new cheap joy and a divine voice leaping from their brains. How [1855: brains: How] beautiful is candor! [1868: candour!] All

347. candor.] 1868: candour.

348. world, and] 1881 and 1855: world and

352. state, or * * * states, a] 1868 and 1855: state or the whole republic of states a

353. despised—and] 1881: despised . . . and] 1855: despised . . . . and

354. fool'd—and] 1881: fooled . . . and] 1855: fooled . . . . and

355. puff—and] 1881: puff . . . and] 1855: puff . . . . and

356. globe, nor] 1855: globe nor

which precedes the birth of babes, nor at any time during the changes of life, nor in any stretch of abeyance or action of vitality, nor in any process of formation or reformation anywhere, a being whose instinct hated the truth.

Extreme caution or prudence, the soundest organic health, large hope and comparison and fondness for women and children, large alimentiveness and destructiveness and causality, with a perfect sense of the oneness of nature, and the propriety of the same spirit applied to human affairs, are called up of the float of the brain of the world to be parts of the greatest poet from his birth out of his mother's womb, and from her birth out of her mother's. Caution seldom goes far enough. It has been thought that the prudent citizen was the citizen who applied himself to solid gains, and did well for himself and for his family, and completed a lawful life without debt or crime. The greatest poet sees and admits these economies as he sees the economies of food and sleep, but has higher notions of prudence than to think he gives much when he gives a few slight attentions at the latch of the gate. The premises of the prudence of life are not the hospitality of it, or the ripeness and harvest of it. Beyond the independence of a little sum laid aside for burial-money, and of a few clap-boards around and shingles overhead on a lot of American soil own'd, and the easy dollars that supply the year's plain clothing and meals, the melancholy prudence of the abandonment of such a great being as a man is, to the toss and pallor of years of money-making, with all their

356. satellite, nor in that] 1881, 1868, and 1855: satellite, or [1868 and 1855: satellite or] star, nor upon the asteroids, nor in any part of ethereal space, nor in the midst of density, nor under the fluid wet of the sea, nor in that

358. life, nor in any] 1881, 1868, and 1855: life, nor in that condition that follows what we term death, nor in any

358. action of] 1881, 1868, and 1855: action afterward of

362. comparison and] 1881: comparison, and

364. nature, and] 1881 and 1855: nature and

364–365. affairs, are] 1881: affairs . . . these are] 1868: affairs—these are] 1855: affairs . . these are

366–367. birth * * * womb, and * * * Caution] 1881 and 1855: birth * * * womb and * * * Caution] 1868: birth. Caution

369. gains, and] 1881 and 1855: gains and

369. and for his family, and] 1881: and for his family and] 1868: and his family, and] 1855: and his family and

374. of it, or] 1881 and 1855: of it or

376. clap-boards] 1868 and 1855: clapboards

379. is, to] 1881, 1868, and 1855: is to

379. money-making, with] 1881 and 1868: moneymaking, with] 1855: money-making with

380. nights, and] 1855: nights and

380. underhand] 1881, 1868, and 1855: underhanded

381. parlors] 1881 and 1868: parlours

scorching days and icy nights, and all their stifling deceits and underhand dodgings, or infinitesimals of parlors, or shameless stuffing while others starve, and all the loss of the bloom and odor of the earth, and of the flowers and atmosphere, and of the sea, and of the true taste of the women and men you pass or have to do with in youth or middle age, and the issuing sickness and desperate revolt at the close of a life without elevation or naïveté, (even if you have achiev'd a secure 10,000 a year, or election to Congress or the Governorship,) and the ghastly chatter of a death without serenity or majesty, is the great fraud upon modern civilization and forethought, blotching the surface and system which civilization undeniably drafts, and moistening with tears the immense features it spreads and spreads with such velocity before the reach'd kisses of the soul.

Ever the right explanation remains to be made about prudence. The prudence of the mere wealth and respectability of the most esteem'd life appears too faint for the eye to observe at all, when little and large alike drop quietly aside at the thought of the prudence suitable for immortality. What is the wisdom that fills the thinness of a year, or seventy or eighty years—to the wisdom spaced out by ages, and coming back at a certain time with strong reinforcements and rich presents, and the clear faces of wedding-guests as far as you can look, in every direction, running gaily toward you? Only the soul is of itself—all else has reference to what ensues. All that a person does or thinks is of consequence. Nor can the

382. starve, and] 1881: starve . . . and] 1868: starve,—and] 1855: starve . . and
382. odor] 1881 and 1868: odour
382. earth, and] 1881 and 1855: earth and
383. atmosphere, and of the sea, and] 1881 and 1855: atmosphere and of the sea, and [1855: sea and]
386–387. naïveté, * * * and] 1881 and 1868: naïveté, and] 1855: naivete, and
388. majesty, is] 1868: majesty,—is
389. forethought, blotching] 1868: forethought; blotching
391–393. of the soul.
Ever the right] 1881, 1868, and 1855: of the soul. . . . Still [1868: soul. Still; 1855: soul. . . Still] the right [Same paragraph continued in 1881, 1868, 1855.]
395. all, when] 1881, 1868, and 1855: all when
397. is thc wisdom] 1881, 1868, and 1855: is wisdom
397. year, or] 1881: year, of] 1868 and 1855: year or
398. years—to the wisdom] 1881: years, of wisdom] 1868: years, to wisdom] 1855: years to wisdom
398. ages, and] 1881 and 1855: ages and
399. presents, and] 1868 and 1855: presents and
400. look, in every direction, running] 1868 and 1855: look in every direction running
401. itself—all] 1881: itself . . . all] 1855: itself . . . . all
402. After "of consequence." *SDC* deletes the remaining eleven lines of page 24 of the 1881 text and the first ten lines of page 25. For the deleted passage, with variants in 1868 and 1855 in brackets, see Appendix I, *4*.

push of charity or personal force ever be anything else than the profoundest reason, whether it brings argument to hand or no. No specification is necessary—to add or subtract or divide is in vain. Little or big, learn'd or unlearn'd, white or black, legal or illegal, sick or well, from the first inspiration down the windpipe to the last expiration out of it, all that a male or female does that is vigorous and benevolent and clean is so much sure profit to him or her in the unshakable order of the universe, and through the whole scope of it forever. The prudence of the greatest poet answers at last the craving and glut of the soul, puts off nothing, permits no let-up for its own case or any case, has no particular sabbath or judgment day, divides not the living from the dead, or the righteous from the unrighteous, is satisfied with the present, matches every thought or act by its correlative, and knows no possible forgiveness or deputed atonement.

The direct trial of him who would be the greatest poet is to-day. If he does not flood himself with the immediate age as with vast oceanic tides —if he be not himself the age transfigur'd, and if to him is not open'd the eternity which gives similitude to all periods and locations and processes, and animate and inanimate forms, and which is the bond of time, and rises up from its inconceivable vagueness and infiniteness in the swimming shapes of to-day, and is held by the ductile anchors of life, and makes the

405. necessary—to] 1881: necessary . . . to] 1855: necessary . . to

409. universe, and] 1881, 1868, and 1855: universe and

410. forever.] 1881: for ever.

410. After "forever." SDC deletes the remaining twelve lines of page 25, and all except the last eight lines of page 26, of the text of 1881. For the deleted passage, with variants in 1868 and 1855 in brackets, see Appendix I, 5.

411. soul, puts off] 1881, 1868, and 1855: soul, is not contemptuous of less ways of prudence if they conform to its ways, puts off

412–413. sabbath or judgment day] 1868: Sabbath or judgment-day] 1855: sabbath or judgment-day

413. dead, or] 1881, 1868, and 1855: dead or

415. correlative, and knows] 1881, 1868, and 1855: correlative, knows

416. SDC deletes the first eleven lines of page 27, text of 1881, which in earlier texts form the conclusion of the sentence and paragraph which SDC ends with the word "atonement." For the deleted passage, with variants in 1868 and 1855 shown in brackets, see Appendix I, 6.

416. to-day] 1855: today

417–418. tides—if he be] 1881 and 1855: tides . . . and [1855: tides . . . . . and] if he does not attract his own land body [1855: bady] and soul to himself, and [1855: himself and] hand on its neck with incomparable love, and [1855: love and] plunge his semitic muscle into its merits and demerits . . . and if he be] 1868: tides—and if he does not attract his own land body and soul to himself, and hang on its neck with incomparable love—and if he be

418. transfigur'd, and] 1881: transfigured . . . and] 1868: transfigured—and] 1855: transfigured . . . . and

419–420. processes, and] 1881, 1868, and 1855: processes and

422. shapes of to-day] 1868: shape of to-day] 1855: shape of today

present spot the passage from what was to what shall be, and commits itself to the representation of this wave of an hour, and this one of the sixty beautiful children of the wave—let him merge in the general run, and wait his development.

Still the final test of poems, or any character or work, remains. The prescient poet projects himself centuries ahead, and judges performer or performance after the changes of time. Does it live through them? Does it still hold on untired? Will the same style, and the direction of genius to similar points, be satisfactory now? Have the marches of tens and hundreds and thousands of years made willing detours to the right hand and the left hand for his sake? Is he beloved long and long after he is buried? Does the young man think often of him? and the young woman think often of him? and do the middle-aged and the old think of him?

A great poem is for ages and ages in common, and for all degrees and complexions, and all departments and sects, and for a woman as much as a man, and a man as much as a woman. A great poem is no finish to a man or woman, but rather a beginning. Has any one fancied he could sit at last under some due authority, and rest satisfied with explanations, and realize, and be content and full? To no such terminus does the greatest poet bring—he brings neither cessation nor shelter'd fatness and ease.

424. hour, and] 1881 and 1855: hour and

425–426. run, and] 1881, 1868, and 1855: run and

426–427. development.
Still the] 1881: development. . . . Still the] 1868: development. . . . . . Still, the] 1855: developement. . . . . Still the [After "development." 1881, 1868, and 1855 continue the same paragraph.]

427. poems, * * * remains] 1881, 1868, and 1855: poems or any character of work remains

428. ahead, and] 1881 and 1855: ahead and

430. style, and] 1881 and 1855: style and

431. points, be] 1881 and 1855: points be

431. now? Have the marches] 1881, 1868, and 1855: now? Has no new discovery in science or [1868: science, or] arrival at superior planes of thought and judgment and behaviour fixed him, or lies so [1868: behaviour, fixed him or his so; 1855: behaviour fixed him or his so] that either can be looked down upon? Have the marches

435. middle-aged] 1881: middle aged] 1855: middleaged

436. ages in common, and] 1868: ages, in common, and] 1855: ages and ages in common and

437. complexions, and] 1855: complexions and

437. sects, and] 1855: sects and

438. man, and] 1855: man and

439. woman, but] 1881 and 1855: woman but

440. authority, and] 1881 and 1855: authority and

440–441. explanations, and realize, and] 1881 and 1855: explanations and realize and] 1868: explanations, and realize and

442. bring—he] 1881 and 1855: bring . . . he

The touch of him, like Nature, tells in action. Whom he takes he takes with firm sure grasp into live regions previously unattain'd—thenceforward is no rest—they see the space and ineffable sheen that turn the old spots and lights into dead vacuums. Now there shall be a man cohered out of tumult and chaos—the elder encourages the younger and shows him how—they two shall launch off fearlessly together till the new world fits an orbit for itself, and looks unabash'd on the lesser orbits of the stars, and sweeps through the ceaseless rings, and shall never be quiet again.

There will soon be no more priests. Their work is done. A new order shall arise, and they shall be the priests of man, and every man shall be his own priest. They shall find their inspiration in real objects to-day, symptoms of the past and future. They shall not deign to defend immortality or God, or the perfection of things, or liberty, or the exquisite beauty and reality of the soul. They shall arise in America, and be responded to from the remainder of the earth.

The English language befriends the grand American expression—it is brawny enough, and limber and full enough. On the tough stock of a race who through all change of circumstance was never without the idea of political liberty, which is the animus of all liberty, it has attracted the

443. him, like Nature, tells] 1881, 1868, and 1855: him tells

444–445. unattain'd—thenceforward is no rest—they] 1881: unattained . . . thenceforward is no rest . . . they] 1868: unattained. Thenceforward is no rest: they] 1855: unattained . . . . thenceforward is no rest . . . . they

446. vacuums. Now there] 1881, 1868, and 1855: vacuums. The companion of him beholds the birth and progress of stars and [1868: stars, and] learns one of the meanings. Now there

447. chaos—the] 1881: chaos . . . the] 1868: chaos. The] 1855: chaos . . . . the

448. how—they] 1881 and 1855: how . . . they] 1868: how: they

449. itself, and] 1881 and 1855: itself and

449–450. stars, and] 1855: stars and

450. rings, and] 1855: rings and

451. done. A new order] 1881, 1868, and 1855: done. They may wait awhile . . . perhaps [1868: awhile—perhaps; 1855: awhile . . perhaps] a generation or two . . . dropping [1868: two,—dropping; 1855: two . . dropping] off by degrees. A superior breed shall take their place . . . the [1868: place—the; 1855: place . . . . the] gangs of kosmos and prophets *en masse* [1855: en masse] shall take their place. A new order

452. arise, and] 1881 and 1855: arise and] 1868: arise; and

453. own priest. They] 1881, 1868, and 1855: own priest. The churches built under their umbrage shall be the churches of men and women. Through the divinity of themselves shall the kosmos and the new breed of poets be interpreters of men and women and of all events and things. They

453. to-day] 1855: today

454. future. They] 1881: future . . . They] 1855: future . . . . They

454–455. immortality * * * liberty, or] 1881 and 1855: immortality or God or the perfection of things or liberty or] 1868: immortality, or God, or the perfection of things, or liberty, or

456. America, and] 1881 and 1855: America and

terms of daintier and gayer and subtler and more elegant tongues. It is the powerful language of resistance—it is the dialect of common sense. It is the speech of the proud and melancholy races, and of all who aspire. It is the chosen tongue to express growth, faith, self-esteem, freedom, justice, equality, friendliness, amplitude, prudence, decision, and courage. It is the medium that shall wellnigh express the inexpressible.

No great literature, nor any like style of behavior or oratory, or social intercourse or household arrangements, or public institutions, or the treatment by bosses of employ'd people, nor executive detail, or detail of the army and navy, nor spirit of legislation or courts, or police or tuition or architecture, or songs or amusements, can long elude the jealous and passionate instinct of American standards. Whether or no the sign appears from the mouths of the people, it throbs a live interrogation in every freeman's and freewoman's heart, after that which passes by, or this built to remain. Is it uniform with my country? Are its disposals without ignominious distinctions? Is it for the ever-growing communes of brothers and lovers, large, well united, proud, beyond the old models, generous beyond all models? Is it something grown fresh out of the fields, or drawn from the sea for use to me to-day here? I know that what answers for me,

458. expression—it] 1881: expression . . . it] 1855: expression . . . . it
459. enough, and] 1881 and 1855: enough and
459. enough. On] 1881: enough . . . on
460. who through] 1868: who, through
460. circumstance was] 1868: circumstance, was] 1855: circumstances was
463. resistance—it] 1881 and 1855: resistance . . . it
464. races, and] 1881 and 1855: races and
465–466. growth, * * * decision, and] 1855: growth faith self-esteem freedom justice equality friendliness amplitude prudence decision and
467. wellnigh] 1881, 1868, and 1855: well nigh
468. literature, nor] 1881 and 1855: literature nor
468. behavior or oratory, or] 1881, 1868, and 1855: behaviour or oratory or
469. arrangements, or] 1881, 1868, and 1855: arrangements or
469. institutions, or] 1881, 1868, and 1855: institutions or
470. by bosses] 1881: of bosses
470. detail, or] 1881 and 1855: detail or
471–472. legislation * * * or songs or amusements, can] 1881 and 1855: legislation or courts of police [1855: or police] or tuition or architecture or songs or amusements or the costumes of young men, can] 1868: legislation, or courts or police, or tuition or architecture, or songs or amusements, or the costumes of young men, can
475. heart, after] 1881, 1868, and 1855: heart after
475. by, or] 1881 and 1855: by or
477. ever-growing] 1881: ever growing] 1868 and 1855: evergrowing
478. well united] 1868 and 1855: well-united
479. fields, or] 1881 and 1855: fields or
480. sea for use to me to-day here?] 1881 and 1855: sea for use to me to-day [1855: today] here?] 1868: sea, for use to me, to-day, here?
480–481. me, * * * must] 1881 and 1855: me an American must] 1868: me, an American, must

an American, in Texas, Ohio, Canada, must answer for any individual or nation that serves for a part of my materials. Does this answer? Is it for the nursing of the young of the republic? Does it solve readily with the sweet milk of the nipples of the breasts of the Mother of Many Children?

America prepares with composure and good-will for the visitors that have sent word. It is not intellect that is to be their warrant and welcome. The talented, the artist, the ingenious, the editor, the statesman, the erudite, are not unappreciated—they fall in their place and do their work. The soul of the nation also does its work. It rejects none, it permits all. Only toward the like of itself will it advance half way. An individual is as superb as a nation when he has the qualities which make a superb nation. The soul of the largest and wealthiest and proudest nation may well go half-way to meet that of its poets.

Preface, 1872,

to "As a Strong Bird on Pinions Free,"
(now "Thou Mother with thy Equal Brood,"
in permanent ed'n.)

The impetus and ideas urging me, for some years past, to an utterance, or attempt at utterance, of New World songs, and an epic of Democracy, having already had their publish'd expression, as well as I can expect to give it, in "Leaves of Grass," the present and any future pieces from me

482. answer? Is it] 1881, 1868, and 1855: answer? or is it without reference to universal needs? or sprung of the needs of the less developed society of special ranks? or old needs of pleasure overlaid by modern science or forms? [1868 and 1855: and forms?] Does this acknowledge liberty with audible and absolute acknowledgment, and set slavery at nought for life and death? Will it help breed one goodshaped and wellhung man, [1868: goodshaped man,] and a woman to be his perfect and independent mate? Does it improve manners? Is it

483–484. milk * * * Children?] 1881 and 1855: milk of the nipples of the breasts of the mother of many children?] 1868: milk of the breasts of the mother of many children?

484. After "Many Children?" SDC deletes the last four lines of the paragraph and the first five lines of the next paragraph, at the end of page 30 of the 1881 text. For these lines, with 1868 and 1855 variants in brackets, see Appendix I, 7.

485. good-will] 1868 and 1855: goodwill

488. erudite, are] 1881: erudite . . . they are] 1868: erudite—they are] 1855: erudite . . they are

489. its work. It rejects] 1881, 1868, and 1855: its work. No disguise can pass on it . . . no [1868: on it—no; 1855: on it . . no] disguise can conceal from it. It rejects

490. Only toward the like] 1881, 1868, and 1855: Only toward as good as itself and toward the like

490. half way] 1868 and 1855: half-way

are really but the surplusage forming after that volume, or the wake eddying behind it. I fulfill'd in that an imperious conviction, and the commands of my nature as total and irresistible as those which make the sea flow, or the globe revolve. But of this supplementary volume, I confess I am not so certain. Having from early manhood abandon'd the business pursuits and applications usual in my time and country, and obediently yielded myself up ever since to the impetus mention'd, and to the work of expressing those ideas, it may be that mere habit has got dominion of me, when there is no real need of saying any thing further. But what is life but an experiment? and mortality but an exercise? with reference to results beyond. And so shall my poems be. If incomplete here, and superfluous there, *n'importe*—the earnest trial and persistent exploration shall at least be mine, and other success failing shall be success enough. I have been more anxious, anyhow, to suggest the songs of vital endeavor and manly evolution, and furnish something for races of outdoor athletes, than to make perfect rhymes, or reign in the parlors. I ventur'd from the beginning my own way, taking chances—and would keep on venturing.

I will therefore not conceal from any persons, known or unknown to me, who take an interest in the matter, that I have the ambition of devoting yet a few years to poetic composition. The mighty present age! To absorb and express in poetry, anything of it—of its world—America—cities and States—the years, the events of our Nineteenth century—the rapidity of movement—the violent contrasts, fluctuations of light and shade, of hope and fear—the entire revolution made by science in the poetic

493. After "of its poets." 1881, 1868, and 1855 have the following four sentences to end the Preface: "The signs are effectual. There is no fear of mistake. If the one is true the [1868: true, the] other is true. The proof of a poet is that his country absorbs him as affectionately as he has absorbed it."

Preface, 1872, to "As a Strong Bird on Pinions Free."

Printed in SDC from the clipped or unbound sheets of either TR or the small volume *As a Strong Bird on Pinions Free and Other Poems* (1872), for which the preface was originally written. The contents of this volume were bound in as a component of TR without revision or change in pagination. Revisions for SDC were made, with few exceptions, in black ink. Reprinted in SDC Glasgow, and CPP 1888, from the SDC plates, without change. It was omitted in DVOP. In the collation the text of 1872 and 1876 is identified as TR.

4. "Leaves of Grass,"] *TR:* LEAVES OF GRASS,
13. further. But] *TR:* further. . . . But
17. failing shall] *TR:* failing, shall
18. endeavor and] *TR:* endeavor, and
20–21. beginning my] *TR:* beginning, my
23. take an interest] *TR:* take interest
24. composition. The] *TR:* composition. . . . The
24–25. absorb and] *TR:* absorb, and
25. anything] *TR:* any thing

method—these great new underlying facts and new ideas rushing and spreading everywhere;—truly a mighty age! As if in some colossal drama, acted again like those of old under the open sun, the Nations of our time, and all the characteristics of Civilization, seem hurrying, stalking across, flitting from wing to wing, gathering, closing up, toward some long-prepared, most tremendous denouement. Not to conclude the infinite scenas of the race's life and toil and happiness and sorrow, but haply that the boards be clear'd from oldest, worst incumbrances, accumulations, and Man resume the eternal play anew, and under happier, freer auspices. To me, the United States are important because in this colossal drama they are unquestionably designated for the leading parts, for many a century to come. In them history and humanity seem to seek to culminate. Our broad areas are even now the busy theatre of plots, passions, interests, and suspended problems, compared to which the intrigues of the past of Europe, the wars of dynasties, the scope of kings and kingdoms, and even the development of peoples, as hitherto, exhibit scales of measurement comparatively narrow and trivial. And on these areas of ours, as on a stage, sooner or later, something like an *eclaircissement* of all the past civilization of Europe and Asia is probably to be evolved.

The leading parts. Not to be acted, emulated here, by us again, that role till now foremost in history—not to become a conqueror nation, or to achieve the glory of mere military, or diplomatic, or commercial superiority—but to become the grand producing land of nobler men and women—of copious races, cheerful, healthy, tolerant, free—to become the most friendly nation, (the United States indeed)—the modern composite nation, form'd from all, with room for all, welcoming all immigrants—accepting the work of our own interior development, as the work fitly filling ages and ages to come;—the leading nation of peace, but neither ignorant nor incapable of being the leading nation of war;—not the man's nation only, but the woman's nation—a land of splendid mothers, daughters, sisters, wives.

Our America to-day I consider in many respects as but indeed a vast seething mass of *materials*, ampler, better, (worse also,) than previously known—eligible to be used to carry towards its crowning stage, and build for good, the great ideal nationality of the future, the nation of the body

1*n*. achievements] *TR:* achievement

38. auspices. To] *TR:* auspices. . . . To
39. drama they] *TR:* drama, they
48. parts. Not] *TR:* parts. . . . Not
49. history—not] *TR:* History—Not
52. free—to] *TR:* free—To
62. towards] *TR:* toward

and the soul,*—no limit here to land, help, opportunities, mines, products, demands, supplies, &c.;—with (I think) our political organization, National, State, and Municipal, permanently establish'd, as far ahead as we can calculate—but, so far, no social, literary, religious, or esthetic organizations, consistent with our politics, or becoming to us—which organizations can only come, in time, through great democratic ideas, religion—through science, which now, like a new sunrise, ascending, begins to illuminate all—and through our own begotten poets and literatuses. (The moral of a late well-written book on civilization seems to be that the only real foundation-walls and bases—and also *sine qua non* afterward—of true and full civilization, is the eligibility and certainty of boundless products for feeding, clothing, sheltering everybody—perennial fountains of physical and domestic comfort, with intercommunication, and with civil and ecclesiastical freedom—and that then the esthetic and mental business will take care of itself. Well, the United States have establish'd this basis, and upon scales of extent, variety, vitality, and continuity, rivaling those of Nature; and have now to proceed to build an edifice upon it. I say this edifice is only to be fitly built by new literatures, especially the poetic. I say a modern image-making creation is indispensable to fuse and express the modern political and scientific creations—and then the trinity will be complete.)

When I commenced, years ago, elaborating the plan of my poems, and continued turning over that plan, and shifting it in my mind through many years, (from the age of twenty-eight to thirty-five,) experimenting much, and writing and abandoning much, one deep purpose underlay the others, and has underlain it and its execution ever since—and that has been the religious purpose. Amid many changes, and a formulation taking

* The problems of the achievements of this crowning stage through future first-class National Singers, Orators, Artists, and others—of creating in literature an *imaginative* New World, the correspondent and counterpart of the current Scientific and Political New Worlds,—and the perhaps distant, but still delightful prospect, (for our children, if not in our own day,) of delivering America, and, indeed, all Christian lands everywhere, from the thin moribund and watery, but appallingly extensive nuisance of conventional poetry—by putting something really alive and substantial in its place—I have undertaken to grapple with, and argue, in the preceding "Democratic Vistas."

9*n*. in the preceding "Democratic Vistas."] *TR:* in DEMOCRATIC VISATAS.

63. good, the] *TR:* good the
69. through great] *TR:* through native schools or teachers of great
71. literatuses. (The] *TR:* Literatuses. . . . (The
75. everybody] *TR:* every body
77. freedom—and] *TR:* freedom;—and
78. itself. Well,] *TR:* itself. . . . Well,

far different shape from what I at first supposed, this basic purpose has never been departed from in the composition of my verses. Not of course to exhibit itself in the old ways, as in writing hymns or psalms with an eye to the church-pew, or to express conventional pietism, or the sickly yearnings of devotees, but in new ways, and aiming at the widest sub-bases and inclusions of humanity, and tallying the fresh air of sea and land. I will see, (said I to myself,) whether there is not, for my purposes as poet, a religion, and a sound religious germenancy in the average human race, at least in their modern development in the United States, and in the hardy common fibre and native yearnings and elements, deeper and larger, and affording more profitable returns, than all mere sects or churches—as boundless, joyous, and vital as Nature itself—a germenancy that has too long been unencouraged, unsung, almost unknown. With science, the old theology of the East, long in its dotage, begins evidently to die and disappear. But (to my mind) science—and may be such will prove its principal service—as evidently prepares the way for One indescribably grander—Time's young but perfect offspring—the new theology—heir of the West—lusty and loving, and wondrous beautiful. For America, and for to-day, just the same as any day, the supreme and final science is the science of God—what we call science being only its minister—as Democracy is, or shall be also. And a poet of America (I said) must fill himself with such thoughts, and chant his best out of them. And as those were the convictions and aims, for good or bad, of "Leaves of Grass," they are no less the intention of this volume. As there can be, in my opinion, no sane and complete personality, nor any grand and electric nationality, without the stock element of religion imbuing all the other elements, (like heat in chemistry, invisible itself, but the life of all visible life,) so there can be no poetry worthy the name without that element behind all. The time has certainly come to begin to discharge the idea of religion, in the United States, from mere ecclesiasticism, and from Sundays and churches and church-going, and assign it to that general position, chiefest, most indispensable, most exhilarating, to which the others are to be adjusted, inside of all human character, and education, and affairs. The people, especially the young men and women of America, must begin to learn that religion, (like poetry,) is something far, far different from what they supposed. It is, indeed, too important to the

102. itself—a] *TR:* itself—A
103. unknown. With] *TR:* unknown. . . . With
111. is, or] *TR:* is or
112–113. them. And] *TR:* them. . . . . . And
113–114. "Leaves of Grass,"] *TR:* Leaves of Grass,
115. personality, nor] *TR:* Personality—nor

power and perpetuity of the New World to be consign'd any longer to the churches, old or new, Catholic or Protestant—Saint this, or Saint that. It must be consign'd henceforth to democracy *en masse*, and to literature. It must enter into the poems of the nation. It must make the nation.

The Four Years' War is over—and in the peaceful, strong, exciting, fresh occasions of to-day, and of the future, that strange, sad war is hurrying even now to be forgotten. The camp, the drill, the lines of sentries, the prisons, the hospitals,—(ah! the hospitals!)—all have passed away—all seem now like a dream. A new race, a young and lusty generation, already sweeps in with oceanic currents, obliterating the war, and all its scars, its mounded graves, and all its reminiscences of hatred, conflict, death. So let it be obliterated. I say the life of the present and the future makes undeniable demands upon us each and all, south, north, east, west. To help put the United States (even if only in imagination) hand in hand, in one unbroken circle in a chant—to rouse them to the unprecedented grandeur of the part they are to play, and are even now playing—to the thought of their great future, and the attitude conform'd to it—especially their great esthetic, moral, scientific future, (of which their vulgar material and political present is but as the preparatory tuning of instruments by an orchestra,) these, as hitherto, are still, for me, among my hopes, ambitions.

"Leaves of Grass," already publish'd, is, in its intentions, the song of a great composite *democratic individual*, male or female. And following on and amplifying the same purpose, I suppose I have in my mind to run through the chants of this volume, (if ever completed,) the thread-voice, more or less audible, of an aggregated, inseparable, unprecedented, vast, composite, electric *democratic nationality*.

Purposing, then, to still fill out, from time to time through years to come, the following volume, (unless prevented,) I conclude this preface to the first instalment of it, pencil'd in the open air, on my fifty-third birth-day, by wafting to you, dear reader, whoever you are, (from amid the fresh scent of the grass, the pleasant coolness of the forenoon breeze, the lights and shades of tree-boughs silently dappling and playing around me, and the notes of the cat-bird for undertone and accompaniment,) my true good-will and love. W.W.

Washington, D. C., May 31, 1872.

119. all. The] *TR:* all. . . . . . The
128–129. that. It] *TR:* that. . . . It
135–136. and lusty generation] *TR:* and living generation
136. the war] *TR:* that war
140. west. To] *TR:* West. . . . To
141. chant—to] *TR:* chant—To
148. "Leaves of Grass,"] *TR:* LEAVES OF GRASS,

Preface, 1876,
to the two-volume Centennial Edition of L. of G. and "Two Rivulets."

At the eleventh hour, under grave illness, I gather up the pieces of prose and poetry left over since publishing, a while since, my first and main volume, "Leaves of Grass"—pieces, here, some new, some old—nearly all of them (sombre as many are, making this almost death's book) composed in by-gone atmospheres of perfect health—and preceded by the freshest collection, the little "Two Rivulets," now send them out, embodied in the present melange, partly as my contribution and outpouring to celebrate, in some sort, the feature of the time, the first centennial of our New World nationality—and then as chyle and nutriment to that moral, indissoluble union, equally representing all, and the mother of many coming centennials.

And e'en for flush and proof of our America—for reminder, just as much, or more, in moods of towering pride and joy, I keep my special chants of death and immortality* to stamp the coloring-finish of all,

* Passage to India.—As in some ancient legend-play, to close the plot and the hero's career, there is a farewell gathering on ship's deck and on shore, a loosing of hawsers and ties, a spreading of sails to the wind—a starting out on unknown seas, to fetch up no one knows whither—to return no more—and the curtain falls, and there is the end of it—so I have reserv'd that poem, with its cluster, to finish and explain much that, without them, would not be explain'd, and to take leave, and escape for good, from all that

5*n*. more—and] *TR:* more—And
5*n*. it—so] *TR:* it—So
8*n*. "Passage to India,"] *TR: Passage to India,*

Preface, 1876, to the Centennial Edition.

Printed in *SDC* from clippings of pages (or proof pages) 5–14 of *TR* in which this preface first appeared. Revisions, with few exceptions, were made in black ink. Reprinted in *SDC* Glasgow and *CPP* from plates of *SDC;* omitted in *DVOP*. Rough draft MS fragments are preserved in the Trent Collection, Duke University, and in the Feinberg Collection, but they are not sufficiently complete to be of value in the collation. The following extracts, with minor variations, were printed in an anonymous prepublication review of *TR*, entitled "Walt Whitman's Poems," probably written by Whitman (see "Walt Whitman to Whitelaw Reid," by Edwin H. Miller, *SB*, VIII, 1956, 242–249), in *NYTR*, February 19, 1876: lines 1–11, the first paragraph; the first sentence of the third paragraph, lines 17–20, and the third and fourth sentences following in *TR*, which were deleted in *SDC* (see note on lines 21–22 below); a whole paragraph and parts of two others near the end, lines 88–113 and 118–123. (See also "The Real War Will Never Get in the Books," and Ap-

present and past. For terminus and temperer to all, they were originally written; and that shall be their office at the last.

For some reason—not explainable or definite to my own mind, yet secretly pleasing and satisfactory to it—I have not hesitated to embody in, and run through the volume, two altogether distinct veins, or strata—politics for one, and for the other, the pensive thought of immortality. Thus, too, the prose and poetic, the dual forms of the present book. The volume, therefore, after its minor episodes, probably divides into these two, at first sight far diverse, veins of topic and treatment. Three points, in especial, have become very dear to me, and all through I seek to make them again and again, in many forms and repetitions, as will be seen: 1. That the true growth-characteristics of the democracy of the New World are henceforth to radiate in superior literary, artistic and religious expressions, far more than in its republican forms, universal suffrage, and frequent elections, (though these are unspeakably important.) 2. That the vital political mission of the United States is, to practically solve and settle the problem of two sets of rights—the fusion, thorough compatibility and junction of individual State prerogatives, with the indispensable necessity of centrality and Oneness—the national identity power—the sovereign Union, relentless, permanently comprising all, and over all, and

has preceded them. (Then probably "Passage to India," and its cluster, are but freer vent and fuller expression to what, from the first, and so on throughout, more or less lurks in my writings, underneath every page, every line, everywhere.)

I am not sure but the last inclosing sublimation of race or poem is, what it thinks of death. After the rest has been comprehended and said, even the grandest—after those contributions to mightiest nationality, or to sweetest

12*n*. is, what] *TR:* is, What
13*n*. death. After] *TR:* Death. . . . . . . After
14*n*. grandest—after] *TR:* grandest—After

pendix XI, *1*, in *Prose 1892*, I; and in this volume "Ventures, on an Old Theme," "Lacks and Wants Yet," and "Freedom.")

3. "Leaves of Grass"] *TR:* LEAVES OF GRASS
5. and preceded] *TR:* and, preceded
6. "Two Rivulets," now] *TR:* TWO RIVULETS, and by this rambling Prefatory gossip,* now
6. The footnote to which the asterisk refers is also omitted in *SDC*. It is as follows: " *This Preface is not only for the present collection, but, in a sort, for all my writings, both Volumes." [That is, *TR* and *LG* 1876.—ED.]
21–22. book. The volume] *TR:* book. . . . . . The pictures from the Hospitals during the War, in *Memoranda*, I have also decided to include. Though they differ in character and composition from the rest of my pieces, yet I feel that that they ought to go with them, and must do so. . . . . The present Volume
23. Between "and treatment." and "Three points" *TR* has several lines omitted in *SDC*. See Appendix VIII, *2*.
29. important.) 2.] *TR:* important) . . . . . . 2.

in that never yielding an inch: then 3d. Do we not, amid a general malaria of fogs and vapors, our day, unmistakably see two pillars of promise, with grandest, indestructible indications—one, that the morbid facts of

song, or to the best personalism, male or female, have been glean'd from the rich and varied themes of tangible life, and have been fully accepted and sung, and the pervading fact of visible existence, with the duty it devolves, is rounded and apparently completed, it still remains to be really completed by suffusing through the whole and several, that other pervading invisible fact, so large a part, (is it not the largest part?) of life here, combining the rest, and furnishing, for person or State, the only permanent and unitary meaning to all, even the meanest life, consistently with the dignity of the universe, in Time. As from the eligibility to this thought, and the cheerful conquest of this fact, flash forth the first distinctive proofs of the soul, so to me, (extending it only a little further,) the ultimate Democratic purports, the ethereal and spiritual ones, are to concentrate here, and as fixed stars, radiate hence. For, in my opinion, it is no less than this idea of immortality, above all other ideas, that is to enter into, and vivify, and give crowning religious stamp, to democracy in the New World.

It was originally my intention, after chanting in "Leaves of Grass" the songs of the body and existence, to then compose a further, equally needed volume, based on those convictions of perpetuity and conservation which, enveloping all precedents, make the unseen soul govern absolutely at last. I meant, while in a sort continuing the theme of my first chants, to shift the slides, and exhibit the problem and paradox of the same ardent and fully appointed personality entering the sphere of the resistless gravitation of spiritual law, and with cheerful face estimating death, not at all as the cessation, but as somehow what I feel it must be, the entrance upon by far the greatest part of existence, and something that life is at least as much for, as it is for itself. But the full construction of such a work is beyond my powers, and must remain for some bard in the future. The physical and the sensuous, in themselves or in their immediate continuations, retain holds upon me which I think are never entirely releas'd; and those holds I have not only not denied, but hardly wish'd to weaken.

Meanwhile, not entirely to give the go-by to my original plan, and far more to avoid a mark'd hiatus in it, than to entirely fulfil it, I end my books with thoughts, or radiations from thoughts, on death, immortality, and a free en-

23*n*. Time. As from] *TR:* Time. . . . . . As, from
30*n*. "Leaves of Grass"] *TR:* LEAVES OF GRASS
39*n*. After "for itself." *TR* begins a new paragraph.
40*n*. work is] *TR:* work (even if I lay the foundation, or give impetus to it) is
51*n*. recollate] *TR:* re-collate
52*n*. press, in] *TR:* press, (much the same, I transcribe my *Memoranda* following, of gloomy times out of the War, and Hospitals, in
61*n*–62*n*. influence] *TR:* influences
62*n*. "Leaves of Grass."] *TR:* LEAVES OF GRASS.

35. inch: then 3d.] *TR:* inch. . . . . . . then 3d.
37. one] *TR:* One

American politics and society everywhere are but passing incidents and flanges of our unbounded impetus of growth? weeds, annuals, of the rank, rich soil—not central, enduring, perennial things? The other, that all the

trance into the spiritual world. In those thoughts, in a sort, I make the first steps or studies toward the mighty theme, from the point of view necessitated by my foregoing poems, and by modern science. In them I also seek to set the key-stone to my democracy's enduring arch. I recollate them now, for the press, in order to partially occupy and offset days of strange sickness, and the heaviest affliction and bereavement of my life; and I fondly please myself with the notion of leaving that cluster to you, O unknown reader of the future, as "something to remember me by," more especially than all else. Written in former days of perfect health, little did I think the pieces had the purport that now, under present circumstances, opens to me.

[As I write these lines, May 31, 1875, it is again early summer—again my birth-day—now my fifty-sixth. Amid the outside beauty and freshness, the sunlight and verdure of the delightful season, O how different the moral atmosphere amid which I now revise this Volume, from the jocund influence surrounding the growth and advent of "Leaves of Grass." I occupy myself, arranging these pages for publication, still envelopt in thoughts of the death two years since of my dear Mother, the most perfect and magnetic character, the rarest combination of practical, moral and spiritual, and the least selfish, of all and any I have ever known—and by me O so much the most deeply loved—and also under the physical affliction of a tedious attack of paralysis, obstinately lingering and keeping its hold upon me, and quite suspending all bodily activity and comfort.]

Under these influences, therefore, I still feel to keep "Passage to India" for last words even to this centennial dithyramb. Not as, in antiquity, at highest festival of Egypt, the noisome skeleton of death was sent on exhibition to the revelers, for zest and shadow to the occasion's joy and light—but as the marble statue of the normal Greeks at Elis, suggesting death in the form of a beautiful and perfect young man, with closed eyes, leaning on an inverted torch—emblem of rest and aspiration after action—of crown and point which all lives and poems should steadily have reference to, namely, the justified and noble termination of our identity, this grade of it, and outlet-preparation to another grade.

67*n*. loved—and] *TR:* loved. . . . . . . and

69*n*. After "comfort." before the closing bracket *TR* has the following lines, omitted in *SDC:* ". . . . . . I see now, much clearer than ever—perhaps these experiences were needed to show—how much my former poems, the bulk of them, are indeed the expression of health and strength, and sanest, joyfulest life."

70*n*. "Passage to India"] *TR: Passage to India*

73*n*. revelers] *TR:* revellers

77*n*. In *TR* the letter "j" in "justified," coming at the beginning of a line, did not print, and the copy has a blank space there.

39. growth? weeds] *TR:* growth—weeds

40. things? The other] *TR:* things?—The Other

hitherto experience of the States, their first century, has been but preparation, adolescence—and that this Union is only now and henceforth, (*i.e.* since the secession war,) to enter on its full democratic career?

Of the whole, poems and prose, (not attending at all to chronological order, and with original dates and passing allusions in the heat and impression of the hour, left shuffled in, and undisturb'd,) the chants of "Leaves of Grass," my former volume, yet serve as the indispensable deep soil, or basis, out of which, and out of which only, could come the roots and stems more definitely indicated by these later pages. (While that volume radiates physiology alone, the present one, though of the like origin in the main, more palpably doubtless shows the pathology which was pretty sure to come in time from the other.)

In that former and main volume, composed in the flush of my health and strength, from the age of 30 to 50 years, I dwelt on birth and life, clothing my ideas in pictures, days, transactions of my time, to give them positive place, identity—saturating them with that vehemence of pride and audacity of freedom necessary to loosen the mind of still-to-be-form'd America from the accumulated folds, the superstitions, and all the long, tenacious and stifling anti-democratic authorities of the Asiatic and European past—my enclosing purport being to express, above all artificial regulation and aid, the eternal bodily composite, cumulative, natural character of one's self.*

* Namely, a character, making most of common and normal elements, to the superstructure of which not only the precious accumulations of the learning and experiences of the Old World, and the settled social and municipal necessities and current requirements, so long a-building, shall still faithfully contribute, but which at its foundations and carried up thence, and receiving its impetus from the democratic spirit, and accepting its gauge in all departments from the democratic formulas, shall again directly be vitalized by the perennial influences of Nature at first hand, and the old heroic stamina of Nature, the strong air of prairie and mountain, the dash of the briny sea, the primary antiseptics—of the passions, in all their fullest heat and potency, of courage, rankness, amativeness, and of immense pride. Not to lose at all, therefore, the benefits of artificial progress and civilization, but to re-occupy for Western tenancy the oldest though ever-fresh fields, and reap from them the

80*n*. *Namely] *TR:* *LEAVES OF GRASS.—Namely
90*n*. pride. Not] *TR:* pride . . . . Not
96*n*. "Leaves of Grass" is, I hope,] *TR:* LEAVES OF GRASS is, I think,
99*n*. animalism. While] *TR:* animalism . . . . While

47. "Leaves of Grass,"] *TR:* LEAVES OF GRASS,
61–62. eternal . . . one's self.*] *TR:* eternal Bodily Character of One's-Self.*
61–62. After "One's-Self.* " *TR* has three paragraphs omitted in *SDC.* See Ap-

Estimating the American Union as so far, and for some time to come, in its yet formative condition, I bequeath poems and essays as nutriment and influences to help truly assimilate and harden, and especially to furnish something toward what the States most need of all, and which seems to me yet quite unsupplied in literature, namely, to show them, or begin to show them, themselves distinctively, and what they are for. For though perhaps the main points of all ages and nations are points of resemblance, and, even while granting evolution, are substantially the same, there are some vital things in which this Republic, as to its individualities, and as a compacted Nation, is to specially stand forth, and culminate modern humanity. And these are the very things it least morally and mentally knows—(though, curiously enough, it is at the same time faithfully acting upon them.)

I count with such absolute certainty on the great future of the United States—different from, though founded on, the past—that I have always invoked that future, and surrounded myself with it, before or while singing my songs. (As ever, all tends to followings—America, too, is a prophecy. What, even of the best and most successful, would be justified by itself alone? by the present, or the material ostent alone? Of men or States, few realize how much they live in the future. That, rising like pinnacles, gives its main significance to all You and I are doing today. Without it, there were little meaning in lands or poems—little purport in

savage and sane nourishment indispensable to a hardy nation, and the absence of which, threatening to become worse and worse, is the most serious lack and defect to-day of our New World literature.

Not but what the brawn of "Leaves of Grass" is, I hope, thoroughly spiritualized everywhere, for final estimate, but, from the very subjects, the direct effect is a sense of the life, as it should be, of flesh and blood, and physical urge, and animalism. While there are other themes, and plenty of abstract thoughts and poems in the volume—while I have put in it passing and rapid but actual glimpses of the great struggle between the nation and the slave-power, (1861–'65,) as the fierce and bloody panorama of that contest unroll'd itself: while the whole book, indeed, revolves around that four years' war, which, as I was in the midst of it, becomes, in "Drum-Taps," pivotal to the rest entire—and here and there, before and afterward, not a few epi-

100*n*. volume . . . passing] *TR:* Volume—While I have put in it (supplemented in the present Work by my prose *Memoranda,*) passing

103*n*. itself: while] *TR:* itself—While

104*n*. "Drum-Taps,"] *TR: Drum-Taps,*

105*n*. entire—and] *TR:* entire—follow'd by *Marches now the War is Over*—and

pendix, VIII, 3.

63. I bequeath] *TR:* I therefore now bequeath

79. songs. (As] *TR:* Songs. . . . (As

sodes and speculations—*that*—namely, to make a type-portrait for living, active, worldly, healthy personality, objective as well as subjective, joyful and potent, and modern and free, distinctively for the use of the United States, male and female, through the long future—has been, I say, my general object. (Probably, indeed, the whole of these varied songs, and all my writings, both volumes, only ring changes in some sort, on the ejaculation, How vast, how eligible, how joyful, how real, is a human being, himself or herself.)

Though from no definite plan at the time, I see now that I have unconsciously sought, by indirections at least as much as directions, to express the whirls and rapid growth and intensity of the United States, the prevailing tendency and events of the Nineteenth century, and largely the spirit of the whole current world, my time; for I feel that I have partaken of that spirit, as I have been deeply interested in all those events, the closing of long-stretch'd eras and ages, and, illustrated in the history of the United States, the opening of larger ones. (The death of President Lincoln, for instance, fitly, historically closes, in the civilization of feudalism, many old influences—drops on them, suddenly, a vast, gloomy, as it were, separating curtain.)

Since I have been ill, (1873–74–75,) mostly without serious pain, and with plenty of time and frequent inclination to judge my poems, (never composed with eye on the book-market, nor for fame, nor for any pecuniary profit,) I have felt temporary depression more than once, for fear that in "Leaves of Grass" the *moral* parts were not sufficiently pronounc'd. But in my clearest and calmest moods I have realized that as those "Leaves," all and several, surely prepare the way for, and necessitate morals, and are adjusted to them, just the same as Nature does and is, they are what, consistently with my plan, they must and probably should be. (In a certain sense, while the Moral is the purport and last intelligence of all Nature, there is absolutely nothing of the moral in the works, or laws, or shows of Nature. Those only lead inevitably to it—begin and necessitate it.)

Then I meant "Leaves of Grass," as publish'd, to be the Poem of average Identity, (of *yours*, whoever you are, now reading these lines.) A man is not greatest as victor in war, nor inventor or explorer, nor even in science, or in his intellectual or artistic capacity, or exemplar in some vast benevolence. To the highest democratic view, man is most acceptable in living well the practical life and lot which happens to him as ordinary farmer, sea-farer, mechanic, clerk, laborer, or driver—upon and from which position as a central basis or pedestal, while performing its labors, and his duties as citizen, son, husband,

122*n*. After "separating curtain." and inside the closing mark of parenthesis, *TR* has the following sentence to close the paragraph, omitted in *SDC:* "The world's entire dramas afford none more indicative—none with folds more tragic, or more sombre or far spreading."

126*n*–127*n*. "Leaves of Grass"] *TR:* LEAVES OF GRASS

128*n*. "Leaves,"] *TR:* LEAVES

131*n*. be. (In] *TR:* be. . . . . . . (In

135*n*. "Leaves of Grass,"] *TR:* LEAVES OF GRASS

135*n*–136*n*. of average . . . A man] *TR:* of Identity, (of *Yours*, whoever you are, now reading these lines) . . . . . . For genius must realize that, precious as it may be, there is something far more precious, namely, simple Identity, One's-self. A man

139*n*. the practical] *TR:* the average, practical

father and employ'd person, he preserves his physique, ascends, developing, radiating himself in other regions—and especially where and when, (greatest of all, and nobler than the proudest mere genius or magnate in any field,) he fully realizes the conscience, the spiritual, the divine faculty, cultivated well, exemplified in all his deeds and words, through life, uncompromising to the end—a flight loftier than any of Homer's or Shakspere's—broader than all poems and bibles—namely, Nature's own, and in the midst of it, Yourself, your own Identity, body and soul. (All serves, helps—but in the centre of all, absorbing all, giving, for your purpose, the only meaning and vitality to all, master or mistress of all, under the law, stands Yourself.) To sing the Song of that law of average Identity, and of Yourself, consistently with the divine law of the universal, is a main intention of those "Leaves."

Something more may be added—for, while I am about it, I would make a full confession. I also sent out "Leaves of Grass" to arouse and set flowing in men's and women's hearts, young and old, endless streams of living, pulsating love and friendship, directly from them to myself, now and ever. To this terrible, irrepressible yearning, (surely more or less down underneath in most human souls)—this never-satisfied appetite for sympathy, and this boundless offering of sympathy—this universal democratic comradeship—this old, eternal, yet ever-new interchange of adhesiveness, so fitly emblematic of America—I have given in that book, undisguisedly, declaredly, the openest expression. Besides, important as they are in my purpose as emotional expressions for humanity, the special meaning of the "Calamus" cluster of "Leaves of Grass," (and more or less running through the book, and cropping out in "Drum-Taps,") mainly resides in its political significance. In my opinion, it is by a fervent, accepted development of comradeship, the beautiful and sane affection of man for man, latent in all the young fellows, north and south, east and west—it is by this, I say, and by what goes directly and indirectly along with it, that the United States of the future, (I cannot too often repeat,) are to be most effectually welded together, intercalated, anneal'd into a living union.

Then, for enclosing clue of all, it is imperatively and ever to be borne in mind that "Leaves of Grass" entire is not to be construed as an intellectual or scholastic effort or poem mainly, but more as a radical utterance out of the Emotions and the Physique—an utterance adjusted to, perhaps born of, Democracy and the Modern—in its very nature regardless of the old conventions, and, under the great laws, following only its own impulses.

152*n*. Yourself.) To] *TR:* Yourself.) . . . . . To
153*n*. that law] *TR:* that divine law
154*n*. "Leaves."] *TR:* LEAVES.
156*n*. "Leaves of Grass"] *TR:* LEAVES OF GRASS
157*n*. old, endless] *TR:* old, (my present and future readers,) endless
163*n*. After "expression." and before "Besides" in the text of the note in *TR*, three sentences, completing the paragraph in *TR*, are omitted in *SDC*. See Appendix VIII, *4*.
165*n*–167*n*. "Calamus" cluster . . . in "Drum-Taps,")] *TR: Calamus* cluster of LEAVES OF GRASS, (and more or less running through that book, and cropping out in *Drum-Taps.*)
174*n*. "Leaves of Grass"] *TR:* LEAVES OF GRASS
175*n*–176*n*. of the Emotions] *TR:* of the abysms of the Soul, the Emotions
177*n*. and the Modern—in] *TR:* and Modern Science, and in

human lives. All ages, all Nations and States, have been such prophecies. But where any former ones with prophecy so broad, so clear, as our times, our lands—as those of the West?)

Without being a scientist, I have thoroughly adopted the conclusions of the great savans and experimentalists of our time, and of the last hundred years, and they have interiorly tinged the chyle of all my verse, for purposes beyond. Following the modern spirit, the real poems of the present, ever solidifying and expanding into the future, must vocalize the vastness and splendor and reality with which scientism has invested man and the universe, (all that is called creation,) and must henceforth launch humanity into new orbits, consonant with that vastness, splendor, and reality, (unknown to the old poems,) like new systems of orbs, balanced upon themselves, revolving in limitless space, more subtle than the stars. Poetry, so largely hitherto and even at present wedded to children's tales, and to mere amorousness, upholstery and superficial rhyme, will have to accept, and, while not denying the past, nor the themes of the past, will be revivified by this tremendous innovation, the kosmic spirit, which must henceforth, in my opinion, be the background and underlying impetus, more or less visible, of all first-class songs.

Only, (for me, at any rate, in all my prose and poetry,) joyfully accepting modern science, and loyally following it without the slightest hesitation, there remains ever recognized still a higher flight, a higher fact, the eternal soul of man, (of all else too,) the spiritual, the religious—which it is to be the greatest office of scientism, in my opinion, and of future poetry also, to free from fables, crudities and superstitions, and launch forth in renew'd faith and scope a hundred fold. To me, the worlds of religiousness, of the conception of the divine, and of the ideal, though mainly latent, are just as absolute in humanity and the universe as the world of chemistry, or anything in the objective worlds. To me

The prophet and the bard,
Shall yet maintain themselves—in higher circles yet,
Shall mediate to the modern, to democracy—interpret yet to them,
God and eidólons.

85. lives. All] *TR:* lives . . . . . . All
113. anything] *TR:* any thing
114. The *TR* "Preface" has "Prophet" and "Bard," but all texts of the poem "Eidólons" have lower case initials.
115. Both the *TR* "Preface" and *TR* "Eidólons" have the dash, but all later texts of "Eidólons" substitute a comma.
116. All texts, including the *TR* "Preface," have initial capitals in "modern" and

To me, the crown of savantism is to be, that it surely opens the way for a more splendid theology, and for ampler and diviner songs. No year, nor even century, will settle this. There is a phase of the real, lurking behind the real, which it is all for. There is also in the intellect of man, in time, far in prospective recesses, a judgment, a last appellate court, which will settle it.

In certain parts in these flights, or attempting to depict or suggest them, I have not been afraid of the charge of obscurity, in either of my two volumes—because human thought, poetry or melody, must leave dim escapes and outlets—must possess a certain fluid, aerial character, akin to space itself, obscure to those of little or no imagination, but indispensable to the highest purposes. Poetic style, when address'd to the soul, is less definite form, outline, sculpture, and becomes vista, music, half-tints, and even less than half-tints. True, it may be architecture; but again it may be the forest wild-wood, or the best effect thereof, at twilight, the waving oaks and cedars in the wind, and the impalpable odor.

Finally, as I have lived in fresh lands, inchoate, and in a revolutionary age, future-founding, I have felt to identify the points of that age, these lands, in my recitatives, altogether in my own way. Thus my form has strictly grown from my purports and facts, and is the analogy of them. Within my time the United States have emerged from nebulous vagueness and suspense, to full orbic, (though varied,) decision—have done the deeds and achiev'd the triumphs of half a score of centuries—and are henceforth to enter upon their real history—the way being now, (*i.e.* since the result of the Secession War,) clear'd of death-threatening impedimenta, and the free areas around and ahead of us assured and certain, which were not so before—(the past century being but preparations, trial voyages and experiments of the ship, before her starting out upon deep water.)

In estimating my volumes, the world's current times and deeds, and their spirit, must be first profoundly estimated. Out of the hundred years just ending, (1776–1876,) with their genesis of inevitable wilful events, and new experiments and introductions, and many unprecedented things of war and peace, (to be realized better, perhaps only realized, at the re-

"democracy"; *TR* "Preface" and *TR* "Eidólons" have the dash after "democracy," but all texts of "Eidólons" after 1876 substitute a comma.

117. The *TR* "Eidólons" has a comma after "God." The *TR* "Preface" and all later texts of the poem omit the comma. The *TR* "Preface" and *TR* "Eidólons" have an initial capital in "eidólons"; all later texts substitute a lower case initial.

132. effect] *TR:* effects

137–138. them. Within] *TR:* them. . . . . . . Within

150. new experiments and introductions] *TR:* new introductions

move of a century hence;) out of that stretch of time, and especially out of the immediately preceding twenty-five years, (1850–75,) with all their rapid changes, innovations, and audacious movements—and bearing their own inevitable wilful birth-marks—the experiments of my poems too have found genesis.

W. W.

Poetry To-day in America—Shakspere—The Future.

Strange as it may seem, the topmost proof of a race is its own born poetry. The presence of that, or the absence, each tells its story. As the flowering rose or lily, as the ripen'd fruit to a tree, the apple or the peach, no matter how fine the trunk, or copious or rich the branches and foliage, here waits *sine qua non* at last. The stamp of entire and finish'd greatness to any nation, to the American Republic among the rest, must be sternly withheld till it has put what it stands for in the blossom of original, first-class poems. No imitations will do.

And though no *esthetik* worthy the present condition or future certainties of the New World seems to have been outlined in men's minds, or has been generally called for, or thought needed, I am clear that until the United States have just such definite and native expressers in the highest artistic fields, their mere political, geographical, wealth-forming, and even intellectual eminence, however astonishing and predominant, will constitute but a more and more expanded and well-appointed body, and perhaps brain, with little or no soul. Sugar-coat the grim truth as we may, and ward off with outward plausible words, denials, explanations, to the mental inward perception of the land this blank is plain; a barren void exists. For the meanings and maturer purposes of these States are not the

152. of a century hence;) out] *TR:* of another Century hence)—Out
155. birth-marks—the experiments of my] *TR:* birth-marks—my

Poetry To-Day in America—Shakspere—the Future.

This essay is printed in *SDC* from clipped pages 195–210 of *NAR* for February, 1881, Vol. 132, where it has the title "The Poetry of the Future." Revisions are mostly in pencil; a very few in black and red ink. It was first reprinted in *SDC;* omitted in *DVOP.* The MS in the Feinberg Collection is obviously an early draft and is not collated here with the printed texts.

7. has put] *NAR:* has expressed itself, and put
10. been outlined] *NAR:* been even outlined
10. After the word "minds," *NAR* has an asterisk referring to the following footnote at the bottom of the page, omitted in *SDC:* "In 1850, Emerson said earnestly to Miss Bremer, in response to her praises: 'No, you must not be too good-natured. We

constructing of a new world of politics merely, and physical comforts for the million, but even more determinedly, in range with science and the modern, of a new world of democratic sociology and imaginative literature. If the latter were not establish'd for the States, to form their only permanent tie and hold, the first-named would be of little avail.

With the poems of a first-class land are twined, as weft with warp, its types of personal character, of individuality, peculiar, native, its own physiognomy, man's and woman's, its own shapes, forms, and manners, fully justified under the eternal laws of all forms, all manners, all times. The hour has come for democracy in America to inaugurate itself in the two directions specified—autochthonic poems and personalities—born expressers of itself, its spirit alone, to radiate in subtle ways, not only in art, but the practical and familiar, in the transactions between employers and employ'd persons, in business and wages, and sternly in the army and navy, and revolutionizing them. I find nowhere a scope profound enough, and radical and objective enough, either for aggregates or individuals. The thought and identity of a poetry in America to fill, and worthily fill, the great void, and enhance these aims, electrifying all and several, involves the essence and integral facts, real and spiritual, of the whole land, the whole body. What the great sympathetic is to the congeries of bones, joints, heart, fluids, nervous system and vitality, constituting, launching forth in time and space a human being—aye, an immortal soul—such relation, and no less, holds true poetry to the single personality, or to the nation.

Here our thirty-eight States stand to-day, the children of past precedents, and, young as they are, heirs of a very old estate. One or two points we will consider, out of the myriads presenting themselves. The feudalism of the British Islands, illustrated by Shakspere—and by his

have not yet any poetry which can be said to represent the mind of our world. The poet of America is not yet come. When he comes, he will sing quite differently.' "

14–15. constitute but a more] *NAR:* constitute (as I have before likened it) a more

18. plain; a barren] *NAR:* plain. A barren

23. were not establish'd for the States, to form] *NAR:* were not carried out and established to form

28–29. times. The hour] *NAR:* times.
I say the hour

34. After "revolutionizing them." *NAR* begins a new paragraph.

37–38. aims . . . involves] *NAR:* aims, involves

39–40. bones, . . . vitality,] *NAR:* bones and joints, and heart and fluids and nervous system, and vitality,

41–42. soul—such . . . holds true] *NAR:* soul—in such relation, and no less, stands true

47. Shakspere—and] *NAR:* Shakespeare, and

legitimate followers, Walter Scott and Alfred Tennyson—with all its tyrannies, superstitions, evils, had most superb and heroic permeating veins, poems, manners; even its errors fascinating. It almost seems as if only that feudalism in Europe, like slavery in our own South, could outcrop types of tallest, noblest personal character yet—strength and devotion and love better than elsewhere—invincible courage, generosity, aspiration, the spines of all. Here is where Shakspere and the others I have named perform a service incalculably precious to our America. Politics, literature, and everything else, centers at last in perfect *personnel*, (as democracy is to find the same as the rest;) and here feudalism is unrival'd—here the rich and highest-rising lessons it bequeaths us—a mass of foreign nutriment, which we are to work over, and popularize and enlarge, and present again in our own growths.

Still there are pretty grave and anxious drawbacks, jeopardies, fears. Let us give some reflections on the subject, a little fluctuating, but starting from one central thought, and returning there again. Two or three curious results may plow up. As in the astronomical laws, the very power that would seem most deadly and destructive turns out to be latently conservative of longest, vastest future births and lives. We will for once briefly examine the just-named authors solely from a Western point of view. It may be, indeed, that we shall use the sun of English literature, and the brightest current stars of his system, mainly as pegs to hang some cogitations on, for home inspection.

As depicter and dramatist of the passions at their stormiest outstretch, though ranking high, Shakspere (spanning the arch wide enough) is equal'd by several, and excell'd by the best old Greeks, (as Æschylus.) But in portraying mediæval European lords and barons, the arrogant port, so dear to the inmost human heart, (pride! pride! dearest, perhaps, of all—touching us, too, of the States closest of all—closer than love,) he stands alone, and I do not wonder he so witches the world.

From first to last, also, Walter Scott and Tennyson, like Shakspere, exhale that principle of caste which we Americans have come on earth to destroy. Jefferson's verdict on the Waverley novels was that they turn'd

48. Tennyson—with] *NAR:* Tennyson, with
50. manners; even] *NAR:* manners—even
54, 72, and 78. Shakspere] *NAR:* Shakespeare
58–59. mass of foreign nutriment] *NAR:* mass of precious, though foreign, nutriment
60. in our own growths.] *NAR:* in Western growths.
66. lives. We will for once] *NAR:* lives.
Let us for once
74. mediæval European . . . so dear] *NAR:* mediæval lords and barons, the arrogant port and stomach so dear

and condens'd brilliant but entirely false lights and glamours over the lords, ladies, and aristocratic institutes of Europe, with all their measureless infamies, and then left the bulk of the suffering, down-trodden people contemptuously in the shade. Without stopping to answer this hornet-stinging criticism, or to repay any part of the debt of thanks I owe, in common with every American, to the noblest, healthiest, cheeriest romancer that ever lived, I pass on to Tennyson, his works.

Poetry here of a very high (perhaps the highest) order of verbal melody, exquisitely clean and pure, and almost always perfumed, like the tuberose, to an extreme of sweetness—sometimes not, however, but even then a camellia of the hot-house, never a common flower—the verse of inside elegance and high-life; and yet preserving amid all its super-delicatesse a smack of outdoors and outdoor folk. The old Norman lordhood quality here, too, cross'd with that Saxon fiber from which twain the best current stock of England springs—poetry that revels above all things in traditions of knights and chivalry, and deeds of derring-do. The odor of English social life in its highest range—a melancholy, affectionate, very manly, but dainty breed—pervading the pages like an invisible scent; the idleness, the traditions, the mannerisms, the stately *ennui;* the yearning of love, like a spinal marrow, inside of all; the costumes, brocade and satin; the old houses and furniture—solid oak, no mere veneering—the moldy secrets everywhere; the verdure, the ivy on the walls, the moat, the English landscape outside, the buzzing fly in the sun inside the window pane. Never one democratic page; nay, not a line, not a word; never free and *naïve* poetry, but involv'd, labor'd, quite sophisticated—even when the theme is ever so simple or rustic, (a shell, a bit of sedge, the commonest love-passage between a lad and lass,) the handling of the rhyme all showing the scholar and conventional gentleman; showing the laureate, too, the *attaché* of the throne, and most excellent, too; nothing better through the volumes than the dedication "to the Queen" at the beginning, and the other fine dedication, "these to his memory" (Prince Albert's,) preceding "Idylls of the King."

Such for an off-hand summary of the mighty three that now, by the

80. Jefferson's verdict on] *NAR:* Jefferson's criticism on
82. ladies, and] *NAR:* ladies, courts, and
87. Tennyson, his] *NAR:* Tennyson and his
91–92. of inside . . . and] *NAR:* of elegance and high-life, and
93. folk. The] *NAR:* folk—The
98. the pages like] *NAR:* the books like
100. costumes, brocade] *NAR:* costumes, old brocade
110. "to] *NAR:* "To
111. "these to his memory"] *NAR:* "These to his Memory"

women, men, and young folk of the fifty millions given these States by their late census, have been and are more read than all others put together.

We hear it said, both of Tennyson and another current leading literary illustrator of Great Britain, Carlyle—as of Victor Hugo in France—that not one of them is personally friendly or admirant toward America; indeed, quite the reverse. *N'importe.* That they (and more good minds than theirs) cannot span the vast revolutionary arch thrown by the United States over the centuries, fix'd in the present, launch'd to the endless future; that they cannot stomach the high-life-below-stairs coloring all our poetic and genteel social status so far—the measureless viciousness of the great radical Republic, with its ruffianly nominations and elections; its loud, ill-pitch'd voice, utterly regardless whether the verb agrees with the nominative; its fights, errors, eructations, repulsions, dishonesties, audacities; those fearful and varied and long-continued storm and stress stages (so offensive to the well-regulated college-bred mind) wherewith Nature, history, and time block out nationalities more powerful than the past, and to upturn it and press on to the future;—that they cannot understand and fathom all this, I say, is it to be wonder'd at? Fortunately, the gestation of our thirty-eight empires (and plenty more to come) proceeds on its course, on scales of area and velocity immense and absolute as the globe, and, like the globe itself, quite oblivious even of great poets and thinkers. But we can by no means afford to be oblivious of them.

The same of feudalism, its castles, courts, etiquettes, personalities. However they, or the spirits of them hovering in the air, might scowl and glower at such removes as current Kansas or Kentucky life and forms, the latter may by no means repudiate or leave out the former. Allowing all the evil that it did, we get, here and to-day, a balance of good out of its reminiscence almost beyond price.

Am I content, then, that the general interior chyle of our republic should be supplied and nourish'd by wholesale from foreign and antagonistic sources such as these? Let me answer that question briefly:

Years ago I thought Americans ought to strike out separate, and have expressions of their own in highest literature. I think so still, and more decidedly than ever. But those convictions are now strongly temper'd by some additional points, (perhaps the results of advancing age, or the reflections of invalidism.) I see that this world of the West, as part of all, fuses inseparably with the East, and with all, as time does—the ever new, yet old, old human race—"the same subject continued," as the novels of

116. and another current] *NAR:* and the other current
136. etiquettes, personalities] *NAR:* etiquettes, wars, personalities

our grandfathers had it for chapter-heads. If we are not to hospitably receive and complete the inaugurations of the old civilizations, and change their small scale to the largest, broadest scale, what on earth are we for?

The currents of practical business in America, the rude, coarse, tussling facts of our lives, and all their daily experiences, need just the precipitation and tincture of this entirely different fancy world of lulling, contrasting, even feudalistic, anti-republican poetry and romance. On the enormous outgrowth of our unloos'd individualities, and the rank self-assertion of humanity here, may well fall these grace-persuading, *recherché* influences. We first require that individuals and communities shall be free; then surely comes a time when it is requisite that they shall not be too free. Although to such results in the future I look mainly for a great poetry native to us, these importations till then will have to be accepted, such as they are, and thankful they are no worse. The inmost spiritual currents of the present time curiously revenge and check their own compell'd tendency to democracy, and absorption in it, by mark'd leanings to the past—by reminiscences in poems, plots, operas, novels, to a far-off, contrary, deceased world, as if they dreaded the great vulgar gulf tides of to-day. Then what has been fifty centuries growing, working in, and accepted as crowns and apices for our kind, is not going to be pulled down and discarded in a hurry.

It is, perhaps, time we paid our respects directly to the honorable party, the real object of these preambles. But we must make *reconnaissance* a little further still. Not the least part of our lesson were to realize the curiosity and interest of friendly foreign experts,* and how our situation looks to them. "American poetry," says the London "Times,"† "is "the poetry of apt pupils, but it is afflicted from first to last with a fatal "want of raciness. Bryant has been long passed as a poet by Professor

* A few years ago I saw the question, "Has America produced any great poem?" announced as prize-subject for the competition of some university in Northern Europe. I saw the item in a foreign paper and made a note of it; but being taken down with paralysis, and prostrated for a long season, the matter slipp'd away, and I have never been able since to get hold of any essay presented for the prize, or report of the discussion, nor to learn for certain whether there was any essay or discussion, nor can I now remember the place. It may have been Upsala, or possibly Heidelberg. Perhaps some German or Scandinavian can give particulars. I think it was in 1872.

† In a long and prominent editorial, at the time, on the death of William Cullen Bryant.

165. After "worse." *NAR* begins a new paragraph.

187–200. These lines, through the sentence ending "English born." constitute in *NAR* an indented paragraph, set in smaller type.

"Longfellow; but in Longfellow, with all his scholarly grace and tender "feeling, the defect is more apparent than it was in Bryant. Mr. Lowell "can overflow with American humor when politics inspire his muse; but in "the realm of pure poetry he is no more American than a Newdigate "prize-man. Joaquin Miller's verse has fluency and movement and har-"mony, but as for the thought, his songs of the sierras might as well have "been written in Holland."

Unless in a certain very slight contingency, the "Times" says: "American verse, from its earliest to its latest stages, seems an exotic, "with an exuberance of gorgeous blossom, but no principle of reproduc-"tion. That is the very note and test of its inherent want. Great poets are "tortured and massacred by having their flowers of fancy gathered and "gummed down in the *hortus siccus* of an anthology. American poets "show better in an anthology than in the collected volumes of their works. "Like their audience they have been unable to resist the attraction of the "vast orbit of English literature. They may talk of the primeval forest, "but it would generally be very hard from internal evidence to detect "that they were writing on the banks of the Hudson rather than on those "of the Thames. . . . . In fact, they have caught the English tone and "air and mood only too faithfully, and are accepted by the superficially "cultivated English intelligence as readily as if they were English born. "Americans themselves confess to a certain disappointment that a literary "curiosity and intelligence so diffused [as in the United States] have "not taken up English literature at the point at which America has re-"ceived it, and carried it forward and developed it with an independent "energy. But like reader like poet. Both show the effects of having come "into an estate they have not earned. A nation of readers has required of "its poets a diction and symmetry of form equal to that of an old literature "like that of Great Britain, which is also theirs. No ruggedness, however "racy, would be tolerated by circles which, however superficial their cul-"ture, read Byron and Tennyson."

The English critic, though a gentleman and a scholar, and friendly withal, is evidently not altogether satisfied, (perhaps he is jealous,) and winds up by saying: "For the English language to have been enriched

194. audience they] *NAR:* audience, they

198. Thames. . . . . In] *NAR:* Thames. . . . In

201–210. These lines, beginning with "Americans" and continuing to the end of the paragraph, constitute in *NAR* an indented paragraph, set in smaller type.

213–215. The quoted sentence is printed as an indented paragraph, in the smaller type, in *NAR*.

215–216. This sentence is an indented paragraph in *NAR*.

225–226. future, (a phrase open to sharp criticism, and not satisfactory to me, but significant,] *NAR:* future (the phrase is open to sharp criticism, and is not satis-

"with a national poetry which was not English but American, would have "been a treasure beyond price." With which, as whet and foil, we shall proceed to ventilate more definitely certain no doubt willful opinions.

Leaving unnoticed at present the great masterpieces of the antique, or anything from the middle ages, the prevailing flow of poetry for the last fifty or eighty years, and now at its height, has been and is (like the music) an expression of mere surface melody, within narrow limits, and yet, to give it its due, perfectly satisfying to the demands of the ear, of wondrous charm, of smooth and easy delivery, and the triumph of technical art. Above all things it is fractional and select. It shrinks with aversion from the sturdy, the universal, and the democratic.

The poetry of the future, (a phrase open to sharp criticism, and not satisfactory to me, but significant, and I will use it)—the poetry of the future aims at the free expression of emotion, (which means far, far more than appears at first,) and to arouse and initiate, more than to define or finish. Like all modern tendencies, it has direct or indirect reference continually to the reader, to you or me, to the central identity of everything, the mighty Ego. (Byron's was a vehement dash, with plenty of impatient democracy, but lurid and introverted amid all its magnetism; not at all the fitting, lasting song of a grand, secure, free, sunny race.) It is more akin, likewise, to outside life and landscape, (returning mainly to the antique feeling,) real sun and gale, and woods and shores—to the elements themselves—not sitting at ease in parlor or library listening to a good tale of them, told in good rhyme. Character, a feature far above style or polish—a feature not absent at any time, but now first brought to the fore—gives predominant stamp to advancing poetry. Its born sister, music, already responds to the same influences. "The music of the present, "Wagner's, Gounod's, even the later Verdi's, all tends toward this free "expression of poetic emotion, and demands a vocalism totally unlike that "required for Rossini's splendid roulades, or Bellini's suave melodies."

Is there not even now, indeed, an evolution, a departure from the masters? Venerable and unsurpassable after their kind as are the old works, and always unspeakably precious as studies, (for Americans more than any other people,) is it too much to say that by the shifted combina-

factory to me, but is significant,

240–243. The sentence in quotation marks is printed as an indented paragraph in *NAR*. It is a slightly revised sentence from a newspaper clipping introduced into the Feinberg MS. The source of the clipping cannot be determined.

240–241. present, Wagner's] Clip.: present—Wagner's

241. Verdi's, all] Clip.: Verdi's—all

241. toward this free] Clip.: toward the free

243. Clip. has a semicolon after "melodies". In the Feinberg MS Whitman writes after the last word of the clipping "and poetry the same."

tions of the modern mind the whole underlying theory of first-class verse has changed? "Formerly, during the period term'd classic," says Sainte-Beuve, "when literature was govern'd by recognized rules, he was con-"sider'd the best poet who had composed the most perfect work, the most "beautiful poem, the most intelligible, the most agreeable to read, the "most complete in every respect,—the Æneid, the Gerusalemme, a fine "tragedy. To-day, something else is wanted. For us the greatest poet is he "who in his works most stimulates the reader's imagination and reflection, "who excites him the most himself to poetize. The greatest poet is not he "who has done the best; it is he who suggests the most; he, not all of "whose meaning is at first obvious, and who leaves you much to desire, to "explain, to study, much to complete in your turn."

The fatal defects our American singers labor under are subordination of spirit, an absence of the concrete and of real patriotism, and in excess that modern æsthetic contagion a queer friend of mine calls the *beauty disease.* "The immoderate taste for beauty and art," says Charles Baudelaire, "leads men into monstrous excesses. In minds imbued with a frantic greed for the beautiful, all the balances of truth and justice disappear. There is a lust, a disease of the art faculties, which eats up the moral like a cancer."

Of course, by our plentiful verse-writers there is plenty of service perform'd, of a kind. Nor need we go far for a tally. We see, in every polite circle, a class of accomplish'd, good-natured persons, ("society," in fact, could not get on without them,) fully eligible for certain problems, times, and duties—to mix eggnog, to mend the broken spectacles, to decide whether the stew'd eels shall precede the sherry or the sherry the stew'd eels, to eke out Mrs. A. B.'s parlor-tableaux with monk, Jew, lover, Puck, Prospero, Caliban, or what not, and to generally contribute and gracefully adapt their flexibilities and talents, in those ranges, to the world's service. But for real crises, great needs and pulls, moral or physical, they might as well have never been born.

Or the accepted notion of a poet would appear to be a sort of male odalisque, singing or piano-playing a kind of spiced ideas, second-hand reminiscences, or toying late hours at entertainments, in rooms stifling with fashionable scent. I think I haven't seen a new-publish'd, healthy, bracing, simple lyric in ten years. Not long ago, there were verses in each of three

249–259. This quotation is a translation of a passage in the second of two papers on "Les Cinq Derniers Mois de la Vie de Racine," in Sainte-Beuve's *Nouveaux Lundis*, Vol. x, pp. 390–391. Volume x was first published in Paris in 1868. Whitman must have copied the passage from an unsigned review of that volume in the section of "Critical Notices" of *NAR* Vol. 108 (January, 1869), pp. 296–299. The lines as

fresh monthlies, from leading authors, and in every one the whole central *motif* (perfectly serious) was the melancholiness of a marriageable young woman who didn't get a rich husband, but a poor one!

Besides its tonic and *al fresco* physiology, relieving such as this, the poetry of the future will take on character in a more important respect. Science, having extirpated the old stock-fables and superstitions, is clearing a field for verse, for all the arts, and even for romance, a hundred-fold ampler and more wonderful, with the new principles behind. Republicanism advances over the whole world. Liberty, with Law by her side, will one day be paramount—will at any rate be the central idea. Then only—for all the splendor and beauty of what has been, or the polish of what is—then only will the true poets appear, and the true poems. Not the satin and patchouly of to-day, not the glorification of the butcheries and wars of the past, nor any fight between Deity on one side and somebody else on the other—not Milton, not even Shakspere's plays, grand as they are. Entirely different and hitherto unknown classes of men, being authoritatively called for in imaginative literature, will certainly appear. What is hitherto most lacking, perhaps most absolutely indicates the future. Democracy has been hurried on through time by measureless tides and winds, resistless as the revolution of the globe, and as far-reaching and rapid. But in the highest walks of art it has not yet had a single representative worthy of it anywhere upon the earth.

Never had real bard a task more fit for sublime ardor and genius than to sing worthily the songs these States have already indicated. Their origin, Washington, '76, the picturesqueness of old times, the war of 1812 and the sea-fights; the incredible rapidity of movement and breadth of area—to fuse and compact the South and North, the East and West, to express the native forms, situations, scenes, from Montauk to California, and from the Saguenay to the Rio Grande—the working out on such gigantic scales, and with such a swift and mighty play of changing light and shade, of the great problems of man and freedom,—how far ahead of the stereotyped plots, or gem-cutting, or tales of love, or wars of mere ambition! Our history is so full of spinal, modern, germinal subjects—one above all. What the ancient siege of Illium, and the puissance of Hector's and Agamemnon's warriors proved to Hellenic art and literature, and all art and literature since, may prove the war of at-

translated in *NAR* are correctly quoted by Whitman except that in line 249 he wrote "period term'd classic" where *NAR* has "period called classic."

263–267. The source of this quotation in the translated works of Baudelaire available to Whitman has not been located. The quotation is not in the Feinberg MS.

274–275. Jew, lover, Puck] *NAR:* Jew, Turk, lover, Romeo, Puck

298 and 370. Shakspere's] *NAR:* Shakespeare's

tempted secession of 1861–'65 to the future æsthetics, drama, romance, poems of the United States.

Nor could utility itself provide anything more practically serviceable to the hundred millions who, a couple of generations hence, will inhabit within the limits just named, than the permeation of a sane, sweet, autochthonous national poetry—must I say of a kind that does not now exist? but which, I fully believe, will in time be supplied on scales as free as Nature's elements. (It is acknowledged that we of the States are the most materialistic and money-making people ever known. My own theory, while fully accepting this, is that we are the most emotional, spiritualistic, and poetry-loving people also.)

Infinite are the new and orbic traits waiting to be launch'd forth in the firmament that is, and is to be, America. Lately, I have wonder'd whether the last meaning of this cluster of thirty-eight States is not only practical fraternity among themselves—the only real *union*, (much nearer its accomplishment, too, than appears on the surface)—but for fraternity over the whole globe—that dazzling, pensive dream of ages! Indeed, the peculiar glory of our lands, I have come to see, or expect to see, not in their geographical or republican greatness, nor wealth or products, nor military or naval power, nor special, eminent names in any department, to shine with, or outshine, foreign special names in similar departments,—but more and more in a vaster, saner, more surrounding Comradeship, uniting closer and closer not only the American States, but all nations, and all humanity. That, O poets! is not that a theme worth chanting, striving for? Why not fix your verses henceforth to the gauge of the round globe? the whole race? Perhaps the most illustrious culmination of the modern may thus prove to be a signal growth of joyous, more exalted bards of adhesiveness, identically one in soul, but contributed by every nation, each after its distinctive kind. Let us, audacious, start it. Let the diplomats, as ever, still deeply plan, seeking advantages, proposing treaties between governments, and to bind them, on paper: what I seek is different, simpler. I would inaugurate from America, for this purpose, new formulas—international poems. I have thought that the invisible root out of which the poetry deepest in, and dearest to, humanity grows, is Friendship. I have thought that both in patriotism and song (even amid their grandest shows past) we have adhered too long to petty limits, and that the time has come to enfold the world.

Not only is the human and artificial world we have establish'd in the

342. more surrounding Comradeship] *NAR:* more splendid Comradeship
345. After "whole race?" *NAR* begins a new paragraph.
349. diplomats] *NAR:* diplomates

West a radical departure from anything hitherto known—not only men and politics, and all that goes with them—but Nature itself, in the main sense, its construction, is different. The same old font of type, of course, but set up to a text never composed or issued before. For Nature consists not only in itself, objectively, but at least just as much in its subjective reflection from the person, spirit, age, looking at it, in the midst of it, and absorbing it—faithfully sends back the characteristic beliefs of the time or individual—takes, and readily gives again, the physiognomy of any nation or literature—falls like a great elastic veil on a face, or like the molding plaster on a statue.

What is Nature? What were the elements, the invisible backgrounds and eidólons of it, to Homer's heroes, voyagers, gods? What all through the wanderings of Virgil's Æneas? Then to Shakspere's characters—Hamlet, Lear, the English-Norman kings, the Romans? What was Nature to Rousseau, to Voltaire, to the German Goethe in his little classical court gardens? In those presentments in Tennyson (see the "Idyls of the King"—what sumptuous, perfumed, arras-and-gold Nature, inimitably described, better than any, fit for princes and knights and peerless ladies —wrathful or peaceful, just the same—Vivien and Merlin in their strange dalliance, or the death-float of Elaine, or Geraint and the long journey of his disgraced Enid and himself through the wood, and the wife all day driving the horses,) as in all the great imported art-works, treatises, systems, from Lucretius down, there is a constantly lurking, often pervading something, that will have to be eliminated, as not only unsuited to modern democracy and science in America, but insulting to them, and disproved by them.*

Still, the rule and demesne of poetry will always be not the exterior, but interior; not the macrocosm, but microcosm; not Nature, but Man. I haven't said anything about the imperative need of a race of giant bards in the future, to hold up high to eyes of land and race the eternal antiseptic models, and to dauntlessly confront greed, injustice, and all forms of that wiliness and tyranny whose roots never die—(my opinion is,

* Whatever may be said of the few principal poems—or their best passages—it is certain that the overwhelming mass of poetic works, as now absorb'd into human character, exerts a certain constipating, repressing, in-door, and artificial influence, impossible to elude—seldom or never that freeing, dilating, joyous one, with which uncramp'd Nature works on every individual without exception.

369. eidólons] *NAR:* eidolons
383. them.*] [The footnote to which the reference is made here (lines 12*n*–17*n*) does not appear in *NAR.*]
389. die—(my] *NAR:* die (my

that after all the rest is advanced, *that* is what first-class poets are for; as, to their days and occasions, the Hebrew lyrists, Roman Juvenal, and doubtless the old singers of India, and the British Druids)— to counteract dangers, immensest ones, already looming in America—measureless corruption in politics—what we call religion, a mere mask of wax or lace;—for *ensemble*, that most cankerous, offensive of all earth's shows—a vast and varied community, prosperous and fat with wealth of money and products and business ventures—plenty of mere intellectuality too—and then utterly without the sound, prevailing, moral and æsthetic health-action beyond all the money and mere intellect of the world.

Is it a dream of mine that, in times to come, west, south, east, north, will silently, surely arise a race of such poets, varied, yet one in soul—nor only poets, and of the best, but newer, larger prophets—larger than Judea's, and more passionate—to meet and penetrate those woes, as shafts of light the darkness?

As I write, the last fifth of the nineteenth century is enter'd upon, and will soon be waning. Now, and for a long time to come, what the United States most need, to give purport, definiteness, reason why, to their unprecedented material wealth, industrial products, education by rote merely, great populousness and intellectual activity, is the central, spinal reality, (or even the idea of it,) of such a democratic band of native-born-and-bred teachers, artists, *littérateurs*, tolerant and receptive of importations, but entirely adjusted to the West, to ourselves, to our own days, combinations, differences, superiorities. Indeed, I am fond of thinking that the whole series of concrete and political triumphs of the Republic are mainly as bases and preparations for half a dozen future poets, ideal personalities, referring not to a special class, but to the entire people, four or five millions of square miles.

Long, long are the processes of the development of a nationality. Only to the rapt vision does the seen become the prophecy of the unseen.*

* Is there not such a thing as the philosophy of American history and politics? And if so, what is it? . . . Wise men say there are two sets of wills to

19*n*. if so, what is it? . . . Wise] *NAR:* if so—what is it? . . . . Wise] *MDW:*

390–391. for; as,] *NAR:* for, as,
392. Druids)—to] *NAR:* Druids),—to
394. politics—what] *NAR:* politics; what
395. lace;—for] *NAR:* lace; for
413. days, combinations] *NAR:* days, purports, combinations
415. dozen future] *NAR:* dozen first-rate future
419. The seven paragraphs of the footnote, lines 18*n*–92*n*, were first printed in

Democracy, so far attending only to the real, is not for the real only, but the grandest ideal—to justify the modern by that, and not only to equal, but to become by that superior to the past. On a comprehensive summing up of the processes and present and hitherto condition of the United States, with reference to their future, and the indispensable precedents to it, my point, below all surfaces, and subsoiling them, is, that the bases and prerequisites of a leading nationality are, first, at all hazards, freedom, worldly wealth and products on the largest and most varied scale, common education and intercommunication, and, in general, the passing through of just the stages and crudities we have passed or are passing through in the United States.

Then, perhaps, as weightiest factor of the whole business, and of the main outgrowths of the future, it remains to be definitely avow'd that the native-born middle-class population of quite all the United States—the average of farmers and mechanics everywhere—the real, though latent and silent bulk of America, city or country, presents a magnificent mass of material, never before equaled on earth. It is this material, quite unexpress'd by literature or art, that in every respect insures the future of the republic. During the Secession War I was with the armies, and saw the rank and file, North and South, and studied them for four years. I have never had the least doubt about the country in its essential future since.

Meantime, we can (perhaps) do no better than to saturate ourselves with, and continue to give imitations, yet awhile, of the æsthetic models, supplies, of that past and of those lands we spring from. Those wondrous stores, reminiscences, floods, currents! Let them flow on, flow hither freely. And let the sources be enlarged, to include not only the works of British origin, as now, but stately and devout Spain, courteous France, profound Germany, the manly Scandinavian lands, Italy's art race, and always the mystic Orient. Remembering that at present, and doubtless long ahead, a

nations and to persons—one set that acts and works from explainable motives —from teaching, intelligence, judgment, circumstance, caprice, emulation,

if so—what is it? . . . . Wise

MDW, and at the end of the note in *NAR* is the credit line: "*From my 'Memoranda of the War.'*" The seven paragraphs consist of paragraphs 3–5, 7–8, and 11–12 under the heading "Future History of the United States," etc., *MDW* "Notes," pp. 66–68. For paragraphs 1–2, 6, and 9–10 under the same heading, see *Prose 1892*, I, Appendix XI, 10–12.

424–425. to it, my point] *NAR:* to it, I say I am fully content. My point

443. awhile] *NAR:* a while

449. After "mystic Orient." *NAR* begins a new paragraph.

greed, &c.—and then another set, perhaps deep, hidden, unsuspected, yet often more potent than the first, refusing to be argued with, rising as it were out of abysses, resistlessly urging on speakers, doers, communities, unwitting to themselves—the poet to his fieriest words—the race to pursue its loftiest ideal. Indeed, the paradox of a nation's life and career, with all its wondrous contradictions, can probably only be explain'd from these two wills, sometimes conflicting, each operating in its sphere, combining in races or in persons, and producing strangest results.

Let us hope there is (indeed, can there be any doubt there is?) this great unconscious and abysmic second will also running through the average nationality and career of America. Let us hope that, amid all the dangers and defections of the present, and through all the processes of the conscious will, it alone is the permanent and sovereign force, destined to carry on the New World to fulfill its destinies in the future—to resolutely pursue those destinies, age upon age; to build, far, far beyond its past vision, present thought; to form and fashion, and for the general type, men and women more noble, more athletic than the world has yet seen; to gradually, firmly blend, from all the States, with all varieties, a friendly, happy, free, religious nationality—a nationality not only the richest, most inventive, most productive and materialistic the world has yet known, but compacted indissolubly, and out of whose ample and solid bulk, and giving purpose and finish to it, conscience, morals, and all the spiritual attributes, shall surely rise, like spires above some group of edifices, firm-footed on the earth, yet scaling space and heaven.

Great as they are, and greater far to be, the United States, too, are but a series of steps in the eternal process of creative thought. And here is, to my mind, their final justification, and certain perpetuity. There is in that sublime process, in the laws of the universe—and, above all, in the moral law—something that would make unsatisfactory, and, even vain and contemptible, all the triumphs of war, the gains of peace, and the proudest worldly grandeur of all the nations that have ever existed, or that (ours included) now exist, except that we constantly see, through all their worldly career, however struggling and blind and lame, attempts, by all ages, all peoples, according to their development, to reach, to press, to progress on, and ever farther on, to more and more advanced ideals.

The glory of the republic of the United States, in my opinion, is to be that, emerging in the light of the modern and the splendor of science, and solidly

24*n*. communities, unwitting] *MDW:* communities, Nations, unwitting

25*n*–26*n*. ideal. Indeed,] *NAR:* ideal. . . . Indeed,] *MDW:* ideal. . . . . . Indeed

30*n*. there is (indeed] *MDW:* there is, (Indeed

36*n*. age; to] *MDW:* age—to

36*n*. thought; to] *MDW:* thought—to

38*n*. seen; to] *MDW:* seen—to

41*n*. known, but] *MDW:* known—but

44*n*. After "space and heaven." *MDW* has the paragraph beginning "No more" which *NAR* and *SDC* transfer to a later position beginning with line 71*n*.

45*n*. are, and] *MDW:* are, therefore, and

54*n*. on, and ever farther] *NAR* and *MDW:* on, and farther

based on the past, it is to cheerfully range itself, and its politics are henceforth to come, under those universal laws, and embody them, and carry them out, to serve them. And as only that individual becomes truly great who understands well that, while complete in himself in a certain sense, he is but a part of the divine, eternal scheme, and whose special life and laws are adjusted to move in harmonious relations with the general laws of Nature, and especially with the moral law, the deepest and highest of all, and the last vitality of man or state—so the United States may only become the greatest and the most continuous, by understanding well their harmonious relations with entire humanity and history, and all their laws and progress, sublimed with the creative thought of Deity, through all time, past, present, and future. Thus will they expand to the amplitude of their destiny, and become illustrations and culminating parts of the cosmos, and of civilization.

No more considering the States as an incident, or series of incidents, however vast, coming accidentally along the path of time, and shaped by casual emergencies as they happen to arise, and the mere result of modern improvements, vulgar and lucky, ahead of other nations and times, I would finally plant, as seeds, these thoughts or speculations in the growth of our republic—that it is the deliberate culmination and result of all the past—that here, too, as in all departments of the universe, regular laws (slow and sure in planting, slow and sure in ripening) have controll'd and govern'd, and will yet control and govern; and that those laws can no more be baffled or steer'd clear of, or vitiated, by chance, or any fortune or opposition, than the laws of winter and summer, or darkness and light.

The summing up of the tremendous moral and military perturbations of 1861–5, and their results—and indeed of the entire hundred years of the past of our national experiment, from its inchoate movement down to the present day (1780–1881)—is, that they all now launch the United States fairly forth, consistently with the entirety of civilization and humanity, and in main sort the representative of them, leading the van, leading the fleet of the modern and democratic, on the seas and voyages of the future.

And the real history of the United States—starting from that great convulsive struggle for unity, the secession war, triumphantly concluded, and *the South* victorious after all—is only to be written at the remove of hundreds, perhaps a thousand, years hence.

60*n*. them. And] *NAR:* them. . . . And] *MDW:* them. . . . . . . And
61*n*. that, while] *MDW:* that, (while
61*n*. sense, he] *MDW:* sense,) he
64*n*–65*n*. or state—so the United States may] *NAR* and *MDW:* or State—so those nations, and so the United States, may
67*n*. progress, sublimed] *NAR* and *MDW:* progress, and sublimed
69*n*. become illustrations] *NAR* and *MDW:* become splendid illustrations
71*n*. the States] *MDW:* the United States
77*n*. in planting, slow] *NAR* and *MDW:* in acting, slow
79*n*. govern; and] *NDW:* govern—and
82*n*. The summing up] *MDW:* Yes: The summing-up
84*n*–85*n*. present day (1780–1881)] *MDW:* present day, (1775–1876)
90*n*. unity, the secession war, triumphantly] *MDW:* Unity, triumphantly

certain humility would well become us. The course through time of highest civilization, does it not wait the first glimpse of our contribution to its cosmic train of poems, bibles, first-class structures, perpetuities—Egypt and Palestine and India—Greece and Rome and mediæval Europe—and so onward? The shadowy procession is not a meagre one, and the standard not a low one. All that is mighty in our kind seems to have already trod the road. Ah, never may America forget her thanks and reverence for samples, treasures such as these—that other life-blood, inspiration, sunshine, hourly in use to-day, all days, forever, through her broad demesne!

All serves our New World progress, even the bafflers, headwinds, cross-tides. Through many perturbations and squalls, and much backing and filling, the ship, upon the whole, makes unmistakably for her destination. Shakspere has served, and serves, may-be, the best of any.

For conclusion, a passing thought, a contrast, of him who, in my opinion, continues and stands for the Shaksperean cultus at the present day among all English-writing peoples—of Tennyson, his poetry. I find it impossible, as I taste the sweetness of those lines, to escape the flavor, the conviction, the lush-ripening culmination, and last honey of decay (I dare not call it rottenness) of that feudalism which the mighty English dramatist painted in all the splendors of its noon and afternoon. And how they are chanted—both poets! Happy those kings and nobles to be so sung, so told! To run their course—to get their deeds and shapes in lasting pigments—the very pomp and dazzle of the sunset!

Meanwhile, democracy waits the coming of its bards in silence and in twilight—but 'tis the twilight of the dawn.

452. bibles, first-class structures] *NAR:* bibles, structures
455. mighty in] *NAR:* mighty or precious in
455–456. have already trod] *NAR:* have trod
463. Shakspere] *NAR:* Shakespeare
465. Shaksperean] *NAR:* Shakespearean
467. of those lines] *NAR:* of these lines
475. *NAR* has the name "Walt Whitman" at the end of the article.

A Memorandum at a Venture.

Printed in SDC, except for the second epigraph (lines 3–10), from clippings of irregular length of what appears to be the galley proof, or perhaps the broadside offprint, of the article of the same title in *NAR*, CXXIV (June, 1882), 546–550. It was first reprinted in *SDC;* omitted in *DVOP*. A twelve-page autograph MS of the article, probably the one from which the *NAR* printer's copy was made, exists in the Feinberg Collection. This MS (here designated FMS) is collated with the printed texts.

1–2. This quotation is drawn from Alfred Sensier's *Jean-François Millet, Peasant and Painter*, translated by Helena de Kay (New York, 1881); previously printed

A Memorandum at a Venture.

"All is proper to be express'd, provided our aim is only high enough."—*J. F. Millet.*

"The candor of science is the glory of the modern. It does not hide and repress; it confronts, turns on the light. It alone has perfect faith—faith not in a part only, but all. Does it not undermine the old religious standards? Yes, in God's truth, by excluding the devil from the theory of the universe—by showing that evil is not a law in itself, but a sickness, a perversion of the good, and the other side of the good—that in fact all of humanity, and of everything, is divine in its bases, its eligibilities."

Shall the mention of such topics as I have briefly but plainly and resolutely broach'd in the "Children of Adam" section of "Leaves of Grass" be admitted in poetry and literature? Ought not the innovation to be put down by opinion and criticism? and, if those fail, by the District Attorney? True, I could not construct a poem which declaredly took, as never before, the complete human identity, physical, moral, emotional, and intellectual, (giving precedence and compass in a certain sense to the first,) nor fulfil that *bona fide* candor and entirety of treatment which was a part of my purpose, without comprehending this section also. But I would entrench myself more deeply and widely than that. And while I do not ask any man to indorse my theory, I confess myself anxious that what I sought to write and express, and the ground I built on, shall be at least partially understood, from its own platform. The best way seems to me to confront the question with entire frankness.

There are, generally speaking, two points of view, two conditions of

in five installments in *Scribner's Monthly* from September, 1880, to January, 1881. The complete sentence reads: "We can start from any point and arrive at the sublime, and all is proper to be expressed, provided our aim is high enough." Its source was an unpublished manuscript found among Millet's papers at his death in January, 1875. An article on Whitman by E. C. Stedman appeared in *Scribner's* for November, 1880. In the MS the first word, "all," does not have an initial capital, nor does the MS contain the word "only" before "high."

3–9. This quotation sounds like Whitman in style but its source has not so far been determined. It is printed in *SDC* from an autograph MS in pencil. It does not appear in *NAR*.

9. its eligibilities] FMS: its best eligibilities

10. the mention] FMS: the open mention

11. the "Children of Adam" section] FMS: the *Calamus* section

11–12. of "Leaves of Grass"] FMS: of my *Leaves of Grass*

14–18. This sentence, beginning "True," is not in FMS.

17. fulfil] *NAR:* fulfill

24–25. view, . . . world's] FMS: view for the world's

the world's attitude toward these matters; the first, the conventional one of good folks and good print everywhere, repressing any direct statement of them, and making allusions only at second or third hand—(as the Greeks did of death, which, in Hellenic social culture, was not mention'd point-blank, but by euphemisms.) In the civilization of to-day, this condition—without stopping to elaborate the arguments and facts, which are many and varied and perplexing—has led to states of ignorance, repressal, and cover'd over disease and depletion, forming certainly a main factor in the world's woe. A non-scientific, non-æsthetic, and eminently non-religious condition, bequeath'd to us from the past, (its origins diverse, one of them the far-back lessons of benevolent and wise men to restrain the prevalent coarseness and animality of the tribal ages—with Puritanism, or perhaps Protestantism itself for another, and still another specified in the latter part of this memorandum)—to it is probably due most of the ill births, inefficient maturity, snickering pruriency, and of that human pathologic evil and morbidity which is, in my opinion, the keel and reason-why of every evil and morbidity. Its scent, as of something sneaking, furtive, mephitic, seems to lingeringly pervade all modern literature, conversation, and manners.

The second point of view, and by far the largest—as the world in working-day dress vastly exceeds the world in parlor toilette—is the one of common life, from the oldest times down, and especially in England, (see the earlier chapters of "Taine's English Literature," and see Shakspere almost anywhere,) and which our age to-day inherits from riant stock, in the wit, or what passes for wit, of masculine circles, and in erotic stories and talk, to excite, express, and dwell on, that merely sensual voluptuousness which, according to Victor Hugo, is the most universal trait of all ages, all lands. This second condition, however bad, is at any

27. hand—(as] *NAR:* hand (as] FMS: hand, (as

28–29. was not mention'd] FMS: was never mentioned

31. are . . . perplexing] FMS: are varied and perplexing and many

31–33. ignorance, . . . a main] FMS: ignorance, depravity, repressal, and covered-up morbidity in certain departments forming probably a main

33. non-æsthetic] FMS: non-artistic

34. past, (its] *NAR:* past (its] FMS: past, its

36–38. ages—with Puritanism, . . . another specified] FMS: ages,—cause Puritanism, with perhaps Protestantism for another cause, and still another attitude specified

38–39. memorandum)—to . . . most] *NAR:* memorandum), to . . . most] FMS: memorandum,) it causes, in my opinion, much or most

39–40. and of that . . . morbidity. Its] FMS: and that bodily evil which is probably the keel and foundation of every evil. Its

42. mephitic, . . . pervade all] FMS: mephitic, lingeringly pervades all

rate like a disease which comes to the surface, and therefore less dangerous than a conceal'd one.

The time seems to me to have arrived, and America to be the place, for a new departure—a third point of view. The same freedom and faith and earnestness which, after centuries of denial, struggle, repression, and martyrdom, the present day brings to the treatment of politics and religion, must work out a plan and standard on this subject, not so much for what is call'd society, as for thoughtfulest men and women, and thoughtfulest literature. The same spirit that marks the physiological author and demonstrator on these topics in his important field, I have thought necessary to be exemplified, for once, in another certainly not less important field.

In the present memorandum I only venture to indicate that plan and view—decided upon more than twenty years ago, for my own literary action, and formulated tangibly in my printed poems—(as Bacon says an abstract thought or theory is of no moment unless it leads to a deed or work done, exemplifying it in the concrete)—that the sexual passion in itself, while normal and unperverted, is inherently legitimate, creditable, not necessarily an improper theme for poet, as confessedly not for scientist—that, with reference to the whole construction, organism, and intentions of "Leaves of Grass," anything short of confronting that theme, and making myself clear upon it, as the enclosing basis of everything, (as the sanity of everything was to be the atmosphere of the poems,) I should beg the question in its most momentous aspect, and the superstructure that follow'd, pretensive as it might assume to be, would all rest on a poor foundation, or no foundation at all. In short, as the assumption of the sanity of birth, Nature and humanity, is the key to any true theory of life and the universe—at any rate, the only theory out of

45. working-day dress] FMS: working dress

45–46. toilette—is the one of common] FMS: toilette—that of common

49–50. in erotic stories] FMS: in sensuous stories

50–52. dwell on, . . . all lands.] FMS: dwell on mere sensual voluptousness, perhaps the most universal trait of all ages and lands.

52–54. This sentence does not appear in FMS.

56. departure—a third] FMS: departure on the subject—a third

61–64. This sentence does not appear in FMS.

65. In the . . . venture to] FMS: In this memorandum I only design to

68. tangibly in] FMS: tangibly and practically in

67–68. says an . . . theory is] FMS: says a thought or theory in the abstract is

69–93. After the words "concrete)—that" these lines are missing in FMS, of which the eighth page ends in the middle of a sentence and the next page begins with the sentence beginning "Might not" in line 93.

74. enclosing] *NAR:* inclosing

which I wrote—it is, and must inevitably be, the only key to "Leaves of Grass," and every part of it. *That*, (and not a vain consistency or weak pride, as a late "Springfield Republican" charges,) is the reason that I have stood out for these particular verses uncompromisingly for over twenty years, and maintain them to this day. *That* is what I felt in my inmost brain and heart, when I only answer'd Emerson's vehement arguments with silence, under the old elms of Boston Common.

Indeed, might not every physiologist and every good physician pray for the redeeming of this subject from its hitherto relegation to the tongues and pens of blackguards, and boldly putting it for once at least, if no more, in the demesne of poetry and sanity—as something not in itself gross or impure, but entirely consistent with highest manhood and womanhood, and indispensable to both? Might not only every wife and every mother—not only every babe that comes into the world, if that were possible—not only all marriage, the foundation and *sine qua non* of the civilized state—bless and thank the showing, or taking for granted, that motherhood, fatherhood, sexuality, and all that belongs to them, can be asserted, where it comes to question, openly, joyously, proudly, "without shame or the need of shame," from the highest artistic and human considerations—but, with reverence be it written, on such attempt to justify the base and start of the whole divine scheme in humanity, might not the Creative Power itself deign a smile of approval?

To the movement for the eligibility and entrance of women amid new spheres of business, politics, and the suffrage, the current prurient, conventional treatment of sex is the main formidable obstacle. The rising tide of "woman's rights," swelling and every year advancing farther and farther, recoils from it with dismay. There will in my opinion be no general progress in such eligibility till a sensible, philosophic, democratic method is substituted.

The whole question—which strikes far, very far deeper than most people have supposed, (and doubtless, too, something is to be said on all sides,) is peculiarly an important one in art—is first an ethic, and then

82. After "part of it." *NAR* begins a new paragraph.
82. *That*, (and] *NAR:* That (and
85. *That*] *NAR:* That
95–96. of the civilized state—bless and thank] FMS: of every civilized state—thank and bless
96–102. In lieu of these lines, beginning with the word "granted," FMS has the following, ending the paragraph: "granted, resolutely maintain and justify the base and start of the whole divine scheme in humanity; might not the Creative Power itself deign a smile of approval?"
99–100. and human considerations] *NAR:* and sociologic considerations
103–109. This entire paragraph is missing in FMS.

still more an æsthetic one. I condense from a paper read not long since at Cheltenham, England, before the "Social Science Congress," to the Art Department, by P.H. Rathbone of Liverpool, on the "Undraped Figure in Art," and the discussion that follow'd:

> "When coward Europe suffer'd the unclean Turk to soil the sacred shores of Greece by his polluting presence, civilization and morality receiv'd a blow from which they have never entirely recover'd, and the trail of the serpent has been over European art and European society ever since. The Turk regarded and regards women as animals without soul, toys to be play'd with or broken at pleasure, and to be hidden, partly from shame, but chiefly for the purpose of stimulating exhausted passion. Such is the unholy origin of the objection to the nude as a fit subject for art; it is purely Asiatic, and though not introduced for the first time in the fifteenth century, is yet to be traced to the source of all impurity—the East. Although the source of the prejudice is thoroughly unhealthy and impure, yet it is now shared by many pure-minded and honest, if somewhat uneducated, people. But I am prepared to maintain that it is necessary for the future of English art and of English morality that the right of the nude to a place in our galleries should be boldly asserted; it must, however, be the nude as represented by thoroughly trained artists, and with a pure and noble ethic purpose. The human form, male and female, is the type and standard of all beauty of form and proportion, and it is necessary to be thoroughly familiar with it in order safely to judge of all beauty which consists of form and proportion. To women it is most necessary that they should become thoroughly imbued with the knowledge of the ideal female form, in order that they should recognize the perfection of it at once, and without effort, and so far as possible avoid deviations from the ideal. Had this been the case in times past, we should not have had to deplore the distortions effected by tight-lacing, which destroy'd the figure and ruin'd the health of so many of the last generation. Nor should we have had the scandalous dresses alike of society and the stage. The extreme development of the low dresses which obtain'd some years ago, when the stays crush'd up the breasts into suggestive prominence, would surely have been check'd, had the eye of the public been properly educated by familiarity with the exquisite beauty of line of a well-shaped bust. I might show how thorough acquaintance with the ideal nude foot would

110–113. In lieu of this sentence, FMS has the following sentence: "The whole question, (which strikes much deeper than at first thought would be supposed and doubtless something is to be said on all sides,) is peculiarly important in Art,—is first ethic, and then an aesthetic one."

117–173. This long quotation is not in FMS. It was presumably a newspaper clipping, revised by Whitman, which he sent to *NAR* with the MS.

117–164. This portion of the quotation in *NAR* is enclosed in single quotation marks inside the double quotation marks used for the entire extract.

141. After the word "tight-lacing" the proof clipping has "(cheers)" which Whitman deletes. It does not appear in the text of *NAR*.

147, 151. After "well-shaped bust." and after "ungainly attitude." the proof clipping has "(cheers)". Whitman deletes both and they do not appear in the text of *NAR*.

probably have much modified the foot-torturing boots and high heels, which wring the foot out of all beauty of line, and throw the body forward into an awkward and ungainly attitude.

"It is argued that the effect of nude representation of women upon young men is unwholesome, but it would not be so if such works were admitted without question into our galleries, and became thoroughly familiar to them. On the contrary, it would do much to clear away from healthy-hearted lads one of their sorest trials—that prurient curiosity which is bred of prudish concealment. Where there is mystery there is the suggestion of evil, and to go to a theatre, where you have only to look at the stalls to see one-half of the female form, and to the stage to see the other half undraped, is far more pregnant with evil imaginings than the most objectionable of totally undraped figures. In French art there have been questionable nude figures exhibited; but the fault was not that they were nude, but that they were the portraits of ugly immodest women."

Some discussion follow'd. There was a general concurrence in the principle contended for by the reader of the paper. Sir Walter Stirling maintain'd that the perfect male figure, rather than the female, was the model of beauty. After a few remarks from Rev. Mr. Roberts and Colonel Oldfield, the Chairman regretted that no opponent of nude figures had taken part in the discussion. He agreed with Sir Walter Stirling as to the male figure being the most perfect model of proportion. He join'd in defending the exhibition of nude figures, but thought considerable supervision should be exercised over such exhibitions.

No, it is not the picture or nude statue or text, with clear aim, that is indecent; it is the beholder's own thought, inference, distorted construction. True modesty is one of the most precious of attributes, even virtues, but in nothing is there more pretense, more falsity, than the needless assumption of it. Through precept and consciousness, man has long

175. indecent; it] FMS: indecent—it
177. pretense] FMS: pretence
177–178. than the needless assumption of it.] FMS: than its assumption.
178. After "assumption of it." FMS begins a new paragraph.
180–181. the spinal meaning] FMS: the meaning
181. text, *God overlook'd all that He had made*] *NAR:* text, God overlooked all that He had made] FMS: text, God weighed all that He had made
182. apex of the whole—humanity—with its] FMS: apex of the universe, humanity, its
183. *and behold, it was very good.*] *NAR* and FMS: and pronounced it *very good.*
184–191. Of this paragraph FMS has only the first sentence, which does not begin a new paragraph but concludes one, and the essay, as follows: "Does not any thing short of that point of view, when you come to look at it profoundly, impugn the theory of Creation from the outset?"
187. centre] *NAR:* center

Death of Abraham Lincoln.

Printed in *SDC* from two sets of clippings. Lines 1–144 and 272–353 are

enough realized how bad he is. I would not so much disturb or demolish that conviction, only to resume and keep unerringly with it the spinal meaning of the Scriptural text, *God overlook'd all that He had made*, (including the apex of the whole—humanity—with its elements, passions, appetites,) *and behold, it was very good.*

Does not anything short of that third point of view, when you come to think of it profoundly and with amplitude, impugn Creation from the outset? In fact, however overlaid, or unaware of itself, does not the conviction involv'd in it perennially exist at the centre of all society, and of the sexes, and of marriage? Is it not really an intuition of the human race? For, old as the world is, and beyond statement as are the countless and splendid results of its culture and evolution, perhaps the best and earliest and purest intuitions of the human race have yet to be develop'd.

Death of Abraham Lincoln.

LECTURE *deliver'd in New York, April 14, 1879— in Philadelphia, '80—in Boston, '81.*

How often since that dark and dripping Saturday—that chilly April day, now fifteen years bygone—my heart has entertain'd the dream, the wish, to give of Abraham Lincoln's death, its own special thought and memorial. Yet now the sought-for opportunity offers, I find my notes incompetent, (why, for truly profound themes, is statement so idle? why does the right phrase never offer?) and the fit tribute I dream'd of, waits unprepared as ever. My talk here indeed is less because of itself or anything in it, and nearly altogether because I feel a desire, apart from

printed from what appear to be proof sheets of large size with large type prepared by Whitman for public reading. (These proof sheets are identical with those boxed with other Lincoln material in the Whitman Collection of the Library of Congress.) The first paragraph, lines 1–22, was printed after the date of his first lecture, April 14, 1879, but before his lecture at Association Hall, Philadelphia, April 15, 1880; since in line 2 he says the day of Lincoln's death is "now fifteen years bygone." Lines 165–308 are printed from clippings of *MDW*, *TR*, pp. 46–49. Except for lines 1–22 and paragraph 16, lines 250–266 (omitted though it had been twice published before), the entire lecture was published under the title "A Poet on the Platform" in *NYTR*, April 15, 1879. All of lines 145–271 except one paragraph, lines 161–171 had been previously published in "Abraham Lincoln's Death," *NYS*, February 12, 1876. Lines 25–40 had been published as part of paragraph 12 of "Ten Years," First Paper, *NYWG*, January 24, 1874. Lines 44–108 had been twice published before they appeared in *NYTR*, once as a footnote in *MDW*, *TR*, pp. 22–23, and earlier in a section subtitled "Abraham Lincoln—My First Sight and Impression of Him" (paragraphs 15–20) of "Ten Years," First Paper, *NYWG*. The lecture was reprinted in *CPP* and *CPW*, but omitted in *DVOP*. All texts are here collated.

any talk, to specify the day, the martyrdom. It is for this, my friends, I have call'd you together. Oft as the rolling years bring back this hour, let it again, however briefly, be dwelt upon. For my own part, I hope and desire, till my own dying day, whenever the 14th or 15th of April comes, to annually gather a few friends, and hold its tragic reminiscence. No narrow or sectional reminiscence. It belongs to these States in their entirety—not the North only, but the South—perhaps belongs most tenderly and devoutly to the South, of all; for there, really, this man's birth-stock. There and thence his antecedent stamp. Why should I not say that thence his manliest traits—his universality—his canny, easy ways and words upon the surface—his inflexible determination and courage at heart? Have you never realized it, my friends, that Lincoln, though grafted on the West, is essentially, in personnel and character, a Southern contribution?

And though by no means proposing to resume the Secession war tonight, I would briefly remind you of the public conditions preceding that contest. For twenty years, and especially during the four or five before the war actually began, the aspect of affairs in the United States, though without the flash of military excitement, presents more than the survey of a battle, or any extended campaign, or series, even of Nature's convulsions. The hot passions of the South—the strange mixture at the North of inertia, incredulity, and conscious power—the incendiarism of the abolitionists—the rascality and *grip* of the politicians, unparallel'd in any

11–12. and desire, till] Proof: and intend, till

23. And though] *NYTR* and Proof: Though

23. Before the paragraph beginning in this line, *NYTR* has the following introductory paragraph not in Proof:

"The poet Walt Whitman made his beginning as a lecturer last night, at Steck Hall, in Fourteenth-st. His subject was the death of President Lincoln. He reads from notes, sitting in a chair, as he is still much disabled from paralysis. He desires engagements as a reader of his own poems and as a lecturer. The following was last night's discourse:"

24. you of] *NYTR* and Proof: you, my friends, of

25. years, and] *NYWG:* years preceding the war, and

25–26. five . . . aspect] *NYWG:* five immediately before its opening, the aspect

27. the flash] *NYWG:* the keenness and flash

27. presents more] *NYWG:* presents to any man of thoughtfulness, or artistic perceptions, more

29–35. These two sentences are not in *NYWG.*

31. *grip*] *NYTR:* grip

35. equinox. In politics, what can] Proof: equinox. In politics, what can] *NYTR:* equinox. What could] (Proof begins a new paragraph with "In politics" and *NYTR* begins a new paragraph with "What could".)

36. Presidentiads] *NYTR:* Presidentials

36–40. than . . . aristocracies.] *NYWG:* than the fetid condition of everything from 1840 to '60, especially under Fillmore's and Buchanan's administrations. These

land, any age. To these I must not omit adding the honesty of the essential bulk of the people everywhere—yet with all the seething fury and contradiction of their natures more arous'd than the Atlantic's waves in wildest equinox. In politics, what can be more ominous, (though generally unappreciated then)—what more significant than the Presidentiads of Fillmore and Buchanan? proving conclusively that the weakness and wickedness of elected rulers are just as likely to afflict us here, as in the countries of the Old World, under their monarchies, emperors, and aristocracies. In that Old World were everywhere heard underground rumblings, that died out, only to again surely return. While in America the volcano, though civic yet, continued to grow more and more convulsive—more and more stormy and threatening.

In the height of all this excitement and chaos, hovering on the edge at first, and then merged in its very midst, and destined to play a leading part, appears a strange and awkward figure. I shall not easily forget the first time I ever saw Abraham Lincoln. It must have been about the 18th or 19th of February, 1861. It was rather a pleasant afternoon, in New York city, as he arrived there from the West, to remain a few hours, and then pass on to Washington, to prepare for his inauguration. I saw him in Broadway, near the site of the present Post-office. He came down, I think from Canal street, to stop at the Astor House. The broad spaces, sidewalks, and street in the neighborhood, and for some distance, were crowded with solid masses of people, many thousands. The omnibuses and

two Presidentiads—and perhaps one other—prove conclusively that the weakness and wickedness of elected rulers, backed by our great parties, are just as likely to afflict us, here, (but to be met and remedied,) as the same evils in the countries of the old world, under their monarchies, emperors, and aristocracies.

38. rulers are] *NYTR:* rulers, backed by our great parties, are

40–43. For these two sentences *NYWG* has the following: "The Slave power had complete possession of the helm, and was evidently determined on its own tack. All the moral convictions of the best portion of the Nation were outraged. A powerful faction, ruling the North, was art and part with the Slaveocracy, and stood then and stands to-day, just as responsible for the Rebellion." (Cf. also "Origins of Attempted Secession," lines 8–9.)

41. only to again surely return] *NYTR:* only again surely to return

43. After "threatening." Proof has the following sentence-paragraph deleted in *SDC* and *NYTR:* "Who, I say, can ever paint those years? those peace campaigns preceding, and more lucid and terrible than any war?"

44–46. This sentence, a separate paragraph in *NYTR*, Proof, and *NYWG*, is omitted in *MDW* and *TR*.

44. the height of] *NYWG:* the midst of

47. I ever saw] *TR* and *NYWG:* I saw

48. pleasant afternoon] Proof, *TR*, and *NYWG:* pleasant spring afternoon

49. as he arrived there from] *NYTR:* as he arrived here from] *TR* and *NYWG:* as Lincoln arrived there from

49. West, to remain a] *TR* and *NYWG:* West to stop a

51. He came down] *TR* and *NYWG:* He had come down

other vehicles had all been turn'd off, leaving an unusual hush in that busy part of the city. Presently two or three shabby hack barouches made their way with some difficulty through the crowd, and drew up at the Astor House entrance. A tall figure step'd out of the centre of these barouches, paus'd leisurely on the sidewalk, look'd up at the granite walls and looming architecture of the grand old hotel—then, after a relieving stretch of arms and legs, turn'd round for over a minute to slowly and good-humoredly scan the appearance of the vast and silent crowds. There were no speeches—no compliments—no welcome—as far as I could hear, not a word said. Still much anxiety was conceal'd in that quiet. Cautious persons had fear'd some mark'd insult or indignity to the President-elect—for he possess'd no personal popularity at all in New York city, and very little political. But it was evidently tacitly agreed that if the few political supporters of Mr. Lincoln present would entirely abstain from any demonstration on their side, the immense majority, who were any thing but supporters, would abstain on their side also. The result was a sulky, unbroken silence, such as certainly never before characterized so great a New York crowd.

Almost in the same neighborhood I distinctly remember'd seeing Lafayette on his visit to America in 1825. I had also personally seen and heard, various years afterward, how Andrew Jackson, Clay, Webster, Hungarian Kossuth, Filibuster Walker, the Prince of Wales on his visit, and other celebres, native and foreign, had been welcom'd there—all that indescribable human roar and magnetism, unlike any other sound in the universe—the glad exulting thunder-shouts of countless unloos'd throats of men! But on this occasion, not a voice—not a sound. From the top of an omnibus, (driven up one side, close by, and block'd by the curbstone and the crowds,) I had, I say, a capital view of it all, and especially of Mr. Lincoln, his look and gait—his perfect composure and coolness—his

55. had all been] *TR* and *NYWG:* had been all
58. step'd] *NYTR* and *NYWG:* stepped
59. the granite] *NYTR*, Proof, *TR*, and *NYWG:* the dark granite
62–95. These lines are quite different from the corresponding passage in *TR* and in *NYWG* (17–18 and part of 16). See Appendix v, *1*.
101–108. This paragraph is omitted in *TR*, but in *NYWG* it consists of two paragraphs (19 and 20) immediately following the passage quoted in Appendix v, *1*.
75. heard, various years afterward, how] *NYTR* and Proof: heard how
77. celebres] *NYTR:* célèbres
77. there—all] *NYTR* and Proof: there, at various times—all
79. universe—the] *NYTR:* universe, the
80. After "not a sound." *NYTR* and Proof begin a new paragraph.
86. face, black] *NYTR* and Proof: face, his black
90. Shakspere] *NYTR:* Shakspeare
101–103. These two sentences are enclosed in parentheses in *NYWG* and constitute a separate paragraph.

unusual and uncouth height, his dress of complete black, stovepipe hat push'd back on the head, dark-brown complexion, seam'd and wrinkled yet canny-looking face, black, bushy head of hair, disproportionately long neck, and his hands held behind as he stood observing the people. He look'd with curiosity upon that immense sea of faces, and the sea of faces return'd the look with similar curiosity. In both there was a dash of comedy, almost farce, such as Shakspere puts in his blackest tragedies. The crowd that hemm'd around consisted I should think of thirty to forty thousand men, not a single one his personal friend—while I have no doubt, (so frenzied were the ferments of the time,) many an assassin's knife and pistol lurk'd in hip or breast-pocket there, ready, soon as break and riot came.

But no break or riot came. The tall figure gave another relieving stretch or two of arms and legs; then with moderate pace, and accompanied by a few unknown looking persons, ascended the portico-steps of the Astor House, disappear'd through its broad entrance—and the dumb-show ended.

I saw Abraham Lincoln often the four years following that date. He changed rapidly and much during his Presidency—but this scene, and him in it, are indelibly stamped upon my recollection. As I sat on the top of my omnibus, and had a good view of him, the thought, dim and inchoate then, has since come out clear enough, that four sorts of genius, four mighty and primal hands, will be needed to the complete limning of this man's future portrait—the eyes and brains and finger-touch of Plutarch and Eschylus and Michel Angelo, assisted by Rabelais.

And now—(Mr. Lincoln passing on from this scene to Washington, where he was inaugurated, amid armed cavalry, and sharpshooters at every point—the first instance of the kind in our history—and I hope it will be the last)—now the rapid succession of well-known events, (too

101. saw . . . that date.] Proof: saw Abraham Lincoln often the four or five years following that date.] *NYWG:* saw Lincoln often the three or four years following this date.

102–103. scene, and him in it, are] *NYWG:* scene and his portrait, as he looked, and moved, and stood in it, as above given, are

103–105. As I sat . . . enough, that four] *NYWG:* But of Abraham Lincoln, (the thought, as I had a good sight of him there in Broadway, from the top of an omnibus, driven up one side and blocked in, was dim and inchoate, but received its negative even then, and has now come out clear and definite enough,) four

106–107. of this man's future] *NYWG:* of his future

108. Eschylus and Michel] *NYTR:* Aeschylus and Michael

109–249 and 267–271. These lines in *NYTR* have the subtitle "The War and the murder."

109. now—(Mr.] *NYTR:* now (Mr.

111–112. history—and . . . last)—now] *NYTR:* history, and . . . last), now] Proof: history—and . . . last)—Now

well known—I believe, these days, we almost hate to hear them mention'd)—the national flag fired on at Sumter—the uprising of the North, in paroxysms of astonishment and rage—the chaos of divided councils—the call for troops—the first Bull Run—the stunning cast-down, shock, and dismay of the North—and so in full flood the Secession war. Four years of lurid, bleeding, murky, murderous war. Who paint those years, with all their scenes?—the hard-fought engagements—the defeats, plans, failures—the gloomy hours, days, when our Nationality seem'd hung in pall of doubt, perhaps death—the Mephistophelean sneers of foreign lands and attachés—the dreaded Scylla of European interference, and the Charybdis of the tremendously dangerous latent strata of secession sympathizers throughout the free States, (far more numerous than is supposed)—the long marches in summer—the hot sweat, and many a sunstroke, as on the rush to Gettysburg in '63—the night battles in the woods, as under Hooker at Chancellorsville—the camps in winter—the military prisons—the hospitals—(alas! alas! the hospitals.)

The Secession war? Nay, let me call it the Union war. Though whatever call'd, it is even yet too near us—too vast and too closely overshadowing—its branches unform'd yet, (but certain,) shooting too far into the future—and the most indicative and mightiest of them yet ungrown. A great literature will yet arise out of the era of those four years, those scenes—era compressing centuries of native passion, first-class pictures, tempests of life and death—an inexhaustible mine for the histories, drama, romance, and even philosophy, of peoples to come—indeed the verteber of poetry and art, (of personal character too,) for all future America—far more grand, in my opinion, to the hands capable of it, than Homer's siege of Troy, or the French wars to Shakspere.

112–113. There are no marks of parenthesis in *NYTR*.

114. Sumter] Proof: Sumpter

117. North—and] *NYTR:* North: and

127. Chancellorsville—the] *NYTR* and Proof: Chancellorsville (a strange episode) —the

132. After "ungrown." *NYTR* and Proof begin a new paragraph.

133. will yet arise] Proof: will arise

139. Shakspere] *NYTR:* Shakespeare

141. After "myself to." *NYTR* begins a new paragraph.

143–144. memoranda, written at the time, and] *NYTR* and Proof: memoranda, already published, written at the time on the spot, and

145. The subtitle "*Murder of President Lincoln.*" at the beginning of this line in the proof has been cut away. Here begins the section of the lecture first published in *NYS* for February 12, 1876. The paragraph in *NYS* introducing the essay, not reprinted, is as follows:

"To-day is the anniversary of President Lincoln's birth. If he had lived till now he would have been sixty-six years old. The following vivid description of the scenes

But I must leave these speculations, and come to the theme I have assign'd and limited myself to. Of the actual murder of President Lincoln, though so much has been written, probably the facts are yet very indefinite in most persons' minds. I read from my memoranda, written at the time, and revised frequently and finally since.

The day, April 14, 1865, seems to have been a pleasant one throughout the whole land—the moral atmosphere pleasant too—the long storm, so dark, so fratricidal, full of blood and doubt and gloom, over and ended at last by the sun-rise of such an absolute National victory, and utter break-down of Secessionism—we almost doubted our own senses! Lee had capitulated beneath the apple-tree of Appomattox. The other armies, the flanges of the revolt, swiftly follow'd. And could it really be, then? Out of all the affairs of this world of woe and failure and disorder, was there really come the confirm'd, unerring sign of plan, like a shaft of pure light—of rightful rule—of God? So the day, as I say, was propitious. Early herbage, early flowers, were out. (I remember where I was stopping at the time, the season being advanced, there were many lilacs in full bloom. By one of those caprices that enter and give tinge to events without being at all a part of them, I find myself always reminded of the great tragedy of that day by the sight and odor of these blossoms. It never fails.)

But I must not dwell on accessories. The deed hastens. The popular afternoon paper of Washington, the little "Evening Star," had spatter'd all over its third page, divided among the advertisements in a sensational manner, in a hundred different places, *The President and his Lady will be at the Theatre this evening. . . .* (Lincoln was fond of the theatre. I have myself seen him there several times. I remember thinking how

at Ford's Theatre at the time of the assassination, from a forthcoming book by Walt Whitman, has never before been published:"

149. break-down of Secessionism] *NYTR:* break-down of secession] *TR* and *NYS:* breaking-down of Secessionism

150–155. These five sentences, beginning "Lee had" and ending "was propitious." are omitted in *NYTR*.

151. follow'd. And] *TR:* follow'd. . . . . . . And

151. *NYS* begins a new paragraph after "follow'd."

152–153. woe . . . disorder, was] *TR* and *NYS:* woe and passion, of failure and disorder and dismay, was

154. God? So] *TR:* God? . . . . So

154–160. These lines, a separate paragraph, in *NYS* follow rather than precede the paragraph beginning "But I must".

162. paper of Washington, the] *NYS:* paper, the

162. "Evening Star,"] *NYTR*, *TR*, and *NYS: Evening Star*,

164–165. *NYTR* and *NYS* use roman type in quotation marks in place of italics.

165. *evening. . . .* (Lincoln] *TR: evening. . . . . .* (Lincoln] *NYTR* and *NYS:* evening." (Lincoln

funny it was that he, in some respects the leading actor in the stormiest drama known to real history's stage through centuries, should sit there and be so completely interested and absorb'd in those human jack-straws, moving about with their silly little gestures, foreign spirit, and flatulent text.)

On this occasion the theatre was crowded, many ladies in rich and gay costumes, officers in their uniforms, many well-known citizens, young folks, the usual clusters of gas-lights, the usual magnetism of so many people, cheerful, with perfumes, music of violins and flutes—(and over all, and saturating all, that vast, vague wonder, *Victory*, the nation's victory, the triumph of the Union, filling the air, the thought, the sense, with exhilaration more than all music and perfumes.)

The President came betimes, and, with his wife, witness'd the play from the large stage-boxes of the second tier, two thrown into one, and profusely draped with the national flag. The acts and scenes of the piece—one of those singularly written compositions which have at least the merit of giving entire relief to an audience engaged in mental action or business excitements and cares during the day, as it makes not the slightest call on either the moral, emotional, esthetic, or spiritual nature—a piece, ("Our American Cousin,") in which, among other characters, so call'd, a Yankee, certainly such a one as was never seen, or the least like it ever seen, in North America, is introduced in England, with a varied fol-de-rol of talk, plot, scenery, and such phantasmagoria as goes to make up a modern popular drama—had progress'd through perhaps a couple of its acts, when in the midst of this comedy, or non-such, or whatever it is to be call'd, and to offset it, or finish it out, as if in Nature's and the great Muse's mockery of those poor mimes, came interpolated that scene, not really or exactly to be described at all, (for on the many hundreds who were there it seems to this hour to have left a passing blur, a dream, a blotch)—and yet partially to be described as I now proceed to give it. There is a scene in the play representing a modern parlor, in which two

167. he] *TR:* He

167. the stormiest] *TR* and *NYS:* the greatest and stormiest

178. all music and perfumes.)] *TR* and *NYS:* all perfumes

181–196. These lines, beginning with "The acts" and continuing through the sentence ending "to give it." do not appear in *NYTR.*

182. singularly written compositions] *NYS:* singularly witless compositions

191. comedy, or non-such] *TR* and *NYS:* comedy, or tragedy or non-such

193. of those . . . interpolated] *TR:* of those poor mimes, comes interpolated] *NYS:* of these poor mimes, comes interpolated

195. left a] *TR* and *NYS:* left little but a

196. give it. There is] *NYTR:* National Flag. There is] Proof and *TR:* give it. . . . . . There is] *NYS:* give it. There is] [After "give it." *NYS* begins a new paragraph.]

unprecedented English ladies are inform'd by the impossible Yankee that he is not a man of fortune, and therefore undesirable for marriage-catching purposes; after which, the comments being finish'd, the dramatic trio make exit, leaving the stage clear for a moment. At this period came the murder of Abraham Lincoln. Great as all its manifold train, circling round it, and stretching into the future for many a century, in the politics, history, art, &c., of the New World, in point of fact the main thing, the actual murder, transpired with the quiet and simplicity of any commonest occurrence—the bursting of a bud or pod in the growth of vegetation, for instance. Through the general hum following the stage pause, with the change of positions, came the muffled sound of a pistol-shot, which not one-hundredth part of the audience heard at the time—and yet a moment's hush—somehow, surely, a vague startled thrill—and then, through the ornamented, draperied, starr'd and striped space-way of the President's box, a sudden figure, a man, raises himself with hands and feet, stands a moment on the railing, leaps below to the stage, (a distance of perhaps fourteen or fifteen feet,) falls out of position, catching his boot-heel in the copious drapery, (the American flag,) falls on one knee, quickly recovers himself, rises as if nothing had happen'd, (he really sprains his ankle, but unfelt then)—and so the figure, Booth, the murderer, dress'd in plain black broadcloth, bare-headed, with full, glossy, raven hair, and his eyes like some mad animal's flashing with light and resolution, yet with a certain strange calmness, holds aloft in one hand a large knife—walks along not much back from the footlights—turns fully toward the audience his face of statuesque beauty, lit by those basilisk eyes, flashing with desperation, perhaps insanity—launches out in a firm and steady voice the words *Sic semper tyrannis*—and then walks with neither slow nor very rapid pace diagonally across to the back of the stage, and disappears. (Had not all this terrible scene—making the mimic ones preposterous—had it not all been rehears'd, in blank, by Booth, beforehand?)

A moment's hush—a scream—the cry of *murder*—Mrs. Lincoln lean-

198. by the impossible] *NYTR:* by an impossible] *TR* and *NY:* by the unprecedented and impossible
201. moment. At this] *TR* and *NYS:* moment. There was a pause, a hush as it were. At this
202. Great as all its] *NYTR*, *TR*, and *NYS:* Great as that was, with all its
207. After "for instance." *NYS* begins a new paragraph.
208. positions, came] *NYTR:* positions came] *TR* and *NYS:* positions, &c., came
214–215. in the copious] *NYTR:* in a copious
218. with full, glossy] *NYTR*, *TR*, and *NYS:* with a full head of glossy
220. certain strange calmness] *NYTR:* certain calmness
225–226. disappears. (Had] *NYTR* and *TR:* disappears . . . . (Had
228. hush—a scream] *TR* and *NYS:* hush, incredulous—a scream
228. *murder*] *NYTR* and *TR: Murder*] *NYS:* murder

ing out of the box, with ashy cheeks and lips, with involuntary cry, pointing to the retreating figure, *He has kill'd the President.* And still a moment's strange, incredulous suspense—and then the deluge!—then that mixture of horror, noises, uncertainty—(the sound, somewhere back, of a horse's hoofs clattering with speed)—the people burst through chairs and railings, and break them up—there is inextricable confusion and terror—women faint—quite feeble persons fall, and are trampled on—many cries of agony are heard—the broad stage suddenly fills to suffocation with a dense and motley crowd, like some horrible carnival—the audience rush generally upon it, at least the strong men do—the actors and actresses are all there in their play-costumes and painted faces, with mortal fright showing through the rouge—the screams and calls, confused talk—redoubled, trebled—two or three manage to pass up water from the stage to the President's box—others try to clamber up—&c., &c.

In the midst of all this, the soldiers of the President's guard, with others, suddenly drawn to the scene, burst in—(some two hundred altogether)—they storm the house, through all the tiers, especially the upper ones, inflamed with fury, literally charging the audience with fix'd bayonets, muskets and pistols, shouting *Clear out! clear out! you sons of* ——. . . . . Such the wild scene, or a suggestion of it rather, inside the play-house that night.

Outside, too, in the atmosphere of shock and craze, crowds of people, fill'd with frenzy, ready to seize any outlet for it, come near committing murder several times on innocent individuals. One such case was especially exciting. The infuriated crowd, through some chance, got started against one man, either for words he utter'd, or perhaps without any cause at all, and were proceeding at once to actually hang him on a neighboring lamp-post, when he was rescued by a few heroic policemen, who placed him in their midst, and fought their way slowly and amid

230. *He has kill'd the President.* And] *NYTR* and *TR: He has* kill'd the President. . . . . And] *NYS:* "He has killed the President.["] And

234. them up—there is] *NYTR*, *TR*, and *NYS:* them up—that noise adds to the queerness of the scene—there is

238. it, at] *NYTR*, *TR*, and *NYS:* it—at

240. rouge—the] *NYTR*, *TR*, and *NYS:* rouge, some trembling—some in tears—the

258. station house. It] *TR:* Station House . . . . It

264. made a] *TR* and *NYS:* made indeed a

250–266. These lines do not appear in *NYTR*.

267. in the midst of that pandemonium, infuriated] *NYTR:* in that night-pandemonium of senseless hate, infuriated] *TR* and *NYS:* in the midst of that night-pandemonium of senseless hate, infuriated

271. After "on the lips." *TR* has a series of periods and continues with the following three sentences to complete the paragraph, which *NYS* prints as a separate para-

great peril toward the station house. It was a fitting episode of the whole affair. The crowd rushing and eddying to and fro—the night, the yells, the pale faces, many frighten'd people trying in vain to extricate themselves—the attack'd man, not yet freed from the jaws of death, looking like a corpse—the silent, resolute, half-dozen policemen, with no weapons but their little clubs, yet stern and steady through all those eddying swarms—made a fitting side-scene to the grand tragedy of the murder. They gain'd the station house with the protected man, whom they placed in security for the night, and discharged him in the morning.

And in the midst of that pandemonium, infuriated soldiers, the audience and the crowd, the stage, and all its actors and actresses, its paint-pots, spangles, and gas-lights—the life blood from those veins, the best and sweetest of the land, drips slowly down, and death's ooze already begins its little bubbles on the lips.

Thus the visible incidents and surroundings of Abraham Lincoln's murder, as they really occur'd. Thus ended the attempted secession of these States; thus the four years' war. But the main things come subtly and invisibly afterward, perhaps long afterward—neither military, political, nor (great as those are,) historical. I say, certain secondary and indirect results, out of the tragedy of this death, are, in my opinion, greatest. Not the event of the murder itself. Not that Mr. Lincoln strings the principal points and personages of the period, like beads, upon the single string of his career. Not that his idiosyncrasy, in its sudden appearance and disappearance, stamps this Republic with a stamp more mark'd and enduring than any yet given by any one man—(more even than Washington's;)—but, join'd with these, the immeasurable value and meaning of that whole tragedy lies, to me, in senses finally dearest to a nation, (and here all our own)—the imaginative and artistic senses—the literary and dramatic ones. Not in any common or low meaning of those terms, but a

graph, as follows: "Such, hurriedly sketch'd, were the accompaniments of the death of President Lincoln. So suddenly and in murder and horror unsurpass'd he was taken from us. But his death was painless." This paragraph was cut away in the clipping of *TR*, p. 49, together with the next paragraph, in brackets, which had been previously used in the section dated April 16, 1865, and subtitled "Death of President Lincoln." (See that section in *Prose 1892*, I.)

272–353. These lines in *NYTR* have the subtitle "Results of the Tragedy."

272. of Abraham Lincoln's] *NYTR* and Proof: of President Lincoln's

273–274. secession of these States; thus] *NYTR:* secessions of these States. Thus] Proof: Secession of These States. Thus

277. of the tragedy] *NYTR* and Proof: of the war, and out of the tragedy

282–283. Washington's;)—but] *NYTR:* Washington's). But] Proof: Washington's;)—But

285. and artistic] *NYTR* and Proof: and the artistic

285–286. and dramatic] *NYTR* and Proof: and the dramatic

meaning precious to the race, and to every age. A long and varied series of contradictory events arrives at last at its highest poetic, single, central, pictorial denouement. The whole involved, baffling, multiform whirl of the secession period comes to a head, and is gather'd in one brief flash of lightning-illumination—one simple, fierce deed. Its sharp culmination, and as it were solution, of so many bloody and angry problems, illustrates those climax-moments on the stage of universal Time, where the historic Muse at one entrance, and the tragic Muse at the other, suddenly ringing down the curtain, close an immense act in the long drama of creative thought, and give it radiation, tableau, stranger than fiction. Fit radiation—fit close! How the imagination—how the student loves these things! America, too, is to have them. For not in all great deaths, nor far or near—not Cæsar in the Roman senate-house, or Napoleon passing away in the wild night-storm at St. Helena—not Paleologus, falling, desperately fighting, piled over dozens deep with Grecian corpses—not calm old Socrates, drinking the hemlock—outvies that terminus of the secession war, in one man's life, here in our midst, in our own time—that seal of the emancipation of three million slaves—that parturition and delivery of our at last really free Republic, born again, henceforth to commence its career of genuine homogeneous Union, compact, consistent with itself.

Nor will ever future American Patriots and Unionists, indifferently over the whole land, or North or South, find a better moral to their lesson. The final use of the greatest men of a Nation is, after all, not with reference to their deeds in themselves, or their direct bearing on their times or lands. The final use of a heroic-eminent life—especially of a heroic-eminent death—is its indirect filtering into the nation and the race, and to give, often at many removes, but unerringly, age after age, color and fibre to the personalism of the youth and maturity of that age, and of mankind. Then there is a cement to the whole people, subtler, more underlying, than any thing in written constitution, or courts or armies—namely, the cement of a death identified thoroughly with that people, at its head, and for its sake. Strange, (is it not?) that battles, martyrs, agonies, blood, even assassination, should so condense—perhaps only really, lastingly condense—a Nationality.

300. Paleologus] *NYTR:* Palaeologus] Proof: Paleolagus

304–305. our at . . . henceforth] *NYTR* and Proof: our new-born, at last really free Republic, henceforth

306. compact, consistent] Proof: compact, untied consistent

308. better moral to] *NYTR* and Proof: better seal to

330–336. These lines, beginning with "But Lincoln", do not appear in *NYTR.*

331. autochthonic. (Sometimes] Proof: autochthonic. Sometimes

I repeat it—the grand deaths of the race—the dramatic deaths of every nationality—are its most important inheritance-value—in some respects beyond its literature and art—(as the hero is beyond his finest portrait, and the battle itself beyond its choicest song or epic.) Is not here indeed the point underlying all tragedy? the famous pieces of the Grecian masters —and all masters? Why, if the old Greeks had had this man, what trilogies of plays—what epics—would have been made out of him! How the rhapsodes would have recited him! How quickly that quaint tall form would have enter'd into the region where men vitalize gods, and gods divinify men! But Lincoln, his times, his death—great as any, any age— belong altogether to our own, and are autochthonic. (Sometimes indeed I think our American days, our own stage—the actors we know and have shaken hands, or talk'd with—more fateful than any thing in Eschylus— more heroic than the fighters around Troy—afford kings of men for our Democracy prouder than Agamemnon—models of character cute and hardy as Ulysses—deaths more pitiful than Priam's.)

When, centuries hence, (as it must, in my opinion, be centuries hence before the life of these States, or of Democracy, can be really written and illustrated,) the leading historians and dramatists seek for some personage, some special event, incisive enough to mark with deepest cut, and mnemonize, this turbulent Nineteenth century of ours, (not only these States, but all over the political and social world)—something, perhaps, to close that gorgeous procession of European feudalism, with all its pomp and caste-prejudices, (of whose long train we in America are yet so inextricably the heirs)—something to identify with terrible identification, by far the greatest revolutionary step in the history of the United States, (perhaps the greatest of the world, our century)—the absolute extirpation and erasure of slavery from the States—those historians will seek in vain for any point to serve more thoroughly their purpose, than Abraham Lincoln's death.

Dear to the Muse—thrice dear to Nationality—to the whole human race—precious to this Union—precious to Democracy—unspeakably and forever precious—their first great Martyr Chief.

334–335. Troy—afford . . . prouder] Proof: Troy: afford kings of men, (at least, for our Democracy) prouder

336. than Priam's.)] Proof: than Priam's—afford, too, (as all history for future use is resolv'd into persons,) central figures, illustrators, in whom our whirling periods shall concentrate—the best future Art and Poetry find themes—and around which the whole age shall turn.

340. with deepest] *NYTR:* with the deepest

344–345. The marks of parenthesis do not appear in *NYTR.*

Two Letters.

1. To—— — ——(London, England.)

CAMDEN, N. J., U. S. AMERICA, *March 17, 1876.*

DEAR FRIEND:—Yours of the 28th Feb. receiv'd, and indeed welcom'd. I am jogging along still about the same in physical condition—still certainly no worse, and I sometimes lately suspect rather better, or at any rate more adjusted to the situation. Even begin to think of making some move, some change of base, &c.: the doctors have been advising it for over two years, but I haven't felt to do it yet. My paralysis does not lift—I cannot walk any distance—I still have this baffling, obstinate, apparently chronic affection of the stomachic apparatus and liver: yet I get out of doors a little every day—write and read in moderation—appetite sufficiently good—(eat only very plain food, but always did that)—digestion tolerable—spirits unflagging. I have told you most of this before, but suppose you might like to know it all again, up to date. Of course, and pretty darkly coloring the whole, are bad spells, prostrations, some pretty grave ones, intervals—and I have resign'd myself to the certainty of permanent incapacitation from solid work: but things may continue at least in this half-and-half way for months, even years.

My books are out, the new edition; a set of which, immediately on receiving your letter of 28th, I have sent you, (by mail, March 15,) and I suppose you have before this receiv'd them. My dear friend, your offers of help, and those of my other British friends, I think I fully appreciate, in the right spirit, welcome and acceptive—leaving the matter altogether in your and their hands, and to your and their convenience, discretion, leisure, and nicety. Though poor now, even to penury, I have not so far been deprived of any physical thing I need or wish whatever, and I feel confident I shall not in the future. During my employment of seven years or

Two Letters.

These letters are also included in their proper place in *The Correspondence of Walt Whitman*, edited by Edwin H. Miller.

The first letter, to W. M. Rossetti, dated March 17, 1876, was printed in SDC from a large printed sheet, apparently an offprint, and revised in black ink. The title and date in the MS were written in black ink on a strip of paper pasted to the top of the printed sheet. The title is "*To* —— — —— (*London, England.*)," omitting the name of the addressee. This letter was omitted in DVOP.

The second letter, to Dr. I. Fitzgerald Lee, dated December 20, 1881, was

more in Washington after the war (1865–72) I regularly saved part of my wages: and, though the sum has now become about exhausted by my expenses of the last three years, there are already beginning at present welcome dribbles hitherward from the sales of my new edition, which I just job and sell, myself, (all through this illness, my book-agents for three years in New York successively, badly cheated me,) and shall continue to dispose of the books myself. And *that* is the way I should prefer to glean my support. In that way I cheerfully accept all the aid my friends find it convenient to proffer.

To repeat a little, and without undertaking details, understand, dear friend, for yourself and all, that I heartily and most affectionately thank my British friends, and that I accept their sympathetic generosity in the same spirit in which I believe (nay, know) it is offer'd—that though poor I am not in want—that I maintain good heart and cheer; and that by far the most satisfaction to me (and I think it can be done, and believe it will be) will be to live, as long as possible, on the sales, by myself, of my own works, and perhaps, if practicable, by further writings for the press.

W. W.

I am prohibited from writing too much, and I must make this candid statement of the situation serve for all my dear friends over there.

2. *To — ——— —— (Dresden, Saxony.)*

CAMDEN, *New Jersey, U. S. A., Dec. 20, '81.*

DEAR SIR:—Your letter asking definite endorsement to your translation of my "*Leaves of Grass*" into Russian is just received, and I hasten to answer it. Most warmly and willingly I consent to the translation, and waft a prayerful *God speed* to the enterprise.

You Russians and we Americans! Our countries so distant, so unlike at first glance—such a difference in social and political conditions, and our respective methods of moral and practical development the last hundred years;—and yet in certain features, and vastest ones, so resem-

printed from three pages of autograph MS, written in black ink and substantially revised in the same. The top of the first sheet, which probably contained the name of the addressee, was cut away and a strip pasted on with the title "To — ——— —— (*Dresden, Germany*)" in the same ink. "Germany" was changed to "Saxony," presumably in the proof. On the third sheet the original signature appears to have been "Walt W." or "Whitman." This was erased and "W. W." written over it in heavy ink. Below the initials the MS has the following words written in pencil and crossed out in black ink: "go on with your translation. I send you a book by this mail—advise me from time to time—address me here." This letter was printed in *DVOP*, but after "Notes Left Over," with no change except the omission of Whitman's initials at the end.

bling each other. The variety of stock-elements and tongues, to be resolutely fused in a common identity and union at all hazards—the idea, perennial through the ages, that they both have their historic and divine mission—the fervent element of manly friendship throughout the whole people, surpass'd by no other races—the grand expanse of territorial limits and boundaries—the unform'd and nebulous state of many things, not yet permanently settled, but agreed on all hands to be the preparations of an infinitely greater future—the fact that both People have their independent and leading positions to hold, keep, and if necessary, fight for, against the rest of the world—the deathless aspirations at the inmost centre of each great community, so vehement, so mysterious, so abysmic—are certainly features you Russians and we Americans possess in common.

As my dearest dream is for an internationality of poems and poets, binding the lands of the earth closer than all treaties and diplomacy—As the purpose beneath the rest in my book is such hearty comradeship, for individuals to begin with, and for all the nations of the earth as a result—how happy I should be to get the hearing and emotional contact of the great Russian peoples.

To whom, now and here, (addressing you for Russia and Russians, and empowering you, should you see fit, to print the present letter, in your book, as a preface,) I waft affectionate salutation from these shores, in America's name. W. W.

Notes Left Over.

NATIONALITY—(AND YET.)

It is more and more clear to me that the main sustenance for highest separate personality, these States, is to come from that general sustenance of the aggregate, (as air, earth, rains, give sustenance to a tree)—and that such personality, by democratic standards, will only be fully coherent, grand and free, through the cohesion, grandeur and freedom of the common aggregate, the Union. Thus the existence of the

Notes Left Over.

These miscellaneous notes were first collected and given their group title in SDC 1882. They were reprinted from the same plates in SDC Glasgow 1883, CPP 1888, and CPW 1892. They were also reprinted, but not from the same plates, in DVOP 1888. In the present edition they are reprinted under the same group title and subtitles as in SDC 1882 and later editions.

NATIONALITY—(AND YET.)

Printed in SDC from three clippings of the lower parts of pages 23, 24, and 25

true American continental solidarity of the future, depending on myriads of superb, large-sized, emotional and physically perfect individualities, of one sex just as much as the other, the supply of such individualities, in my opinion, wholly depends on a compacted imperial ensemble. The theory and practice of both sovereignties, contradictory as they are, are necessary. As the contripetal law were fatal alone, or the centrifugal law deadly and destructive alone, but together forming the law of eternal kosmical action, evolution, preservation, and life—so, by itself alone, the fullness of individuality, even the sanest, would surely destroy itself. This is what makes the importance to the identities of these States of the thoroughly fused, relentless, dominating Union—a moral and spiritual idea, subjecting all the parts with remorseless power, more needed by American democracy than by any of history's hitherto empires or feudalities, and the *sine qua non* of carrying out the republican principle to develop itself in the New World through hundreds, thousands of years to come.

Indeed, what most needs fostering through the hundred years to come, in all parts of the United States, north, south, Mississippi valley, and Atlantic and Pacific coasts, is this fused and fervent identity of the individual, whoever he or she may be, and wherever the place, with the idea and fact of AMERICAN TOTALITY, and with what is meant by the Flag, the stars and stripes. We need this conviction of nationality as a faith, to be absorb'd in the blood and belief of the people everywhere, south, north, west, east, to emanate in their life, and in native literature and art. We want the germinal idea that America, inheritor of the past, is the custodian of the future of humanity. Judging from history, it is some such moral and spiritual ideas appropriate to them, (and such ideas only,) that have made the profoundest glory and endurance of nations in the past. The races of Judea, the classic clusters of Greece and Rome, and the feudal and ecclesiastical clusters of the Middle Ages, were each and all vitalized by their separate distinctive ideas, ingrain'd in them, redeeming many sins, and indeed, in a sense, the principal reason-why for their whole career.

Then, in the thought of nationality especially for the United States,

of *TR*. All texts are here collated. In *TR* the title is at the beginning of the first line.

6. Union. Thus] *TR:* Union . . . . Thus

7. American continental] *TR:* American, Continental

18. idea, subjecting] *TR:* Idea—subjecting

20–21. develop] *TR:* develope

23. needs fostering] *TR:* needs development through

28. stripes. We] *TR:* Stripes . . . . We

32. humanity. Judging] *TR:* Humanity . . . . . . Judging

and making them original, and different from all other countries, another point ever remains to be consider'd. There are two distinct principles —aye, paradoxes—at the life-fountain and life-continuation of the States; one, the sacred principle of the Union, the right of ensemble, at whatever sacrifice—and yet another, an equally sacred principle, the right of each State, consider'd as a separate sovereign individual, in its own sphere. Some go zealously for one set of these rights, and some as zealously for the other set. We must have both; or rather, bred out of them, as out of mother and father, a third set, the perennial result and combination of both, and neither jeopardized. I say the loss or abdication of one set, in the future, will be ruin to democracy just as much as the loss of the other set. The problem is, to harmoniously adjust the two, and the play of the two. [Observe the lesson of the divinity of Nature, ever checking the excess of one law, by an opposite, or seemingly opposite law—generally the other side of the same law.] For the theory of this Republic is, not that the General government is the fountain of all life and power, dispensing it forth, around, and to the remotest portions of our territory, but that THE PEOPLE are, represented in both, underlying both the General and State governments, and consider'd just as well in their individualities and in their separate aggregates, or States, as consider'd in one vast aggregate, the Union. This was the original dual theory and foundation of the United States, as distinguish'd from the feudal and ecclesiastical single idea of monarchies and papacies, and the divine rights of kings. (Kings have been of use, hitherto, as representing the idea of the identity of nations. But, to American democracy, *both* ideas must be fulfill'd, and in my opinion the loss of vitality of either one will indeed be the loss of vitality of the other.)

EMERSON'S BOOKS, (THE SHADOWS OF THEM.)

In the regions we call Nature, towering beyond all measurement,

42. consider'd. There] *CPW*, *CPP*, and *SDC:* considered. There] MS of *SDC:* consider'd. There] *TR:* consider'd. . . . . . . There [the reading of the MS and *TR* is restored. The printing of *SDC*, *CPP*, and *CPW* is probably a typographical error.—ED.]
53. two. [Observe] *TR:* two. . . . . . . [Observe
53. divinity of Nature] *TR:* divinity in Nature
55. law.] For] *TR:* law.] . . . . . . For
60–61. aggregate, the Union.] *TR:* Aggregate, as the Union.
63–64. kings. (Kings] *TR:* kings. . . . . . . (Kings

EMERSON'S BOOKS, (THE SHADOWS OF THEM.)

Printed in *SDC* from clippings of an article by the same title in *BLW* for May 22, 1880 (Vol. 11, pp. 177–178). This number of *BLW* was devoted to the celebration of Emerson's birthday, and contained articles also by G. W. Cooke, G. W. Curtis, F. H. Hedge, and others. Portions of Whitman's article were re-

with infinite spread, infinite depth and height—in those regions, including Man, socially and historically, with his moral-emotional influences—how small a part, (it came in my mind to-day,) has literature really depicted—even summing up all of it, all ages. Seems at its best some little fleet of boats, hugging the shores of a boundless sea, and never venturing, exploring the unmapp'd—never, Columbus-like, sailing out for New Worlds, and to complete the orb's rondure. Emerson writes frequently in the atmosphere of this thought, and his books report one or two things from that very ocean and air, and more legibly address'd to our age and American polity than by any man yet. But I will begin by scarifying him—thus proving that I am not insensible to his deepest lessons. I will consider his books from a democratic and western point of view. I will specify the shadows on these sunny expanses. Somebody has said of heroic character that "wherever the tallest peaks are present, must inevitably be deep chasms and valleys." Mine be the ungracious task (for reasons) of leaving unmention'd both sunny expanses and sky-reaching heights, to dwell on the bare spots and darknesses. I have a theory that no artist or work of the very first class may be or can be without them.

First, then, these pages are perhaps too perfect, too concentrated. (How good, for instance, is good butter, good sugar. But to be eating nothing but sugar and butter all the time! even if ever so good.) And though the author has much to say of freedom and wildness and simplicity and spontaneity, no performance was ever more based on artificial scholarships and decorums at third or fourth removes, (he calls it culture,) and built up from them. It is always a *make*, never an unconscious *growth*. It is the porcelain figure or statuette of lion, or stag, or Indian hunter—and a very choice statuette too—appropriate for the rosewood or marble bracket of parlor or library; never the animal itself, or the hunter himself. Indeed, who wants the real animal or hunter? What would that do amid astral and bric-a-brac and tapestry, and ladies and gentlemen

printed in NYTR, May 15, 1882, as "A Democratic Criticism. By Walt Whitman," which was the first of two short pieces under the general title "Emerson's Books and Home." [The second piece, "The Home of the Sage of Concord," was reprinted from the Boston *Herald;* the author's name is not mentioned, but presumably it was not by Whitman.] The texts collated here are those of BLW, NYTR, SDC, and later texts.

1–12. Omitted in NYTR through the sentence ending "deepest lessons."

2. those regions] *BLW:* those vast regions

12–30. The passage beginning "I will" and ending "the hunter himself." is the first portion reprinted in NYTR.

16–17. task (for reasons) of] *NYTR:* task for reasons of

20. perfect, too] BLW and *NYTR:* perfect—too

26. *make*] *NYTR:* make

27. *growth*] *NYTR:* growth

30–58. These lines, beginning "Indeed" and ending "of all." are omitted in NYTR.

talking in subdued tones of Browning and Longfellow and art? The least suspicion of such actual bull, or Indian, or of Nature carrying out itself, would put all those good people to instant terror and flight.

Emerson, in my opinion, is not most eminent as poet or artist or teacher, though valuable in all those. He is best as critic, or diagnoser. Not passion or imagination or warp or weakness, or any pronounced cause or specialty, dominates him. Cold and bloodless intellectuality dominates him. (I know the fires, emotions, love, egotisms, glow deep, perennial, as in all New Englanders—but the façade hides them well—they give no sign.) He does not see or take one side, one presentation only or mainly, (as all the poets, or most of the fine writers anyhow)—he sees all sides. His final influence is to make his students cease to worship anything—almost cease to believe in anything, outside of themselves. These books will fill, and well fill, certain stretches of life, certain stages of development—are, (like the tenets or theology the author of them preach'd when a young man,) unspeakably serviceable and precious as a stage. But in old or nervous or solemnest or dying hours, when one needs the impalpably soothing and vitalizing influences of abysmic Nature, or its affinities in literature or human society, and the soul resents the keenest mere intellection, they will not be sought for.

For a philosopher, Emerson possesses a singularly dandified theory of manners. He seems to have no notion at all that manners are simply the signs by which the chemist or metallurgist knows his metals. To the profound scientist, all metals are profound, as they really are. The little one, like the conventional world, will make much of gold and silver only. Then to the real artist in humanity, what are called bad manners are often the most picturesque and significant of all. Suppose these books becoming absorb'd, the permanent chyle of American general and particular character—what a well-wash'd and grammatical, but bloodless and helpless, race we should turn out! No, no, dear friend; though the States want scholars, undoubtedly, and perhaps want ladies and gentlemen who use the bath frequently, and never laugh loud, or talk wrong, they don't want scholars, or ladies and gentlemen, at the expense of all the rest. They want good farmers, sailors, mechanics, clerks, citizens—perfect business and social relations—perfect fathers and mothers. If we could

58. After "significant of all." *BLW* begins a new paragraph.

58–61. The sentence beginning "Suppose" is inserted in *NYTR* at this point, but not to begin a paragraph as it does in *BLW*.

61–104. This passage, beginning with "No, no," and continuing to the end of the section in *SDC*, is omitted in *NYTR*.

71. provided on] *BLW:* provided for, and on

only have these, or their approximations, plenty of them, fine and large and sane and generous and patriotic, they might make their verbs disagree from their nominatives, and laugh like volleys of musketeers, if they should please. Of course these are not all America wants, but they are first of all to be provided on a large scale. And, with tremendous errors and escapades, this, substantially, is what the States seem to have an intuition of, and to be mainly aiming at. The plan of a select class, superfined, (demarcated from the rest,) the plan of Old World lands and literatures, is not so objectionable in itself, but because it chokes the true plan for us, and indeed is death to it. As to such special class, the United States can never produce any equal to the splendid show, (far, far beyond comparison or competition here,) of the principal European nations, both in the past and at the present day. But an immense and distinctive commonalty over our vast and varied area, west and east, south and north—in fact, for the first time in history, a great, aggregated, real PEOPLE, worthy the name, and made of develop'd heroic individuals, both sexes—is America's principal, perhaps only, reason for being. If ever accomplish'd, it will be at least as much, (I lately think, doubly as much,) the result of fitting and democratic sociologies, literatures and arts—if we ever get them—as of our democratic politics.

At times it has been doubtful to me if Emerson really knows or feels what Poetry is at its highest, as in the Bible, for instance, or Homer or Shakspere. I see he covertly or plainly likes best superb verbal polish, or something old or odd—Waller's "Go, lovely rose," or Lovelace's lines "to Lucasta"—the quaint conceits of the old French bards, and the like. Of *power* he seems to have a gentleman's admiration—but in his inmost heart the grandest attribute of God and Poets is always subordinate to the octaves, conceits, polite kinks, and verbs.

The reminiscence that years ago I began like most youngsters to have a touch (though it came late, and was only on the surface) of Emerson-on-the-brain—that I read his writings reverently, and address'd him in print as "Master," and for a month or so thought of him as such—I retain not only with composure, but positive satisfaction. I have noticed that most young people of eager minds pass through this stage of exercise.

The best part of Emersonianism is, it breeds the giant that destroys

73–74. superfined, . . . the plan] *BLW:* super-refined, the plan

79. But an immense] *BLW:* But the production of an immense

90–91. lines "to Lucasta"—the] *BLW:* lines "To Lucusta"—the] *SDC* and all later texts: lines "to Lucusta"—the] [Since this is either a printer's error or an error in Whitman's spelling, the correct spelling of "Lucasta" is here restored.—ED.]

93. attribute] *SDC:* attributes

itself. Who wants to be any man's mere follower? lurks behind every page. No teacher ever taught, that has so provided for his pupil's setting up independently—no truer evolutionist.

VENTURES, ON AN OLD THEME.

A DIALOGUE—*One party says*—We arrange our lives—even the best and boldest men and women that exist, just as much as the most limited—with reference to what society conventionally rules and makes right. We retire to our rooms for freedom; to undress, bathe, unloose everything in freedom. These, and much else, would not be proper in society.

Other party answers—Such is the rule of society. Not always so, and considerable exceptions still exist. However, it must be called the general rule, sanction'd by immemorial usage, and will probably always remain so.

First party—Why not, then, respect it in your poems?

Answer—One reason, and to me a profound one, is that the soul of a man or woman demands, enjoys compensation in the highest directions for this very restraint of himself or herself, level'd to the average, or rather mean, low, however eternally practical, requirements of society's intercourse. To balance this indispensable abnegation, the free minds of poets relieve themselves, and strengthen and enrich mankind with free flights in all the directions not tolerated by ordinary society.

First party—But must not outrage or give offence to it.

Answer—No, not in the deepest sense—and do not, and cannot. The vast averages of time and the race *en masse* settle these things. Only

104. The last two sentences completing this paragraph in *BLW* and two additional paragraphs completing the article in *BLW* are omitted in *SDC* and all subsequent texts. *NYTR* has the two sentences omitted from the last paragraph of *SDC* and the final paragraph of the article in *BLW*, but omits all the paragraph next preceding the last of *BLW*. For the portions of *BLW* omitted from *SDC*, with variants in *NYTR* inserted in brackets, see Appendix IX, *1*.

VENTURES, ON AN OLD THEME.

Printed in *SDC* from five clippings and two pages of autograph MS in ink. The first portion, under the subhead "A Dialogue," is from a clipping of Whitman's article "A Christmas Garland," published in the Christmas Number, 1874, of *NYDG*. Whitman's new subtitle in *SDC*, "Ventures, on an Old Theme," was written in black ink on a strip of white paper pasted above the clipping. Of the second portion, under the subhead "New Poetry," part is from three clippings of *TR*, pp. 28–30, part from a clipping of "A Christmas Garland," and part from the autograph MS. The Christmas Number, 1874, of *NYDG* is now apparently lost, but Emory Holloway reprinted Number, 1874, of *NYDG* is now apparently lost, but Emory Holloway reprinted in in *UPP* (II, 53–58) the portions of the prose in "A Christmas Garland" that Whitman himself did not reprint. (See Appendix VI and VI, *4*.) Inadvertently, Holloway reprinted in *UPP* two paragraphs that appear in *SDC*. One of these was reprinted as

understand that the conventional standards and laws proper enough for ordinary society apply neither to the action of the soul, nor its poets. In fact the latter know no laws but the laws of themselves, planted in them by God, and are themselves the last standards of the law, and its final exponents—responsible to Him directly, and not at all to mere etiquette. Often the best service that can be done to the race, is to lift the veil, at least for a time, from these rules and fossil-etiquettes.

NEW POETRY—*California, Canada, Texas*—In my opinion the time has arrived to essentially break down the barriers of form between prose and poetry. I say the latter is henceforth to win and maintain its character regardless of rhyme, and the measurement-rules of iambic, spondee, dactyl, &c., and that even if rhyme and those measurements continue to furnish the medium for inferior writers and themes, (especially for persiflage and the comic, as there seems henceforward, to the perfect taste, something inevitably comic in rhyme, merely in itself, and anyhow,) the truest and greatest *Poetry*, (while subtly and necessarily always rhythmic, and distinguishable easily enough,) can never again, in the English language, be express'd in arbitrary and rhyming metre, any more than the greatest eloquence, or the truest power and passion. While admitting that the venerable and heavenly forms of chiming versification have in their time play'd great and fitting parts—that the pensive complaint, the ballads, wars, amours, legends of Europe, &c., have, many of them, been inimitably render'd in rhyming verse—that there have been very illustrious poets whose shapes the mantle of such verse has beautifully and appropriately envelopt —and though the mantle has fallen, with perhaps added beauty, on some

lines 63–72 of this section; the other was reprinted as lines 35–44 of "Final Confessions—Literary Tests" (*q.v.* in *Prose 1892*, I).

1–27. These lines, under the subhead "A Dialogue," first appearing in the Christmas 1874 *NYDG*, were not reprinted until *SDC* 1882.

3. society conventionally rules] *NYDG:* society rules

10. Why not] *DVOP:* Why, not

13. level'd] *NYDG:* levelled

21. the conventional standards] *NYDG:* the standards

24. God, and] *NYDG:* God; and

25. *NYDG* ends the sentence and the paragraph with the word "exponents."

25–27. On the clipping, Whitman changed the period to a dash after "exponents" and added these three lines in ink.

28–62. Printed from clippings of the lower parts of *TR*, pp. 28–30. These lines were printed, with minor variations, in an anonymous prepublication review of *TR* entitled "Walt Whitman's Poems," probably written by Whitman, in *NYTR*, February 19, 1876. (See "Walt Whitman to Whitelaw Reid," by Edwin H. Miller, *SB*, VIII, 1956, 242–249. See also notes on "Preface, 1876.")

28. In place of this line, *TR* has a number of lines crossed out on the clipping. See Appendix VIII, 8.

36. *Poetry*] *TR:* POETRY

39. passion. While] *TR:* passion. . . . . . . In my opinion, I say, while

of our own age—it is, notwithstanding, certain to me, that the day of such conventional rhyme is ended. In America, at any rate, and as a medium of highest æsthetic practical or spiritual expression, present or future, it palpably fails, and must fail, to serve. The Muse of the Prairies, of California, Canada, Texas, and of the peaks of Colorado, dismissing the literary, as well as social etiquette of over-sea feudalism and caste, joyfully enlarging, adapting itself to comprehend the size of the whole people, with the free play, emotions, pride, passions, experiences, that belong to them, body and soul—to the general globe, and all its relations in astronomy, as the savans portray them to us—to the modern, the busy Nineteenth century, (as grandly poetic as any, only different,) with steamships, railroads, factories, electric telegraphs, cylinder presses—to the thought of the solidarity of nations, the brotherhood and sisterhood of the entire earth—to the dignity and heroism of the practical labor of farms, factories, foundries, workshops, mines, or on shipboard, or on lakes and rivers—resumes that other medium of expression, more flexible, more eligible—soars to the freer, vast, diviner heaven of prose.

Of poems of the third or fourth class, (perhaps even some of the second,) it makes little or no difference who writes them—they are good enough for what they are; nor is it necessary that they should be actual emanations from the personality and life of the writers. The very reverse sometimes gives piquancy. But poems of the first class, (poems of the depth, as distinguished from those of the surface,) are to be sternly tallied with the poets themselves, and tried by them and their lives. Who wants a glorification of courage and manly defiance from a coward or a sneak?—a ballad of benevolence or chastity from some rhyming hunks, or lascivious, glib *roué?*

In these States, beyond all precedent, poetry will have to do with actual facts, with the concrete States, and—for we have not much more than begun—with the definitive getting into shape of the Union. Indeed I sometimes think *it* alone is to define the Union, (namely, to give it artistic character, spirituality, dignity.) What American humanity is most

49–50. Prairies, . . . the peaks] *TR:* Prairies, and of the Peaks

58. earth—to] *TR:* Earth—To

63–72. Printed in *SDC* from a clipping of *NYDG*, Christmas Number, as explained above.

63–64. Of poems . . . the second,)] *NYDG:* OF POEMS of the third or fourth class (perhaps even some of the second),

67. class, (poems] *NYDG:* class (poems

68. surface,) are] *NYDG:* surface) are

73–89. Printed for the first time in *SDC* from two holograph MS pages, the first of which consists of four pieces of white paper, in black ink, posted on a gray base sheet; the second (the last three lines) in pencil on two narrow strips of white paper pasted on a gray sheet.

in danger of is an overwhelming prosperity, "business" worldliness, materialism: what is most lacking, east, west, north, south, is a fervid and glowing Nationality and patriotism, cohering all the parts into one. Who may fend that danger, and fill that lack in the future, but a class of loftiest poets?

If the United States haven't grown poets, on any scale of grandeur, it is certain they import, print, and read more poetry than any equal number of people elsewhere—probably more than all the rest of the world combined.

Poetry (like a grand personality) is a growth of many generations—many rare combinations.

To have great poets, there must be great audiences, too.

BRITISH LITERATURE.

To avoid mistake, I would say that I not only commend the study of this literature, but wish our sources of supply and comparison vastly enlarged. American students may well derive from all former lands—from forenoon Greece and Rome, down to the perturb'd medieval times, the Crusades, and so to Italy, the German intellect—all the older literatures, and all the newer ones—from witty and warlike France, and markedly, and in many ways, and at many different periods, from the enterprise and soul of the great Spanish race—bearing ourselves always courteous, always deferential, indebted beyond measure to the mother-world, to all its nations dead, as all its nations living—the offspring, this America of ours, the daughter, not by any means of the British isles exclusively, but of the continent, and all continents. Indeed, it is time we should realize and fully fructify those germs we also hold from Italy, France, Spain, especially in the best imaginative productions of those lands, which are, in many ways, loftier and subtler than the English, or British, and indispensable to complete our service, proportions, education, reminiscences, &c. . . . The British element these States hold, and have always held, enormously beyond its fit proportions. I have already spoken

BRITISH LITERATURE.

Printed in *SDC* from three clippings from the "General Notes" to *DV*, pp. 80–82. Whitman probably used clippings or remaining unbound sheets from *DV* 1871, or else some sheets left over from the first printing of *TR* (the 100 copies having the label "Centennial Edition"). In *DV* 1871 and in all the copies of the Centennial Edition examined, there is no apostrophe after the final "s" in "Cervantes" (line 34). In all other copies of *TR* examined, the apostrophe is printed. The clipped page used by Whitman in his printer's copy for *SDC* does not have the apostrophe. The second clipping is a complete page and is longer than the pages of the bound volume of *TR*, which had been cut.

17. &c. . . . The] *TR* and *DV:* &c. . . . .The

of Shakspere. He seems to me of astral genius, first class, entirely fit for feudalism. His contributions, especially to the literature of the passions, are immense, forever dear to humanity—and his name is always to be reverenced in America. But there is much in him ever offensive to democracy. He is not only the tally of feudalism, but I should say Shakspere is incarnated, uncompromising feudalism, in literature. Then one seems to detect something in him—I hardly know how to describe it—even amid the dazzle of his genius; and, in inferior manifestations, it is found in nearly all leading British authors. (Perhaps we will have to import the words Snob, Snobbish, &c., after all.) While of the great poems of Asian antiquity, the Indian epics, the book of Job, the Ionian Iliad, the unsurpassedly simple, loving, perfect idyls of the life and death of Christ, in the New Testament, (indeed Homer and the Biblical utterances intertwine familiarly with us, in the main,) and along down, of most of the characteristic, imaginative or romantic relics of the continent, as the Cid, Cervantes' Don Quixote, &c., I should say they substantially adjust themselves to us, and, far off as they are, accord curiously with our bed and board to-day, in New York, Washington, Canada, Ohio, Texas, California—and with our notions, both of seriousness and of fun, and our standards of heroism, manliness, and even the democratic requirements—those requirements are not only not fulfilled in the Shaksperean productions, but are insulted on every page.

I add that—while England is among the greatest of lands in political freedom, or the idea of it, and in stalwart personal character, &c.—the spirit of English literature is not great, at least is not greatest—and its products are no models for us. With the exception of Shakspere, there is no first-class genius in that literature—which, with a truly vast amount of value, and of artificial beauty, (largely from the classics,) is almost always material, sensual, not spiritual—almost always congests, makes plethoric, not frees, expands, dilates—is cold, anti-democratic, loves to be sluggish and stately, and shows much of that characteristic of vulgar per-

19, 23, and 44. Shakspere] *TR* and *DV:* Shakespeare
34. Cervantes'] *TR* and *DV:* Cervantes
36. to-day, in New York, Washington] *TR* and *DV:* to-day, in 1870, in Brooklyn, Washington
39. Shaksperean] *DVOP:* Shaksperian] *TR* and *DV:* Shakesperean
45. genius in that] *TR* and *DV:* genius, or approaching to first-class, in that
52. pervades it; it is] *TR* and *DV:* pervades it;—it is
58. *TR* and *DV* continue the paragraph after "wo." with several lines deleted in *SDC*. See Appendix IV, 7.

sons, the dread of saying or doing something not at all improper in itself, but unconventional, and that may be laugh'd at. In its best, the sombre pervades it; it is moody, melancholy, and, to give it its due, expresses, in characters and plots, those qualities, in an unrival'd manner. Yet not as the black thunderstorms, and in great normal, crashing passions, of the Greek dramatists—clearing the air, refreshing afterward, bracing with power; but as in Hamlet, moping, sick, uncertain, and leaving ever after a secret taste for the blues, the morbid fascination, the luxury of wo. . . .

I strongly recommend all the young men and young women of the United States to whom it may be eligible, to overhaul the well-freighted fleets, the literatures of Italy, Spain, France, Germany, so full of those elements of freedom, self-possession, gay-heartedness, subtlety, dilation, needed in preparations for the future of the States. I only wish we could have really good translations. I rejoice at the feeling for Oriental researches and poetry, and hope it will go on.

DARWINISM—(THEN FURTHERMORE.)

Running through prehistoric ages—coming down from them into the daybreak of our records, founding theology, suffusing literature, and so brought onward—(a sort of verteber and marrow to all the antique races and lands, Egypt, India, Greece, Rome, the Chinese, the Jews, &c., and giving cast and complexion to their art, poems, and their politics as well as ecclesiasticism, all of which we more or less inherit,) appear those venerable claims to origin from God himself, or from gods and goddesses —ancestry from divine beings of vaster beauty, size, and power than ours. But in current and latest times, the theory of human origin that seems to have most made its mark, (curiously reversing the antique,) is that we have come on, originated, developt, from monkeys, baboons—a theory more significant perhaps in its indirections, or what it necessitates, than it is even in itself. (Of the twain, far apart as they seem, and angrily

DARWINISM—(THEN FURTHERMORE.)

Printed in *SDC* from pages 26–27 of *TR*, where it was published for the first time. The pages of this MS have a deeper margin at the foot than the pages of the bound volume, suggesting either untrimmed pages or page proofs.

1. In *TR* the title appears at the beginning of the first line, as follows: ORIGINS —*Darwinism*—(*Then Furthermore.*)—
1. prehistoric] *TR:* pre-historic
2. daybreak] *TR:* day-break
9. ours. But] *TR:* ours. . . . . But
11–12. baboons—a theory] *TR:* baboons. . . . . . a theory
13. After "in itself." *TR* begins a new paragraph.
13. (Of the twain] *TR:* (Of the foregoing speculations twain

as their conflicting advocates to-day oppose each other, are not both theories to be possibly reconciled, and even blended? Can we, indeed, spare either of them? Better still, out of them is not a third theory, the real one, or suggesting the real one, to arise?)

Of this old theory, evolution, as broach'd anew, trebled, with indeed all-devouring claims, by Darwin, it has so much in it, and is so needed as a counterpoise to yet widely prevailing and unspeakably tenacious, enfeebling superstitions—is fused, by the new man, into such grand, modest, truly scientific accompaniments—that the world of erudition, both moral and physical, cannot but be eventually better'd and broaden'd in its speculations, from the advent of Darwinism. Nevertheless, the problem of origins, human and other, is not the least whit nearer its solution. In due time the Evolution theory will have to abate its vehemence, cannot be allow'd to dominate every thing else, and will have to take its place as a segment of the circle, the cluster—as but one of many theories, many thoughts, of profoundest value—and re-adjusting and differentiating much, yet leaving the divine secrets just as inexplicable and unreachable as before—may-be more so.

Then furthermore—What is finally to be done by priest or poet—and by priest or poet only—amid all the stupendous and dazzling novelties of our century, with the advent of America, and of science and democracy—remains just as indispensable, after all the work of the grand astronomers, chemists, linguists, historians, and explorers of the last hundred years—and the wondrous German and other metaphysicians of that time—and will continue to remain, needed, America and here, just the same as in the world of Europe, or Asia, of a hundred, or a thousand, or several thousand years ago. I think indeed *more* needed, to furnish statements from the present points, the added arriere, and the unspeakably immenser vistas of to-day. Only the priests and poets of the modern, at least as exalted as any in the past, fully absorbing and appreciating the results of the past, in the commonalty of all humanity, all time, (the main

24. speculations, from] *TR:* speculations—from
42. to-day. Only] *TR:* to-day. . . . . . .Only
48. After "forms" *TR* has a series of seven periods and continues in the same paragraph.
51. its] [Printed "its" in *TR*, but changed to "it's," obviously through a typographical error that Whitman overlooked, in *SDC* and so reprinted in *SDC* Glasgow, *CPP*, *DVOP*, and *CPW* 1892; here corrected.—ED.]

"SOCIETY."

Printed in *SDC* from pages 79–80 of *DV*, the first subdivision of "General Notes." As in the case of "British Literature" above, Whitman used either some unbound sheets or clippings from *DV* 1871 or unbound sheets from the batch used

results already, for there is perhaps nothing more, or at any rate not much, strictly new, only more important modern combinations, and new relative adjustments,) must indeed recast the old metal, the already achiev'd material, into and through new moulds, current forms.

Meantime, the highest and subtlest and broadest truths of modern science wait for their true assignment and last vivid flashes of light—as Democracy waits for its—through first-class metaphysicians and speculative philosophs—laying the basements and foundations for those new, more expanded, more harmonious, more melodious, freer American poems.

"SOCIETY."

I have myself little or no hope from what is technically called "Society" in our American cities. New York, of which place I have spoken so sharply, still promises something, in time, out of its tremendous and varied materials, with a certain superiority of intuitions, and the advantage of constant agitation, and ever new and rapid dealings of the cards. Of Boston, with its circles of social mummies, swathed in cerements harder than brass—its bloodless religion, (Unitarianism,) its complacent vanity of scientism and literature, lots of grammatical correctness, mere knowledge, (always wearisome, in itself)—its zealous abstractions, ghosts of reforms—I should say, (ever admitting its business powers, its sharp, almost demoniac, intellect, and no lack, in its own way, of courage and generosity)—there is, at present, little of cheering, satisfying sign. In the West, California, &c., "society" is yet unform'd, puerile, seemingly unconscious of anything above a driving business, or to liberally spend the money made by it, in the usual rounds and shows.

Then there is, to the humorous observer of American attempts at fashion, according to the models of foreign courts and saloons, quite a comic side—particularly visible at Washington city—a sort of high-life-below-stairs business. As if any farce could be funnier, for instance, than

for the 100 copies of the "Centennial Edition" of *TR* which were still uncorrected and just slightly different in text from the regular edition of *TR*. It is certain that the sheets were not cut from a bound volume of *TR* because the first of the two pages of "Society" used in the printer's copy is a full page and is longer than the pages of the bound volume of *TR*, which had been cut. Evidence that these pages were from the lot printed originally for *DV* 1871 is seen in the fact that the word "puerile" (line 13) is correctly spelled in the regular 1876 edition of *TR* but is spelled "peurile" in *DV* 1871 and in the Centennial Edition of *TR*.

1. The subtitle "Society." was at the beginning of the first line in *TR* and *DV*.

13. puerile. [So printed in the regular edition of *TR* and in all subsequent printings, but misprinted "peurile" in *DV* 1871 and in all copies examined of the Centennial Edition of *TR*.]

18–19. high-life-below-stairs] *TR* and *DV:* high life below stairs

the scenes of the crowds, winter nights, meandering around our Presidents and their wives, cabinet officers, western or other Senators, Representatives, &c.; born of good laboring mechanic or farmer stock and antecedents, attempting those full-dress receptions, finesse of parlors, foreign ceremonies, etiquettes, &c.

Indeed, consider'd with any sense of propriety, or any sense at all, the whole of this illy-play'd fashionable play and display, with their absorption of the best part of our wealthier citizens' time, money, energies, &c., is ridiculously out of place in the United States. As if our proper man and woman, (far, far greater words than "gentleman" and "lady,") could still fail to see, and presently achieve, not this spectral business, but something truly noble, active, sane, American—by modes, perfections of character, manners, costumes, social relations, &c., adjusted to standards, far, far different from those.

Eminent and liberal foreigners, British or continental, must at times have their faith fearfully tried by what they see of our New World personalities. The shallowest and least American persons seem surest to push abroad, and call without fail on well-known foreigners, who are doubtless affected with indescribable qualms by these queer ones. Then, more than half of our authors and writers evidently think it a great thing to be "aristocratic," and sneer at progress, democracy, revolution, &c. If some international literary snobs' gallery were establish'd, it is certain that America could contribute at least her full share of the portraits, and some very distinguish'd ones. Observe that the most impudent slanders, low insults, &c., on the great revolutionary authors, leaders, poets, &c., of Europe, have their origin and main circulation in certain circles here. The treatment of Victor Hugo living, and Byron dead, are samples. Both deserving so well of America, and both persistently attempted to be soil'd here by unclean birds, male and female.

Meanwhile I must still offset the like of the foregoing, and all it infers, by the recognition of the fact, that while the surfaces of current society here show so much that is dismal, noisome, and vapory, there are, beyond question, inexhaustible supplies, as of true gold ore, in the mines of America's general humanity. Let us, not ignoring the dross, give fit stress to these precious immortal values also. Let it be distinctly admitted, that

33. those.] *TR* and *DV:* those!
34. Eminent] *TR* and *DV:* —Eminent
49. Meanwhile I] *TR* and *DV:*—Meanwhile, I
58. *the People*] *TR* and *DV:* THE PEOPLE
61. aesthetic] *TR* and *DV:* esthetic
66. tending—and] *TR* and *DV:* tending—And

—whatever may be said of our fashionable society, and of any foul fractions and episodes—only here in America, out of the long history and manifold presentations of the ages, has at last arisen, and now stands, what never before took positive form and sway, *the People*—and that view'd en masse, and while fully acknowledging deficiencies, dangers, faults, this people, inchoate, latent, not yet come to majority, nor to its own religious, literary, or æsthetic expression, yet affords, to-day, an exultant justification of all the faith, all the hopes and prayers and prophecies of good men through the past—the stablest, solidest-based government of the world—the most assured in a future—the beaming Pharos to whose perennial light all earnest eyes, the world over, are tending—and that already, in and from it, the democratic principle, having been mortally tried by severest tests, fatalities of war and peace, now issues from the trial, unharm'd, trebly-invigorated, perhaps to commence forthwith its finally triumphant march around the globe.

THE TRAMP AND STRIKE QUESTIONS.

Part of a Lecture proposed, (never deliver'd.)

Two grim and spectral dangers—dangerous to peace, to health, to social security, to progress—long known in concrete to the governments of the Old World, and there eventuating, more than once or twice, in dynastic overturns, bloodshed, days, months, of terror—seem of late years to be nearing the New World, nay, to be gradually establishing themselves among us. What mean these phantoms here? (I personify them in fictitious shapes, but they are very real.) Is the fresh and broad demesne of America destined also to give them foothold and lodgment, permanent domicile?

Beneath the whole political world, what most presses and perplexes to-day, sending vastest results affecting the future, is not the abstract question of democracy, but of social and economic organization, the treatment of working-people by employers, and all that goes along with it—not only the wages-payment part, but a certain spirit and principle, to vivify anew these relations; all the questions of progress, strength, tariffs, finance, &c., really evolving themselves more or less directly out of the

THE TRAMP AND STRIKE QUESTIONS.

Printed in *SDC* from six pages of autograph MS made up of ten or twelve scraps of paper of different sizes pasted on larger sheets. Title in red ink, top of first page. The rest in black ink except two scraps on the fourth page and the last small scrap on the sixth page, which are in pencil. Revisions in black ink. An ink blot in the upper left hand part of the first MS scrap obscures several words.

7. There is no period in the MS after the word "real" before the final parenthesis.

Poverty Question, ("the Science of Wealth," and a dozen other names are given it, but I prefer the severe one just used.) I will begin by calling the reader's attention to a thought upon the matter which may not have struck you before—the wealth of the civilized world, as contrasted with its poverty—what does it derivatively stand for, and represent? A rich person ought to have a strong stomach. As in Europe the wealth of to-day mainly results from, and represents, the rapine, murder, outrages, treachery, hoggishness, of hundreds of years ago, and onward, later, so in America, after the same token—(not yet so bad, perhaps, or at any rate not so palpable—we have not existed long enough—but we seem to be doing our best to make it up.)

Curious as it may seem, it is in what are call'd the poorest, lowest characters you will sometimes, nay generally, find glints of the most sublime virtues, eligibilities, heroisms. Then it is doubtful whether the State is to be saved, either in the monotonous long run, or in tremendous special crises, by its good people only. When the storm is deadliest, and the disease most imminent, help often comes from strange quarters—(the homœopathic motto, you remember, *cure the bite with a hair of the same dog.*)

The American Revolution of 1776 was simply a great strike, successful for its immediate object—but whether a real success judged by the scale of the centuries, and the long-striking balance of Time, yet remains to be settled. The French Revolution was absolutely a strike, and a very terrible and relentless one, against ages of bad pay, unjust division of wealth-products, and the hoggish monopoly of a few, rolling in superfluity, against the vast bulk of the work-people, living in squalor.

If the United States, like the countries of the Old World, are also to grow vast crops of poor, desperate, dissatisfied, nomadic, miserably-waged populations, such as we see looming upon us of late years—steadily, even if slowly, eating into them like a cancer of lungs or stomach—then our republican experiment, notwithstanding all its surface-successes, is at heart an unhealthy failure.

Feb., '79.—I saw to-day a sight I had never seen before—and it amazed, and made me serious; three quite good-looking American men,

33. imminent,] MS: immanent, [Correction presumably made in proof.]
34. homœopathic] MS: homoepath's [Correction presumably made in proof.]
38. long-striking] MS: long striking
38. Time, yet] MS: Time—yet
42. work-people] MS: work people

DEMOCRACY IN THE NEW WORLD.

Printed in *SDC* from two clippings of paragraphs 6–9 under the general

of respectable personal presence, two of them young, carrying chiffonier-bags on their shoulders, and the usual long iron hooks in their hands, plodding along, their eyes cast down, spying for scraps, rags, bones, &c.

DEMOCRACY IN THE NEW WORLD,

estimated and summ'd-up to-day, having thoroughly justified itself the past hundred years, (as far as growth, vitality and power are concern'd,) by severest and most varied trials of peace and war, and having establish'd itself for good, with all its necessities and benefits, for time to come, is now to be seriously consider'd also in its pronounc'd and already developt dangers. While the battle was raging, and the result suspended, all defections and criticisms were to be hush'd, and everything bent with vehemence unmitigated toward the urge of victory. But that victory settled, new responsibilities advance. I can conceive of no better service in the United States, henceforth, by democrats of thorough and heart-felt faith, than boldly exposing the weakness, liabilities and infinite corruptions of democracy. By the unprecedented opening-up of humanity en-masse in the United States, the last hundred years, under our institutions, not only the good qualities of the race, but just as much the bad ones, are prominently brought forward. Man is about the same, in the main, whether with despotism, or whether with freedom.

"The ideal form of human society," Canon Kingsley declares, "is democracy. A nation—and were it even possible, a whole world—of free men, lifting free foreheads to God and Nature; calling no man master, for One is their master, even God; knowing and doing their duties toward the Maker of the universe, and therefore to each other; not from fear, nor calculation of profit or loss, but because they have seen the beauty of righteousness, and trust, and peace; because the law of God is in their hearts. Such a nation—such a society—what nobler conception of moral existence can we form? Would not that, indeed, be the kingdom of God come on earth?"

To this faith, founded in the ideal, let us hold—and never abandon or lose it. Then what a spectacle is *practically* exhibited by our American democracy to-day!

heading "Thoughts for the Centennial" from the lower parts of *TR*, pp. 18–19. In *TR* there is no separate title, but the first word of the first line, "Democracy," is printed in capital letters. For the new title Whitman underlines the words "Democracy in the New World."

7–8. everything] *TR:* every thing
12. democracy. By the] *TR:* Democracy . . . . . . By the
27. in the ideal, let us] *TR:* in the Practical as well as the Ideal, let us
28. lose it. Then] *TR:* lose it! . . . . . . Then

FOUNDATION STAGES—THEN OTHERS.

Though I think I fully comprehend the absence of moral tone in our current politics and business, and the almost entire futility of absolute and simple honor as a counterpoise against the enormous greed for worldly wealth, with the trickeries of gaining it, all through society our day, I still do not share the depression and despair on the subject which I find possessing many good people. The advent of America, the history of the past century, has been the first general aperture and opening-up to the average human commonalty, on the broadest scale, of the eligibilities to wealth and worldly success and eminence, and has been fully taken advantage of; and the example has spread hence, in ripples, to all nations. To these eligibilities—to this limitless aperture, the race has tended, en-masse, roaring and rushing and crude, and fiercely, turbidly hastening—and we have seen the first stages, and are now in the midst of the result of it all, so far. But there will certainly ensue other stages, and entirely different ones. In nothing is there more evolution than the American mind. Soon, it will be fully realized that ostensible wealth and money-making, show, luxury, &c., imperatively necessitate something beyond—namely, the sane, eternal moral and spiritual-esthetic attributes, elements. (We cannot have even that realization on any less terms than the price we are now paying for it.) Soon, it will be understood clearly, that the State cannot flourish, (nay, cannot exist,) without those elements. They will gradually enter into the chyle of sociology and literature. They will finally make the blood and brawn of the best American individualities of both sexes—and thus, with them, to a certainty, (through these very processes of to-day,) dominate the New World.

GENERAL SUFFRAGE, ELECTIONS, &C.

It still remains doubtful to me whether these will ever secure, officially, the best wit and capacity—whether, through them, the first-class genius of America will ever personally appear in the high political sta-

FOUNDATION STAGES—THEN OTHERS.

Printed in *SDC* from two clippings (paragraph 10 of "Thoughts for the Centennial") from the lower parts of *TR*, pp. 19–20. In *TR* there is no separate title, but the first word of the first line is printed in capital letters, as in the preceding paragraph. The new title is inserted in red ink.

14. so far. But] *TR:* so far. . . . But

GENERAL SUFFRAGE, ELECTIONS, &C.

Printed in *SDC* from a clipping of the middle part of page 83 of *DV* "General

tions, the Presidency, Congress, the leading State offices, &c. Those offices, or the candidacy for them, arranged, won, by caucusing, money, the favoritism or pecuniary interest of rings, the superior manipulation of the ins over the outs, or the outs over the ins, are, indeed, at best, the mere business agencies of the people, are useful as formulating, neither the best and highest, but the average of the public judgment, sense, justice, (or sometimes want of judgment, sense, justice.) We elect Presidents, Congressmen, &c., not so much to have them consider and decide for us, but as surest practical means of expressing the will of majorities on mooted questions, measures, &c.

As to general suffrage, after all, since we have gone so far, the more general it is, the better. I favor the widest opening of the doors. Let the ventilation and area be wide enough, and all is safe. We can never have a born penitentiary-bird, or panel-thief, or lowest gambling-hell or groggery keeper, for President—though such may not only emulate, but get, high offices from localities—even from the proud and wealthy city of New York.

WHO GETS THE PLUNDER?

The protectionists are fond of flashing to the public eye the glittering delusion of great money-results from manufactures, mines, artificial exports—so many millions from this source, and so many from that—such a seductive, unanswerable show—an immense revenue of annual cash from iron, cotton, woollen, leather goods, and a hundred other things, all bolstered up by "protection." But the really important point of all is, *into whose pockets does this plunder really go?* It would be some excuse and satisfaction if even a fair proportion of it went to the masses of laboring-men—resulting in homesteads to such, men, women, children—myriads of actual homes in fee simple, in every State, (not the false glamour of the stunning wealth reported in the census, in the statistics, or tables in the newspapers,) but a fair division and generous average to those workmen and workwomen—*that* would be something. But the fact

Notes," where it was printed for the first time. The title has been removed from the first line and centered on the page. The text is identical in all printed versions.

WHO GETS THE PLUNDER?

Printed in *SDC* from an autograph MS of three pages consisting of white sheets written in black ink and pasted on gray base sheets. The title is inserted in red ink at the top of the first gray sheet. Revisions are in black ink. These scraps were originally meant to be included in the section on "The Tramp and Strike Questions," since that title is written at the top of the first white sheet and crossed out. The MS is printed in *SDC* as revised except for the insertion of two or three commas and the insertion of ",in" between "census" and "the statistics" in line 11.

itself is nothing of the kind. The profits of "protection" go altogether to a few score select persons—who, by favors of Congress, State legislatures, the banks, and other special advantages, are forming a vulgar aristocracy, full as bad as anything in the British or European castes, of blood, or the dynasties there of the past. As Sismondi pointed out, the true prosperity of a nation is not in the great wealth of a special class, but is only to be really attain'd in having the bulk of the people provided with homes or land in fee simple. This may not be the best show, but it is the best reality.

FRIENDSHIP, (THE REAL ARTICLE.)

Though Nature maintains, and must prevail, there will always be plenty of people, and good people, who cannot, or think they cannot, see anything in that last, wisest, most envelop'd of proverbs, "Friendship rules the World." Modern society, in its largest vein, is essentially intellectual, infidelistic—secretly admires, and depends most on, pure compulsion or science, its rule and sovereignty—is, in short, in "cultivated" quarters, deeply Napoleonic.

"Friendship," said Bonaparte, in one of his lightning-flashes of candid garrulity, "Friendship is but a name. I love no one—not even my brothers; Joseph perhaps a little. Still, if I do love him, it is from habit, because he is the eldest of us. Duroc? Ay, him, if any one, I love in a sort—but why? He suits me; he is cool, undemonstrative, unfeeling—has no weak affections—never embraces any one—never weeps."

I am not sure but the same analogy is to be applied, in cases, often seen, where, with an extra development and acuteness of the intellectual faculties, there is a mark'd absence of the spiritual, affectional, and sometimes, though more rarely, the highest æsthetic and moral elements of cognition.

FRIENDSHIP, (THE REAL ARTICLE.)

Printed in *SDC* from a clipping of the Christmas Number, 1874, of *NYDG*. This was the third section of Whitman's "A Christmas Garland," following a section with the line heading "Genius—Victor Hugo—George Sand—Emerson" that was not reprinted in Whitman's lifetime (see Appendix VI, *1*) and the poem "The Ox Tamer" (reprinted in *TR*, p. 27). This section on "Friendship" was not reprinted in *TR*. It was included in *DVOP*.

1. In *NYDG* the title was included in the first line, with only the first word in capital letters.

5. admires, and depends most on, pure] *NYDG:* admires and depends on pure

LACKS AND WANTS YET.

Printed in *SDC* from two clippings of paragraphs 4 and 5 of "Thoughts for

LACKS AND WANTS YET.

Of most foreign countries, small or large, from the remotest times known, down to our own, each has contributed after its kind, directly or indirectly, at least one great undying song, to help vitalize and increase the valor, wisdom, and elegance of humanity, from the points of view attain'd by it up to date. The stupendous epics of India, the holy Bible itself, the Homeric canticles, the Nibelungen, the Cid Campeador, the Inferno, Shakspere's dramas of the passions and of the feudal lords, Burns's songs, Goethe's in Germany, Tennyson's poems in England, Victor Hugo's in France, and many more, are the widely various yet integral signs or landmarks, (in certain respects the highest set up by the human mind and soul, beyond science, invention, political amelioration, &c.,) narrating in subtlest, best ways, the long, long routes of history, and giving identity to the stages arrived at by aggregate humanity, and the conclusions assumed in its progressive and varied civilizations. . . . Where is America's art-rendering, in any thing like the spirit worthy of herself and the modern, to these characteristic immortal monuments? So far, our Democratic society, (estimating its various strata, in the mass, as one,) possesses nothing—nor have we contributed any characteristic music, the finest tie of nationality—to make up for that glowing, blood-throbbing, religious, social, emotional, artistic, indefinable, indescribably beautiful charm and hold which fused the separate parts of the old feudal societies together, in their wonderful interpenetration, in Europe and Asia, of love, belief, and loyalty, running one way like a living weft—and picturesque responsibility, duty, and blessedness, running like a warp the other way. (In the Southern States, under slavery, much of the same.) . . . In coincidence, and as things now exist in the States, what is more terrible, more alarming, than the total want of any such fusion and mutuality of love, belief, and rapport of interest, between the comparatively few successful rich, and the great

the Centennial" from the lower parts of *TR*, pp. 16–17. The title was inserted in red ink at the top of the first clipping. For the omitted third paragraph, which is introductory to the two paragraphs here clipped, see Appendix VIII, *6*. Paragraphs 3, 4, and 5 were printed in an anonymous prepublication review of *TR* entitled "Walt Whitman's Poems," probably written by Whitman (see "Walt Whitman to Whitelaw Reid," by Edwin H. Miller, *SB*, VIII, 1956, 242–249), in *NYTR*, February 19, 1876; see also notes to "Preface, 1876"). The fourth paragraph is preceded by the numeral "1." and the fifth paragraph by the numeral "2." Both numerals are deleted in the MS. For the first two paragraphs of "Thoughts for the Centennial," see the section subtitled "Little or Nothing New, After All."

16. After "monuments?" *TR* begins a new paragraph.
16. far, our] *TR:* far, in America, our
21. together, in] *TR:* together in
24. duty, and] *TR:* duty and

masses of the unsuccessful, the poor? As a mixed political and social question, is not this full of dark significance? Is it not worth considering as a problem and puzzle in our democracy—an indispensable want to be supplied?

RULERS STRICTLY OUT OF THE MASSES.

In the talk (which I welcome) about the need of men of training, thoroughly school'd and experienced men, for statesmen, I would present the following as an offset. It was written by me twenty years ago—and has been curiously verified since:

I say no body of men are fit to make Presidents, Judges, and Generals, unless they themselves supply the best specimens of the same; and that supplying one or two such specimens illuminates the whole body for a thousand years. I expect to see the day when the like of the present personnel of the governments, Federal, State, municipal, military, and naval, will be look'd upon with derision, and when qualified mechanics and young men will reach Congress and other official stations, sent in their working costumes, fresh from their benches and tools, and returning to them again with dignity. The young fellows must prepare to do credit to this destiny, for the stuff is in them. Nothing gives place, recollect, and never ought to give place, except to its clean superiors. There is more rude and undevelopt

29. poor? As] *TR:* poor? . . . . . . As

RULERS STRICTLY OUT OF THE MASSES.

The first two paragraphs (lines 1–26) were printed in *SDC* from two paragraphs with the present subtitle at the bottom of *TR*, p. 30. The third paragraph (lines 27–32), not previously published, was printed from an autograph MS. The first two paragraphs were reprinted in *TR* from a section with the same subtitle in Whitman's "A Christmas Garland," *NYDG*, Christmas Number, 1874. The second paragraph (lines 5–26) was originally part of "The Eighteenth Presidency!" This political tract, written in 1856 and perhaps printed about the same time, has survived in several sets of proofs, but was not published in Whitman's lifetime. It has since been published several times; its first publication was in a French magazine in 1926. (See Edward F. Grier's preface to his edition of the pamphlet, University of Kansas Press, 1956.) At least two sets of the proofs show revisions, but Whitman's text of *TR* and *NYDG* agree with the unrevised proof sheets in the Library of Congress. The entire section was reprinted in *DVOP*. For purposes of collation Professor Grier's text of "The Eighteenth Presidency!" is here used. Since the Christmas Number, 1874, of *NYDG* is not available, and no clipping of it exists, apparently, "A Christmas Garland" is collated in the text of *UPP*, supplemented by Professor Holloway's notes made at the time he was preparing *UPP* for the press.

4. verified since:] *TR* and *NYDG:* verified since by the advent of Abraham Lincoln:

5–8. The first sentence of this paragraph was originally drawn from the first paragraph of a section of "The Eighteenth Presidency!" that has the subtitle "Has Much Been Done in the Theory of These States?" The first of that paragraph, omitted in *NYDG* and *TR*, is as follows: "Very good; more remains. Who is satisfied with the theory, or a parade of the theory? I say, delay not, come quickly to its most courageous facts and illustrations." (Grier, p. 20.)

bravery, friendship, conscientiousness, clear-sightedness, and practical genius for any scope of action, even the broadest and highest, now among the American mechanics and young men, than in all the official persons in these States, legislative, executive, judicial, military, and naval, and more than among all the literary persons. I would be much pleased to see some heroic, shrewd, fully-inform'd, healthy-bodied, middle-aged, beard-faced American blacksmith or boatman come down from the West across the Alleghanies, and walk into the Presidency, dress'd in a clean suit of working attire, and with the tan all over his face, breast, and arms; I would certainly vote for that sort of man, possessing the due requirements, before any other candidate.

(The facts of rank-and-file workingmen, mechanics, Lincoln, Johnson, Grant, Garfield, brought forward from the masses and placed in the Presidency, and swaying its mighty powers with firm hand—really with more sway than any king in history, and with better capacity in using that sway—can we not see that these facts have bearings far, far beyond their political or party ones?)

MONUMENTS—THE PAST AND PRESENT.

If you go to Europe, (to say nothing of Asia, more ancient and massive still,) you cannot stir without meeting venerable mementos—cathe-

8. After "thousand years." the text of "Eighteenth Presidency!" begins a new paragraph.

8–9. personnel] *TR: personnel*

16. Professor Grier notes that in one set of proofs, now in the collection of Mr. Charles E. Feinberg, which he designates "F2," the words "friendship" and "clear-sightedness" are deleted.

21. Professor Grier notes that in "F2," the words "fully-informed," and "middle-aged, beard-faced" are deleted.

26. After "candidate." the following sentence in "Eighteenth Presidency!" continuing and ending the paragraph, is omitted in all later texts: "Such is the thought that must become familiar to you, whoever you are, and to the people of These States; and must eventually take shape in action."

26. After "candidate." *NYDG*, according to Mr. Holloway's notes, continues with the following two sentences, which are the beginning of the paragraph of "Eighteenth Presidency!" next following the paragraph ending with the sentence quoted above, and which were not included in *TR* or any later text: "At present, we are environed with nonsense under the name of respectability. Everywhere lowers that stifling atmosphere that makes all the millions of farmers and mechanics of These States the helpless supplejacks of a comparatively few politicians." (In *DV*, lines 751–753, the following similar sentence occurs: "I have noticed how the millions of sturdy farmers and mechanics are thus helpless supple-jacks of comparatively few politicians." See notes to *DV*.)

MONUMENTS—THE PAST AND PRESENT.

Printed in *SDC* from two clippings of *TR*, pp. 21–22. The title is inserted in red ink. This is paragraph 10 under the general heading "Thoughts for the Centennial."

1. If you go] *TR:* IF YOU GO

drals, ruins of temples, castles, monuments of the great, statues and paintings, (far, far beyond anything America can ever expect to produce,) haunts of heroes long dead, saints, poets, divinities, with deepest associations of ages. But here in the New World, while *those* we can never emulate, we have *more* than those to build, and far more greatly to build. (I am not sure but the day for conventional monuments, statues, memorials, &c., has pass'd away—and that they are henceforth superfluous and vulgar.) An enlarged general superior humanity, (partly indeed resulting from those,) we are to build. European, Asiatic greatness are in the past. Vaster and subtler, America, combining, justifying the past, yet works for a grander future, in living democratic forms. (Here too are indicated the paths for our national bards.) Other times, other lands, have had their missions—Art, War, Ecclesiasticism, Literature, Discovery, Trade, Architecture, &c., &c.—but that grand future is the enclosing purport of the United States.

LITTLE OR NOTHING NEW, AFTER ALL.

How small were the best thoughts, poems, conclusions, except for a certain invariable resemblance and uniform standard in the final thoughts, theology, poems, &c., of all nations, all civilizations, all centuries and times. Those precious legacies—accumulations! They come to us from the far-off—from all eras, and all lands—from Egypt, and India, and Greece, and Rome—and along through the middle and later ages, in the grand monarchies of Europe—born under far different institutes and conditions from ours—but out of the insight and inspiration of the same old humanity—the same old heart and brain—the same old countenance yearningly,

4. anything] *TR:* any thing
6. ages. But] *TR:* ages......But
9-10. vulgar.) An] *TR:* vulgar.)......An
14. bards.) Other] *TR:* bards.).....Other
16. but that grand future is] *TR:* but *that* is

LITTLE OR NOTHING NEW, AFTER ALL.

Printed in *SDC* from a clipping of the latter part of the first paragraph and all of the second paragraph, *TR*, p. 15 (see Appendix VIII, 5), which are the first of a series of twelve connected paragraphs (pp. 15–22) under the general heading, "Thoughts For The Centennial.—" The new title for *SDC* is inserted in red ink. Of the remaining ten paragraphs, seven appear in *SDC*. (See preceding notes on "Democracy in the New World," "Foundation States—Then Others," "Lacks and Wants Yet," and "Monuments—the Past and Present.") Omitted from *SDC*, in addition to the first part of the first paragraph of "Lacks and Wants Yet," already noted, are the two short paragraphs at the bottom of *TR*, p. 22. For these two paragraphs, which were printed in Whitman's anonymous review of *TR* under the heading "Walt Whitman's Poems," in *NYTR*, February 19, 1876 ("Walt Whitman to Whitelaw Reid," *SB*, VIII, 1956, 242–249), see Appendix VIII, 7.

1. How] *TR:* how

pensively, looking forth. What we have to do to-day is to receive them cheerfully, and to give them ensemble, and a modern American and democratic physiognomy.

A LINCOLN REMINISCENCE.

As is well known, story-telling was often with President Lincoln a weapon which he employ'd with great skill. Very often he could not give a point-blank reply or comment—and these indirections, (sometimes funny, but not always so,) were probably the best responses possible. In the gloomiest period of the war, he had a call from a large delegation of bank presidents. In the talk after business was settled, one of the big Dons asked Mr. Lincoln if his confidence in the permanency of the Union was not beginning to be shaken—whereupon the homely President told a little story: "When I was a young man in Illinois," said he, "I boarded for a time with a deacon of the Presybterian church. One night I was roused from my sleep by a rap at the door, and I heard the deacon's voice exclaiming, 'Arise, Abraham! the day of judgment has come!' I sprang from my bed and rushed to the window, and saw the stars falling in great showers; but looking back of them in the heavens I saw the grand old constellations, with which I was so well acquainted, fixed and true in their places. Gentlemen, the world did not come to an end then, nor will the Union now."

FREEDOM.

It is not only true that most people entirely misunderstand Freedom, but I sometimes think I have not yet met one person who rightly understands it. The whole Universe is absolute Law. Freedom only opens entire

1. conclusions, except] *TR:* conclusions and products, except
3. After "and times." *TR* begins a new paragraph.
5–6. Greece, and Rome] *TR:* Greece and Rome
10. forth. What] *TR:* forth......Strictly speaking, they are indeed none of them new, and are indeed not ours originally—ours, however, by inheritance. What] [The omitted sentence is not deleted in the MS, hence must have been deleted in the proof.—ED.]

A LINCOLN REMINISCENCE.

Printed in *SDC* from an autograph MS page consisting of a full sheet and an added strip at the bottom, written in black ink, and not drastically revised. Title in red ink.

FREEDOM.

Printed in *SDC* from two clippings of *TR*, pp. 31–32, where the same title is used, but at the beginning of the first line. This appeared, with minor variations, in an anonymous prepublication review of *TR*, entitled "Walt Whitman's Poems" (see "Walt Whitman to Whitelaw Reid," by Edwin H. Miller, *SB*, VIII, 1956, 242–249.)

3. it. The] *TR:* it........The

activity and license *under the law.* To the degraded or undevelopt—and even to too many others—the thought of freedom is a thought of escaping from law—which, of course, is impossible. More precious than all worldly riches is Freedom—freedom from the painful constipation and poor narrowness of ecclesiasticism—freedom in manners, habiliments, furniture, from the silliness and tyranny of local fashions—entire freedom from party rings and mere conventions in Politics—and better than all, a general freedom of One's-Self from the tyrannic domination of vices, habits, appetites, under which nearly every man of us, (often the greatest brawler for freedom,) is enslaved. Can we attain such enfranchisement—the true Democracy, and the height of it? While we are from birth to death the subjects of irresistible law, enclosing every movement and minute, we yet escape, by a paradox, into true free will. Strange as it may seem, we only attain to freedom by a knowledge of, and implicit obedience to, Law. Great —unspeakably great—is the Will! the free Soul of man! At its greatest, understanding and obeying the laws, it can then, and then only, maintain true liberty. For there is to the highest, that law as absolute as any—more absolute than any—the Law of Liberty. The shallow, as intimated, consider liberty a release from all law, from every constraint. The wise see in it, on the contrary, the potent Law of Laws, namely, the fusion and combination of the conscious will, or partial individual law, with those universal, eternal, unconscious ones, which run through all Time, pervade history, prove immortality, give moral purpose to the entire objective world, and the last dignity to human life.

BOOK-CLASSES—AMERICA'S LITERATURE.

For certain purposes, literary productions through all the recorded ages may be roughly divided into two classes. The first consisting of only a score or two, perhaps less, of typical, primal, representative works, dif-

6. After "impossible." *TR* begins a new paragraph.
12. brawler] *TR:* bawler [Change not made in MS.]
13. After "enslaved." *TR* begins a new paragraph.
14. After "height of it." *TR* begins a new paragraph.
20. liberty. For] *TR:* liberty........For

BOOK-CLASSES—AMERICA'S LITERATURE.

Printed in *SDC* from an autograph MS page consisting of two sheets of odd sizes written in black ink. The title in red ink appears in the upper left hand corner.

9. After "only to them." the MS has the following two sentences lined out and omitted from *SDC:* "In other words criticism falls powerless before them. The second class only are always tried, and to be properly tried, by the technical laws and fashions of a time or country, and are to fail or succeed thereby."

10–13. If Whitman was thinking of Margaret Fuller's essay "American Literature" (*Papers on Literature and Art*, 1846), as seems probable, he quoted incor-

ferent from any before, and embodying in themselves their own main laws and reasons for being. Then the second class, books and writings innumerable, incessant—to be briefly described as radiations or offshoots, or more or less imitations of the first. The works of the first class, as said, have their own laws, and may indeed be described as making those laws, and amenable only to them. The sharp warning of Margaret Fuller, unquell'd for thirty years, yet sounds in the air; "It does not follow that because the United States print and read more books, magazines, and newspapers than all the rest of the world, that they really have, therefore, a literature."

OUR REAL CULMINATION.

The final culmination of this vast and varied Republic will be the production and perennial establishment of millions of comfortable city homesteads and moderate-sized farms, healthy and independent, single separate ownership, fee simple, life in them complete but cheap, within reach of all. Exceptional wealth, splendor, countless manufactures, excess of exports, immense capital and capitalists, the five-dollar-a-day hotels well fill'd, artificial improvements, even books, colleges, and the suffrage—all, in many respects, in themselves, (hard as it is to say so, and sharp as a surgeon's lance,) form, more or less, a sort of anti-democratic disease and monstrosity, except as they contribute by curious indirections to that culmination—seem to me mainly of value, or worth consideration, only with reference to it.

There is a subtle something in the common earth, crops, cattle, air, trees, &c., and in having to do at first hand with them, that forms the only purifying and perennial element for individuals and for society. I must confess I want to see the agricultural occupation of America at first hand permanently broaden'd. Its gains are the only ones on which God seems to

rectly. There is nothing in the essay about the quantity of books and magazines read in this country. The first two paragraphs of her essay read as follows:

"Some thinkers may object to this essay, that we are about to write of that which has as yet no existence.

For it does not follow because many books are written by persons born in America that there exists an American literature. Books which imitate or represent the thought and life of Europe do not constitute an American literature. Before such can exist, an original idea must animate this nation and fresh currents of life must call into life fresh thoughts along its shores." (Cf. "American National Literature," *GBF*, lines 142–145.)

OUR REAL CULMINATION.

The first paragraph was printed from an autograph MS page consisting of three gray sheets of odd sizes pasted together, with writing in black ink. The title in red ink. There is no MS for the second paragraph, which must have been inserted in the proof.

smile. What others—what business, profit, wealth, without a taint? What fortune else—what dollar—does not stand for, and come from, more or less imposition, lying, unnaturalness?

AN AMERICAN PROBLEM.

One of the problems presented in America these times is, how to combine one's duty and policy as a member of associations, societies, brotherhoods or what not, and one's obligations to the State and Nation, with essential freedom as an individual personality, without which freedom a man cannot grow or expand, or be full, modern, heroic, democratic, American. With all the necessities and benefits of association, (and the world cannot get along without it,) the true nobility and satisfaction of a man consist in his thinking and acting for himself. The problem, I say, is to combine the two, so as not to ignore either.

THE LAST COLLECTIVE COMPACTION.

I like well our polyglot construction-stamp, and the retention thereof, in the broad, the tolerating, the many-sided, the collective. All nations here—a home for every race on earth. British, German, Scandinavian, Spanish, French, Italian—papers published, plays acted, speeches made, in all languages—on our shores the crowning resultant of those distillations, decantations, compactions of humanity, that have been going on, on trial, over the earth so long.

AN AMERICAN PROBLEM.

Printed in SDC from an autograph MS page, a white sheet, in pencil with revisions in black ink. The title is written in red ink in the upper left-hand corner of the sheet as if it were added at the time the MSS were assembled.

THE LAST COLLECTIVE COMPACTION.

Printed from an autograph MS consisting of a single sheet of white paper, written in black ink, with the title in red ink on a separate strip of paper and pasted across the top of the page.

The Appendix of SDC, "Pieces in Early Youth," has been omitted from this edition of *Prose Works 1892*. It is included in another volume of the *Collected Writings* entitled *The Early Poems and the Fiction*, edited by Thomas L. Brasher.

November Boughs.

Whitman's *Commonplace Book*, now in the Feinberg Collection, shows that NB, a collection of prose and verse, was copyrighted in September and published by David McKay in Philadelphia before October 7, 1888. Parts of the prose selections had been included in DVOP, published in London by Walter Scott, earlier presumably, since Whitman's preface to DVOP is dated April, 1888. All of NB was re-

November Boughs.

Our Eminent Visitors Past, Present and Future.

Welcome to them each and all! They do good—the deepest, widest, most needed good—though quite certainly not in the ways attempted—which have, at times, something irresistibly comic. What can be more farcical, for instance, than the sight of a worthy gentleman coming three or four thousand miles through wet and wind to speak complacently and at great length on matters of which he both entirely mistakes or knows nothing—before crowds of auditors equally complacent, and equally at fault?

Yet welcome and thanks, we say, to those visitors we have, and have had, from abroad among us—and may the procession continue! We have had Dickens and Thackeray, Froude, Herbert Spencer, Oscar Wilde, Lord Coleridge—soldiers, savants, poets—and now Matthew Arnold and Irving the actor. Some have come to make money—some for a "good time"—some to help us along and give us advice—and some undoubtedly to investigate, *bona fide*, this great problem, democratic America, looming upon the world

printed from the same plates without revision in CPP, which came from the press shortly after NB, not later than December, 1888. All of the prose pages of NB were reprinted in CPW 1892, apparently from the same plates, without change except repagination. Of the MS from which NB was printed, only the section on Elias Hicks, now in the Feinberg Collection, has been available for collation. Most of the corrected galleys have survived and are now in the Feinberg Collection. All changes in the galleys are noted in the collation except Whitman's correction of printer's errors. Details of previous publication are given in the headnote for each separate title.

Our Eminent Visitors.

Originally published under the same title in CR for November 17, 1883 (III, 459–460); revised and reprinted in NB. Reprinted in DVOP from the text of CR.

2. needed good] *CR:* needed, good
3. times, something] DVOP and *CR:* times, to the appreciative nostril, a scent of something
3. What can be more] DVOP and *CR:* Can there be anything more
7. nothing—before crowds of] DVOP and *CR:* nothing, before a crowd of
9. those visitors we have] DVOP and *CR:* those we have
10. had, from abroad among] DVOP and *CR:* had, among
13. Coleridge . . . and] DVOP and *CR:* Coleridge—and

with such cumulative power through a hundred years, now with the evident intention (since the Secession War) to stay, and take a leading hand, for many a century to come, in civilization's and humanity's eternal game. But alas! that very investigation—the method of that investigation—is where the deficit most surely and helplessly comes in. Let not Lord Coleridge and Mr. Arnold (to say nothing of the illustrious actor) imagine that when they have met and survey'd the etiquettical gatherings of our wealthy, distinguish'd and sure-to-be-put-forward-on-such-occasions citizens (New York, Boston, Philadelphia, &c., have certain stereotyped strings of them, continually lined and paraded like the lists of dishes at hotel tables—you are sure to get the same over and over again—it is very amusing)—and the bowing and introducing, the receptions at the swell clubs, the eating and drinking and praising and praising back—and the next day riding about Central Park, or doing the "Public Institutions"—and so passing through, one after another, the full-dress coteries of the Atlantic cities, all grammatical and cultured and correct, with the toned-down manners of the gentlemen, and the kid-gloves, and luncheons and finger-glasses—Let not our eminent visitors, we say, suppose that, by means of these experiences, they have "seen America," or captur'd any distinctive clew or purport thereof. Not a bit of it. Of the pulse-beats that lie within and vitalize this Commonweal to-day—of the hard-pan purports and idiosyncrasies pursued faithfully and triumphantly by its bulk of men North and South, generation after generation, superficially unconscious of their own aims, yet none the less pressing onward with deathless intuition—those coteries do not furnish the faintest scintilla. In the Old World the best flavor and significance of a race may possibly need to be look'd for in its "upper classes," its gentries, its court, its *état major*. In the United States the rule is revers'd. Besides (and a point, this, perhaps deepest of all,) the special marks of our grouping and design are not going to be understood in a hurry. The lesson and scanning right on the ground are difficult; I was going to say they are impossible to foreigners—but I have occasionally found the clearest appreciation of all, coming from far-off quarters. Surely

16–17. with the evident] *DVOP* and *CR:* with evident
19. alas! . . . the] *DVOP* and *CR:* alas! in that very investigation—at any rate the
25. of dishes] *DVOP* and *CR:* of dinner dishes
32. finger-glasses—Let] *DVOP:* finger-glasses.—Let] *CR:* finger-glasses. Let [Revised on the galley.]
33–34. that . . . they] *CR:* that they
37–38. men North and South, generation] *DVOP* and *CR:* men, generation
39. intuition—those] *DVOP* and *CR:* intuition age after age—those
43. Besides . . . special] *DVOP* and *CR:* Besides, the special
45. difficult; I] *DVOP* and *CR:* difficult, I
51–52. Delmonico's, . . . guests:] *DVOP* and *CR:* Delmonico's:

nothing could be more apt, not only for our eminent visitors present and to come, but for home study, than the following editorial criticism of the London *Times* on Mr. Froude's visit and lectures here a few years ago, and the culminating dinner given at Delmonico's, with its brilliant array of guests:

> "We read the list," says the *Times*, "of those who assembled to do honor to Mr. Froude: there were Mr. Emerson, Mr. Beecher, Mr. Curtis, Mr. Bryant; we add the names of those who sent letters of regret that they could not attend in person—Mr. Longfellow, Mr. Whittier. They are names which are well known—almost as well known and as much honor'd in England as in America; and yet what must we say in the end? The American people outside this assemblage of writers is something vaster and greater than they, singly or together, can comprehend. It cannot be said of any or all of them that they can speak for their nation. We who look on at this distance are able perhaps on that account to see the more clearly that there are qualities of the American people which find no representation, no voice, among these their spokesmen. And what is true of them is true of the English class of whom Mr. Froude may be said to be the ambassador. Mr. Froude is master of a charming style. He has the gift of grace and the gift of sympathy. Taking any single character as the subject of his study, he may succeed after a very short time in so comprehending its workings as to be able to present a living figure to the intelligence and memory of his readers. But the movements of a nation, *the voiceless purpose of a people which cannot put its own thoughts into words, yet acts upon them in each successive generation*—these things do not lie within his grasp. . . . The functions of literature such as he represents are limited in their action; the influence he can wield is artificial and restricted, and, while he and his hearers please and are pleas'd with pleasant periods, the great mass of national life will flow around them unmov'd in its tides by action as powerless as that of the dwellers by the shore to direct the currents of the ocean."

A thought, here, that needs to be echoed, expanded, permanently treasur'd by our literary classes and educators. (The gestation, the youth, the knitting preparations, are now over, and it is full time for definite purpose, result.) How few think of it, though it is the impetus and back-

53–78. [It has not been determined what issue of the *Times* contains this criticism, nor whether Whitman found it there or quoted in some American journal. Froude gave five lectures in New York in October and November, 1872, on Irish history. The last of this series, "Ireland Since the Union," was published in the second volume of *Short Studies on Great Subjects* (4 vols., 1876), pp. 515–562. —ED.]

72. *generation*—these] CR: *generation*,—these

73. grasp. . . . The] CR: grasp. . . . . . The

76. the great] [CR and DVOP read "the great". This was printed "his great" in NB and later texts, obviously a typographical error which is here corrected.—ED.]

80–82. The sentence in parentheses is not in CR; it appeared for the first time in the text of NB.

ground of our whole Nationality and popular life. In the present brief memorandum I very likely for the first time awake "the intelligent reader" to the idea and inquiry whether there isn't such a thing as the distinctive genius of our democratic New World, universal, immanent, bringing to a head the best experience of the past—not specially literary or intellectual—not merely "good," (in the Sunday School and Temperance Society sense,) —some invisible spine and great sympathetic to these States, resident only in the average people, in their practical life, in their physiology, in their emotions, in their nebulous yet fiery patriotism, in the armies (both sides) through the whole Secession War—an identity and character which indeed so far "finds no voice among their spokesmen."

To my mind America, vast and fruitful as it appears to-day, is even yet, for its most important results, entirely in the tentative state; its very formation-stir and whirling trials and essays more splendid and picturesque, to my thinking, than the accomplish'd growths and shows of other lands, through European history, or Greece, or all the past. Surely a New World literature, worthy the name, is not to be, if it ever comes, some fiction, or fancy, or bit of sentimentalism or polish'd work merely by itself, or in abstraction. So long as such literature is no born branch and offshoot of the Nationality, rooted and grown from its roots, and fibred with its fibre, it can never answer any deep call or perennial need. Perhaps the untaught Republic is wiser than its teachers. The best literature is always a result of something far greater than itself—not the hero, but the portrait of the hero. Before there can be recorded history or poem there must be the transaction. Beyond the old masterpieces, the Iliad, the interminable Hindu epics, the Greek tragedies, even the Bible itself, range the immense facts of what must have preceded them, their *sine qua non*—the veritable poems and masterpieces, of which, grand as they are, the word-statements are but shreds and cartoons.

For to-day and the States, I think the vividest, rapidest, most stupendous processes ever known, ever perform'd by man or nation, on the largest scales and in countless varieties, are now and here presented. Not as our

85. whether there isn't] *DVOP:* whether where isn't [An obvious error.]
86. our democratic New] *DVOP* and *CR:* our New
88. not merely] *DVOP* and *CR:* not even merely
95–98. In *DVOP* and *CR* there is a period after "state", and the rest of the sentence, beginning "Its", is made into a separate sentence and enclosed in parentheses.
104. is wiser than] *DVOP* and *CR:* is deeper, wiser, than
105. itself—not] *DVOP* and *CR:* itself—is not
110. which, . . . are] *DVOP* and *CR:* which these are
123. meaning—Such] *DVOP* and *CR:* meaning—such [Revised on the galley.]
134–137. from Victor Hugo—or Thomas . . . would ensue?] *DVOP* and *CR:* from Thomas Carlyle. Castelar, Tennyson, Victor Hugo—were they and we to come

poets and preachers are always conventionally putting it—but quite different. Some colossal foundry, the flaming of the fire, the melted metal, the pounding trip-hammers, the surging crowds of workmen shifting from point to point, the murky shadows, the rolling haze, the discord, the crudeness, the deafening din, the disorder, the dross and clouds of dust, the waste and extravagance of material, the shafts of darted sunshine through the vast open roof-scuttles aloft—the mighty castings, many of them not yet fitted, perhaps delay'd long, yet each in its due time, with definite place and use and meaning—Such, more like, is a symbol of America.

After all of which, returning to our starting-point, we reiterate, and in the whole Land's name, a welcome to our eminent guests. Visits like theirs, and hospitalities, and hand-shaking, and face meeting face, and the distant brought near—what divine solvents they are! Travel, reciprocity, "interviewing," intercommunion of lands—what are they but Democracy's and the highest Law's best aids? O that our own country—that every land in the world—could annually, continually, receive the poets, thinkers, scientists, even the official magnates, of other lands, as honor'd guests. O that the United States, especially the West, could have had a good long visit and explorative jaunt, from the noble and melancholy Tourguéneff, before he died—or from Victor Hugo—or Thomas Carlyle. Castelar, Tennyson, any of the two or three great Parisian essayists—were they and we to come face to face, how is it possible but that the right understanding would ensue?

The Bible As Poetry.

I suppose one cannot at this day say anything new, from a literary point of view, about those autochthonic bequests of Asia—the Hebrew Bible, the mighty Hindu epics, and a hundred lesser but typical works; (not now definitely including the Iliad—though that work was certainly of

face to face, how is it possible but that the right and amicable understanding would ensue?

154. In *CR* Whitman's name appears at the end of the article.

The Bible As Poetry.

Originally published as an essay by the same title in *CR* for February 3, 1883 (III, 39–40); revised and reprinted in *NB*. The text in *NB* begins with the second paragraph of the essay as printed in *CR*. The first paragraph of the *CR* text is the last paragraph in *NB*. The piece is not included in *DVOP*.

Asiatic genesis, as Homer himself was—considerations which seem curiously ignored.) But will there ever be a time or place—ever a student, however modern, of the grand art, to whom those compositions will not afford profounder lessons than all else of their kind in the garnerage of the past? Could there be any more opportune suggestion, to the current popular writer and reader of verse, what the office of poet was in primeval times—and is yet capable of being, anew, adjusted entirely to the modern?

All the poems of Orientalism, with the Old and New Testaments at the centre, tend to deep and wide, (I don't know but the deepest and widest,) psychological development—with little, or nothing at all, of the mere æsthetic, the principal verse-requirement of our day. Very late, but unerringly, comes to every capable student the perception that it is not in beauty, it is not in art, it is not even in science, that the profoundest laws of the case have their eternal sway and outcropping.

In his discourse on "Hebrew Poets" De Sola Mendes said: "The fundamental feature of Judaism, of the Hebrew nationality, was religion; its poetry was naturally religious. Its subjects, God and Providence, the convenants with Israel, God in Nature, and as reveal'd, God the Creator and Governor, Nature in her majesty and beauty, inspired hymns and odes to Nature's God. And then the checker'd history of the nation furnish'd allusions, illustrations, and subjects for epic display—the glory of the sanctuary, the offerings, the splendid ritual, the Holy City, and lov'd Palestine with its pleasant valleys and wild tracts." Dr. Mendes said "that rhyming was not a characteristic of Hebrew poetry at all. Metre was not a necessary mark of poetry. Great poets discarded it; the early Jewish poets knew it not."

Compared with the famed epics of Greece, and lesser ones since, the spinal supports of the Bible are simple and meagre. All its history, biography, narratives, etc., are as beads, strung on and indicating the eternal thread of the Deific purpose and power. Yet with only deepest faith for impetus, and such Deific purpose for palpable or impalpable theme, it often transcends the masterpieces of Hellas, and all masterpieces. The metaphors daring beyond account, the lawless soul, extravagant by our standards, the glow of love and friendship, the fervent kiss— nothing in argument or logic, but unsurpass'd in proverbs, in religious ecstacy, in suggestions of common mortality and death, man's great equalizers—the spirit everything, the ceremonies and forms of the churches nothing, faith

15. æsthetic] *CR:* esthetic [Revised on the galley.]

19–30. Whitman's source for this quotation has not been identified. It may have been taken from a newspaper report of a lecture. Dr. Frederic de Sola Mendes was a learned rabbi of New York City who about this time undertook to found an agricultural village alliance for Jewish refugees from Russia near Vineland, N. J., about

limitless, its immense sensuousness immensely spiritual—an incredible, all-inclusive non-worldliness and dew-scented illiteracy (the antipodes of our Nineteenth Century business absorption and morbid refinement)—no hair-splitting doubts, no sickly sulking and sniffling, no "Hamlet," no "Adonais," no "Thanatopsis," no "In Memoriam."

The culminated proof of the poetry of a country is the quality of its personnel, which, in any race, can never be really superior without superior poems. The finest blending of individuality with universality (in my opinion nothing out of the galaxies of the "Iliad," or Shakspere's heroes, or from the Tennysonian "Idyls," so lofty, devoted and starlike,) typified in the songs of those old Asiatic lands. Men and women as great columnar trees. Nowhere else the abnegation of self towering in such quaint sublimity; nowhere else the simplest human emotions conquering the gods of heaven, and fate itself. (The episode, for instance, toward the close of the "Mahabharata"—the journey of the wife Savitri with the god of death, Yama,

"One terrible to see—blood-red his garb,
His body huge and dark, bloodshot his eyes,
Which flamed like suns beneath his turban cloth,
Arm'd was he with a noose,"

who carries off the soul of the dead husband, the wife tenaciously following, and—by the resistless charm of perfect poetic recitation!—eventually redeeming her captive mate.)

I remember how enthusiastically William H. Seward, in his last days, once expatiated on these themes, from his travels in Turkey, Egypt, and Asia Minor, finding the oldest Biblical narratives exactly illustrated there to-day with apparently no break or change along three thousand years—the veil'd women, the costumes, the gravity and simplicity, all the manners just the same. The veteran Trelawney said he found the only real *nobleman* of the world in a good average specimen of the mid-aged or elderly Oriental. In the East the grand figure, always leading, is the *old man*, majestic, with flowing beard, paternal, etc. In Europe and America, it is, as we know, the young fellow—in novels, a handsome and interesting hero, more or less juvenile—in operas, a tenor with blooming cheeks, black mustache, superficial animation, and perhaps good lungs, but no more depth than skim-milk. But reading folks probably get their information of those Bible areas and current peoples, as depicted in print by English and

thirty miles south of Camden.

58–61. The source of this quotation has not been identified. The verses may be Whitman's own roughened adaptation of Sir Edwin Arnold's verse rendition of "Savitri; or Love and Death," in *Indian Idylls, from the Sanscrit of the Mahabharata* (Boston, 1883), p. 34.

French cads, the most shallow, impudent, supercilious brood on earth.

I have said nothing yet of the cumulus of associations (perfectly legitimate parts of its influence, and finally in many respects the dominant parts,) of the Bible as a poetic entity, and of every portion of it. Not the old edifice only—the congeries also of events and struggles and surroundings, of which it has been the scene and motive—even the horrors, dreads, deaths. How many ages and generations have brooded and wept and agonized over this book! What untellable joys and ecstasies—what support to martyrs at the stake—from it. (No really great song can ever attain full purport till long after the death of its singer—till it has accrued and incorporated the many passions, many joys and sorrows, it has itself arous'd.) To what myriads has it been the shore and rock of safety—the refuge from driving tempest and wreck! Translated in all languages, how it has united this diverse world! Of civilized lands to-day, whose of our retrospects has it not interwoven and link'd and permeated? Not only does it bring us what is clasp'd within its covers; nay, that is the least of what it brings. Of its thousands, there is not a verse, not a word, but is thick-studded with human emotions, successions of fathers and sons, mothers and daughters, of our own antecedents, inseparable from that background of us, on which, phantasmal as it is, all that we are to-day inevitably depends—our ancestry, our past.

Strange, but true, that the principal factor in cohering the nations, eras and paradoxes of the globe, by giving them a common platform of two or three great ideas, a commonalty of origin, and projecting cosmic brotherhood, the dream of all hope, all time—that the long trains, gestations, attempts and failures, resulting in the New World, and in modern solidarity and politics—are to be identified and resolv'd back into a collection of old poetic lore, which, more than any one thing else, has been the axis of civilization and history through thousands of years—and except for which this America of ours, with its polity and essentials, could not now be existing.

No true bard will ever contravene the Bible. If the time ever comes when iconoclasm does its extremest in one direction against the Books of the Bible in its present form, the collection must still survive in another,

82. every portion of] *CR:* every book of

109. After "the Bible." *CR* continues, completing the paragraph with the following sentence, omitted in *NB* and later texts: "Coming steadily down from the past, like a ship, through all perturbations, all ebbs and flows, all time, it is to-day his art's chief reason for being."

109–118. All this paragraph, except the first sentence, is from the first paragraph of the article in the *CR* text.

110–111. against . . . the collection] *CR:* against this Book, the collection

113–114. and definite element-principle] *CR:* and definitive element-principle

and dominate just as much as hitherto, or more than hitherto, through its divine and primal poetic structure. To me, that is the living and definite element-principle of the work, evolving everything else. Then the continuity; the oldest and newest Asiatic utterance and character, and all between, holding together, like the apparition of the sky, and coming to us the same. Even to our Nineteenth Century here are the fountain heads of song.

Father Taylor (and Oratory.)

I have never heard but one essentially perfect orator—one who satisfied those depths of the emotional nature that in most cases go through life quite untouch'd, unfed—who held every hearer by spells which no conventionalist, high or low—nor any pride or composure, nor resistance of intellect—could stand against for ten minutes.

And by the way, is it not strange, of this first-class genius in the rarest and most profound of humanity's arts, that it will be necessary, (so nearly forgotten and rubb'd out is his name by the rushing whirl of the last twenty-five years,) to first inform current readers that he was an orthodox minister, of no particular celebrity, who during a long life preach'd especially to Yankee sailors in an old fourth-class church down by the wharves in Boston—had practically been a sea-faring man through his earlier years—and died April 6, 1871, "just as the tide turn'd, going out with the ebb as an old salt should"? His name is now comparatively unknown, outside of Boston—and even there, (though Dickens, Mr. Jameson, Dr. Bartol and Bishop Haven have commemorated him,) is mostly but a reminiscence.

During my visits to "the Hub," in 1859 and '60 I several times saw and heard Father Taylor. In the spring or autumn, quiet Sunday forenoons, I liked to go down early to the quaint ship-cabin-looking church where the old man minister'd—to enter and leisurely scan the building, the low ceiling, every thing strongly timber'd (polish'd and rubb'd apparently,) the dark rich colors, the gallery, all in half-light—and smell the aroma of old

118. In *CR* Whitman's name appears at the end of the essay.

Father Taylor (and Oratory.)

Printed in *NB* from the article "Father Taylor and Oratory," published in *CEN*, February, 1887 (Vol. 33, pp. 583–584), which is here collated with the later texts. The piece is not in *DVOP*.

22. half-light—and] *CEN:* half-light, and

wood—to watch the auditors, sailors, mates, "matlows," officers, singly or in groups, as they came in—their physiognomies, forms, dress, gait, as they walk'd along the aisles,—their postures, seating themselves in the rude, roomy, undoor'd, uncushion'd pews—and the evident effect upon them of the place, occasion, and atmosphere.

The pulpit, rising ten or twelve feet high, against the rear wall, was back'd by a significant mural painting, in oil—showing out its bold lines and strong hues through the subdued light of the building—of a stormy sea, the waves high-rolling, and amid them an old-style ship, all bent over, driving through the gale, and in great peril—a vivid and effectual piece of limning, not meant for the criticism of artists (though I think it had merit even from that standpoint,) but for its effect upon the congregation, and what it would convey to them.

Father Taylor was a moderate-sized man, indeed almost small, (reminded me of old Booth, the great actor, and my favorite of those and preceding days,) well advanced in years, but alert, with mild blue or gray eyes, and good presence and voice. Soon as he open'd his mouth I ceas'd to pay any attention to church or audience, or pictures or lights and shades; a far more potent charm entirely sway'd me. In the course of the sermon, (there was no sign of any MS., or reading from notes,) some of the parts would be in the highest degree majestic and picturesque. Colloquial in a severe sense, it often lean'd to Biblical and oriental forms. Especially were all allusions to ships and the ocean and sailors' lives, of unrival'd power and life-likeness. Sometimes there were passages of fine language and composition, even from the purist's point of view. A few arguments, and of the best, but always brief and simple. One realized what grip there might have been in such words-of-mouth talk as that of Socrates and Epictetus. In the main, I should say, of any of these discourses, that the old Demosthenean rule and requirement of "action, action, action," first in its inward and then (very moderate and restrain'd) its outward sense, was the quality that had leading fulfilment.

I remember I felt the deepest impression from the old man's prayers, which invariably affected me to tears. Never, on similar or any other occasions, have I heard such impassion'd pleading—such human-harassing

23. wood—to] *CEN:* wood, to
24. in—their] *CEN:* in, their
25. aisles,—their] *CEN:* aisles, their
26. pews—and] *CEN:* pews, and
48–49. This sentence is not in *CEN*. It appears in *NB* for the first time.
51–52. then (very moderate and restrain'd) its] *CEN:* then its
53. fulfilment] *CEN:* fulfillment

reproach (like Hamlet to his mother, in the closet)—such probing to the very depths of that latent conscience and remorse which probably lie somewhere in the background of every life, every soul. For when Father Taylor preach'd or pray'd, the rhetoric and art, the mere words, (which usually play such a big part) seem'd altogether to disappear, and the *live feeling* advanced upon you and seiz'd you with a power before unknown. Everybody felt this marvelous and awful influence. One young sailor, a Rhode Islander, (who came every Sunday, and I got acquainted with, and talk'd to once or twice as we went away,) told me, "that must be the Holy Ghost we read of in the Testament."

I should be at a loss to make any comparison with other preachers or public speakers. When a child I had heard Elias Hicks—and Father Taylor (though so different in personal appearance, for Elias was of tall and most shapely form, with black eyes that blazed at times like meteors,) always reminded me of him. Both had the same inner, apparently inexhaustible, fund of latent volcanic passion—the same tenderness, blended with a curious remorseless firmness, as of some surgeon operating on a belov'd patient. Hearing such men sends to the winds all the books, and formulas, and polish'd speaking, and rules of oratory.

Talking of oratory, why is it that the unsophisticated practices often strike deeper than the train'd ones? Why do our experiences perhaps of some local country exhorter—or often in the West or South at political meetings—bring the most definite results? In my time I have heard Webster, Clay, Edward Everett, Phillips, and such *célébrès;* yet I recall the minor but life-eloquence of men like John P. Hale, Cassius Clay, and one or two of the old abolition "fanatics" ahead of all those stereotyped fames. Is not—I sometimes question—the first, last, and most important quality of all, in training for a "finish'd speaker," generally unsought, unreck'd of, both by teacher and pupil? Though maybe it cannot be taught, anyhow. At any rate, we need to clearly understand the distinction between oratory and elocution. Under the latter art, including some of high order, there is indeed no scarcity in the United States, preachers, lawyers, actors, lecturers, &c. With all, there seem to be few real orators—almost none.

I repeat, and would dwell upon it (more as suggestion than mere fact)

55. on similar or any other] *CEN:* on any similar or other
68. Hicks—and] *CEN:* Hicks, and
72. of latent volcanic] *CEN:* of volcanic
79. most definite results] *CEN:* most rapid results
80. yet I recall] *CEN:* yet for effect and permanence I recall
86. to clearly understand] *CEN:* to understand
88. States, preachers] *CEN:* States,—preachers
88–89. lawyers, actors, lecturers] *CEN:* lawyers, lecturers

—among all the brilliant lights of bar or stage I have heard in my time (for years in New York and other cities I haunted the courts to witness notable trials, and have heard all the famous actors and actresses that have been in America the past fifty years) though I recall marvellous effects from one or other of them, I never had anything in the way of vocal utterance to shake me through and through, and become fix'd, with its accompaniments, in my memory, like those prayers and sermons—like Father Taylor's personal electricity and the whole scene there—the prone ship in the gale, and dashing wave and foam for background—in the little old sea-church in Boston, those summer Sundays just before the Secession War broke out.

The Spanish Element in Our Nationality.

[Our friends at Santa Fé, New Mexico, have just finish'd their long drawn out anniversary of the 333d year of the settlement of their city by the Spanish. The good, gray Walt Whitman was asked to write them a poem in commemoration. Instead he wrote them a letter as follows: —*Philadelphia Press*, August 5, 1883.]

CAMDEN, NEW JERSEY, *July* 20, 1883.

To Messrs. Griffin, Martinez, Prince, and other Gentlemen at Santa Fé:

DEAR SIRS:—Your kind invitation to visit you and deliver a poem for the 333d Anniversary of founding Santa Fé has reach'd me so late that I have to decline, with sincere regret. But I will say a few words off hand.

We Americans have yet to really learn our own antecedents, and sort them, to unify them. They will be found ampler than has been supposed, and in widely different sources. Thus far, impress'd by New England writers and schoolmasters, we tacitly abandon ourselves to the notion that our United States have been fashion'd from the British Islands only, and essentially form a second England only—which is a very great mistake.

91. time (for] *CEN:* time—for
94. years) though] *CEN:* years—though
94. marvellous] *CEN:* marvelous

The Spanish Element in Our Nationality.

First published in *PP*, Sunday, August 5, 1883, and then in *CR*, August 11, 1883. These texts are here collated with later texts. The piece is not in *DVOP*.

1–5. In lieu of this headnote and the title, *CR* has the following:
"Walt Whitman on the Santa Fé Celebration.

Many leading traits for our future national personality, and some of the best ones, will certainly prove to have originated from other than British stock. As it is, the British and German, valuable as they are in the concrete, already threaten excess. Or rather, I should say, they have certainly reach'd that excess. To-day, something outside of them, and to counterbalance them, is seriously needed.

The seething materialistic and business vortices of the United States, in their present devouring relations, controlling and belittling everything else, are, in my opinion, but a vast and indispensable stage in the new world's development, and are certainly to be follow'd by something entirely different—at least by immense modifications. Character, literature, a society worthy the name, are yet to be establish'd, through a nationality of noblest spiritual, heroic and democratic attributes—not one of which at present definitely exists—entirely different from the past, though unerringly founded on it, and to justify it.

To that composite American identity of the future, Spanish character will supply some of the most needed parts. No stock shows a grander historic retrospect—grander in religiousness and loyalty, or for patriotism, courage, decorum, gravity and honor. (It is time to dismiss utterly the illusion-compound, half raw-head-and-bloody-bones and half Mysteries-of-Udolpho, inherited from the English writers of the past 200 years. It is time to realize—for it is certainly true—that there will not be found any more cruelty, tyranny, superstition, &c., in the *résumé* of past Spanish history than in the corresponding *résumé* of Anglo-Norman history. Nay, I think there will not be found so much.)

Then another point, relating to American ethnology, past and to come, I will here touch upon at a venture. As to our aboriginal or Indian population—the Aztec in the South, and many a tribe in the North and West—I know it seems to be agreed that they must gradually dwindle as time rolls on, and in a few generations more leave only a reminiscence, a blank. But I am not at all clear about that. As America, from its many far-back sources and current supplies, develops, adapts, entwines, faithfully

Walt Whitman was invited by the Tertio-Millennial Anniversary Association of Santa Fé, New Mexico, to read a poem at the recent memorial celebration in that ancient town. His reply is given below. The memorial exercises, it may be said incidentally, are soon to be repeated."

In *PP* the headnote is identical with that of *NB* except that it omits "New Mexico" in line 1 and adds before the colon in line 4: "—which is now printed for the first time".

6–8. This date line and salutation are omitted in *CR*.

9. *CR* begins a new paragraph with "Your kind".

40, 41. *résumé*] *CR:* résumé] *PP:* resume

49. sources and current supplies, develops] *CR:* sources and currents, supplies, develops

identifies its own—are we to see it cheerfully accepting and using all the contributions of foreign lands from the whole outside globe—and then rejecting the only ones distinctively its own—the autochthonic ones?

As to the Spanish stock of our Southwest, it is certain to me that we do not begin to appreciate the splendor and sterling value of its race element. Who knows but that element, like the course of some subterranean river, dipping invisibly for a hundred or two years, is now to emerge in broadest flow and permanent action?

If I might assume to do so, I would like to send you the most cordial, heartfelt congratulations of your American fellow-countrymen here. You have more friends in the Northern and Atlantic regions than you suppose, and they are deeply interested in the development of the great Southwestern interior, and in what your festival would arouse to public attention.

Very respectfully, &c.,

WALT WHITMAN.

What Lurks behind Shakspere's Historical Plays?

We all know how much *mythus* there is in the Shakspere question as it stands to-day. Beneath a few foundations of proved facts are certainly engulf'd far more dim and elusive ones, of deepest importance—tantalizing and half suspected—suggesting explanations that one dare not put in plain statement. But coming at once to the point, the English historical plays are to me not only the most eminent as dramatic performances (my maturest judgment confirming the impressions of my early years, that the distinctiveness and glory of the Poet reside not in his vaunted dramas of the passions, but those founded on the contests of English dynasties, and the French wars,) but form, as we get it all, the chief in a complexity of puzzles. Conceiv'd out of the fullest heat and pulse of European feudalism—personifying in unparallel'd ways the mediæval aristocracy, its towering spirit of ruthless and gigantic caste, with its own peculiar air and arrogance (no mere imitation)—only one of the "wolfish earls" so plenteous in the plays themselves, or some born descendant and knower, might seem to be the true author of those amazing works—works in some respect greater than anything else in recorded literature.

What Lurks behind Shakspere's Historical Plays?

First published in *CR*, September 27, 1884. In the title, *CR* has the spelling "Shakspeare's." Reprinted in *DVOP* from *CR*.

14. arrogance (no mere imitation)—] *CR:* arrogance, no mere imitation—

The start and germ-stock of the pieces on which the present speculation is founded are undoubtedly (with, at the outset, no small amount of bungling work) in "Henry VI." It is plain to me that as profound and forecasting a brain and pen as ever appear'd in literature, after floundering somewhat in the first part of that trilogy—or perhaps draughting it more or less experimentally or by accident—afterward developed and defined his plan in the Second and Third Parts, and from time to time, thenceforward, systematically enlarged it to majestic and mature proportions in "Richard II," "Richard III," "King John," "Henry IV," "Henry V," and even in "Macbeth," "Coriolanus" and "Lear." For it is impossible to grasp the whole cluster of those plays, however wide the intervals and different circumstances of their composition, without thinking of them as, in a free sense, the result of an *essentially controling plan.* What was that plan? Or, rather, what was veil'd behind it?—for to me there was certainly something so veil'd. Even the episodes of Cade, Joan of Arc, and the like (which sometimes seem to me like interpolations allow'd,) may be meant to foil the possible sleuth, and throw any too 'cute pursuer off the scent. In the whole matter I should specially dwell on, and make much of, that inexplicable element of every highest poetic nature which causes it to cover up and involve its real purpose and meanings in folded removes and far recesses. Of this trait—hiding the nest where common seekers may never find it—the Shaksperean works afford the most numerous and mark'd illustrations known to me. I would even call that trait the leading one through the whole of those works.

All the foregoing to premise a brief statement of how and where I get my new light on Shakspere. Speaking of the special English plays, my friend William O'Connor says:

> They seem simply and rudely historical in their motive, as aiming to give in the rough a tableau of warring dynasties,—and carry to me a lurking sense of being in aid of some ulterior design, probably well enough understood in that age, which perhaps time and criticism will reveal. . . . . Their atmosphere is one of barbarous and tumultuous gloom,—they do not make us love the times they limn, ... and it is impossible to believe that the greatest of the Elizabethan men could have sought to indoctrinate the age with the love of feudalism which his own drama in its entirety, if the view taken of it herein be true, certainly and subtly saps and mines.

27. "Macbeth," "Coriolanus" and "Lear."] *DVOP* and *CR:* 'Macbeth' and 'Lear.'
30. *controling*] *DVOP* and *CR: controlling*
39 and 66. Shaksperean] *DVOP:* Shaksperian] *CR:* Shakspearean
43. Shakspere] *CR:* Shakspeare

Reading the just-specified plays in the light of Mr. O'Connor's suggestion, I defy any one to escape such new and deep utterance-meanings, like magic ink, warm'd by the fire, and previously invisible. Will it not indeed be strange if the author of "Othello" and "Hamlet" is destin'd to live in America, in a generation or two, less as the cunning draughtsman of the passions, and more as putting on record the first full exposé—and by far the most vivid one, immeasurably ahead of doctrinaires and economists—of the political theory and results, or the reason-why and necessity for them which America has come on earth to abnegate and replace?

The summary of my suggestion would be, therefore, that while the more the rich and tangled jungle of the Shaksperean area is travers'd and studied, and the more baffled and mix'd, as so far appears, becomes the exploring student (who at last surmises everything, and remains certain of nothing,) it is possible a future age of criticism, diving deeper, mapping the land and lines freer, completer than hitherto, may discover in the plays named the scientific (Baconian?) inauguration of modern Democracy—furnishing realistic and first-class artistic portraitures of the mediæval world, the feudal personalities, institutes, in their morbid accumulations, deposits, upon politics and sociology,—may penetrate to that hard-pan, far down and back of the ostent of to-day, on which (and on which only) the progressism of the last two centuries has built this Democracy which now holds secure lodgment over the whole civilized world.

Whether such was the unconscious, or (as I think likely) the more or less conscious, purpose of him who fashion'd those marvellous architectonics, is a secondary question.

A Thought on Shakspere.

The most distinctive poems—the most permanently rooted and with heartiest reason for being—the copious cycle of Arthurian legends, or the almost equally copious Charlemagne cycle, or the poems of the Cid, or

55. plays] CPW, CPP, and NB: play] DVOP and CR: plays] [Since the reference is definitely to "English plays" in line 43, the reading of CPW, CPP, and NB must be an error; the correct reading is here restored.—ED.]

62–63. results, or the reason-why and necessity for them which] DVOP and CR: results which

A Thought on Shakspere.

First published in CR, August 14, 1886; reprinted in DVOP from CR. All

Scandinavian Eddas, or Nibelungen, or Chaucer, or Spenser, or *bona fide* Ossian, or Inferno—probably had their rise in the great historic perturbations, which they came in to sum up and confirm, indirectly embodying results to date. Then however precious to "culture," the grandest of those poems, it may be said, preserve and typify results offensive to the modern spirit, and long past away. To state it briefly, and taking the strongest examples, in Homer lives the ruthless military prowess of Greece, and of its special god-descended dynastic houses; in Shakspere the dragon-rancors and stormy feudal splendor of mediæval caste.

Poetry, largely consider'd, is an evolution, sending out improved and ever-expanded types—in one sense, the past, even the best of it, necessarily giving place, and dying out. For our existing world, the bases on which all the grand old poems were built have become vacuums—and even those of many comparatively modern ones are broken and half-gone. For us to-day, not their own intrinsic value, vast as that is, backs and maintains those poems—but a mountain-high growth of associations, the layers of successive ages. Everywhere—their own lands included—(is there not something terrible in the tenacity with which the one book out of millions holds its grip?)—the Homeric and Virgilian works, the interminable ballad-romances of the middle ages, the utterances of Dante, Spenser, and others, are upheld by their cumulus-entrenchment in scholarship, and as precious, always welcome, unspeakably valuable reminiscences.

Even the one who at present reigns unquestion'd—of Shakspere—for all he stands for so much in modern literature, he stands entirely for the mighty æsthetic sceptres of the past, not for the spiritual and democratic, the sceptres of the future. The inward and outward characteristics of Shakspere are his vast and rich variety of persons and themes, with his wondrous delineation of each and all—not only limitless funds of verbal and pictorial resource, but great excess, superfœtation—mannerism, like a fine, aristocratic perfume, holding a touch of musk (Euphues, his mark)—with boundless sumptuousness and adornment, real velvet and gems, not shoddy nor paste—but a good deal of bombast and fustian—(certainly some terrific mouthing in Shakspere!)

printed texts and also the available portion of the galley proof are collated.

4. Nibelungen] DVOP and CR: Niebelungen] [Revised on the galley proof.]

4–5. or *bona fide* Ossian] DVOP and CR: or Ossian

5. in the great] DVOP and CR: in great

7. date. Then however] DVOP and CR: date. However

11–12. houses; in . . . caste.] DVOP and CR: houses;—in Shakspere, [CR: Shakspeare,] the 'dragon-rancors and stormy feudal splendor of mediaeval caste.' [Throughout the essay CR uses the spelling "Shakspeare."—ED.]

Superb and inimitable as all is, it is mostly an objective and physiological kind of power and beauty the soul finds in Shakspere—a style supremely grand of the sort, but in my opinion stopping short of the grandest sort, at any rate for fulfilling and satisfying modern and scientific and democratic American purposes. Think, not of growths as forests primeval, or Yellowstone geysers, or Colorado ravines, but of costly marble palaces, and palace rooms, and the noblest fixings and furniture, and noble owners and occupants to correspond—think of carefully built gardens from the beautiful but sophisticated gardening art at its best, with walks and bowers and artificial lakes, and appropriate statue-groups and the finest cultivated roses and lilies and japonicas in plenty—and you have the tally of Shakspere. The low characters, mechanics, even the loyal henchmen—all in themselves nothing—serve as capital foils to the aristocracy. The comedies (exquisite as they certainly are) bringing in admirably portray'd common characters, have the unmistakable hue of plays, portraits, made for the divertisement only of the élite of the castle, and from its point of view. The comedies are altogether non-acceptable to America and Democracy.

But to the deepest soul, it seems a shame to pick and choose from the riches Shakspere has left us—to criticise his infinitely royal, multiform quality—to gauge, with optic glasses, the dazzle of his sun-like beams.

The best poetic utterance, after all, can merely hint, or remind, often very indirectly, or at distant removes. Aught of real perfection, or the solution of any deep problem, or any completed statement of the moral, the true, the beautiful, eludes the greatest, deftest poet—flies away like an always uncaught bird.

Robert Burns As Poet and Person.

What the future will decide about Robert Burns and his works—what place will be assign'd them on that great roster of geniuses and genius which can only be finish'd by the slow but sure balancing of the

43. or Yellowstone geysers] *DVOP* and *CR:* or Yosemite geysers
48. finest cultivated roses] *DVOP* and *CR:* finest roses
50–51. serve as capital] *CR:* serve us capital
63. After this line, ending the article, *CR* has Whitman's name.

Robert Burns As Poet and Person.

The earliest version of this essay was published with the title "Robert Burns" in *CR*, December 16, 1882. In a revised and expanded version, it was published with

centuries with their ample average—I of course cannot tell. But as we know him, from his recorded utterances, and after nearly one century, and its diligence of collections, songs, letters, anecdotes, presenting the figure of the canny Scotchman in a fullness and detail wonderfully complete, and the lines mainly by his own hand, he forms to-day, in some respects, the most interesting personality among singers. Then there are many things in Burns's poems and character that specially endear him to America. He was essentially a Republican—would have been at home in the Western United States, and probably become eminent there. He was an average sample of the good-natured, warm-blooded, proud-spirited, amative, alimentive, convivial, young and early-middle-aged man of the decent-born middle classes everywhere and any how. Without the race of which he is a distinct specimen, (and perhaps his poems) America and her powerful Democracy could not exist to-day—could not project with unparallel'd historic sway into the future.

Perhaps the peculiar coloring of the era of Burns needs always first to be consider'd. It included the times of the '76–'83 Revolution in America, of the French Revolution, and an unparallel'd chaos development in Europe and elsewhere. In every department, shining and strange names, like stars, some rising, some in meridian, some declining—Voltaire, Franklin, Washington, Kant, Goethe, Fulton, Napoleon, mark the era. And while so much, and of grandest moment, fit for the trumpet of the world's fame, was being transacted—that little tragi-comedy of R. B.'s life and death was going on in a country by-place in Scotland!

Burns's correspondence, generally collected and publish'd since his death, gives wonderful glints into both the amiable and weak (and worse than weak) parts of his portraiture, habits, good and bad luck, ambition and associations. His letters to Mrs. Dunlop, Mrs. McLehose, (Clarinda,) Mr. Thompson, Dr. Moore, Robert Muir, Mr. Cunningham, Miss Margaret Chalmers, Peter Hill, Richard Brown, Mrs. Riddel, Robert Ainslie, and Robert Graham, afford valuable lights and shades to the outline, and with numerous others, help to a touch here, and fill-in there, of poet and poems. There are suspicions, it is true, of "the Genteel Letter-

its present title in *DVOP*, and again with a few revisions in *NAR* in November, 1886 (Vol. 143, pp. 427–435). All these texts are collated. The proofs have only a few marks for the correction of typographical errors.

1–51. These three paragraphs appeared for the first time in *DVOP*.

6. collections, songs] *NAR* and *DVOP:* collections, personal songs.

19. Burns needs] *NAR* and *DVOP:* Burns, in the world's history, biography and civilization, needs

21–22. chaos development] *NAR* and *DVOP:* chaos-development

25. of grandest moment] *NAR* and *DVOP:* of moment

32. Mr. Thompson] *DVOP:* Mr. Thomson

Writer," with scraps and words from "the Manual of French Quotations," and, in the love-letters, some hollow mouthings. Yet we wouldn't on any account lack the letters. A full and true portrait is always what is wanted; veracity at every hazard. Besides, do we not all see by this time that the story of Burns, even for its own sake, requires the record of the whole and several, with nothing left out? Completely and every point minutely told out its fullest, explains and justifies itself—(as perhaps almost any life does.) He is very close to the earth. He pick'd up his best words and tunes directly from the Scotch home-singers, but tells Thompson they would not please his, T's, "learn'd lugs," adding, "I call them simple—you would pronounce them silly." Yes, indeed; the idiom was undoubtedly his happiest hit. Yet Dr. Moore, in 1789, writes to Burns, "If I were to offer an opinion, it would be that in your future productions you should abandon the Scotch stanza and dialect, and adopt the measure and language of modern English poetry"!

As the 128th birth-anniversary of the poet draws on, (January, 1887,) with its increasing club-suppers, vehement celebrations, letters, speeches, and so on—(mostly, as William O'Connor says, from people who would not have noticed R. B. at all during his actual life, nor kept his company, or read his verses, on any account)—it may be opportune to print some leisurely-jotted notes I find in my budget. I take my observation of the Scottish bard by considering him as an individual amid the crowded clusters, galaxies, of the old world—and fairly inquiring and suggesting what out of these myriads he too may be to the Western Republic. In the first place no poet on record so fully bequeaths his own personal magnetism,* nor illustrates more pointedly how one's verses, by time and reading,

* Probably no man that ever lived—a friend has made the statement—was so fondly loved, both by men and women, as Robert Burns. The reason is not hard to find: he had a real heart of flesh and blood beating in his bosom;

1n–15n. The source of this footnote has not been identified.

40. do we not] *NAR* and *DVOP:* do not we

42–43. Completely . . . explains] *NAR* and *DVOP:* Completely and minutely told, it fullest explains

45–46. Thompson] *DVOP:* Thomson

46. his, T's,] *NAR* and *DVOP:* his, (T.'s),

47. silly." Yes, indeed; the idiom] *NAR* and *DVOP:* silly." As before said, the Scotch idiom

48–51. In *NAR* and *DVOP* this sentence is enclosed in parentheses.

52–53. As the 128th . . . its increasing] *CR:* As the 124th birth-anniversary of Burns draws pretty close (January, 1883) with its ever-increasing

56. account)—it] *CR:* account) it

56–57. some . . . find] *CR:* some jottings I find

58. bard by] *CR:* bard not so much from the zealous points of view of his clannish and foreign race (for to America, he and all of them, are they not foreigners and

can so curiously fuse with the versifier's own life and death, and give final light and shade to all.

I would say a large part of the fascination of Burns's homely, simple dialect-melodies is due, for all current and future readers, to the poet's personal "errors," the general bleakness of his lot, his ingrain'd pensiveness, his brief dash into dazzling, tantalizing, evanescent sunshine—finally culminating in those last years of his life, his being taboo'd and in debt, sick and sore, yaw'd as by contending gales, deeply dissatisfied with everything, most of all with himself—high-spirited too—(no man ever really higher-spirited than Robert Burns.) I think it a perfectly legitimate part too. At any rate it has come to be an impalpable aroma through which only both the songs and their singer must henceforth be read and absorb'd. Through that view-medium of misfortune—of a noble spirit in low environments, and of a squalid and premature death—we view the undoubted facts, (giving, as we read them now, a sad kind of pungency,) that Burns's were, before all else, the lyrics of illicit loves and carousing intoxication. Perhaps even it is this strange, impalpable *post-mortem* comment and influence referr'd to, that gives them their contrast, attraction, making the zest of their author's after fame. If he had lived steady, fat, moral, comfortable, well-to-do years, on his own grade, (let alone, what of course was out of the question, the ease and velvet and rosewood and copious royalties of Tennyson or Victor Hugo or Longfellow,) and died well-ripen'd and respectable, where could have come in that burst of passionate sobbing and remorse which well'd forth instantly and generally in Scotland, and soon follow'd everywhere among English-speaking races, on the announcement of his death? and which,

you could almost hear it throb. "Some one said, that if you had shaken hands with him his hand would have burnt yours. The gods, indeed, made him poetical, but Nature had a hand in him first. His heart was in the right place;

clannish enough?) but by

60. of these . . . be to] *NAR*, *DVOP*, and *CR:* of those myriads he too may be to us, to

60–61. In the first place no poet] *CR:* No poet

63–64. give final light] *NAR* and *DVOP:* give light] *CR:* give immortal light

65. I would say] *CR:* I say

66–67. to the poet's personal "errors,"] *CR:* to that reminiscence of the personnel of the poet—his "errors,"

68–69. sunshine—finally] *NAR:* sunshine; finally

69. in those last years of] *CR:* in the last year or two of

74–75. be read and absorb'd. Through] *NAR* and *DVOP:* be received. Through] *CR:* be received. If he had lived] [*CR* begins a new paragraph with "If he had lived".]

75–81. These two sentences, beginning "Through" and ending "fame." before the sentence beginning "If he had lived" are not in *CR*.

81. attraction, making the zest] *NAR* and *DVOP:* attraction, the zest

88. death? and] *NAR* and *DVOP:* death, and

with no sign of stopping, only regulated and vein'd with fitting appreciation, flows deeply, widely yet?

Dear Rob! manly, witty, fond, friendly, full of weak spots as well as strong ones—essential type of so many thousands—perhaps the average, as just said, of the decent-born young men and the early mid-aged, not only of the British Isles, but America, too, North and South, just the same. I think, indeed, one best part of Burns is the unquestionable proof he presents of the perennial existence among the laboring classes, especially farmers, of the finest latent poetic elements in their blood. (How clear it is to me that the common soil has always been, and is now, thickly strewn with just such gems.) He is well-called the *Ploughman.* "Holding the plough," said his brother Gilbert, "was the favorite situation with Robert for poetic compositions; and some of his best verses were produced while he was at that exercise." "I must return to my humble station, and woo my rustic muse in my wonted way, at the plough-tail." 1787, to the Earl of Buchan. He has no high ideal of the poet or the poet's office; indeed quite a low and contracted notion of both:

"Fortune! if thou'll but gie me still
Hale breeks, a scone, and whiskey gill,
An' rowth o' rhyme to rave at will,
Tak' a' the rest."

See also his rhym'd letters to Robert Graham invoking patronage; "one stronghold," Lord Glencairn, being dead, now these appeals to

he did not pile up cantos of poetic diction; he pluck'd the mountain daisy under his feet; he wrote of field-mouse hurrying from its ruin'd dwelling. He held the plough or the pen with the same firm, manly grasp. And he was loved. The simple roll of the women who gave him their affection and their sympathy would make a long manuscript; and most of these were of such noble worth that, as Robert Chambers says, 'their character may stand as a testimony in favor of that of Burns.' " [As I understand, the foregoing is from an extremely rare book publish'd my M'Kie, in Kilmarnock. I find the whole beautiful paragraph in a capital paper on Burns, by Amelia Barr.]

9*n*–13*n*. *NAR*, *DVOP*, and *CR* have double quotation marks after "grasp." and

92. average, as just said, of] *CR:* average of
95. same. I think, indeed, one] *CR:* same. Indeed one
97. finest latent] *CR:* finest and noblest latent
98. the common soil] *CR:* the average soil
99. the *Ploughman*] *NAR*, *DVOP*, and *CR: the Ploughman*
101. compositions; and] *NAR*, *DVOP*, and *CR:* compositions, and
103. plough-tail." 1787,] *NAR*, *DVOP*, and *CR:* plough-tail."—1787,
104–127. These lines, beginning "He has", are not in *CR*.

"Fintra, my other stay," (with in one letter a copious shower of vituperation generally.) In his collected poems there is no particular unity, nothing that can be called a leading theory, no unmistakable spine or skeleton. Perhaps, indeed, their very desultoriness is the charm of his songs: "I take up one or another," he says in a letter to Thompson, "just as the bee of the moment buzzes in my bonnet-lug."

Consonantly with the customs of the time—yet markedly inconsistent in spirit with Burns's own case, (and not a little painful as it remains on record, as depicting some features of the bard himself,) the relation called *patronage* existed between the nobility and gentry on one side, and literary people on the other, and gives one of the strongest side-lights to the general coloring of poems and poets. It crops out a good deal in Burns's Letters, and even necessitated a certain flunkeyism on occasions, through life. It probably, with its requirements, (while it help'd in money and countenance) did as much as any one cause in making that life a chafed and unhappy one, ended by a premature and miserable death.

Yes, there is something about Burns peculiarly acceptable to the concrete, human points of view. He poetizes work-a-day agricultural labor and life, (whose spirit and sympathies, as well as practicalities, are much the same everywhere,) and treats fresh, often coarse, natural occurrences, loves, persons, not like many new and some old poets in a genteel style of gilt and china, or at second or third removes, but in their own born atmosphere, laughter, sweat, unction. Perhaps no one ever sang "lads and lasses"—that universal race, mainly the same, too, all ages, all lands —down on their own plane, as he has. He exhibits no philosophy worth mentioning; his morality is hardly more than parrot-talk—not bad or deficient, but cheap, shopworn, the platitudes of old aunts and uncles to the youngsters (be good boys and keep your noses clean.) Only when he gets at Poosie Nansie's, celebrating the "barley bree," or among tramps, or democratic bouts and drinking generally,

("Freedom and whiskey gang thegither,")

double quotation marks around the quotation from Robert Chambers. This was obviously an error, corrected in *NB*.

107. scone, and whiskey] *NAR* and *DVOP:* scone, an' whiskey
115. is the charm] *NAR* and *DVOP:* is one charm
116. Thompson] *DVOP:* Thomson
123. poets.] *NAR* and *DVOP:* poet.
128. Yes, there is] *CR:* Indeed there is
129. poetizes work-a-day agricultural] *CR:* poetizes decent average agricultural
136. has. He] *DVOP:* has. The surge and swell of animal appetites, the masculinity over all, is in his utterances from first to last. He

we have, in his own unmistakable color and warmth, those interiors of rake-helly life and tavern fun—the cantabile of jolly beggars in highest jinks—lights and groupings of rank glee and brawny amorousness, outvying the best painted pictures of the Dutch school, or any school.

By America and her democracy such a poet, I cannot too often repeat, must be kept in loving remembrance; but it is best that discriminations be made. His admirers (as at those anniversary suppers, over the "hot Scotch") will not accept for their favorite anything less than the highest rank, alongside of Homer, Shakspere, etc. Such, in candor, are not the true friends of the Ayrshire bard, who really needs a different place quite by himself. The Iliad and the Odyssey express courage, craft, full-grown heroism in situations of danger, the sense of command and leadership, emulation, the last and fullest evolution of self-poise as in kings, and god-like even while animal appetites. The Shaksperean compositions, on vertebers and framework of the primary passions, portray (essentially the same as Homer's,) the spirit and letter of the feudal world, the Norman lord, ambitious and arrogant, taller and nobler than common men—with much underplay and gusts of heat and cold, volcanoes and stormy seas. Burns (and some will say to his credit) attempts none of these themes. He poetizes the humor, riotous blood, sulks, amorous torments, fondness for the tavern and for cheap objective nature, with disgust at the grim and narrow ecclesiasticism of his time and land, of a young farmer on a bleak and hired farm in Scotland, through the years and under the circumstances of the British politics of that time, and of his short personal career as author, from 1783 to 1796. He is intuitive and affectionate, and just emerged or emerging from the shackles of the kirk, from poverty, ignorance, and from his own rank appetites—(out of which latter, however, he never extricated himself.) It is to be said that amid not a little smoke and gas in his poems, there is in almost every piece a spark of fire,

144. beggars in] *CR:* beggars carousing in

146. After "any school." *CR* has the following sentence (not in later texts) to end the paragraph: "(His many sentimental songs of love-sickness doubtless express, after a sort, the temporary disease of young farmers and mechanics in that condition—but, without getting on stilts, either aesthetic or moral, I doubt if they are poetry in any high sense.)"

147. poet, . . . repeat,] *CR:* poet, I repeat,

155–156. emulation, . . . god-like] *CR:* emulation, and god-like

156. Shaksperean] *NAR* and *DVOP:* Shaksperian] *CR:* Shakspearian

157–158. portray . . . spirit] *DVOP:* portray, (essentially the same as Homer's, and with that certain heroic ecstasy, which, or the suggestion of which, is never absent in the works of the masters—I find it plainly in Walter Scott and Tennyson), the spirit] *CR:* portray the spirit

167. 1783] *CR:* 1785

169. own rank appetites] *NAR*, *DVOP*, and *CR:* own low appetites

and now and then the real afflatus. He has been applauded as democratic, and with some warrant; while Shakspere, and with the greatest warrant, has been called monarchical or aristocratic (which he certainly is.) But the splendid personalizations of Shakspere, formulated on the largest, freest, most heroic, most artistic mould, are to me far dearer as lessons, and more precious even as models for Democracy, than the humdrum samples Burns presents. The motives of some of his effusions are certainly discreditable personally—one or two of them markedly so. He has, moreover, little or no spirituality. This last is his mortal flaw and defect, tried by highest standards. The ideal he never reach'd (and yet I think he leads the way to it.) He gives melodies, and now and then the simplest and sweetest ones; but harmonies, complications, oratorios in words, never. (I do not speak this in any deprecatory sense. Blessed be the memory of the warm-hearted Scotchman for what he has left us, just as it is!) He likewise did not know himself, in more ways than one. Though so really free and independent, he prided himself in his songs on being a reactionist and a Jacobite—on persistent sentimental adherency to the cause of the Stuarts—the weakest, thinnest, most faithless, brainless dynasty that ever held a throne.

Thus, while Burns is not at all great for New World study, in the sense that Isaiah and Eschylus and the book of Job are unquestionably great—is not to be mention'd with Shakspere—hardly even with current Tennyson or our Emerson—he has a nestling niche of his own, all fragrant, fond, and quaint and homely—a lodge built near but outside the mighty temple of the gods of song and art—those universal strivers, through their works of harmony and melody and power, to ever show or intimate man's crowning, last, victorious fusion in himself of Real and Ideal. Precious, too—fit and precious beyond all singers, high or low—will Burns ever be to the native Scotch, especially to the working-classes

169–170. The marks of parenthesis are omitted in *CR*.
171. in almost every] *CR:* in every
178–179. This sentence, beginning "The motives", does not appear in *CR*.
180. This last is] *CR:* This is
185. the warm-hearted] *CR:* the manly and warm-hearted
188. *CR* has a period after "Jacobite" and omits the remainder of the sentence.
189. cause] *NAR* and *DVOP:* "cause"
191. not at . . . study, in] *CR:* not only not great (for New World study, like all the rest of them), in
192. Eschylus] *NAR*, *DVOP*, and *CR:* Æschylus
193–194. with current Tennyson or our Emerson] *CR:* with our current Tennyson or Emerson
198–199. Ideal. Precious too—fit] *CR:* Ideal. Finally, and most precious, however—fit [*CR* begins a new paragraph with "Finally".]
200. to the] *CR:* to all the

of North Britain; so intensely one of them, and so racy of the soil, sights, and local customs. He often apostrophizes Scotland, and is, or would be, enthusiastically patriotic. His country has lately commemorated him in a statue.* His aim is declaredly to be 'a Rustic Bard.' His poems were all written in youth or young manhood, (he was little more than a young man when he died.) His collected works in giving everything, are nearly one half first drafts. His brightest hit is his use of the Scotch patois, so full of terms flavor'd like wild fruits or berries. Then I should make an allowance to Burns which cannot be made for any other poet. Curiously even the frequent crudeness, haste, deficiencies, (flatness and puerilities by no means absent) prove upon the whole not out of keeping in any comprehensive collection of his works, heroically printed, 'following copy,' every piece, every line according to originals. Other poets might tremble for such boldness, such rawness. In 'this odd-kind chiel' such points hardly mar the rest. Not only are they in consonance with the underlying spirit of the pieces, but complete the full abandon and veracity of the farm-fields and the home-brew'd flavor of the Scotch vernacular. (Is there not often something in the very neglect, unfinish, careless nudity, slovenly hiatus, coming from intrinsic genius, and not 'put on,' that secretly pleases the soul more than the wrought and re-wrought polish of the most perfect verse?) Mark the native spice and untranslatable twang in the very names of his songs—"O for ane and twenty, Tam," "John Barleycorn," "Last May a braw Wooer," "Rattlin roarin Willie," "O wert thou in the cauld, cauld blast," "Gude e'en to you, Kimmer," "Merry hae I been teething a Heckle," "O lay thy loof in mine, lass," and others.

The longer and more elaborated poems of Burns are just such as would please a natural but homely taste, and cute but average intellect, and are inimitable in their way. The "Twa Dogs," (one of the best) with

* The Dumfries statue of Robert Burns was successfully unveil'd April 1881 by Lord Roseberry, the occasion having been made national in its character. Before the ceremony, a large procession paraded the streets of the town, all the trades and societies of that part of Scotland being represented, at the head of which went dairymen and ploughmen, the former driving their carts and being accompanied by their maids. The statue is of Sicilian marble. It

16*n*–17*n*. unveil'd April 1881 by] *CR:* unveiled last April by

201. soil, sights] *CR:* soil, history, sights
203–204. has lately commemorated him in a statue.*] *CR:* has commemorated him in bronze.*
204. His aim is] *CR:* His aim or ideal is
207. half first] *CR:* half crudities and first
208. wild fruits or] *NAR*, *DVOP*, and *CR:* wild fruit or
208–238. These lines, beginning "Then I" and ending "and raciness." do not ap-

the conversation between Cesar and Luath, the "Brigs of Ayr," "the Cotter's Saturday Night," "Tam O'Shanter"—all will be long read and re-read and admired, and ever deserve to be. With nothing profound in any of them, what there is of moral and plot has an inimitably fresh and racy flavor. If it came to question, Literature could well afford to send adrift many a pretensive poem, and even book of poems, before it could spare these compositions.

Never indeed was there truer utterance in a certain range of idiosyncracy than by this poet. Hardly a piece of his, large or small, but has "snap" and raciness. He puts in cantering rhyme (often doggerel) much cutting irony and idiomatic ear-cuffing of the kirk-deacons—drily good-natured addresses to his cronies, (he certainly would not stop us if he were here this moment, from classing that "to the De'il" among them)—"to Mailie and her Lambs," "to auld Mare Maggie," "to a Mouse,"

"Wee, sleekit, cowrin, tim'rous beastie:"

"to a Mountain Daisy," "to a Haggis," "to a Louse," "to the Toothache," etc.—and occasionally to his brother bards and lady or gentleman patrons, often with strokes of tenderest sensibility, idiopathic humor, and genuine poetic imagination—still oftener with shrewd, original, sheeny, steel-flashes of wit, home-spun sense, or lance-blade puncturing. Then, strangely, the basis of Burns's character, with all its fun and manliness, was hypochondria, the blues, palpable enough in "Despondency," "Man was made to Mourn," "Address to Ruin," a "Bard's Epitaph," &c. From such deep-down elements sprout up, in very contrast and paradox, those riant utterances of which a superficial reading will not detect the hidden foundation. Yet nothing is clearer to me than the black and desperate background behind those pieces—as I shall now specify them.

rests on a pedestal of gray stone five feet high. The poet is represented as sitting easily on an old tree root, holding in his left hand a cluster of daisies. His face is turn'd toward the right shoulder, and the eyes gaze into the distance. Near by lie a collie dog, a broad bonnet half covering a well-thumb'd song-book, and a rustic flageolet. The costume is taken from the Nasmyth portrait, which has been follow'd for the features of the face.

17*n*. Roseberry] *NAR* and *DVOP:* Rosebery
19*n*. represented, at] *NAR*, *DVOP*, and *CR:* represented, and at

pear in *CR*.
214. 'this odd-kind chiel'] *NAR* and *DVOP:* 'This odd kind chiel'
229. Cesar] *DVOP:* Cæsar
248–249. puncturing. Then, . . . Burns's character] *CR:* puncturing. The basis of his character
253. riant] *NAR:* *riant*
255–256. them. I find] *CR:* them, for conclusion. To tell, or repeat, the last truth

I find his most characteristic, Nature's masterly touch and luxuriant life-blood, color and heat, not in "Tam O'Shanter," "the Cotter's Saturday Night," "Scots wha hae," "Highland Mary," "the Twa Dogs," and the like, but in "the Jolly Beggars," "Rigs of Barley," "Scotch Drink," "the Epistle to John Rankine," "Holy Willie's Prayer," and in "Halloween," (to say nothing of a certain cluster, known still to a small inner circle in Scotland, but, for good reasons, not published anywhere.) In these compositions, especially the first, there is much indelicacy (some editions flatly leave it out,) but the composer reigns alone, with handling free and broad and true, and is an artist. You may see and feel the man indirectly in his other verses, all of them, with more or less life-likeness—but these I have named last call out pronouncedly in his own voice,

"I, Rob, am here."

Finally, in any summing-up of Burns, though so much is to be said in the way of fault-finding, drawing black marks, and doubtless severe literary criticism—(in the present outpouring I have 'kept myself in,' rather than allow'd any free flow)—after full retrospect of his works and life, the aforesaid 'odd-kind chiel' remains to my heart and brain as almost the tenderest, manliest, and (even if contradictory) dearest flesh-and-blood figure in all the streams and clusters of by-gone poets.

A Word about Tennyson.

Beautiful as the song was, the original 'Locksley Hall' of half a century ago was essentially morbid, heart-broken, finding fault with

concerning this poet's work, I find [*CR* begins a new paragraph with the sentence beginning "To tell".]

256–257. luxuriant life-blood,] *CR:* luxuriant life, blood,

258. "Scots wha hae,"] *CPW*, *NB*, *NAR* and *CR:* "Scots who hae,"] *DVOP:* "Scots wha hae," [Apparently a typographical error; here corrected.—ED.]

258. "Highland Mary," "the Twa Dogs,"] *NAR* and *DVOP:* "Highland Mary," "the Twa' Dogs,"] *CR:* "Highland Mary," or "The Twa' Dogs,"

259–262. "Scotch Drink," . . . anywhere.) In] *NAR* and *DVOP:* "Scotch Drink," "the Epistle to John Rankine," "Holy Willie's Prayer," and in "Halloween," &c. In] *CR:* "Scotch Drink," "Halloween," etc. In

269–275. These lines do not appear in *CR*. Whitman's name appears just after the quotation "I, Rob, am here."

273. the aforesaid 'odd-kind chiel'] *NAR:* the 'odd kind chiel'] *DVOP:* the 'odd-kind chiel'

274. manliest, and (even] *NAR* and *DVOP:* manliest, (even

275. After this line *NAR* has Whitman's name.

A Word about Tennyson.

First published in *CR*, January 1, 1887; reprinted in *DVOP* from *CR*, and in

everything, especially the fact of money's being made (as it ever must be, and perhaps should be) the paramount matter in worldly affairs;

> Every door is barr'd with gold, and opens but to golden keys.

First, a father, having fallen in battle, his child (the singer)

> Was left a trampled orphan, and a selfish uncle's ward.

Of course love ensues. The woman in the chant or monologue proves a false one; and as far as appears the ideal of woman, in the poet's reflections, is a false one—at any rate for America. Woman is *not* 'the lesser man.' (The heart is not the brain.) The best of the piece of fifty years since is its concluding line:

> For the mighty wind arises roaring seaward and I go.

Then for this current 1886–7, a just-out sequel, which (as an apparently authentic summary says) 'reviews the life of mankind during the past sixty years, and comes to the conclusion that its boasted progress is of doubtful credit to the world in general and to England in particular. A cynical vein of denunciation of democratic opinions and aspirations runs throughout the poem in mark'd contrast with the spirit of the poet's youth.' Among the most striking lines of this sequel are the following:

> Envy wears the mask of love, and, laughing sober fact to scorn,
> Cries to weakest as to strongest, 'Ye are equals, equal born,'
> Equal-born! Oh yes, if yonder hill be level with the flat.
> Charm us, orator, till the lion look no larger than the cat:
> Till the cat, through that mirage of overheated language, loom
> Larger than the lion,—Demos end in working its own doom.

* * * * * * * * * * * * * * * * * * * *

> Tumble Nature heel o'er head, and, yelling with the yelling street,
> Set the feet above the brain, and swear the brain is in the feet.

NB, presumably from *DVOP*. An autograph MS of seven pages, written in black ink, seems to have been the copy from which the text of *CR* was printed. This MS, now in the Trent Collection of the Duke University Library, is here referred to as DMS.

4. *DVOP* has a period after "affairs".

7. Was left] DMS: was left] [The line properly begins "I was".]

10. one—at] *DVOP*, *CR*, and DMS: one, at

15–31. These lines, beginning " 'reviews," are printed in *CR* from an unidentified newspaper clipping pasted to page 2 of DMS.

19–20. spirit of the poet's youth] Clipping before revision: spirit of the Locksley Hall" of the poet's youth

20. lines of this sequel are] Clipping before revision: lines are

21–31. From "Locksley Hall Sixty Years After," text of Tennyson's *Poetical Works* (Boston, 1887), the first collected edition in which it appeared. Tennyson uses initial capitals in the following words: Love, Weakest, Strongest, Orator, Lion, Cat, and Nature, as well as in the words in which Whitman uses the initial capital. In Tennyson's text the couplets are spaced out, not printed solid as here. The first six lines quoted by Whitman are 111–116 of the poem, and the last four lines are 137–140. Whitman made no changes in the verses on the newspaper clipping.

26. This line is badly mangled in all the texts. *CPW*, *CPP*, and *NB* read: Larger

Bring the old dark ages back, without the faith, without the hope
Beneath the State, the Church, the Throne, and roll their ruins down the slope.

I should say that all this is a legitimate consequence of the tone and convictions of the earlier standards and points of view. Then some reflections, down to the hard-pan of this sort of thing.

The course of progressive politics (democracy) is so certain and resistless, not only in America but in Europe, that we can well afford the warning calls, threats, checks, neutralizings, in imaginative literature, or any department, of such deep-sounding and high-soaring voices as Carlyle's and Tennyson's. Nay, the blindness, excesses, of the prevalent tendency—the dangers of the urgent trends of our times—in my opinion, need such voices almost more than any. I should, too, call it a signal instance of democratic humanity's luck that it has such enemies to contend with—so candid, so fervid, so heroic. But why do I say enemies? Upon the whole is not Tennyson—and was not Carlyle (like an honest and stern physician)—the true friend of our age?

Let me assume to pass verdict, or perhaps momentary judgment, for the United States on this poet—a remov'd and distant position giving some advantages over a nigh one. What is Tennyson's service to his race, times, and especially to America? First, I should say—or at least not forget—his personal character. He is not to be mention'd as a rugged, evolutionary, aboriginal force—but (and a great lesson is in it) he has been consistent throughout with the native, healthy, patriotic spinal element and promptings of himself. His moral line is local and conventional, but it is vital and genuine. He reflects the upper-crust of his time, its pale cast of thought—even its *ennui*. Then the simile of my friend John Burroughs is entirely true, 'his glove is a glove of silk, but the hand is a hand of iron.' He shows how one can be a royal laureate, quite elegant and 'aristocratic,' and a little queer and affected, and at the same time perfectly manly and natural. As to his non-democracy, it fits him well, and I like him the better for it. I guess we all like to have (I am sure I do) some one who presents those sides of a thought, or possibility, different from our

than the lion Demo—end in working its own doom.] *DVOP*, *CR*, and DMS read: Larger than the lion Demos—end in working its own doom.] Tennyson's reading is restored in the present edition, except that in conformity with Whitman's practice in the other lines, the word "lion" is given a lower case initial.

26–27. Between these two lines *CR* (but no other text) has a line of asterisks to indicate a series of lines omitted. These are restored in the present edition.

41. enemies?] *DVOP*, *CR*, and DMS: enemy?

46–47. DMS encloses in parentheses the words beginning "a remov'd" and ending "nigh one."

own—different and yet with a sort of home-likeness—a tartness and contradiction offsetting the theory as we view it, and construed from tastes and proclivities not at all his own.

To me, Tennyson shows more than any poet I know (perhaps has been a warning to me) how much there is in finest verbalism. There is such a latent charm in mere words, cunning collocations, and in the voice ringing them, which he has caught and brought out, beyond all others—as in the line,

And hollow, hollow, hollow, all delight,

in 'The Passing of Arthur,' and evidenced in 'The Lady of Shalott,' 'The Deserted House,' and many other pieces. Among the best (I often linger over them again and again) are 'Lucretius,' 'The Lotos Eaters,' and 'The Northern Farmer.' His mannerism is great, but it is a noble and welcome mannerism. His very best work, to me, is contain'd in the books of 'The Idyls of the King,' and all that has grown out of them. Though indeed we could spare nothing of Tennyson, however small or however peculiar—not 'Break, Break,' nor 'Flower in the Crannied Wall,' nor the old, eternally-told passion of 'Edward Gray:'

Love may come and love may go,
  And fly like a bird from tree to tree.
But I will love no more, no more
  Till Ellen Adair come back to me.

Yes, Alfred Tennyson's is a superb character, and will help give illustriousness, through the long roll of time, to our Nineteenth Century. In its bunch of orbic names, shining like a constellation of stars, his will be one of the brightest. His very faults, doubts, swervings, doublings upon himself, have been typical of our age. We are like the voyagers of a ship, casting off for new seas, distant shores. We would still dwell in the old suffocating and dead haunts, remembering and magnifying their pleasant experiences only, and more than once impell'd to jump ashore before it is too late, and stay where our fathers stay'd, and live as they lived.

48–49. say—or at least not forget—his] *DVOP*, *CR*, and DMS: say, his
49. *ennui*] DMS (unrevised): ennui
51. native, healthy] *DVOP*, *CR*, and DMS: native, personal, healthy
63. all his own.] *DVOP* and *CR:* all our own.
66. collocations] *CPW*, *NB*, and *CR:* collocutions] [DMS has the correct spelling; the printer's error is here corrected.]
73. After 'The Northern Farmer' DMS begins a new paragraph.
75. the King,' and all] *DVOP*, *CR*, and DMS: the King,' all of them, and all
80–81. Tennyson has a colon at the end of the second quoted line and a comma at the end of the third. DMS has no punctuation at the end of either line.

May-be I am non-literary and non-decorous (let me at least be human, and pay part of my debt) in this word about Tennyson. I want him to realize that here is a great and ardent Nation that absorbs his songs, and has a respect and affection for him personally, as almost for no other foreigner. I want this word to go to the old man at Farringford as conveying no more than the simple truth; and that truth (a little Christmas gift) no slight one either. I have written impromptu, and shall let it all go at that. The readers of more than fifty millions of people in the New World not only owe to him some of their most agreeable and harmless and healthy hours, but he has enter'd into the formative influences of character here, not only in the Atlantic cities, but inland and far West, out in Missouri, in Kansas, and away in Oregon, in farmer's house and miner's cabin.

Best thanks, anyhow, to Alfred Tennyson—thanks and appreciation in America's name.

Slang in America.

View'd freely, the English language is the accretion and growth of every dialect, race, and range of time, and is both the free and compacted composition of all. From this point of view, it stands for Language in the largest sense, and is really the greatest of studies. It involves so much; is indeed a sort of universal absorber, combiner, and conqueror. The scope of its etymologies is the scope not only of man and civilization, but the history of Nature in all departments, and of the organic Universe, brought up to date; for all are comprehended in words, and their backgrounds. This is when words become vitaliz'd, and stand for things, as they unerringly and soon come to do, in the mind that enters on their study with fitting spirit, grasp, and appreciation.

Slang, profoundly consider'd, is the lawless germinal element, below all words and sentences, and behind all poetry, and proves a certain perennial rankness and protestantism in speech. As the United States inherit by far their most precious possession—the language they talk and write—from the Old World, under and out of its feudal institutes, I will

101–102. agreeable and harmless and healthy] DVOP and CR: agreeable and healthy
107. DMS has "Walt Whitman" at the end.

Slang in America.
Reprinted in NB from NAR, November, 1885 (CXLI, 431–435), where it was

allow myself to borrow a simile even of those forms farthest removed from American Democracy. Considering Language then as some mighty potentate, into the majestic audience-hall of the monarch ever enters a personage like one of Shakspere's clowns, and takes position there, and plays a part even in the stateliest ceremonies. Such is Slang, or indirection, an attempt of common humanity to escape from bald literalism, and express itself illimitably, which in highest walks produces poets and poems, and doubtless in pre-historic times gave the start to, and perfected, the whole immense tangle of the old mythologies. For, curious as it may appear, it is strictly the same impulse-source, the same thing. Slang, too, is the wholesome fermentation or eructation of those processes eternally active in language, by which froth and specks are thrown up, mostly to pass away; though occasionally to settle and permanently chrystallize.

To make it plainer, it is certain that many of the oldest and solidest words we use, were originally generated from the daring and license of slang. In the processes of word-formation, myriads die, but here and there the attempt attracts superior meanings, becomes valuable and indispensable, and lives forever. Thus the term *right* means literally only straight. *Wrong* primarily meant twisted, distorted. *Integrity* meant oneness. *Spirit* meant breath, or flame. A *supercilious* person was one who rais'd his eyebrows. To *insult* was to leap against. If you *influenc'd* a man, you but flow'd into him. The Hebrew word which is translated *prophesy* meant to bubble up and pour forth as a fountain. The enthusiast bubbles up with the Spirit of God within him, and it pours forth from him like a fountain. The word prophecy is misunderstood. Many suppose that it is limited to mere prediction; that is but the lesser portion of prophecy. The greater work is to reveal God. Every true religious enthusiast is a prophet.

Language, be it remember'd, is not an abstract construction of the learn'd, or of dictionary makers, but is something arising out of the work, needs, ties, joys, affections, tastes, of long generations of humanity, and has its bases broad and low, close to the ground. Its final decisions are made by the masses, people nearest the concrete, having most to do with actual land and sea. It impermeates all, the Past as well as the Present,

first published.

2–3. and is both the free and compacted composition] *NAR:* and is the culling and composition

10. and soon] *NAR:* and very soon

13–14. certain perennial] *NAR:* certain freedom and perennial

40. *prophesy*] *NAR:* prophesy

and is the grandest triumph of the human intellect. "Those mighty works of art," says Addington Symonds, "which we call languages, in the construction of which whole peoples unconsciously co-operated, the forms of which were determin'd not by individual genius, but by the instincts of successive generations, acting to one end, inherent in the nature of the race—Those poems of pure thought and fancy, cadenced not in words, but in living imagery, fountainheads of inspiration, mirrors of the mind of nascent nations, which we call Mythologies—these surely are more marvellous in their infantine spontaneity than any more mature production of the races which evolv'd them. Yet we are utterly ignorant of their embryology; the true science of Origins is yet in its cradle."

Daring as it is to say so, in the growth of Language it is certain that the retrospect of slang from the start would be the recalling from their nebulous conditions of all that is poetical in the stores of human utterance. Moreover, the honest delving, as of late years, by the German and British workers in comparative philology, has pierc'd and dispers'd many of the falsest bubbles of centuries; and will disperse many more. It was long recorded that in Scandinavian mythology the heroes in the Norse Paradise drank out of the skulls of their slain enemies. Later investigation proves the word taken for skulls to mean *horns* of beasts slain in the hunt. And what reader had not been exercis'd over the traces of that feudal custom, by which *seigneurs* warm'd their feet in the bowels of serfs, the abdomen being open'd for the purpose? It now is made to appear that the serf was only required to submit his unharm'd abdomen as a foot cushion while his lord supp'd, and was required to chafe the legs of the seigneur with his hands.

It is curiously in embryons and childhood, and among the illiterate, we always find the groundwork and start, of this great science, and its noblest products. What a relief most people have in speaking of a man not by his true and formal name, with a "Mister" to it, but by some odd or homely appellative. The propensity to approach a meaning not directly and squarely, but by circuitous styles of expression, seems indeed a born quality of the common people everywhere, evidenced by nick-names, and the inveterate determination of the masses to bestow sub-titles, sometimes ridiculous, sometimes very apt. Always among the soldiers during the Secession War, one heard of "Little Mac" (Gen. McClellan), or of "Uncle Billy" (Gen. Sherman.) "The old man" was, of course, very common. Among the rank and file, both armies, it was very general to speak of the different States they came from by their slang names. Those from

78. is curiously in] *NAR:* is in

Maine were call'd Foxes; New Hampshire, Granite Boys; Massachusetts, Bay Staters; Vermont, Green Mountain Boys; Rhode Island, Gun Flints; Connecticut, Wooden Nutmegs; New York, Knickerbockers; New Jersey, Clam Catchers; Pennsylvania, Logher Heads; Delaware, Muskrats; Maryland, Claw Thumpers; Virginia, Beagles; North Carolina, Tar Boilers; South Carolina, Weasels; Georgia, Buzzards; Louisiana, Creoles; Alabama, Lizzards; Kentucky, Corn Crackers; Ohio, Buckeyes; Michigan, Wolverines; Indiana, Hoosiers; Illinois, Suckers; Missouri, Pukes; Mississippi, Tad Poles; Florida, Fly up the Creeks; Wisconsin, Badgers; Iowa, Hawkeyes; Oregon, Hard Cases. Indeed I am not sure but slang names have more than once made Presidents. "Old Hickory," (Gen. Jackson) is one case in point. "Tippecanoe, and Tyler too," another.

I find the same rule in the people's conversations everywhere. I heard this among the men of the city horse-cars, where the conductor is often call'd a "snatcher" (i. e. because his characteristic duty is to constantly pull or snatch the bell-strap, to stop or go on.) Two young fellows are having a friendly talk, amid which, says 1st conductor, "What did you do before you was a snatcher?" Answer of 2d conductor, "Nail'd." (Translation of answer: "I work'd as carpenter.") What is a "boom"? says one editor to another. "Esteem'd contemporary," says the other, "a boom is a bulge." "Barefoot whiskey" is the Tennessee name for the undiluted stimulant. In the slang of the New York common restaurant waiters a plate of ham and beans is known as "stars and stripes," codfish balls as "sleeve-buttons," and hash as "mystery."

The Western States of the Union are, however, as may be supposed, the special areas of slang, not only in conversation, but in names of localities, towns, rivers, etc. A late Oregon traveller says:

> "On your way to Olympia by rail, you cross a river called the Shookum-Chuck; your train stops at places named Newaukum, Tumwater, and Toutle; and if you seek further you will hear of whole counties labell'd Wahkiakum, or Snohomish, or Kitsar, or Klikatat; and Cowlitz, Hookium, and Nenolelops greet and offend you. They complain in Olympia that Washington Territory gets but little immigration; but what wonder? What man, having the whole American continent to choose from, would willingly date his letters from the county of Snohomish or bring up his children in the city of Nenolelops? The village of Tumwater is, as I am ready to bear witness, very pretty indeed; but surely an emigrant would think twice before he establish'd himself either there or at Toutle. Seattle is sufficiently barbarous; Stelicoom is no better; and I suspect that the Northern Pacific Railroad terminus has been fixed at Tacoma because it

118–132. The source of this quotation has not been identified.

is one of the few places on Puget Sound whose name does not inspire horror."

Then a Nevada paper chronicles the departure of a mining party from Reno: "The toughest set of roosters that ever shook the dust off any town left Reno yesterday for the new mining district of Cornucopia. They came here from Virginia. Among the crowd were four New York cock-fighters, two Chicago murderers, three Baltimore bruisers, one Philadelphia prize-fighter, four San Francisco hoodlums, three Virginia beats, two Union Pacific roughs, and two check guerrillas." Among the far-west newspapers, have been, or are, *The Fairplay* (Colorado) *Flume*, *The Solid Muldoon*, of Ouray, *The Tombstone Epitaph*, of Nevada, *The Jimplecute*, of Texas, and *The Bazoo*, of Missouri. Shirttail Bend, Whiskey Flat, Puppytown, Wild Yankee Ranch, Squaw Flat, Rawhide Ranch, Loafer's Ravine, Squitch Gulch, Toenail Lake, are a few of the names of places in Butte county, Cal.

Perhaps indeed no place or term gives more luxuriant illustrations of the fermentation processes I have mention'd, and their froth and specks, than those Mississippi and Pacific coast regions, at the present day. Hasty and grotesque as are some of the names, others are of an appropriateness and originality unsurpassable. This applies to the Indian words, which are often perfect. Oklahoma is proposed in Congress for the name of one of our new Territories. Hog-eye, Lick-skillet, Rake-pocket and Steal-easy are the names of some Texan towns. Miss Bremer found among the aborigines the following names: *Men's*, Horn-point; Round-Wind; Stand-and-look-out; The-Cloud-that-goes-aside; Iron-toe; Seek-the-sun; Iron-flash; Red-bottle; White-spindle; Black-dog; Two-feathers-of-honor; Gray-grass; Bushy-tail; Thunder-face; Go-on-the-burning-sod; Spirits-of-the-dead. *Women's*, Keep-the-fire; Spiritual-woman; Second-daughter-of-the-house; Blue-bird.

Certainly philologists have not given enough attention to this element and its results, which, I repeat, can probably be found working every where to-day, amid modern conditions, with as much life and activity as in far-back Greece or India, under prehistoric ones. Then the wit—the rich flashes of humor and genius and poetry—darting out often from a gang of laborers, railroad-men, miners, drivers or boatmen! How often

134. dust off any] *NAR:* dust of any
175. Walt Whitman's name is at the end of the article in *NAR.*

An Indian Bureau Reminiscence.

First published in *BM*, February, 1884; reprinted in *To-Day, the Monthly Magazine of Scientific Socialism* (London, May, 1884); reprinted in *NB*, probably

have I hover'd at the edge of a crowd of them, to hear their repartees and impromptus! You get more real fun from half an hour with them than from the books of all "the American humorists."

The science of language has large and close analogies in geological science, with its ceaseless evolution, its fossils, and its numberless submerged layers and hidden strata, the infinite go-before of the present. Or, perhaps Language is more like some vast living body, or perennial body of bodies. And slang not only brings the first feeders of it, but is afterward the start of fancy, imagination and humor, breathing into its nostrils the breath of life.

An Indian Bureau Reminiscence.

After the close of the Secession War in 1865, I work'd several months (until Mr. Harlan turn'd me out for having written "Leaves of Grass") in the Interior Department at Washington, in the Indian Bureau. Along this time there came to see their Great Father an unusual number of aboriginal visitors, delegations for treaties, settlement of lands, &c.— some young or middle-aged, but mainly old men, from the West, North, and occasionally from the South—parties of from five to twenty each—the most wonderful proofs of what Nature can produce, (the survival of the fittest, no doubt—all the frailer samples dropt, sorted out by death)—as if to show how the earth and woods, the attrition of storms and elements, and the exigencies of life at first hand, can train and fashion men, indeed *chiefs*, in heroic massiveness, imperturbability, muscle, and that last and highest beauty consisting of strength—the full exploitation and fruitage of a human identity, not from the culmination-points of "culture" and artificial civilization, but tallying our race, as it were, with giant, vital, gnarl'd, enduring trees, or monoliths of separate hardiest rocks, and humanity holding its own with the best of the said trees or rocks, and outdoing them.

There were Omahas, Poncas, Winnebagoes, Cheyennes, Navahos, Apaches, and many others. Let me give a running account of what I see and hear through one of these conference collections at the Indian Bureau,

from BM.
1. 1865] *To-Day* and BM: '65
2. for having written] *To-Day* and BM: for writing
6. young or middle-aged] *To-Day* and BM: young and middle-aged
7. South—parties] *To-Day* and BM: South—several hundreds of them, in parties
14. culmination-points] *To-Day* and BM: culmination-point
19. Winnebagoes . . . and] *To-Day* and BM: Winnebagoes, and
21. these conference collections at] *To-Day* and BM: these exhibitions at

going back to the present tense. Every head and face is impressive, even artistic; Nature redeems herself out of her crudest recesses. Most have red paint on their cheeks, however, or some other paint. ("Little Hill" makes the opening speech, which the interpreter translates by scraps.) Many wear head tires of gaudy-color'd braid, wound around thickly—some with circlets of eagles' feathers. Necklaces of bears' claws are plenty around their necks. Most of the chiefs are wrapt in large blankets of the brightest scarlet. Two or three have blue, and I see one black. (A wise man call'd "the Flesh" now makes a short speech, apparently asking something. Indian Commissioner Dole answers him, and the interpreter translates in scraps again.) All the principal chiefs have tomahawks or hatchets, some of them very richly ornamented and costly. Plaid shirts are to be observ'd—none too clean. Now a tall fellow, "Hole-in-the-Day," is speaking. He has a copious head-dress composed of feathers and narrow ribbon, under which appears a countenance painted all over a bilious yellow. Let us note this young chief. For all his paint, "Hole-in-the-Day" is a handsome Indian, mild and calm, dress'd in drab buckskin leggings, dark gray surtout, and a soft black hat. His costume will bear full observation, and even fashion would accept him. His apparel is worn loose and scant enough to show his superb physique, especially in neck, chest, and legs. ("The Apollo Belvidere!" was the involuntary exclamation of a famous European artist when he first saw a full-grown young Choctaw.)

One of the red visitors—a wild, lean-looking Indian, the one in the black woolen wrapper—has an empty buffalo head, with the horns on, for his personal surmounting. I see a markedly Bourbonish countenance among the chiefs—(it is not very uncommon among them, I am told.) Most of them avoided resting on chairs during the hour of their "talk" in the Commissioner's office; they would sit around on the floor, leaning against something, or stand up by the walls, partially wrapt in their blankets. Though some of the young fellows were, as I have said, magnificent and beautiful animals, I think the palm of unique picturesqueness, in body, limb, physiognomy, etc., was borne by the old or elderly chiefs, and the wise men.

My here-alluded-to experience in the Indian Bureau produced one very definite conviction, as follows: There is something about these aboriginal Americans, in their highest characteristic representations, es-

22–23. impressive, even artistic; Nature] *To-Day* and *BM:* impressive; Nature
37. chief. For] *To-Day* and *BM:* chief however. For
45. woolen] *To-Day:* woollen
70–71. personality, dignity, heroic] *To-Day:* personality, heroic

sential traits, and the ensemble of their physique and physiognomy—something very remote, very lofty, arousing comparisons with our own civilized ideals—something that our literature, portrait painting, etc., have never caught, and that will almost certainly never be transmitted to the future, even as a reminiscence. No biographer, no historian, no artist, has grasp'd it—perhaps could not grasp it. It is so different, so far outside our standards of eminent humanity. Their feathers, paint—even the empty buffalo skull—did not, to say the least, seem any more ludicrous to me than many of the fashions I have seen in civilized society. I should not apply the word savage (at any rate, in the usual sense) as a leading word in the description of those great aboriginal specimens, of whom I certainly saw many of the best. There were moments, as I look'd at them or studied them, when our own exemplification of personality, dignity, heroic presentation anyhow (as in the conventions of society, or even in the accepted poems and plays,) seem'd sickly, puny, inferior.

The interpreters, agents of the Indian Department, or other whites accompanying the bands, in positions of responsibility, were always interesting to me; I had many talks with them. Occasionally I would go to the hotels where the bands were quarter'd, and spend an hour or two informally. Of course we could not have much conversation—though (through the interpreters) more of this than might be supposed—sometimes quite animated and significant. I had the good luck to be invariably receiv'd and treated by all of them in their most cordial manner.

[*Letter to W. W. from an artist, B. H., who has been much among the American Indians:*]

"I have just receiv'd your little paper on the Indian delegations. In the fourth paragraph you say that there is something about the essential traits of our aborigines which 'will almost certainly never be transmitted to the future.' If I am so fortunate as to regain my health I hope to weaken the force of that statement, at least in so far as my talent and training will permit. I intend to spend some years among them, and shall endeavor to perpetuate on canvas some of the finer types, both men and women, and some of the characteristic features of their life. It will certainly be well worth the while. My artistic enthusiasm was never so thoroughly stirr'd up as by the Indians. They certainly have more of beauty, dignity and

71–72. The parenthetical phrase is not in *To-Day* or BM.
80. cordial manner.] *To-Day* and BM: cordial and accepted manner.
80. After this line Whitman's name appears in *To-Day*, but in BM it is printed under the title.
81–107. These lines are not in *To-Day* or BM.

nobility mingled with their own wild individuality, than any of the other indigenous types of man. Neither black nor Afghan, Arab nor Malay (and I know them all pretty well) can hold a candle to the Indian. All of the other aboriginal types seem to be more or less distorted from the model of perfect human form—as we know it—the blacks, thin-hipped, with bulbous limbs, not well mark'd; the Arabs large-jointed, &c. But I have seen many a young Indian as perfect in form and feature as a Greek statue—very different from a Greek statue, of course, but as satisfying to the artistic perceptions and demand.

"And the worst, or perhaps the best of it all is that it will require an artist—and a good one—to record the real facts and impressions. Ten thousand photographs would not have the value of one really finely felt painting. Color is all-important. No one but an artist knows how much. An Indian is only half an Indian without the blue-black hair and the brilliant eyes shining out of the wonderful dusky ochre and rose complexion."

Some Diary Notes at Random.

Negro Slaves in New York.—I can myself almost remember negro slaves in New York State, as my grandfather and great-grandfather (at West Hills, Suffolk County, New York) own'd a number. The hard labor of the farm was mostly done by them, and on the floor of the big kitchen, toward sundown, would be squatting a circle of twelve or fourteen "pickaninnies," eating their supper of pudding (Indian corn mush) and milk. A friend of my grandfather, named Wortman, of Oyster Bay, died in 1810, leaving ten slaves. Jeanette Treadwell, the last of them, died suddenly in Flushing last Summer (1884,) at the age of ninety-four years. I remember "old Mose," one of the liberated West Hills slaves, well. He was very genial, correct, manly, and cute, and a great friend of my childhood.

Canada Nights.—*Late in August.*—Three wondrous nights. Effects of moon, clouds, stars, and night-sheen, never surpass'd. I am out every night, enjoying all. The sunset begins it. (I have said already how long evening lingers here.) The moon, an hour high just after eight, is past her half, and looks somehow more like a human face up there than ever before. As it grows later, we have such gorgeous and broad cloud-effects, with

Some Diary Notes at Random.

First published in *BM*, December, 1885, from which the text of *NB* was probably reprinted.

3. County, New York) own'd] *BM:* County, Long Island) owned

Luna's tawny halos, silver edgings—great fleeces, depths of blue-black in patches, and occasionally long, low bars hanging silently a while, and then gray bulging masses rolling along stately, sometimes in long procession. The moon travels in Scorpion to-night, and dims all the stars of that constellation except fiery Antares, who keeps on shining just to the big one's side.

COUNTRY DAYS AND NIGHTS.—*Sept.* 30, '82, 4.30 A.M.—I am down in Camden County, New Jersey, at the farm-house of the Staffords—have been looking a long while at the comet—have in my time seen longer-tail'd ones, but never one so pronounc'd in cometary character, and so spectral-fierce—so like some great, pale, living monster of the air or sea. The atmosphere and sky, an hour or so before sunrise, so cool, still, translucent, give the whole apparition to great advantage. It is low in the east. The head shows about as big as an ordinary good-sized saucer—is a perfectly round and defined disk—the tail some sixty or seventy feet—not a stripe, but quite broad, and gradually expanding. Impress'd with the silent, inexplicably emotional sight, I linger and look till all begins to weaken in the break of day.

October 2.—The third day of mellow, delicious, sunshiny weather. I am writing this in the recesses of the old woods, my seat on a big pine log, my back against a tree. Am down here a few days for a change, to bask in the Autumn sun, to idle lusciously and simply, and to eat hearty meals, especially my breakfast. Warm mid-days—the other hours of the twenty-four delightfully fresh and mild—cool evenings, and early mornings perfect. The scent of the woods, and the peculiar aroma of a great yet unreap'd maize-field near by—the white butterflies in every direction by day—the golden-rod, the wild asters, and sunflowers—the song of the katydid all night.

Every day in Cooper's Woods, enjoying simple existence and the passing hours—taking short walks—exercising arms and chest with the saplings, or my voice with army songs or recitations. A perfect week for weather; seven continuous days bright and dry and cool and sunny. The nights splendid, with full moon—about 10 the grandest of star-shows up in the east and south, Jupiter, Saturn, Capella, Aldebaran, and great Orion. Am feeling pretty well—am outdoors most of the time, absorbing the days and nights all I can.

24–25. I am down . . . Staffords—have] *BM:* I have
81–82. of our great cities—aye] *BM:* of this city—aye
91. is, a few miles] *BM:* is, forty or fifty miles
96. Spent most of the day] *BM:* Spent half a day

Central Park Notes.—*American Society from a Park Policeman's Point of View.*—Am in New York City, upper part—visit Central Park almost every day (and have for the last three weeks) off and on, taking observations or short rambles, and sometimes riding around. I talk quite a good deal with one of the Park policemen, C. C., up toward the Ninetieth street entrance. One day in particular I got him a-going, and it proved deeply interesting to me. Our talk floated into sociology and politics. I was curious to find how these things appear'd on their surfaces to my friend, for he plainly possess'd sharp wits and good nature, and had been seeing, for years, broad streaks of humanity somewhat out of my latitude. I found that as he took such appearances the inward caste-spirit of European "aristocracy" pervaded rich America, with cynicism and artificiality at the fore. Of the bulk of official persons, Executives, Congressmen, Legislators, Aldermen, Department heads, etc., etc., or the candidates for those positions, nineteen in twenty, in the policeman's judgment, were just players in a game. Liberty, Equality, Union, and all the grand words of the Republic, were, in their mouths, but lures, decoys, chisel'd likenesses of dead wood, to catch the masses. Of fine afternoons, along the broad tracks of the Park, for many years, had swept by my friend, as he stood on guard, the carriages, etc., of American Gentility, not by dozens and scores, but by hundreds and thousands. Lucky brokers, capitalists, contractors, grocery-men, successful political strikers, rich butchers, dry goods' folk, &c. And on a large proportion of these vehicles, on panels or horse-trappings, were conspicuously borne *heraldic family crests.* (Can this really be true?) In wish and willingness (and if that were so, what matter about the reality?) titles of nobility, with a court and spheres fit for the capitalists, the highly educated, and the carriage-riding classes—to fence them off from "the common people"—were the heart's desire of the "good society" of our great cities—aye, of North and South.

So much for my police friend's speculations—which rather took me aback—and which I have thought I would just print as he gave them (as a doctor records symptoms.)

Plate Glass Notes.—*St. Louis, Missouri, November,* '79.—What do you think I find manufactur'd out here—and of a kind the clearest and largest, best, and the most finish'd and luxurious in the world—and with ample demand for it too? *Plate glass!* One would suppose that was the last dainty outcome of an old, almost effete-growing civilization; and yet here it is, a few miles from St. Louis, on a charming little river, in the wilds of the West, near the Mississippi. I went down that way to-day by the Iron

Mountain Railroad—was switch'd off on a side-track four miles through woods and ravines, to Swash Creek, so-call'd, and there found Crystal City, and immense Glass Works, built (and evidently built to stay) right in the pleasant rolling forest. Spent most of the day, and examin'd the inexhaustible and peculiar sand the glass is made of—the original whity-gray stuff in the banks—saw the melting in the pots (a wondrous process, a real poem) —saw the delicate preparation the clay material undergoes for these great pots (it has to be kneaded finally by human feet, no machinery answering, and I watch'd the picturesque bare-legged Africans treading it)—saw the molten stuff (a great mass of a glowing pale yellow color) taken out of the furnaces (I shall never forget that Pot, shape, color, concomitants, more beautiful than any antique statue,) pass'd into the adjoining casting-room, lifted by powerful machinery, pour'd out on its bed (all glowing, a newer, vaster study for colorists, indescribable, a pale red-tinged yellow, of tarry consistence, all lambent,) roll'd by a heavy roller into rough plate glass, I should say ten feet by fourteen, then rapidly shov'd into the annealing oven, which stood ready for it. The polishing and grinding rooms afterward—the great glass slabs, hundreds of them, on their flat beds, and the see-saw music of the steam machinery constantly at work polishing them—the myriads of human figures (the works employ'd 400 men) moving about, with swart arms and necks, and no superfluous clothing—the vast, rude halls, with immense play of shifting shade, and slow-moving currents of smoke and steam, and shafts of light, sometimes sun, striking in from above with effects that would have fill'd Michel Angelo with rapture.

Coming back to St. Louis this evening, at sundown, and for over an hour afterward, we follow'd the Mississippi, close by its western bank, giving me an ampler view of the river, and with effects a little different from any yet. In the eastern sky hung the planet Mars, just up, and of a very clear and vivid yellow. It was a soothing and pensive hour—the spread of the river off there in the half-light—the glints of the down-bound steamboats plodding along—and that yellow orb (apparently twice as large and significant as usual) above the Illinois shore. (All along, these nights, nothing can exceed the calm, fierce, golden, glistening domination of Mars over all the stars in the sky.)

As we came nearer St. Louis, the night having well set in, I saw some (to me) novel effects in the zinc smelting establishments, the tall chimneys belching flames at the top, while inside through the openings at the façades of the great tanks burst forth (in regular position) hundreds of fierce tufts of a peculiar blue (or green) flame, of a purity and intensity, like electric lights—illuminating not only the great buildings themselves, but far and near outside, like hues of the aurora borealis, only more vivid. (So that—remembering the Pot from the crystal furnace—my jaunt seem'd to give me new revelations in the color line.)

Some War Memoranda.

JOTTED DOWN AT THE TIME.

I find this incident in my notes (I suppose from "chinning" in hospital with some sick or wounded soldier who knew of it):

When Kilpatrick and his forces were cut off at Brandy Station (last of September, '63, or thereabouts,) and the bands struck up "Yankee Doodle," there were not cannon enough in the Southern Confederacy to keep him and them "in." It was when Meade fell back. K. had his large cavalry division (perhaps 5000 men,) but the rebs, in superior force, had surrounded them. Things look'd exceedingly desperate. K. had two fine bands, and order'd them up immediately; they join'd and play'd "Yankee Doodle" with a will! It went through the men like lightning—but to inspire, not to unnerve. Every man seem'd a giant. They charged like a cyclone, and cut their way out. Their loss was but 20. It was about two in the afternoon.

WASHINGTON STREET SCENES.

April 7, 1864.—WALKING DOWN PENNSYLVANIA AVENUE.—Warmish forenoon, after the storm of the past few days. I see, passing up, in the broad space between the curbs, a big squad of a couple of hundred conscripts, surrounded by a strong cordon of arm'd guards, and others interspers'd between the ranks. The government has learn'd caution from its experiences; there are many hundreds of "bounty jumpers," and already, as I am told, eighty thousand deserters! Next (also passing up the Avenue,) a cavalry company, young, but evidently well drill'd and service-harden'd men. Mark the upright posture in their saddles, the bronz'd and bearded young faces, the easy swaying to the motions of the horses, and the carbines by their right knees; handsome and reckless, some eighty of them, riding with rapid gait, clattering along. Then the tinkling bells of passing cars, the many shops (some with large show-windows, some with swords, straps for the shoulders of different ranks, hat-cords with acorns, or other insignia,) the military patrol marching along, with the orderly or second-

Some War Memoranda.

First published in *NAR*, January, 1887 (CXLIV, 55–60, from which the text of *NB* was probably reprinted.

lieutenant stopping different ones to examine passes—the forms, the faces, all sorts crowded together, the worn and pale, the pleas'd, some on their way to the railroad depot going home, the cripples, the darkeys, the long trains of government wagons, or the sad strings of ambulances conveying wounded—the many officers' horses tied in front of the drinking or oyster saloons, or held by black men or boys, or orderlies.

THE 195TH PENNSYLVANIA.

Tuesday, Aug. 1, 1865.—About 3 o'clock this afternoon (sun broiling hot) in Fifteenth street, by the Treasury building, a large and handsome regiment, 195th Pennsylvania, were marching by—as it happen'd, receiv'd orders just here to halt and break ranks, so that they might rest themselves awhile. I thought I never saw a finer set of men—so hardy, candid, bright American looks, all weather-beaten, and with warm clothes. Every man was home-born. My heart was much drawn toward them. They seem'd very tired, red, and streaming with sweat. It is a one-year regiment, mostly from Lancaster County, Pa.; have been in Shenandoah Valley. On halting, the men unhitch'd their knapsacks, and sat down to rest themselves. Some lay flat on the pavement or under trees. The fine physical appearance of the whole body was remarkable. Great, very great, must be the State where such young farmers and mechanics are the practical average. I went around for half an hour and talk'd with several of them, sometimes squatting down with the groups.

LEFT-HAND WRITING BY SOLDIERS.

April 30, 1866.—Here is a single significant fact, from which one may judge of the character of the American soldiers in this just concluded war: A gentleman in New York City, a while since, took it into his head to collect specimens of writing from soldiers who had lost their right hands in battle, and afterwards learn'd to use the left. He gave public notice of his desire, and offer'd prizes for the best of these specimens. Pretty soon they began to come in, and by the time specified for awarding the prizes three hundred samples of such left-hand writing by maim'd soldiers had arrived.

I have just been looking over some of this writing. A great many of the specimens are written in a beautiful manner. All are good. The writing in nearly all cases slants backward instead of forward. One piece

7. men,) but the rebs] *NAR:* men,) and the rebs
10. will!] *NAR:* will.

of writing, from a soldier who had lost both arms, was made by holding the pen in his mouth.

CENTRAL VIRGINIA IN '64.

Culpeper, where I am stopping, looks like a place of two or three thousand inhabitants. Must be one of the pleasantest towns in Virginia. Even now, dilapidated fences, all broken down, windows out, it has the remains of much beauty. I am standing on an eminence overlooking the town, though within its limits. To the west the long Blue Mountain range is very plain, looks quite near, though from 30 to 50 miles distant, with some gray splashes of snow yet visible. The show is varied and fascinating. I see a great eagle up there in the air sailing with pois'd wings, quite low. Squads of red-legged soldiers are drilling; I suppose some of the new men of the Brooklyn 14th; they march off presently with muskets on their shoulders. In another place, just below me, are some soldiers squaring off logs to build a shanty—chopping away, and the noise of the axes sounding sharp. I hear the bellowing, unmusical screech of the mule. I mark the thin blue smoke rising from camp fires. Just below me is a collection of hospital tents, with a yellow flag elevated on a stick, and moving languidly in the breeze. Two discharged men (I know them both) are just leaving. One is so weak he can hardly walk; the other is stronger, and carries his comrade's musket. They move slowly along the muddy road toward the depot. The scenery is full of breadth, and spread on the most generous scale (everywhere in Virginia this thought fill'd me.) The sights, the scenes, the groups, have been varied and picturesque here beyond description, and remain so.

I heard the men return in force the other night—heard the shouting, and got up and went out to hear what was the matter. That night scene of so many hundred tramping steadily by, through the mud (some big flaring torches of pine knots,) I shall never forget. I like to go to the paymaster's tent, and watch the men getting paid off. Some have furloughs, and start at once for home, sometimes amid great chaffing and blarneying. There is every day the sound of the wood-chopping axe, and the plentiful sight of negroes, crows, and mud. I note large droves and pens of cattle. The teamsters have camps of their own, and I go often among them. The officers occasionally invite me to dinner or supper at headquarters. The fare is plain, but you get something good to drink, and plenty of it. Gen. Meade is absent; Sedgwick is in command.

76. sounding sharp.] *NAR:* sounding good.

PAYING THE 1ST U. S. C. T.

One of my war time reminiscences comprises the quiet side scene of a visit I made to the First Regiment U. S. Color'd Troops, at their encampment, and on the occasion of their first paying off, July 11, 1863. Though there is now no difference of opinion worth mentioning, there was a powerful opposition to enlisting blacks during the earlier years of the secession war. Even then, however, they had their champions. "That the color'd race," said a good authority, "is capable of military training and efficiency, is demonstrated by the testimony of numberless witnesses, and by the eagerness display'd in the raising, organizing, and drilling of African troops. Few white regiments make a better appearance on parade than the First and Second Louisiana Native Guards. The same remark is true of other color'd regiments. At Milliken's Bend, at Vicksburg, at Port Hudson, on Morris Island, and wherever tested, they have exhibited determin'd bravery, and compell'd the plaudits alike of the thoughtful and thoughtless soldiery. During the siege of Port Hudson the question was often ask'd those who beheld their resolute charges, how the 'niggers' behav'd under fire; and without exception the answer was complimentary to them. 'O, tip-top!' 'first-rate!' 'bully!' were the usual replies." But I did not start out to argue the case—only to give my reminiscence literally, as jotted on the spot at the time.

I write this on Mason's (otherwise Analostan) Island, under the fine shade trees of an old white stucco house, with big rooms; the white stucco house, originally a fine country seat (tradition says the famous Virginia Mason, author of the Fugitive Slave Law, was born here.) I reach'd the spot from my Washington quarters by ambulance up Pennsylvania avenue, through Georgetown, across the Aqueduct bridge, and around through a cut and winding road, with rocks and many bad gullies not lacking. After reaching the island, we get presently in the midst of the camp of the 1st Regiment U. S. C. T. The tents look clean and good; indeed, altogether, in locality especially, the pleasantest camp I have yet seen. The spot is umbrageous, high and dry, with distant sounds of the city, and the puffing steamers of the Potomac, up to Georgetown and back again. Birds are singing in the trees, the warmth is endurable here in this moist shade, with the fragrance and freshness. A hundred rods across is Georgetown. The river between is swell'd and muddy from the late rains up country. So quiet here, yet full of vitality, all around in the far distance glimpses, as I sweep my eye, of hills, verdure-clad, and with

114. fire; and] *NAR:* fire, and

plenteous trees; right where I sit, locust, sassafras, spice, and many other trees, a few with huge parasitic vines; just at hand the banks sloping to the river, wild with beautiful, free vegetation, superb weeds, better, in their natural growth and forms, than the best garden. Lots of luxuriant grape vines and trumpet flowers; the river flowing far down in the distance.

Now the paying is to begin. The Major (paymaster) with his clerk seat themselves at a table—the rolls are before them—the money box is open'd—there are packages of five, ten, twenty-five cent pieces. Here comes the first Company (B), some 82 men, all blacks. Certes, we cannot find fault with the appearance of this crowd—negroes though they be. They are manly enough, bright enough, look as if they had the soldier-stuff in them, look hardy, patient, many of them real handsome young fellows. The paying, I say, has begun. The men are march'd up in close proximity. The clerk calls off name after name, and each walks up, receives his money, and passes along out of the way. It is a real study, both to see them come close, and to see them pass away, stand counting their cash—(nearly all of this company get ten dollars and three cents each.) The clerk calls George Washington. That distinguish'd personage steps from the ranks, in the shape of a very black man, good sized and shaped, and aged about 30, with a military moustache; he takes his "ten three," and goes off evidently well pleas'd. (There are about a dozen Washingtons in the company. Let us hope they will do honor to the name.) At the table, how quickly the Major handles the bills, counts without trouble, everything going on smoothly and quickly. The regiment numbers to-day about 1,000 men (including 20 officers, the only whites.)

Now another company. These get $5.36 each. The men look well. They, too, have great names; besides the Washingtons aforesaid, John Quincy Adams, Daniel Webster, Calhoun, James Madison, Alfred Tennyson, John Brown, Benj. G. Tucker, Horace Greeley, etc. The men step off aside, count their money with a pleas'd, half-puzzled look. Occasionally, but not often, there are some thoroughly African physiognomies, very black in color, large, protruding lips, low forehead, etc. But I have to say that I do not see one utterly revolting face.

Then another company, each man of this getting $10.03 also. The pay proceeds very rapidly (the calculation, roll-signing, etc., having been arranged before hand.) Then some trouble. One company, by the rigid

193–194. Potomac; the] *NAR:* Potomac, the
197. stopt] *NAR:* stopped
199. Whitman's name is printed at the end of the article in *NAR.*

rules of official computation, gets only 23 cents each man. The company (K) is indignant, and after two or three are paid, the refusal to take the paltry sum is universal, and the company marches off to quarters unpaid.

Another company (I) gets only 70 cents. The sullen, lowering, disappointed look is general. Half refuse it in this case. Company G, in full dress, with brass scales on shoulders, look'd, perhaps, as well as any of the companies—the men had an unusually alert look.

These, then, are the black troops,—or the beginning of them. Well, no one can see them, even under these circumstances—their military career in its novitiate—without feeling well pleas'd with them.

As we enter'd the island, we saw scores at a little distance, bathing, washing their clothes, etc. The officers, as far as looks go, have a fine appearance, have good faces, and the air military. Altogether it is a significant show, and brings up some "abolition" thoughts. The scene, the porch of an Old Virginia slave-owner's house, the Potomac rippling near, the Capitol just down three or four miles there, seen through the pleasant blue haze of this July day.

After a couple of hours I get tired, and go off for a ramble. I write these concluding lines on a rock, under the shade of a tree on the banks of the island. It is solitary here, the birds singing, the sluggish muddy-yellow waters pouring down from the late rains of the upper Potomac; the green heights on the south side of the river before me. The single cannon from a neighboring fort has just been fired, to signal high noon. I have walk'd all around Analostan, enjoying its luxuriant wildness, and stopt in this solitary spot. A water snake wriggles down the bank, disturb'd, into the water. The bank near by is fringed with a dense growth of shrubbery, vines, etc.

Five Thousand Poems.

There have been collected in a cluster nearly five thousand big and little American poems—all that diligent and long-continued research could lay hands on! The author of 'Old Grimes is Dead' commenced it, more than fifty years ago; then the cluster was pass'd on and accumulated by C. F. Harris; then further pass'd on and added to by the late Senator

Five Thousand Poems.

First published in CR, April 16, 1887. Reprinted in DVOP from CR. The text of NB was presumably reprinted from DVOP. Galley proof in the Feinberg Collection.

Anthony, from whom the whole collection has been bequeath'd to Brown University. A catalogue (such as it is) has been made and publish'd of these five thousand poems—and is probably the most curious and suggestive part of the whole affair. At any rate it has led me to some abstract reflection like the following.

I should like, for myself, to put on record my devout acknowledgment not only of the great masterpieces of the past, but of the benefit of *all* poets, past and present, and of *all* poetic utterance—in its entirety the dominant moral factor of humanity's progress. In view of that progress, and of evolution, the religious and æsthetic elements, the distinctive and most important of any, seem to me more indebted to poetry than to all other means and influences combined. In a very profound sense *religion is the poetry of humanity.* Then the points of union and rapport among all the poems and poets of the world, however wide their separations of time and place and theme, are much more numerous and weighty than the points of contrast. Without relation as they may seem at first sight, the whole earth's poets and poetry—*en masse*—the Oriental, the Greek, and what there is of Roman—the oldest myths—the interminable ballad-romances of the Middle Ages—the hymns and psalms of worship—the epics, plays, swarms of lyrics of the British Islands, or the Teutonic old or new—or modern French—or what there is in America, Bryant's, for instance, or Whittier's or Longfellow's—the verse of all tongues and ages, all forms, all subjects, from primitive times to our own day inclusive—really combine in one aggregate and electric globe or universe, with all its numberless parts and radiations held together by a common centre or verteber. To repeat it, all poetry thus has (to the point of view comprehensive enough) more features of resemblance than difference, and becomes essentially, like the planetary globe itself, compact and orbic and whole. Nature seems to sow countless seeds—makes incessant crude

10. reflection] DVOP and CR: reflections

17–18. *religion is the poetry of humanity.*] DVOP and CR: religion *is* the poetry of humanity.

34. After "and whole." DVOP and CR have the following two sentences, omitted in NB and later texts: "Even science has sometimes to vail or bow her majestic head to her imaginative sister. That there should be a good deal of waste land and many sterile spots is doubtless an inherent necessity of the case—perhaps that the greater part of the rondure should be waste (at least until brought out, discovered)."

36. CR has Walt Whitman's name at the end.

The Old Bowery.

Published for the first time as "Booth and 'The Bowery,'" with the subtitles "New-York Theatres Forty Years Ago. Walt Whitman Recalls His Youthful

attempts—thankful to get now and then, even at rare and long intervals, something approximately good.

The Old Bowery.

A Reminiscence of New York Plays and Acting Fifty Years Ago.

In an article not long since, "Mrs. Siddons as Lady Macbeth," in "The Nineteenth Century," after describing the bitter regretfulness to mankind from the loss of those first-class poems, temples, pictures, gone and vanish'd from any record of men, the writer (Fleeming Jenkin) continues:

> If this be our feeling as to the more durable works of art, what shall we say of those triumphs which, by their very nature, last no longer than the action which creates them—the triumphs of the orator, the singer or the actor? There is an anodyne in the words, "must be so," "inevitable," and there is even some absurdity in longing for the impossible. This anodyne and our sense of humor temper the unhappiness we feel when, after hearing some great performance, we leave the theatre and think, "Well, this great thing has been, and all that is now left of it is the feeble print upon my brain, the little thrill which memory will send along my nerves, mine and my neighbors, as we live longer the print and thrill must be feebler, and when we pass away the impress of the great artist will vanish from the world." The regret that a great art should in its nature be trasitory, explains the lively interest which many feel in reading anecdotes or descriptions of a great actor.

All this is emphatically my own feeling and reminiscence about the best dramatic and lyric artists I have seen in bygone days—for instance, Marietta Alboni, the elder Booth, Forrest, the tenor Bettini, the baritone Badiali, "old man Clarke"—(I could write a whole paper on the latter's

Impressions," in NYTR, Sunday, August 16, 1885. The text of NB was presumably reprinted from NYTR. The piece is not in DVOP. The Feinberg Collection contains galley proofs of the last half of the article, NB, pp. 90–92.

1–2. The article referred to has as subtitle "From Contemporary Notes by George Joseph Bell," and was published in the February Number, 1878, III, 296–313. In NYTR "Lady Macbeth" and "The Nineteenth Century" are printed in italics. (Names of characters are in italics throughout NYTR.)

4. any record] NYTR: any knowledge or record

6–19. In NYTR these lines are in quotation marks and not indented. In *Nineteenth Century*, Jenkin's sentence continues for two lines after "great actor."

15. neighbors, as] NYTR and *Nineteenth Century:* neighbors'; as

21. bygone] NYTR: by-gone

22. Alboni, the elder] NYTR: Alboni, Fanny Kemble, the elder

23–25. NYTR omits the marks of parenthesis after and before the dashes.

peerless rendering of the Ghost in "Hamlet" at the Park, when I was a young fellow)—an actor named Ranger, who appear'd in America forty years ago in *genre* characters) Henry Placide, and many others. But I will make a few memoranda at least of the best one I knew.

For the elderly New Yorker of to-day, perhaps, nothing were more likely to start up memories of his early manhood than the mention of the Bowery and the elder Booth. At the date given, the more stylish and select theatre (prices, 50 cents pit, $1 boxes) was "The Park," a large and well-appointed house on Park Row, opposite the present Post-office. English opera and the old comedies were often given in capital style; the principal foreign stars appear'd here, with Italian opera at wide intervals. The Park held a large part in my boyhood's and young manhood's life. Here I heard the English actor, Anderson, in "Charles de Moor," and in the fine part of "Gisippus." Here I heard Fanny Kemble, Charlotte Cushman, the Seguins, Daddy Rice, Hackett as Falstaff, Nimrod Wildfire, Rip Van Winkle, and in his Yankee characters. (See pages 19, 20, *Specimen Days.*) It was here (some years later than the date in the headline) I also heard Mario many times, and at his best. In such parts as Gennaro, in "Lucrezia Borgia," he was inimitable—the sweetest of voices, a pure tenor, of considerable compass and respectable power. His wife, Grisi, was with him, no longer first-class or young—a fine Norma, though, to the last.

Perhaps my dearest amusement reminiscences are those musical ones. I doubt if ever the senses and emotions of the future will be thrill'd as were the auditors of a generation ago by the deep passion of Alboni's contralto (at the Broadway Theatre, south side, near Pearl street)—or by the trumpet notes of Badiali's baritone, or Bettini's pensive and incomparable tenor in Fernando in "Favorita," or Marini's bass in "Faliero," among the Havana troupe, Castle Garden.

But getting back more specifically to the date and theme I started from—the heavy tragedy business prevail'd more decidedly at the Bowery Theatre, where Booth and Forrest were frequently to be heard. Though Booth *pere*, then in his prime, ranging in age from 40 to 44 years (he was born in 1796,) was the loyal child and continuer of the traditions of orthodox English play-acting, he stood out "himself alone"

26. characters; Henry Placide, and] *NYTR:* characters, and

29–30. than the mention . . . Booth.] *NYTR:* than the head-line of this article.

36–38. These lines are not in *NYTR.*

41. headline) I also heard] *NYTR:* head-line) I heard

46–52. This paragraph is omitted in *NYTR*, where an ellipsis is marked by a series of three spaced periods after "to the last." in line 45.

61–64. The source of this quotation has not been identified.

in many respects beyond any of his kind on record, and with effects and ways that broke through all rules and all traditions. He has been well describ'd as an actor "whose instant and tremendous concentration of passion in his delineations overwhelm'd his audience, and wrought into it such enthusiasm that it partook of the fever of inspiration surging through his own veins." He seems to have been of beautiful private character, very honorable, affectionate, good-natured, no arrogance, glad to give the other actors the best chances. He knew all stage points thoroughly, and curiously ignored the mere dignities. I once talk'd with a man who had seen him do the Second Actor in the mock play to Charles Kean's Hamlet in Baltimore. He was a marvellous linguist. He play'd Shylock once in London, giving the dialogue in Hebrew, and in New Orleans Oreste (Racine's "Andromaque") in French. One trait of his habits, I have heard, was strict vegetarianism. He was exceptionally kind to the brute creation. Every once in a while he would make a break for solitude or wild freedom, sometimes for a few hours, sometimes for days. (He illustrated Plato's rule that to the forming an artist of the very highest rank a dash of insanity or what the world calls insanity is indispensable.) He was a small-sized man—yet sharp observers noticed that however crowded the stage might be in certain scenes, Booth never seem'd overtopt or hidden. He was singularly spontaneous and fluctuating; in the same part each rendering differ'd from any and all others. He had no stereotyped positions and made no arbitrary requirements on his fellow-preformers.

As is well known to old play-goers, Booth's most effective part was Richard III. Either that, or Iago, or Shylock, or Pescara in "The Apostate," was sure to draw a crowded house. (Remember heavy pieces were much more in demand those days than now.) He was also unapproachably grand in Sir Giles Overreach, in "A New Way to Pay Old Debts," and the principal character in "The Iron Chest."

In any portraiture of Booth, those years, the Bowery Theatre, with its leading lights, and the lessee and manager, Thomas Hamblin, cannot be left out. It was at the Bowery I first saw Edwin Forrest (the play was John Howard Payne's "Brutus, or the Fall of Tarquin," and it affected me for weeks; or rather I might say permanently filter'd into my whole nature,) then in the zenith of his fame and ability. Sometimes (perhaps

66. actors the best chances.] *NYTR:* actors any good chances.
74–76. In *NYTR* the entire sentence is not in parentheses, but only the clause "or what the world calls insanity".
77. man—yet] *NYTR:* man, yet
82–87. This paragraph is omitted in *NYTR*, where an ellipsis is marked by a series of three spaced periods after "fellow-performers."
89. the lessee and manager] *NYTR:* the manager

a veteran's benefit night,) the Bowery would group together five or six of the first-class actors of those days—Booth, Forrest, Cooper, Hamblin, and John R. Scott, for instance. At that time and here George Jones ("Count Joannes") was a young, handsome actor, and quite a favorite. I remember seeing him in the title role in "Julius Cæsar," and a capital performance it was.

To return specially to the manager. Thomas Hamblin made a first-rate foil to Booth, and was frequently cast with him. He had a large, shapely, imposing presence, and dark and flashing eyes. I remember well his rendering of the main role in Maturin's "Bertram, or the Castle of St. Aldobrand." But I thought Tom Hamblin's best acting was in the comparatively minor part of Faulconbridge in "King John"—he himself evidently revell'd in the part, and took away the house's applause from young Kean (the King) and Ellen Tree (Constance,) and everybody else on the stage—some time afterward at the Park. Some of the Bowery actresses were remarkably good. I remember Mrs. Pritchard in "Tour de Nesle," and Mrs. McClure in "Fatal Curiosity," and as Millwood in "George Barnwell." (I wonder what old fellow reading these lines will recall the fine comedietta of "The Youth That Never Saw a Woman," and the jolly acting in it of Mrs. Herring and old Gates.)

The Bowery, now and then, was the place, too, for spectacular pieces, such as "The Last Days of Pompeii," "The Lion-Doom'd" and the yet undying "Mazeppa." At one time "Jonathan Bradford, or the Murder at the Roadside Inn," had a long and crowded run; John Sefton and his brother William acted in it. I remember well the Frenchwoman Celeste, a splendid pantomimist, and her emotional "Wept of the Wishton-Wish." But certainly the main "reason for being" of the Bowery Theatre those years was to furnish the public with Forrest's and Booth's performances—the latter having a popularity and circles of enthusiastic admirers and critics fully equal to the former—though people were divided as always. For some reason or other, neither Forrest nor Booth would accept engagements at the more fashionable theatre, the Park. And it is a curious reminiscence, but a true one, that both these great actors and their performances were taboo'd by "polite society" in New York and Boston at the time—probably as being too robustuous. But no such scruples affected the Bowery.

104–108. This sentence is enclosed in parentheses in *NYTR*, in addition to the words enclosed in parentheses in *NB*.

109–110. de Nesle] *NYTR:* d'Nesle

110. and as Millwood] *NYTR:* and *Millwood*

111–113. This sentence is not enclosed in parentheses in *NYTR*.

Recalling from that period the occasion of either Forrest or Booth, any good night at the old Bowery, pack'd from ceiling to pit with its audience mainly of alert, well dress'd, full-blooded young and middle-aged men, the best average of American-born mechanics—the emotional nature of the whole mass arous'd by the power and magnetism of as mighty mimes as ever trod the stage—the whole crowded auditorium, and what seeth'd in it, and flush'd from its faces and eyes, to me as much a part of the show as any—bursting forth in one of those long-kept-up tempests of hand-clapping peculiar to the Bowery—no dainty kid-glove business, but electric force and muscle from perhaps 2000 full-sinew'd men—(the inimitable and chromatic tempest of one of those ovations to Edwin Forrest, welcoming him back after an absence, comes up to me this moment)—Such sounds and scenes as here resumed will surely afford to many old New Yorkers some fruitful recollections.

I can yet remember (for I always scann'd an audience as rigidly as a play) the faces of the leading authors, poets, editors, of those times—Fenimore Cooper, Bryant, Paulding, Irving, Charles King, Watson Webb, N. P. Willis, Hoffman, Halleck, Mumford, Morris, Leggett, L. G. Clarke, R. A. Locke and others, occasionally peering from the first tier boxes; and even the great National Eminences, Presidents Adams, Jackson, Van Buren and Tyler, all made short visits there on their Eastern tours.

Awhile after 1840 the character of the Bowery as hitherto described completely changed. Cheap prices and vulgar programmes came in. People who of after years saw the pandemonium of the pit and the doings on the boards must not gauge by them the times and characters I am describing. Not but what there was more or less rankness in the crowd even then. For types of sectional New York those days—the streets East of the Bowery, that intersect Division, Grand, and up to Third Avenue—types that never found their Dickens, or Hogarth, or Balzac, and have pass'd away unportraitured—the young shipbuilders, cartmen, butchers, firemen (the old-time "soap-lock" or exaggerated "Mose" or "Sikesey," of Chanfrau's plays,) they, too, were always to be seen in these audiences, racy of the East River and the Dry Dock. Slang, wit, occasional shirt sleeves, and a picturesque freedom of looks and manners, with a rude good-nature and restless movement, were generally noticeable. Yet there never were audiences that paid a good actor or an interesting play the

123. former—though] *NYTR:* former, though
128. robustuous.] *NYTR:* robustious.
131. the old Bowery] Galley before revision: the Bowery
142. moment)—Such] *NYTR:* moment)—such
153. of after years] *NYTR:* of later years

compliment of more sustain'd attention or quicker rapport. Then at times came the exceptionally decorous and intellectual congregations I have hinted at; for the Bowery really furnish'd plays and players you could get nowhere else. Notably, Booth always drew the best hearers; and to a specimen of his acting I will now attend in some detail.

I happen'd to see what has been reckon'd by experts one of the most marvelous pieces of histrionism ever known. It must have been about 1834 or '35. A favorite comedian and actress at the Bowery, Thomas Flynn and his wife, were to have a joint benefit, and, securing Booth for Richard, advertised the fact many days before-hand. The house fill'd early from top to bottom. There was some uneasiness behind the scenes, for the afternoon arrived, and Booth had not come from down in Maryland, where he lived. However, a few minutes before ringing-up time he made his appearance in lively condition.

After a one-act farce over, as contrast and prelude, the curtain rising for the tragedy, I can, from my good seat in the pit, pretty well front, see again Booth's quiet entrance from the side, as, with head bent, he slowly and in silence, (amid the tempest of boisterous hand-clapping,) walks down the stage to the footlights with that peculiar and abstracted gesture, musingly kicking his sword, which he holds off from him by its sash. Though fifty years have pass'd since then, I can hear the clank, and feel the perfect following hush of perhaps three thousand people waiting. (I never saw an actor who could make more of the said hush or wait, and hold the audience in an indescribable, half-delicious, half-irritating suspense.) And so throughout the entire play, all parts, voice, atmosphere, magnetism, from

"Now is the winter of our discontent,"

to the closing death fight with Richmond, were of the finest and grandest. The latter character was play'd by a stalwart young fellow named Ingersoll. Indeed, all the renderings were wonderfully good. But the great spell cast upon the mass of hearers came from Booth. Especially was the dream scene very impressive. A shudder went through every nervous system in the audience; it certainly did through mine.

Without question Booth was royal heir and legitimate representative

180. farce over] *NYTR:* farce is over

181. rising for the tragedy, I can, from] *NYTR:* rises for the tragedy. I can (from

183–184. slowly and . . . hand-clapping,) walks] Galley before revision: slowly and . . . hand-clappings,) walks] *NYTR:* slowly walks

187. perfect following hush] *NYTR:* perfect hush

of the Garrick-Kemble-Siddons dramatic traditions; but he vitalized and gave an unnamable *race* to those traditions with his own electric personal idiosyncrasy. (As in all art-utterance it was the subtle and powerful something *special to the individual* that really conquer'd.)

To me, too, Booth stands for much else besides theatricals. I consider that my seeing the man those years glimps'd for me, beyond all else, that inner spirit and form—the unquestionable charm and vivacity, but intrinsic sophistication and artificiality—crystallizing rapidly upon the English stage and literature at and after Shakspere's time, and coming on accumulatively through the seventeenth and eighteenth centuries to the beginning, fifty or forty years ago, of those disintegrating, decomposing processes now authoritatively going on. Yes; although Booth must be class'd in that antique, almost extinct school, inflated, stagy, rendering Shakspere (perhaps inevitably, appropriately) from the growth of arbitrary and often cockney conventions, his genius was to me one of the grandest revelations of my life, a lesson of artistic expression. The words fire, energy, *abandon*, found in him unprecedented meanings. I never heard a speaker or actor who could give such a sting to hauteur or the taunt. I never heard from any other the charm of unswervingly perfect vocalization without trenching at all on mere melody, the province of music.

So much for a Thespian temple of New York fifty years since, where "sceptred tragedy went trailing by" under the gaze of the Dry Dock youth, and both players and auditors were of a character and like we shall never see again. And so much for the grandest histrion of modern times, as near as I can deliberately judge (and the phrenologists put my "caution" at 7)—grander, I believe, than Kean in the expression of electric passion, the prime eligibility of the tragic artist. For though those brilliant years had many fine and even magnificent actors, undoubtedly at Booth's death (in 1852) went the last and by far the noblest Roman of them all.

204. *NYTR* continues the same paragraph.
204. too, Booth stands] *NYTR:* too, he stands
208. Shakspere's] *NYTR:* Shakespeare's
213. Shakspere] *NYTR:* Shakespeare
220. The *NYTR* article ends with this paragraph, with Whitman's name following.
226. "caution" at 7)] Galley before revision: "caution" &c. at 7)

Notes to Late English Books.

"SPECIMEN DAYS IN AMERICA," LONDON EDITION, JUNE, 1887. PREFACE TO THE READER IN THE BRITISH ISLANDS.

If you will only take the following pages, as you do some long and gossippy letter written for you by a relative or friend traveling through distant scenes and incidents, and jotting them down lazily and informally, but ever veraciously (with occasional diversions of critical thought about somebody or something,) it might remove all formal or literary impediments at once, and bring you and me close together in the spirit in which the jottings were collated to be read. You have had, and have, plenty of public events and facts and general statistics of America;—in the following book is a common individual New World *private life*, its birth and growth, its struggles for a living, its goings and comings and observations (or representative portions of them) amid the United States of America the last thirty or forty years, with their varied war and peace, their local coloring, the unavoidable egotism, and the lights and shades and sights and joys and pains and sympathies common to humanity. Further introductory light may be found in the paragraph, "A Happy Hour's Command," and the bottom note belonging to it, at the beginning of the book. I have said in the text that if I were required to give good reason-for-being of "Specimen Days," I should be unable to do so. Let me fondly hope that it has at least the reason and excuse of such off-hand gossippy letter as just alluded to, portraying American life-sights and incidents as they actually occurred—their presentation, making additions as far as it goes, to the simple experience and association of your soul, from a comrade soul;—and that also, in the volume, as below any page of mine, anywhere, ever remains, for seen or unseen basis-phrase, GOOD-WILL BETWEEN THE COMMON PEOPLE OF ALL NATIONS.

ADDITIONAL NOTE, 1887, TO ENGLISH EDITION "SPECIMEN DAYS."

As I write these lines I still continue living in Camden, New Jersey, America. Coming this way from Washington City, on my road to the sea-

Notes to Late English Books.

The first of these items (lines 1–25) was first published as "Preface to the Reader in the British Islands" at the beginning of SDA, the second (lines 26–68) first appeared as "Additional Note. *Written 1887 for the English Edition*," at the end of SDA, and the third (lines 69–100) first appeared as the Preface to DVOP. No MS version is known to the present editor. All of "Preface to the Reader in the

shore (and a temporary rest, as I supposed) in the early summer of 1873, I broke down disabled, and have dwelt here, as my central residence, all the time since—almost 14 years. In the preceding pages I have described how, during those years, I partially recuperated (in 1876) from my worst paralysis by going down to Timber Creek, living close to Nature, and domiciling with my dear friends, George and Susan Stafford. From 1877 or '8 to '83 or '4 I was well enough to travel around, considerably—journey'd westward to Kansas, leisurely exploring the Prairies, and on to Denver and the Rocky Mountains; another time north to Canada, where I spent most of the summer with my friend Dr. Bucke, and jaunted along the great lakes, and the St. Lawrence and Saguenay rivers; another time to Boston, to properly print the final edition of my poems (I was there over two months, and had a "good time.") I have so brought out the completed "Leaves of Grass" during this period; also "Specimen Days," of which the foregoing is a transcript; collected and re-edited the "Democratic Vistas" cluster (see companion volume to the present)—commemorated Abraham Lincoln's death, on the successive anniversaries of its occurrence, by delivering my lecture on it ten or twelve times; and "put in," through many a month and season, the aimless and resultless ways of most human lives.

Thus the last 14 years have pass'd. At present (end-days of March, 1887—I am nigh entering my 69th year) I find myself continuing on here, quite dilapidated and even wreck'd bodily from the paralysis, &c. —but in *good heart* (to use a Long Island country phrase,) and with about the same mentality as ever. The worst of it is, I have been growing feebler quite rapidly for a year, and now can't walk around—hardly from one room to the next. I am forced to stay in-doors and in my big chair nearly all the time. We have had a sharp, dreary winter too, and it has pinch'd me. I am alone most of the time; every week, indeed almost every day, write some—reminiscences, essays, sketches, for the magazines; and read, or rather I should say dawdle over books and papers a good deal—spend half the day at that.

Nor can I finish this note without putting on record—wafting over sea from hence—my deepest thanks to certain friends and helpers (I would specify them all and each by name, but imperative reasons, outside of my

British Islands" and the first three paragraphs of "Additional Note" (lines 1–68) were reprinted in *NB* without change. After line 68 *SDA* has two concluding paragraphs not reprinted in *NB* at this point because they are partly identical with "A Backward Glance O'er Travel'd Roads," lines 437–453 and 502–505, *q.v.* The "Preface" to *DVOP* (lines 69–100) was reprinted in *NB* without change. The galley proofs for *NB* in the Feinberg Collection show no revisions.

own wishes, forbid,) in the British Islands, as well as in America. Dear, even in the abstract, is such flattering unction always no doubt to the soul! Nigher still, if possible, I myself have been, and am to-day indebted to such help for my very sustenance, clothing, shelter, and continuity. And I would not go to the grave without briefly, but plainly, as I here do, acknowledging—may I not say even glorying in it?

PREFACE TO "DEMOCRATIC VISTAS" WITH OTHER PAPERS.—ENGLISH EDITION.

Mainly I think I should base the request to weigh the following pages on the assumption that they present, however indirectly, some views of the West and Modern, or of a distinctly western and modern (American) tendency, about certain matters.

Then, too, the pages include (by attempting to illustrate it,) a theory herein immediately mentioned. For another and different point of the issue, the Enlightenment, Democracy and Fair-show of the bulk, the common people of America (from sources representing not only the British Islands, but all the world,) means, at least, eligibility to Enlightenment, Democracy and Fair-show for the bulk, the common people of all civilized nations.

That positively "the dry land has appeared," at any rate, is an important fact.

America is really the great test or trial case for all the problems and promises and speculations of humanity, and of the past and present.

I say, too, we* are not to look so much to changes, ameliorations, and adaptations in Politics as to those of Literature and (thence) domestic Sociology. I have accordingly in the following melange introduced many themes besides political ones.

Several of the pieces are ostensibly in explanation of my own writings; but in that very process they best include and set forth their side of principles and generalities pressing vehemently for consideration our age.

* We who, in many departments, ways, make *the building up of the masses*, by *building up grand individuals*, our shibboleth: and in brief that is the marrow of this book.

Abraham Lincoln.

First published, without separate title, in *RAL* (pp. 469–475), edited by Allen Thorndike Rice (New York, 1886). Rice was then general editor of *NAR*. It does not appear in *DVOP*. Whether the text of *NB* was printed from MS or clippings of *RAL* is not known. The galley proof for *NB* in the Feinberg Collection shows no revision except as mentioned in the collation.

1. give—were . . . lacking—even] *RAL:* give even

Upon the whole, it is on the atmosphere they are born in, and, (I hope) give out, more than any specific piece or trait, I would care to rest.

I think Literature—a new, superb, democratic literature—is to be the medicine and lever, and (with Art) the chief influence in modern civilization. I have myself not so much made a dead set at this theory, or attempted to present it directly, as admitted it to color and sometimes dominate what I had to say. In both Europe and America we have serried phalanxes who promulge and defend the political claims: I go for an equal force to uphold the other.

WALT WHITMAN.

CAMDEN, NEW JERSEY, *April*, 1888.

Abraham Lincoln.

Glad am I to give—were anything better lacking—even the most brief and shorn testimony of Abraham Lincoln. Everything I heard about him authentically, and every time I saw him (and it was my fortune through 1862 to '65 to see, or pass a word with, or watch him, personally, perhaps twenty or thirty times,) added to and anneal'd my respect and love at the moment. And as I dwell on what I myself heard or saw of the mighty Westerner, and blend it with the history and literature of my age, and of what I can get of all ages, and conclude it with his death, it seems like some tragic play, superior to all else I know—vaster and fierier and more convulsionary, for this America of ours, than Eschylus or Shakspere ever drew for Athens or for England. And then the Moral permeating, underlying all! the Lesson that none so remote—none so illiterate—no age, no class—but may directly or indirectly read!

Abraham Lincoln's was really one of those characters, the best of which is the result of long trains of cause and effect—needing a certain spaciousness of time, and perhaps even remoteness, to properly enclose them—having unequal'd influence on the shaping of this Republic (and

2. testimony of] *RAL:* testimony in memory of

5. *RAL* has an asterisk after "times" and a footnote beginning as follows: * "From my Note-book in 1864, at Washington City, I find this memorandum, under date of August 12:" Then follows the description, with some variations, that Whitman first used in an article in *NYT*, August 16, 1863, and later in *MDW* (pp. 22–24) and in *SDC* (pp. 43–44). For collation see notes on the section "Abraham Lincoln," *Prose 1892*, I.

11. Shakspere] *RAL:* Shakspeare

therefore the world) as to-day, and then far more important in the future. Thus the time has by no means yet come for a thorough measurement of him. Nevertheless, we who live in his era—who have seen him, and heard him, face to face, and are in the midst of, or just parting from, the strong and strange events which he and we have had to do with—can in some respects bear valuable, perhaps indispensable testimony concerning him.

I should first like to give a very fair and characteristic likeness of Lincoln, as I saw him and watch'd him one afternoon in Washington, for nearly half an hour, not long before his death. It was as he stood on the balcony of the National Hotel, Pennsylvania Avenue, making a short speech to the crowd in front, on the occasion either of a set of new colors presented to a famous Illinois regiment, or of the daring capture, by the Western men, of some flags from "the enemy," (which latter phrase, by the by, was not used by him at all in his remarks.) How the picture happen'd to be made I do not know, but I bought it a few days afterward in Washington, and it was endors'd by every one to whom I show'd it. Though hundreds of portraits have been made, by painters and photographers, (many to pass on, by copies, to future times,) I have never seen one yet that in my opinion deserv'd to be called a perfectly *good likeness;* nor do I believe there is really such a one in existence. May I not say too, that, as there is no entirely competent and emblematic likeness of Abraham Lincoln in picture or statue, there is not—perhaps cannot be—any fully appropriate literary statement or summing-up of him yet in existence?

The best way to estimate the value of Lincoln is to think what the condition of America would be to-day, if he had never lived—never been President. His nomination and first election were mainly accidents, experiments. Severely view'd, one cannot think very much of American Political Parties, from the beginning, after the Revolutionary War, down to the present time. Doubtless, while they have had their uses—have been and are "the grass on which the cow feeds"—and indispensable economies of growth—it is undeniable that under flippant names they have merely identified temporary passions, or freaks, or sometimes

25. give a] *RAL:* give what I call a

25–42. This was a photograph by Brady. Whitman's copy is in the Feinberg Collection. It is reprinted in *RAL* between pages 470 and 471.

42. existence?] *RAL:* existence.

56–57. Saxon, and Franklin—of the] *RAL:* Saxon and Franklin of the

60. European, was quite thoroughly Western] *RAL:* European, far more Western,

prejudice, ignorance, or hatred. The only thing like a great and worthy idea vitalizing a party, and making it heroic, was the enthusiasm in '64 for re-electing Abraham Lincoln, and the reason behind that enthusiasm.

How does this man compare with the acknowledg'd "Father of his country?" Washington was model'd on the best Saxon, and Franklin—of the age of the Stuarts (rooted in the Elizabethan period)—was essentially a noble Englishman, and just the kind needed for the occasions and the times of 1776–'83. Lincoln, underneath his practicality, was far less European, was quite thoroughly Western, original, essentially non-conventional, and had a certain sort of out-door or prairie stamp. One of the best of the late commentators on Shakspere, (Professor Dowden,) makes the height and aggregate of his quality as a poet to be, that he thoroughly blended the ideal with the practical or realistic. If this be so, I should say that what Shakspere did in poetic expression, Abraham Lincoln essentially did in his personal and official life. I should say the invisible foundations and vertebra of his character, more than any man's in history, were mystical, abstract, moral and spiritual—while upon all of them was built, and out of all of them radiated, under the control of the average of circumstances, what the vulgar call *horse-sense*, and a life often bent by temporary but most urgent materialistic and political reasons.

He seems to have been a man of indomitable firmness (even obstinacy) on rare occasions, involving great points; but he was generally very easy, flexible, tolerant, almost slouchy, respecting minor matters. I note that even those reports and anecdotes intended to level him down, all leave the tinge of a favorable impression of him. As to his religious nature, it seems to me to have certainly been of the amplest, deepest-rooted, loftiest kind.

Already a new generation begins to tread the stage, since the persons and events of the Secession War. I have more than once fancied to myself the time when the present century has closed, and a new one open'd, and the men and deeds of that contest have become somewhat vague and mythical—fancied perhaps in some great Western city, or group collected together, or public festival, where the days of old, of 1863 and '4 and '5 are discuss'd—some ancient soldier sitting in the background as the talk

62 and 65. Shakspere] *RAL:* Shakespeare

74. tolerant, almost slouchy, respecting] *RAL:* tolerant, respecting

77–78. deepest-rooted, loftiest kind.] *RAL:* deepest-rooted kind.

78. After this line Whitman deletes, in the galley proof, the following paragraph: "But I do not care to dwell on the features presented so many times, and that will readily occur to every one in recalling Abraham Lincoln and his era. It is more from the wish—and it no doubt actuates others—to bring for our own sake, some record, however incompetent—some leaf or little wreath to place, as on a grave."

goes on, and betraying himself by his emotion and moist eyes—like the journeying Ithacan at the banquet of King Alcinoüs, when the bard sings the contending warriors and their battles on the plains of Troy:

"So from the sluices of Ulysses' eyes
Fast fell the tears, and sighs succeeded sighs."

I have fancied, I say, some such venerable relic of this time of ours, preserv'd to the next or still the next generation of America. I have fancied, on such occasion, the young men gathering around; the awe, the eager questions: "What! have you seen Abraham Lincoln—and heard him speak—and touch'd his hand? Have you, with your own eyes, look'd on Grant, and Lee, and Sherman?"

Dear to Democracy, to the very last! And among the paradoxes generated by America, not the least curious was that spectacle of all the kings and queens and emperors of the earth, many from remote distances, sending tributes of condolence and sorrow in memory of one rais'd through the commonest average of life—a rail-splitter and flat-boatman!

Consider'd from contemporary points of view—who knows what the future may decide?—and from the points of view of current Democracy and The Union, (the only thing like passion or infatuation in the man was the passion for the Union of These States,) Abraham Lincoln seems to me the grandest figure yet, on all the crowded canvas of the Nineteenth Century.

[*From the New Orleans Picayune, Jan. 25, 1887.*]

New Orleans in 1848.

Walt Whitman Gossips of His Sojourn Here Years Ago as a Newspaper Writer. Notes of His Trip Up the Mississippi and to New York.

Among the letters brought this morning (Camden, New Jersey, Jan. 15, 1887,) by my faithful post-office carrier, J. G., is one as follows:

89–90. The lines, correctly quoted, are from Pope's translation of the *Odyssey*, near the end of Book VIII.

94. RAL has a period after "questions".

107. RAL has Whitman's name after this line.

New Orleans in 1848.

First published in NOP, January 25, 1887, under the same title and headlines. Not in DVOP. Whether the text of NB was printed from MS or clippings of NOP is

"New Orleans, Jan. 11, '87.—We have been informed that when you were younger and less famous than now, you were in New Orleans and perhaps have helped on the *Picayune*. If you have any remembrance of the *Picayune's* young days, or of journalism in New Orleans of that era, and would put it in writing (verse or prose) for the *Picayune's* fiftieth year edition, Jan. 25, we shall be pleased," etc.

In response to which: I went down to New Orleans early in 1848 to work on a daily newspaper, but it was not the *Picayune*, though I saw quite a good deal of the editors of that paper, and knew its personnel and ways. But let me indulge my pen in some gossipy recollections of that time and place, with extracts from my journal up the Mississippi and across the great lakes to the Hudson.

Probably the influence most deeply pervading everything at that time through the United States, both in physical facts and in sentiment, was the Mexican War, then just ended. Following a brilliant campaign (in which our troops had march'd to the capital city, Mexico, and taken full possession,) we were returning after our victory. From the situation of the country, the city of New Orleans had been our channel and *entrepot* for everything, going and returning. It had the best news and war correspondents; it had the most to say, through its leading papers, the *Picayune* and *Delta* especially, and its voice was readiest listen'd to; from it "Chapparal" had gone out, and his army and battle letters were copied everywhere, not only in the United States, but in Europe. Then the social cast and results; no one who has never seen the society of a city under similar circumstances can understand what a strange vivacity and *rattle* were given throughout by such a situation. I remember the crowds of soldiers, the gay young officers, going or coming, the receipt of important news, the many discussions, the returning wounded, and so on.

I remember very well seeing Gen. Taylor with his staff and other officers at the St. Charles Theatre one evening (after talking with them during the day.) There was a short play on the stage, but the principal performance was of Dr. Colyer's troupe of "Model Artists," then in the full tide of their popularity. They gave many fine groups and solo shows.

not known. Galley proofs for *NB* in the Feinberg Collection are collated with the published texts.

1–2. morning (Camden, New Jersey, Jan. 15, 1887,)] *NOP:* morning (Jan. 15, 1887.)

5. The names of newspapers, *Picayune* and *Crescent*, are regularly italicized in *NB*, but not in *NOP.*

17. then just ended.] *NOP:* then near its end.

23. *Picayune* and *Delta* especially] *NOP:* Picayune especially

34. was of Dr.] *NOP:* was from Dr.

The house was crowded with uniforms and shoulder-straps. Gen. T. himself, if I remember right, was almost the only officer in civilian clothes; he was a jovial, old, rather stout, plain man, with a wrinkled and dark-yellow face, and, in ways and manners, show'd the least of conventional ceremony or etiquette I ever saw; he laugh'd unrestrainedly at everything comical. (He had a great personal resemblance to Fenimore Cooper, the novelist, of New York.) I remember Gen. Pillow and quite a cluster of other militaires also present.

One of my choice amusements during my stay in New Orleans was going down to the old French Market, especially of a Sunday morning. The show was a varied and curious one; among the rest, the Indian and negro hucksters with their wares. For there were always fine specimens of Indians, both men and women, young and old. I remember I nearly always on these occasions got a large cup of delicious coffee with a biscuit, for my breakfast, from the immense shining copper kettle of a great Creole mulatto woman (I believe she weigh'd 230 pounds.) I never have had such coffee since. About nice drinks, anyhow, my recollection of the "cobblers" (with strawberries and snow on top of the large tumblers,) and also the exquisite wines, and the perfect and mild French brandy, help the regretful reminiscence of my New Orleans experiences of those days. And what splendid and roomy and leisurely bar-rooms! particularly the grand ones of the St. Charles and St. Louis. Bargains, auctions, appointments, business conferences, &c., were generally held in the spaces or recesses of these bar-rooms.

I used to wander a midday hour or two now and then for amusement on the crowded and bustling levees, on the banks of the river. The diagonally wedg'd-in boats, the stevedores, the piles of cotton and other merchandise, the carts, mules, negroes, etc., afforded never-ending studies and sights to me. I made acquaintances among the captains, boatmen, or other characters, and often had long talks with them—sometimes finding a real rough diamond among my chance encounters. Sundays I sometimes went forenoons to the old Catholic Cathedral in the French quarter. I used to walk a good deal in this arrondissement; and I have deeply regretted since that I did not cultivate, while I had such a good opportunity, the chance of better knowledge of French and Spanish Creole New Orleans people. (I have an idea that there is much and of importance about the Latin race contributions to American nationality

38–39. dark-yellow face] *NOP:* dark yellow face
39. manners, show'd the least] *NOP:* manners, the least
41–42. This sentence, beginning "He had", is not enclosed in parentheses in *NOP.*
58–59. in the . . . these] *NOP:* in these] (Revision made on the galley proof.)

in the South and Southwest that will never be put with sympathetic understanding and tact on record.)

Let me say, for better detail, that through several months (1848) I work'd on a new daily paper, *The Crescent;* my situation rather a pleasant one. My young brother, Jeff, was with me; and he not only grew very homesick, but the climate of the place, and especially the water, seriously disagreed with him. From this and other reasons (although I was quite happily fix'd) I made no very long stay in the South. In due time we took passage northward for St. Louis in the "Pride of the West" steamer, which left her wharf just at dusk. My brother was unwell, and lay in his berth from the moment we left till the next morning; he seem'd to me to be in a fever, and I felt alarm'd. However, the next morning he was all right again, much to my relief.

Our voyage up the Mississippi was after the same sort as the voyage, some months before, down it. The shores of this great river are very monotonous and dull—one continuous and rank flat, with the exception of a meagre stretch of bluff, about the neighborhood of Natchez, Memphis, etc. Fortunately we had good weather, and not a great crowd of passengers, though the berths were all full. The "Pride" jogg'd along pretty well, and put us into St. Louis about noon Saturday. After looking around a little I secured passage on the steamer "Prairie Bird," (to leave late in the afternoon,) bound up the Illinois River to La Salle, where we were to take canal for Chicago. During the day I rambled with my brother over a large portion of the town, search'd after a refectory, and, after much trouble, succeeded in getting some dinner.

Our "Prairie Bird" started out at dark, and a couple of hours after there was quite a rain and blow, which made them haul in along shore and tie fast. We made but thirty miles the whole night. The boat was excessively crowded with passengers, and had withal so much freight that we could hardly turn around. I slept on the floor, and the night was uncomfortable enough. The Illinois River is spotted with little villages with big names, Marseilles, Naples, etc.; its banks are low, and the vegetation excessively rank. Peoria, some distance up, is a pleasant town; I went over the place; the country back is all rich land, for sale cheap. Three or four miles from P., land of the first quality can be bought for $3 or $4 an acre. (I am transcribing from my notes written at the time.)

Arriving at La Salle Tuesday morning, we went on board a canal-

66. among my chance] *NOP:* among such chance

73. Southwest that] *NOP:* Southwest that I have grown to think highly of and that

73–74. put with . . . tact on] *NOP:* put on [Revision made on the galley proof.]

81. *NOP* omits quotation marks enclosing all names of ships.

boat, had a detention by sticking on a mud bar, and then jogg'd along at a slow trot, some seventy of us, on a moderate-sized boat. (If the weather hadn't been rather cool, particularly at night, it would have been insufferable.) Illinois is the most splendid agricultural country I ever saw; the land is of surpassing richness; the place par excellence for farmers. We stopt at various points along the canal, some of them pretty villages.

It was 10 o'clock A.M. when we got in Chicago, too late for the steamer; so we went to an excellent public house, the "American Temperance," and I spent the time that day and till next morning, looking around Chicago.

At 9 the next forenoon we started on the "Griffith" (on board of which I am now inditing these memoranda,) up the blue waters of Lake Michigan. I was delighted with the appearance of the towns along Wisconsin. At Milwaukee I went on shore, and walk'd around the place. They say the country back is beautiful and rich. (It seems to me that if we should ever remove from Long Island, Wisconsin would be the proper place to come to.) The towns have a remarkable appearance of good living, without any penury or want. The country is so good naturally, and labor is in such demand.

About 5 o'clock one afternoon I heard the cry of "a woman overboard." It proved to be a crazy lady, who had become so from the loss of her son a couple of weeks before. The small boat put off, and succeeded in picking her up, though she had been in the water 15 minutes. She was dead. Her husband was on board. They went off at the next stopping place. While she lay in the water she probably recover'd her reason, as she toss'd up her arms and lifted her face toward the boat.

Sunday Morning, June 11.—We pass'd down Lake Huron yesterday and last night, and between 4 and 5 o'clock this morning we ran on the "flats," and have been vainly trying, with the aid of a steam tug and a lumbering lighter, to get clear again. The day is beautiful and the water clear and calm. Night before last we stopt at Mackinaw, (the island and town,) and I went up on the old fort, one of the oldest stations in the Northwest. We expect to get to Buffalo by to-morrow. The tug has fasten'd lines to us, but some have been snapt and the others have no effect. We seem to be firmly imbedded in the sand. (With the exception

117–118. *NOP* omits quotation marks around "American Temperance."

119. After "Chicago." *NOP* has the following sentence to end the paragraph: "The city is a fine one, and has every appearance of thrift."

128. After "in such demand." *NOP* continues with three paragraphs (13–15), omitted in *NB*. These three paragraphs were first condensed to two in the printing of *NB*, as shown by the galley proof, and then deleted; the galley readings, when

of a larger boat and better accommodations, it amounts to about the same thing as a becalmment I underwent on the Montauk voyage, East Long Island, last summer.) Later.—We are off again—expect to reach Detroit before dinner.

We did not stop at Detroit. We are now on Lake Erie, jogging along at a good round pace. A couple of hours since we were on the river above. Detroit seem'd to me a pretty place and thrifty. I especially liked the looks of the Canadian shore opposite and of the little village of Windsor, and, indeed, all along the banks of the river. From the shrubbery and the neat appearance of some of the cottages, I think it must have been settled by the French. While I now write we can see a little distance ahead the scene of the battle between Perry's fleet and the British during the last war with England. The lake looks to me a fine sheet of water. We are having a beautiful day.

June 12.—We stopt last evening at Cleveland, and though it was dark, I took the opportunity of rambling about the place; went up in the heart of the city and back to what appear'd to be the court-house. The streets are unusually wide, and the buildings appear to be substantial and comfortable. We went down through Main Street and found, some distance along, several squares of ground very prettily planted with trees and looking attractive enough. Return'd to the boat by way of the lighthouse on the hill.

This morning we are making for Buffalo, being, I imagine, a little more than half across Lake Erie. The water is rougher than on Michigan or Huron. (On St. Clair it was smooth as glass.) The day is bright and dry, with a stiff head wind.

We arriv'd in Buffalo on Monday evening; spent that night and a portion of next day going round the city exploring. Then got in the cars and went to Niagara; went under the falls—saw the whirlpool and all the other sights.

Tuesday night started for Albany; travel'd all night. From the time daylight afforded us a view of the country all seem'd very rich and well cultivated. Every few miles were large towns or villages.

Wednesday late we arriv'd at Albany. Spent the evening in exploring. There was a political meeting (Hunker) at the capitol, but I pass'd it by.

different from *NOP*, are inserted in brackets. See Appendix XIII, 1.

129. 5 o'clock one afternoon] *NOP:* 5 o'clock this afternoon [Revision made on the galley proof.]

136. Sunday Morning, June 11.—We pass'd] *NOP:* Sunday Morning, June 11.—On a sandbar, in the St. Clair flats, where we have been stuck for a couple of hours.
We passed

Next morning I started down the Hudson in the "Alida;" arriv'd safely in New York that evening.

Small Memoranda.

Thousands lost—here one or two preserv'd.

Attorney General's Office, *Washington, Aug. 22, 1865.*—As I write this, about noon, the suite of rooms here is fill'd with southerners, standing in squads, or streaming in and out, some talking with the Pardon Clerk, some waiting to see the Attorney General, others discussing in low tones among themselves. All are mainly anxious about their pardons. The famous 13th exception of the President's Amnesty Proclamation of ———, makes it necessary that every secessionist, whose property is worth $20,-000 or over, shall get a special pardon, before he can transact any legal purchase, sale, &c. So hundreds and thousands of such property owners have either sent up here, for the last two months, or have been, or are now coming personally here, to get their pardons. They are from Virginia, Georgia, Alabama, Mississippi, North and South Carolina, and every southern State. Some of their written petitions are very abject. Secession officers of the rank of Brigadier General, or higher, also need these special pardons. They also come here. I see streams of the $20,000 men, (and some women,) every day. I talk now and then with them, and learn much that is interesting and significant. All the southern women that come (some splendid specimens, mothers, &c.) are dress'd in deep black.

Immense numbers (several thousands) of these pardons have been pass'd upon favorably; the Pardon Warrants (like great deeds) have been issued from the State Department, on the requisition of this office. But for some reason or other, they nearly all yet lie awaiting the President's signature. He seems to be in no hurry about it, but lets them wait.

The crowds that come here make a curious study for me. I get along, very sociably, with any of them—as I let them do all the talking; only now and then I have a long confab, or ask a suggestive question or two.

If the thing continues as at present, the property and wealth of the Southern States is going to legally rest, for the future, on these pardons.

181. After this line *NOP* has Walt Whitman's name to end the article.

Small Memoranda.

All of this section, except the last item, "The Place Gratitude Fills in a Fine Character," seems to have been published for the first time in *NB*. The galley proof is in the Feinberg Collection and is here collated with the published texts.

Every single one is made out with the condition that the grantee shall respect the abolition of slavery, and never make an attempt to restore it.

Washington, Sept. 8, 9, *&c.*, 1865.—The arrivals, swarms, &c., of the $20,000 men seeking pardons, still continue with increas'd numbers and pertinacity. I yesterday (I am a clerk in the U. S. Attorney General's office here) made out a long list from Alabama, nearly 200, recommended for pardon by the Provisional Governor. This list, in the shape of a requisition from the Attorney General, goes to the State Department. There the Pardon Warrants are made out, brought back here, and then sent to the President, where they await his signature. He is signing them very freely of late.

The President, indeed, as at present appears, has fix'd his mind on a very generous and forgiving course toward the return'd secessionists. He will not countenance at all the demand of the extreme Philo-African element of the North, to make the right of negro voting at elections a condition and *sine qua non* of the reconstruction of the United States south, and of their resumption of co-equality in the Union.

A glint inside of Abraham Lincoln's Cabinet appointments. One item of many.—While it was hanging in suspense who should be appointed Secretary of the Interior, (to take the place of Caleb Smith,) the choice was very close between Mr. Harlan and Col. Jesse K. Dubois, of Illinois. The latter had many friends. He was competent, he was honest, and he was a *man*. Mr. Harlan, in the race, finally gain'd the Methodist interest, and got himself to be consider'd as identified with it; and his appointment was apparently ask'd for by that powerful body. Bishop Simpson, of Philadelphia, came on and spoke for the selection. The President was much perplex'd. The reasons for appointing Col. Dubois were very strong, almost insuperable—yet the argument for Mr. Harlan, under the adroit position he had plac'd himself, was heavy. Those who press'd him adduc'd the magnitude of the Methodists as a body, their loyalty, more general and genuine than any other sect—that they represented the West, and had a right to be heard—that all or nearly all the other great denominations had their representatives in the heads of the government—that they as a body and the great sectarian power of the West, formally ask'd

17–18. The words in parentheses were inserted in the galley proof.
26. The words "have a long confab, or" were inserted in the galley proof.
32. of the $20,000] Galley proof before revision: of $20,000
32. continue] Galley proof before revision: continues
54. for the selection] Galley proof after revision: for the H. selection] Galley proof before revision: for the appointment

Mr. Harlan's appointment—that he was of them, having been a Methodist minister—that it would not do to offend them, but was highly necessary to propitiate them.

Mr. Lincoln thought deeply over the whole matter. He was in more than usual tribulation on the subject. Let it be enough to say that though Mr. Harlan finally receiv'd the Secretaryship, Col. Dubois came as near being appointed as a man could, and not be. The decision was finally made one night about 10 o'clock. Bishop Simpson and other clergymen and leading persons in Mr. Harlan's behalf, had been talking long and vehemently with the President. A member of Congress who was pressing Col. Dubois's claims, was in waiting. The President had told the Bishop that he would make a decision that evening, and that he thought it unnecessary to be press'd any more on the subject. That night he call'd in the M. C. above alluded to, and said to him: "Tell Uncle Jesse that I want to give him this appointment, and yet I cannot. I will do almost anything else in the world for him I am able. I have thought the matter all over, and under the circumstances think the Methodists too good and too great a body to be slighted. They have stood by the government, and help'd us their very best. I have had no better friends; and as the case stands, I have decided to appoint Mr. Harlan."

NOTE TO A FRIEND.

[*Written on the fly-leaf of a copy of "Specimen Days," sent to Peter Doyle, at Washington, June, 1883.*]

Pete, do you remember—(of course you do—I do well)—those great long jovial walks we had at times for years, (1866–'72) out of Washington City—often moonlight nights—'way to "Good Hope";—or, Sundays, up and down the Potomac shores, one side or the other, sometimes ten miles at a stretch? Or when you work'd on the horse-cars, and I waited for you, coming home late together—or resting and chatting at the Market, corner 7th Street and the Avenue, and eating those nice musk or watermelons? Or during my tedious sickness and first paralysis ('73) how you used to come to my solitary garret-room and make up my bed, and enliven me, and chat for an hour or so—or perhaps go out and get the medicines Dr. Drinkard had order'd for me—before you went on duty? ....Give my love to dear Mrs. and Mr. Nash, and tell them I have not forgotten them, and never will. W. W.

98. forgotten them, and] Galley proof before revision: forgotten, and

106–131. This item was first published with the title "A Poet's Prose: the Place Walt Whitman Thinks Gratitude Fills in a Fine Character," in *PP*, November 27, 1884, and was not reprinted before *NB*.

WRITTEN IMPROMPTU IN AN ALBUM.

GERMANTOWN, PHILA., Dec. 26, '83.

In memory of these merry Christmas days and nights—to my friends Mr. and Mrs. Williams, Churchie, May, Gurney, and little Aubrey.........A heavy snow-storm blocking up everything, and keeping us in. But souls, hearts, thoughts, unloos'd. And so—one and all, little and big—hav'n't we had a good time? W. W.

From the Philadelphia Press, Nov. 27, 1884, (*Thanksgiving number.*)
THE PLACE GRATITUDE FILLS IN A FINE CHARACTER.

Scene.—A large family supper party, a night or two ago, with voices and laughter of the young, mellow faces of the old, and a by-and-by pause in the general jovialty. "Now, Mr. Whitman," spoke up one of the girls, "what have you to say about Thanksgiving? Won't you give us a sermon in advance, to sober us down?" The sage nodded smilingly, look'd a moment at the blaze of the great wood fire, ran his forefinger right and left through the heavy white moustache that might have otherwise impeded his voice, and began: "Thanksgiving goes probably far deeper than you folks suppose. I am not sure but it is the source of the highest poetry—as in parts of the Bible. Ruskin, indeed, makes the central source of all great art to be praise (gratitude) to the Almighty for life, and the universe with its objects and play of action.

"We Americans devote an official day to it every year; yet I sometimes fear the real article is almost dead or dying in our self-sufficient, independent Republic. Gratitude, anyhow, has never been made half enough of by the moralists; it is indispensable to a complete character, man's or woman's—the disposition to be appreciative, thankful. That is the main matter, the element, inclination—what geologists call the *trend.* Of my own life and writings I estimate the giving thanks part, with what it infers, as essentially the best item. I should say the quality of gratitude rounds the whole emotional nature; I should say love and faith would quite lack vitality without it. There are people—shall I call them even religious people, as things go?—who have no such trend to their disposition."

117–119. This sentence is not in *PP*.
125. element, inclination—what] *PP:* element—what
131. After "disposition." *PP* has this sentence, omitted in *NB*, to end the paragraph: "I pity 'em." Whitman's name appears at the end of the article in *PP*.

Last of the War Cases

Memorandized at the time, Washington, 1865–'66.

[Of reminiscences of the Secession War, after the rest is said, I have thought it remains to give a few special words—in some respects at the time the typical words of all, and most definite—of the samples of the kill'd and wounded in action, and of soldiers who linger'd afterward, from these wounds, or were laid up by obstinate disease or prostration. The general statistics have been printed already, but can bear to be briefly stated again. There were over 3,000,000 men (for all periods of enlistment, large and small) furnish'd to the Union army during the war, New York State furnishing over 500,000, which was the greatest number of any one State. The losses by disease, wounds, kill'd in action, accidents, &c., were altogether about 600,000, or approximating to that number. Over 4,000,000 cases were treated in the main and adjudicatory army hospitals. The number sounds strange, but it is true. More than two-thirds of the deaths were from prostration or disease. To-day there lie buried over 300,000 soldiers in the various National army Cemeteries, more than half of them (and that is really the most significant and eloquent bequest of the War) mark'd "unknown." In full mortuary statistics of the war, the greatest deficiency arises from our not having

Last of the War Cases.

Reprinted in NB from an article entitled "Army Hospitals and Cases. Memoranda at the Time, 1863–66," in CEN, October, 1888 (Vol. 36, pp. 825–830). Parts of the article had been included in SDC, but these were omitted in NB (see notes on lines 138 and 181 below). The galley proofs are in the Feinberg Collection.

1–2. said, I have thought it] *CEN:* said, it

2–3. respects at the time the] *CEN:* respects the

3. most definite—of the samples of] *CEN:* most definitive—of the army hospitals and samples of those that filled them, of

5. by obstinate disease] *CEN:* by disease

6. have been] *CEN:* have perhaps been

6. but can] *CEN:* but, as introductory to the incidents I am going to describe, they can

7. 3,000,000 men] *CEN:* 2,000,000 men

9. furnishing over 500,000] *CEN:* furnishing nearly 500,000

11. about 600,000] *CEN:* about 300,000

12. Over 4,000,000 cases] *CEN:* Over 6,000,000 cases

12–13. the main and adjudicatory army] *CEN:* the army

16–17. The words in parentheses are not in CEN.

20. helps conceal] *CEN:* helps to conceal

21. places; it] *CEN:* places. It

21–22. The words in parentheses are not in CEN.

22–23. died, largely . . . And now,] *CEN:* died in the hands of the enemy.* And now,

the rolls, even as far as they were kept, of most of the Southern military prisons—a gap which probably both adds to, and helps conceal, the indescribable horrors of those places; it is, however, (restricting one vivid point only) certain that over 30,000 Union soldiers, died, largely of actual starvation, in them. And now, leaving all figures and their "sum totals," I feel sure a few genuine memoranda of such things—some cases jotted down '64, '65, and '66—made at the time and on the spot, with all the associations of those scenes and places brought back, will not only go directest to the right spot, but give a clearer and more actual sight of that period, than anything else. Before I give the last cases I begin with verbatim extracts from letters home to my mother in Brooklyn, the second year of the war.—W. W.]

Washington, Oct. 13, 1863.—There has been a new lot of wounded and sick arriving for the last three days. The first and second days, long strings of ambulances with the sick. Yesterday the worst, many with bad and bloody wounds, inevitably long neglected. I thought I was cooler and more used to it, but the sight of some cases brought tears into my eyes. I had the luck yesterday, however, to do lots of good. Had provided many nourishing articles for the men for another quarter, but, fortunately, had my stores where I could use them at once for these new-comers, as they arrived, faint, hungry, fagg'd out from their journey, with soil'd clothes, and all bloody. I distributed these articles, gave partly to the

23. The asterisk in CEN refers to the following footnote, omitted in NB:
"The latest official compilation (1885) shows the Union mortality to have been 359, 528, of whom 29,498 died in Southern prisons.—Editor."

24–25. things—some . . . made] CEN: things, made

25–26. spot, . . . places] CEN: spot, defective as they are, but with all the associations of those persons, scenes, and places

27–28. sight of that] CEN: sight of "army hospitals and cases" during that

28. else. Before . . . I] CEN: else. I

31–51. These two paragraphs are a revision of the second paragraph of Whitman's letter to his mother on October 13, 1863. (See Letter 88, *The Correspondence of Walt Whitman*, edited by Edwin H. Miller, I, 165–166.) The published text of this letter in Miller's edition, abbreviated CWW, is here collated with other texts.

31–32. In place of the first sentence CWW has: "There is a new lot of wounded now again. They have been arriving, sick & wounded, for three days—"

32. The first and second days, long] CWW: First long

33. Yesterday the worst, many] CWW: But yesterday many

34. wounds, inevitably long neglected. I] CWW: wounds, poor fellows. I

35. some cases brought] CWW: some of them brought

36–40. For these two sentences CWW has: "Mother, I had the good luck yesterday to do quite a great deal of good—I had provided a lot of nourishing things for the men, but for another quarter—but I had them where I could use them immediately for these new wounded as they came in faint & hungry, & fagged out with a long rough journey, all dirty & torn, & many pale as ashes, & all bloody—"

40. distributed these articles, gave] CWW: distributed my stores, gave

nurses I knew, or to those in charge. As many as possible I fed myself. Then I found a lot of oyster soup handy, and bought it all at once.

It is the most pitiful sight, this, when the men are first brought in, from some camp hospital broke up, or a part of the army moving. These who arrived yesterday are cavalry men. Our troops had fought like devils, but got the worst of it. They were Kilpatrick's cavalry; were in the rear, part of Meade's retreat, and the reb cavalry, knowing the ground and taking a favorable opportunity, dash'd in between, cut them off, and shell'd them terribly. But Kilpatrick turn'd and brought them out mostly. It was last Sunday. (One of the most terrible sights and tasks is of such receptions.)

Oct. 27, 1863.—If any of the soldiers I know (or their parents or folks) should call upon you—as they are often anxious to have my address in Brooklyn—you just use them as you know how, and if you happen to have pot-luck, and feel to ask them to take a bite, don't be afraid to do so. I have a friend, Thomas Neat, 2d N. Y. Cavalry, wounded in leg, now home in Jamaica, on furlough; he will probably call. Then possibly a Mr. Haskell, or some of his folks, from western New York: he had a son died here, and I was with the boy a good deal. The old man and his wife

41. knew, or . . . possible I] *CWW:* knew that were just taking charge of them —& as many as I could I
42. Then I] *CWW:* Then besides I
42. and bought it] *CWW:* & I procured it
43. *CWW* continues in the same paragraph.
43–46. For these three sentences *CWW* has: "Mother, it is the most pitiful sight I think when first the men are brought in—I have to bustle round, to keep from crying—they are such rugged young men—all these just arrived are cavalry men—Our troops got the worst of it, but fought like devils."
46. They were] *CWW:* Our men engaged were
46. cavalry; were] *CWW:* cavalry. They were
46–47. rear, part] *CWW:* rear as part
47–49. cavalry, knowing . . . and shell'd] *CWW:* cavalry cut in between & cut them off & [attacked] them & shelled
49. Kilpatrick turn'd and brought] *CWW:* Kilpatrick brought
49–50. mostly. It was] *CWW:* mostly—this was
50–51. This sentence is not in *CWW*, and it is not in *CEN*.
52–63. This paragraph is a revision of the third paragraph of Whitman's letter to his mother on October 27, 1863 (*CWW*, I, 172–174). The published text in Miller's edition, cited above, is here collated with other texts.
52–53. If any . . . should call] *CWW:* Mother, if any of my soldier boys should ever call
53–54. *CWW* has parentheses where *NB* and *CEN* have dashes.
54. how, and] *CWW:* how to without ceremony, &
55–56. so. . . . Thomas Neat] *CWW:* so—there is one very good boy, Thos Neat
56–57. leg, now . . . call. Then] *CWW:* leg—he is now home on furlough, his folks live I think in Jamaica, he is a noble boy, he may call upon you, (I gave him here $1 toward buying his crutches &c.)—I like him very much—Then
58. New York: he] *CWW:* New York, may call—he

have written me and ask'd me my Brooklyn address; he said he had children in New York, and was occasionally down there. (When I come home I will show you some of the letters I get from mothers, sisters, fathers, &c. They will make you cry.)

How the time passes away! To think it is over a year since I left home suddenly—and have mostly been down in front since. The year has vanish'd swiftly, and oh, what scenes I have witness'd during that time! And the war is not settled yet; and one does not see anything certain, or even promising, of a settlement. But I do not lose the solid feeling, in myself, that the Union triumph is assured, whether it be sooner or whether it be later, or whatever roundabout way we may be led there; and I find I don't change that conviction from any reverses we meet, nor delays, nor blunders. One realizes here in Washington the great labors, even the negative ones, of Lincoln; that it is a big thing to have just kept the United States from being thrown down and having its throat cut. I have not waver'd or had any doubt of the issue, since Gettysburg.

8th September, '63.—Here, now, is a specimen army hospital case: Lorenzo Strong, Co. A, 9th United States Cavalry, shot by a shell last Sunday; right leg amputated on the field. Sent up here Monday night,

59. here, and I] *CWW:* here, a very fine boy. I

59. with the boy a good deal. The] *CWW:* with him a good deal, & the

60. Brooklyn address] *CWW:* address in Brooklyn

61–63. These two sentences are not enclosed in parentheses in *CEN*. *CWW* begins the first sentence "Mother" and has dashes in place of parentheses.

64–75. This paragraph is from the last paragraph of the same letter.

64–66. For these three sentences *CWW* has the following: "Well, dear Mother, how the time passes away—to think it will soon be a year I have been away—it has passed away very swiftly somehow to me—O what things I have witnessed during that time—I shall never forget them—"

67–69. anything certain . . . Union triumph] *CWW:* any thing at all certain about the settlement yet, but I have finally got for good I think into the feeling that our triumph

70. we may be led] *CWW:* we are led

71–73. nor delays, nor blunders. One realizes here in Washington the great labors, even the negative [*CEN:* even negative] ones, of Lincoln; that it is a big] *CWW:* or any delays or government blunders—there are blunders enough, heaven knows, but I am thankful things have gone on as well for us as they have—thankful the ship rides safe & sound at all—then I have finally made up my mind that Mr Lincoln has done as good as a human man could do—I still think him a pretty big President—I realize here in Washington that it has been a big

74–75. cut. I . . . since Gettysburg.] *CWW:* cut—& now I have no doubt it will throw down secession & cut its throat—& I have not had any doubt since Gettysburgh—

76–99. If this paragraph is from a letter by Whitman to his mother, the letter has not been printed and is not mentioned in Miller's checklist.

76. *8th September*, '63.] *CEN: 18th September, 1863.*

77. 9th United States Cavalry, shot] *CEN:* 9th New York Cavalry (his brother, Horace L. Strong, Rochester, N. Y.), shot

14th. Seem'd to be doing pretty well till Wednesday noon, 16th, when he took a turn for the worse, and a strangely rapid and fatal termination ensued. Though I had much to do, I staid and saw all. It was a death-picture characteristic of these soldiers' hospitals—the perfect specimen of physique, one of the most magnificent I ever saw—the convulsive spasms and working of muscles, mouth, and throat. There are two good women nurses, one on each side. The doctor comes in and gives him a little chloroform. One of the nurses constantly fans him, for it is fearfully hot. He asks to be rais'd up, and they put him in a half-sitting posture. He call'd for "Mark" repeatedly, half-deliriously, all day. Life ebbs, runs now with the speed of a mill race; his splendid neck, as it lays all open, works still, slightly; his eyes turn back. A religious person coming in offers a prayer, in subdued tones, bent at the foot of the bed; and in the space of the aisle, a crowd, including two or three doctors, several students, and many soldiers, has silently gather'd. It is very still and warm, as the struggle goes on, and dwindles, a little more, and a little more—and then welcome oblivion, painlessness, death. A pause, the crowd drops away, a white bandage is bound around and under the jaw, the propping pillows are removed, the limpsy head falls down, the arms are softly placed by the side, all composed, all still,—and the broad white sheet is thrown over everything.

April 10, 1864.—Unusual agitation all around concentrated here. Exciting times in Congress. The Copperheads are getting furious, and want to recognize the Southern Confederacy. "This is a pretty time to talk

82. hospitals—the] *CEN:* hospitals: the
83. physique, one] *CEN:* physique,—one
91. tones, . . . bed; and] *CEN:* tones; around the foot of the bed, and [Change made in galley proof.]
100–133. These lines are from Whitman's letter to his mother April 10, 1864; the second paragraph is an addition to this letter written April 12. (See *CWW*, I, 209–210.) Whitman does not use the first paragraph and the first three lines of the second paragraph of the letter.
100–101. For the first two sentences *CWW* has: "there are exciting times in Congress—" and has "the" before "Copperheads".
102–104. In place of this sentence with quotation *CWW* has the following after the word "Confederacy" without quotation marks: "—this is a pretty time to talk of recognizing such villains after what they have done, and after what has transpired the last three years—"
105. Fredericksburg] *CWW:* Fredericksburgh
106. that had pass'd] *CEN* and *CWW:* that has passed
106. away. The] *CWW:* away, the
107. on. I] *CWW:* on—& I
107. go in the ranks myself if] *CWW:* go myself in the ranks if
108. than as at] *CWW:* than at
109. *CWW* has a dash after "it is" and ends the paragraph.
109–111. This sentence, beginning "Then" is not in *CWW*.

of recognizing such ——," said a Pennsylvania officer in hospital to me to-day, "after what has transpired the last three years." After first Fredericksburg I felt discouraged myself, and doubted whether our rulers could carry on the war. But that had pass'd away. The war *must* be carried on. I would willingly go in the ranks myself if I thought it would profit more than as at present, and I don't know sometimes but I shall, as it is. Then there is certainly a strange, deep, fervid feeling form'd or arous'd in the land, hard to describe or name; it is not a majority feeling, but it will make itself felt. M., you don't know what a nature a fellow gets, not only after being a soldier a while, but after living in the sights and influences of the camps, the wounded, &c.—a nature he never experienced before. The stars and stripes, the tune of Yankee Doodle, and similar things, produce such an effect on a fellow as never before. I have seen them bring tears on some men's cheeks, and others turn pale with emotion. I have a little flag (it belong'd to one of our cavalry regiments,) presented to me by one of the wounded; it was taken by the secesh in a fight, and rescued by our men in a bloody skirmish following. It cost three men's lives to get back that four-by-three flag—to tear it from the breast of a dead rebel—for *the name* of getting their little "rag" back again. The man that secured it was very badly wounded, and they let him keep it. I was with him a good deal; he wanted to give me some keepsake, he said,—he didn't expect to live,—so he gave me that flag. The best of it all is, dear M., there isn't a regiment, cavalry or infantry, that wouldn't do the like, on the like occasion.

111. M.,] *CWW:* Mother,
111. a nature a] *CWW:* a feeling a
112. gets, not . . . living in] *CWW:* gets after being in
113. the camps, . . . nature he] *CWW:* the camp, the Army, the wounded &c.—he gets to have a deep feeling he
114. before. The stars and stripes, the] *CWW:* before—the flag, the
115. produce . . . before. I] *CWW:* produce an effect on a fellow never such before—I
116. seen them bring tears on some men's] *CWW:* seen some bring tears on the men's
116–117. pale with emotion. I] *CWW:* pale, under such circumstances—I
119. a fight] *CWW:* a cavalry fight
119–120. bloody skirmish following. It] *CWW:* bloody little skirmish, it
120. get back . . . tear it] *CWW:* get one little flag, four by three—our men rescued it, & tore it
121. rebel—for] *CWW:* rebel—all that just for
121–122. little "rag" back again. The man] *CWW:* little banner back again—this man
123–124. me some keepsake, he] *CWW:* me something he
124–125. me that flag. The best of it all ["all" inserted in the galley proof] is, dear M., there] *CWW:* me the little banner as a keepsake—I mention this, Mother, to show you a specimen of the feeling—there

April 12.—I will finish my letter this morning; it is a beautiful day. I was up in Congress very late last night. The House had a very excited night session about expelling the men that proposed recognizing the Southern Confederacy. You ought to hear (as I do) the soldiers talk; they are excited to madness. We shall probably have hot times here, not in the military fields alone. The body of the army is true and firm as the North Star.

May 6, '64.—M., the poor soldier with diarrhœa, is still living, but, oh, what a looking object! Death would be a relief to him—he cannot last many hours. Cunningham, the Ohio soldier, with leg amputated at thigh, has pick'd up beyond expectation; now looks indeed like getting well. (He died a few weeks afterward.) The hospitals are very full. I am very well indeed. Hot here to-day.

May 23, '64.—Sometimes I think that should it come when it *must*, to fall in battle, one's anguish over a son or brother kill'd might be temper'd with much to take the edge off. Lingering and extreme suffering from wounds or sickness seem to me far worse than death in battle. I can honestly say the latter has no terrors for me, as far as I myself am concern'd. Then I should say, too, about death in war, that our feelings and

127. April 12.—I] *CWW:* Tuesday morning April 12th Mother, I
127–128. day. I] *CWW:* day to-day—I
128. night. The House] *CWW:* night, the house
129. that proposed recognizing the] *CWW:* that want to recognize the
130. hear (as I do) the] *CWW:* hear the
132–133. the military . . . North Star.] *CWW:* the Army alone—the soldiers are true as the north star—
133. The last seven or eight sentences of the letter, which are personal, are omitted in *CEN* and *NB*.
134–139. These lines are a revision of the following paragraph, the fifth, of Whitman's letter to his mother dated May 6, 1864; Miller's text, cited above:

"Mother, the poor soldier with diarrhea is still living, but O what a looking object, death would be a boon to him, he cannot last many hours—Cunningham, the Ohio boy with leg amputated at thigh, has picked up beyond expectation, now looks altogether like getting well—the hospitals are very full—I am very well indeed—pretty warm here to-day—"

137–138. The sentence in parentheses is placed in brackets in *CEN*.
138. After "full." *CEN* has an asterisk referring to a long footnote on page 827, omitted in *NB*. The first part of the note is reprinted from "Hospitals Ensemble," the second from "Summer of 1864," in the text of *SDC*, without significant changes. (See these sections in *Prose 1892*, I.)
140–164. These lines are from the second paragraph of Whitman's letter to his brother, Thomas Jefferson Whitman, May 23, 1864, *CWW*, I, 225.
140. *must*, to] *CWW: must* be, to
141. might be] *CWW:* would be
142–143. This sentence beginning "Lingering" is not in *CWW*.
144. say the latter has] *CWW:* say it has

imaginations make a thousand times too much of the whole matter. Of the many I have seen die, or known of, the past year, I have not seen or known one who met death with terror. In most cases I should say it was a welcome relief and release.

Yesterday I spent a good part of the afternoon with a young soldier of seventeen, Charles Cutter, of Lawrence City, Massachusetts, 1st Massachusetts Heavy Artillery, Battery M. He was brought to one of the hospitals mortally wounded in abdomen. Well, I thought to myself, as I sat looking at him, it ought to be a relief to his folks if they could see how little he really suffer'd. He lay very placid, in a half lethargy, with his eyes closed. As it was extremely hot, and I sat a good while silently fanning him, and wiping the sweat, at length he open'd his eyes quite wide and clear, and look'd inquiringly around. I said, "What is it, my boy? Do you want anything?" He answer'd quietly, with a good-natured smile, "Oh, nothing; I was only looking around to see who was with me." His mind was somewhat wandering, yet he lay in an evident peacefulness that sanity and health might have envied. I had to leave for other engagements. He died, I heard afterward, without any special agitation, in the course of the night.

144–145. me, as far . . . war, that] *CWW:* me, if I had to be hit in battle, as far as I myself am concerned—it would be a noble & manly death, & in the best cause—then one finds, as I have the past year, that

147–148. or known . . . one] *CWW:* or heard of *one*

148. with terror.] *CWW:* with any terror—

148–149. This last sentence of the paragraph is not in *CWW.*

150. Yesterday I] *CWW:* Yesterday afternoon I

151. seventeen, Charles] *CWW:* 17, named Charles

151–152. Lawrence City, Massachusetts, 1st Massachusetts Heavy Artillery, Battery M. He] *CEN:* Lawrence, Massachusetts (1st Massachusetts Heavy Artillery, Battery M); he] *CWW:* Lawrence City, Mass, 1st Mass heavy artillery, battery M—he

154. folks if] *CWW:* folks after all, if

155. he really suffer'd. He] *CWW:* he suffered—he

156–157. closed. As . . . silently fanning] *CWW:* closed, it was very warm, & I sat a long while fanning

158–159. *CWW* has no quotation marks in these lines.

158–159. my boy? Do] *CWW:* my dear, do

159. He answer'd quietly] *CWW:* —he said quietly

160. "Oh, nothing;] *CWW:* O nothing,

161–164. For these last three sentences of the paragraph, *CWW* has the following: "—his mind was somewhat wandering, yet he lay so peaceful, in his dying condition—he seemed to be a real New England country boy, so good natured, with a pleasant homely way, & quite a fine looking boy—without any doubt he died in course of night—" [He did not die that night but about ten days later, as appears from Whitman's letter to his mother June 3, which Whitman either did not have at hand or forgot to consult.—ED.]

Washington, May 26, '63.—M., I think something of commencing a series of lectures, readings, talks, &c., through the cities of the North, to supply myself with funds for hospital ministrations. I do not like to be so beholden to others; I need a pretty free supply of money, and the work grows upon me, and fascinates me. It is the most magnetic as well as terrible sight: the lots of poor wounded and helpless men depending so much, in one ward or another, upon my soothing or talking to them, or rousing them up a little, or perhaps petting, or feeding them their dinner or supper (here is a patient, for instance, wounded in both arms,) or giving some trifle for a novelty or change—anything, however trivial, to break the monotony of those hospital hours.

It is curious: when I am present at the most appalling scenes, deaths, operations, sickening wounds (perhaps full of maggots,) I keep cool and do not give out or budge, although my sympathies are very much excited; but often, hours afterward, perhaps when I am home, or out walking alone, I feel sick, and actually tremble, when I recall the case again before me.

Sunday afternoon, opening of 1865.—Pass'd this afternoon among a collection of unusually bad cases, wounded and sick Secession soldiers, left upon our hands. I spent the previous Sunday afternoon there also. At that time two were dying. Two others have died during the week. Several of them are partly deranged. I went around among them elaborately. Poor boys, they all needed to be cheer'd up. As I sat down by any particular one, the eyes of all the rest in the neighboring cots would fix upon me, and remain steadily riveted as long as I sat within their

165–175. This paragraph is part of the last paragraph of Whitman's letter to his mother dated June 9, 1863 (not May 26, the date in line 165). This is Letter 53 in *CWW*, I, 109.

165. In *CWW* the paragraph begins "M., I think".

166. lectures, . . . the cities] *CWW:* lectures & readings &c. through different cities

167. for hospital ministrations. I] *CWW:* for my Hospital & Soldiers visits—as I

168. be so beholden to others; I] *CWW:* be beholden to the medium of others—I

168. pretty free supply of money, and the] *CWW:* pretty large supply of money &c. to do the good I would Like to—& the

169. me. It] *CWW:* me—it

169–175. For these lines *CWW* has the following: "—it is the most affecting thing you ever see, the lots of poor sick & wounded young men that depend so much, in one ward or another, upon my petting or soothing or feeding, sitting by them & feeding them their dinner or supper, some are quite helpless—some wounded in both arms—or giving some trifle (for a novelty or a change, it isn't for the value of it,) or stopping a little while with them—nobody will do but me—"

176–181. This paragraph, though under the same date as the preceding, is drawn from the fifth paragraph of Whitman's letter to his mother dated October 6,

sight. Nobody seem'd to wish anything special to eat or drink. The main thing ask'd for was postage stamps, and paper for writing. I distributed all the stamps I had. Tobacco was wanted by some.

One call'd me over to him and ask'd me in a low tone what denomination I belong'd to. He said he was a Catholic—wish'd to find some one of the same faith—wanted some good reading. I gave him something to read, and sat down by him a few minutes. Moved around with a word for each. They were hardly any of them personally attractive cases, and no visitors come here. Of course they were all destitute of money. I gave small sums to two or three, apparently the most needy. The men are from quite all the Southern States, Georgia, Mississippi, Louisiana, &c.

Wrote several letters. One for a young fellow named Thomas J. Byrd, with a bad wound and diarrhœa. Was from Russell county, Alabama; been out four years. Wrote to his mother; had neither heard from her nor written to her in nine months. Was taken prisoner last Christmas, in Tennessee; sent to Nashville, then to Camp Chase, Ohio, and kept there a long time; all the while not money enough to get paper and postage stamps. Was paroled, but on his way home the wound took gangrene; had diarrhœa also; had evidently been very low. Demeanor cool, and patient. A dark-skinn'd, quaint young fellow, with strong Southern idiom; no education.

Another letter for John W. Morgan, aged 18, from Shellot, Brunswick county, North Carolina; been out nine months; gunshot wound in right leg, above knee; also diarrhœa; wound getting along well; quite a gentle, affectionate boy; wish'd me to put in the letter for his mother to kiss his

1863. This is Letter 83 in CWW, I, 157.

176. It is curious: when] CWW: —it is curious—when

176. appalling scenes, deaths,] CWW: appaling things, deaths,

177–178. I keep . . . budge, although] CWW: I do not fail, although

178–179. excited; but] CWW: excited, but keep singularly cool—but

180–181. recall the case again before me.] CWW: recal the thing & have it in my mind again before me—

181. After this line CEN has the following sentence, in brackets, omitted from NB: "The following memoranda describe some of the last cases and hospital scenes of the war, from my own observation."

Following this bracketed sentence, CEN has a paragraph with the side head *Two brothers, one South, one North.—May 28–29, 1865.* This paragraph is identical, except for minor changes in punctuation, with the section "Two Brothers, One South, One North," in SDC, pp. 74–75, and is omitted in NB. (See *Prose 1892*, I.)

182–319. These lines were published for the first time in CEN, though they are obviously related to notes published in MDW, pp. 53–55 and reprinted in later texts.

182. *Sunday afternoon, opening of* 1865.—Pass'd] CEN: *Sunday Afternoon, July* 30.—Passed

186. deranged. I went around among them] CEN: deranged. To-day I went around them [Change made in galley proof.]

little brother and sister for him. [I put strong envelopes on these, and two or three other letters, directed them plainly and fully, and dropt them in the Washington post-office the next morning myself.]

The large ward I am in is used for Secession soldiers exclusively. One man, about forty years of age, emaciated with diarrhœa, I was attracted to, as he lay with his eyes turn'd up, looking like death. His weakness was so extreme that it took a minute or so, every time, for him to talk with anything like consecutive meaning; yet he was evidently a man of good intelligence and education. As I said anything, he would lie a moment perfectly still, then, with closed eyes, answer in a low, very slow voice, quite correct and sensible, but in a way and tone that wrung my heart. He had a mother, wife, and child living (or probably living) in his home in Mississippi. It was long, long since he had seen them. Had he caus'd a letter to be sent them since he got here in Washington? No answer. I repeated the question, very slowly and soothingly. He could not tell whether he had or not—things of late seem'd to him like a dream. After waiting a moment, I said: "Well, I am going to walk down the ward a moment, and when I come back you can tell me. If you have not written, I will sit down and write." A few minutes after I return'd; he said he remember'd now that some one had written for him two or three days before. The presence of this man impress'd me profoundly. The flesh was all sunken on face and arms; the eyes low in their sockets and glassy, and with purple rings around them. Two or three great tears silently flow'd out from the eyes, and roll'd down his temples (he was doubtless unused to be spoken to as I was speaking to him.) Sickness, imprisonment, exhaustion, &c., had conquer'd the body, yet the mind held mastery still, and call'd even wandering remembrance back.

There are some fifty Southern soldiers here; all sad, sad cases. There is a good deal of scurvy. I distributed some paper, envelopes, and postage stamps, and wrote addresses full and plain on many of the envelopes.

I return'd again Tuesday, August 1, and moved around in the same manner a couple of hours.

September 22, '65.—Afternoon and evening at Douglas Hospital to see a friend belonging to 2d New York Artillery (Hiram W. Frazee, Serg't,) down with an obstinate compound fracture of left leg receiv'd in one of the last battles near Petersburg. After sitting a while with him, went through several neighboring wards. In one of them found an old acquaintance transferr'd here lately, a rebel prisoner, in a dying condition. Poor fellow, the look was already on his face. He gazed long at me. I ask'd him if he knew me. After a moment he utter'd something, but inarticulately. I have seen him off and on for the last five months. He has suffer'd very much; a bad wound in left leg, severely fractured, several operations, cuttings, extractions of bone, splinters, &c. I remember he seem'd to me, as I used to talk with him, a fair specimen of the main strata of the Southerners, those without property or education, but still with the stamp which comes from freedom and equality. I liked him; Jonathan Wallace, of Hurd Co., Georgia, age 30 (wife, Susan F. Wallace, Houston, Hurd Co., Georgia.) [If any good soul of that county should see this, I hope he will send her this word.] Had a family; had not heard from them since taken prisoner, now six months. I had written for him, and done trifles for him, before he came here. He made no outward show, was mild in his talk and behavior, but I knew he worried much inwardly. But now all would be over very soon. I half sat upon the little stand near the head of the bed. Wallace was somewhat restless. I placed my hand lightly on his forehead and face, just sliding it over the surface. In a moment or so he fell into a calm, regular-breathing lethargy or sleep, and remain'd so while I sat there. It was dark, and the lights were lit. I hardly know why (death seem'd hovering near,) but I stay'd nearly an hour. A Sister of Charity, dress'd in black, with a broad white linen bandage around her head and under her chin, and a black crape over all and flowing down from her head in long wide pieces, came to him, and moved around the bed. She bow'd low and solemn to me. For some time she moved around there noiseless as a ghost, doing little things for the dying man.

December, '65.—The only remaining hospital is now "Harewood," out in the woods, northwest of the city. I have been visiting there regularly every Sunday, during these two months.

January 24, '66.—Went out to Harewood early to-day, and remain'd all day.

Sunday, *February* 4, 1866.—Harewood Hospital again. Walk'd out this afternoon (bright, dry, ground frozen hard) through the woods. Ward 6 is fill'd with blacks, some with wounds, some ill, two or three with limbs frozen. The boys made quite a picture sitting round the stove. Hardly any can read or write. I write for three or four, direct envelopes, give some tobacco, &c.

Joseph Winder, a likely boy, aged twenty-three, belongs to 10th Color'd Infantry (now in Texas;) is from Eastville, Virginia. Was a slave; belong'd to Lafayette Homeston. The master was quite willing he should leave. Join'd the army two years ago; has been in one or two battles. Was sent to hospital with rheumatism. Has since been employ'd as cook. His

263. her this word.] CEN: her word.

parents at Eastville; he gets letters from them, and has letters written to them by a friend. Many black boys left that part of Virginia and join'd the army; the 10th, in fact, was made up of Virginia blacks from thereabouts. As soon as discharged is going back to Eastville to his parents and home, and intends to stay there.

Thomas King, formerly 2d District Color'd Regiment, discharged soldier, Company E, lay in a dying condition; his disease was consumption. A Catholic priest was administering extreme unction to him. (I have seen this kind of sight several times in the hospitals; it is very impressive.)

Harewood, April 29, 1866. *Sunday afternoon.*—Poor Joseph Swiers, Company H, 155th Pennsylvania, a mere lad (only eighteen years of age;) his folks living in Reedsburgh, Pennsylvania. I have known him now for nearly a year, transferr'd from hospital to hospital. He was badly wounded in the thigh at Hatcher's Run, February 6, '65.

James E. Ragan, Atlanta, Georgia; 2d United States Infantry. Union folks. Brother impress'd, deserted, died; now no folks, left alone in the world, is in a singularly nervous state; came in hospital with intermittent fever.

Walk slowly around the ward, observing, and to see if I can do anything. Two or three are lying very low with consumption, cannot recover; some with old wounds; one with both feet frozen off, so that on one only the heel remains. The supper is being given out: the liquid call'd tea, a thick slice of bread, and some stew'd apples.

That was about the last I saw of the regular army hospitals.

NOTES (*such as they are*) *founded on* *Elias Hicks.*

Here is a portrait of E. H. from life, by Henry Inman, in New York, about 1827 or '28. The painting was finely copperplated in 1830, and the present is a fac simile. Looks as I saw him in the following narrative.

The time was signalized by the *separation* of the Society of Friends, so

319. Whitman's name appears at the end of the article in *CEN.*

Elias Hicks.

Printed in *NB* from the autograph MS, written in black ink and pencil, and from marked passages of *Journal of the Life and Religious Labours of Elias Hicks. Written by Himself.* Hicks's *Journal* was first published in 1832 and was reprinted several times. In the collation it is abbreviated *HJ.* The MS, with directions to the printer, is in the Feinberg Collection, and is collated here with the printed texts, including the galley proof and page proof. The portrait is from the engraving of a portrait by Henry Inman, probably the one sent to Whitman while he was in Canada, during the summer of 1880, by Mrs. E. S. L., of Detroit (see "Reminiscence

greatly talked of—and continuing yet—but so little really explain'd. (All I give of this separation is in a Note following.)

[This portrait appears in the Illustrations section of the present text, which begins opposite page 710. *Ed.*]

Prefatory Note.—As myself a little boy hearing so much of E. H., at that time, long ago, in Suffolk and Queens and Kings Counties—and more than once personally seeing the old man—and my dear, dear father and mother faithful listeners to him at the meetings—I remember how I dream'd to write perhaps a piece about E. H. and his look and discourses, however long afterward—for my parents' sake—and the dear Friends too! And the following is what has at last but all come out of it—the feeling and intention never forgotten yet!

There is a sort of nature of persons I have compared to little rills of water, fresh, from perennial springs—(and the comparison is indeed an appropriate one)—persons not so very plenty, yet some few certainly of them running over the surface and area of humanity, all times, all lands. It is a specimen of this class I would now present. I would sum up in E. H., and make his case stand for the class, the sort, in all ages, all lands, sparse, not numerous, yet enough to irrigate the soil—enough to prove the inherent moral stock and irrepressible devotional aspirations growing indigenously of themselves, always advancing, and never utterly gone under or lost.

Always E. H. gives the service of pointing to the fountain of all naked theology, all religion, all worship, all the truth to which you are possibly eligible—namely in *yourself* and your inherent relations. Others talk of Bibles, saints, churches, exhortations, vicarious atonements—the canons outside of yourself and apart from man—E. H. to the religion inside of man's very own nature. This he incessantly labors to kindle, nourish, educate, bring forward and strengthen. He is the most *democratic* of the religionists—the prophets.

I have no doubt that both the curious fate and death of his four sons, and the facts (and dwelling on them) of George Fox's strange early life, and permanent "conversion," had much to do with the peculiar and sombre ministry and style of E. H. from the first, and confirmed him all through. One must not be dominated by the man's almost absurd saturation in cut and dried biblical phraseology, and in ways, talk, and standard, regardful mainly of the one need he dwelt on, above all the rest. This main need he drove home to the soul; the canting and sermonizing soon exhale away to any auditor that realizes what E. H. is for and after. The present paper, (a broken memorandum of his formation, his earlier life,) is the cross-notch that rude wanderers make in the woods, to remind them afterward of some matter of first-rate importance and full investigation. (Remember too, that E. H. was a *thorough believer in the Hebrew Scriptures*, in his way.)

The following are really but disjointed fragments recall'd to serve and eke out here the lank printed pages of what I commenc'd unwittingly two months ago. Now,

of Elias Hicks," *Prose 1892*, I).

2–3. personally . . . father] MS: personally seeing and hearing the old man—and my father [Revisions on galley proof.]

5–6. my parents' . . . too!] MS: my dear parents' sake—and the Friends' too. [Revisions on galley proof.]

6. last but all come] MS: last all but come [Revisions on galley proof.]

13–15. These lines, beginning with "all lands," are missing from the MS.

23–34. These lines, not in the original MS nor in the first proof, were written in black ink on a separate sheet and attached to the corrected proof with directions to insert before the paragraph beginning "The following."

28. talk, and standard] MS: talk, standard

as I am well in for it, comes an old attack, the sixth or seventh recurrence, of my war-paralysis, dulling me from putting the notes in shape, and threatening any further action, head or body.

—*W. W., Camden, N. J., July, 1888.*

To begin with, my theme is comparatively featureless. The great historian has pass'd by the life of Elias Hicks quite without glance or touch. Yet a man might commence and overhaul it as furnishing one of the amplest historic and biography's backgrounds. While the foremost actors and events from 1750 to 1830 both in Europe and America were crowding each other on the world's stage—While so many kings, queens, soldiers, philosophs, musicians, voyagers, littérateurs, enter one side, cross the boards, and disappear—amid loudest reverberating names—Frederick the Great, Swedenborg, Junius, Voltaire, Rousseau, Linneus, Herschel—curiously contemporary with the long life of Goethe—through the occupancy of the British throne by George the Third—amid stupendous visible political and social revolutions, and far more stupendous invisible moral ones—while the many quarto volumes of the Encyclopædia Française are being published at fits and intervals, by Diderot, in Paris—while Haydn and Beethoven and Mozart and Weber are working out their harmonic compositions—while Mrs. Siddons and Talma and Kean are acting—while Mungo Park explores Africa, and Capt. Cook circumnavigates the globe—through all the fortunes of the American Revolution, the beginning, continuation and end, the battle of Brooklyn, the surrender at Saratoga, the final peace of '83—through the lurid tempest of the French Revolution, the execution of the king and queen, and the Reign of Terror—through the whole of the meteor-career of Napoleon—through all Washington's, Adams's, Jefferson's, Madison's, and Monroe's Presidentiads—amid so many flashing lists of names, (indeed there seems hardly, in any department, any end to them, Old World or New,) Franklin, Sir Joshua Reynolds, Mirabeau, Fox, Nelson, Paul Jones, Kant, Fichte, and Hegel, Fulton, Walter Scott, Byron, Mesmer, Champollion—Amid pictures that dart upon me even as I speak, and glow and mix and coruscate and fade like aurora boreales—Louis the 16th threaten'd by the mob, the trial of Warren Hastings, the death-bed of Robert Burns, Wellington at Waterloo, Decatur capturing the Macedonian, or the sea-fight between the Chesapeake and the Shannon—During all these whiles, I say, and though on a far different grade,

39. After this line MS has simply "W. W." Whitman deleted the initials on the galley proof and wrote in the subscription as it now stands.
51. George the Third] MS: George Third

running parallel and contemporary with all—a curious quiet yet busy life centred in a little country village on Long Island, and within sound on still nights of the mystic surf-beat of the sea. About this life, this Personality—neither soldier, nor scientist, nor littérateur—I propose to occupy a few minutes in fragmentary talk, to give some few melanges, disconnected impressions, statistics, resultant groups, pictures, thoughts of him, or radiating from him.

Elias Hicks was born March 19, 1748, in Hempstead township, Queens county, Long Island, New York State, near a village bearing the old Scripture name of Jericho, (a mile or so north and east of the present Hicksville, on the L. I. Railroad.) His father and mother were Friends, of that class working with their own hands, and mark'd by neither riches nor actual poverty. Elias as a child and youth had small education from letters, but largely learn'd from Nature's schooling. He grew up even in his ladhood a thorough gunner and fisherman. The farm of his parents lay on the south or sea-shore side of Long Island, (they had early removed from Jericho,) one of the best regions in the world for wild fowl and for fishing. Elias became a good horseman, too, and knew the animal well, riding races; also a singer, fond of "vain songs," as he afterwards calls them; a dancer, too, at the country balls. When a boy of 13 he had gone to live with an elder brother; and when about 17 he changed again and went as apprentice to the carpenter's trade. The time of all this was before the Revolutionary War, and the locality 30 to 40 miles from New York city. My great-grandfather, Whitman, was often with Elias at these periods, and at merry-makings and sleigh-rides in winter over "the plains."

How well I remember the region—the flat plains of the middle of Long Island, as then, with their prairie-like vistas and grassy patches in every direction, and the 'kill-calf' and herds of cattle and sheep. Then the South Bay and shores and the salt meadows, and the sedgy smell, and numberless little bayous and hummock-islands in the waters, the habitat of every sort of fish and aquatic fowl of North America. And the bay men—a strong, wild, peculiar race—now extinct, or rather entirely changed. And the beach outside the sandy bars, sometimes many miles at a stretch, with their old history of wrecks and storms—the weird, white-gray beach—not without its tales of pathos—tales, too, of grandest heroes and heroisms.

In such scenes and elements and influences—in the midst of Nature

69. aurora] MS: aurorora
77. soldier, nor scientist, nor littérateur] MS: soldier's, no scientist's, nor littérateur's
78–79. melanges, disconnected] MS: melanged disconnected

and along the shores of the sea—Elias Hicks was fashion'd through boyhood and early manhood, to maturity. But a moral and mental and emotional change was imminent. Along at this time he says:

> My apprenticeship being now expir'd, I gradually withdrew from the company of my former associates, became more acquainted with Friends, and was more frequent in my attendance of meetings; and although this was in some degree profitable to me, yet I made but slow progress in my religious improvement. The occupation of part of my time in fishing and fowling had frequently tended to preserve me from falling into hurtful associations; but through the rising intimations and reproofs of divine grace in my heart, I now began to feel that the manner in which I sometimes amus'd myself with my gun was not without sin; for although I mostly preferr'd going alone, and while waiting in stillness for the coming of the fowl, my mind was at times so taken up in divine meditations, that the opportunities were seasons of instruction and comfort to me; yet, on other occasions, when accompanied by some of my acquaintances, and when no fowls appear'd which would be useful to us after being obtain'd, we sometimes, from wantonness or for mere diversion, would destroy the small birds which could be of no service to us. This cruel procedure affects my heart while penning these lines.

In his 23d year Elias was married, by the Friends' ceremony, to Jemima Seaman. His wife was an only child; the parents were well off for common people, and at their request the son-in-law mov'd home with them and carried on the farm—which at their decease became his own, and he liv'd there all his remaining life. Of this matrimonial part of his career, (it continued, and with unusual happiness, for 58 years,) he says, giving the account of his marriage:

> On this important occasion, we felt the clear and consoling evidence of divine truth, and it remain'd with us as a seal upon our spirits, strengthening us mutually to bear, with becoming fortitude, the vicissitudes and trials which fell to our lot, and of which we had a large share in passing through this probationary state. My wife, although not of a very strong constitution, liv'd to be the mother of eleven children, four sons and seven daughters. Our second daughter, a very lovely, promising child, died when young, with the small-pox, and the youngest was not living at its birth. The rest all arriv'd to years of discretion, and afforded us considerable comfort, as they prov'd to be in a good degree dutiful children.

114–130. Printed from a marked passage of *HJ*, pp. 12–13.

118. improvement. The] *HJ:* improvement, until several years after I had entered into a married state. The

130. After "lines." *HJ* has a semicolon and continues the sentence.

131. 23d year] MS: 22d year

136. 58 years,)] MS: 60 years,)

138–166. These lines were printed from a marked passage of *HJ*, p. 14, beginning

All our sons, however, were of weak constitutions, and were not able to take care of themselves, being so enfeebl'd as not to be able to walk after the ninth or tenth year of their age. The two eldest died in the fifteenth year of their age, the third in his seventeenth year, and the youngest was nearly nineteen when he died. But, although thus helpless, the innocency of their lives, and the resign'd cheerfulness of their dispositions to their allotments, made the labor and toil of taking care of them agreeable and pleasant; and I trust we were preserv'd from murmuring or repining, believing the dispensation to be in wisdom, and according to the will and gracious disposing of an all-wise providence, for purposes best known to himself. And when I have observ'd the great anxiety and affliction which many parents have with undutiful children who are favor'd with health, especially their sons, I could perceive very few whose troubles and exercises, on that account, did not far exceed ours. The weakness and bodily infirmity of our sons tended to keep them much out of the way of the troubles and temptations of the world; and we believ'd that in their death they were happy, and admitted into the realms of peace and joy: a reflection, the most comfortable and joyous that parents can have in regard to their tender offspring.

Of a serious and reflective turn, by nature, and from his reading and surroundings, Elias had more than once markedly devotional inward intimations. These feelings increas'd in frequency and strength, until soon the following:

About the twenty-sixth year of my age I was again brought, by the operative influence of divine grace, under deep concern of mind; and was led, through adorable mercy, to see, that although I had ceas'd from many sins and vanities of my youth, yet there were many remaining that I was still guilty of, which were not yet aton'd for, and for which I now felt the judgments of God to rest upon me. This caus'd me to cry earnestly to the Most High for pardon and redemption, and he graciously condescended to hear my cry, and to open a way before me, wherein I must walk, in order to experience reconciliation with him; and as I abode in watchfulness and deep humiliation before him, light broke forth out of obscurity, and my darkness became as the noon-day. I began to have openings leading to the ministry, which brought me under close exercise and deep travail of spirit; for although I had for some time spoken on subjects of business in monthly and preparative meetings, yet the prospect of opening my mouth in public meetings was a close trial; but I endeavor'd to keep my mind quiet and resign'd to the heavenly call, if it

in the middle of a paragraph, with only very minor changes in punctuation.

168–169. once . . . intimations.] MS: one markedly devotional intimation.

171–196. Printed from a marked passage of *HJ*, pp. 15–16, beginning in the middle of a paragraph.

171. About] *HJ:* But, about

181. After "noon-day." Whitman omits two sentences in *HJ*.

181. I began] *HJ:* About this time, I began

should be made clear to me to be my duty. Nevertheless, as I was, soon after, sitting in a meeting, in much weightiness of spirit, a secret, though clear, intimation accompanied me to speak a few words, which were then given to me to utter, yet fear so prevail'd, that I did not yield to the intimation. For this omission, I felt close rebuke, and judgment seem'd, for some time, to cover my mind; but as I humbl'd myself under the Lord's mighty hand, he again lifted up the light of his countenance upon me, and enabl'd me to renew covenant with him, that if he would pass by this my offence, I would, in future, be faithful, if he should again require such a service of me.

The Revolutionary War following, tried the sect of Friends more than any. The difficulty was to steer between their convictions at patriots, and their pledges of non-warring peace. Here is the way they solv'd the problem:

A war, with all its cruel and destructive effects, having raged for several years between the British Colonies in North America and the mother country, Friends, as well as others, were expos'd to many severe trials and sufferings; yet, in the colony of New York, Friends, who stood faithful to their principles, and did not meddle in the controversy, had, after a short period at first, considerable favor allow'd them. The yearly meeting was held steadily, during the war, on Long Island, where the king's party had the rule; yet Friends from the Main, where the American army ruled, had free passage through both armies to attend it, and any other meetings they were desirous of attending, except in a few instances. This was a favor which the parties would not grant to their best friends, who were of a warlike disposition; which shows what great advantages would redound to mankind, were they all of this pacific spirit. I pass'd myself through the lines of both armies six times during the war, without molestation, both parties generally receiving me with openness and civility; and although I had to pass over a tract of country, between the two armies, sometimes more than thirty miles in extent, and which was much frequented by robbers, a set, in general, of cruel, unprincipled banditti, issuing out from both parties, yet, excepting once, I met with no interruption even from them. But although Friends in general experienc'd many favors and deliverances, yet those scenes of war and confusion occasion'd many trials and provings in various ways to the faithful. One circumstance I am willing to mention, as it caus'd me considerable exercise and concern. There was a large cellar under the new meeting-house belonging to Friends in New York, which was generally let as a store. When the king's troops enter'd the city, they took possession of it for the purpose of depositing their warlike stores; and ascertaining what Friends had the care of letting it, their commissary came forward and offer'd to

201–273. Printed from a marked passage of *HJ*, pp. 16–18.

pay the rent; and those Friends, for want of due consideration, accepted it. This caus'd great uneasiness to the concern'd part of the Society, who apprehended it not consistent with our peaceable principles to receive payment for the depositing of military stores in our houses. The subject was brought before the yearly meeting in 1779, and engag'd its careful attention; but those Friends, who had been active in the reception of the money, and some few others, were not willing to acknowledge their proceedings to be inconsistent, nor to return the money to those from whom it was receiv'd; and in order to justify themselves therein, they referr'd to the conduct of Friends in Philadelphia in similar cases. Matters thus appearing very difficult and embarrassing, it was unitedly concluded to refer the final determination thereof to the yearly meeting of Pennsylvania; and several Friends were appointed to attend that meeting in relation thereto, among whom I was one of the number. We accordingly set out on the 9th day of the 9th month, 1779, and I was accompanied from home by my beloved friend John Willis, who was likewise on the appointment. We took a solemn leave of our families, they feeling much anxiety at parting with us, on account of the dangers we were expos'd to, having to pass not only the lines of the two armies, but the deserted and almost uninhabited country that lay between them, in many places the grass being grown up in the streets, and many houses desolate and empty. Believing it, however, my duty to proceed in the service, my mind was so settled and trust-fix'd in the divine arm of power, that faith seem'd to banish all fear, and cheerfulness and quiet resignation were, I believe, my constant companions during the journey. We got permission, with but little difficulty, to pass the outguards of the king's army at Kingsbridge, and proceeded to Westchester. We afterwards attended meetings at Harrison's Purchase, and Oblong, having the concurrence of our monthly meeting to take some meetings in our way, a concern leading thereto having for some time previously attended my mind. We pass'd from thence to Nine Partners, and attended their monthly meeting, and then turn'd our faces towards Philadelphia, being join'd by several others of the Committee. We attended New Marlborough, Hardwick, and Kingswood meetings on our journey, and arriv'd at Philadelphia on the 7th day of the week, and 25th of 9th month, on which day we attended the yearly meeting of Ministers and Elders, which began at the eleventh hour. I also attended all the sittings of the yearly meeting until the 4th day of the next week, and was then so indispos'd with a fever, which had been increasing on me for several days, that I was not able to attend after that time. I was therefore not present when the subject was discuss'd, which came from our yearly meeting; but I was inform'd by my companion, that it was a very solemn opportunity, and the matter was resulted in advising that the money should be return'd into the office from whence it was receiv'd, accompanied with our reasons for so doing: and this was accordingly done by the direction of our yearly meeting the next year.

261. Kingswood] *HJ:* Kingwood

Then, season after season, when peace and Independence reign'd, year following year, this remains to be (1791) a specimen of his personal labors:

> I was from home on this journey four months and eleven days; rode about one thousand five hundred miles, and attended forty-nine particular meetings among Friends, three quarterly meetings, six monthly meetings, and forty meetings among other people.

And again another experience:

> In the forepart of this meeting, my mind was reduc'd into such a state of great weakness and depression, that my faith was almost ready to fail, which produc'd great searchings of heart, so that I was led to call in question all that I had ever before experienc'd. In this state of doubting, I was ready to wish myself at home, from an apprehension that I should only expose myself to reproach, and wound the cause I was embark'd in; for the heavens seem'd like brass, and the earth as iron; such coldness and hardness, I thought, could scarcely have ever been experienc'd before by any creature, so great was the depth of my baptism at this time; nevertheless, as I endeavor'd to quiet my mind, in this conflicting dispensation, and be resign'd to my allotment, however distressing, towards the latter part of the meeting a ray of light broke through the surrounding darkness, in which the Shepherd of Israel was pleas'd to arise, and by the light of his glorious countenance, to scatter those clouds of opposition. Then ability was receiv'd, and utterance given, to speak of his marvellous works in the redemption of souls, and to open the way of life and salvation, and the mysteries of his glorious kingdom, which are hid from the wise and prudent of this world, and reveal'd only unto those who are reduc'd into the state of little children and babes in Christ.

And concluding another jaunt in 1794:

> I was from home in this journey about five months, and travell'd by land and water about two thousand two hundred and eighty-three miles; having visited all the meetings of Friends in the New England states, and many meetings amongst those of other professions; and also visited many meetings, among Friends and others, in the upper part of our own yearly meeting; and found real peace in my labors.

Another 'tramp' in 1798:

> I was absent from home in this journey about five months and two weeks, and rode about sixteen hundred miles, and attended about one hundred and forty-three meetings.

277–280. From *HJ*, p. 38.
282–300. From *HJ*, middle part of a paragraph, pp. 45–46.
291. endeavor'd] *HJ:* endeavoured
302–307. From *HJ*, p. 53.
309–311. From *HJ*, p. 81.

Here are some memoranda of 1813, near home:

> First day. Our meeting this day pass'd in silent labor. The cloud rested on the tabernacle; and, although it was a day of much rain outwardly, yet very little of the dew of Hermon appear'd to distil among us. Nevertheless, a comfortable calm was witness'd towards the close, which we must render to the account of unmerited mercy and love.
>
> Second day. Most of this day was occupied in a visit to a sick friend, who appear'd comforted therewith. Spent part of the evening in reading part of Paul's Epistle to the Romans.
>
> Third day. I was busied most of this day in my common vocations. Spent the evening principally in reading Paul. Found considerable satisfaction in his first epistle to the Corinthians; in which he shows the danger of some in setting too high a value on those who were instrumental in bringing them to the knowledge of the truth, without looking through and beyond the instrument, to the great first cause and Author of every blessing, to whom all the praise and honor are due.
>
> Fifth day, 1st of 4th month. At our meeting to-day found it, as usual, a very close steady exercise to keep the mind center'd where it ought to be. What a multitude of intruding thoughts imperceptibly, as it were, steal into the mind, and turn it from its proper object, whenever it relaxes its vigilance in watching against them. Felt a little strength, just at the close, to remind Friends of the necessity of a steady perseverance, by a recapitulation of the parable of the unjust judge, showing how men ought always to pray, and not to faint.
>
> Sixth day. Nothing material occurr'd, but a fear lest the cares of the world should engross too much of my time.
>
> Seventh day. Had an agreeable visit from two ancient friends, whom I have long lov'd. The rest of the day I employ'd in manual labor, mostly in gardening.

But we find if we attend to records and details, we shall lay out an endless task. We can briefly say, summarily, that his whole life was a long religious missionary life of method, practicality, sincerity, earnestness, and pure piety—as near to his time here, as one in Judea, far back—or in any life, any age. The reader who feels interested must get—with all its dryness and mere dates, absence of emotionality or literary quality, and whatever abstract attraction (with even a suspicion of cant, sniffling,) the "Journal of the Life and Religious Labours of Elias Hicks, written by himself," at some Quaker book-store. (It is from this headquarters I have extracted the preceding quotations.) During E. H.'s matured life,

313–340. From *HJ*, pp. 132–133.
313. labor.] *HJ:* labour.
314. tabernacle; and] *HJ:* tabernacle: and
316. close, which] *HJ:* close; which
341–460. Printed from the autograph MS.

continued from fifty to sixty years—while working steadily, earning his living and paying his way without intermission—he makes, as previously memorandised, several hundred preaching visits, not only through Long Island, but some of them away into the Middle or Southern States, or north into Canada, or the then far West—extending to thousands of miles, or filling several weeks and sometimes months. These religious journeys—scrupulously accepting in payment only his transportation from place to place, with his own food and shelter, and never receiving a dollar of money for "salary" or preaching—Elias, through good bodily health and strength, continues till quite the age of eighty. It was thus at one of his latest jaunts in Brooklyn city I saw and heard him. This sight and hearing shall now be described.

Elias Hicks was at this period in the latter part (November or December) of 1829. It was the last tour of the many missions of the old man's life. He was in the 81st year of his age, and a few months before he had lost by death a beloved wife with whom he had lived in unalloyed affection and esteem for 58 years. (But a few months after this meeting Elias was paralyzed and died.) Though it is sixty years ago since—and I a little boy at the time in Brooklyn, New York—I can remember my father coming home toward sunset from his day's work as carpenter, and saying briefly, as he throws down his armful of kindling-blocks with a bounce on the kitchen floor, "Come, mother, Elias preaches to-night." Then my mother, hastening the supper and the table-cleaning afterward, gets a neighboring young woman, a friend of the family, to step in and keep house for an hour or so—puts the two little ones to bed—and as I had been behaving well that day, as a special reward I was allow'd to go also.

We start for the meeting. Though, as I said, the stretch of more than half a century has pass'd over me since then, with its war and peace, and all its joys and sins and deaths (and what a half century! how it comes up sometimes for an instant, like the lightning flash in a storm at night!) I can recall that meeting yet. It is a strange place for religious devotions. Elias preaches anywhere—no respect to buildings—private or public houses, school-rooms, barns, even theatres—anything that will accommodate. This time it is in a handsome ball-room, on Brooklyn Heights, overlooking New York, and in full sight of that great city, and its North and East Rivers fill'd with ships—is (to specify more particularly) the

350. extracted the] MS (unrevised): extracted from the
365. 81st year] MS: 82d year [Changed on the galley proof.]
367–368. MS has no marks of parenthesis.
406. between 80 and 81 years] MS: between 75 and 80 years] [Changed in galley proof to "between 79 and 80," and in page proof to the present reading. From this

second story of "Morrison's Hotel," used for the most genteel concerts, balls, and assemblies—a large, cheerful, gay-color'd room, with glass chandeliers bearing myriads of sparkling pendants, plenty of settees and chairs, and a sort of velvet divan running all round the side-walls. Before long the divan and all the settees and chairs are fill'd; many fashionables out of curiosity; all the principal dignitaries of the town, Gen. Jeremiah Johnson, Judge Furman, George Hall, Mr. Willoughby, Mr. Pierrepont, N. B. Morse, Cyrus P. Smith, and F. C. Tucker. Many young folks too; some richly dress'd women; I remember I noticed with one party of ladies a group of uniform'd officers, either from the U. S. Navy Yard, or some ship in the stream, or some adjacent fort. On a slightly elevated platform at the head of the room, facing the audience, sit a dozen or more Friends, most of them elderly, grim, and with their broad-brimm'd hats on their heads. Three or four women, too, in their characteristic Quaker costumes and bonnets. All still as the grave.

At length after a pause and stillness becoming almost painful, Elias rises and stands for a moment or two without a word. A tall, straight figure, neither stout nor very thin, dress'd in drab cloth, clean-shaved face, forehead of great expanse, and large and clear black eyes,* long or middling-long white hair; he was at this time between 80 and 81 years of age, his head still wearing the broad-brim. A moment looking around the audience with those piercing eyes, amid the perfect stillness. (I can almost see him and the whole scene now.) Then the words come from his lips, very emphatically and slowly pronounc'd, in a resonant, grave, melodious voice, *What is the chief end of man?* I was told in my early youth, *it was to glorify God and seek and enjoy him forever.*

I cannot follow the discourse. It presently becomes very fervid, and in the midst of its fervor he takes the broad-brim hat from his head, and almost dashing it down with violence on the seat behind, continues with uninterrupted earnestness. But, I say, I cannot repeat, hardly suggest his sermon. Though the differences and disputes of the formal division of the Society of Friends were even then under way, he did not allude to them at all. A pleading, tender, nearly agonizing conviction, and magnetic

* In Walter Scott's reminiscences he speaks of Burns as having the most eloquent, glowing, flashing, illuminated dark-orbed eyes he ever beheld in a human face; and I think Elias Hicks's must have been like them.

and other evidence, such as the last paragraph of the "Prefatory Note," it seems probable that Whitman wrote this page and much of the rest of his MS (nearly all in pencil) before consulting *HJ* for details.—ED.]

411–412. In the MS the entire sentence beginning "I was told" was underlined. Revised in the galley proof.

stream of natural eloquence, before which all minds and natures, all emotions, high or low, gentle or simple, yielded entirely without exception, was its cause, method, and effect. Many, very many were in tears. Years afterward in Boston, I heard Father Taylor, the sailor's preacher, and found in his passionate unstudied oratory the resemblance to Elias Hicks's —not argumentative or intellectual, but so penetrating—so different from anything in the books—(different as the fresh air of a May morning or sea-shore breeze from the atmosphere of a perfumer's shop.) While he goes on he falls into the nasality and sing-song tone sometimes heard in such meetings; but in a moment or two more, as if recollecting himself, he breaks off, stops, and resumes in a natural tone. This occurs three or four times during the talk of the evening, till all concludes.

Now and then, at the many scores and hundreds—even thousands—of his discourses—as at this one—he was very mystical and radical,† and had much to say of "the light within." Very likely this same *inner light*, (so dwelt upon by newer men, as by Fox and Barclay at the beginning, and all Friends and deep thinkers since and now,) is perhaps only another name for the religious conscience. In my opinion they have all diagnos'd, like superior doctors, the real inmost disease of our times, probably any times. Amid the huge inflammation call'd society, and that other inflammation call'd politics, what is there to-day of moral power and ethic sanity as antiseptic to them and all? Though I think the essential elements of the moral nature exist latent in the good average people of the United States of today, and sometimes break out strongly, it is certain that any mark'd or dominating National Morality (if I may use the phrase) has not only not yet been develop'd, but that—at any rate when the point of view is turn'd on business, politics, competition, practical

† The true Christian religion, (such was the teaching of Elias Hicks,) consists neither in rites or Bibles or sermons or Sundays—but in noiseless secret ecstasy and unremitted aspiration, in purity, in a good practical life, in charity to the poor and toleration to all. He said, "A man may keep the Sabbath, may belong to a church and attend all the observances, have regular family prayer, keep a well-bound copy of the Hebrew Scriptures in a conspicuous place in his house, and yet not be a truly religious person at all."

2n. glowing, flashing] MS (unrevised): glowering flashing
5*n.* Bibles] MS (unrevised): bibles

435. by newer men] MS (before revision in ink): by Elias Hicks

449. and verified it] MS: and restated it [The printer erroneously set up "and retard it". Revised on the galley proof.]

452. doctrine of creeds, Bibles] MS: dicta of creeds, bibles [The printer erroneously set up "doctor" for "dicta"; revised on the galley proof.]

life, and in character and manners in our New World—there seems to be a hideous depletion, almost absence, of such moral nature. Elias taught throughout, as George Fox began it, or rather reiterated and verified it, the Platonic doctrine that the ideals of character, of justice, of religious action, whenever the highest is at stake, are to be conform'd to no outside doctrine of creeds, Bibles, legislative enactments, conventionalities, or even decorums, but are to follow the inward Deity-planted law of the emotional soul. In this only the true Quaker, or Friend, has faith; and it is from rigidly, perhaps strainingly carrying it out, that both the Old and New England records of Quakerdom show some unseemly and insane acts.

In one of the lives of Ralph Waldo Emerson is a list of lessons or instructions, ("seal'd orders" the biographer calls them,) prepar'd by the sage himself for his own guidance. Here is one:

> Go forth with thy message among thy fellow-creatures; teach them that they must trust themselves as guided by that inner light which dwells with the pure in heart, to whom it was promis'd of old that they shall see God.

How thoroughly it fits the life and theory of Elias Hicks. Then in Omar Khayyam:

> I sent my soul through the Invisible,
> Some letter of that after-life to spell,
>   And by-and-by my soul return'd to me,
> And answer'd, "I myself am Heaven and Hell."

Indeed, of this important element of the theory and practice of Quakerism, the difficult-to-describe "Light within" or "Inward Law, by

E. believ'd little in a church as organiz'd—even his own—with houses, ministers, or with salaries, creeds, Sundays, saints, Bibles, holy festivals, &c. But he believ'd always in the universal church, in the soul of man, invisibly rapt, ever-waiting, ever-responding to universal truths.—He was fond of pithy proverbs. He said, "It matters not where you live, but how you live." He said once to my father, "They talk of the devil—I tell thee, Walter, there is no worse devil than man."

6*n*. ecstasy] MS (unrevised): extasy
13*n*–14*n*. invisibly rapt] MS (unrevised): invisible rapt

461–464. These lines were printed from a newspaper clipping pasted between the penciled lines. Their source has not been identified.

467–470. This is quatrain number LXVI of the *Rubáiyát*. [In *NB* and later texts, the second line is incorrectly indented like the fourth line. In the MS lines 1, 2, and 4 are aligned, and line 3 is indented; on the authority of the MS, the error is corrected in the present edition.—ED.]

which all must be either justified or condemn'd," I will not undertake where so many have fail'd—the task of making the statement of it for the average comprehension. We will give, partly for the matter and partly as specimen of his speaking and writing style, what Elias Hicks himself says in allusion to it—one or two of very many passages. Most of his discourses, like those of Epictetus and the ancient peripatetics, have left no record remaining—they were extempore, and those were not the times of reporters. Of one, however, deliver'd in Chester, Pa., toward the latter part of his career, there is a careful transcript; and from it (even if presenting you a sheaf of hidden wheat that may need to be pick'd and thrash'd out several times before you get the grain,) we give the following extract:

"I don't want to express a great many words; but I want you to be call'd home to the substance. For the Scriptures, and all the books in the world, can do no more; Jesus could do no more than to recommend to this Comforter, which was the light in him. 'God is light, and in him is no darkness at all; and if we walk in the light, as he is in the light, we have fellowship one with another.' Because the light is one in all, and therefore it binds us together in the bonds of love; for it is not only light, but love—that love which casts out all fear. So that they who dwell in God dwell in love, and they are constrain'd to walk in it; and if they 'walk in it, they have fellowship one with another, and the blood of Jesus Christ his Son cleanseth us from all sin.'

"But what blood, my friends? Did Jesus Christ, the Saviour, ever have any material blood? Not a drop of it, my friends—not a drop of it. That blood which cleanseth from the life of all sin, was the life of the soul of Jesus. The soul of man has no material blood; but as the outward material blood, created from the dust of the earth, is the life of these bodies of flesh, so with respect to the soul, the immortal and invisible spirit, its blood is that life which God breath'd into it.

"As we read, in the beginning, that 'God form'd man of the dust of

481–483. The words in parenthesis, not in the MS, are inserted in the galley proof.

485–505. Printed from the MS, evidently a fair copy for the printer in black ink. The source of the quotation has not been identified.

495. his Son] MS (unrevised): his son

505. soul.' He] MS: soul'—He

508–547. Printed from the MS, a fair copy in black ink. Since this quotation is from the letter to Hugh Judge, of Ohio, dated "*Jericho, 2d mo. 14th*, 1830," and printed in the appendix to *HJ*, pp. 439–442, it may be supposed that Whitman copied it out before his illness compelled him to resort to marking passages in *HJ* for the printer. The *HJ* text is included in the collation, as well as the MS.

508. query, What] *HJ:* query, what

508. answer, It] *HJ:* answer, it

the ground, and breath'd into him the breath of life, and man became a living soul.' He breath'd into that soul, and it became alive to God."

Then, from one of his many letters, for he seems to have delighted in correspondence:

"Some may query, What is the cross of Christ? To these I answer, It is the perfect law of God, written on the tablet of the heart, and in the heart of every rational creature, in such indelible characters that all the power of mortals cannot erase nor obliterate it. Neither is there any power or means given or dispens'd to the children of men, but this inward law and light, by which the true and saving knowledge of God can be obtain'd. And by this inward law and light, all will be either justified or condemn'd, and all made to know God for themselves, and be left without excuse, agreeably to the prophecy of Jeremiah, and the corroborating testimony of Jesus in his last counsel and command to his disciples, not to depart from Jerusalem till they should receive power from on high; assuring them that they should receive power, when they had receiv'd the pouring forth of the spirit upon them, which would qualify them to bear witness of him in Judea, Jerusalem, Samaria, and to the uttermost parts of the earth; which was verified in a marvellous manner on the day of Pentecost, when thousands were converted to the Christian faith in one day.

"By which it is evident that nothing but this inward light and law, as it is heeded and obey'd, ever did, or ever can, make a true and real Christian and child of God. And until the professors of Christianity agree to lay aside all their non-essentials in religion, and rally to this unchangeable foundation and standard of truth, wars and fightings, confusion and error, will prevail, and the angelic song cannot be heard in our land—that of 'glory to God in the highest, and on earth peace and good will to men.'

"But when all nations are made willing to make this inward law and light the rule and standard of all their faith and works, then we shall be brought to know and believe alike, that there is but one Lord, one

509. God, written] *HJ:* God written
513. light, by] *HJ:* light by
515. all made] *HJ:* all be made
518. till] *HJ:* until
525. After "one day." *HJ* continues in the same paragraph.
525. evident that] *HJ:* evident, that
526. can, make] *HJ:* can make
530. error, will] *HJ:* error will
530. land—that] *HJ:* land, that
531. MS does not close the quotation after "men."
532. After "to men." *HJ* continues in the same paragraph.
533. light the] *HJ* and MS: light, the

faith, and but one baptism; one God and Father, that is above all, through all, and in all.

"And then will all those glorious and consoling prophecies recorded in the scriptures of truth be fulfill'd—'He,' the Lord, 'shall judge among the nations, and shall rebuke many people; and they shall beat their swords into ploughshares, and their spears into pruning-hooks; nation shall not lift up the sword against nation, neither shall they learn war any more. The wolf also shall dwell with the lamb; and the cow and the bear shall feed; and the lion shall eat straw like the ox; and the sucking child shall play on the hole of the asp, and the wean'd child put his hand on the cockatrice's den. They shall not hurt nor destroy in all my holy mountain; for the earth,' that is our earthly tabernacle, 'shall be full of the knowledge of the Lord, as the waters cover the sea.'"

The exposition in the last sentence, that the terms of the texts are not to be taken in their literal meaning, but in their spiritual one, and allude to a certain wondrous exaltation of the body, through religious influences, is significant, and is but one of a great number of instances of much that is obscure, to "the world's people," in the preachings of this remarkable man.

Then a word about his physical oratory, connected with the preceding.

536. After "in all" *HJ* has a semicolon and continues in the same sentence.
537. prophecies recorded] *HJ:* prophecies, recorded
538. fulfill'd—'He,' the] *HJ:* fulfilled. Isaiah ii. 4, "He," the
539. and shall rebuke many people; and] *HJ:* and rebuke many people: and
540. ploughshares, and] *HJ:* ploughshares and
540. pruning-hooks; nation] *HJ:* pruning-hooks: nation
541. up the sword] *HJ:* up sword
541. nation, neither] *HJ:* nation; neither
542. more. The] MS: more.—The] *HJ:* more." Isaiah xi. "The
542. lamb; and the cow] *HJ:* lamb, and the leopard shall lie down with the kid; and the calf, and the young lion, and the fatling together; and a little child shall lead them. And the cow
543. feed; and the lion] *HJ:* feed; their young ones shall lie down together; and the lion
543. ox; and] *HJ:* ox. And
545. den. They] MS: den.—They
546. mountain; for] *HJ:* mountain: for
548–553. These lines are also copied in black ink in a fair hand, and on a separate sheet.
554–580. These lines were printed from a sheet written in pencil, with a printed clipping from the poem pasted between lines in the middle.
554–555. Part of these two lines, crowded in at the top of the page, is blotted and illegible in the MS.
557. The word "constitutional" is inserted in the MS in black ink.
561. The words "inherent knowledge, intuition" are inserted in the MS in black ink.

If there is, as doubtless there is, an unnameable something behind oratory, a fund within or atmosphere without, deeper than art, deeper even than proof, that unnameable constitutional something Elias Hicks emanated from his very heart to the hearts of his audience, or carried with him, or probed into, and shook and arous'd in them—a sympathetic germ, probably rapport, lurking in every human eligibility, which no book, no rule, no statement has given or can give inherent knowledge, intuition—not even the best speech, or best put forth, but launch'd out only by powerful human magnetism:

Unheard by sharpest ear—unform'd in clearest eye, or cunningest mind,
Nor lore, nor fame, nor happiness, nor wealth,
And yet the pulse of every heart and life throughout the world, incessantly,
Which you and I, and all, pursuing ever, ever miss;
Open, but still a secret—the real of the real—an illusion;
Costless, vouchsafed to each, yet never man the owner;
Which poets vainly seek to put in rhyme—historians in prose;
Which sculptor never chisel'd yet, nor painter painted;
Which vocalist never sung, nor orator nor actor ever utter'd.

That remorse, too, for a mere worldly life—that aspiration towards the ideal, which, however overlaid, lies folded latent, hidden, in perhaps

564–572. A clipping of lines 2–10 of Whitman's "A Riddle Song." This poem was first published in the spring of 1880, for in a letter to Burroughs, May 9, 1880 (as quoted by Clara Barrus in *Whitman and Burroughs, Comrades*, page 191) Whitman wrote: "I suppose you saw my Riddle Song in the first number of Sunnyside Press—if not, I can send you the 'Progress' with it in." [The clipping seems to be from neither of these periodicals, but from a proof made, perhaps, for the convenience of the printers. The poem was reprinted in LG (1881), somewhat revised. I have found no record of the periodical *Sunnyside Press*, and I do not know exactly when the poem appeared in the *Progress*, a Philadelphia weekly published from 1879 to 1885 by Whitman's friend, Col. John W. Forney, who also published PP.—ED.]

564. ear-unform'd] LG 1881: ear, unform'd

564. eye, or cunningest mind,] LG 1881: eye or cunningest mind,] Clipping: eye, or cunningest mind;

565. lore, nor] LG 1881: lore nor

565. happiness, nor] LG 1881: happiness nor

566. world, incessantly,] LG 1881: world incessantly,] Clipping: world, incessantly;

567. and I . . . miss;] LG 1881: and I and all pursuing ever ever miss,

568. Open . . . illusion;] LG 1881: Open but still a secret, the real of the real, an illusion,

569. owner;] LG 1881: owner,

570. rhyme—historians in prose;] LG 1881: rhyme, historians in prose,

571. painted;] LG 1881: painted,

572. utter'd.] LG 1881: utter'd,] Clipping: utter'd;

573. After "utter'd;" MS continues the same sentence in pencil: "—that remorse," etc.

every character. More definitely, as near as I remember (aided by my dear mother long afterward,) Elias Hicks's discourse there in the Brooklyn ball-room, was one of his old never-remitted appeals to that moral mystical portion of human nature, *the inner light*. But it is mainly for the scene itself, and Elias's *personnel*, that I recall the incident.

Soon afterward the old man died:

> On first day morning, the 14th of 2d month (February, 1830) he was engaged in his room, writing to a friend, until a little after ten o'clock, when he return'd to that occupied by the family, apparently just attack'd by a paralytic affection, which nearly deprived him of the use of his right side, and of the power of speech. Being assisted to a chair near the fire, he manifested by signs, that the letter which he had just finish'd, and which had been dropp'd by the way, should be taken care of; and on its being brought to him, appear'd satisfied, and manifested a desire that all should sit down and be still, seemingly sensible that his labours were brought to a close, and only desirous of quietly waiting the final change. The solemn composure at this time manifest in his countenance, was very impressive, indicating that he was sensible the time of his departure was at hand, and that the prospect of death brought no terrors with it. During his last illness, his mental faculties were occasionally obscured, yet he was at times enabled to give satisfactory evidence to those around him, that all was well, and that he felt nothing in his way.
>
> His funeral took place on fourth day, the 3d of 3d month. It was attended by a large concourse of Friends and others, and a solid meeting was held on the occasion; after which, his remains were interr'd in Friends' burial-ground at this place (Jericho, Queens County, New York.)

I have thought (even presented so incompletely, with such fearful hiatuses, and in my own feebleness and waning life) one might well memorize this life of Elias Hicks. Though not eminent in literature or politics or inventions or business, it is a token of not a few, and is significant. Such men do not cope with statesmen or soldiers—but I have thought they deserve to be recorded and kept up as a sample—that this one specially does. I have already compared it to a little flowing liquid rill of Nature's life, maintaining freshness. As if, indeed, under the

581–596. From a marked paragraph of *HJ* (appendix), pp. 449–450.

581. month (February, 1830,) he] *HJ* (appendix): month last, he

597–600. Printed from another marked paragraph of *HJ* (appendix), page 450, the second following "in his way." though Whitman presents them as if they were consecutive.

600. *HJ* ends the paragraph with "place." The next paragraph, concluding the "Memorial of Jericho Monthly Meeting of Friends Concerning our Ancient Friend Elias Hicks" (pp. 444–450), is as follows: "Signed by direction and on behalf of Jericho Monthly Meeting, held 4th month, 15th, 1830. Willet Robbins, Abigail

smoke of battles, the blare of trumpets, and the madness of contending hosts—the screams of passion, the groans of the suffering, the parching of struggles of money and politics, and all hell's heat and noise and competition above and around—should come melting down from the mountains from sources of unpolluted snows, far up there in God's hidden, untrodden recesses, and so rippling along among us low in the ground, at men's very feet, a curious little brook of clear and cool, and ever-healthy, ever-living water.

Note.—The Separation.—The division vulgarly call'd between Orthodox and Hicksites in the Society of Friends took place in 1827, '8 and '9. Probably it had been preparing some time. One who was present has since described to me the climax, at a meeting of Friends in Philadelphia crowded by a great attendance of both sexes, with Elias as principal speaker. In the course of his utterance or argument he made use of these words: "The blood of Christ—the blood of Christ—why, my friends, the actual blood of Christ in itself was no more effectual than the blood of bulls and goats—not a bit more—not a bit." At these words, after a momentary hush, commenced a great tumult. Hundreds rose to their feet. . . . Canes were thump'd upon the floor. From all parts of the house angry mutterings. Some left the place, but more remain'd, with exclamations, flush'd faces and eyes. This was the definite utterance, the overt act, which led to the separation. Families diverg'd—even husbands and wives, parents and children, were separated.

Of course what Elias promulg'd spread a great commotion among the Friends. Sometimes when he presented himself to speak in the meeting, there would be opposition—this led to angry words, gestures, unseemly noises, recriminations. Elias, at such times, was deeply affected—the tears roll'd in streams down his cheeks—he silently waited the close of the dispute. "Let the Friend speak; let the Friend speak!" he would say when his supporters in the meeting tried to bluff off some violent orthodox person objecting to the new doctrinaire. But he never recanted.

A reviewer of the old dispute and separation made the following

Hicks, *Clerks.*"

601–616. Printed from a page of the autograph MS composed of three strips, written in pencil, pasted together, or, probably, a revised draft of this page.

604. a token of] MS: a sample of [Change made in page proof.]

605. with statesmen or soldiers—but] MS: with the statesman's or soldier's—but [Change made in page proof.]

617–737. Not in the MS in the Feinberg Collection, except the few fragments indicated. These addenda to "Elias Hicks" were apparently sent to the printer with the MS of "George Fox (and Shakspere)" for they are set up on the same series of galleys. Both galley proof and page proof are collated.

comments on them in a paper ten years ago: "It was in America, where there had been no persecution worth mentioning since Mary Dyer was hang'd on Boston Common, that about fifty years ago differences arose, singularly enough upon doctrinal points of the divinity of Christ and the nature of the atonement. Whoever would know how bitter was the controversy, and how much of human infirmity was found to be still lurking under broad-brim hats and drab coats, must seek for the information in the Lives of Elias Hicks and of Thomas Shillitoe, the latter an English Friend, who visited us at this unfortunate time, and who exercised his gifts as a peacemaker with but little success. The meetings, according to his testimony, were sometimes turn'd into mobs. The disruption was wide, and seems to have been final. Six of the ten yearly meetings were divided; and since that time various sub-divisions have come, four or five in number. There has never, however, been anything like a repetition of the excitement of the Hicksite controversy; and Friends of all kinds at present appear to have settled down into a solid, steady, comfortable state, and to be working in their own way without troubling other Friends whose ways are different."

Note.—Old persons, who heard this man in his day, and who glean'd impressions from what they saw of him, (judg'd from their own points of view,) have, in their conversation with me, dwelt on another point. They think Elias Hicks had a large element of personal ambition, the pride of leadership, of establishing perhaps a sect that should reflect his own name, and to which he should give especial form and character. Very likely. Such indeed seems the means, all through progress and civilization, by which strong men and strong convictions achieve anything definite. But the basic foundation of Elias was undoubtedly genuine religious fervor. He was like an old Hebrew prophet. He had the spirit of one, and

641–658. The source of this quotation has not been identified.

659–668. From an unnumbered MS page, mostly in black ink. The word "*Note*" is not in the MS.

659. heard this man] MS: heard Elias

659–660. glean'd impressions from] MS: gleaned their impressions directly from

660–661. The words in parenthesis are not in the MS.

662. think Elias Hicks had] MS: think he had

662–663. pride . . . perhaps] MS: pride of establishing leadership, perhaps

664. he should . . . character.] MS: he himself should give acknowledged form & character.

665. indeed seems the] MS: indeed is the

666–667. anything definite. But] MS: anything. But

668–669. These two sentences, beginning "He was like", are written in pencil on a strip pasted to the bottom of the sheet in black ink.

in his later years look'd like one. What Carlyle says of John Knox will apply to him:

> "He is an instance to us how a man, by sincerity itself, becomes heroic; it is the grand gift he has. We find in him a good, honest, intellectual talent, no transcendent one;—a narrow, inconsiderable man, as compared with Luther; but in heartfelt instinctive adherence to truth, in *sincerity* as we say, he has no superior; nay, one might ask, What equal he has? The heart of him is of the true Prophet cast. 'He lies there,' said the Earl of Morton at Knox's grave, 'who never fear'd the face of man.' He resembles, more than any of the moderns, an old Hebrew Prophet. The same inflexibility, intolerance, rigid, narrow-looking adherence to God's truth."

A Note yet. The United States to-day.—While under all previous conditions (even convictions) of society, Oriental, Feudal, Ecclesiastical, and in all past (or present) Despotisms, through the entire past, there existed, and exists yet, in ally and fusion with them, and frequently forming the main part of them, certain churches, institutes, priesthoods, fervid beliefs, &c., practically promoting religious and moral action to the fullest degrees of which humanity there under circumstances was capable, and often conserving all there was of justice, art, literature, and good manners—it is clear I say, that, under the Democratic Institutes of the United States, now and henceforth, there are no equally genuine fountains of fervid beliefs, adapted to produce similar moral and religious results, according to our circumstances. I consider that the churches, sects, pulpits, of the present day, in the United States, exist not by any solid convictions, but by a sort of tacit, supercilious, scornful sufferance. Few speak openly—none officially—against them. But the ostent continuously imposing, who is not aware that any such living fountains of belief in them are now utterly ceas'd and departed from the minds of men?

669. in his later years] MS: in old age
671–680. These lines are from "The Hero as Priest," in Carlyle's *On Heroes, Hero-Worship, and the Heroic in History* (1841), p. 171, which is included in the collation.
672. heroic;] Carlyle: heroic:
672. in him a] Carlyle: in Knox a
672. Carlyle has no comma after "good" or "honest".
674. Luther;] Carlyle: Luther:
677. Knox's grave] Carlyle: his grave
678. old Hebrew Prophet] Carlyle: Old-Hebrew Prophet
680. After "truth" Carlyle has a comma and continues the sentence.
681–697. The MS for this paragraph is missing.
695. the ostent] Galley proof before revision: extent
697. Period after "of men" changed to a question mark in the page proof.

A Lingering Note.—In the making of a full man, all the other consciences, (the emotional, courageous, intellectual, esthetic, &c.,) are to be crown'd and effused by the religious conscience. In the higher structure of a human self, or of community, the Moral, the Religious, the Spiritual, is strictly analogous to the subtle vitalization and antiseptic play call'd Health in the physiologic structure. To person or State, the main verteber (or rather *the* verteber) is Morality. That is indeed the only real vitalization of character, and of all the supersensual, even heroic and artistic portions of man or nationality. It is to run through and knit the superior parts, and keep man or State vital and upright, as health keeps the body straight and blooming. Of course a really grand and strong and beautiful character is probably to be slowly grown, and adjusted strictly with reference to itself, its own personal and social sphere—with (paradox though it may be) the clear understanding that the conventional theories of life, worldly ambition, wealth, office, fame, &c., are essentially but glittering mayas, delusions.

Doubtless the greatest scientists and theologians will sometimes find themselves saying, It isn't only those who know most, who contribute most to God's glory. Doubtless these very scientists at times stand with bared heads before the humblest lives and personalities. For there is something greater (is there not?) than all the science and poems of the world—above all else, like the stars shining eternal—above Shakspere's plays, or Concord philosophy, or art of Angelo or Raphael—something that shines elusive, like beams of Hesperus at evening—high above all the vaunted wealth and pride—prov'd by its practical outcropping in life, each case after its own concomitants—the intuitive blending of divine love and faith in a human emotional character—blending for all, for the unlearn'd, the common, and the poor.

I don't know in what book I once read, (possibly the remark has been made in books, all ages,) that no life ever lived, even the most uneventful, but, probed to its centre, would be found in itself as subtle a drama as any that poets have ever sung, or playwrights fabled. Often, too, in size and

698–737. A rough draft, a single page, mostly in black ink, exists for lines 698–708 (ending with "blooming."), but no MS for the rest. At the top of the page, before the indented sentence beginning "In the making," the following is written in pencil, as if it was meant to introduce the first sentence, but it is not in the printed text: "If there is one final lesson in history what is it? it is that".

698. man, all] MS: man, or Nation, all

700. and effused by the] MS: and suffused with the

700–701. of a human self, or of community, the] MS: of every human identity, or of communities, the

701–702. Religious, the Spiritual, is strictly analogous] MS: Religious, is fully analogous

weight, that life suppos'd obscure. For it isn't only the palpable stars; astronomers say there are dark, or almost dark, unnotic'd orbs and suns, (like the dusky companion of Sirius, seven times as large as our own sun,) rolling through space, real and potent as any—perhaps the most real and potent. Yet none recks of them. In the bright lexicon we give the spreading heavens, they have not even names. Amid ceaseless sophistications all times, the soul would seem to glance yearningly around for such contrasts—such cool, still offsets.

GEORGE FOX (AND SHAKSPERE.)

While we are about it, we must almost inevitably go back to the origin of the Society of which Elias Hicks has so far prov'd to be the most mark'd individual result. We must revert to the latter part of the 16th, and all, or nearly all of that 17th century, crowded with so many important historical events, changes, and personages. Throughout Europe, and especially in what we call our Mother Country, men were unusually arous'd—(some would say demented.) It was a special age of the insanity of witch-trials and witch-hangings. In one year 60 were hung for witchcraft in one English county alone. It was peculiarly an age of military-religious conflict. Protestantism and Catholicism were wrestling like giants for the mastery, straining every nerve. Only to think of it—that age! its events, persons—Shakspere just dead, (his folios publish'd, complete)—Charles 1st, the shadowy spirit and the solid block! To sum up all, it was *the age of Cromwell!*

As indispensable foreground, indeed, for Elias Hicks, and perhaps *sine qua non* to an estimate of the kind of man, we must briefly transport ourselves back to the England of that period. As I say, it is the time of tremendous moral and political agitation; ideas of conflicting forms, governments, theologies, seethe and dash like ocean storms, and ebb and flow like mighty tides. It was, or had been, the time of the long feud between the Parliament and the Crown. In the midst of the sprouts, began George Fox—born eight years after the death of Shakspere. He was the son of a

703–704. To person . . . is Morality.] MS: Person or State, the main verteber is the Moral one.

704–705. indeed . . . character] MS: indeed the vitalization of character

705–706. the supersensual . . . or nationality.] MS: the super-sensual portion of man or Nationality.

707. keep . . . upright] MS: keep them alive & upright

735. names] Galley proof before revision: name

GEORGE FOX (AND SHAKSPERE.)

This section, probably intended to be a subdivision of "Elias Hicks," was published for the first time in *NB*. The MS from which it was printed is not avail-

weaver, himself a shoemaker, and was "converted" before the age of 20. But O the sufferings, mental and physical, through which those years of the strange youth pass'd! He claim'd to be sent by God to fulfil a mission. "I come," he said, "to direct people to the spirit that gave forth the Scriptures." The range of his thought, even then, cover'd almost every important subject of after times, anti-slavery, women's rights, &c. Though in a low sphere, and among the masses, he forms a mark'd feature in the age.

And how, indeed, beyond all any, that stormy and perturb'd age! The foundations of the old, the superstitious, the conventionally poetic, the credulous, all breaking—the light of the new, and of science and democracy, definitely beginning—a mad, fierce, almost crazy age! The political struggles of the reigns of the Charleses, and of the Protectorate of Cromwell, heated to frenzy by theological struggles. Those were the years following the advent and practical working of the Reformation—but Catholicism is yet strong, and yet seeks supremacy. We think our age full of the flush of men and doings, and culminations of war and peace; and so it is. But there could hardly be a grander and more picturesque and varied age than that.

Born out of and in this age, when Milton, Bunyan, Dryden and John Locke were still living—amid the memories of Queen Elizabeth and James First, and the events of their reigns—when the radiance of that galaxy of poets, warriors, statesmen, captains, lords, explorers, wits and gentlemen, that crowded the courts and times of those sovereigns still fill'd the atmosphere—when America commencing to be explor'd and settled commenc'd also to be suspected as destin'd to overthrow the old standards and calculations—when Feudalism, like a sunset, seem'd to gather all its glories, reminiscences, personalisms, in one last gorgeous effort, before the advance of a new day, a new incipient genius—amid the social and domestic circles of that period—indifferent to reverberations that seem'd enough to wake the dead, and in a sphere far from the

able, though notes and clippings on which it must have been partly based are in the Feinberg Collection. Both galley proof and page proof are collated, but they show no changes except the correction of printer's errors. Also collated are two pages of MS, abbreviated FMS, rough draft fragments, in the Feinberg Collection.

42–57. These lines exist in rough draft on two pages, in black ink.

42. age, when] FMS: age—when

44–45. the radiance . . . statesmen] FMS: the immediate radiance of that vast galaxy of poets, statesmen

46. courts and times of] FMS: courts of

47–49. atmosphere . . . Feudalism] FMS: atmosphere—when Feudalism

50. glories . . . in] FMS: glories its Personalisms, & reminiscences in

pageants of the court, the awe of any personal rank or charm of intellect, or literature, or the varying excitement of Parliamentarian or Royalist fortunes—this curious young rustic goes wandering up and down England.

George Fox, born 1624, was of decent stock, in ordinary lower life—as he grew along toward manhood, work'd at shoemaking, also at farm labors—loved to be much by himself, half-hidden in the woods, reading the Bible—went about from town to town, dress'd in leather clothes—walk'd much at night, solitary, deeply troubled ("the inward divine teaching of the Lord")—sometimes goes among the ecclesiastical gatherings of the great professors, and though a mere youth bears bold testimony—goes to and fro disputing—(must have had great personality)—heard the voice of the Lord speaking articulately to him, as he walk'd in the fields—feels resistless commands not to be explain'd, but follow'd, to abstain from taking off his hat, to say *Thee* and *Thou*, and not bid others Good morning or Good evening—was illiterate, could just read and write—testifies against shows, games, and frivolous pleasures—enters the courts and warns the judges that they see to doing justice—goes into public houses and market-places, with denunciations of drunkenness and money-making—rises in the midst of the church-services, and gives his own explanations of the ministers' explanations, and of Bible passages and texts—sometimes for such things put in prison, sometimes struck fiercely on the mouth on the spot, or knock'd down, and lying there beaten and bloody—was of keen wit, ready to any question with the most apropos of answers—was sometimes press'd for a soldier, (*him* for a soldier!)—was indeed terribly buffeted; but goes, goes, goes—often sleeping outdoors, under hedges, or hay stacks—forever taken before justices—improving such, and all occasions, to *bear testimony*, and give good advice—still enters the "steeple-houses," (as he calls churches,) and though often dragg'd out and whipt till he faints away, and lies like one dead, when he comes-to—stands up again, and offering himself all bruis'd and

51–57. After "before the advance" FMS has, instead of the *NB* text, the following: "of a new genius, its enemy & destined conqueror,—we behold bred from & acting amid the social and domestic customs of that period, and in a sphere far, far from the pageants of the Court, the awe of personal rank or genius, or the excitements of royalists or Parliamentarian fortunes—a curious young rustic, a dreamer, after tending sheep & cobbling shoes awhile, now wandering to and fro in England." In revising these lines, Whitman marked for deletion everything after "we behold" up to and including "fortunes—" and added after "England.": "Indifferent to all those reverberations that seemed enough to wake the dead, far from the sphere of courts or armies, he—"

57–151. The MS from which these lines were printed in *NB* are unavailable, perhaps lost.

bloody, cries out to his tormenters, "Strike—strike again, here where you have not yet touch'd! my arms, my head, my cheeks."—Is at length arrested and sent up to London, confers with the Protector, Cromwell,—is set at liberty, and holds great meetings in London.

Thus going on, there is something in him that fascinates one or two here, and three or four there, until gradually there were others who went about in the same spirit, and by degrees the Society of Friends took shape, and stood among the thousand religious sects of the world. Women also catch the contagion, and go round, often shamefully misused. By such contagion these ministerings, by scores, almost hundreds of poor travelling men and women, keep on year after year, through ridicule, whipping, imprisonment, &c.—some of the Friend-ministers emigrate to New England—where their treatment makes the blackest part of the early annals of the New World. Some were executed, others maim'd, par-burnt, and scourg'd—two hundred die in prison—some on the gallows, or at the stake.

George Fox himself visited America, and found a refuge and hearers, and preach'd many times on Long Island, New York State. In the village of Oysterbay they will show you the rock on which he stood, (1672,) addressing the multitude, in the open air—thus rigidly following the fashion of apostolic times.—(I have heard myself many reminiscences of him.) Flushing also contains (or contain'd—I have seen them) memorials of Fox, and his son, in two aged white-oak trees, that shaded him while he bore his testimony to people gather'd in the highway.—Yes, the American Quakers were much persecuted—almost as much, by a sort of consent of all the other sects, as the Jews were in Europe in the middle ages. In New England, the cruelest laws were pass'd, and put in execution against them. As said, some were whipt—women the same as men. Some had their ears cut off—others their tongues pierc'd with hot irons—others their faces branded. Worse still, a woman and three men had been hang'd, (1660.)—Public opinion, and the statutes, join'd together, in an odious union, Quakers, Baptists, Roman Catholics and Witches.—Such a fragmentary sketch of George Fox and his time—and the advent of 'the Society of Friends' in America.

Strange as it may sound, Shakspere and George Fox, (think of them! compare them!) were born and bred of similar stock, in much the same surroundings and station in life—from the same England—and at a similar period. One to radiate all of art's, all literature's splendor—a splendor so dazzling that he himself is almost lost in it, and his contemporaries the same—his fictitious Othello, Romeo, Hamlet, Lear, as real as any lords of England or Europe then and there—more real to us, the mind sometimes thinks, than the man Shakspere himself. Then the other —may we indeed name him the same day? What is poor plain George Fox compared to William Shakspere—to fancy's lord, imagination's heir? Yet George Fox stands for something too—a thought—the thought that wakes in silent hours—perhaps the deepest, most eternal thought latent in the human soul. This is the thought of God, merged in the thoughts of moral right and the immortality of identity. Great, great is this thought —aye, greater than all else. When the gorgeous pageant of Art, refulgent in the sunshine, color'd with roses and gold—with all the richest mere poetry, old or new, (even Shakspere's)—with all that statue, play, painting, music, architecture, oratory, can effect, ceases to satisfy and please—When the eager chase after wealth flags, and beauty itself becomes a loathing—and when all worldly or carnal or esthetic, or even scientific values, having done their office to the human character, and minister'd their part to its development—then, if not before, comes forward this over-arching thought, and brings its eligibilities, germinations. Most neglected in life of all humanity's attributes, easily cover'd with crust, deluded and abused, rejected, yet the only certain source of what all are seeking, but few or none find—in it I for myself clearly see the first, the last, the deepest depths and highest heights of art, of literature, and of the purposes of life. I say whoever labors here, makes contributions here, or best of all sets an incarnated example here, of life or death, is dearest to humanity—remains after the rest are gone. And here, for these purposes, and up to the light that was in him, the man Elias Hicks—as the man George Fox had done years before him—lived long, and died, faithful in life, and faithful in death.

Good-Bye My Fancy.

An Old Man's Rejoinder.

In the domain of Literature loftily consider'd (an accomplish'd and veteran critic in his just out work* now says,) 'the kingdom of the Father has pass'd; the kingdom of the Son is passing; the kingdom of the Spirit begins.' Leaving the reader to chew on and extract the juice and meaning of this, I will proceed to say in melanged form what I have had brought out by the English author's essay (he discusses the poetic art mostly) on my own, real, or by him supposed, views and purports. If I give any an-

* Two new volumes, 'Essays Speculative and Suggestive,' by John Addington Symonds. One of the Essays is on 'Democratic Art,' in which I and my books are largely alluded to and cited and dissected. It is this part of the vols. that has caused the off-hand lines above—(first thanking Mr. S. for his invariable courtesy of personal treatment).

5*n*. After "treatment)." the footnote in CR continues with the following, cut away in the clipping: "The Essays are remarkably fine specimens of type, paper and press-work—Chapman & Hall their English publishers—and jobb'd here by Scribners, New York."

Good-Bye My Fancy.

GBF, a collection of prose and verse, was published by David McKay of Philadelphia in 1891. Whitman's *Commonplace Book* shows that on May 17 he was finishing the proofs and that on May 18 he applied for the copyright. The MS from which it was printed, now in the Feinberg Collection, consists of printed clippings, autograph MSS, and one typescript. GBF contained nothing that Whitman had previously published in a volume of his collected writings. All of the prose in GBF except "Preface Note to 2d Annex," which went into the 1891–92 edition of LG, was reprinted in CPW 1892 from the same plates, without change except repagination. The two poems, together with the footnote to the second one, in GBF, p. 28, and the four short poems in GBF, p. 44, although reprinted in CPW (p. 484 and p. 500), are omitted in this volume of the *Collected Writings* since they have their proper place in the volumes containing LG. In this collation, the terms "MS" and "clipping," unless otherwise specified, refer to the printer's copy in the Feinberg Collection. Details of previous publication, if any, are given in the headnote for each separate title.

An Old Man's Rejoinder.

Printed in GBF from clippings of the article of the same title in CR, August 16, 1890.

swers to him, or explanations of what my books intend, they will be not direct but indirect and derivative. Of course this brief jotting is personal. Something very like querulous egotism and growling may break through the narrative (for I have been and am rejected by all the great magazines, carry now my 72d annual burden, and have been a paralytic for 18 years.)

No great poem or other literary or artistic work of any scope, old or new, can be essentially consider'd without weighing first the age, politics (or want of politics) and aim, visible forms, unseen soul, and current times, out of the midst of which it rises and is formulated: as the Biblic canticles and their days and spirit—as the Homeric, or Dante's utterance, or Shakspere's, or the old Scotch or Irish ballads, or Ossian, or Omar Khayyam. So I have conceiv'd and launch'd, and work'd for years at, my 'Leaves of Grass'—personal emanations only at best, but with specialty of emergence and background—the ripening of the nineteenth century, the thought and fact and radiation of individuality, of America, the Secession war, and showing the democratic conditions supplanting everything that insults them or impedes their aggregate way. Doubtless my poems illustrate (one of novel thousands to come for a long period) those conditions; but 'democratic art' will have to wait long before it is satisfactorily formulated and defined—if it ever is.

I will now for one indicative moment lock horns with what many think the greatest thing, the question of art, so-call'd. I have not seen without learning something therefrom, how, with hardly an exception, the poets of this age devote themselves, always mainly, sometimes altogether, to fine rhyme, spicy verbalism, the fabric and cut of the garment, jewelry, *concetti*, style, art. To-day these adjuncts are certainly the effort, beyond all else. Yet the lesson of Nature undoubtedly is, to proceed with single purpose toward the result necessitated, and for which the time has arrived, utterly regardless of the outputs of shape, appearance or criticism, which are always left to settle themselves. I have not only not bother'd much about style, form, art, etc., but confess to more or less apathy (I believe I have sometimes caught myself in decided aversion) toward them throughout, asking nothing of them but negative advantages—that they should never impede me, and never under any circumstances, or for their own purposes only, assume any mastery over me.

From the beginning I have watch'd the sharp and sometimes heavy and deep-penetrating objections and reviews against my work, and I hope entertain'd and audited them; (for I have probably had an advantage

18. Shakspere's] *CR:* Shakespeare's
45. them; (for] *CR:* them (for

in constructing from a central and unitary principle since the first, but at long intervals and stages—sometimes lapses of five or six years, or peace or war.) Ruskin, the Englishman, charges as a fearful and serious lack that my poems have no humor. A profound German critic complains that, compared with the luxuriant and well-accepted songs of the world, there is about my verse a certain coldness, severity, absence of spice, polish, or of consecutive meaning and plot. (The book is autobiographic at bottom, and may-be I do not exhibit and make ado about the stock passions: I am partly of Quaker stock.) Then E. C. Stedman finds (or found) mark'd fault with me because while celebrating the common people *en masse*, I do not allow enough heroism and moral merit and good intentions to the choicer classes, the college-bred, the *état-major*. It is quite probable that S. is right in the matter. In the main I myself look, and have from the first look'd, to the bulky democratic *torso* of the United States even for esthetic and moral attributes of serious account—and refused to aim at or accept anything less. If America is only for the rule and fashion and small typicality of other lands (the rule of the *état-major*) it is not the land I take it for, and should to-day feel that my literary aim and theory had been blanks and misdirections. Strictly judged, most modern poems are but larger or smaller lumps of sugar, or slices of toothsome sweet cake—even the banqueters dwelling on those glucose flavors as a main part of the dish. Which perhaps leads to something: to have great heroic poetry we need great readers—a heroic appetite and audience. Have we at present any such?

Then the thought at the centre, never too often repeated. Boundless material wealth, free political organization, immense geographic area, and unprecedented 'business' and products—even the most active intellect and 'culture'—will not place this Commonwealth of ours on the topmost range of history and humanity—or any eminence of 'democratic art' —to say nothing of its pinnacle. Only the production (and on the most copious scale) of loftiest moral, spiritual and heroic personal illustrations —a great native Literature headed with a Poetry stronger and sweeter than any yet. If there can be any such thing as a kosmic modern and original song, America needs it, and is worthy of it.

In my opinion to-day (bitter as it is to say so) the outputs through civilized nations everywhere from the great words Literature, Art, Religion, etc., with their conventional administerers, stand squarely in the way of what the vitalities of those great words signify, more than they really

66. sweet cake] *CR:* sweetcake

80–81. In my opinion . . . the great] *CR:* In my opinion to-day, what is meant through civilized nations everywhere by the great

prepare the soil for them—or plant the seeds, or cultivate or garner the crop. My own opinion has long been, that for New World service our ideas of beauty (inherited from the Greeks, and so on to Shakspere—*query*—perverted from them?) need to be radically changed, and made anew for to-day's purposes and finer standards. But if so, it will all come in due time—the real change will be an autochthonic, interior, constitutional, even local one, from which our notions of beauty (lines and colors are wondrous lovely, but character is lovelier) will branch or offshoot.

So much have I now rattled off (old age's garrulity,) that there is not space for explaining the most important and pregnant principle of all, *viz.*, that *Art is one*, is not partial, but includes all times and forms and sorts—is not exclusively aristocratic or democratic, or oriental or occidental. My favorite symbol would be a good font of type, where the impeccable long-primer rejects nothing. Or the old Dutch flour-miller who said, 'I never bother myself what road the folks come—I only want good wheat and rye.'

The font is about the same forever. Democratic art results of democratic development, from tinge, true nationality, belief, in the one setting up from it.

Old Poets.

Poetry (I am clear) is eligible of something far more ripen'd and ample, our lands and pending days, than it has yet produced from any utterance old or new. Modern or new poetry, too, (viewing or challenging it with severe criticism,) is largely a void—while the very cognizance, or even suspicion of that void, and the need of filling it, proves a certainty of the hidden and waiting supply. Leaving other lands and languages to speak for themselves, we can abruptly but deeply suggest it best from our own—going first to oversea illustrations, and standing on them. Think of Byron, Burns, Shelley, Keats, (even first-raters, "the brothers of the radiant summit," as William O'Connor calls them,) as having done only their precursory and 'prentice work, and all their best and real poems being left yet unwrought, untouch'd. Is it difficult to imagine ahead of us and them, evolv'd from them, poesy completer far than any they them-

84. them—for] *CR:* them, or
86. Shakspere] *CR:* Shakespeare
94. *viz.*, that] *CR: viz.:* that
100–101. of democratic] *CR:* of the democratic
102. *CR* has Whitman's name at the end.

selves fulfill'd? One has in his eye and mind some very large, very old, entirely sound and vital tree or vine, like certain hardy, ever-fruitful specimens in California and Canada, or down in Mexico, (and indeed in all lands) beyond the chronological records—illustrations of growth, continuity, power, amplitude and *exploitation*, almost beyond statement, but proving fact and possibility, outside of argument.

Perhaps, indeed, the rarest and most blessed quality of transcendent noble poetry—as of law, and of the profoundest wisdom and æstheticism—is, (I would suggest,) from sane, completed, vital, capable old age. The final proof of song or personality is a sort of matured, accreted, superb, evoluted, almost divine, impalpable diffuseness and atmosphere or invisible magnetism, dissolving and embracing all—and not any special achievement of passion, pride, metrical form, epigram, plot, thought, or what is call'd beauty. The bud of the rose or the half-blown flower is beautiful, of course, but only the perfected bloom or apple or finish'd wheat-head is beyond the rest. Completed fruitage like this comes (in my opinion) to a grand age, in man or woman, through an essentially sound continuated physiology and psychology (both important) and is the culminating glorious aureole of all and several preceding. Like the tree or vine just mention'd, it stands at last in a beauty, power and productiveness of its own, above all others, and of a sort and style uniting all criticisms, proofs and adherences.

Let us diversify the matter a little by portraying some of the American poets from our own point of view.

Longfellow, reminiscent, polish'd, elegant, with the air of finest conventional library, picture-gallery or parlor, with ladies and gentlemen in them, and plush and rosewood, and ground-glass lamps, and mahogany and ebony furniture, and a silver inkstand and scented satin paper to write on.

Whittier stands for morality (not in any all-accepting philosophic or Hegelian sense, but) filter'd through a Puritanical or Quaker filter—is incalculably valuable as a genuine utterance, (and the finest,)—with many local and Yankee and *genre* bits—all hued with anti-slavery coloring—(the *genre* and anti-slavery contributions all precious—all help.) Whittier's is rather a grand figure, but pretty lean and ascetic—no Greek—

Old Poets.

Printed in GBF from clippings of the galley proof of the article of the same title in NAR, CLI (November, 1890), 610–614.

4. a void] CPW and GBF: a-void] NAR: a void] [An obvious error in printing GBF; corrected in the present edition.—ED.]

25. all—and] NAR: all, and

not universal and composite enough (don't try—don't wish to be) for ideal Americanism. Ideal Americanism would take the Greek spirit and law, and democratize and scientize and (thence) truly Christianize them for the whole, the globe, all history, all ranks and lands, all facts, all good and bad. (Ah this *bad*—this nineteen-twentieths of us all! What a stumbling-block it remains for poets and metaphysicians—what a chance (the strange, clear-as-ever inscription on the old dug-up tablet) it offers yet for being translated—what can be its purpose in the God-scheme of this universe, and all?)

Then William Cullen Bryant—meditative, serious, from first to last tending to threnodies—his genius mainly lyrical—when reading his pieces who could expect or ask for more magnificent ones than such as "The Battle-Field," and "A Forest Hymn"? Bryant, unrolling, prairie-like, notwithstanding his mountains and lakes—moral enough (yet worldly and conventional)—a naturalist, pedestrian, gardener and fruiter—well aware of books, but mixing to the last in cities and society. I am not sure but his name ought to lead the list of American bards. Years ago I thought Emerson pre-eminent (and as to the last polish and intellectual cuteness may-be I think so still)—but, for reasons, I have been gradually tending to give the file-leading place for American native poesy to W. C. B.

Of Emerson I have to confirm my already avow'd opinion regarding his highest bardic and personal attitude. Of the galaxy of the past—of Poe, Halleck, Mrs. Sigourney, Allston, Willis, Dana, John Pierpont, W. G. Simms, Robert Sands, Drake, Hillhouse, Theodore Fay, Margaret Fuller, Epes Sargent, Boker, Paul Hayne, Lanier, and others, I fitly in essaying such a theme as this, and reverence for their memories, may at least give a heart-benison on the list of their names.

Time and New World humanity having the venerable resemblances more than anything else, and being "the same subject continued," just here in 1890, one gets a curious nourishment and lift (I do) from all those grand old veterans, Bancroft, Kossuth, von Moltke—and such typical specimen-reminiscences as Sophocles and Goethe, genius, health, beauty of person, riches, rank, renown and length of days, all combining and centering in one case.

Above everything, what could humanity and literature do without the mellow, last-justifying, averaging, bringing-up of many, many years—a great old age amplified? Every really first-class production has likely to

70. have to] *NAR:* have already to
81. specimen-reminiscences as] *NAR:* specimens as

pass through the crucial tests of a generation, perhaps several generations. Lord Bacon says the first sight of any work really new and first-rate in beauty and originality always arouses something disagreeable and repulsive. Voltaire term'd the Shaksperean works "a huge dunghill"; Hamlet he described (to the Academy, whose members listen'd with approbation) as "the dream of a drunken savage, with a few flashes of beautiful thoughts." And not the Ferney sage alone; the orthodox judges and law-givers of France, such as La Harpe, J. L. Geoffroy, and Chateaubriand, either join'd in Voltaire's verdict, or went further. Indeed the classicists and regulars there still hold to it. The lesson is very significant in all departments. People resent anything new as a personal insult. When umbrellas were first used in England, those who carried them were hooted and pelted so furiously that their lives were endanger'd. The same rage encounter'd the attempt in theatricals to perform women's parts by real women, which was publicly consider'd disgusting and outrageous. Byron thought Pope's verse incomparably ahead of Homer and Shakspere. One of the prevalent objections, in the days of Columbus was, the learn'd men boldly asserted that if a ship should reach India she would never get back again, because the rotundity of the globe would present a kind of mountain, up which it would be impossible to sail even with the most favorable wind.

"Modern poets," says a leading Boston journal, "enjoy longevity. Browning lived to be seventy-seven. Wordsworth, Bryant, Emerson, and Longfellow were old men. Whittier, Tennyson, and Walt Whitman still live." Started out by that item on Old Poets and Poetry for chyle to inner American sustenance—I have thus gossipp'd about it all, and treated it from my own point of view, taking the privilege of rambling wherever the talk carried me. Browning is lately dead; Bryant, Emerson and Longfellow have not long pass'd away; and yes, Whittier and Tennyson remain, over eighty years old—the latter having sent out not long since a fresh volume, which the English-speaking Old and New Worlds are yet reading. I have already put on record my notions of T. and his effusions: they are very attractive and flowery to me—but flowers, too, are at least as profound as anything; and by common consent T. is settled as the poetic cream-skimmer of our age's melody, *ennui* and polish—a verdict in which I agree, and should say that nobody (not even Shakspere) goes deeper in those exquisitely touch'd and half-hidden hints and indirections left like faint perfumes in the crevices of his lines. Of Browning

83. centering] *NAR:* centring
90. Shaksperean] *NAR:* Shakespearean
103, 122, and 150. Shakspere] *NAR:* Shakespeare

I don't know enough to say much; he must be studied deeply out, too, and quite certainly repays the trouble—but I am old and indolent, and cannot study (and never did.)

Grand as to-day's accumulative fund of poetry is, there is certainly something unborn, not yet come forth, different from anything now formulated in any verse, or contributed by the past in any land—something waited for, craved, hitherto non-express'd. What it will be, and how, no one knows. It will probably have to prove itself by itself and its readers. One thing, it must run through entire humanity (this new word and meaning Solidarity has arisen to us moderns) twining all lands like a divine thread, stringing all beads, pebbles or gold, from God and the soul, and like God's dynamics and sunshine illustrating all and having reference to all. From anything like a cosmical point of view, the entirety of imaginative literature's themes and results as we get them to-day seems painfully narrow. All that has been put in statement, tremendous as it is, what is it compared with the vast fields and values and varieties left unreap'd? Of our own country, the splendid races North or South, and especially of the Western and Pacific regions, it sometimes seems to me their myriad noblest Homeric and Biblic elements are all untouch'd, left as if ashamed of, and only certain very minor occasional *delirium tremens* glints studiously sought and put in print, in short tales, "poetry" or books.

I give these speculations, or notions, in all their audacity, for the comfort of thousands—perhaps a majority of ardent minds, women's and young men's—who stand in awe and despair before the immensity of suns and stars already in the firmament. Even in the Iliad and Shakspere there is (is there not?) a certain humiliation produced to us by the absorption of them, unless we sound in equality, or above them, the songs due our own democratic era and surroundings, and the full assertion of ourselves. And in vain (such is my opinion) will America seek sucessfully to tune any superb national song unless the heart-strings of the people start it from their own breasts—to be return'd and echoed there again.

156. The article in NAR ends with this line. GBF and CPW continue with the poems "Ship Ahoy!" and "For Queen Victoria's Birthday" and a footnote to the latter; all omitted in this volume.

American National Literature.

Printed in GBF from clippings of the galley proof or an offprint of the article "Have We a National Literature?" in NAR, CLII (March, 1891), 332–338. At the

American National Literature.
Is there any such thing—or can there ever be?

So you want an essay about American National Literature, (tremendous and fearful subject!) do you?* Well, if you will let me put down some melanged cogitations regarding the matter, hap-hazard, and from my own points of view, I will try. Horace Greeley wrote a book named "Hints toward Reforms," and the title-line was consider'd the best part of all. In the present case I will give a few thoughts and suggestions, of good and ambitious intent enough anyhow—first reiterating the question right out plainly: American National Literature—is there distinctively any such thing, or can there ever be? First to me comes an almost indescribably august form, the People, with varied typical shapes and attitudes—then the divine mirror, Literature.

As things are, probably no more puzzling question ever offer'd itself than (going back to old Nile for a trope,) What bread-seeds of printed mentality shall we cast upon America's waters, to grow and return after many days? Is there for the future authorship of the United States any better way than submission to the teeming facts, events, activities, and importations already vital through and beneath them all? I have often ponder'd it, and felt myself disposed to let it go at that. Indeed, are not those facts and activities and importations potent and certain to fulfil themselves all through our Commonwealth, irrespective of any attempt from individual guidance? But allowing all, and even at that, a good part of the matter being honest discussion, examination, and earnest personal presentation, we may even for sanitary exercise and contact plunge boldly into the spread of the many waves and cross-tides, as follows. Or, to change the figure, I will present my varied little collation (what is our Country itself but an infinitely vast and varied collation?) in the hope that the show itself indicates a duty getting more and more incumbent every day.

In general, civilization's totality or real representative National Litera-

* The essay was for the *North American Review*, in answer to the formal request of the editor. It appear'd in March, 1891.

1*n*–2*n*. The footnote was inserted in ink.

top of the first clipping, the new title, and the italicized line beneath it, were inserted in ink. Below this insertion the following printed lines were lined out in ink:

"*From the North American Review, March, 1891*
Have We a National Literature?
By Walt Whitman"

25. varied little collation] *NAR:* varied collation

ture formates itself (like language, or "the weather") not from two or three influences, however important, nor from any learned syllabus, or criticism, or what ought to be, nor from any minds or advice of toploftical quarters—and indeed not at all from the influences and ways ostensibly supposed (though they too are adopted, after a sort)—but slowly, slowly, curiously, from many more and more, deeper mixings and siftings (especially in America) and generations and years and races, and what largely appears to be chance—but is not chance at all. First of all, for future National Literature in America, New England (the technically moral and schoolmaster region, as a cynical fellow I know calls it) and the three or four great Atlantic-coast cities, highly as they to-day suppose they dominate the whole, will have to haul in their horns. *Ensemble* is the tap-root of National Literature. America is become already a huge world of peoples, rounded and orbic climates, idiocrasies, and geographies—forty-four Nations curiously and irresistibly blent and aggregated in ONE NATION, with one imperial language, and one unitary set of social and legal standards over all—and (I predict) a yet to be National Literature. (In my mind this last, if it ever comes, is to prove grander and more important for the Commonwealth than its politics and material wealth and trade, vast and indispensable as those are.)

Think a moment what must, beyond peradventure, be the real permanent sub-bases, or lack of them. Books profoundly consider'd show a great nation more than anything else—more than laws or manners. (This is, of course, probably the deep-down meaning of that well-buried but ever-vital platitude, Let me sing the people's songs, and I don't care who makes their laws.) Books too reflect humanity *en masse*, and surely show them splendidly, or the reverse, and prove or celebrate their prevalent traits (these last the main things.) Homer grew out of and has held the ages, and holds to-day, by the universal admiration for personal prowess, courage, rankness, *amour propre*, leadership, inherent in the whole human race. Shakspere concentrates the brilliancy of the centuries of feudalism on the proud personalities they produced, and paints the amorous passion. The books of the Bible stand for the final superiority of devout emotions over the rest, and of religious adoration, and ultimate absolute justice, more powerful than haughtiest kings or millionaires or majorities.

What the United States are working out and establishing needs imperatively the connivance of something subtler than ballots and legislators. The Goethean theory and lesson (if I may briefly state it so) of the exclusive sufficiency of artistic, scientific, literary equipment to the character,

37. the technically moral] *NAR:* the specially moral
51. than laws] *NAR:* than their laws

irrespective of any strong claims of the political ties of nation, state, or city, could have answer'd under the conventionality and pettiness of Weimar, or the Germany, or even Europe, of those times; but it will not do for America to-day at all. We have not only to exploit our own theory above any that has preceded us, but we have entirely different, and deeper-rooted, and infinitely broader themes.

When I have had a chance to see and observe a sufficient crowd of American boys or maturer youths or well-grown men, all the States, as in my experiences in the Secession War among the soldiers, or west, east, north, or south, or my wanderings and loiterings through cities (especially New York and in Washington,) I have invariably found coming to the front three prevailing personal traits, to be named here for brevity's sake under the heads Good-Nature, Decorum, and Intelligence. (I make Good-Nature first, as it deserves to be—it is a splendid resultant of all the rest, like health or fine weather.) Essentially these lead the inherent list of the high average personal born and bred qualities of the young fellows everywhere through the United States, as any sharp observer can find out for himself. Surely these make the vertebral stock of superbest and noblest nations! May the destinies show it so forthcoming. I mainly confide the whole future of our Commonwealth to the fact of these three bases. Need I say I demand the same in the elements and spirit and fruitage of National Literature?

Another, perhaps a born root or branch, comes under the words *Noblesse Oblige*, even for a national rule or motto. My opinion is that this foregoing phrase, and its spirit, should influence and permeate official America and its representatives in Congress, the Executive Departments, the Presidency, and the individual States—should be one of their chiefest mottoes, and be carried out practically. (I got the idea from my dear friend the democratic Englishwoman, Mrs. Anne Gilchrist, now dead. "The beautiful words *Noblesse Oblige*," said she to me once, "are not best for some develop'd gentleman or lord, but some rich and develop'd nation—and especially for your America.")

Then another and very grave point (for this discussion is deep, deep—not for trifles, or pretty seemings.) I am not sure but the establish'd and old (and superb and profound, and, one may say, needed as old) conception of Deity as mainly of moral constituency (goodness, purity, sinlessness, &c.) has been undermined by nineteenth-century ideas and science. What does this immense and almost abnormal development of Philanthropy mean among the moderns? One doubts if there ever will come a day when the

53. sing the people's] *NAR:* sing a people's
59 and 119. Shakspere] *NAR:* Shakespeare

moral laws and moral standards will be supplanted as over all: while time proceeds (I find it so myself) they will probably be intrench'd deeper and expanded wider. Then the expanded scientific and democratic and truly philosophic and poetic quality of modernism demands a Deific identity and scope superior to all limitations, and essentially including just as well the so-call'd evil and crime and criminals—all the malformations, the defective and abortions of the universe.

Sometimes the bulk of the common people (who are far more 'cute than the critics suppose) relish a well-hidden allusion or hint carelessly dropt, faintly indicated, and left to be disinterr'd or not. Some of the very old ballads have delicious morsels of this kind. Greek Aristophanes and Pindar abounded in them. (I sometimes fancy the old Hellenic audiences must have been as generally keen and knowing as any of their poets.) Shakspere is full of them. Tennyson has them. It is always a capital compliment from author to reader, and worthy the peering brains of America. The mere smartness of the common folks, however, does not need encouraging, but qualities more solid and opportune.

What are now deepest wanted in the States as roots for their literature are Patriotism, Nationality, Ensemble, or the ideas of these, and the uncompromising genesis and saturation of these. Not the mere bawling and braggadocio of them, but the radical emotion-facts, the fervor and perennial fructifying spirit at fountain-head. And at the risk of being misunderstood I should dwell on and repeat that a great imaginative *literatus* for America can never be merely good and moral in the conventional method. Puritanism and what radiates from it must always be mention'd by me with respect; then I should say, for this vast and varied Commonwealth, geographically and artistically, the puritanical standards are constipated, narrow, and non-philosophic.

In the main I adhere to my positions in "Democratic Vistas," and especially to my summing-up of American literature as far as to-day is concern'd. In Scientism, the Medical Profession, Practical Inventions, and Journalism, the United States have press'd forward to the glorious front rank of advanced civilized lands, as also in the popular dissemination of printed matter (of a superficial nature perhaps, but that is an indispensable preparatory stage,) and have gone in common education, so-call'd, far beyond any other land or age. Yet the high-pitch'd taunt of Margaret Fuller, forty years ago, still sounds in the air: "It does not follow, because

109. the expanded scientific] *NAR:* the scientific

117–118. Pindar abounded] *NAR:* Pindar must have abounded

143–145. The quotation was adapted, perhaps, from the second paragraph of Margaret Fuller's essay "American Literature" (*Papers on Literature and Art,*

the United States print and read more books, magazines, and newspapers than all the rest of the world, that they really have therefore a literature." For perhaps it is not alone the free schools and newspapers, nor railroads and factories, nor all the iron, cotton, wheat, pork, and petroleum, nor the gold and silver, nor the surplus of a hundred or several hundred millions, nor the Fourteenth and Fifteenth Amendments, nor the last national census, that can put this Commonweal high or highest on the cosmical scale of history. Something else is indispensable. All that record is lofty, but there is a loftier.

The great current points are perhaps simple, after all: first, that the highest developments of the New World and Democracy, and probably the best society of the civilized world all over, are to be only reach'd and spinally nourish'd (in my notion) by a new evolutionary sense and treatment; and, secondly, that the evolution-principle, which is the greatest law through nature, and of course in these States, has now reach'd us markedly for and in our literature.

In other writings I have tried to show how vital to any aspiring Nationality must ever be its autochthonic song, and how for a really great people there can be no complete and glorious Name, short of emerging out of and even rais'd on such born poetic expression, coming from its own soil and soul, its area, spread, idiosyncrasies, and (like showers of rain, originally rising impalpably, distill'd from land and sea,) duly returning there again. Nor do I forget what we all owe to our ancestry; though perhaps we are apt to forgive and bear too much for that alone.

One part of the national American literatus's task is (and it is not an easy one) to treat the old hereditaments, legends, poems, theologies, and even customs, with fitting respect and toleration, and at the same time clearly understand and justify, and be devoted to and exploit our own day, its diffused light, freedom, responsibilities, with all it necessitates, and that our New-World circumstances and stages of development demand and make proper. For American literature we want mighty authors, *not* even Carlyle- and Heine-like, born and brought up in (and more or less essentially partaking and giving out) that vast abnormal ward or hysterical sick-chamber which in many respects Europe, with all its glories, would seem to be. The greatest feature in current poetry (perhaps in literature anyhow) is the almost total lack of first-class power, and simple, natural health, flourishing and produced at first hand, typifying our own era. Mod-

1846). The same quotation, with a slight variation, was used by Whitman in the section of "Collect," "Book Classes—America's Literature," *q.v.*

165. born poetic expression] *NAR:* born expression

180. poetry (perhaps in] *NAR:* poetry (in

ern verse generally lacks quite altogether the modern, and is oftener possess'd in spirit with the past and feudal, dressed may-be in late fashions. For novels and plays often the plots and surfaces are contemporary—but the spirit, even the fun, is morbid and effete.

There is an essential difference between the Old and New. The poems of Asia and Europe are rooted in the long past. They celebrate man and his intellections and relativenesses as they have been. But America, in as high a strain as ever, is to sing them all as they are and are to be. (I know, of course, that the past is probably a main factor in what we are and know and must be.) At present the States are absorb'd in business, money-making, politics, agriculture, the development of mines, intercommunications, and other material attents—which all shove forward and appear at their height—as, consistently with modern civilization, they must be and should be. Then even these are but the inevitable precedents and providers for home-born, transcendent, democratic literature—to be shown in superior, more heroic, more spiritual, more emotional, personalities and songs. A national literature is, of course, in one sense, a great mirror or reflector. There must however be something before—something to reflect. I should say now, since the Secession War, there has been, and to-day unquestionably exists, that something.

Certainly, anyhow, the United States do not so far utter poetry, first-rate literature, or any of the so-call'd arts, to any lofty admiration or advantage—are not dominated or penetrated from actual inherence or plain bent to the said poetry and arts. Other work, other needs, current inventions, productions, have occupied and to-day mainly occupy them. They are very 'cute and imitative and proud—can't bear being left too glaringly away far behind the other high-class nations—and so we set up some home "poets," "artists," painters, musicians, *literati*, and so forth, all our own (thus claim'd.) The whole matter has gone on, and exists to-day, probably as it should have been, and should be; as, for the present, it must be. To all which we conclude, and repeat the terrible query: American National Literature—is there distinctively any such thing, or can there ever be?

182. hand, typifying] NAR: hand, and typifying
200. must however be] NAR: must be
214. At the end of the article NAR has Whitman's name.

Gathering the Corn.

Printed in GBF from two newspaper clippings. The article first appeared under the same title in NYTR, October 24, 1878, but the clippings are of later date and from a different paper, not identified.

1. "*Last of October.*" is inserted in ink on the clipping.

3. Now, or of late, all] NYTR: Now, all

5–6. The line arrangement is the same on the clipping as in GBF. NYTR has a period after "notice" and makes the quotation the first sentence of a new paragraph.

Gathering the Corn.

Last of October.—Now mellow, crisp Autumn days, bright moonlight nights, and gathering the corn—"cutting up," as the farmers call it. Now, or of late, all over the country, a certain green and brown-drab eloquence seeming to call out, "You that pretend to give the news, and all that's going, why not give us a notice?" Truly, O fields, as for the notice,

"Take, we give it willingly."

Only we must do it our own way. Leaving the domestic, dietary, and commercial parts of the question (which are enormous, in fact, hardly second to those of any other of our great soil-products), we will just saunter down a lane we know, on an average West Jersey farm, and let the fancy of the hour itemize America's most typical agricultural show and specialty.

Gathering the Corn—the British call it Maize, the old Yankee farmer Indian Corn. The great plumes, the ears well-envelop'd in their husks, the long and pointed leaves, in summer, like green or purple ribands, with a yellow stem-line in the middle, all now turn'd dingy; the sturdy stalks, and the rustling in the breeze—the breeze itself well tempering the sunny noon —The varied reminiscences recall'd—the ploughing and planting in spring —(the whole family in the field, even the little girls and boys dropping seed in the hill)—the gorgeous sight through July and August—the walk and observation early in the day—the cheery call of the robin, and the low whirr of insects in the grass—the Western husking party, when ripe—the November moonlight gathering, and the calls, songs, laughter of the young fellows.

Not to forget, hereabouts, in the Middle States, the old worm fences, with the gray rails and their scabs of moss and lichen—those old rails, weather beaten, but strong yet. Why not come down from literary dignity, and confess we are sitting on one now, under the shade of a great walnut

The quotation is the second line of the sixth and last stanza of "The Passage," by Johann L. Uhland; Whitman changes "I give" to "we give." Longfellow included the poem in his *Poets and Poetry of Europe* (1845 and later), where he credits the translation to an anonymous article in the *Edinburgh Review*, October, 1832. The entire stanza, somewhat altered, was copied by Whitman at an early date and is preserved in *Notes & Fragments*, p. 43, where Dr. Bucke mistakenly attributes Whitman's version to a different translation.

7. it our] *NYTR:* it in our
14. leaves . . . ribands] *NYTR:* leaves, like green brocade ribands
21–22. the November moonlight] *NYTR:* the moonlight
24. hereabouts, . . . the old] *NYTR:* hereabout, the old
26. yet. Why] Clipping and *NYTR:* yet! Why [Change made in proof.]

tree? Why not confide that these lines are pencill'd on the edge of a woody bank, with a glistening pond and creek seen through the trees south, and the corn we are writing about close at hand on the north? Why not put in the delicious scent of the "life everlasting" that yet lingers so profusely in every direction—the chromatic song of the one persevering locust (the insect is scarcer this fall and the past summer than for many years) beginning slowly, rising and swelling to much emphasis, and then abruptly falling—so appropriate to the scene, so quaint, so racy and suggestive in the warm sunbeams, we could sit here and look and listen for an hour? Why not even the tiny, turtle-shaped, yellow-back'd, black-spotted lady-bug that has lit on the shirt-sleeve of the arm inditing this? Ending our list with the fall-drying grass, the Autumn days themselves,

"Sweet days; so cool, so calm, so bright,"

(yet not so cool either, about noon)—the horse-mint, the wild carrot, the mullein, and the bumble-bee.

How the half-mad vision of William Blake—how the far freer, far firmer fantasy that wrote "Midsummer Night's Dream"—would have revell'd night or day, and beyond stint, in one of our American corn fields! Truly, in color, outline, material and spiritual suggestiveness, where any more inclosing theme for idealist, poet, literary artist?

What we have written has been at noon day—but perhaps better still (for this collation,) to steal off by yourself these fine nights, and go slowly, musingly down the lane, when the dry and green-gray frost-touch'd leaves seem whisper-gossipping all over the field in low tones, as if every hill had something to say—and you sit or lean recluse near by, and inhale that rare,

31–32. that yet lingers . . . the chromatic] *NYTR:* that grows so profusely in every direction—the swarms of white and straw-colored butterflies—the chromatic
36. Why not] *NYTR:* Why, not
37. lady-bug] Clipping: Lady Bug] *NYTR:* Lady's Bug
38. inditing this?] *NYTR:* indicting this!
39. the Autumn days] *NYTR:* the October days
40–41. Clipping sets off the quoted line, but begins a new paragraph with "(Yet not". *NYTR* has a period after "themselves" and makes a separate paragraph beginning "(Yet not", as in the clipping. The quotation, slightly altered by Whitman, is from the first stanza of "Virtue," in *The Temple*, by George Herbert. The line in Herbert's poem reads: "Sweet day, so cool, so calm, so bright,".
42. bumble-bee.] *NYTR:* bumble-bees.
44. "Midsummer] Clipping and *NYTR:* "Mid-summer [Changed in the proof.]
49. Words in parenthesis inserted in ink on the clipping.
49. fine nights] *NYTR:* fine Autumn nights
50. green-gray frost-touch'd leaves] *NYTR:* green-gray leaves
53. the gather'd plant] *NYTR:* the plant
58–59. and over head the] Clipping and *NYTR:* and at the meridian the
59. rare well-shadow'd hour!] Clipping and *NYTR:* rare hour!

rich, ripe and peculiar odor of the gather'd plant which comes out best only to the night air. The complex impressions of the far-spread fields and woods in the night, are blended mystically, soothingly, indefinitely, and yet palpably to you (appealing curiously, perhaps mostly, to the sense of smell.) All is comparative silence and clear-shadow below, and the stars are up there with Jupiter lording it over westward; sulky Saturn in the east, and over head the moon. A rare well-shadow'd hour! By no means the least of the eligibilities of the gather'd corn!

A Death-Bouquet.

Pick'd Noontime, Early January, 1890.

DEATH—too great a subject to be treated so—indeed the greatest subject—and yet I am giving you but a few random lines about it—as one writes hurriedly the last part of a letter to catch the closing mail. Only I trust the lines, especially the poetic bits quoted, may leave a lingering odor of spiritual heroism afterward. For I am probably fond of viewing all really great themes indirectly, and by side-ways and suggestions. Certain music from wondrous voices or skilful players—then poetic glints still more—put the soul in rapport with death, or toward it. Hear a strain from Tennyson's late "Crossing the Bar":

"Twilight and evening bell,
And after that the dark!
And may there be no sadness of farewell,
When I embark;

60. gather'd corn!] Clipping and *NYTR:* gathered Corn, this last—and probably here for the first time put on record.

60. *NYTR* has the name "Walt Whitman" at the end of the article.

A Death-Bouquet.

Printed in *GBF* from three typewritten sheets, the first cut at the bottom, the second at both top and bottom, and the third cut or torn irregularly at the bottom. A cancelled memorandum in ink at the top of the first sheet reads: "Sent to Franklin File 1285 Broadway, New York January '90 (paid $10)". [Franklin Fyles, dramatic critic of *NYS*, copyrighted several plays under the name of Franklin File.—ED.] Under the subtitle, "By Walt Whitman" is typed and then cancelled in ink. Whitman's *Commonplace Book* records a letter from Whitman to Franklin File of *NYS*, January 8, 1890, but the letter, if sent, is not known to exist. W. S. Kennedy says (*The Fight of a Book*, p. 241) this piece was published in *PP*, February 2, 1890. The present editor has failed to find this article in either *PP* or *NYS*. The MS contains some of the page proof.]

2. Between "lines" and "about", the typescript has two or three words so heavily crossed out in black ink that they are now illegible.

10–17. The third and fourth stanzas of the poem, correctly quoted.

"For tho' from out our bourne of Time and Place
The floods may bear me far,
I hope to see my Pilot face to face
When I have crost the bar."

Am I starting the sail-craft of poets in line? Here then a quatrain of Phrynichus long ago to one of old Athens' favorites:

"Thrice-happy Sophocles! in good old age,
Bless'd as a man, and as a craftsman bless'd,
He died; his many tragedies were fair,
And fair his end, nor knew he any sorrow."

Certain music, indeed, especially voluntaries by a good player, at twilight—or idle rambles alone by the shore, or over prairie or on mountain road, for that matter—favor the right mood. Words are difficult—even impossible. No doubt any one will recall ballads or songs or hymns (may-be instrumental performances) that have arous'd so curiously, yet definitely, the thought of death, the mystic, the after-realm, as no statement or sermon could—and brought it hovering near.

A happy (to call it so) and easy death is at least as much a physiological result as a psychological one. The foundation of it really begins before birth, and is thence directly or indirectly shaped and affected, even constituted, (the base stomachic) by every thing from that minute till the time of its occurrence. And yet here is something (Whittier's "Burning Driftwood") of an opposite coloring:

"I know the solemn monotone
Of waters calling unto me;
I know from whence the airs have blown,
That whisper of the Eternal Sea;
As low my fires of driftwood burn,
I hear that sea's deep sounds increase,

19. Athens'] Typescript: Athens's [Revised in page proof.]

20–23. Whitman's source for this quatrain has not been identified.

24–30. These lines, not in the typescript, are inserted in ink in the page proof and printed without change.

34. The words in parenthesis inserted in ink in the typescript.

37–44. The last two stanzas of Whittier's "Burning Drift-Wood." Whittier's text has no punctuation at the end of the third line, has a period after the fourth line, and a hyphen in "drift-wood" in the fifth line. Whitman's semicolon in the fourth line is inserted in ink on the typescript.

48. After "such is" Whitman inserts "at all" in ink in the typescript.

53. After "even gone.)" typescript continues in the same paragraph.

56–64. These lines are all of Whitman's poem "Now Finalè to the Shore" except the first line, which is crossed out in the typescript. The lines in *LG* (1881 and 1892) differ as follows: in line 2 (the first line quoted) *LG* has no punctuation after "life" and "finalè" and a comma at the end of the line; in line 3 *LG* has a comma after "depart" and after "store"; in line 6 *LG* has a semicolon after "returning"; in line 7 *LG* has no punctuation except a comma at the end; in line 8 *LG* has a comma after "friends" and at the end of the line; and in line 10 *LG* has no punctuation except

And, fair in sunset light, discern
Its mirage-lifted Isles of Peace."

Like an invisible breeze after a long and sultry day, death sometimes sets in at last, soothingly and refreshingly, almost vitally. In not a few cases the termination even appears to be a sort of ecstasy. Of course there are painful deaths, but I do not believe such is at all the general rule. Of the many hundreds I myself saw die in the fields and hospitals during the Secession War the cases of mark'd suffering or agony *in extremis* were very rare. (It is a curious suggestion of immortality that the mental and emotional powers remain to their clearest through all, while the senses of pain and flesh-volition are blunted or even gone.)

Then to give the following, and cease before the thought gets thread-bare:

"Now, land and life, finalè, and farewell!
Now Voyager depart! (much, much for thee is yet in store;)
Often enough hast thou adventur'd o'er the seas,
Cautiously cruising, studying the charts,
Duly again to port and hawser's tie returning.
—But now obey thy cherish'd, secret wish,
Embrace thy friends—leave all in order;
To port and hawser's tie no more returning,
Depart upon thy endless cruise, old Sailor!"

Some Laggards Yet.

THE PERFECT HUMAN VOICE.

Stating it briefly and pointedly I should suggest that the human voice is a cultivation or form'd growth on a fair native foundation. This

a period at the end.

Some Laggards Yet.

The seven prose pieces included in *GBF* under this general heading (through "Gay-Heartedness") are collated as separate sections since they have very little in common. The general title was inserted in ink in the page proof. For the somewhat haphazard construction of the group, see below, notes on "Splinters."

THE PERFECT HUMAN VOICE.

Printed in *GBF* from a printed clipping, presumably from Munyon's *Illustrated World* (Philadelphia), October, 1890 (VI, 2), where it had the title "The Human Voice." This periodical is not available; collation is with the clipping in the copy for *GBF*, checked with a transcript made by Professor Emory Holloway from a clipping he saw many years ago in the Harned Collection. The word "Perfect" in the title was inserted in ink on the page proof. The words "By Walt Whitman" under the title are lined out on the clipping.

1–2. the human voice] Clipping: the voice

foundation probably exists in nine cases out of ten. Sometimes nature affords the vocal organ in perfection, or rather I would say near enough to whet one's appreciation and appetite for a voice that might be truly call'd perfection. To me the grand voice is mainly physiological—(by which I by no means ignore the mental help, but wish to keep the emphasis where it belongs.) Emerson says *manners* form the representative apex and final charm and captivation of humanity: but he might as well have changed the typicality to voice.

Of course there is much taught and written about elocution, the best reading, speaking, etc., but it finally settles down to *best* human vocalization. Beyond all other power and beauty, there is something in the quality and power of the right voice (*timbre* the schools call it) that touches the soul, the abysms. It was not for nothing that the Greeks depended, at their highest, on poetry's and wisdom's vocal utterance by *tete-a-tete* lectures—(indeed all the ancients did.)

Of celebrated people possessing this wonderful vocal power, patent to me, in former days, I should specify the contralto Alboni, Elias Hicks, Father Taylor, the tenor Bettini, Fanny Kemble, and the old actor Booth, and in private life many cases, often women. I sometimes wonder whether the best philosophy and poetry, or something like the best, after all these centuries, perhaps waits to be rous'd out yet, or suggested, by the perfect physiological human voice.

SHAKSPERE FOR AMERICA.

Let me send you a supplementary word to that "view" of Shakspere attributed to me, publish'd in your July number,* and so courteously

* This bit was in "Poet-lore" monthly for September, 1890.

4\. enough to] Clipping: enough thither to
7\. the mental] Clipping: the normal and mental
9\. humanity: but] Clipping: humanity—but
12\. it finally settles] Clipping: it all settles
12\. to *best* human] Clipping: to good human [Changed on page proof.]
14\. Words in parentheses were inserted in ink on the clipping.
15\. abysms.] Clipping: abysm.
16–17. lectures—(indeed] Clipping: lectures (indeed
19\. me, in] Clipping: me in
19\. Alboni] Clipping: Albani [Obviously a misprint.]
23\. centuries, perhaps waits] Clipping: centuries, waits
23–24. perfect physiological human] Clipping: perfect human

SHAKSPERE FOR AMERICA.

Printed in *GBF* from an offprint of "Shakespeare in America," *P-L*, September 15, 1890. Whitman changes "Shakespeare" to "Shakspere" and deletes the credit line on the *P-L* offprint. Whitman's article is in response to or comment on the article by Jonathan Trumbull, "Walt Whitman's View of Shakespeare," in *P-L*, July 15, 1890, which quotes from "A Backward Glance" and from "A Thought on

worded by the reviewer (thanks! dear friend.) But you have left out what, perhaps, is the main point, as follows:

"Even the one who at present reigns unquestion'd—of Shakspere—for all he stands for so much in modern literature, he stands entirely for the mighty æsthetic sceptres of the past, not for the spiritual and democratic, the sceptres of the future." (See pp. 55–56 in "November Boughs," and also some of my further notions on Shakspere.)

The Old World (Europe and Asia) is the region of the poetry of concrete and real things,—the past, the æsthetic, palaces, etiquette, the literature of war and love, the mythological gods, and the myths anyhow. But the New World (America) is the region of the future, and its poetry must be spiritual and democratic. Evolution is not the rule in Nature, in Politics, and Inventions only, but in Verse. I know our age is greatly materialistic, but it is greatly spiritual, too, and the future will be, too. Even what we moderns have come to mean by *spirituality* (while including what the Hebraic utterers, and mainly perhaps all the Greek and other old typical poets, and also the later ones, meant) has so expanded and color'd and vivified the comprehension of the term, that it is quite a different one from the past. Then science, the final critic of all, has the casting vote for future poetry.

"UNASSAIL'D RENOWN."

The N. Y. *Critic*, Nov: 24, 1889, propounded a circular to several persons, and giving the responses, says, "Walt Whitman's views [as follow] are, naturally, more radical than those of any other contributor to the discussion":

Shakspere," *q.v.*, in NB. Trumbull also published "The Whitman-Shakespeare Question" in *P-L*, December 15, 1891.

1. Before this line Whitman lines out "To the Editors of Poet-Lore—"

1, 5, and 9. Shakspere] *P-L:* Shakespeare

5. *P-L* inserts commas before the dashes; they were not in *NB*.

"UNASSAIL'D RENOWN."

Printed in *GBF* from a clipping of *CR*, November 24, 1888, where it is without title, one of a number of solicited comments; Whitman's title is inserted in ink. On the larger sheet to which the clipping is pasted, Whitman wrote the title, "American Poetry," and the comment: "An English writer had an article named 'Has America Produced a Poet?' in an American magazine for October, 1888, whereupon the N. Y. *Critic*, Nov. 24, 1889 [An error for 1888.—ED.], propounded a circular to several persons, and giving responses, says,". All this is deleted except what remains in lines 1–2. The article referred to was by Edmund Gosse, in the *Forum* (VI, 176–186), and was in turn suggested by E. C. Stedman's *Poets of America* (1885). In *CR*, October 13, 1888, the leading article discussed Gosse's essay.

2–4. The sentence in quotation marks is the first paragraph of the *CR* clipping. The words in brackets (line 3) were inserted in ink.

Briefly to answer impromptu your request of Oct: 19—the question whether I think any American poet not now living deserves a place among the thirteen "English inheritors of unassail'd renown" (Chaucer, Spenser, Shakspere, Milton, Dryden, Pope, Gray, Burns, Wordsworth, Coleridge, Byron, Shelley and Keats,)—and which American poets would be truly worthy, &c. Though to me the *deep* of the matter goes down, down beneath. I remember the London *Times* at the time, in opportune, profound and friendly articles on Bryant's and Longfellow's deaths, spoke of the embarrassment, warping effect, and confusion on America (her poets and poetic students) "coming in possession of a great estate they had never lifted a hand to form or earn"; and the further contingency of "the English language ever having annex'd to it a lot of first-class Poetry that would be American, not European"—proving then something precious over all, and beyond valuation. But perhaps that is venturing outside the question. Of the thirteen British immortals mention'd—after placing Shakspere on a sort of pre-eminence of fame not to be invaded yet—the names of Bryant, Emerson, Whittier and Longfellow (with even added names, sometimes Southerners, sometimes Western or other writers of only one or two pieces,) deserve in my opinion an equally high niche of renown as belongs to any on the dozen of that glorious list.

INSCRIPTION FOR A LITTLE BOOK ON GIORDANO BRUNO.

As America's mental courage (the thought comes to me to-day) is so indebted, above all current lands and peoples, to the noble army of Old-World martyrs past, how incumbent on us that we clear those martyrs' lives and names, and hold them up for reverent admiration, as well as beacons. And typical of this, and standing for it and all perhaps, Giordano

5. Oct: 19—the question] *CR:* Oct: 19—to answer the question

INSCRIPTION FOR A LITTLE BOOK ON GIORDANO BRUNO.

Printed in *GBF* from what appears to be a proof sheet; the printing, in italics, is centered on the page. The book was *Giordano Bruno: Philosopher and Martyr*, by David Garrison Brinton and Thomas Davidson (Philadelphia, 1890), and consisted of two addresses delivered in Philadelphia early in 1890. At the top the notation in ink, "March 14 '90 for an Inscription, first page", is crossed out; below that, also in ink, the present title for *GBF* is written. Below the printed inscription "Walt Whitman" is crossed out and "W. W." written in. The "Inscription" appeared in the volume, signed "Walt Whitman." At the left, the second numeral in the date is deleted so that it is illegible and "4" written in the margin.

5. beacons. And] Proof sheet: beacons; and

SPLINTERS.

This section and the two following were printed in *GBF* from autograph MS

Bruno may well be put, to-day and to come, in our New World's thankfulest heart and memory.

February 24th, 1890. W. W.
Camden, N. J.

SPLINTERS.

While I stand in reverence before the fact of Humanity, the People, I will confess, in writing my L of G, the least consideration out of all that has had to do with it has been the consideration of "the public"—at any rate as it now exists. Strange as it may sound for a democrat to say so, I am clear that no free and original and lofty-soaring poem, or one ambitious of those achievements, can possibly be fulfill'd by any writer who has largely in his thought *the public*—or the question, What will establish'd literature—What will the current authorities say about it?

As far as I have sought any, not the best laid out garden or parterre has been my model—but Nature has been. I know that in a sense the garden is nature too, but I had to choose—I could not give both. Besides the gardens are well represented in poetry; while Nature (in letter and in spirit, in the divine essence,) little if at all.

Certainly, (while I have not hit it by a long shot,) I have aim'd at the most ambitious, the best—and sometimes feel to advance that aim (even with all its arrogance) as the most redeeming part of my books. I have never so much cared to feed the esthetic or intellectual palates—but if I could arouse from its slumbers that elegibility in every soul for its own true exercise! if I could only wield that lever!

Out from the well-tended concrete and the physical—and in them and from them only—radiate the spiritual and heroic.

pages not originally arranged under the general title "Some Laggards Yet," but added in the MS after "Last Saved Items" and given their present position after first page proof was set. On proof page 41, below "Inscription For a Little Book on Giordano Bruno," Whitman directed the printer: "see copy A B & C to fill out this and p. 42 also." A and B are the two MS pages of "Splinters," and C has several short poems, omitted in this edition. At the top of A this endorsement: "This copy (A, B, C,) to fill out pages 41 and 42—put C copy or let it run over so as to fill out p. 42, say 2/3ds if it will—(I can take out or add to)." Each MS page consists of several strips pasted together. Below the page proof of "Splinters" he directs the printer: "set up the copy D E and F sent herewith, & fill out this & page 43 and 44 & let me have proofs of the pages (I will expand or contract as needed)—of course the successive page numbers will have to be changed."

2. confess, in] MS: confess that in [Change must have been made on galley proof.)

20–21. and from them] MS: and of them [Change made on page proof.]

Undoubtedly many points belonging to this essay—perhaps of the greatest necessity, fitness and importance to it—have been left out or forgotten. But the amount of the whole matter—poems, preface and everything—is merely to make one of those little punctures or eye-lets the actors possess in the theatre-curtains to look out upon "the house"—one brief, honest, living glance.

HEALTH, (OLD STYLE.)

In that condition the whole body is elevated to a state by others unknown—inwardly and outwardly illuminated, purified, made solid, strong, yet buoyant. A singular charm, more than beauty, flickers out of, and over, the face—a curious transparency beams in the eyes, both in the iris and the white—the temper partakes also. Nothing that happens—no event, rencontre, weather, etc.—but it is confronted—nothing but is subdued into sustenance—such is the marvellous transformation from the old timorousness and the old process of causes and effects. Sorrows and disappointments cease—there is no more borrowing trouble in advance. A man realizes the venerable myth—he is a god walking the earth, he sees new eligibilities, powers and beauties everywhere; he himself has a new eyesight and hearing. The play of the body in motion takes a previously unknown grace. Merely *to move* is then a happiness, a pleasure—to breathe, to see, is also. All the beforehand gratifications, drink, spirits, coffee, grease, stimulants, mixtures, late hours, luxuries, deeds of the night, seem as vexatious dreams, and now the awakening;—many fall into their natural places, wholesome, conveying diviner joys.

What I append—Health, old style—I have long treasur'd—found originally in some scrap-book fifty years ago—a favorite of mine (but quite a glaring contrast to my present bodily state:)

On a high rock above the vast abyss,
  Whose solid base tumultuous waters lave;
Whose airy high-top balmy breezes kiss,
  Fresh from the white foam of the circling wave—

There ruddy Health, in rude majestic state,
  His clust'ring forelock combatting the winds—
Bares to each season's change his breast elate,
  And still fresh vigor from th' encounter finds:

HEALTH, (OLD STYLE.)

Printed in *GBF* from two autograph pages with newspaper clippings attached. D has lines 1–32 and E has lines 33–68. The source of the poem has not been identified.

With mighty mind to every fortune braced,
To every climate each corporeal power,
And high-proof heart, impenetrably cased,
He mocks the quick transitions of the hour.

Now could he hug bleak Zembla's bolted snow,
Now to Arabia's heated deserts turn,
Yet bids the biting blast more fiercely blow,
The scorching sun without abatement burn.

There this bold Outlaw, rising with the morn,
His sinewy functions fitted for the toil,
Pursues, with tireless steps, the rapturous horn,
And bears in triumph back the shaggy spoil.

Or, on his rugged range of towering hills,
Turns the stiff glebe behind his hardy team;
His wide-spread heaths to blithest measures tills,
And boasts the joys of life are not a dream!

Then to his airy hut, at eve, retires,
Clasps to his open breast his buxom spouse,
Basks in his faggot's blaze, his passions fires,
And strait supine to rest unbroken bows.

On his smooth forehead, Time's old annual score,
Tho' left to furrow, yet disdains to lie;
He bids weak sorrow tantalize no more,
And puts the cup of care contemptuous by.

If, from some inland height, that, skirting, bears
Its rude encroachments far into the vale,
He views where poor dishonor'd nature wears
On her soft cheek alone the lily pale;

How will he scorn alliance with the race,
Those aspin shoots that shiver at a breath;
Children of sloth, that danger dare not face,
And find in life but an extended death:

Then from the silken reptiles will he fly,
To the bold cliff in bounding transports run,
And stretch'd o'er many a wave his ardent eye,
Embrace the enduring Sea-Boy as his son!

12. The words "in motion" are set off by commas in the MS; presumably revised in proof.
21–60. These ten stanzas are from printed clippings.
61–68. These two stanzas are in Whitman's autograph.

Yes! thine alone—from pain, from sorrow free,
The lengthen'd life with peerless joys replete;
Then let me, Lord of Mountains, share with thee
The hard, the early toil—the relaxation sweet.

GAY-HEARTEDNESS.

Walking on the old Navy Yard bridge, Washington, D. C., once with a companion, Mr. Marshall, from England, a great traveler and observer, as a squad of laughing young black girls pass'd us—then two copper-color'd boys, one good-looking lad 15 or 16, barefoot, running after —"What *gay creatures* they all appear to be," said Mr. M. Then we fell to talking about the general lack of buoyant animal spirits. "I think," said Mr. M., "that in all my travels, and all my intercourse with people of every and any class, especially the cultivated ones, (the literary and fashionable folks,) I have never yet come across what I should call a really GAY-HEARTED MAN."

It was a terrible criticism—cut into me like a surgeon's lance. Made me silent the whole walk home.

Memoranda.

[Let me indeed turn upon myself a little of the light I have been so fond of casting on others.

Of course these few exceptional later mems are far far short of one's concluding history or thoughts or life—giving only a hap-hazard pinch of all. But the old Greek proverb put it, "Anybody who really has a good quality" (or bad one either, I guess) "has *all*." There's something in the proverb; but you mustn't carry it too far.

1*n*. Footnote inserted in ink.

GAY-HEARTEDNESS.

Printed in *GBF* from an autograph page consisting of two sheets pasted together. This must be page F of the MS, though it is not so marked. This is the last section under the general title "Some Laggards Yet."

12. *GBF* and *CPW* continue after this line with four short poems (copy C of the MS), omitted in this volume, to wit: "As in a Swoon," "L of G," "After the Argument," and "For Us Two, Reader Dear."

Memoranda.

This is the general title for the remaining seventeen items in *GBF*. In the MS the first page of this group was numbered 63 and it followed next after "Inscription for a Little Book on Giordano Bruno."

1–18. Printed from an autograph page consisting of several strips pasted together.

I will not reject any theme or subject because the treatment is too personal. As my stuff settles into shape, I am told (and sometimes myself discover, uneasily, but feel all right about it in calmer moments) it is mainly autobiographic, and even egotistic after all—which I finally accept, and am contented so.

If this little volume betrays, as it doubtless does, a weakening hand, and decrepitude, remember it is knit together out of accumulated sickness, inertia, physical disablement, acute pain, and listlessness. My fear will be that at last my pieces show indooredness, and being chain'd to a chair—as never before. Only the resolve to keep up, and on, and to add a remnant, and even perhaps obstinately see what failing powers and decay may contribute too, have produced it.

And now as from some fisherman's net hauling all sorts, and disbursing the same.]

A WORLD'S SHOW.

New York, Great Exposition open'd in 1853.—I went a long time (nearly a year)—days and nights—especially the latter—as it was finely lighted, and had a very large and copious exhibition gallery of paintings (shown at best at night, I tho't)—hundreds of pictures from Europe, many masterpieces—all an exhaustless study—and, scatter'd thro' the building, sculptures, single figures or groups—among the rest, Thorwaldsen's "Apostles," colossal in size—and very many fine bronzes, pieces of plate from English silversmiths, and curios from everywhere abroad—with woods from all lands of the earth—all sorts of fabrics and products and handiwork from the workers of all nations.

NEW YORK—THE BAY—THE OLD NAME.

Commencement of a gossipy travelling letter in a New York city paper, May 10, 1879.—My month's visit is about up; but before I get back to Camden let me print some jottings of the last four weeks. Have you not, reader dear, among your intimate friends, some one, temporarily absent,

4. or life—giving only] *GBF* and *CPW:* or life-giving—only] [The reading in *GBF* is an uncorrected printer's error, for the MS is very clear and the printed version makes no sense. Corrected in the present edition.—ED.]

A WORLD'S SHOW.

Printed in *GBF* from a page of autograph MS. Whitman directs the printer to change the title on the MS to a side head; the new centered title, not in the MS, was inserted in the page proof. Otherwise the MS seems to have been printed without change, though the writing is obscure in places.

NEW YORK—THE BAY—THE OLD NAME.

Printed in *GBF* from clippings of the first four paragraphs of Whitman's "Broadway Revisited," *NYTR*, May 10, 1879. (For Whitman's use of the rest of this article, see *Prose 1892*, I, Appendix XIX.) The section title, not in the MS, was inserted in the page proof.

1–2. The side head in italics was inserted in ink.

whose letters to you, avoiding all the big topics and disquisitions, give only minor, gossipy sights and scenes—just as they come—subjects disdain'd by solid writers, but interesting to you because they were such as happen to everybody, and were the moving entourage to your friend—to his or her steps, eyes, mentality? Well, with an idea something of that kind, I suppose, I set out on the following hurrygraphs of a breezy early-summer visit to New-York City and up the North River—especially at present of some hours along Broadway.

What I came to New York for.—To try the experiment of a lecture—to see whether I could stand it, and whether an audience could—was my specific object. Some friends had invited me—it was by no means clear how it would end—I stipulated that they should get only a third-rate hall, and not sound the advertising trumpets a bit—and so I started. I much wanted something to do for occupation, consistent with my limping and paralyzed state. And now, since it came off, and since neither my hearers nor I myself really collaps'd at the aforesaid lecture, I intend to go up and down the land (in moderation,) seeking whom I may devour, with lectures, and reading of my own poems—short pulls, however—never exceeding an hour.

Crossing from Jersey City, 5 to 6 p. m.—The city part of the North River with its life, breadth, peculiarities—the amplitude of sea and wharf, cargo and commerce—one don't realize them till one has been away a long time and, as now returning, (crossing from Jersey City to Desbrosses-st.,) gazes on the unrivall'd panorama, and far down the thin-vapor'd vistas of the bay, toward the Narrows—or northward up the Hudson—or on the ample spread and infinite variety, free and floating, of the more immediate views—a countless river series—everything moving, yet so easy, and such plenty of room! Little, I say, do folks here appreciate the most ample, eligible, picturesque bay and estuary surroundings in the world! This is the third time such a conviction has come to me after absence, returning to New-York, dwelling on its magnificent entrances—approaching the city by them from any point.

6. come—subjects] NYTR: come—reminiscences subjects
10. following hurrygraphs] NYTR: following mems and hurrygraphs
13. This side head in italics was a center head in capitals in NYTR.
15. me—it was] NYTR: me—I was
22–23. NYTR has marks of parenthesis before "short" and after "hour."
24. "Crossing from Jersey City" was the center head, in capitals, in NYTR. The side head in NYTR was "*April* 9, 5 *to* 6 *p.m.*—". The date was lined out in the MS.
37–41. This paragraph was enclosed in parentheses in NYTR.

A SICK SPELL.

Printed in GBF from a page of autograph MS, in ink, without revisions of con-

More and more, too, the *old name* absorbs into me—MANNAHATTA, "the place encircled by many swift tides and sparkling waters." How fit a name for America's great democratic island city! The word itself, how beautiful! how aboriginal! how it seems to rise with tall spires, glistening in sunshine, with such New World atmosphere, vista and action!

A SICK SPELL.

Christmas Day, 25th Dec., 1888.—Am somewhat easier and freer to-day and the last three days—sit up most of the time—read and write, and receive my visitors. Have now been in-doors sick for seven months—half of the time bad, bad, vertigo, indigestion, bladder, gastric, head trouble, inertia—Dr. Bucke, Dr. Osler, Drs. Wharton and Walsh—now Edward Wilkins my help and nurse. A fine, splendid, sunny day. My "November Boughs" is printed and out; and my "Complete Works, Poems and Prose," a big volume, 900 pages, also. It is ab't noon, and I sit here pretty comfortable.

TO BE PRESENT ONLY.

At the Complimentary Dinner, Camden, New Jersey, May 31, 1889.—Walt Whitman said:

My friends, though announced to give an address, there is no such intention. Following the impulse of the spirit, (for I am at least half of Quaker stock) I have obey'd the command to come and look at you, for a minute, and show myself, face to face; which is probably the best I can do. But I have felt no command to make a speech; and shall not therefore attempt any. All I have felt the imperative conviction to say I have already printed in my books of poems or prose; to which I refer any who may be curious. And so, hail and farewell. Deeply acknowledging this deep compliment, with my best respects and love to you personally—to Camden—to New-Jersey, and to all represented here—you must excuse me from any word further.

sequence, except that the title was inserted in the page proof.

TO BE PRESENT ONLY.

Printed in *GBF* from what appears to be a proof sheet, the printing in the center of a sheet identical with the preceding MS page; probably prepared for reading. Whitman directs that the title on the proof sheet be made a side head. The new centered title, not in the MS, must have been inserted in the printer's proof.

3–4. This sentence was inserted in ink.

5. you, for] Proof sheet (before revision): you, my friends, for

F'm Pall-Mall Gazette, London, England, Feb. 8, 1890.
"INTESTINAL AGITATION."

Mr. Ernest Rhys has just receiv'd an interesting letter from Walt Whitman, dated "Camden, January 22, 1890." The following is an extract from it:

I am still here—no very mark'd or significant change or happening—fairly buoyant spirits, &c.—but surely, slowly ebbing. At this moment sitting here, in my den, Mickle Street, by the oakwood fire, in the same big strong old chair with wolf-skin spread over back—bright sun, cold, dry winter day. America continues—is generally busy enough all over her vast demesnes (intestinal agitation I call it,) talking, plodding, making money, every one trying to get on—perhaps to get towards the top—but no special individual signalism—(just as well, I guess.)

"WALT WHITMAN'S LAST 'PUBLIC.'"

The gay and crowded audience at the Art Rooms, Philadelphia, Tuesday night, April 15, 1890, says a correspondent of the Boston *Transcript*, April 19, might not have thought that W. W. crawl'd out of a sick bed a few hours before crying,

Dangers retreat when boldly they're confronted,

and went over, hoarse and half blind, to deliver his memoranda and essay on the death of Abraham Lincoln, on the twenty-fifth anniversary of that tragedy. He led off with the following new paragraph:

"Of Abraham Lincoln, bearing testimony twenty-five years after his death—and of that death—I am now my friends before you. Few realize the days, the great historic and esthetic personalities, with him in the centre, we pass'd through. Abraham Lincoln, familiar, our own, an Illinoisian, modern, yet tallying ancient Moses, Joshua, Ulysses, or later

"INTESTINAL AGITATION."

Printed in GBF from two small clippings of the *Pall Mall Gazette*, February 8, 1890, as shown by Whitman's endorsement. The GBF subtitle is not in the MS, and must have been inserted in the proof. The name "Walt Whitman" at the bottom of the second clipping is deleted.

"WALT WHITMAN'S LAST 'PUBLIC.'"

Printed in GBF from a clipping of the *Pall Mall Gazette*, May 24, 1890, where it has the same title. Revisions were made in ink on the clipping. W. S. Kennedy says that Whitman sent the MS to Kennedy's paper, the Boston *Transcript*, with the request that it be returned to him, and that he returned it after its publication on April 19, 1890, under the head "Walt Whitman Tuesday Night." (*The Fight of a*

Cromwell, and grander in some respects than any of them; Abraham Lincoln, that makes the like of Homer, Plutarch, Shakspere, eligible our day or any day. My subject this evening for forty or fifty minutes' talk is the death of this man, and how that death will really filter into America. I am not going to tell you anything new; and it is doubtless nearly altogether because I ardently wish to commemorate the hour and martyrdom and name I am here. Oft as the rolling years bring back this hour, let it again, however briefly, be dwelt upon. For my own part I hope and intend till my own dying day, whenever the 14th or 15th of April comes, to annually gather a few friends and hold its tragic reminiscence. No narrow or sectional reminiscence. It belongs to these States in their entirety—not the North only, but the South—perhaps belongs most tenderly and devoutly to the South, of all; for there really this man's birthstock; there and then his antecedent stamp. Why should I not say that thence his manliest traits, his universality, his canny, easy ways and words upon the surface—his inflexible determination at heart? Have you ever realized it, my friends, that Lincoln, though grafted on the West, is essentially in personnel and character a Southern contribution?"

The most of the poet's address was devoted to the actual occurrences and details of the murder. We believe the delivery on Tuesday was Whitman's thirteenth of it. The old poet is now physically wreck'd. But his voice and magnetism are the same. For the last month he has been under a severe attack of the lately prevailing influenza, the grip, in accumulation upon his previous ailments, and, above all, that terrible paralysis, the bequest of Secession War times. He was dress'd last Tuesday night in an entire suit of French Canadian grey wool cloth, with broad shirt collar, with no necktie; long white hair, red face, full beard and moustache, and look'd as though he might weigh two hundred pounds. He had to be help'd and led every step. In five weeks more he will begin his seventy-second year. He is still writing a little.

Book for the World, p. 270.) The *Transcript* text is here collated with the clipping before revision and with the text of GBF and CPW.

1. At the beginning of the line, Whitman deletes: "We take the following from the *Camden Post*." This sentence is not in the *Transcript*.

2–3. night, April 15, 1890, says . . . April 19, might] Clipping: night, April 15, says . . . April 19, might] *Transcript:* night last, April 15, might

3–4. that W. W. crawl'd] Clipping and *Transcript:* that he crawled

11. the days] Clipping and *Transcript:* the great days

12–13. Illinoisian] Clipping: Illinosian] *Transcript:* Illinoisan

15. Shakspere] Clipping and *Transcript:* Shakspeare

32. the poet's address was] Clipping and *Transcript:* the piece was

39. of French Canadian] *Transcript:* of fresh Canadian

43. a little.] Clipping and *Transcript:* a little, and a poem from him is expected in the forthcoming *Century*.

From the Camden Post, N. J., June 2, 1890.

INGERSOLL'S SPEECH.

He attends and makes a speech at the celebration of Walt Whitman's birthday.—Walt Whitman is now in his seventy-second year. His younger friends, literary and personal, men and women, gave him a complimentary supper last Saturday night, to note the close of his seventy-first year, and the late curious and unquestionable "boom" of the old man's wide-spreading popularity, and that of his "Leaves of Grass." There were thirty-five in the room, mostly young, but some old, or beginning to be. The great feature was Ingersoll's utterance. It was probably, in its way, the most admirable specimen of modern oratory hitherto delivered in the English language, immense as such praise may sound. It was 40 to 50 minutes long, altogether without notes, in a good voice, low enough and not too low, style easy, rather colloquial (over and over again saying "you" to Whitman who sat opposite,) sometimes markedly impassion'd, once or twice humorous—amid his whole speech, from interior fires and volition, pulsating and swaying like a first-class Andalusian dancer.

And such a critical dissection, and flattering summary! The Whitmanites for the first time in their lives were fully satisfied; and that is saying a good deal, for they have not put their claims low, by a long shot. Indeed it was a tremendous talk! Physically and mentally Ingersoll (he had been working all day in New York, talking in court and in his office,) is now at his best, like mellow'd wine, or a just ripe apple; to the artist-sense, too, looks at his best—not merely like a bequeath'd Roman bust or fine smooth marble Cicero-head, or even Greek Plato; for he is modern and vital and vein'd and American, and (far more than the age knows,) justifies us all.

We cannot give a full report of this most remarkable talk and supper (which was curiously conversational and Greek-like) but must add the following significant bit of it.

After the speaking, and just before the close, Mr. Whitman reverted to

INGERSOLL'S SPEECH.

Printed from a clipping of the Camden *Post*, June 2, 1890; title same as in *GBF*. The line in italics above the title was inserted in ink on the clipping. Revisions in ink on the clipping.

1–2. In the clipping the first sentence reads: "He attends the celebration of Walt Whitman's Seventy-second Birthday." Whitman directs the printer to make the revised sentence a sidehead.

6. thirty-five] Clipping: fifty or sixty [Revision, not on the clipping, presumably on the proof.]

10–11. was 40 to 50 . . . in a] Clipping: was 40 minutes long, in a

12. easy, rather] Clipping: easy, altogether without mannerism, rather

13. sometimes markedly impassion'd] Clipping: sometimes impassioned

14. humorous—amid] Clipping: humerous, amid

21–22. too, . . . not] Clipping: too looks at his best, not

24. far] Clipping: for

Colonel Ingersoll's tribute to his poems, pronouncing it the cap-sheaf of all commendation that he had ever receiv'd. Then, his mind still dwelling upon the Colonel's religious doubts, he went on to say that what he himself had in his mind when he wrote "Leaves of Grass" was not only to depict American life, as it existed, and to show the triumphs of science, and the poetry in common things, and the full of an individual democratic humanity, for the aggregate, but also to show that there was behind all something which rounded and completed it. "For what," he ask'd, "would this life be without immortality? It would be as a locomotive, the greatest triumph of modern science, with no train to draw after it. If the spiritual is not behind the material, to what purpose is the material? What is this world without a further Divine purpose in it all?"

Colonel Ingersoll repeated his former argument in reply.

FEELING FAIRLY.

Friday, July 27, 1890.—Feeling fairly these days, and even jovial—sleep and appetite good enough to be thankful for—had a dish of Maryland blackberries, some good rye bread and a cup of tea, for my breakfast—relish'd all—fine weather—bright sun to-day—pleasant north-west breeze blowing in the open window as I sit here in my big rattan chair—two great fine roses (white and red, blooming, fragrant, sent by mail by W. S. K. and wife, Mass.) are in a glass of water on the table before me.

Am now in my 72d year.

OLD BROOKLYN DAYS.

It must have been in 1822 or '3 that I first came to live in Brooklyn. Lived first in Front street, not far from what was then call'd "the New Ferry," wending the river from the foot of Catharine (or Main) street to New York City.

I was a little child (was born in 1819,) but tramp'd freely about the neighborhood and town, even then; was often on the aforesaid New Ferry;

25. remarkable talk and supper] Clipping: remarkable supper
29. the cap-sheaf of] Clipping: the culmination of
34–35. individual democratic humanity] Clipping: individual humanity
38. draw after it.] Clipping: draw.

FEELING FAIRLY.

Printed from the lower half of an autograph sheet, torn across the middle. The title was inserted on the page proof.

5. rattan] MS: ratan [Corrected on proof.]

OLD BROOKLYN DAYS.

Printed in *GBF* from two clippings of *NYMJ*, August 3, 1890. Most revisions were made on the clippings. Under the title in *NYMJ* appears "By Walt Whitman, 'The Good Gray Poet.'" This is lined out in ink.

2. Lived] *NYMJ:* I lived [Revision on page proof.]
3. wending the river from] *NYMJ:* wending from

remember how I was petted and deadheaded by the gatekeepers and deck-hands (all such fellows are kind to little children,) and remember the horses that seem'd to me so queer as they trudg'd around in the central houses of the boats, making the water-power. (For it was just on the eve of the steam-engine, which was soon after introduced on the ferries.) Edward Copeland (afterward Mayor) had a grocery store then at the corner of Front and Catharine streets.

Presently we Whitmans all moved up to Tillary street, near Adams, where my father, who was a carpenter, built a house for himself and us all. It was from here I 'assisted' the personal coming of Lafayette in 1824–5 to Brooklyn. He came over the Old Ferry, as the now Fulton Ferry (partly navigated quite up to that day by 'horse boats,' though the first steamer had begun to be used hereabouts) was then call'd, and was receiv'd at the foot of Fulton street. It was on that occasion that the corner-stone of the Apprentices' Library, at the corner of Cranberry and Henry streets—since pull'd down—was laid by Lafayette's own hands. Numerous children arrived on the grounds, of whom I was one, and were assisted by several gentlemen to safe spots to view the ceremony. Among others, Lafayette, also helping the children, took me up—I was five years old, press'd me a moment to his breast—gave me a kiss and set me down in a safe spot. Lafayette was at that time between sixty-five and seventy years of age, with a manly figure and a kind face.

TWO QUESTIONS.

An editor of (or in) a leading monthly magazine (Harper's Monthly, July, 1890,) asks: "A hundred years from now will W. W. be popularly rated a great poet—or will he be forgotten?" . . . A mighty ticklish question—which can only be left for a hundred years hence—per-

2n. there—went] *TT:* there; went

11–13. This sentence was a separate paragraph in *NYMJ*.
14–15. street, near Adams, where] *NYMJ:* street, where
16. I 'assisted' the personal] *NYMJ:* I visited, and will describe the personal
17. After "Brooklyn." *NYMJ* begins a new paragraph.
17. the now] *NYMJ:* the new [Revision on page proof.]
20. After "street." *NYMJ* begins a new paragraph.
24. After "ceremony." *NYMJ* begins a new paragraph.
26. After "spot." *NYMJ* begins a new paragraph.
28. After "kind face." *NYMJ* concludes with two paragraphs not reprinted in *GBF*. A passage very similar to them, drawn from an earlier unidentified newspaper, appears in *SDC*, in the footnote to "Printing Office.—Old Brooklyn." *Prose 1892*, I, *q.v.*) The two paragraphs are printed in Appendix XIV, *1*, collated with the text of the clipping used in *SDC*.

TWO QUESTIONS.

Printed from an autograph MS page made up of four strips; all in ink. In the "Editor's Easy Chair" (*Harper's Magazine*, LXXXI, 311), in an article commenting

haps more than that. But whether W. W. has been mainly rejected by his own times is an easier question to answer.

All along from 1860 to '91, many of the pieces in L of G, and its annexes, were first sent to publishers or magazine editors before being printed in the L, and were peremptorily rejected by them, and sent back to their author. The "Eidōlons" was sent back by Dr. H., of "Scribner's Monthly" with a lengthy, very insulting and contemptuous letter. "To the Sun-Set Breeze," was rejected by the editor of "Harper's Monthly" as being "an improvisation" only. "On, on ye jocund twain" was rejected by the "Century" editor as being personal merely. Several of the pieces went the rounds of all the monthlies, to be thus summarily rejected.

June, '90.—The———rejects and sends back my little poem, so I am now set out in the cold by every big magazine and publisher, and may as well understand and admit it—which is just as well, for I find I am palpably losing my sight and ratiocination.

PREFACE TO A VOLUME OF ESSAYS AND TALES BY WM. D. O'CONNOR, PUB'D POSTHUMOUSLY IN 1891.

A hasty memorandum, not particularly for Preface to the following tales, but to put on record my respect and affection for as sane, beautiful, cute, tolerant, loving, candid and free and fair-intention'd a nature as ever vivified our race.

In Boston, 1860, I first met WILLIAM DOUGLAS O'CONNOR.* As I

* Born Jan. 2d, 1832. When grown, lived several years in Boston, and edited journals and magazines there—went about 1861 to Washington, D. C., and became a U. S. clerk, first in the Light-House Bureau, and then in the U. S. Life-Saving Service, in which branch he was Assistant Superintendent for many years—sicken'd in 1887—died there at Washington, May 9th, 1889.

3*n*. Light-House] *TT:* Lighthouse

on the remark of Sydney Smith in the *Edinburgh Review* in 1820, "who reads an American book?" the editor says: "There is no critic living who can foretell whether a hundred years hence our good friend Walt Whitman will be accepted as a great poet or have fallen into the limbo where the vast throng of Kettell's poets lie." George William Curtis conducted the "Easy Chair" in 1890. In 1829 Samuel Kettell published *Specimens of American Poetry*, in three volumes.

PREFACE TO A VOLUME, OF ESSAYS AND TALES.

Printed in *GBF* from what appears to be a specially printed sheet, or broadside, with two columns of print. Page proof of *GBF* is preserved also with the revised broadside. This preface was written for the posthumous volume by William D. O'Connor, *Three Tales*, copyright 1891, but dated on the title page, 1892. *Three Tales* appeared after *GBF*. The title on the broadside is simply "Preface," as in O'Connor's book. Along the margin Whitman writes and directs the printer to add to the title in italics: "*—to the first page or two of a volume of essays and tales by Wm D. O'Connor, pub'd posthumously in 1891.*" In the page proof Whitman deletes "the first page or two of" before "a volume." The text in *Three Tales*, abbreviated *TT*, is collated with others.

saw and knew him then, in his 29th year, and for twenty-five further years along, he was a gallant, handsome, gay-hearted, fine-voiced, glowing-eyed man; lithe-moving on his feet, of healthy and magnetic atmosphere and presence, and the most welcome company in the world. He was a thorough-going anti-slavery believer, speaker and writer, (doctrinaire,) and though I took a fancy to him from the first, I remember I fear'd his ardent abolitionism—was afraid it would probably keep us apart. (I was a decided and out-spoken anti-slavery believer myself, then and always; but shy'd from the extremists, the red-hot fellows of those times.) O'C. was then correcting the proofs of *Harrington*, an eloquent and fiery novel he had written, and which was printed just before the commencement of the Secession War. He was already married, the father of two fine little children, and was personally and intellectually the most attractive man I had ever met.

Last of '62 I found myself led towards the war-field—went to Washington City—(to become absorb'd in the armies, and in the big hospitals, and to get work in one of the Departments,)—and there I met and resumed friendship, and found warm hospitality from O'C. and his noble New England wife. They had just lost by death their little child-boy, Philip; and O'C. was yet feeling serious about it. The youngster had been vaccinated against the threatening of small-pox which alarm'd the city; but somehow it led to worse results than it was intended to ward off—or at any rate O'C. thought that proved the cause of the boy's death. He had one child left, a fine bright little daughter, and a great comfort to her parents. (Dear Jeannie! She grew up a most accomplish'd and superior young woman—declined in health, and died about 1881.)

On through for months and years to '73 I saw and talk'd with O'C. almost daily. I had soon got employment, first for a short time in the Indian Bureau (in the Interior Department,) and then for a long while in the Attorney General's Office. The Secession War, with its tide of varying fortunes, excitements—President Lincoln and the daily sight of him—the doings in Congress and at the State Capitals—the news from the fields and

6–7. years along, he] Broadside and *TT:* years, he
14. shy'd] *TT:* shied
15. *Harrington*] *TT:* "Harrington"
19. After "met." Broadside and *TT* continue in the same paragraph, but the paragraph symbol is inserted on the broadside in ink.
23. his noble New] *TT:* his New
24–31. After "wife." *TT* omits the remainder of this paragraph.
32. On . . . '73] Broadside and *TT:* On through to '73
38–39. governments . . . with a] Broadside and *TT:* governments, with a
42. O'C.] *TT:* O'Connor
42–43. first-class public] Broadside and *TT:* first-class orator or public
44. This sentence, not in *TT*, is inserted on the broadside in ink, but with "that" instead of "a" before "strange." It was changed on the page proof.

campaigns, and from foreign governments—my visits to the Army Hospitals, daily and nightly, soon absorbing everything else,—with a hundred matters, occurrences, personalities,—(Greeley, Wendell Phillips, the parties, the Abolitionists, &c.)—were the subjects of our talk and discussion. I am not sure from what I heard then, but O'C. was cut out for a first-class public speaker or forensic advocate. No audience or jury could have stood out against him. He had a strange charm of physiologic voice. He had a power and sharp-cut faculty of statement and persuasiveness beyond any man's else. I know it well, for I have felt it many a time. If not as orator, his forte was as critic, newer, deeper than any: also, as literary author. One of his traits was that while he knew all, and welcom'd all sorts of great *genre* literature, all lands and times, from all writers and artists, and not only tolerated each, and defended every attack'd literary person with a skill or heart-catholicism that I never saw equal'd—invariably advocated and excused them—he kept an idiosyncrasy and identity of his own very mark'd, and without special tinge or undue color from any source. He always applauded the freedom of the masters, whence and whoever. I remember his special defences of Byron, Burns, Poe, Rabelais, Victor Hugo, George Sand, and others. There was always a little touch of pensive cadence in his superb voice; and I think there was something of the same sadness in his temperament and nature. Perhaps, too, in his literary structure. But he was a very buoyant, jovial, good-natured companion.

So much for a hasty melanged reminiscence and note of William O'Connor, my dear, dear friend, and staunch, (probably my staunchest) literary believer and champion from the first, and throughout without halt or demur, for twenty-five years. No better friend—none more reliable through this life of one's ups and downs. On the occurrence of the latter he would be sure to make his appearance on the scene, eager, hopeful, full of fight like a perfect knight of chivalry. For he was a born sample here in the 19th century of the flower and symbol of olden time first-class knighthood. Thrice blessed be his memory! W. W.

50–51. skill or] Broadside: skill and [Revised on galley proof.]
53. or undue color] Broadside before revision: or color
54. applauded the freedom of the masters] Broadside and *TT:* applauded the [Revised on the broadside.]
58. nature. Perhaps] *TT:* nature,—perhaps
61. staunch] *TT:* stanch
61. staunchest] *TT:* stanchest
66–68. For this sentence, beginning "For," the broadside and *TT* have: "For he was a sample of the flower and symbol of olden time first-class knighthood here in the 19th [*TT:* nineteenth] century."
68. *TT* has a period after "memory".
68. Broadside and *TT* have "Walt Whitman" at the end; on the broadside this is lined out and "W. W." written in ink.

F'm the Engineering Record, New York, Dec. 13, 1890.

AN ENGINEER'S OBITUARY.

THOMAS JEFFERSON WHITMAN was born July 18, 1833, in Brooklyn, N. Y., from a father of English stock, and mother (Louisa Van Velsor) descended from Dutch (Holland) immigration. His early years were spent on Long Island, either in the country or Brooklyn. As a lad he show'd a tendency for surveying and civil engineering, and about at 19 went with Chief Kirkwood, who was then prospecting and outlining for the great city water-works. He remain'd at that construction throughout, was a favorite and confidant of the Chief, and was successively promoted. He continued also under Chief Moses Lane. He married in 1859, and not long after was invited by the Board of Public Works of St. Louis, Missouri, to come there and plan and build a new and fitting water-works for that great city. Whitman accepted the call, and moved and settled there, and had been a resident of St. Louis ever since. He plann'd and built the works, which were very successful, and remain'd as superintendent and chief for nearly 20 years.

Of the last six years he has been largely occupied as consulting engineer (divested of his cares and position in St. Louis,) and has engaged in public constructions, bridges, sewers, &c., West and Southwest, and especially the Memphis, Tenn., city water-works.

Thomas J. Whitman was a theoretical and practical mechanic of superior order, founded in the soundest personal and professional integrity. He was a great favorite among the young engineers and students; not a few of them yet remaining in Kings and Queens Counties, and New York City, will remember "Jeff," with old-time good-will and affection. He was mostly self-taught, and was a hard student.

He had been troubled of late years from a bad throat and from gastric

AN ENGINEER'S OBITUARY.

Printed in *GBF* from a clipping of *ER*, December 13, 1890, with corrections in ink. Immediately preceding this obituary in *ER* is a paragraph under the heading: "Thomas Jefferson Whitman," as follows:

"The tribute we publish this week by the venerable poet Walt Whitman to the memory of his brother, the late Thomas Jefferson Whitman, the eminent civil engineer, whose death we noticed in a recent issue, will, we believe, excite the sympathetic interest of our readers."

Whitman directs the printer to put the credit line in italics under the title, not over it as in *GBF*.

12. and had been] *ER:* and has been [Not revised on the clipping.]
20. Thomas J.] *ER:* Thomas Jefferson
27. tending on] *ER:* tending to [Not revised on the clipping.]
46–47. Allegheny Mountains] *ER:* Alleghenies [Revised on the clipping.]
48. Rivers, from Cairo to] *ER:* Rivers to [Revised on the clipping.]

affection, tending on typhoid, and had been rather seriously ill with the last malady, but was getting over the worst of it, when he succumb'd under a sudden and severe attack of the heart. He died at St. Louis, November 25, 1890, in his 58th year. Of his family, the wife died in 1873, and a daughter, Mannahatta, died two years ago. Another daughter, Jessie Louisa, the only child left, is now living in St. Louis.

[When Jeff was born I was in my 15th year, and had much care of him for many years afterward, and he did not separate from me. He was a very handsome, healthy, affectionate, smart child, and would sit on my lap or hang on my neck half an hour at a time. As he grew a big boy he liked outdoor and water sports, especially boating. We would often go down summers to Peconic Bay, east end of Long Island, and over to Shelter Island. I loved long rambles, and he carried his fowling-piece. O, what happy times, weeks! Then in Brooklyn and New York City he learn'd printing, and work'd awhile at it; but eventually (with my approval) he went to employment at land surveying, and merged in the studies and work of topographical engineer; this satisfied him, and he continued at it. He was of noble nature from the first; very good-natured, very plain, very friendly. O, how we loved each other—how many jovial good times we had! Once we made a long trip from New York City down over the Alleghany Mountains (the National Road) and via the Ohio and Mississippi Rivers, from Cairo to New Orleans.]

God's blessing on your name and memory, dear brother Jeff!

W. W.

OLD ACTORS, SINGERS, SHOWS, &c., IN NEW YORK.

Flitting mention—(with much left out.)

Seems to me I ought acknowledge my debt to actors, singers, public speakers, conventions, and the Stage in New York, my youthful days, from

49. The name "Walt Whitman" is lined out in ink and "W. W." written in.

OLD ACTORS, SINGERS, SHOWS &c., IN NEW YORK.

Printed in *GBF* from three autograph pages and two printed pages, apparently clippings from a galley, cut to allow the insertion of the autograph pages; there is no record of previous publication. These pages are numbered A to E. In the printer's copy they follow the last numbered pages of the MS (pp. 76–79, "Some Personal and Old-Age Jottings"), and several sheets of page proof of earlier pages of *GBF*. Pages A and E are printed; B, C, and D are autograph pages. On A the original title, in large capitals, was "Old Actors and Singers," and below it, in smaller capitals, was "Flitting Mention By Walt Whitman." All this is crossed out and the *GBF* title and subtitle are written in ink above it. Revisions are in ink on the printed pages. The page proof of this section is not with the copy.

1–2. singers, . . . and the] Clipping before revision: singers, and the

2. New York, . . . from] Clipping before revision: New York, from

1835 onward—say to '60 or '61—and to plays and operas generally. (Which nudges a pretty big disquisition: of course it should be all elaborated and penetrated more deeply—but I will here give only some flitting mentionings of my youth.) Seems to me now when I look back, the Italian contralto Marietta Alboni (she is living yet, in Paris, 1891, in good condition, good voice yet, considering) with the then prominent histrions Booth, Edwin Forrest, and Fanny Kemble and the Italian singer Bettini, have had the deepest and most lasting effect upon me. I should like well if Madame Alboni and the old composer Verdi, (and Bettini the tenor, if he is living) could know how much noble pleasure and happiness they gave me, and how deeply I always remember them and thank them to this day. For theatricals in literature and doubtless upon me personally, including opera, have been of course serious factors. (The experts and musicians of my present friends claim that the new Wagner and his pieces belong far more truly to me, and I to them. Very likely. But I was fed and bred under the Italian dispensation, and absorb'd it, and doubtless show it.)

As a young fellow, when possible I always studied a play or libretto quite carefully over, by myself, (sometimes twice through) before seeing it on the stage; read it the day or two days before. Tried both ways—not reading some beforehand; but I found I gain'd most by getting that sort of mastery first, if the piece had depth. (Surface effects and glitter were much less thought of I am sure those times.) There were many fine old plays, neither tragedies nor comedies—the names of them quite unknown to today's current audiences. "All is not Gold that Glitters," in which Charlotte Cushman had a superbly enacted part, was of that kind. C. C., who revel'd in them, was great in such pieces; I think better than in the heavy popular roles.

We had some fine music those days. We had the English opera of "Cinderella" (with Henry Placide as the pompous old father, an unsurpassable bit of comedy and music.) We had Bombastes Furioso. Must have been in 1844 (or '5) I saw Charles Kean and Mrs. Kean (Ellen Tree)—saw them in the Park in Shakspere's "King John." He, of course, was the chief character. She play'd *Queen Constance*. Tom Hamblin was

7. yet, in Paris, 1891] Clipping before revision: yet, 1891

11–12. On the clipping, added in ink: "and Brignoli" after "Bettini"; "s" to "tenor," and "they are" in place of "he is." None of these revisions, however, appear in *GBF*, which follows the printed copy.

12. much noble pleasure] Clipping (unrevised): much pleasure

15. opera . . . factors.] Clipping (unrevised): opera, has been of course a serious factor.

15–18. The lines in parentheses were inserted in ink on a strip of paper pasted to the right margin of the galley.

27. C. C.] Clipping before revision: Charlotte Cushman

Faulconbridge, and probably the best ever on the stage. It was an immense show-piece, too; lots of grand set scenes and fine armor-suits and all kinds of appointments imported from London (where it had been first render'd.) The large brass bands—the three or four hundred "supes"—the interviews between the French and English armies—the talk with *Hubert* (and the hot irons)—the delicious acting of *Prince Arthur* (Mrs. Richardson, I think)—and all the fine *blare* and court pomp—I remember to this hour. The death-scene of the King in the orchard of Swinstead Abbey, was very effective. Kean rush'd in, gray-pale and yellow, and threw himself on a lounge in the open. His pangs were horribly realistic. (He must have taken lessons in some hospital.)

Fanny Kemble play'd to wonderful effect in such pieces as "Fazio, or the Italian wife." The turning-point was jealousy. It was a rapid-running, yet heavy-timber'd, tremendous wrenching, passionate play. Such old pieces always seem'd to me built like an ancient ship of the line, solid and lock'd from keel up—oak and metal and knots. One of the finest characters was a great court lady, *Aldabella*, enacted by Mrs. Sharpe. O how it all entranced us, and knock'd us about, as the scenes swept on like a cyclone!

Saw Hackett at the old Park many times, and remember him well. His renderings were first-rate in everything. He inaugurated the true "Rip Van Winkle," and look'd and acted and dialogued it to perfection (he was of Dutch breed, and brought up among old Holland descendants in Kings and Queens counties, Long Island.) The play and the acting of it have been adjusted to please popular audiences since; but there was in that original performance certainly something of a far higher order, more art, more reality, more resemblance, a bit of fine pathos, a lofty *brogue*, beyond anything afterward.

One of my big treats was the rendering at the old Park of Shakspere's "Tempest" in musical version. There was a very fine instrumental band, not numerous, but with a capital leader. Mrs. Austin was the *Ariel*, and Peter Richings the *Caliban;* both excellent. The drunken song of the latter has probably been never equal'd. The perfect actor Clarke (old Clarke) was *Prospero*.

34 and 63. Shakspere's] Clipping before revision: Shakespeare's

41. irons)—the] GBF and CPW: irons) the] [Since the clipping has the dash, which is not deleted, the omission seems to be a printer's error uncorrected; because the sentence structure requires it, the dash is restored in the present edition.—ED.]

42. *blare*] Clipping: *blaze* [The "r" is crossed out on the clipping and "z" written in the margin. Since the sentence makes good sense either way, the reading of GBF and CPW is retained in this edition.—ED.]

51. from keel] Clipping before revision: from her keel

68. The galley is cut after this line; examination of the cut suggests that the next line on the galley before cutting was the present line 135.

Yes; there were in New York and Brooklyn some fine nontechnical singing performances, concerts, such as the Hutchinson band, three brothers, and the sister, the red-cheek'd New England carnation, sweet Abby; sometimes plaintive and balladic—sometimes anti-slavery, anti-calomel, and comic. There were concerts by Templeton, Russell, Dempster, the old Alleghanian band, and many others. Then we had lots of "negro minstrels," with capital character songs and voices. I often saw Rice the original "Jim Crow" at the old Park Theatre filling up the gap in some short bill—and the wild chants and dances were admirable—probably ahead of anything since. Every theatre had some superior voice, and it was common to give a favorite song between the acts. "The Sea" at the bijou Olympic, (Broadway near Grand,) was always welcome from a little Englishman named Edwin, a good balladist. At the Bowery the loves of "Sweet William,"

"When on the Downs the fleet was moor'd,"

always bro't an encore, and sometimes a treble.

I remember Jenny Lind and heard her (1850 I think) several times. She had the most brilliant, captivating, popular musical style and expression of any one known; (the canary, and several other sweet birds are wondrous fine—but there is something in song that goes deeper—isn't there?)

The great "Egyptian Collection" was well up in Broadway, and I got quite acquainted with Dr. Abbott, the proprietor—paid many visits there, and had long talks with him, in connection with my readings of many books and reports on Egypt—its antiquities, history, and how things and the scenes really look, and what the old relics stand for, as near as we can now get. (Dr. A. was an Englishman of say 54—had been settled in Cairo as physician for 25 years, and all that time was collecting these relics, and sparing no time or money seeking and getting them. By advice and for a change of base for himself, he brought the collection to America. But the whole enterprise was a fearful disappointment, in the pay and commercial part.) As said, I went to the Egyptian Museum many many times; sometimes had it all to myself—delved at the formidable catalogue—and on several occasions had the invaluable personal talk, correction, illustration and guidance of Dr. A. himself. He was very kind and helpful to me in

69–134. These lines printed from three autograph pages, in ink, numbered B, C, and D. The first sheet, B, has at the top the words "Before the War", with directions to the printer to make the letters "nonp caps." This is all crossed out. Perhaps, when he wrote these pages, Whitman intended to let them follow the printed part as a separate subdivision.

those studies and examinations; once, by appointment, he appear'd in full and exact Turkish (Cairo) costume, which long usage there had made habitual to him.

One of the choice places of New York to me then was the "Phrenological Cabinet" of Fowler & Wells, Nassau street near Beekman. Here were all the busts, examples, curios and books of that study obtainable. I went there often, and once for myself had a very elaborate and leisurely examination and "chart of bumps" written out (I have it yet,) by Nelson Fowler (or was it Sizer?) there.

And who remembers the renown'd New York "Tabernacle" of those days "before the war"? It was on the east side of Broadway, near Pearl street—was a great turtle-shaped hall, and you had to walk back from the street entrance, thro' a long wide corridor to get to it—was very strong—had an immense gallery—altogether held three or four thousand people. Here the huge annual conventions of the windy and cyclonic "reformatory societies" of those times were held—especially the tumultuous Anti-Slavery ones. I remember hearing Wendell Phillips, Emerson, Cassius Clay, John P. Hale, Beecher, Fred Douglas, the Burleighs, Garrison, and others. Sometimes the Hutchinsons would sing—very fine. Sometimes there were angry rows. A chap named Isaiah Rhynders, a fierce politician of those days, with a band of robust supporters, would attempt to contradict the speakers and break up the meetings. But the Anti-Slavery, and Quaker, and Temperance, and Missionary and other conventicles and speakers were tough, tough, and always maintained their ground, and carried out their programs fully. I went frequently to these meetings, May after May—learn'd much from them—was sure to be on hand when J. P. Hale or Cash Clay made speeches.

There were also the smaller and handsome halls of the Historical and Athenæum Societies up on Broadway. I very well remember W. C. Bryant lecturing on Homœopathy in one of them, and attending two or three addresses by R. W. Emerson in the other.

There was a series of plays and dramatic *genre* characters by a gentleman bill'd as Ranger—very fine, better than merely technical, full of exquisite shades, like the light touches of the violin in the hands of a master. There was the actor Anderson, who brought us Gerald Griffin's "Gisippus," and play'd it to admiration. Among the actors of those times I recall:

74–75. "negro minstrels"] Clipping before revision: "nigger-minstrels"
92. connection] MS unrevised: connexion
121. Burleighs, Garrison, and] Clipping unrevised: Burleighs, Pillsbury, and
123. Isaiah Rhynders] Clipping unrevised: Isaac Rhynders
135–176. Printed from the lower part of the cut galley, page E.
135. and dramatic *genre*] Clipping before revision: and *genre*

Cooper, Wallack, Tom Hamblin, Adams (several), Old Gates, Scott, Wm. Sefton, John Sefton, Geo. Jones, Mitchell, Seguin, Old Clarke, Richings, Fisher, H. Placide, T. Placide, Thorne, Ingersoll, Gale (Mazeppa) Edwin, Horncastle. Some of the women hastily remember'd were: Mrs. Vernon, Mrs. Pritchard, Mrs. McClure, Mary Taylor, Clara Fisher, Mrs. Richardson, Mrs. Flynn. Then the singers, English, Italian and other: Mrs. Wood, Mrs. Seguin, Mrs. Austin, Grisi, La Grange, Steffanone, Bosio, Truffi, Parodi, Vestvali, Bertucca, Jenny Lind, Gazzaniga, Laborde. And the opera men: Bettini, Badiali, Marini, Mario, Brignoli, Amodio, Beneventano, and many, many others whose names I do not at this moment recall.

In another paper I have described the elder Booth, and the Bowery Theatre of those times. Afterward there was the Chatham. The elder Thorne, Mrs. Thorne, William and John Sefton, Kirby, Brougham, and sometimes Edwin Forrest himself play'd there. I remember them all, and many more, and especially the fine theatre on Broadway near Pearl, in 1855 and '6.

There were very good circus performances, or horsemanship, in New York and Brooklyn. Every winter in the first-named city, a regular place in the Bowery, nearly opposite the old theatre; fine animals and fine riding, which I often witness'd. (Remember seeing near here, a young, fierce, splendid lion, presented by an African Barbary Sultan to President Andrew Jackson. The gift comprised also a lot of jewels, a fine steel sword, and an Arab stallion; and the lion was made over to a show-man.)

If it is worth while I might add that there was a small but well-appointed amateur-theatre up Broadway, with the usual stage, orchestra, pit, boxes, &c., and that I was myself a member for some time, and acted parts in it several times—"second parts" as they were call'd. Perhaps it too was a lesson, or help'd that way; at any rate it was full of fun and enjoyment.

And so let us turn off the gas. Out in the brilliancy of the footlights—

143. After "Horncastle." clipping before revision begins a new paragraph.
145. After "Flynn." clipping before revision begins a new paragraph.
148. After "Laborde." clipping before revision begins a new paragraph.
148. The name "Brignoli" is inserted on the clipping in ink.
174. part—But then] Clipping before revision: part—and then

SOME PERSONAL AND OLD-AGE JOTTINGS.

Printed from what appear to be clippings of galley sheets of the same article as published in *LIP*, March, 1891, under the title "Some Personal and Old-Age Memoranda." The text of the galleys is printed in *LIP* without significant change. Whitman's revisions for printing in *GBF* appear on these clippings in ink. An early autograph MS of seven pages exists in the Feinberg Collection, but it is not sufficiently finished to be here collated.

filling the attention of perhaps a crowded audience, and making many a breath and pulse swell and rise—O so much passion and imparted life! —over and over again, the season through—walking, gesticulating, singing, reciting his or her part—But then sooner or later inevitably wending to the flies or exit door—vanishing to sight and ear—and never materializing on this earth's stage again!

SOME PERSONAL AND OLD-AGE JOTTINGS.

Anything like unmitigated acceptance of my *Leaves of Grass* book, and heart-felt response to it, in a popular however faint degree, bubbled forth as a fresh spring from the ground in England in 1876. The time was a critical and turning point in my personal and literary life. Let me revert to my memorandum book, Camden, New Jersey, that year, fill'd with addresses, receipts, purchases, &c., of the two volumes pub'd then by myself—the *Leaves*, and the *Two Rivulets*—some home customers for them, but mostly from the British Islands. I was seriously paralyzed from the Secession war, poor, in debt, was expecting death, (the doctors put four chances out of five against me,)—and I had the books printed during the lingering interim to occupy the tediousness of glum days and nights. Curiously, the sale abroad proved prompt, and what one might call copious: the names came in lists and the money with them, by foreign mail. The price was $10 a set. Both the cash and the emotional cheer were deep medicines; many paid double or treble price, (Tennyson and Ruskin did,) and many sent kind and eulogistic letters; ladies, clergymen, social leaders, persons of rank, and high officials. Those blessed gales from the British Islands probably (certainly) saved me. Here are some of the names, for I w'd like to preserve them: Wm. M. and D. G. Rossetti, Lord Houghton, Edwd. Dowden, Mrs. Ann Gilchrist, Keningale Cook, Edwd. Carpenter, Therese Simpson, Rob't Buchanan, Alfred Tennyson, John Ruskin, C. G. Oates, E. T. Wilkinson, T. L. Warren, C. W. Reynell, W. B. Scott, A. G. Dew Smith, E. W. Gosse, T. W. Rolleston, Geo.

1. *Leaves of Grass* book] Clipping before revision: *Leaves of Grass* expression
2. degree, bubbled] Clipping before revision: degree, (though a big certificate came early from Emerson,*) bubbled

[The footnote to which the asterisk refers is in two parts, both omitted in *GBF:* the first part is Emerson's letter to Whitman, July 21, 1855, slightly revised in punctuation and paragraphing; for the second part, see Appendix xv, 1.]

3. spring from] Clip. and *LIP:* spring out from
6. the two volumes pub'd] Clip. and *LIP:* the two-volume work published
6–7. myself—the] Clip. and *LIP:* myself, the
8. was seriously paralyzed] Clip. and *LIP:* was paralyzed
9. doctors put] Clip. and *LIP:* doctors candidly put
12–13. copious: the] Clip. and *LIP* copious; the
19. names, . . . them:] Clip. and *LIP:* names:

Wallis, Rafe Leicester, Thos. Dixon, N. MacColl, Mrs. Matthews, R. Hannah, Geo. Saintsbury, R. S. Watson, Godfrey and Vernon Lushington, G. H. Lewes, G. H. Boughton, Geo. Fraser, W. T. Arnold, A. Ireland, Mrs. M. Taylor, M. D. Conway, Benj. Eyre, E. Dannreather, Rev. T. E. Brown, C. W. Sheppard, E. J. A. Balfour, P. B. Marston, A. C. De Burgh, J. H. McCarthy, J. H. Ingram, Rev. R. P. Graves, Lady Mount-temple, F. S. Ellis, W. Brockie, Rev. A. B. Grosart, Lady Hardy, Hubert Herkomer, Francis Hueffer, H. G. Dakyns, R. L. Nettleship, W. J. Stillman, Miss Blind, Madox Brown, H. R. Ricardo, Messrs. O'Grady and Tyrrel; and many, many more.

Severely scann'd, it was perhaps no very great or vehement success; but the tide had palpably shifted at any rate, and the sluices were turn'd into my own veins and pockets. That emotional, audacious, open-handed, friendly-mouth'd just-opportune English action, I say, pluck'd me like a brand from the burning, and gave me life again, to finish my book, since ab't completed. I do not forget it, and shall not; and if I ever have a biographer I charge him to put it in the narrative. I have had the noblest friends and backers in America; Wm. O'Connor, Dr. R. M. Bucke, John Burroughs, Geo. W. Childs, good ones in Boston, and Carnegie and R. G. Ingersoll in New York; and yet perhaps the tenderest and gratefulest breath of my heart has gone, and ever goes, over the sea-gales across the big pond.

About myself at present. I will soon enter upon my 73d year, if I live—have pass'd an active life, as country school-teacher, gardener, printer, carpenter, author and journalist, domicil'd in nearly all the United States and principal cities, North and South—went to the front (moving about and occupied as army nurse and missionary) during the Secession war,

29–30. R. P. Graves, Lady Mount-temple, F. S. Ellis] Clip. (unrevised) and *LIP:* R. P. Graves, Rev. T. E. Brown, F. S. Ellis
39. ab't] *LIP:* about
41. America;] *LIP:* America.
42. R. G.] Clip.: R G
46–177. In the Feinberg Collection there is a typescript (pages numbered 3–13) of these lines revised in Whitman's autograph in black ink. Through line 106 the typescript is written in the third person, changed to first person in revision; from 106 to about 157, it is copied from the autobiographical data on the sheet prepared by Whitman for his "Remembrance Copies" of *MDW* (see, below, note to lines 105–106), and is in the first person; lines 157–165 follow a revision of the remembrance sheet prepared in 1889; lines 165–175 are in the third person and were added in 1891. The revised typescript was probably the copy from which the article in *LIP* was printed. This typescript is collated with the printed texts. Revisions of the typescript are mentioned only when they vary from the text of *GBF*, and simple changes from third to first person are not noted.
46. About . . . will] Typescript: The poet above named will
47. school-teacher, gardener, printer] Clip., *LIP*, and Typescript: school-teacher,

1861 to '65, and in the Virginia hospitals and after the battles of that time, tending the Northern and Southern wounded alike—work'd down South and in Washington city arduously three years—contracted the paralysis which I have suffer'd ever since—and now live in a little cottage of my own, near the Delaware in New Jersey. My chief book, unrhym'd and unmetrical (it has taken thirty years, peace and war, "a borning") has its aim as once said, "to utter the same old human *critter*—but now in Democratic American modern and scientific conditions." Then I have publish'd two prose works "Specimen Days," and a late one "November Boughs." (A little volume "Good-Bye my Fancy" is soon to be out, wh' will finish the matter.) I do not propose here to enter the much-fought field of the literary criticism of any of those works.

But for a few portraiture or descriptive bits. To-day in the upper of a little wooden house of two stories near the Delaware river, east shore, sixty miles up from the sea, is a rather large 20-by-20 low ceiling'd room something like a big old ship's cabin. The floor, three quarters of it with an ingrain carpet, is half cover'd by a deep litter of books, papers, magazines, thrown-down letters and circulars, rejected manuscripts, memoranda, bits of light or strong twine, a bundle to be "express'd," and two or three venerable scrap books. In the room stand two large tables (one of ancient St. Domingo mahogany with immense leaves) cover'd by a jumble of more papers, a varied and copious array of writing materials, several glass and china vessels or jars, some with cologne-water, others with real honey, granulated sugar, a large bunch of beautiful fresh yellow chrysanthemums, some letters and envelopt papers ready for the post office, many photographs, and a hundred indescribable things besides. There are all around many books, some quite handsome editions, some half cover'd

printer

48. domicil'd] Typescript: living

57. as once said] Typescript: as Whitman himself says

59–61. Boughs." (A little . . . out, wh' will finish the matter.) I] Clip. and *LIP:* Boughs." (A little . . . out.) I] Typescript: Boughs," We [Revised to read as *LIP*.]

62. of any of those works.] Clip. and *LIP:* of any of those works; on another page however are printed some fresh poetic pieces of mine. The portrait in this number was taken a year or so ago last summer, and is a pretty good likeness.] Typescript: of those works. On another page however are presented some late poetic pieces of Whitman. The portrait in this number was taken last summer and is a pretty good likeness.] (Revised to read as *LIP* except the last sentence, which shows no revision.)

63. But for] Clip. and *LIP:* Now for [In the typescript, the sentence, as in *LIP*, is inserted in ink.]

66. After "cabin." Typescript begins a new paragraph.

70. room stand two] Typescript: room are two

71. St. Domingo mahogany] Clip., *LIP*, and Typescript: solid mahogany

75. envelopt] Clip., *LIP*, and Typescript: enveloped

by dust, some within reach, evidently used, (good-sized print, no type less than long primer,) some maps, the Bible, (the strong cheap edition of the English crown,) Homer, Shakspere, Walter Scott, Emerson, Ticknor's "Spanish Literature," John Carlyle's Dante, Felton's Greece, George Sand's Consuelo, a very choice little Epictetus, some novels, the latest foreign and American monthlies, quarterlies, and so on. There being quite a strew of printer's proofs and slips, and the daily papers, the place with its quaint old fashion'd calmness has also a smack of something alert and of current work. There are several trunks and depositaries back'd up at the walls; (one well-bound and big box came by express lately from Washington city, after storage there for nearly twenty years.) Indeed the whole room is a sort of result and storage collection of my own past life. I have here various editions of my own writings, and sell them upon request; one is a big volume of complete poems and prose, 1000 pages, autograph, essays, speeches, portraits from life, &c. Another is a little *Leaves of Grass*, latest date, six portraits, morocco bound, in pocket-book form.

Fortunately the apartment is quite roomy. There are three windows in front. At one side is the stove, with a cheerful fire of oak wood, near by a good supply of fresh sticks, whose faint aroma is plain. On another side is the bed with white coverlid and woollen blankets. Toward the windows is a huge arm-chair, (a Christmas present from Thomas Donaldson's young daughter and son, Philadelphia) timber'd as by some stout ship's spars, yellow polish'd, ample, with rattan-woven seat and back, and over the latter a great wide wolf-skin of hairy black and silver, spread to guard against

79. primer,) some maps, the] Typescript: primer) the

80. Shakspere] Clip. (unrevised): Shakspeare

82. Sand's] Clip. (unrevised): Sands' [Typescript omits "George Sand's Consuelo", which was inserted in ink.]

82. In the typescript, "some novels" is inserted in ink.

84. slips, . . . the place] Clip. and *LIP:* slips, the place] Typescript: slips and printer's proofs, the place

87–88. The marks of parenthesis are inserted in the typescript.

89. of result] Typescript (unrevised): of a result

89–90. collection . . . various] Typescript: collection of its owners past life. He has the various

90. sell] Typescript: sells

91. "1000 pages," inserted in typescript in ink.

91. autograph,] Typescript (unrevised): autobiography,

93. date, six portraits, morocco] Typescript: date, morocco

94–95. in front.] Typescript: in the front.

97. with white] Clip., *LIP*, and Typescript: with snow white

97. coverlid] Typescript (unrevised): coverled

97. woollen] Typescript: woolen

97. After "blankets." the following sentence in the typescript is lined out in ink: "As I have often been in his room the whole description is from life."

97. Toward the windows is] Typescript: Towards the windows of the place is

cold and draught. A time-worn look and scent of old oak attach both to the chair and the person occupying it.

But probably (even at the charge of parrot talk) I can give no more authentic brief sketch than "from an old remembrance copy," where I have lately put myself on record as follows: Was born May 31, 1819, in my father's farm-house, at West Hills, L. I., New York State. My parents' folks mostly farmers and sailors— on my father's side, of English—on my mother's, (Van Velsor's) from Hollandic immigration. There was, first and last, a large family of children; (I was the second.) We moved to Brooklyn while I was still a little one in frocks—and there in B. I grew up out of frocks—then as child and boy went to the public schools—then to work in a printing office. When only sixteen or seventeen years old, and for three years afterward, I went to teaching country schools down in Queens and Suffolk counties, Long Island, and "boarded round." Then, returning to New York, work'd as printer and writer, (with an occasional shy at "poetry.")

1848–'9.—About this time—after ten or twelve years of experiences and work and lots of fun in New York and Brooklyn—went off on a leisurely journey and working expedition (my brother Jeff with me) through all the Middle States, and down the Ohio and Mississippi rivers. Lived a while in New Orleans, and work'd there. (Have lived quite a good deal in the Southern States.) After a time, plodded back northward, up the Mississippi, the Missouri, &c., and around to, and by way of, the great lakes, Michigan, Huron and Erie, to Niagara Falls and Lower Canada—finally

99. as by some] Typescript: as from some

100. rattan-woven] Clip. (unrevised) and LIP: ratan-woven] Typescript: satin woven [Revised to "ratan-woven".]

102. draught. A time-worn] Typescript: draught. Strength, plainness; ease and comfort with what may be called a time-worn

102. oak attach] Typescript: oak woods attach

103. After "occupying it." the following sentence in the typescript is lined out: "This is Walt Whitman the poet."

104. But probably . . . can] Clip. and LIP: But probably I can] Typescript: Probably we can [The words in parentheses are inserted in the clipping and do not appear earlier.]

105. sketch than "from] Typescript: sketch of W. W. than the one we get "from

105–106. copy," where . . . as follows:] Typescript: copy", he has lately put on record himself as follows: [Typescript begins a new paragraph after "as follows:".]

105–106. The "remembrance copy" was a sheet, two pages, containing autobiographical data, inserted in certain gift copies of MDW.

113. After "office." the typescript begins a new paragraph.

114. three years] Typescript and Remembrance Copy: two years

118–119. time—after . . . Brooklyn—went] Clip. and LIP: time—after . . . and fun and work in New York and Brooklyn—went] Typescript and Remembrance Copy: time went [Typescript revised to read: "time—after eight or nine years of experiences, and fun and work in New York and Brooklyn—went.]

returning through Central New York, and down the Hudson. 1852–'54—Occupied in house-building in Brooklyn. (For a little while of the first part of that time in printing a daily and weekly paper.)

1855.—Lost my dear father this year by death. . . . Commenced putting *Leaves of Grass* to press, for good—after many MSS. doings and undoings—(I had great trouble in leaving out the stock "poetical" touches—but succeeded at last.) The book has since had some eight hitches or stages of growth, with one annex, (and another to come out in 1891, which will complete it.)

1862.—In December of this year went down to the field of war in Virginia. My brother George reported badly wounded in the Fredericksburg fight. (For 1863 and '64, see *Specimen Days.*) 1865 to '71—Had a place as clerk (till well on in '73) in the Attorney General's Office, Washington. (New York and Brooklyn seem more like *home*, as I was born near, and brought up in them, and lived, man and boy, for 30 years. But I lived some years in Washington, and have visited, and partially lived, in most of the Western and Eastern cities.)

1873.—This year lost, by death, my dear dear mother—and, just before, my sister Martha—the two best and sweetest women I have ever seen or known, or ever expect to see. Same year, February, a sudden climax and prostration from paralysis. Had been simmering inside for several years; broke out during those times temporarily, and then went over. But now a serious attack, beyond cure. Dr. Drinkard, my Washington physician, (and a first-rate one,) said it was the result of too extreme bodily and

126. After "Hudson." the typescript and Remembrance Copy begin a new paragraph.

126. 1852–'54] Typescript (not revised): 1851–'54

130. MSS. doings] Clip. (unrevised), *LIP*, Typescript (unrevised), and Remembrance Copy: MS. doings

132–134. This sentence, a separate paragraph in the typescript, is not in the Remembrance Copy of *MDW* or the revised version of 1889.

137. The sentence in parentheses seems to have been added in a revision before 1891; it is not in the 1889 version.

137. Typescript and Remembrance Copy begin a new paragraph with the new date, "1865 to '71".

139–142. These lines were a separate paragraph in Typescript and Remembrance Copy of 1889.

144–145. Clip. (unrevised), *LIP*, Typescript (unrevised), and Remembrance Copy have marks of parenthesis before "the two" and after "to see." After "to see.)" Typescript and Remembrance Copy begin a new paragraph.

145. year, February, a] Typescript and Remembrance Copy: year, a

151–152. physique . . . ever] Typescript and Remembrance Copy: physique ever

152. 1835 to '72] Typescript and Remembrance Copy: 1840 to 1870

153–154. could there . . . among the sick] Clip., *LIP*, and Typescript (unrevised): could among the sick] Remembrance Copy: could among the suffering and sick

155–156. invulnerable.) . . . completely. Quit] Typescript and Remembrance

emotional strain continued at Washington and "down in front," in 1863, '4 and '5. I doubt if a heartier, stronger, healthier physique, more balanced upon itself, or more unconscious, more sound, ever lived, from 1835 to '72. My greatest call (Quaker) to go around and do what I could there in those war-scenes where I had fallen, among the sick and wounded, was, that I seem'd to be *so strong and well.* (I consider'd myself invulnerable.) But this last attack shatter'd me completely. Quit work at Washington, and moved to Camden, New Jersey—where I have lived since, receiving many buffets and some precious caresses—and now write these lines. Since then, (1874–'91) a long stretch of illness, or half-illness, with occasional lulls. During these latter, have revised and printed over all my books—Bro't out "November Boughs"—and at intervals leisurely and exploringly travel'd to the Prairie States, the Rocky Mountains, Canada, to New York, to my birthplace in Long Island, and to Boston. But physical disability and the war-paralysis above alluded to have settled upon me more and more, the last year or so. Am now (1891) domicil'd, and have been for some years, in this little old cottage and lot in Mickle Street, Camden, with a housekeeper and man nurse. Bodily I am completely disabled, but still write for publication. I keep generally buoyant spirits, write often as there comes any lull in physical sufferings, get in the sun and down to the river whenever I can, retain fair appetite, assimilation and digestion, sensibilities acute as ever, the strength and volition of my right arm good, eyesight dimming, but brain normal, and retain my heart's and soul's unmitigated faith not only in their own original literary plans, but in the essential bulk of Ameri-

Copy: invulnerable.) Quit

157–158. since, . . . now write] Typescript: since, and now, write] Remembrance Copy (1889): since, and now, (September, 1889,) write [After "caresses" (line 158), Clip., *LIP*, and revised Typescript have an asterisk referring to a footnote, deleted in *GBF*, for which see Appendix xv, 2.]

158–159. Since then, (1874–'91) a long] Clip. and *LIP:* Since then, (1874–'90) a long] Typescript after revision: Since then, (1874–'87) a long] Typescript before revision and Remembrance Copy (1889), beginning a new paragraph: (A long

159. with occasional lulls.] Typescript and Remembrance Copy (1889): with some lulls.

161. intervals . . . travel'd] Typescript and Remembrance Copy (1889): intervals travelled

165. Remembrance Copy ends with "so." Typescript begins a new paragraph and continues: "The poet now lived in his little

167. nurse, . . . completely] Typescript: nurse. His body is completely

167. write] Typescript: writes

168. After "publication." Clip., *LIP*, and Typescript (revised for *LIP*) have several lines deleted from *GBF*, for which see Appendix xv, 3.

168. write] Typescript: writes

169. get] Typescript: gets

171. strength and volition of my right] Typescript: strength of his right

172. retain . . . unmitigated] Typescript: retains unmitigated

173. in their own] Typescript: in my own

can humanity east and west, north and south, city and country, through thick and thin, to the last. Nor must I forget, in conclusion, a special, prayerful, thankful God's blessing to my dear firm friends and personal helpers, men and women, home and foreign, old and young.

From the Camden Post, April 16, '91.

OUT IN THE OPEN AGAIN.

Walt Whitman got out in the mid-April sun and warmth of yesterday, propelled in his wheel chair, the first time after four months of imprisonment in his sick room. He has had the worst winter yet, mainly from grippe and gastric troubles, and threaten'd blindness; but keeps good spirits, and has a new little forthcoming book in the printer's hands.

AMERICA'S BULK AVERAGE.

If I were ask'd *persona* to specify the one point of America's people on which I mainly rely, I should say the final average or bulk quality of the whole.

Happy indeed w'd I consider myself to give a fair reflection and representation of even a portion of shows, questions, humanity, events, unfoldings, thoughts, &c. &c. my age in these States.

The great social, political, historic function of my time has been of course the attempted Secession War.

And was there not something grand, and an inside proof of perennial grandeur, in that war! We talk of our age's and the States' materialism—and it is too true. But how amid the whole sordidness—the entire devotion of America, at any price, to pecuniary success, merchandise—disregarding all but business and profit—this war for a bare idea and abstraction—a mere, at bottom, heroic dream and reminiscence—burst forth in its great devouring flame and conflagration quickly and fiercely spreading and raging, and enveloping all, defining in two conflicting ideas—first the

174–175. through thick] Typescript: through (as he calls it) thick

175–177. This sentence, not in the Typescript, was added in ink, followed by "W W".

OUT IN THE OPEN AGAIN.

This section was not in the copy of the MS sent to the printer for *GBF*, either in autograph or as a clipping. Presumably it was inserted in the proof. (See, above, notes on "Splinters," and, below, notes on "America's Bulk Average.")

AMERICA'S BULK AVERAGE.

Printed in *GBF* from a page of autograph MS composed of three strips of paper pasted together, all in ink. This page, though next after 79 in the MS, was numbered "85," presumably at a time when the five lettered pages of "Old Actors

Union cause—second *the other*, a strange deadly interrogation point, hard to define—Can we not now safely confess it? with magnificent rays, streaks of noblest heroism, fortitude, perseverance, and even conscientiousness, through its pervadingly malignant darkness.

What an area and rounded field, upon the whole—the spirit, arrogance, grim tenacity of the South—the long stretches of murky gloom—the general National Will below and behind and comprehending all—not once really wavering, not a day, not an hour—What could be, or ever can be, grander?

As in that war, its four years—as through the whole history and development of the New World—these States through all trials, processes, eruptions, deepest dilemmas, (often straining, tugging at society's heart-strings, as if some divine curiosity would find out how much this democracy could stand,) have so far finally and for more than a century best justified themselves by the average impalpable quality and personality of the bulk, the People *en masse*. . . . I am not sure but my main and chief however indefinite claim for any page of mine w'd be its derivation, or seeking to derive itself, f'm that average quality of the American bulk, the people, and getting back to it again.

LAST SAVED ITEMS

f'm a vast batch left to oblivion.

In its highest aspect, and striking its grandest average, essential Poetry expresses and goes along with essential Religion—has been and is more the adjunct, and more serviceable to that true religion (for of course there is a false one and plenty of it,) than all the priests and creeds and churches that now exist or have ever existed—Even while the temporary prevalent theory and practice of poetry is merely one-side and ornamental and dainty—a love-sigh, a bit of jewelry, a feudal conceit, an ingenious tale or intellectual *finesse*, adjusted to the low taste and calibre that will always

. . . " were meant to follow the last page of "Some Personal and Old Age Jottings," which is 79. The original title was "America's Average." Whitman first inserted the word "Splendid," then crossed it out and wrote "Bulk." It is evident that the finished MS was composed by cutting away parts of three MS pages, pasting them at intervals on a base sheet, and interpolating new matter on the base sheet.

LAST SAVED ITEMS.

Printed from three pages of autograph MS, numbered A, B, and C, next after MS page 85. The first page consists of a small and a large sheet pasted on a larger base sheet; the second page is a single sheet; the third page is composed of seven small strips pasted together to form an extra long page. Between pages B and C of the MS there are a number of unrelated printer's bills and statements of costs, and so on. Apparently Whitman's MS page C was added as an afterthought.

sufficiently generally prevail—(ranges of stairs necessary to ascend the higher.)

The sectarian, church and doctrinal, follies, crimes, fanaticisms, aggregate and individual, so rife all thro' history, are proofs of the radicalness and universality of the indestructible element of humanity's Religion, just as much as any, and are the other side of it. Just as disease proves health, and is the other side of it.........The philosophy of Greece taught normality and the beauty of life. Christianity teaches how to endure illness and death. I have wonder'd whether a third philosophy fusing both, and doing full justice to both, might not be outlined.

It will not be enough to say that no Nation ever achiev'd materialistic, political and money-making successes, with general physical comfort, as fully as the United States of America are to-day achieving them. I know very well that those are the indispensable foundations—the *sine qua non* of moral and heroic (poetic) fruitions to come. For if those pre-successes were all—if they ended at that—if nothing more were yielded than so far appears—a gross materialistic prosperity only—America, tried by subtlest tests, were a failure—has not advanced the standard of humanity a bit further than other nations. Or, in plain terms, has but inherited and enjoy'd the results of ordinary claims and preceding ages.

Nature seem'd to use me a long while—myself all well, able, strong and happy—to portray power, freedom, health. But after a while she seems to fancy, may-be I can see and understand it all better by being deprived of most of those.

How difficult it is to add anything more to literature—and how unsatisfactory for any earnest spirit to serve merely the amusement of the multitude! (It even seems to me, said H. Heine, more invigorating to accomplish something bad than something empty.)

The Highest said: Don't let us begin so low—isn't our range too coarse—too gross?.........The Soul answer'd: No, not when we consider what it is all for—the end involved in Time and Space.

Essentially my own printed records, all my volumes, are doubtless but off-hand utterances f'm Personality, spontaneous, following implicitly the inscrutable command, dominated by that Personality, vaguely even if

30. portray] MS (unrevised): pourtray

40–47. This paragraph, written on a small sheet pasted to the right margin of the base sheet of page C and marked for insertion before the last paragraph, was evidently an afterthought.

decidedly, and with little or nothing of plan, art, erudition, &c. If I have chosen to hold the reins, the mastery, it has mainly been to give the way, the power, the road, to the invisible steeds. (I wanted to see how a Person of America, the last half of the 19th century, w'd appear, put quite freely and fairly in honest type.)

Haven't I given specimen clues, if no more? At any rate I have written enough to weary myself—and I will dispatch it to the printers, and cease. But how much—how many topics, of the greatest point and cogency, I am leaving untouch'd!

ILLUSTRATIONS

1. Photograph by Eakins, 1891; used by Whitman as the frontispiece of *Good-Bye My Fancy*. From the Feinberg Collection.

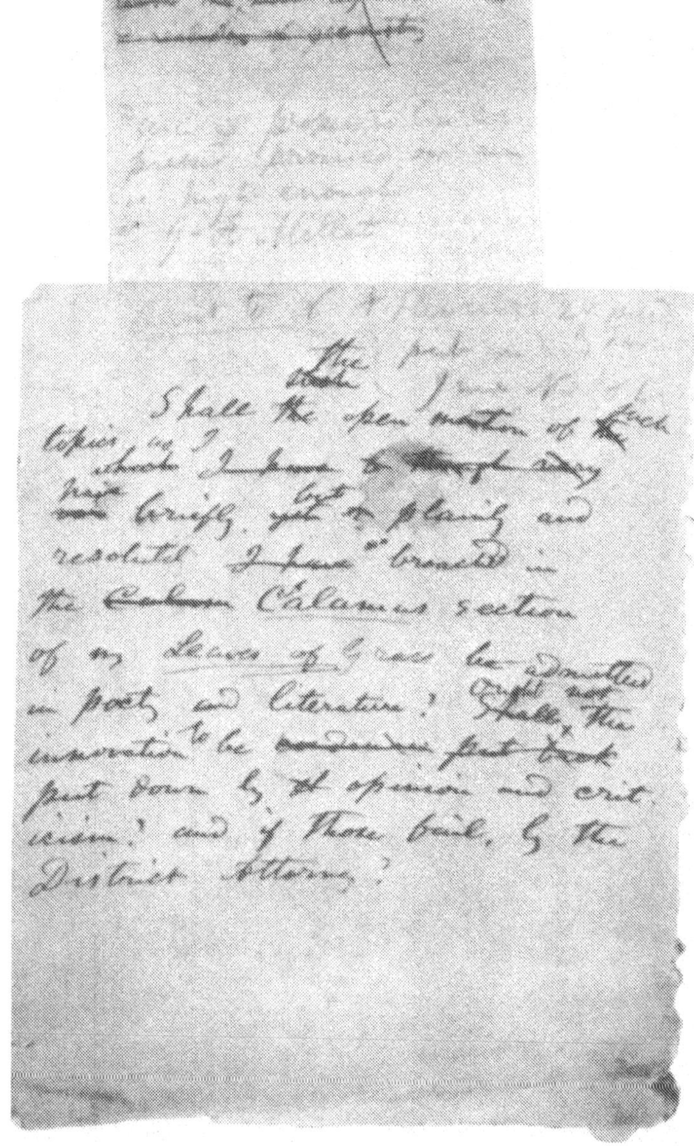

Shall the open mention of such topics as I have briefly yet plainly and resolutely broached in the Calamus section of my Leaves of Grass be admitted in poetry and literature? Ought not the innovation to be put down by the opinion and criticism? and if those fail, by the District Attorney?

2, 3, and 4. Facsimiles of the first three pages of an early manuscript of "A Memorandum at a Venture" (see pages 491–492). From the Feinberg Collection.

But I ~~[illegible]~~ would entrench myself more deeply & widely than that,

And
While

& I do not ask ~~the~~ any man to

~~believe any~~ favor ~~endorse~~ my theory —

I ~~am~~ ~~[illegible]~~ confident ~~[illegible]~~ anxious ask ~~them~~ to &

that what I ~~[illegible]~~ sought to ~~write~~ and express

and the grounds I build on, from its ~~[illegible]~~

shall be ~~at least~~ partially understood,

~~and the grounds I build upon~~

~~that I shall be have a chance~~

~~& that I shall not be~~

~~& that all the din false interfere~~

So far
and ~~Probably the~~ The best way

seems to me to confront the

question with ~~entire~~ perfect ~~candor~~ frankness.
entire

There are, generally speaking, two points of view for the world's attitude toward these matters; the first ~~that of~~ the conventional one ~~society~~, ~~and~~ of good ~~society~~ folks and good ~~literature~~ print ~~all lands almost all ages~~ everywhere, repressing any direct statement of them, and making allusions only at second ~~and~~ or third hand (as the Greeks did of death, which in Hellenic social culture was never mentioned point ~~b~~ blank but by euphemisms.)

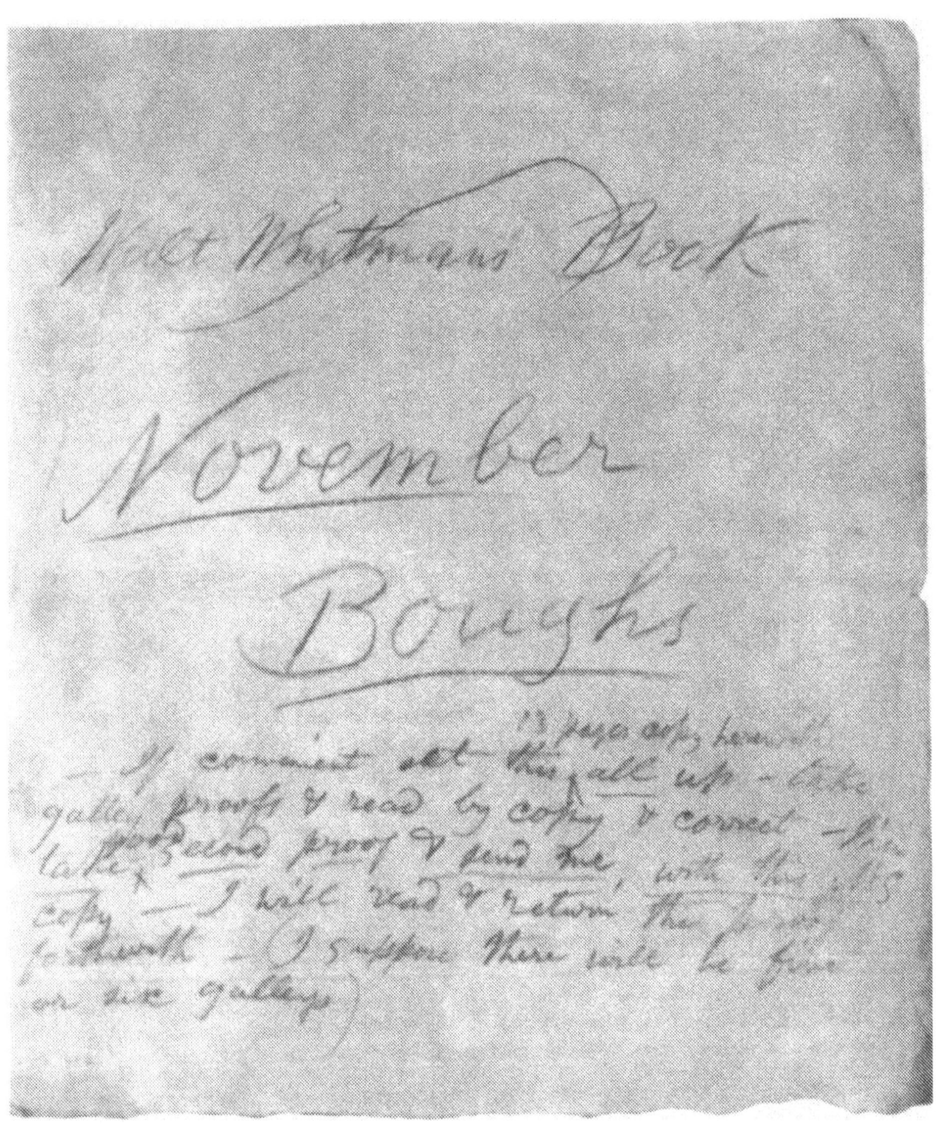

Walt Whitman's Book

November

Boughs

13 pages copy herewith

— If convenient set this all up — take
galley proofs & read by copy & correct — then
take a second proof & send me, with this
copy — I will read & return the proofs
forthwith — (I suppose there will be five
or six galleys)

5. Facsimile of the title page of the manuscript of *November Boughs*, with a note to the printer (see page 541). From the Feinberg Collection.

Elias Hicks

118 *PORTRAIT IN OLD AGE.*

Here is a portrait of E. H. from life, by Henry Inman, in New York, about 1827 or '28. The painting was finely copper-plated in 1830, and the present is a fac simile. Looks as I saw him in the following narrative.

The time was signalized by the *separation* of the Society of Friends, so greatly talked of—and continuing yet—but so little really explain'd. (All I give of this separation is in a Note following.)

BORN . . . . MARCH 19, 1748.

DIED . . . . FEBRUARY 20, 1830.

plate of Elias Hicks
portrait for illustration
Nov: Boughs
with specimen size page

6. Proof page of the plate of Elias Hicks, which appears as page 118 of *November Boughs*, opposite the first page of "Notes (such as they are) founded on Elias Hicks." Whitman's endorsement underneath the portrait was reproduced from a separate manuscript. From the Feinberg Collection.

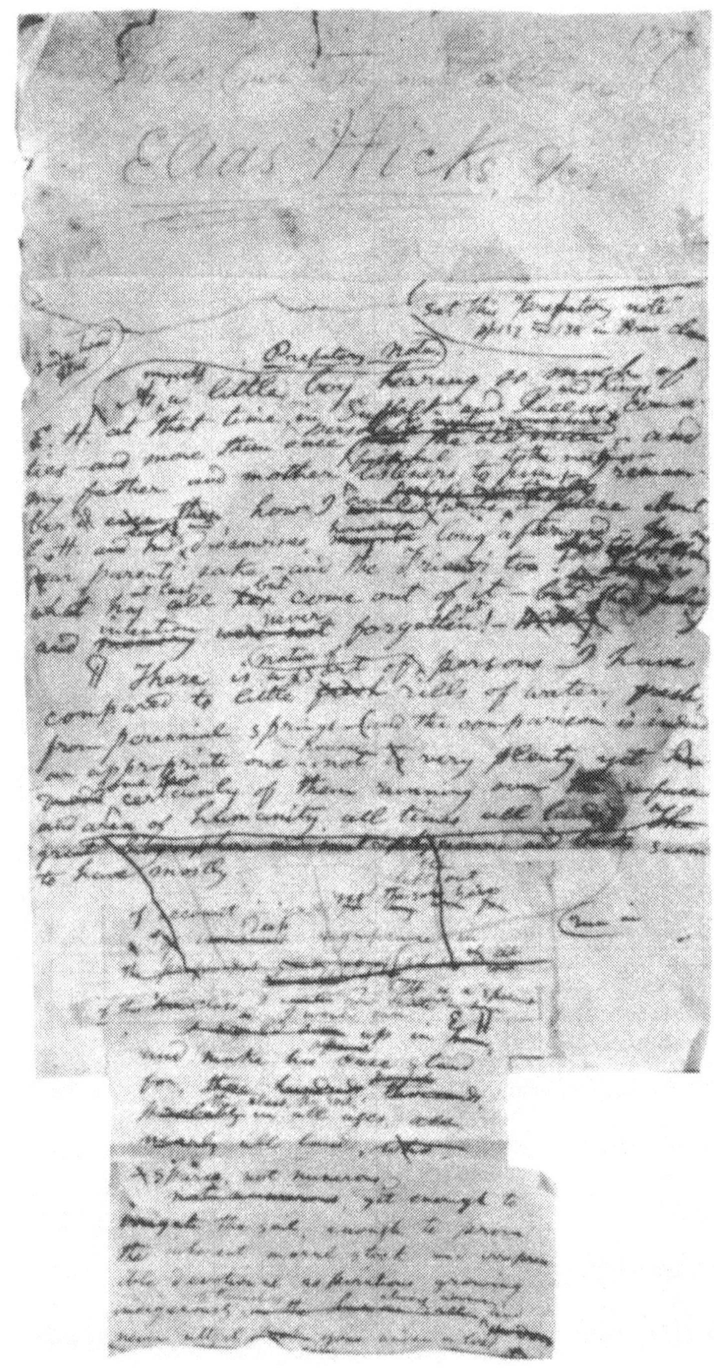

Elias Hicks &c.

Prefatory Note

7. Facsimile of the first page of an early manuscript of "Notes (such as they are) founded on Elias Hicks" (see pages 626–627). From the Feinberg Collection.

Prefaces and Notes Not Included in Complete Prose Works 1892.

A Backward Glance O'er Travel'd Roads.

Perhaps the best of songs heard, or of any and all true love, or life's fairest episodes, or sailors', soldiers' trying scenes on land or sea, is the *résumé* of them, or any of them, long afterwards, looking at the actualities

Prefaces and Notes Not Included in Complete Prose Works 1892.

The reasons for including the seven items in this group are stated in the preface to the present volume. The first five items, all really prefaces or prefatory notes, are arranged in chronological order and should be read in connection with the earlier prefaces in this volume, dated 1855, 1872, and 1876.

A Backward Glance O'er Travel'd Roads.

Printed in NB chiefly from two previously published essays: "My Book and I," LIP, January, 1887 (abbreviated MBI-LIP), and "How I Made a Book," PP, July 11, 1886 (abbreviated HMB-PP). A variant of this essay titled "How Leaves of Grass Was Made" was published in LPM, for June, 1892 (abbreviated HLGM-LPM), with a footnote stating that it was "from his own account of the genesis and purpose of 'Leaves of Grass,' as given in the New York *Star*, in 1885." The present editor has not found the essay in the *Star*. (See also *Walt Whitman's Backward Glances*, edited by Sculley Bradley and John A. Stevenson, p. 6, and Appendix XII of this volume.) A still earlier essay, "A Backward Glance on My Own Road," appeared in CR, January 5, 1884 (abbreviated BG-CR), and was in large part incorporated in the later essays (see Appendix XI). The MS from which this essay was printed is reproduced in *Walt Whitman's Backward Glances*. [The present editor has found the introduction and notes to that volume very helpful; his own notes, however, are based on a first-hand examination of the texts concerned.] MBI was reprinted intact, and HMB was reprinted with thc omission of the first five lines of the last paragraph, and BG was reprinted in a shortened form in DVOP (abbreviations, MBI-DVOP, HMB-DVOP, and BG-DVOP). HLGM-LPM is included in the collation on the assumption that it is an approximate reprinting of an earlier version (in the *Star* or elsewhere) published in Whitman's lifetime but not now available. "A Backward Glance O'er Travel'd Roads" in its final form (abbreviated BG-NB) was reprinted without change from the plates of NB in CPP and in the 1889 and 1892 editions of LG. It was not included in CPW 1892.

All the printed texts above named are collated in the notes. A set of galley proof sheets with a few autograph revisions, now in the Feinberg Collection, is also included in the collation. For paragraphs 1–2, 5, 7–10, and 16 of BG-CR, none of which were reprinted in BG-NB, see Appendix XI, 1–4.

1–270. Printed from the clipped pages of *MBI-LIP*.

1. of songs] *MBI-DVOP* and *MBI-LIP:* of a song

3. the *résumé*] *MBI-DVOP* and *MBI-LIP:* the floating *résumé*

away back past, with all their practical excitations gone. How the soul loves to float amid such reminiscences!

So here I sit gossiping in the early candle-light of old age—I and my book—casting backward glances over our travel'd road. After completing, as it were, the journey—(a varied jaunt of years, with many halts and gaps of intervals—or some lengthen'd ship-voyage, wherein more than once the last hour had apparently arrived, and we seem'd certainly going down—yet reaching port in a sufficient way through all discomfitures at last)—After completing my poems, I am curious to review them in the light of their own (at the time unconscious, or mostly unconscious) intentions, with certain unfoldings of the thirty years they seek to embody. These lines, therefore, will probably blend the weft of first purposes and speculations, with the warp of that experience afterwards, always bringing strange developments.

Result of seven or eight stages and struggles extending through nearly thirty years, (as I nigh my three-score-and-ten I live largely on memory,) I look upon "Leaves of Grass," now finish'd to the end of its opportunities and powers, as my definitive *carte visite* to the coming generations of the New World,* if I may assume to say so. That I have not gain'd the acceptance of my own time, but have fallen back on fond dreams of the future—anticipations—("still lives the song, though Regnar dies")—That from a worldly and business point of view "Leaves of Grass" has been worse than a failure—that public criticism on the book and myself as au-

* When Champollion, on his death-bed, handed to the printer the revised

2*n*. this—it] *MBI-DVOP* and *MBI-LIP:* this,—it

5. to float amid such] *MBI-DVOP* and *MBI-LIP:* to hover over such
8. journey—(a] *MBI-DVOP* and *MBI-LIP:* journey (a
11. down—yet] *MBI-DVOP* and *MBI-LIP:* down, yet
12. After *MBI-DVOP* and *MBI-LIP:* after [Changed in galley proof.]
12. poems, I] *MBI-DVOP* and *MBI-LIP:* poems, and letting an interval elapse to settle them, I
12. review them in] *MBI-DVOP* and *MBI-LIP:* review all in
19. The phrase in parenthesis is not in *MBI-DVOP* or *MBI-LIP.*
22–43. Versions of these lines appear in paragraph 13 of *BG-CR,* 9 of *BG-DVOP,* and 3 of *MBI-LIP* and *MBI-DVOP.*
22–31. For this sentence *BG-CR* and *BG-DVOP* have the following:

"That I have not been accepted during my own time—that the largely prevailing range of criticism on my book has been either mockery or denunciation—and that I, as its author, have been the marked object of two or three (to me pretty serious) official buffetings—is probably no more than I ought to have expected."

23–24. future—anticipations—("still] *MBI-DVOP* and *MBI-LIP:* future ("Still
24. The quotation is from the poem "Alfred the Harper," by John Sterling.
24. —That] *MBI-DVOP* and *MBI-LIP:* ,—that [Changed in galley proof.]

thor of it yet shows mark'd anger and contempt more than anything else—("I find a solid line of enemies to you everywhere,"—letter from W. S. K., Boston, May 28, 1884)—And that solely for publishing it I have been the object of two or three pretty serious special official buffetings—is all probably no more than I ought to have expected. I had my choice when I commenc'd. I bid neither for soft eulogies, big money returns, nor the approbation of existing schools and conventions. As fulfill'd, or partially fulfill'd, the best comfort of the whole business (after a small band of the dearest friends and upholders ever vouchsafed to man or cause—doubtless all the more faithful and uncomprising—this little phalanx!—for being so few) is that, unstopp'd and unwarp'd by any influence outside the soul within me, I have had my say entirely my own way, and put it unerringly on record—the value thereof to be decided by time.

In calculating that decision, William O'Connor and Dr. Bucke are far more peremptory than I am. Behind all else that can be said, I consider "Leaves of Grass" and its theory experimental—as, in the deepest sense, I consider our American republic itself to be, with its theory. (I think I have at least enough philosophy not to be too absolutely certain of any thing, or any results.) In the second place, the volume is a *sortie*—whether to prove triumphant, and conquer its field of aim and escape and construction, nothing less than a hundred years from now can fully answer. I consider the point that I have positively gain'd a hearing, to far more than make up for any and all other lacks and withholdings. Essentially, *that*

proof of his "Egyptian Grammar" he said gayly, "Be careful of this—it is my *carte de visite* to posterity."

26. failure—that public] *MBI-DVOP* and *MBI-LIP:* failure,—that after thirty years of trial public

27. it yet shows] *MBI-DVOP* and *MBI-LIP:* it shows

27–28. else—("I] *MBI-DVOP* and *MBI-LIP:* else ("I

29. 1884)—And] *MBI-DVOP* and *MBI-LIP:* 1884),—and

30. buffetings—is] *MBI-DVOP* and *MBI-LIP:* buffetings,—is

33–39. For this sentence *BG-CR* and *BG-DVOP* have the following: "As now fulfilled after thirty years, the best of the achievement is, that I have had my say entirely my own way, and put it unerringly on record—the value thereof to be decided by time."

35. cause—] *MBI-DVOP* and *MBI-LIP:* cause,—

39. record—] *MBI-DVOP* and *MBI-LIP:* record,—

40. William O'Connor and Dr. Bucke] *BG-DVOP* and *BG-CR:* Dr. Bucke and William O'Connor

41. more peremptory] *BG-DVOP* and *BG-CR:* more definite and peremptory

41–43. For this sentence *BG-DVOP* and *BG-CR* have the following: "I consider the whole thing experimental—as indeed, in a very large sense, I consider the American Republic itself, to be."

43–45. No marks of parenthesis in *MBI-DVOP* and *MBI-LIP;* inserted in galley proof.

45. *sortie*—] *MBI-DVOP* and *MBI-LIP:* *sortie*,—

was from the first, and has remain'd throughout, the main object. Now it seems to be achiev'd, I am certainly contented to waive any otherwise momentous drawbacks, as of little account. Candidly and dispassionately reviewing all my intentions, I feel that they were creditable—and I accept the result, whatever it may be.

After continued personal ambition and effort, as a young fellow, to enter with the rest into competition for the usual rewards, business, political, literary, &c.—to take part in the great *mêlée*, both for victory's prize itself and to do some good—After years of those aims and pursuits, I found myself remaining possess'd, at the age of thirty-one to thirty-three, with a special desire and conviction. Or rather, to be quite exact, a desire that had been flitting through my previous life, or hovering on the flanks, mostly indefinite hitherto, had steadily advanced to the front, defined itself, and finally dominated everything else. This was a feeling or ambition to articulate and faithfully express in literary or poetic form, and uncompromisingly, my own physical, emotional, moral, intellectual, and æsthetic Personality, in the midst of, and tallying, the momentous spirit and facts of its immediate days, and of current America—and to exploit that Personality, identified with place and date, in a far more candid and comprehensive sense than any hitherto poem or book.

Perhaps this is in brief, or suggests, all I have sought to do. Given the Nineteenth Century, with the United States, and what they furnish as area and points of view, "Leaves of Grass" is, or seeks to be, simply a faithful and doubtless self-will'd record. In the midst of all, it gives one man's—the author's—identity, ardors, observations, faiths, and thoughts, color'd hardly at all with any decided coloring from other faiths or other identities. Plenty of songs had been sung—beautiful, matchless songs—adjusted to other lands than these—another spirit and stage of evolution; but I

50–51. it seems to be achiev'd] *MBI-DVOP* and *MBI-LIP:* it is achieved

52–54. This sentence is not in *MBI-DVOP* or *MBI-LIP.*

57. *mêlée*] *BG-LG* 1892: *mèlée*] *BG-LG* 1889: *melée*] *BG-CPP* and *BG-NB: m lée*] *MBI-DVOP* and *MBI-LIP: mêlée* [The *MBI-DVOP* and *MBI-LIP* form was restored in *BG-LG* 1897.—ED.]

58. good—After] *MBI-DVOP* and *MBI-LIP:* good,—after

59. thirty-one to thirty-three] *MBI-DVOP* and *MBI-LIP:* thirty-three to thirty-five

60–61. desire that had been flitting] *MBI-DVOP* and *MBI-LIP:* desire and conviction that had been more or less flitting

64. literary or poetic form] *MBI-DVOP* and *MBI-LIP:* literary form

67–68. Personality . . . in] *MBI–DVOP* and *MBI-LIP:* Personality in

69. hitherto poem or book.] *MBI–DVOP* and *MBI-LIP:* hitherto book.

71. area] *MBI-DVOP:* areas

75–76. any decided . . . identities. Plenty] *MBI-DVOP* and *MBI-LIP:* any coloring from other faiths, other authors, other identities or times. Plenty

77. these—another] *MBI-DVOP* and *MBI-LIP:* these—other days, another

78–79. in, quite . . . to-day.] *MBI-DVOP* and *MBI-LIP:* in, solely with refer-

would sing, and leave or put in, quite solely with reference to America and to-day. Modern science and democracy seem'd to be throwing out their challenge to poetry to put them in its statements in contradistinction to the songs and myths of the past. As I see it now (perhaps too late,) I have unwittingly taken up that challenge and made an attempt at such statements —which I certainly would not assume to do now, knowing more clearly what it means.

For grounds for "Leaves of Grass," as a poem, I abandon'd the conventional themes, which do not appear in it: none of the stock ornamentation, or choice plots of love or war, or high, exceptional personages of Old-World song; nothing, as I may say, for beauty's sake—no legend, or myth, or romance, nor euphemism, nor rhyme. But the broadest average of humanity and its identities in the now ripening Nineteenth Century, and especially in each of their countless examples and practical occupations in the United States to-day.

One main contrast of the ideas behind every page of my verses, compared with establish'd poems, is their different relative attitude towards God, towards the objective universe, and still more (by reflection, confession, assumption, &c.) the quite changed attitude of the ego, the one chanting or talking, towards himself and towards his fellow-humanity. It is certainly time for America, above all, to begin this readjustment in the scope and basic point of view of verse; for everything else has changed. As I write, I see in an article on Wordsworth, in one of the current English magazines, the lines, "A few weeks ago an eminent French critic said that, owing to the special tendency to science and to its all-devouring force, poetry would cease to be read in fifty years." But I anticipate the very contrary. Only a firmer, vastly broader, new area begins to exist—nay, is already form'd—to which the poetic genius must emigrate. Whatever may

ence to America and myself and to-day.

85. as a poem, I abandon'd] *MBI-DVOP* and *MBI-LIP:* as poetry, I have abandoned

93–97. These lines first appeared in the first sentence of paragraph 11 of *BG-CR.*

93. For this line through "verses," *BG-CR* has: "The principal contrast and unlikeness of the personality behind every page of 'Leaves of Grass.' "

94. with establish'd] *BG-CR:* with the personality-sources of established

94–95. is their . . . universe, and] *BG-CR:* is undoubtedly the different relative *attitude* toward the universe, toward humanity, and

96. the quite changed attitude] *BG-CR:* the attitude

97. towards himself and towards his fellow-humanity.] *BG-CR:* toward himself.

99. scope . . . verse; for] *MBI-DVOP* and *MBI-LIP:* scope of verse, for

101–103. Quotation is from "Wordsworth's Relations to Science," by R. Spence Watson; originally in *Macmillan's Magazine* (Vol. 50, p. 202); reprinted in Littell's *Living Age*, Vol. 162, August 2, 1884, quotation on page 300. Whitman is most likely to have seen it in *Living Age.*

102. the special tendency to science] *Living Age:* the specializing tendency of science

have been the case in years gone by, the true use for the imaginative faculty of modern times is to give ultimate vivification to facts, to science, and to common lives, endowing them with the glows and glories and final illustriousness which belong to every real thing, and to real things only. Without that ultimate vivification—which the poet or other artist alone can give—reality would seem incomplete, and science, democracy, and life itself, finally in vain.

Few appreciate the moral revolutions, our age, which have been profounder far than the material or inventive or war-produced ones. The Nineteenth Century, now well towards its close (and ripening into fruit the seeds of the two preceding centuries*)—the uprisings of national masses and shiftings of boundary-lines—the historical and other prominent facts of the United States—the war of attempted Secession—the stormy rush and haste of nebulous forces—never can future years witness more excitement and din of action—never completer change of army front along the whole line, the whole civilized world. For all these new and evolutionary facts, meanings, purposes, new poetic messages, new forms and expressions, are inevitable.

My Book and I—what a period we have presumed to span! those thirty years from 1850 to '80—and America in them! Proud, proud indeed may we be, if we have cull'd enough of that period in its own spirit to worthily waft a few live breaths of it to the future!

Let me not dare, here or anywhere, for my own purposes, or any purposes, to attempt the definition of Poetry, nor answer the question what it is. Like Religion, Love, Nature, while those terms are indispensable, and we all give a sufficiently accurate meaning to them, in my opinion no definition that has ever been made sufficiently encloses the name Poetry;

* The ferment and germination even of the United States to-day, dating back to, and in my opinion mainly founded on, the Elizabethan age in English

6*n*. Shakspere] *MBI-DVOP* and *MBI-LIP:* Shakespeare

117. boundary-lines] *MBI-DVOP:* boundary lines
118. the war of attempted Secession] *MBI-DVOP* and *MBI-LIP:* the Secession War
122. new poetic messages] *MBI-DVOP* and *MBI-LIP:* new messages
128–129. anywhere, . . . definition] *MBI-DVOP* and *MBI-LIP:* anywhere, to attempt any definition
131. them, . . . no] *MBI-DVOP* and *MBI-LIP:* them, no
137–138. always curiously from] *MBI-DVOP* and *MBI-LIP:* always from
139. controling] *MBI-DVOP* and *MBI-LIP:* controlling
141. some fine plot] *MBI-DVOP* and *MBI-LIP:* some plot
141–142. or pensive] *MBI-DVOP* and *MBI-LIP:* or some pensive

nor can any rule or convention ever so absolutely obtain but some great exception may arise and disregard and overturn it.

Also it must be carefully remember'd that first-class literature does not shine by any luminosity of its own; nor do its poems. They grow of circumstances, and are evolutionary. The actual living light is always curiously from elsewhere—follows unaccountable sources, and is lunar and relative at the best. There are, I know, certain controling themes that seem endlessly appropriated to the poets—as war, in the past—in the Bible, religious rapture and adoration—always love, beauty, some fine plot, or pensive or other emotion. But, strange as it may sound at first, I will say there is something striking far deeper and towering far higher than those themes for the best elements of modern song.

Just as all the old imaginative works rest, after their kind, on long trains of presuppositions, often entirely unmention'd by themselves, yet supplying the most important bases of them, and without which they could have had no reason for being, so "Leaves of Grass," before a line was written, presupposed something different from any other, and, as it stands, is the result of such presupposition. I should say, indeed, it were useless to attempt reading the book without first carefully tallying that preparatory background and quality in the mind. Think of the United States to-day—the facts of these thirty-eight or forty empires solder'd in one—sixty or seventy millions of equals, with their lives, their passions, their future—these incalculable, modern, American, seething multitudes around us, of which we are inseparable parts! Think, in comparison, of the petty environage and limited area of the poets of past or present Europe, no matter how great their genius. Think of the absence and ignorance, in all cases hitherto, of the multitudinousness, vitality, and the unprecedented stimu-

history, the age of Francis Bacon and Shakspere. Indeed, when we pursue it, what growth or advent is there that does not date back, back, until lost—perhaps its most tantalizing clues lost—in the receded horizons of the past?

8*n*. the receded horizons] *MBI-DVOP:* the recorded horizons

144. the best elements] *MBI-DVOP* and *MBI-LIP:* the elements
152–158. These lines first used in the third and fourth sentences of *BG-CR*, paragraph 14.
152–153. Think . . . facts] *BG-CR* and *BG-DVOP:* There is always an invisible background to a high-intentioned book—the palimpsest on which every page is written. Apply this to my volume. The facts
153–154. sixty or seventy] *MBI-DVOP*, *MBI-LIP*, *BG-DVOP*, and *BG-CR:* fifty or sixty
155. incalculable . . . seething] *MBI-DVOP* and *MBI-LIP:* incalculable and seething] *BG-DVOP* and *BG-CR:* incalculable areas and seething
155. us, of] *MBI-DVOP*, *MBI-LIP*, *BG-DVOP*, and *BG-CR:* us, and of

lants of to-day and here. It almost seems as if a poetry with cosmic and dynamic features of magnitude and limitlessness suitable to the human soul, were never possible before. It is certain that a poetry of absolute faith and equality for the use of the democratic masses never was.

In estimating first-class song, a sufficient Nationality, or, on the other hand, what may be call'd the negative and lack of it, (as in Goethe's case, it sometimes seems to me,) is often, if not always, the first element. One needs only a little penetration to see, at more or less removes, the material facts of their country and radius, with the coloring of the moods of humanity at the time, and its gloomy or hopeful prospects, behind all poets and each poet, and forming their birth-marks. I know very well that my "Leaves" could not possibly have emerged or been fashion'd or completed, from any other era than the latter half of the Nineteenth Century, nor any other land than democratic America, and from the absolute triumph of the National Union arms.

And whether my friends claim it for me or not, I know well enough, too, that in respect to pictorial talent, dramatic situations, and especially in verbal melody and all the conventional technique of poetry, not only the divine works that to-day stand ahead in the world's reading, but dozens more, transcend (some of them immeasurably transcend) all I have done, or could do. But it seem'd to me, as the objects in Nature, the themes of æstheticism, and all special exploitations of the mind and soul, involve not only their own inherent quality, but the quality, just as inherent and important, of *their point of view*,* the time had come to reflect all themes and things, old and new, in the lights thrown on them by the advent of America

* According to Immanuel Kant, the last essential reality, giving shape

160–162. poetry . . . were] *MBI-DVOP* and *MBI-LIP:* poetry with anything like cosmic features were

163. the democratic masses never] *MBI-DVOP* and *MBI-LIP:* the modern never

171–172. emerged . . . from] *MBI-DVOP* and *MBI-LIP:* emerged from

173. than democratic America] *MBI-DVOP* and *MBI-LIP:* than America

175–201. These lines first appeared as the last part of paragraph 11 of *BG-CR;* omitted in *BG-DVOP.*

175. And whether] *BG-CR:* Whether

175–176. I know . . . that] *BG-CR:* I feel certain that

176. talent, dramatic] *BG-CR:* talent, description, dramatic

178. divine works . . . but] *BG-CR:* divine work already alluded to, but

180–185. seem'd to me . . . new, in] *BG-CR:* seemed to me the time had arrived to reflect those same old themes and things in

186–190. democracy—to . . . literature. Not] *BG-CR:* Democracy—that such illustration, as far as its statement is concerned, is now and here a chief demand of imaginative literature—and that the New World is the most fitting place for its trial, its attempt in original song. Not

188–189. to-day; and] *MBI-DVOP* and *MBI-LIP:* to-day—and

and democracy—to chant those themes through the utterance of one, not only the grateful and reverent legatee of the past, but the born child of the New World—to illustrate all through the genesis and ensemble of to-day; and that such illustration and ensemble are the chief demands of America's prospective imaginative literature. Not to carry out, in the approved style, some choice plot of fortune or misfortune, or fancy, or fine thoughts, or incidents, or courtesies—all of which has been done overwhelmingly and well, probably never to be excell'd—but that while in such æsthetic presentation of objects, passions, plots, thoughts, &c., our lands and days do not want, and probably will never have, anything better than they already possess from the bequests of the past, it still remains to be said that there is even towards all those a subjective and contemporary point of view appropriate to ourselves alone, and to our new genius and environments, different from anything hitherto; and that such conception of current or gone-by life and art is for us the only means of their assimilation consistent with the Western world.

Indeed, and anyhow, to put it specifically, has not the time arrived when, (if it must be plainly said, for democratic America's sake, if for no other) there must imperatively come a readjustment of the whole theory and nature of Poetry? The question is important, and I may turn the argument over and repeat it: Does not the best thought of our day and Republic conceive of a birth and spirit of song superior to anything past or present? To the effectual and moral consolidation of our lands (already, as materially establish'd, the greatest factors in known history, and far, far greater through what they prelude and necessitate, and are to be in future)—to

and significance to all the rest.

191. plot . . . fancy] *MBI-DVOP*, *MBI-LIP*, and *BG-CR:* plot or fancy
191–193. fancy, or fine . . . but that while] *BG-CR:* fancy, nor to portray the passions, or the beautiful, or love, or fine thoughts, or incidents, or aspirations, or courtesies (all of which has been done overwhelmingly and well, probably never to be excelled). But while
197. towards all those] *BG-CR:* toward all these
197. and contemporary point] *MBI-DVOP*, *MBI-LIP*, and *BG-CR:* and democratic point
199. hitherto; and] *MBI-DVOP* and *MBI-LIP:* hitherto, and] *BG-CR:* hitherto—and
199–200. such . . . life] *MBI-DVOP* and *MBI-LIP:* such conception of current life] *BG-CR:* such point of view toward all current life
201. with the Western world.] *BG-CR:* with the modern and scientific spirit, in our Western World.
203–204. when . . . there] *MBI-DVOP* and *MBI-LIP:* when, for highest current and future aims, there
206–207. day and Republic conceive] *MBI-DVOP* and *MBI-LIP:* day conceive
208. of our lands] *MBI-DVOP* and *MBI-LIP:* of America
209. factors] *MBI-DVOP* and *MBI-LIP:* factor

conform with and build on the concrete realities and theories of the universe furnish'd by science, and henceforth the only irrefragable basis for anything, verse included—to root both influences in the emotional and imaginative action of the modern time, and dominate all that precedes or opposes them—is not either a radical advance and step forward, or a new verteber of the best song indispensable?

The New World receives with joy the poems of the antique, with European feudalism's rich fund of epics, plays, ballads—seeks not in the least to deaden or displace those voices from our ear and area—holds them indeed as indispensable studies, influences, records, comparisons. But though the dawn-dazzle of the sun of literature is in those poems for us of to-day—though perhaps the best parts of current character in nations, social groups, or any man's or woman's individuality, Old World or New, are from them—and though if I were ask'd to name the most precious bequest to current American civilization from all the hitherto ages, I am not sure but I would name those old and less old songs ferried hither from east and west—some serious words and debits remain; some acrid considerations demand a hearing. Of the great poems receiv'd from abroad and from the ages, and to-day enveloping and penetrating America, is there one that is consistent with these United States, or essentially applicable to them as they are and are to be? Is there one whose underlying basis is not a denial and insult to democracy? What a comment it forms, anyhow, on this era of literary fulfilment, with the splendid day-rise of science and resuscitation of history, that our chief religious and poetical works are not our own, nor adapted to our light, but have been furnish'd by far-back ages out of their arriere and darkness, or, at most, twilight dimness! What is there in those works that so imperiously and scornfully dominates all our advanced civilization, and culture?

Even Shakspere, who so suffuses current letters and art (which indeed have in most degrees grown out of him,) belongs essentially to the buried past. Only he holds the proud distinction for certain important phases of that past, of being the loftiest of the singers life has yet given voice to. All,

210. they prelude and necessitate, and are] *MBI-DVOP* and *MBI-LIP:* it preludes and necessitates, and is

212. by science] *MBI-DVOP* and *MBI-LIP:* by modern science

212. and henceforth the] *MBI-DVOP* and *MBI-LIP:* and the

214. action . . . dominate] *MBI-DVOP* and *MBI-LIP:* action of our time and any time, and dominate

215. not . . . verteber] *MBI-DVOP* and *MBI-LIP:* not a radically new verteber

218. least] *NB:* last

219. our ear and] *MBI-DVOP* and *MBI-LIP:* our present time and

222. though perhaps the] *MBI-DVOP* and *MBI-LIP:* though the

225. to current American] *MBI-DVOP* and *MBI-LIP:* to American

232–238. These lines appear as paragraph 6 of *BG-CR* and 4 of *BG-DVOP*.

232. it forms . . . era] *BG-DVOP* and *BG-CR:* it is on our era

however, relate to and rest upon conditions, standards, politics, sociologies, ranges of belief, that have been quite eliminated from the Eastern hemisphere, and never existed at all in the Western. As authoritative types of song they belong in America just about as much as the persons and institutes they depict. True, it may be said, the emotional, moral, and æsthetic natures of humanity have not radically changed—that in these the old poems apply to our times and all times, irrespective of date; and that they are of incalculable value as pictures of the past. I willingly make those admissions, and to their fullest extent; then advance the points herewith as of serious, even paramount importance.

I have indeed put on record elsewhere my reverence and eulogy for those never-to-be-excell'd poetic bequests, and their indescribable preciousness as heirlooms for America. Another and separate point must now be candidly stated. If I had not stood before those poems with uncover'd head, fully aware of their colossal grandeur and beauty of form and spirit, I could not have written "Leaves of Grass." My verdict and conclusions as illustrated in its pages are arrived at through the temper and inculcation of the old works as much as through anything else—perhaps more than through anything else. As America fully and fairly construed is the legitimate result and evolutionary outcome of the past, so I would dare to claim for my verse. Without stopping to qualify the averment, the Old World has had the poems of myths, fictions, feudalism, conquest, caste, dynastic wars, and splendid exceptional characters and affairs, which have been great; but the New World needs the poems of realities and science and of the democratic average and basic equality, which shall be greater. In the centre of all, and object of all, stands the Human Being, towards whose heroic and spiritual evolution poems and everything directly or indirectly tend, Old World or New.

Continuing the subject, my friends have more than once suggested—or may be the garrulity of advancing age is possessing me—some further embryonic facts of "Leaves of Grass," and especially how I enter'd upon

234–235. not our . . . but have] *MBI-DVOP* and *MBI-LIP:* not our own, but have] *BG-DVOP* and *BG-CR:* not its own, but have

236. their . . . twilight dimness!] *MBI-DVOP* and *MBI-LIP:* their . . . twilight!] *BG-DVOP* and *BG-CR:* their darkness and ignorance—or, at most, twilight!

237–238. our . . . culture?] *MBI-DVOP*, *MBI-LIP*, *BG-DVOP*, and *BG-CR:* our advancement, boasted civilization, and culture?

239. current letters and] *MBI-DVOP* and *MBI-LIP:* current literature and

240. him,) belongs] *MBI-DVOP* and *MBI-LIP:* him), he too belongs

248. not radically changed] *MBI-DVOP* and *MBI-LIP:* not changed

270. With this line, followed by Whitman's name, ends *MBI-LIP*. *MBI-DVOP* also ends with this line.

271–510. The printer's copy from which these lines were set is not available, per-

them. Dr. Bucke has, in his volume, already fully and fairly described the preparation of my poetic field, with the particular and general plowing, planting, seeding, and occupation of the ground, till everything was fertilized, rooted, and ready to start its own way for good or bad. Not till after all this, did I attempt any serious acquaintance with poetic literature. Along in my sixteenth year I had become possessor of a stout, well-cramm'd one thousand page octavo volume (I have it yet,) containing Walter Scott's poetry entire—an inexhaustible mine and treasury of poetic forage (especially the endless forests and jungles of notes)—has been so to me for fifty years, and remains so to this day.*

Later, at intervals, summers and falls, I used to go off, sometimes for a week at a stretch, down in the country, or to Long Island's seashores—there, in the presence of outdoor influences, I went over thoroughly the Old and New Testaments, and absorb'd (probably to better advantage for me than in any library or indoor room—it makes such difference *where* you read,) Shakspere, Ossian, the best translated versions I could get of Homer, Eschylus, Sophocles, the old German Nibelungen, the ancient Hindoo poems, and one or two other masterpieces, Dante's among them. As it happen'd, I read the latter mostly in an old wood. The Iliad (Buckley's prose version,) I read first thoroughly on the peninsula of Orient, north-east end of Long Island, in a shelter'd hollow of rocks and sand, with the sea on each side. (I have wonder'd since why I was not overwhelm'd by

* Sir Walter Scott's COMPLETE POEMS; especially including BORDER MINSTRELSY; then Sir Tristrem; Lay of the Last Minstrel; Ballads from the German; Marmion; Lady of the Lake; Vision of Don Roderick; Lord of the Isles; Rokeby; Bridal of Triermain; Field of Waterloo; Harold the Dauntless;

11*n*–19*n*. This footnote appeared for the first time in *BG-NB*.

haps has not survived; they were probably printed from clippings of "How I Made a Book," *PP*, July 11, 1886. Most of this part of the essay is in *HMB-DVOP* and *HLGM-LPM*, and brief passages had previously appeared in *BG-CR* and *BG-DVOP*. All texts are collated.

271. Continuing the subject, my friends] *HMB-DVOP*, *HMB-PP*, and *HLGM-LPM:* My friends

271–272. *HLGM-LPM* has marks of parenthesis inside the dashes.

273. and especially how] *HMB-DVOP*, *HMB-PP*, and *HLGM-LPM:* and how

274. has, in his volume, already] *HMB-DVOP*, *HMB-PP*, and *HLGM-LPM:* has already

277–278. This sentence not in *HMB-DVOP* and *HMB-PP*. In place of it *HLGM-LPM* has the sentence: "Not until after this was all settled did I begin any definite and serious acquaintance, or attempt at acquaintance, with poetic literature."

279. *HMB-DVOP* and *HMB-PP* begin a new paragraph with "Along in my".

281. poetic forage] *HMB-DVOP*, *HMB-PP*, and *HLGM-LPM:* poetic study.

284. intervals . . . I] *HMB-DVOP*, *HMB-PP*, and *HLGM-LPM:* intervals, I

those mighty masters. Likely because I read them, as described, in the full presence of Nature, under the sun, with the far-spreading landscape and vistas, or the sea rolling in.)

Toward the last I had among much else look'd over Edgar Poe's poems—of which I was not an admirer, tho' I always saw that beyond their limited range of melody (like perpetual chimes of music bells, ringing from lower *b* flat up to *g*) they were melodious expressions, and perhaps never excell'd ones, of certain pronounc'd phases of human morbidity. (The Poetic area is very spacious—has room for all—has so many mansions!) But I was repaid in Poe's prose by the idea that (at any rate for our occasions, our day) there can be no such thing as a long poem. The same thought had been haunting my mind before, but Poe's argument, though short, work'd the sum out and proved it to me.

Another point had an early settlement, clearing the ground greatly. I saw, from the time my enterprise and questionings positively shaped themselves (how best can I express my own distinctive era and surroundings, America, Democracy?) that the trunk and centre whence the answer was to radiate, and to which all should return from straying however far a distance, must be an identical body and soul, a personality—which personality, after many considerations and ponderings I deliberately settled should be myself—indeed could not be any other. I also felt strongly (whether I have shown it or not) that to the true and full estimate of the

all the Dramas; various Introductions, endless interesting Notes, and Essays on Poetry, Romance, &c.

Lockhart's 1833 (or '34) edition with Scott's latest and copious revisions and annotations. (All the poems were thoroughly read by me, but the ballads of the Border Minstrelsy over and over again.)

285–286. seashores—there] *HLGM-LPM:* seashores; there
289. Shakspere] *HMB-PP:* Shakspeare
289. best translated versions] *HMB-DVOP*, *HMB-PP*, and *HLGM-LPM:* best versions
295–298. These lines not enclosed in parentheses in other texts.
298. After "rolling in." *HLGM-LPM* continues the paragraph with a passage not in other texts. See Appendix XII, 1.
299. For the next three paragraphs *HMB-PP* has the subtitle: "Two Points Early Settled."
300. of which] *HMB-PP* and *HLGM-LPM:* of whom
302. were melodious expressions] *HMB-DVOP*, *HMB-PP*, and *HLGM-LPM:* were expressions
304. spacious . . . has so] *HMB-DVOP*, *HMB-PP*, and *HLGM-LPM:* spacious—has
306. occasions, our] *HMB-DVOP:* occasion, our] *HMB-PP* and *HLGM-LPM:* occasion and our
311. own distinctive era] *HMB-DVOP*, *HMB-PP*, and *HLGM-LPM:* own era
316. After "be any other." *HLGM-LPM* continues the paragraph with a passage not found in any other text. See Appendix XII, 2.
316. I also felt] *HMB-DVOP*, *HMB-PP*, and *HLGM-LPM:* I felt

Present both the Past and the Future are main considerations.

These, however, and much more might have gone on and come to naught (almost positively would have come to naught,) if a sudden, vast, terrible, direct and indirect stimulus for new and national declamatory expression had not been given to me. It is certain, I say, that, although I had made a start before, only from the occurrence of the Secession War, and what it show'd me as by flashes of lightning, with the emotional depths it sounded and arous'd (of course, I don't mean in my own heart only, I saw it just as plainly in others, in millions)—that only from the strong flare and provocation of that war's sights and scenes the final reasons-for-being of an autochthonic and passionate song definitely came forth.

I went down to the war fields in Virginia (end of 1862), lived thenceforward in camp—saw great battles and the days and nights afterward—partook of all the fluctuations, gloom, despair, hopes again arous'd, courage evoked—death readily risk'd—*the cause*, too—along and filling those agonistic and lurid following years, 1863–'64–'65—the real parturition years (more than 1776–'83) of this henceforth homogeneous Union. Without those three or four years and the experiences they gave, "Leaves of Grass" would not now be existing.

But I set out with the intention also of indicating or hinting some point-characteristics which I since see (though I did not then, at least not definitely) were bases and object-urgings toward those "Leaves" from the first. The word I myself put primarily for the description of them as

319. At this point *HLGM-LPM* has the centered divisional number II.

321–322. national declamatory expression] *HMB-DVOP*, *HMB-PP*, and *HLGM-LPM:* national poetic expression

322–323. *HLGM-LPM* has a dash before "although" and before "only".

325. *HLGM-LPM* has a period after "only", possibly a misprint for a comma.

328. autochthonic and passionate song] *HMB-DVOP:* autochthonic American song] *HMB-PP* and *HLGM-LPM:* autochthonic song

328. After "came forth." *HLGM-LPM* continues in the same paragraph.

329. For the next four paragraphs *HMB-PP* has the subtitle "Suggestiveness."

329. fields] *HMB-DVOP*, *HMB-PP*, and *HLGM-LPM:* field

330–331. afterward—partook of all] *HMB-DVOP*, *HMB-PP*, and *HLGM-LPM:* afterward—all

333. lurid following years] *HMB-DVOP*, *HMB-PP*, and *HLGM-LPM:* lurid years

335–336. years . . . would] *HMB-DVOP:* years, my "Leaves of Grass," as they stand, would] *HMB-PP:* years my "Leaves of Grass" would] *HLGM-LPM:* years, and my experience in them, and all that went along with them, and the national victory that ended them, my "Leaves of Grass"—(I don't mean its pictures and pieces in "Drum Taps" only, and parts of its text, but the whole spirit and body as they stand)—would

336. After "existing." *HLGM-LPM* ends the paragraph with the following sentence, not in any other text: "I am fain sometimes to think of the book as a whirling wheel, with the War of 1861–5 as the hub on which it all concentrates and revolves."

they stand at last, is the word Suggestiveness. I round and finish little, if anything; and could not, consistently with my scheme. The reader will always have his or her part to do, just as much as I have had mine. I seek less to state or display any theme or thought, and more to bring you, reader, into the atmosphere of the theme or thought—there to pursue your own flight. Another impetus-word is Comradeship as for all lands, and in a more commanding and acknowledg'd sense than hitherto. Other word-signs would be Good Cheer, Content, and Hope.

The chief trait of any given poet is always the spirit he brings to the observation of Humanity and Nature—the mood out of which he contemplates his subjects. What kind of temper and what amount of faith report these things? Up to how recent a date is the song carried? What the equipment, and special raciness of the singer—what his tinge of coloring? The last value of artistic expressers, past and present—Greek æsthetes, Shakspere—or in our own day Tennyson, Victor Hugo, Carlyle, Emerson—is certainly involv'd in such questions. I say the profoundest service that poems or any other writings can do for their reader is not merely to satisfy the intellect, or supply something polish'd and interesting, nor even to depict great passions, or persons or events, but to fill him with vigorous and clean manliness, religiousness, and give him *good heart* as a radical possession and habit. The educated world seems to have been growing more and more ennuyed for ages, leaving to our time the inheritance of it all. Fortunately there is the original inexhaustible fund of buoyancy, normally

339. and object-urgings] *HMB-DVOP*, *HMB-PP*, and *HLGM-LPM:* and urgings

340–342. This is similar to the first two sentences of paragraph 12 of *BG-CR* (not reprinted in *BG-DVOP*), which are as follows: "The word which I should put primarily as indicating the character of my own poems would be the word Suggestiveness. I round and finish little or nothing; I could not, consistently with my scheme." The third and last sentence of paragraph 12, not printed in any other text, is as follows: "If 'Leaves of Grass' satisfies those who, to use a phrase of Margaret Fuller's, 'expect suggestions only and not fulfilments,' I shall be quite content." [Not an exact quotation, but apparently derived from the first two or three pages of Margaret Fuller's essay on "American Literature," in Vol. II of *Papers on Literature and Art* (1846)—ED.]

345. *HMB-DVOP*, *HMB-PP*, and *HLGM-LPM* begin a new paragraph after "your own flight."

347. After "hitherto." *HLGM-LPM* ends the paragraph with a passage not printed elsewhere. See Appendix XII, 3.

347–348. This sentence is the first of a new paragraph in *HLGM-LPM*, followed by "The chief trait," etc.

355. Shakspere] *HMB-PP:* Shakspeare

356. After "such questions." *HMB-DVOP* and *HMB-PP* begin a new paragraph.

357–358. These lines, beginning "not merely" through "events, but" are enclosed in parentheses in *HLGM-LPM*.

361. ennuyed] *HLGM-LPM:* ennuied

resident in the race, forever eligible to be appeal'd to and relied on.

As for native American individuality, though certain to come, and on a large scale, the distinctive and ideal type of Western character (as consistent with the operative political and even money-making features of United States' humanity in the Nineteenth Century as chosen knights, gentlemen and warriors were the ideals of the centuries of European feudalism) it has not yet appear'd. I have allow'd the stress of my poems from beginning to end to bear upon American individuality and assist it—not only because that is a great lesson in Nature, amid all her generalizing laws, but as counterpoise to the leveling tendencies of Democracy—and for other reasons. Defiant of ostensible literary and other conventions, I avowedly chant "the great pride of man in himself," and permit it to be more or less a *motif* of nearly all my verse. I think this pride indispensable to an American. I think it not inconsistent with obedience, humility, deference, and self-questioning.

Democracy has been so retarded and jeopardized by powerful personalities, that its first instincts are fain to clip, conform, bring in stragglers, and reduce everything to a dead level. While the ambitious thought of my song is to help the forming of a great aggregate Nation, it is, perhaps, altogether through the forming of myriads of fully develop'd and enclosing individuals. Welcome as are equality's and fraternity's doctrines and popular education, a certain liability accompanies them all, as we see. That primal and interior something in man, in his soul's abysms, coloring all, and, by exceptional fruitions, giving the last majesty to him—something continually touch'd upon and attain'd by the old poems and ballads of

364. Five paragraphs of *HMB-PP*, beginning with this line, are under the subtitle "American Character."

364. to come, and on] *HMB-DVOP* and *HMB-PP:* to contain on] *HLGM-LPM:* to command on

367. States'] *HMB-DVOP*, *HMB-PP*, and *HLGM-LPM:* States

368–369. feudalism) it has] *HLGM-LPM:* feudalism) has

370. it—not] *HMB-DVOP* and *HMB-PP:* it—(not] *HLGM-LPM:* it (not

372. but as] *HLGM-LPM:* but) as] [The final mark of parenthesis, which in *HMB-DVOP* and *HMB-PP* might be expected after "but", is omitted; obviously an error.—ED.]

372. leveling] *HMB-DVOP* and *HMB-PP:* levelling

373. After "reasons." *HMB-DVOP* and *HMB-PP* begin a new paragraph.

377. After "self-questioning." *HLGM-LPM* concludes the paragraph with the following sentence, not printed elsewhere: "Indeed, as I now see, part of my object remained throughout, and more decidedly than I was aware at the time, to furnish or suggest, by free cartoon outlinings, a special portraiture, the Western man's and woman's, definite and typical."

382. enclosing] *HLGM-LPM:* inclosing

388. them—modern] *HLGM-LPM:* them, modern

389–390. This sentence is omitted from *HMB-DVOP* and *HMB-PP*. *HLGM-LPM* has the following: "But that appearance is deceptive—or involves, at most, only a passing stage."

feudalism, and often the principal foundation of them—modern science and democracy appear to be endangering, perhaps eliminating. But that forms an appearance only; the reality is quite different. The new influences, upon the whole, are surely preparing the way for grander individualities than ever. To-day and here personal force is behind everything, just the same. The times and depictions from the Iliad to Shakspere inclusive can happily never again be realized—but the elements of courageous and lofty manhood are unchanged.

Without yielding an inch the working-man and working-woman were to be in my pages from first to last. The ranges of heroism and loftiness with which Greek and feudal poets endow'd their god-like or lordly born characters—indeed prouder and better based and with fuller ranges than those—I was to endow the democratic averages of America. I was to show that we, here and to-day, are eligible to the grandest and the best—more eligible now than any times of old were. I will also want my utterances (I said to myself before beginning) to be in spirit the poems of the morning. (They have been founded and mainly written in the sunny forenoon and early midday of my life.) I will want them to be the poems of women entirely as much as men. I have wish'd to put the complete Union of the States in my songs without any preference or partiality whatever. Henceforth, if they live and are read, it must be just as much South as North—just as much along the Pacific as Atlantic—in the valley of the Mississippi, in Canada, up in Maine, down in Texas, and on the shores of Puget Sound.

From another point of view "Leaves of Grass" is avowedly the song of Sex and Amativeness, and even Animality—though meanings that do

390. With "The new influences" *HMB-DVOP* and *HMB-PP* begin a new paragraph.
393. Shakspere] *HMB-PP:* Shakspeare
394. courageous and lofty] *HLGM-LPM:* courageous, lofty
395. After "unchanged." *HLGM-LPM* has two sentences, not reprinted. See Appendix XII, *4*.
396–410. These lines were printed from a clipping of *HMB-PP* found with the galley proof, with revisions in ink.
396. Without . . . working-man] *HMB-DVOP*, *HMB-PP*, and *HLGM-LPM:* Thus the working-man
400. America. I] *HMB-DVOP*, *HMB-PP*, and *HLGM-LPM:* America's men and women. I
403–404. morning. (They have been founded] *HMB-DVOP*, *HMB-PP*, and *HLGM-LPM:* morning. They were founded
405. life.) I] *HMB-DVOP*, *HMB-PP*, and *HLGM-LPM:* life. I
407. any preference or partiality] *HMB-DVOP*, *HMB-PP*, and *HLGM-LPM:* any partiality
408–409. North—just as] *HLGM-LPM:* North—as
409–410. the valley . . . Canada] *HLGM-LPM:* the Mississippi Valley, in Kanada
411. Three paragraphs in *HMB-PP*, beginning with this line, are under the subtitle "Sexuality." At this point *HLGM-LPM* has the divisional number III.
412. of Sex . . . Animality] *HMB-DVOP:* of Sex and Animality] *HMB-PP* and *HLGM-LPM:* of Love, and of Sex and Animality

not usually go along with those words are behind all, and will duly emerge; and all are sought to be lifted into a different light and atmosphere. Of this feature, intentionally palpable in a few lines, I shall only say the espousing principle of those lines so gives breath of life to my whole scheme that the bulk of the pieces might as well have been left unwritten were those lines omitted. Difficult as it will be, it has become, in my opinion, imperative to achieve a shifted attitude from superior men and women towards the thought and fact of sexuality, as an element in character, personality, the emotions, and a theme in literature. I am not going to argue the question by itself; it does not stand by itself. The vitality of it is altogether in its relations, bearings, significance—like the clef of a symphony. At last analogy the lines I allude to, and the spirit in which they are spoken, permeate all "Leaves of Grass," and the work must stand or fall with them, as the human body and soul must remain as an entirety.

Universal as are certain facts and symptoms of communities or individuals all times, there is nothing so rare in modern conventions and poetry as their normal recognizance. Literature is always calling in the doctor for consultation and confession, and always giving evasions and swathing suppressions in place of that "heroic nudity"* on which only a genuine diagnosis of serious cases can be built. And in respect to editions of "Leaves of Grass" in time to come (if there should be such) I take occasion now to confirm those lines with the settled convictions and deliberate re-

* "Nineteenth Century," July, 1883.

416. those lines] *HMB-DVOP*, *HMB-PP*, and *HLGM-LPM:* those few lines

418. After "lines omitted." *HMB-DVOP* and *HMB-PP* begin a new paragraph.

425–426. the human] *HMB-DVOP*, *HMB-PP*, and *HLGM-LPM:* the identified human

426. After "an entirety." *HLGM-LPM* continues in the same paragraph.

431. In all other texts the reference " 'Nineteenth Century,' July, 1883" is inserted in the text in parentheses. The quotation is found on page 126 of the article "The Sirens in Ancient Literature and Art," by Walter Copeland Perry (*Nineteenth Century*, XIV, 109–130), in a sentence describing Odysseus "bound to the mast, and distinguished from his followers by his heroic nudity."

433. "Leaves of Grass"] *HLGM-LPM:* "L. of G."

437. Three paragraphs in *HMB-PP*, beginning with this line, are under the subtitle "Love of Nature."

437. enclosing all, and over] *HMB-PP:* encloses all, and is over] *HLGM-LPM:* incloses all, and is over

437–453. These lines were printed in the fourth paragraph of "Additional Note," *SDA*, pages 311–312; omitted in that section in *NB*.

439. I had had a] *SDA:* I had a

443. ones; to] *HMB-DVOP*, *HMB-PP*, *HLGM-LPM*, and *SDA:* ones. To [After "ones." *HMB-PP* begins a new paragraph.]

443–444. every thought . . . implicit] *HMB-DVOP*, *HMB-PP*, *HLGM-LPM*, and *SDA:* every line should directly or indirectly be an implicit

newals of thirty years, and to hereby prohibit, as far as word of mine can do so, any elision of them.

Then still a purpose enclosing all, and over and beneath all. Ever since what might be call'd thought, or the budding of thought, fairly began in my youthful mind, I had had a desire to attempt some worthy record of that entire faith and acceptance ("to justify the ways of God to man" is Milton's well-known and ambitious phrase) which is the foundation of moral America. I felt it all as positively then in my young days as I do now in my old ones; to formulate a poem whose every thought or fact should directly or indirectly be or connive at an implicit belief in the wisdom, health, mystery, beauty of every process, every concrete object, every human or other existence, not only consider'd from the point of view of all, but of each.

While I can not understand it or argue it out, I fully believe in a clue and purpose in Nature, entire and several; and that invisible spiritual results, just as real and definite as the visible, eventuate all concrete life and all materialism, through Time. My book ought to emanate buoyancy and gladness legitimately enough, for it was grown out of those elements, and has been the comfort of my life since it was originally commenced.

One main genesis-motive of the "Leaves" was my conviction (just as strong to-day as ever) that the crowning growth of the United States is to be spiritual and heroic. To help start and favor that growth—or even to call attention to it, or the need of it—is the beginning, middle and final purpose of the poems. (In fact, when really cipher'd out and summ'd to

447. After "of each." *HMB-DVOP*, *HMB-PP*, *HLGM-LPM*, and *SDA* continue in the same paragraph.

448. in a clue] *HMB-DVOP* and *HMB-PP:* in each clue] *HLGM-LPM:* in each clew

451. My book] *HMB-DVOP*, *HMB-PP*, and *HLGM-LPM:* The book] *SDA:* The book ("Leaves of Grass")

452. gladness legitimately enough, for] *HMB-DVOP*, *HMB-PP*, *HLGM-LPM*, and *SDA:* gladness, too, for

453. After "commenced." *HMB-DVOP*, *HMB-PP*, *HLGM-LPM*, and *SDA* conclude the paragraph with the following sentence, not in *BG-NB:* "I should be willing to jaunt the whole life over again, with all its worldly failures and serious detriments, deficiencies and denials, to get the happiness of retraveling that part of the road."

454. At this point *HLGM-LPM* has the divisional number IV.

454–455. One . . . that the] *HMB-DVOP* and *HMB-PP:* One genesis-motive of the verses was [*HMB-PP:* the "Leaves" was] my conviction that the] *HLGM-LPM:* One genesis motive of the "Leaves" was my conviction that, founded on limitless concrete physical bases, and resting on materialistic and general worldly prosperity, the

456–458. This sentence is not in *HMB-PP*.

458. of the poems.] *HMB-DVOP:* of "Leaves of Grass."

458. After "of the poems." *HLGM-LPM* has three sentences not printed in other texts. See Appendix XII, 5.

458–461. No marks of parenthesis in *HMB-DVOP* and *HMB-PP*. *HLGM-LPM* encloses only the middle part of the sentence.

the last, plowing up in earnest the interminable average fallows of humanity—not "good government" merely, in the common sense—is the justification and main purpose of these United States.)

Isolated advantages in any rank or grace or fortune—the direct or indirect threads of all the poetry of the past—are in my opinion distasteful to the republican genius, and offer no foundation for its fitting verse. Establish'd poems, I know, have the very great advantage of chanting the already perform'd, so full of glories, reminiscences dear to the minds of men. But my volume is a candidate for the future. "All original art," says Taine, anyhow, "is self-regulated, and no original art can be regulated from without; it carries its own counterpoise, and does not receive it from elsewhere—lives on its own blood"—a solace to my frequent bruises and sulky vanity.

As the present is perhaps mainly an attempt at personal statement or illustration, I will allow myself as further help to extract the following anecdote from a book, "Annals of Old Painters," conn'd by me in youth. Rubens, the Flemish painter, in one of his wanderings through the galleries of old convents, came across a singular work. After looking at it thoughtfully for a good while, and listening to the criticisms of his suite of students, he said to the latter, in answer to their questions (as to what school the work implied or belong'd,) "I do not believe the artist, unknown and perhaps no longer living, who has given the world this legacy, ever belong'd to any school, or ever painted anything but this one picture, which is a personal affair—a piece out of a man's life."

"Leaves of Grass" indeed (I cannot too often reiterate) has mainly

459–460. last, plowing . . . sense—is the] *HMB-PP:* last, plowing . . . good government . . . sense, is the] *HLGM-LPM:* last, *that* (not chiefly "good government" in the usual sense, but plowing up in earnest the interminable average fallows of humanity) is the

461. these United States.)] *HMB-DVOP*, *HMB-PP*, and *HLGM-LPM:* these States.

462–471. These lines are not in *HLGM-LPM*. In *HMB-PP* they are the first of three paragraphs under the subtitle "The Past and Future."

467–470. The source of this quotation in Taine's work has not been identified.

469. without; it] *HMB-PP:* without. It

472. At this point *HLGM-LPM* has the division number v.

472. As the] *HLGM-LPM:* Then as the

474. This book has not been identified.

479. belong'd,) "I] *HMB-DVOP*, *HMB-PP*, and *HLGM-LPM:* belonged, etc.): "I

483–489. These lines, through "advance claims." were published for the first time in *BG-NB*.

489–492. This sentence, beginning "No one", was first published as the first of two sentences constituting paragraph 15 of *BG-CR*.

492. After "aestheticism." *HMB-DVOP*, *HMB-PP*, *HLGM-LPM*, and *BG-CR* have the following sentence, not in *BG-NB:* "I hope to go on record for something different—something better, if I may dare to say so." After this sentence *HMB-DVOP*, *HMB-PP*, and *HLGM-LPM* (but not *BG-CR*) have the following, not in *BG-NB* (varia-

been the outcropping of my own emotional and other personal nature—an attempt, from first to last, to put *a Person*, a human being (myself, in the latter half of the Nineteenth Century, in America,) freely, fully and truly on record. I could not find any similar personal record in current literature that satisfied me. But it is not on "Leaves of Grass" distinctively as *literature*, or a specimen thereof, that I feel to dwell, or advance claims. No one will get at my verses who insists upon viewing them as a literary performance, or attempt at such performance, or as aiming mainly toward art or æstheticism.

I say no land or people or circumstances ever existed so needing a race of singers and poems differing from all others, and rigidly their own, as the land and people and circumstances of our United States need such singers and poems to-day, and for the future. Still further, as long as the States continue to absorb and be dominated by the poetry of the Old World, and remain unsupplied with autochthonous song, to express, vitalize and give color to and define their material and political success, and minister to them distinctively, so long will they stop short of first-class Nationality and remain defective.

In the free evening of my day I give to you, reader, the foregoing garrulous talk, thoughts, reminiscences,

> As idly drifting down the ebb,
> Such ripples, half-caught voices, echo from the shore.

Concluding with two items for the imaginative genius of the West, when it worthily rises—First, what Herder taught to the young Goethe,

tions from *HMB-PP* inserted in brackets): "If I rested 'Leaves of Grass' on the usual claims—if I did not feel that the deepest moral, social, political purposes of America are [*HMB-DVOP:* America (aye, of the modern world,) are] the underlying endeavors at least of my pages; that [*HLGM-LPM:* pages—that] the geography and hydrography of this continent, the Prairies, the St. Lawrence, Ohio, the Carolinas, Texas, Missouri are the [*HLGM-LPM:* their] real current concrete—I should not dare to have them put in type and printed and offered for sale." [An autograph direction to the printer on page 18 of the proof shows that the deletion from *BG-NB* above mentioned was made on the plate.—ED.]

493. The last two paragraphs of *HMB-PP* have the subtitle "Parting Words." *HLGM-LPM* continues with the same paragraph.

496. further, as] *HLGM-LPM:* further: as

497. dominated] *HMB-DVOP* and *HMB-PP:* domiciled

502–505. These lines are not in *HMB-DVOP*, but they constitute the last paragraph of "Additional Note" in *SDA* (omitted from that section in *NB*). The verse lines are not in *LG*.

505. half-caught voices, echo] *HMB-PP* and *HLGM-LPM:* half-caught glimpses, echo] *SDA:* half-caught glimpses, echoes

506–510. A version of these lines first appeared in *BG-CR* as the fifth sentence of paragraph 14 and all of paragraph 17; paragraph 17 is a single sentence.

506–507. Concluding . . . First, what] *HMB-DVOP*, *HMB-PP*, and *HLGM-LPM:* I conclude . . . First. what] *BG-CR:* To which I should add what

that really great poetry is always (like the Homeric or Biblical canticles) the result of a national spirit, and not the privilege of a polish'd and select few; Second, that the strongest and sweetest songs yet remain to be sung.

Note at Beginning.

The following volume contains

LEAVES OF GRASS,

with the brief-Annex, SANDS AT SEVENTY, in *November Boughs*,

SPECIMEN DAYS AND COLLECT . . . . and

NOVEMBER BOUGHS,

Revised, corrected, &c., down to date.

(When I had got this volume well under way, I was quite suddenly prostrated by illness—paralysis, continued yet—which will have to serve as excuse for many faults both of omission and commission in it.)

But I would not let the great and momentous Era of these years, these States, slip away without attempting to arrest in a special printed book (as much in spirit as letter, and may-be for the future more than the present,) some few specimens—even vital throbs, breaths—as representations of it all—from my point of view, and right from the midst of it, jotted at the time.

There is a tally-stamp and stage-result of periods and nations, elusive, at second or third hand, often escaping the historian of matter-of-fact—in some sort the nation's spiritual formative ferment or chaos—the getting in of its essence, formulating identity—a law of it, and significant part of its progress. (Of the best of events and facts, even the most important, there are finally not the events and facts only, but something flashing out and fluctuating like tuft-flames or eidólons, from all.) My going up and down amidst these years, and the impromptu jottings of their sights and thoughts, of war and peace, have been in accordance with that law, and probably a result of it. . . . In certain respects, (emotionality, passions, spirituality, the invisible trend,) I therefore launch forth the divisions of

509. of a national] *BG-CR:* of the national

510. few; Second, . . . sung.] *HMB-DVOP*, *HMB-PP*, and *HLGM-LPM:* few; second, . . . sung.] *BG-CR:* I think the best and largest songs yet remain to be sung.

[For that part of "Additional Note" to *SDA* not included in "A Backward Glance O'er Travel'd Roads" see "Notes to Late English Books," lines 26–68.]

Note at Beginning.

Printed in *CPP* from a long autograph MS page in pencil, revised in black ink, now in the Feinberg Collection. This appeared as a preface to *CPP* (1888), and was not reprinted. The printed text follows the revised MS except for minor changes in capitalization, punctuation, and so on. [This and "Note at End" follow "A Back-

the following book as not only a consequent of that period and its influences, but in one sort a History of America, the past 35 years, after the rest, after the adjuncts of that history have been studied and attended to.

Note at End of Complete Poems and Prose.

As I conclude—and (to get typographical correctness,) after running my eyes diligently through the three big divisions of the preceding volume— the interrogative wonder-fancy rises in me whether (if it be not too arrogant to even state it,) the 33 years of my current time, 1855–1888, with their aggregate of our New World doings and people, have not, indeed, created and formulated the foregoing leaves—forcing their utterance as the pages stand—coming actually from the direct urge and developments of those years, and not from any individual epic or lyrical attempts whatever, or from my pen or voice, or any body's special voice. Out of that supposition, the book might assume to be consider'd an autochthonic record and expression, freely render'd, of and out of these 30 to 35 years—of the soul and evolution of America—and of course, by reflection, not ours only, but more or less of the common people of the world. . . . . Seems to me I may dare to claim a deep native tap-root for the book, too, in some sort. I came on the stage too late for personally knowing much of even the lingering Revolutionary worthies—the men of '76. Yet, as a little boy, I have been press'd tightly and lovingly to the breast of Lafayette, (Brooklyn, 1825,) and have talk'd with old Aaron Burr, and also with those who knew Washington and his surroundings, and with original Jeffersonians, and more than one very old soldier and sailor. And in my own day and maturity, my eyes have seen, and ears heard, Lincoln, Grant and Emerson, and my hands have been grasp'd by their hands. Though in a different field and range from most of theirs, I give the foregoing pages as perfectly legitimate, resultant, evolutionary and consistent with them. If these lines should ever reach some reader of a far off future age, let him take them as a missive sent from Abraham Lincoln's fateful age. . . . Repeating,

ward Glance" in the present edition because they properly belong with the prefaces in CPW.—ED.]

Note at End of Complete Poems and Prose.

Printed in CPP from a long autograph MS page, now in the Feinberg Collection, made up of a sheet of original writing in pencil and several strips containing revisions in ink pasted at the top. The printed text varies considerably from the MS.

4. 33 years . . . 1855–1888] MS before revision: 38 years . . . 1850–1888
6. leaves] MS (unrevised): pages
8. attempts] MS (unrevised): attempt
12–13. reflection . . . more or less] MS (unrevised): reflection, more or less
13–38. These lines, beginning "Seems," do not appear in the surviving MS at all.

parrot-like, what in the preceding divisions has been already said, and must serve as a great reason-why of this whole book—1st, That the main part about pronounc'd events and shows, (poems and persons also,) is the point of view from which they are view'd and estimated—and 2d, That I cannot let my momentous, stormy, peculiar Era of peace and war, these States, these years, slip away without arresting some of its specimen events—even its vital breaths—to be portray'd and inscribed from out of the midst of it, from its own days and nights—not so much in themselves, (statistically and descriptively our times are copiously noted and memorandized with an industrial zeal)—but to give from them here their flame-like results in imaginative and spiritual suggestiveness—as they present themselves to me, at any rate, from the point of view alluded to.

Then a few additional words yet to this hurried farewell note. In another sense (the warp crossing the woof, and knitted in,) the book is probably a sort of autobiography; an element I have not attempted to specially restrain or erase. As alluded to at beginning, I had about got the volume well started by the printers, when a sixth recurrent attack of my war-paralysis fell upon me. It has proved the most serious and continued of the whole. I am now uttering *November Boughs*, and printing this book, in my 70th year. To get out the collection—mainly the born results of health, flush life, buoyancy, and happy out-door volition—and to prepare the *Boughs*—have beguiled my invalid months the past summer and fall. ("Are we to be beaten down in our old age?" says one white-hair'd fellow remonstratingly to another in a budget of letters I read last night.) . . . Then I have wanted to leave something markedly *personal*. I have put my name with pen-and-ink with my own hand in the present volume. And from engraved or photo'd portraits taken from life, I have selected some, of different stages, which please me best, (or at any rate displease me least,) and bequeath them at a venture to you, reader, with my love.

W. W., *Nov.* 13, '88.

4*n*. There are 422 pages in this volume, including 404 pages of poems and the 18 pages that comprise this prefatory note and "A Backward Glance O'er Travel'd

Prefatory Note to Leaves of Grass, 1889.

Printed from an autograph MS now in the Feinberg Collection and inserted near the end of *LG* 1889 between the poems and "A Backward Glance O'er Travel'd Roads," which was there reprinted from the plates of *NB*. In *NB* "A Backward Glance" came first in the volume after the title and copyright pages and two pages

Prefatory Note to Leaves of Grass, 1889.

May 31, 1889.
Camden, New Jersey, U. S. America.

To-day completes my three-score-and-ten years—rounds and coheres the successive growths and stages of L. of G. with the following essay and (sort of) testament—my hurried epilogue of intentions-bequest—and gives me the crowning content, (for these lines are written at the last,) of feeling and definitely, perhaps boastfully, reiterating, For good or bad, plain or not-plain, I have held out and now concluded my utterance, entirely its own way; the main wonder being to me, of the foregoing 404 pages entire, amid their many faults and omissions, that (after looking over them leisurely and critically, as the last week, night and day,) they have adhered faithfully to, and carried out, for nearly 40 years, over many gaps, through thick and thin, peace and war, sickness and health, clouds and sunshine, my latent purposes, &c., even as measurably well and far as they do between these covers. (Nature evidently achieves specimens only—plants the seeds of suggestions—is not so intolerant of what is call'd evil—relies on *law* and *character* more than special cases or partialities; and in my little scope I have follow'd or tried to follow the lesson: . . Probably that is about all.)

Yes, to-day finishes my 70th year; and even if but the merest additional preface, (and not plain what tie-together it has with the following *Backward Glance*,) I suppose I must reel out something to celebrate my old birthday anniversary, and for this special edition of the latest completest L. of G. utterance.* Printers send word, too, there is a blank here to be written up—and what with? . . . Probably I may as well transcribe and

* As there are now several editions of L. of G., different texts and dates, I wish to say that I prefer and recommend the present one, complete, for future printing, if there should be any; a copy and fac-simile, indeed, of the text of these 422 pages. The subsequent interval which is so important to form'd and launch'd works, books especially, has pass'd; and waiting till fully after that, I give these concluding words.

Roads." It is a mere coincidence that in the 1891–92 edition of *LG* there are also 422 pages of poems, including the poems in *GBF* and its preface.

of contents, and it was paged 5–18. For *LG* 1889 a new title page was made for "A Backward Glance," and the table of contents was omitted; hence pages 3–4 were available for new material. Whitman apparently wrote this section to fill those two blank pages, but it is also a kind of preface to the volume and is therefore included in this edition with the other prefaces. It was not reprinted.

eke out this note by the following lines of a letter last week to a valued friend who demands to know my current personal condition: . . . "First asking pardon for long neglect—The perfect physical health, strength, buoyancy, (and inward impetus to back them,) which were vouchsafed during my whole life, and especially throughout the Secession War period, (1860 to '66,) seem'd to wane after those years, and were closely track'd by a stunning paralytic seizure, and following physical debility and inertia, (laggardness, torpor, indifference, perhaps laziness,) which put me low in 1873 and '4 and '5—then lifted a little, but have essentially remain'd ever since; several spirts or attacks—five or six of them, one time or another from 1876 onward, but gradually mainly overcome—till now, 1888 and '9, the worst and most obstinate seizure of all. . . . Upon the whole, however, and even at this, and though old and sick, I keep up, maintain fair spirits, partially read and write—have publish'd last and full and revised editions of my poems and prose (records and results of youth and early and mid age—of absolute strength and health—o'erseen now during a lingering ill spell)—But have had a bad year, this last one—have run a varied gauntlet, chronic constipation, and then vertigo, bladder and gastric troubles, and the forementionʼd steady disability and inertia; bequests of the serious paralysis at Washington, D. C., closing the Secession War—that seizure indeed the culmination of much that preceded, and real source of all my woes since. During the past year, and now, with all these, (a body and brain-action dull'd, while the spirit is perhaps willing and live enough,) I get along more contentedly and comfortably than you might suppose—sit here all day in my big, high, strong, rattan-bottom'd chair, (with great wolf-skin spread on the back in cool weather)—as writing to you now on a tablet on my lap, may-be my last missives of love, memories and cheer."

Preface Note to 2d Annex,
Concluding L. of G.—1891.

Had I not better withhold (in this old age and paralysis of me) such little tags and fringe-dots (maybe specks, stains,) as follow a long dusty journey, and witness it afterward? I have probably not been enough afraid of careless touches, from the first—and am not now—nor of parrot-like repetitions—nor platitudes and the commonplace. Perhaps I am too

Preface Note to 2d Annex.

Printed in GBF from four pages of autograph MS, now in the Feinberg Collection, each page consisting of two or three pieces of unequal size, written in

democratic for such avoidances. Besides, is not the verse-field, as originally plann'd by my theory, now sufficiently illustrated—and full time for me to silently retire?—(indeed amid no loud call or market for my sort of poetic utterance.)

In answer, or rather defiance, to that kind of well-put interrogation, here comes this little cluster, and conclusion of my preceding clusters. Though not at all clear that, as here collated, it is worth printing (certainly I have nothing fresh to write)—I while away the hours of my 72d year—hours of forced confinement in my den—by putting in shape this small old age collation:

Last droplets of and after spontaneous rain,
From many limpid distillations and past showers;
(Will they germinate anything? mere exhalations as they all are—the land's and sea's—America's;
Will they filter to any deep emotion? any heart and brain?)

However that may be, I feel like improving to-day's opportunity and wind up. During the last two years I have sent out, in the lulls of illness and exhaustion, certain chirps—lingering-dying ones probably (undoubtedly)—which now I may as well gather and put in fair type while able to see correctly—(for my eyes plainly warn me they are dimming, and my brain more and more palpably neglects or refuses, month after month, even slight tasks or revisions.)

In fact, here I am these current years 1890 and '91, (each successive fortnight getting stiffer and stuck deeper) much like some hard-cased dilapidated grim ancient shell-fish or time-bang'd conch (no legs, utterly non-locomotive) cast up high and dry on the shore-sands, helpless to move anywhere—nothing left but behave myself quiet, and while away the days yet assign'd, and discover if there is anything for the said grim and time-bang'd conch to be got at last out of inherited good spirits and primal buoyant centre-pulses down there deep somewhere within his gray-blurr'd old shell . . . . (Reader, you must allow a little fun here—for one reason there are too many of the following poemets about death, &c., and for another the passing hours (July 5, 1890) are so sunny-fine. And old as I am I feel today almost a part of some frolicsome wave, or for sporting yet like a kid or kitten—probably a streak of physical adjustment and perfection here and now. I believe I have it in me perennially anyhow.)

ink and pasted together. This preface to *GBF* was reprinted without change in the 1891–92 edition of *LG;* it was omitted from *CPW* 1892.

16–20. These lines are not in *LG* and were not reprinted except in the context of this preface.

Then behind all, the deep-down consolation (it is a glum one, but I dare not be sorry for the fact of it in the past, nor refrain from dwelling, even vaunting here at the end) that this late-years palsied old shorn and shell-fish condition of me is the indubitable outcome and growth, now near for 20 years along, of too over-zealous, over-continued bodily and emotional excitement and action through the times of 1862, '3, '4 and '5, visiting and waiting on wounded and sick army volunteers, both sides, in campaigns or contests, or after them, or in hospitals or fields south of Washington City, or in that place and elsewhere—those hot, sad, wrenching times—the army volunteers, all States,—or North or South—the wounded, suffering, dying—the exhausting, sweating summers, marches, battles, carnage—those trenches hurriedly heap'd by the corpse-thousands, mainly unknown—Will the America of the future—will this vast rich Union ever realize what itself cost, back there after all?—those hecatombs of battle-deaths—Those times of which, O far-off reader, this whole book is indeed finally but a reminiscent memorial from thence by me to you?

The Old Man Himself.
A Postscript.

Walt Whitman has a way of putting in his own special word of thanks, his own way, for kindly demonstrations, and may now be considered as appearing on the scene, wheeled at last in his invalid chair, and saying, *propria persona*, Thank you, thank you, my friends all. The living face and voice and emotional pulse only at last hold humanity together; even old poets and their listeners and critics too. One of my dearest objects in my poetic expression has been to combine these Forty-Four United States into One Identity, fused, equal, and independent. My attempt has been mainly of suggestion, atmosphere, reminder, the native and common spirit of all, and perennial heroism. *Walt Whitman.*

44–45. palsied old shorn and shell-fish] MS (unrevised): palsied old bodily old shell-fish

The Old Man Himself. A Postscript.

This paragraph is not in *CPW* 1892, though it was obviously written by Whitman and might appropriately have been included in *GBF*. It was printed at the end of Horace Traubel's article, "Walt Whitman: Poet and Philosopher and Man," in *LIP*, March, 1891. Traubel's article is a summary of Whitman's life and work.

Walt Whitman's Last.

This appeared in *LIP*, August, 1891 (Vol. 48, p. 256), too late to be included in *GBF*, but it is obviously closely related to it, and properly belongs with it in the

Walt Whitman's Last.

Good-Bye My Fancy—concluding Annex to *Leaves of Grass.*

"The Highest said: Don't let us begin so low—isn't our range too coarse—too gross?........The Soul answer'd: No, not when we consider what it is all for—the end involved in Time and Space."—*An item from last page of "Good-Bye."*

H. Heine's first principle of criticising a book was, What motive is the author trying to carry out, or express or accomplish? and the second, Has he achiev'd it?

The theory of my "Leaves of Grass" as a composition of verses has been from first to last, (if I am to give impromptu a hint of the spinal marrow of the business, and sign it with my name,) to thoroughly possess the mind, memory, cognizance of the author himself, with everything beforehand—a full armory of concrete actualities, observations, humanity, past poems, ballads, facts, technique, war and peace, politics, North and South, East and West, nothing too large or too small, the sciences as far as possible—and above all America and the present—after and out of which the subject of the poem, long or short, has been invariably turned over to his Emotionality, even Personality, to be shaped thence; and emerges strictly therefrom, with all its merits and demerits on its head. Every page of my poetic or attempt at poetic utterance therefore smacks of the living physical identity, date, environment, individuality, probably beyond anything known, and in style often offensive to the conventions.

This new last cluster, "Good-Bye my Fancy" follows suit, and yet with a difference. The clef is here changed to its lowest, and the little book is a lot of tremolos about old age, death, and faith. The physical just lingers, but almost vanishes. The book is garrulous, irascible (like old

present edition. The editor of the magazine added the following explanatory note:

"With 'Good-Bye my Fancy' Walt Whitman has rounded out his life-work. This book is his last message, and of course a great deal will be said about it by critics all over the world both in praise and dispraise; but probably nothing that the critics will say will be as interesting as this characteristic utterance upon the book by the poet himself. It is the subjective view as opposed to the objective views of the critics. Briefly Whitman gives as he puts it 'a hint of the spinal marrow of the business,' not only of 'Good-Bye my Fancy' but also of the 'Leaves of Grass.'

"It was only after considerable persuasion on the editor's part that Mr. Whitman consented to write the above. As a concise explanation of the poet's life-work it must have great value to his readers and admirers. After the critics 'have ciphered and ciphered out long' they will probably have nothing better to say."

["Walt Whitman's Last," together with the editorial statement, was included, after *GBF*, in the 1898 edition of *CPW*, published by Small, Maynard & Co.—ED.]

Lear) and has various breaks and even tricks to avoid monotony. It will have to be ciphered and ciphered out long—and is probably in some respects the most curious part of its author's baffling works.

Walt Whitman.

Appendix A

BOOKS AND PERIODICALS FROM WHICH PASSAGES WERE OMITTED IN *SDC*, *NB*, AND *GBF*.

[Much of the material in *Collect*, *November Boughs*, and *Good-Bye My Fancy* had been previously published in books and periodicals, but a number of passages in the earlier texts were omitted in the later volumes. All such passages, if they are too long or too disconnected to be incorporated in the textual notes, are printed in this appendix. For convenience of reference, each separate publication, book or periodical, is given a Roman numeral, and each continuous quoted passage is given an appropriate subordinate Arabic numeral.—ED.]

I *Preface, 1855, to first issue of* Leaves of Grass.

[Reprinted, with revisions, in *Poems of Walt Whitman*, edited by W. M. Rossetti (1868), and in the Trübner pamphlet, *Leaves of Grass. Preface to the Original Edition, 1855* (London, 1881). These three versions will be designated by their dates of publication. Since the Preface of 1855 was printed in SDC from revised sheets of the 1881 pamphlet, the text of 1881 will be quoted for passages omitted in SDC, with variations of 1868 and 1855 inserted in brackets. The leaders, or periods in series, are exactly reproduced.]

1

[A long passage omitted after "races." in line 50.]

Of them a bard is to be commensurate with a people. To him the other continents arrive as contributors ... he [1868: contributions: he; 1855: contributions ... he] gives them reception for their sake and his own sake. His spirit responds to his country's spirit ... he [1868: spirit: he; 1855: spirit ... he] incarnates its geography and natural life and rivers and lakes. Mississippi with annual freshets and changing chutes, Missouri and Columbia, and [1868 and 1855: Columbia and] Ohio and St. Lawrence, with [1868 and 1855: St. Lawrence with] the Falls [1855: falls] and beautiful masculine Hudson, do not embouchure where they spend themselves more than they embouchure into him. The blue breadth over the inland sea of Virginia and Maryland, and [1855: Maryland and] the sea off Massachusetts and Maine, and [1855: Maine and] over Manhattan Bay, and [1868: Bay and; 1855: bay and] over Champlain and Erie, and [1855: Erie and] over Ontario and Huron and Michigan and

Superior, and over the Texan and Mexican and Floridian and Cuban seas, and [1855: seas and] over the seas off California and Oregon, is not tallied by the blue breadth of the waters below more than the breadth of above and below is tallied by him. When the long Atlantic coast stretches longer and [1868: longer, and] the Pacific coast stretches longer, he [1855: longer he] easily stretches with them north or south. He spans between them also from east to west and [1868: west, and] reflects what is between them. On him rise solid growths that offset the growths of pine and cedar and hemlock and live oak [1868: live-oak; 1855: liveoak] and locust and chestnut and cypress and hickory and limetree and cotton-wood and tulip-tree [1855: tuliptree] and cactus and wild-vine [1855: wildvine] and tamarind and persimmon ... and [1868: persimmon, and] tangles as tangled as any cane-break [1855: canebreak] or swamp ... and [1868: swamp, and; 1855: swamp .... and] forests coated with transparent ice, and icicles hanging [1868: ice and icicles, hanging; 1855: ice and icicles hanging] from the boughs and crackling in the wind ... and [1868: wind, and; 1855: wind .... and] sides and peaks of mountains ... and [1868: mountains, and; 1855: mountains .... and] pasturage sweet and free as savannah or upland or prairie ... with [1868: prairie,—with; 1855: prairie .... with] flights and songs and screams that answer those of the wild pigeon [1868: wild-pigeon; 1855: wildpigeon] and high-hold [1855: highhold] and orchard-oriole and coot, and [1868 and 1855: coot and] surf-duck and redshouldered-hawk and fish-hawk and white ibis [1868 and 1855: white-ibis] and Indian-hen [1855: indian-hen] and cat-owl and water-pheasant and qua-bird and pied-sheldrake and blackbird and mocking-bird [1855: mockingbird] and buzzard and condor and night heron [1868 and 1855: night-heron] and eagle. To him the hereditary countenance descends, both [1855: descends both] mother's and father's. To him enter the essences of the real things and past and present events—of the enormous diversity of temperature and agriculture and mines—the tribes of the red aborigines—the weather-beaten [1855: weatherbeaten] vessels entering new ports or [1868: ports, or] making landings on rocky coasts—the first settlements north or south—the rapid stature and muscle—the haughty defiance of '76, and the war and peace and formation of the constitution ... the [1868: constitution—the; 1855: constitution .... the] Union [1868 and 1855: union] always surrounded by blatherers and [1868: blatherers, and] always calm and impregnable—the perpetual coming of immigrants—the wharf-hem'd [1868: wharf-hemmed; 1855: wharfhem'd] cities and superior marine—the unsurveyed interior—the loghouses and clearings and wild animals and hunters and trappers ... the [1868: trappers—the;

1855: trappers .... the] free commerce—the fisheries and whaling, and [1868 and 1855: whaling and] gold-digging—the endless gestation [1868: gestations] of new states—the convening of Congress every December, the members duly coming up from all climates and the uttermost parts ... the [1868: parts—the; 1855: parts .... the] noble character of the young mechanics and of all free American workmen and workwomen ... the [1868: workwomen—the; 1855: workwomen .... the] general ardour [1855: ardor] and friendliness and enterprise—the perfect equality of the female with the male ... the [1868: male—the; 1855: male .... the] large amativeness—the fluid movement of the population—the factories, and [1868 and 1855: factories and] mercantile life and labour-saving [1855: laborsaving] machinery—the Yankee swap—the New York firemen and the target excursion—the Southern [1868 and 1855: southern] plantation life—the character of the north-east [1868 and 1855: northeast] and of the north-west, and south-west [1868 and 1855: northwest and southwest]—slavery, and [1855: slavery and] the tremulous spreading of hands to protect it, and the stern opposition to it which shall never cease till it ceases or [1868: ceases, or] the speaking of tongues and the moving of lips cease.

2

[A passage omitted after "vista." in line 55.]

Here comes one among the well beloved [1868: well-beloved; 1855: wellbeloved] stonecutters, and [1855: stonecutters and] plans with decision and science, and [1855: science and] sees the solid and beautiful forms of the future where there are now no solid forms.

Of all nations, the United States, with [1855: nations the United States with] veins full of poetical stuff, most need poets, and [1868: stuff, most needs poets, and; 1855: stuff most need poets and] will doubtless have the greatest and [1868: greatest, and] use them the greatest. Their Presidents shall not be their common referee so much as their poets shall. Of all mankind the [1868: mankind, the] great poet is the equable man. Not in him but off from him things [1868: in him, but off from him, things] are grotesque or eccentric or [1868: eccentric, or] fail of their sanity. Nothing out of its place is good and [1868: good, and] nothing in its place is bad. He bestows on every object or quality its fit proportions, neither [1855: proportions neither] more nor less. He is the arbiter of the diverse, and [1855: diverse and] he is the key. He is the equalizer of his age and land ... he [1868: land: he; 1855: land .... he] supplies what wants supplying, and [1855: supplying and] checks what wants checking. If peace is the routine, out [1855: routine out] of him speaks the spirit of peace, large, rich, thrifty, building vast and populous cities, encouraging agriculture and the arts and commerce—lighting the study of man, the soul, immortality—federal, state or municipal government, marriage, health, free trade, inter-travel [1868: free-trade, inter-travel; 1855: freetrade, intertravel] by land and sea . . . nothing [1868: sea—nothing; 1855: sea . . . . nothing] too close, nothing too far off . . . the [1868: off,—the] stars not too far off. In war he [1868: In war, he] is the most deadly force of the war. Who recruits him recruits horse and foot . . . he [1868: foot: he] fetches parks of artillery, the [1855: artillery the] best that engineer ever knew. If the time becomes slothful and heavy, he [1855: heavy he] knows how to arouse it . . . he [1868: it: he] can make every word he speaks draw blood.

3

[A long passage omitted after "degrade it." in line 305.]

The attitude of great poets is to cheer up slaves and [1868: slaves, and] horrify despots. The turn of their necks, the sound of their feet, the motions of their wrists, are full of hazard to the one and hope to the other. Come nigh them awhile, and though [1868: awhile, and, though; 1855: awhile and though] they neither speak nor advise, you [1855: speak or advise you] shall learn the faithful American lesson. Liberty is poorly served by men whose good intent is quelled from one failure or two failures or any number of failures, or from the casual indifference or ingratitude of the people, or from the sharp show of the tushes of power, or the bringing to bear soldiers and cannon or any penal statutes. Liberty relies upon itself, invites no one, promises nothing, sits in calmness and light, is positive and composed, and knows no discouragement. The battle rages with many a loud alarm and frequent advance and retreat . . . the [1868: retreat—the; 1855: retreat . . . . the] enemy triumphs . . . the [1868: triumphs—the; 1855: triumphs . . . . the] prison, the handcuffs, the iron necklace and anklet, the scaffold, garrote and leadballs [1868: lead-balls] do their work . . . the [1868: work—the; 1855: work . . . . the] cause is asleep . . . the [1868: asleep—the; 1855: asleep . . . . the] strong throats are choked with their own blood . . . the [1868: blood—the; 1855: blood . . . . the] young men drop their eyelashes toward the ground when they pass each other . . . and [1868 and 1855: other . . . . and] is liberty gone out of that place? No, never. [1855: no never.] When liberty goes it [1868: goes, it] is not the first to go, not [1855: go nor] the second or third to go ... it [1868: go: it; 1855: go .. it] waits for all the rest to go ... it [1868: to go—it; 1855: go .. it] is the last. ... When [1868: last. When; 1855: last. .. When] the memories of the old martyrs are faded utterly away ... when [1868: away—when; 1855: away .... when] the large names of patriots are laughed at in the public halls from the lips of the orators ... when [1868: orators—when; 1855: orators .... when] the boys are no more christened after the same, but [1855: same but] christened after tyrants and traitors instead ... when [1868: instead—when; 1855: instead .... when] the laws of the free are grudgingly permitted and [1868: permitted, and] the laws for informers and blood-money [1855: bloodmoney] are sweet to the taste of the people ... when [1868: people—when; 1855: people .... when] I and you walk abroad upon the earth stung [1868: earth, stung] with compassion at the sight of numberless brothers answering our equal friendship and [1868: friendship, and] calling no man master—and when we are elated with noble joy at the sight of slaves ... when [1868: slaves—when; 1855: slaves .... when] the soul retires in the cool communion of the night and [1868: night, and] surveys its experience, and [1855: experience and] has much ecstasy [1855: extacy] over the word and deed that put back a helpless innocent person into the gripe of the gripers or into any cruel inferiority ... when [1868: inferiority—when; 1855: inferiority .... when] those in all parts of those [1868 and 1855: these] states who could easier realize the true American character but [1868: character, but] do not yet—when the swarms of cringers, suckers, doughfaces, lice of politics, planners of sly involutions for their own preferment to city offices or state legislatures or the judiciary or congress [1868: Congress] or the presidency, [1868: Presidency,] obtain a response of love and natural deference from the people whether [1868: people, whether] they get the offices or no ... when [1868: no—when; 1855: no .... when] it is better to be a bound booby and rogue in office at a high salary than the poorest free mechanic or farmer with [1868: farmer, with] his hat unmoved from his head, and [1855: head and] firm eyes and [1868: eyes, and] a candid and generous heart ... and [1868: heart —and; 1855: heart .... and] when servility by town or state or the federal government or [1868: government, or] any oppression on a large scale or small scale, can [1855: scale can] be tried on without its own punishment following duly after in exact proportion against [1868: proportion, against] the smallest chance of escape ... or [1868: escape—or; 1855: escape .... or] rather when all life and all the souls of men and women are discharged from any part of the earth—then only shall the instinct of liberty be discharged from that part of the earth.

4

[A passage omitted after "consequence." in line 402.]

Not a move can a man or woman make that affects him or her in a day or a month or [1868: month, or] any part of the direct lifetime or the hour of death but [1868: death, but] the same affects him or her onward afterward through the indirect lifetime. The indirect is always as great and real as the direct. The spirit receives from the body just as much as it gives to the body. Not one name of word or deed . . . not of venereal sores or discolorations . . . not the privacy of the onanist . . . not of the putrid [1868: word or deed—not of the putrid; 1855: word or deed . . not of venereal sores or discolorations . . not the privacy of the onanist . . not of the putrid] veins of gluttons or rumdrinkers . . . not [1868: rum-drinkers—not] peculation or cunning, or [1868 and 1855: cunning or] betrayal or murder . . . no [1868: murder—no; 1855: murder . . no] serpentine poison of those that seduce women . . . not [1868: women—not; 1855: women . . not] the foolish yielding of women . . . not prostitution . . . not of any depravity of young men . . . not of the attainment [1868: yielding of women—not of the attainment; 1855: yielding of women . . not prostitution . . not of any depravity of young men . . not of the attainment] of gain by discreditable means . . . not [1868: means—not; 1855: means . . not] any nastiness of appetite . . . nor any [1868: appetite—not any; 1855: appetite . . not any] harshness of officers to men, or [1855: men or] judges to prisoners, or [1855: prisoners or] fathers to sons, or [1855: sons or] sons to fathers, or [1855: fathers or] of husbands to wives, or [1855: wives or] bosses to their boys . . . not [1868: boys—not; 1855: boys . . not] of greedy looks or malignant wishes . . . nor [1868: wishes—nor] any of the wiles practised by people upon themselves . . . ever [1868: themselves—ever] is or ever can be stamped on the programme but [1868: programme, but] it is duly realized and returned, and that returned in further performances . . . and [1868: performances —and] they returned again.

5

[A passage omitted after "forever." in line 410.]

If the savage or felon is wise it [1868: wise, it] is well . . . if [1868: well—if; 1855: well . . . . if] the greatest poet or savan is wise it [1868:

wise, it] is simply the same ... if [1868: same—if] the President or chief justice is wise it [1868: wise, it] is the same ... if [1868: same—if] the young mechanic or farmer is wise it is no more or less ... if the prostitute is wise it is no more or less. The interest [1868: farmer is wise, it is no more or less. The interest] will come round ... all [1868: round—all; 1855: round .. all] will come round. All the best actions of war and peace ... all [1868: peace—all] help given to relatives and strangers and [1868: strangers, and] the poor and old and sorrowful and [1868: sorrowful, and] young children and widows and the sick, and to all shunned persons ... all [1868: persons—all; 1855: persons .. all] furtherance of fugitives and of the escape of slaves ... all [1868: slaves—all; 1855: slaves .. all] the self-denial that stood steady and aloof on wrecks and [1868: wrecks, and] saw others take the seats of the boats ... all [1868: boats—all] offering of substance or life for the good old cause, or for a friend's sake or opinion's sake ... all [1868: sake—all] pains of enthusiasts scoffed at by their neighbours ... all [1868: neighbours—all; 1855: neighbors .. all] the vast sweet love and precious sufferings of mothers ... all [1868: suffering of mothers—all; 1855: suffering of mothers ... all] honest men baffled in strifes recorded or unrecorded ... all [1868: unrecorded—all; 1855: unrecorded .... all] the grandeur and good of the few ancient nations whose fragments of annals we inherit ... and [1868: inherit—and; 1855: inherit .. and] all the good of the hundreds of far mightier and more ancient nations unknown to us by name or date or location ... all [1868: location—all; 1855: location .... all] that was ever manfully begun, whether it succeeded or no ... all [1868: no—all; 1855: not .... all] that has at any time been well suggested out of the divine heart of man or [1868: man, or] by the divinity of his mouth or [1868: mouth, or] by the shaping of his great hands ... and [1868: hands, and; 1855: hands .. and] all that is well thought or done this day on any part of the surface of the globe ... or [1868: globe, or; 1855: globe .. or] on any of the wandering stars or fixed stars by those there as we are here ... or [1868: here—or; 1855: here .. or] that is henceforth to be well thought or done by you whoever [1868: you, whoever] you are, or by any one—these singly and wholly inured at their time and [1868: time, and] inure now and [1868: now, and] will inure always to the identities from which they sprung or shall spring ... Did [1868: spring. Did; 1855: spring. .. Did] you guess any of them lived only its moment? The world does not so exist ... no [1868: exist—no; 1855: exist .. no] parts palpable or impalpable so exist ... no [1868: parts, palpable or impalpable, so exist—no] result exists now without being from its long antecedent result, and that from its antecedent, and so backward without the furthest [1868 and 1855: farthest] mentionable spot coming a bit nearer the beginning than any other spot . . . Whatever [1868 and 1855: spot. . . . . Whatever] satisfies the soul is truth.

6

[A passage, continuing the sentence after "atonement" in line 415.]

atonement . . . knows [1868: atonement—knows; 1855: atonement . . knows that the young man who composedly perilled [1855: periled] his life and lost it has done exceeding well for himself, while the man who has not perilled [1855: periled] his life and [1868: life, and] retains to [1868 and 1855: retains it to] old age in riches and ease has [1868: ease, has] perhaps achieved nothing for himself worth mentioning . . . and [1868: mentioning—and; 1855: mentioning . . and] that only that person has no great prudence to learn who has learnt to prefer real long-lived [1855: longlived] things, and favours [1855: favors] body and soul the same, and perceives the indirect assuredly following the direct, and what evil or good he does leaping onward and waiting to meet him again—and who in his spirit in any emergency whatever neither hurries nor avoids death.

7

[A passage omitted after "Children?" in line 484.]

Has it too the old ever-fresh forbearance and impartiality? Does it look for [1868 and 1855: look with] the same love on the last born and on those hardening toward stature, and on the errant, and on those who disdain all strength of assault outside their [1868 and 1855: outside of their] own?

The poems distilled from other poems will probably pass away. The coward will surely pass away. The expectation of the vital and great can only be satisfied by the demeanour [1855: demeanor] of the vital and great. The swarms [1855 begins a new paragraph with "The swarms"] of the polished deprecating and reflectors and the polite float [1868: polished, deprecating, and reflectors, and the polite, float] off and have [1868 and 1855: and leave] no remembrance.

II "*Democracy.*"

GAL, December, 1867 (IV, 919–933).
[Lines 368 to 893 in the text of *SDC* were drawn from this essay in the composition of the pamphlet *DV* in 1871. One long and one short passage were omitted in *SDC*, in addition to those included in the textual notes.]

1

[A long passage beginning after "Solidarity has arisen." in line 626 was omitted from *DV* 1871 and all later texts.]

How, then (for that shape forebodes the current deluge)—how shall we, good-class folk, meet the rolling, mountainous surges of "swarmery" that already beat upon and threaten to overwhelm us? What disposal, short of wholesale throat-cutting and extermination (which seems not without its advantages), offers, for the countless herds of "hoofs and hobnails," that will somehow, and so perversely get themselves born, and grow up to annoy and vex us? What under heaven is to become of "nigger Cushee," that imbruted and lazy being—now, worst of all, preposterously free? etc. Never before such a yawning gulf; never such danger as now from incarnated Democracy advancing, with the laboring classes at its back. Woe the day; woe the doings, the prospects thereof! England, or any respectable land, giving the least audience to these "servants of mud gods," or, utterly infatuate, extending to them the suffrage, takes swift passage therewith, bound for the infernal pit. Ring the alarum bell! Put the flags at the half mast! Or, rather, let each man spring for the nearest loose spar or plank. The ship is going down!

Be not so moved, not to say distraught, my venerable friend. Spare those spasms of dread and disgust. England, after her much-widened suffrage, as she did before, will still undergo troubles and tribulations, without doubt; but they will be nothing to what (in the judgment of all heads not quite careened and addled), would certainly follow the spirit, carried out in any modern nation, these days, of your appeal or diatribe. Neither by berating them, nor twitting them with their low condition of ignorance and misery, nor by leaving them as they are, nor by turning the screws still tighter, nor by taking even the most favorable chances for 'the noble Few' to come round with relief, will the demon of that "unanimous vulgar" (paying very heavy taxes) be pacified and made harmless any more. Strangely enough, about the only way to really lay the fiend appears to be this very way—the theme of these your ravings. A sort of fate and antique Nemesis, of the highest old Greek tragedy sort, is in it (as in our own Play, or affair, rapidly played of late here in the South, through all the acts—indeed a regular, very wondrous Eschuylean piece—to that old part First, that bound and chained unkillable Prometheus, now, after twenty-three hundred years, very grandly and epico-dramatically supplementing and fully supplying the lost, or never before composed, Second and Third parts). Your noble, hereditary, Anglo-Saxon-Norman institutions (still here so loudly championed and battled for in your argument) having been, through some seven or eight centuries, thriftily engaged in cooking up this mess, have now got to eat it. The only course eligible, it is plain, is to plumply confront, embrace, absorb, swallow (O, big and bitter pill!) the entire British "swarmery," demon, "loud roughs" and all. These ungrateful men, not satisfied with the poor-house for their old age, and the charity-school for their infants, evidently mean business—may-be of bloody kind. By all odds, my friend, the thing to do is to make a flank movement, surround them, disarm them, give them their first degree, incorporate them in the State as voters, and then—wait for the next emergency.

Nor may I permit myself to dismiss this utterance of the eminent person without pronouncing its laboriously-earned and fully-deserved credit for about the highest eminence attained yet, in a certain direction, of any linguistic product, written or spoken, to me known. I have had occasion in my past life (being born, as it were, with propensities, from my earliest years, to attend popular American speech-gatherings, conventions, nominations, camp-meetings, and the like, and also as a reader of newspapers, foreign and domestic)—I therefore know that trial to one's ears and brains from divers creatures, alluded to by sample, and well-hatchelled in this diatribe, crow-cawing the words Liberty, loyalty, human rights, constitutions, etc. I, too, have heard the ceaseless braying, screaming blatancy (on behalf of my own side), making noisiest threats and clatter stand for sense. But I must now affirm that such a comic-painful hullabaloo and vituperative cat-squalling as this about "the Niagara leap," "swarmery," "Orsonism," etc. (meaning, in point, as I make out, simply extending to full-grown British working-folk, farmers, mechanics, clerks, and so on—the "industrial aristocracy," indeed, there named—the privilege of the ballot, or vote, deciding, by popular majorities, who shall be designated to sit in one of the two Houses of Parliament, if it mean anything), I never yet encountered; no, not even in extremest hour of midnight, in whooping Tennessee revival, or Bedlam let loose in crowded, colored Carolina bush-meeting.

But to proceed, and closer to our text.

2

[A passage reprinted in *DV* and *TR*, but omitted in *SDC* after line 655. Variants in *GAL* inserted in brackets.]

There is (turning home again,) a thought or fact, I must not forget—subtle and vast, dear to America, twin-sister of its Democracy—so ligatured indeed to it, that either's death, if not the other's also, would make that other live out life, dragging a corpse, a loathsome horrid tag and burden forever at its feet. What the idea of Messiah was to the ancient race of Israel, through storm and calm, through public glory and their name's humiliation, tenacious, refusing to be argued with, shedding all shafts of ridicule and disbelief, undestroyed by captivities, battles, deaths —for neither scalding blood of war, nor the rotted ichor of peace could ever wash it out, nor has yet—a great Idea, bedded in Judah's heart—source of the loftiest Poetry the world yet knows—continuing the same, though all else varies—the spinal thread of incredible romance of that people's career along five thousand years,—So runs [*GAL:* years—so runs] this thought, this fact, amid our own land's race and history. It is the thought of Oneness, averaging, including all; of Identity—the indissoluble sacred Union [*GAL:* Indissoluble Union] of These States.

III "*Personalism.*"

GAL, May, 1868 (v, 540–547).

[Lines 874 to 1275 of *DV* in the text of *SDC* were drawn from this essay in the composition of the pamphlet *DV* in 1871. Only one passage was omitted in *SDC* except those included in the textual notes.]

1

[A passage omitted from the text of *DV* and *TR*, continuing the paragraph after line 1080.]

Whoso dilates to the idea of the infinite holds the clue of all grandeur, as all meaning. What is here said may be trite; but our current society, with its blare, dandyism, and pettiness—its feasts, presenting infinitudes of little dishes, and so seldom anything large or solid—perpetually needs such hints.

(We should perhaps talk in a still sharper tone, and widely extend our fault-finding, but that we plainly see, even in directions where our scourge might fall the heaviest, only, after all, faults and evils inevitable to the free growth of some of the most precious law-characteristics of our land and age—even those we are here attempting to enforce.)

IV "*Democratic Vistas*" (*1871*).

[Reprinted without change in *TR* (1876).]

1

[Subtitles inserted at intervals in the clipped pages of *DV* prepared for the printing of *SDC*, but cancelled before printing. The number at the left of each subtitle is the line number above which it was inserted in the MS.]

1. Our Real Grandeur Abroad.
34. I Admit Democracy's Dangers.
72. American Arts, Poems, Theology.
99. The Main Organ and Medium.
176. New World Ideas—Representers.
225. The Gravest Question of All.
341. Individualism Versus the Aggregate.
460. The War Proved Democracy.
528. Consideration—Customs—Law—the Esthetic—Cohesion.
621. Our Lesson to Europe.
656. Reformers, Money-Makers, &c.
680. Indefiniteness in 1868.
734. Evil Also Serves.
790. A Thought in My Musings.
831. Far-Stretch, in Distance, Our Vistas.
894. Individuality—Identity—a Mystery—the Centre of All.
992. This "Culture" So Much Wanted.
1044. A Crayon'd, Democratic Personality.
1088. The Element First, Last, Indispensable.
1147. Women—Portraits—Speculation.
1250. Yet We Thank This Culture.
1404. Is Literature Really Advancing?
1460. Facts Beyond Dreams.
1472. America's True Revolutions.
1538. Race & Literature—the Drama—Poetry.
1570. The Drama. [Line 1915 originally began a paragraph; since Whitman ran two paragraphs together, it falls in the middle of a paragraph.]
1626. When the Present Century Closes.
1680. Democracy's Last Real Triumph. [This line originally began a paragraph; it falls in the middle because Whitman ran two paragraphs together.]
1687. Nature as Much Ideal as Real.
1740. A Moral Purpose Behind Everything.
1855. What These Pages Are For, to Suggest Leaders Fit for the Future.
1967. True Use of the Old Theology, Politics, Personal Models.

2 (*A passage omitted after line 655. See Appendix II, 2.*)

3

[A footnote at line 1885, omitted in *SDC*.]

THE LABOR QUESTION.—The immense problem of the relation, adjustment, conflict, between Labor and its status and pay, on the one side, and the Capital of employers on the other side—looming up over These States like an ominous, limitless, murky cloud, perhaps before long to overshadow us all;—the many thousands of decent working-people, through the cities and elsewhere, trying to keep up a good appearance, but living by daily toil, from hand to mouth, with nothing ahead, and no owned homes—the increasing aggregation of capital in the hands of a few—the chaotic confusion of labor in the Southern States, consequent on the abrogation of slavery—the Asiatic immigration on our Pacific side—the advent of new machinery, dispensing more and more with hand-work—the growing, alarming spectacle of countless squads of vagabond children, roaming everywhere the streets and wharves of the great cities, getting trained for thievery and prostitution—the hideousness and squalor of certain quarters of the cities—the advent of late years, and increasing frequency, of these pompous, nauseous, outside shows of vulgar wealth—(What a chance for a new Juvenal!)—wealth acquired perhaps by some quack, some measureless financial rogue, triply brazen in impudence, only shielding himself by his money from a shaved head, a striped dress, and a felon's cell;—and then, below all, the plausible, sugar-coated, but abnormal and sooner or later inevitably ruinous delusion and loss, of our system of inflated paper-money currency, (cause of all conceivable swindles, false standards of value, and principal breeder and bottom of those enormous fortunes for the few, and of poverty for the million)—with that other plausible and sugar-coated delusion, the theory and practice of a protective tariff, still clung to by many;—such, with plenty more, stretching themselves through many a long year, for solution, stand as huge impedimenta of America's progress.

4

[A passage omitted after line 1945.]

To furnish, therefore, something like escape and foil and remedy—to restrain, with gentle but sufficient hand, the terrors of materialistic, intellectual, and democratic civilization—to ascend to more ethereal, yet just as real, atmospheres—to invoke and set forth ineffable portraits of Personal Perfection, (the true, final aim of all,) I say my eyes are fain to behold, though with straining sight—and my spirit to prophecy—far down the vistas of These States, that Order, Class, superber, far more efficient than any hitherto, arising. I say we must enlarge and entirely recast the theory of noble authorship, and conceive and put up as our model, a Literatus—groups, series of Literatuses—not only consistent with modern science, practical, political, full of the arts, of highest erudition—not only possessed by, and possessors of, Democracy even—but with the equal of the burning fire and extasy of Conscience, which have brought down to us, over and through the centuries, that chain of old unparalleled Judean prophets, with their flashes of power, wisdom and poetic beauty, lawless as lightning, indefinite—yet power, wisdom, beauty, above all mere art, and surely, in some respects, above all else we know of mere literature.

5

[A passage omitted after line 1948.]

we now proceed to note, as on the hopeful terraces or platforms of our history, to be enacted, not only amid peaceful growth, but amid all the perturbations, and after not a few departures, filling the vistas then, certain most coveted, stately arrivals.

—A few years, and there will be an appropriate native grand Opera, the lusty and wide-lipp'd offspring of Italian methods. Yet it will be no mere imitation, nor follow precedents, anymore than Nature follows precedents. Vast oval halls will be constructed, on acoustic principles, in cities, where companies of musicians will perform lyrical pieces, born to the people of These States; and the people will make perfect music a part of their lives. Every phase, every trade will have its songs, beautifying those trades. Men on the land will have theirs, and men on the water theirs. Who now is ready to begin that work for America, of composing music fit for us—songs, choruses, symphonies, operas, oratorios, fully identified with the body and soul of The States? music complete in all its appointments, but in some fresh, courageous, melodious, undeniable styles—as all that is ever to permanently satisfy us must be. The composers to make such music are to learn everything that can be possibly learned in the schools and traditions of their art, and then calmly dismiss all traditions from them.

Also, a great breed of orators will one day spread over The United States, and be continued. Blessed are the people where, (the nation's Unity and Identity preserved at all hazards,) strong emergencies, throes, occur. Strong emergencies will continually occur in America, and will be provided for. Such orators are wanted as have never yet been heard upon earth. What specimen have we had where even the physical capacities of the voice have been fully accomplished? I think there would be in the human voice, thoroughly practised and brought out, more seductive pathos than in any organ or any orchestra of stringed instruments, and a ring more impressive than that of artillery.

Also, in a few years, there will be, in the cities of These States, immense Museums, with suites of halls, containing samples and illustrations from all the places and peoples of the earth, old and new. In these halls, in the presence of these illustrations, the noblest savans will deliver lectures to thousands of young men and women, on history, natural history, the sciences, &c. History itself will get released from being that false and distant thing, that fetish it has been. It will become a friend, a venerable teacher, a live being, with hands, voice, presence. It will be disgraceful to a young person not to know chronology, geography, poems, heroes, deeds, and all the former nations, and present ones also—and it will be disgraceful in a teacher to teach any less or more than he believes.

6

[Last paragraph of *DV* before "General Notes."]

Finally, we have to admit, we see, even to-day, and in all these things, the born Democratic taste and will of The United States, regardless of precedent, or of any authority but their own, beginning to arrive, seeking place—which, in due time, they will fully occupy. At first, of course, under current prevalences of theology, conventions, criticism, &c., all appears impracticable—takes chances to be denied and misunderstood. Therewith, of course, murmurers, puzzled persons, supercilious inquirers, (with a mighty stir and noise among these windy little gentlemen that swarm in literature, in the magazines.) But America, advancing steadily, evil as well as good, penetrating deep, without one thought of retraction, ascending, expanding, keeps her course, hundreds, thousands of years.

7

[A passage omitted after line 58 in *SDC* text of "British Literature," after "wo. . . ."; *TR* and *DV*, p. 82.]

(I cannot dismiss English, or British imaginative literature without the cheerful name of Walter Scott. In my opinion he deserves to stand next to Shakespeare. Both are, in their best and absolute quality, continental, not British—both teeming, luxuriant, true to their lands and origin, namely feudality, yet ascending into universalism. Then, I should say, both deserve to be finally considered and construed as shining suns, whom it were ungracious to pick spots upon.)

8

[First paragraph of THE LATE WAR, *TR* and *DV*, p. 82.]

THE LATE WAR.—The secession War in the United States appears to me as the last great material and military outcropping of the Feudal spirit, in our New World history, society, &c. Though it was not certain, hardly probable, that the effort for founding a Slave-Holding power, by breaking up the Union, should be successful, it was urged on by indomitable passion, pride and will. The signal downfall of this effort, the abolition of Slavery, and the extirpation of the Slaveholding Class, (cut out and thrown away like a tumor by surgical operation,) makes incomparably the longest advance for Radical Democracy, utterly removing its only really dangerous impediment, and insuring its progress in the United States—and thence, of course, over the world.—(Our immediate years witness the solution of three vast, life-threatening calculi, in different parts of the world—the removal of serfdom in Russia, slavery in the United States, and of the meanest of Imperialisms in France.)

9

[STATE RIGHTS and LATEST FROM EUROPE, *TR* and *DV*, pp. 83–84.]

STATE RIGHTS.—Freedom, (under the universal laws,) and the fair and uncramped play of Individuality, can only be had at all through strong-knit cohesion, identity. There are, who, talking of the rights of The States, as in separatism and independence, condemn a rigid nationality, centrality. But to my mind, the freedom, as the existence at all, of The States, pre-necessitates such a Nationality, an imperial Union. Thus, it is to serve separatism that we favor generalization, consolidation. It is to give, under the compaction of potent general law, an independent vitality and sway within their spheres, to The States singly, (really just as important a part of our scheme as the sacred Union itself,) that we insist on the preservation of our Nationality forever, and at all hazards. I say neither States, nor any thing like State Rights, could permanently exist on any other terms.

LATEST FROM EUROPE.—As I send my last pages to press (Sept. 19, 1870,) the ocean-cable continuing its daily budget of Franco-German war news—Louis Napoleon a prisoner, (his rat-cunning at an end)—the conquerors advanced on Paris—the French, assuming Republican forms—seeking to negotiate with the King of Prussia, at the head of his armies—"his Majesty," says the despatch, "refuses to treat, on any terms, with a government risen out of Democracy."

Let us note the words, and not forget them. The official relations of Our States, we know, are with the reigning kings, queens, &c., of the Old World. But the only deep, vast, emotional, real affinity of America is with the cause of Popular Government there—and especially in France. O that I could express, in my printed lines, the passionate yearnings, the pulses of sympathy, forever throbbing in the heart of These States, for sake of that—the eager eyes forever turned to that—watching it, struggling, appearing and disappearing, often apparently gone under, yet never to be abandoned, in France, Italy, Spain, Germany, and in the British Islands.

v " 'Tis But Ten Years Since," First Paper.

NYWG, January 24, 1874.

[For most of this article, see Appendix v and textual notes in *Prose 1892*, I. Of the portions found in the present volume, paragraph 9 was used in *MDW* "Notes" (p. 65) and in lines 175–183 of "Origins of Attempted Secession," *q.v.*, paragraph 12 in lines 25–40 of "Death of Abraham Lincoln," *q.v.*, 15–20 in lines 44–108 of "Death of Abraham Lincoln," part of which varies widely in details, as shown in the passage quoted below (v, 1).]

1

[Passage including paragraphs 17–18 and the last part of 16 that differs from the comparable passage of *SDC*, lines 62–95; the text is that of the footnote, *MDW* and *TR*, pp. 22–23, with *NYWG* variants in brackets.]

of the vast and silent crowds—and so, with very moderate pace, and accompanied by a few unknown-looking persons, ascended the portico steps.

The figure, the look, the gait, are distinctly impress'd upon me yet; the unusual and uncouth height, the dress of complete black, the stovepipe hat push'd back on the head, the dark-brown complexion, the seam'd and wrinkled yet canny-looking face, the black, bushy head of hair, the disproportionately long neck, and the hands held behind as he stood observing the people. All [*NYWG:* (beginning a new paragraph after "people.") It was, indeed, a strange scene. All] was comparative and ominous silence. The new comer look'd with curiosity upon that immense sea of faces, and the sea of faces return'd the look with similar curiosity. In both there was a dash of something almost comical. Yet there was much anxiety in certain quarters. Cautious persons had fear'd that there would be some outbreak, some mark'd indignity or insult to the President elect on his passage through the city, for he possess'd no personal popularity in New York, and not much political. No such outbreak or insult, however, occurr'd. Only the silence of the crowd was very significant to those who were accustom'd to the usual demonstrations of New York [*NYWG:* of mass New York] in wild, tumultuous hurrahs—the deafening [*NYWG:* hurrahs. The present was a great contrast to the deafening] tumults of welcome, and the thunder-shouts of pack'd myriads along the whole line of Broadway, receiving Hungarian Kossuth or [*NYWG:* and] Filibuster Walker.

VI "*A Christmas Garland, in Prose and Verse.*"

NYDG, Christmas Number, 1874.

[This article contained two poems, "The Ox Tamer" and "In the Wake Following," both reprinted in TR, the latter with the title "After the Sea Ship," and the rest prose. The prose is arranged under the following side heads, often only the first words of the first sentence in capitals: "Genius—Victor Hugo—George Sand—Emerson": three paragraphs, not reprinted; "Friendship (the Real Article)": three paragraphs, reprinted for the first time in SDC under the same title, *q.v.;* "Rulers Strictly Out of the Masses": two paragraphs, reprinted under the same title in TR and, with a third paragraph added, in SDC, *q.v.;* "A Thought on Culture," not reprinted; "Travel," not reprinted; "A Dialogue": six paragraphs, reprinted for the first time in SDC as the first part of "Ventures, on an Old Theme," *q.v.;* "It Remains," one paragraph, not reprinted; "Has It": reprinted for the first time in SDC in the last paragraph of "Final Confessions—Literary Tests," *q.v.*, *Prose 1892*, I; "Of Poems": reprinted (except the five lines of verse beginning "Go, said the Soul,") for the first time in SDC as lines 63–72 of "Ventures, on an Old Theme," *q.v.;* "A Hint to Preachers and Authors": one paragraph, not reprinted; "Have Normal": two paragraphs, not reprinted; "As If": one paragraph, not reprinted; "In the Statesmanship": two paragraphs, not reprinted; "Transportation, the Mails, &c.": one paragraph, reprinted in TR, p. 31, with the title "Transportation, Expresses, &c.," omitted from *SDC;* "It Is": one paragraph, not reprinted; and "Do We": one paragraph, not reprinted. Since the Christmas Number of *NYDG*, 1874, is lost or misplaced and cannot be located, the text of passages below is that of Emory Holloway's *UPP*, II, 53–58. Each consecutive passage is given an arabic number.]

1

GENIUS—VICTOR HUGO—GEORGE SAND—EMERSON. I call it one of the chief acts of art, and the greatest trick of literary genius (which is a higher sanity of insanity), to hold the reins firmly, and to preserve the mastery in its wildest escapades. Not to deny the most ecstatic and even irregular moods, so called—rather indeed to favor them—at the same time never to be entirely carried away with them, and always feeling, by a fine caution, when and wherein to limit or prune them, and at such times relentlessly applying restraint and negation. Few even of the accepted great artists or writers hit the happy balance of this principle—this paradox. Victor Hugo, for instance, runs off into the craziest, and sometimes (in his novels) most ridiculous and flatulent, literary blotches and excesses, and by almost entire want of prudence allows them to stand. In his poems, his fire and his fine instincts carry the day, even against such faults; and his plays, though sensational, are best of all. But his novels, evidently well meant, in the interest of Democracy, and with a certain grandeur of plots, are frightful and tedious violations of the principle alluded to.

I like Madame Daudevant much better. Her stories are like good air, good associations in real life, and healthy emotional stimuli. She is not continually putting crises in them, but when crises do come they invariably go to the heart. How simply yet profoundly they are depicted—you have to lay down the book and give your emotions room.

Coming, for further illustration, to R. W. Emerson, is not his fault, finally, too great prudence, too rigid a caution? I am not certain it is so. Indeed I have generally felt that Emerson was altogether adjusted to himself, in every attribute, as he should be (as a pine tree is a pine tree, not a quince or a rose bush). But upon the whole, and notwithstanding the many unsurpassed beauties of his poetry first, and prose only second to it, I am disposed to think (picking out spots against the sun) that his constitutional distrust and doubt—almost finical in their nicety—have been too much for him—have not perhaps stopped him short of first-class genius, but have veiled it—have certainly clipped and pruned that free luxuriance of it which only satisfies the soul at last.

2

[Omitted after "Rulers Strictly Out of the Masses."]

A Thought on Culture.—I distinctly admit that, in all fields of life, character and civilization we owe, and doubtless shall ever owe, the broadest, highest, and deepest, not only to science, to aesthetically educated persons. Then, I call attention to the fact that, in certain directions, and those also very important, the most glorious Personalities of America and of the World have been men who talked little, wrote less, possessed no brilliant qualities, and could read and write only.

But, says some one, true Culture, includes all—asks that a man be developed in his full Personality, his animal physique, even his ruggedness and rudeness. This may be the written formula, but does not come out in actual operation. It is like the claims to catholicity which each of the churches makes; but cipher to the results, and they mean just about the narrow specialty which characterizes them (probably good enough, and true enough, as far as it goes), and no genuine catholicity at all.

(But this thought on Culture is by no means the whole question—in fact, is useful only as a check on the morbid and false theory of it.)

Travel.—The argument for travelling abroad is not all on one side. There are pulses of irresistible ardor, with due reasons why they may not be gainsaid. But a calm man of deep vision will find, in this tremendous modern spectacle of America, at least as great sights as anything the foreign world, or the antique, or the relics of the antique, can afford him. Why shall I travel to Rome to see the old pillars of the Forum, only important for those who lived there ages ago? Shall I journey four thousand miles to weigh the ashes of some corpses? Shall I not vivify myself with life here, rushing, tumultous, scornful, masterful, oceanic—greater than ever before known?

Study the past and the foreign in the best books, relics, museums, lectures, pictures. Then, if you have a season or a year to spare, travel in and study your own land.

3

[Omitted after "A Dialogue."]

It remains a question yet whether the America of the future can successfully compete with the mighty accumulations of the Old World, the planners and builders of Asia, Europe, or even Africa, in permanent architecture, monuments, poems, art, &c.; or with current France, England, Germany, and Italy, in philosophy, science, or the first-class literature of philosophy and the sciences—or in courtly manners, ornamentation, costumes, &c. In most of those fields, while our brain in the United States is intelligent and receptive enough, Europe leads, and we still follow, receive, imitate. But there is one field, and the grandest of all, that is left open for our cultus—and that is, to fashion on a free scale for the average masses, and inclusive of all, a splendid and perfect Personality, real men and women without limit—not a special, small class, eminent for grace, erudition, and refinement—not merely the rare (yet inexpressibly valuable) selected specimens of heroes, as depicted in Homer, Shakespeare, &c., with warlike and kingly port—not merely fine specimens of the aristocracy and gentry as in the British islands—but masses of free men and women, gigantic and natural and beautiful and sane and perfect, in their physical, moral, mental, and emotional elements, and filling all the departments of farming and working life.

4

[Omitted after the paragraph beginning "Has It" and the paragraph beginning "Of Poems," which *UPP* prints but which were reprinted in *SDC*, as above.]

A Hint to Preachers and Authors.—Confronting the dangers of the State, the aggregate, by appeals (each writer, each artist after his kind) to the sympathies of Individualism, its pride, love of grand physique, urge of spiritual development, and the need of comrades. There is something immortal, universal, in these sympathies individualized, all men, all ages: something in the human being that will unerringly respond to them.

Have normal belief and simplicity—those old, natural, sterling qualities the individual or the race starts from in childhood, and supposed to be arrived at again, doubly intrenched and confirmed, after the fullest study, travel, observation, and cultivation—have they died out? or rather are they still to remain unborn or ungrown in America?

No one can observe life and society (so-called) in the United States today without seeing that they are penetrated and suffused with suspicion of everybody—a contempt and doubt, and the attribution of meanly selfish motives to everything and everybody—glossed over, it is true, by a general external observance to one's face of politeness and manners—but inwardly incredulous of any soundness, or primal, disinterested virtue among men and women. The same mocking quality shows itself in the journalism of The States, especially in the cities—a supercilious tone runs through all the editorials of the papers, as if the best way to show smartness. It is a taint more offensive in society and the press in America than in any other country.

As IF we had not strained the voting and digestive calibre of American Democracy to the utmost for the last fifty years with the millions of ignorant foreigners, we have now infused a powerful percentage of blacks, with about as much intellect and calibre (in the mass) as so many baboons. But we stood the former trial—solved it—and, though this is much harder, will, I doubt not, triumphantly solve this.

IN THE STATESMANSHIP (or want of Statesmanship) of this Union, the present time, and along henceforth, among the principal points to be borne in mind are the free action of the rights of The States, within their own spheres (Individuality, to stifle which were death), and the rights of minorities—always in danger of being infringed upon by temporary wilful majorities.

We have passed—or nearly passed—the possibility of ruin from insolent State autonomy. The possibility of that insolence now seems to be shifting to the Central Power.

TRANSPORTATION, THE MAILS, &C.—I am not sure but the most typical and representative things in the United States are what are involved in the vast network of Interstate Railroad Lines—our Electric Telegraphs—our Mails (post-office)—and the whole of the mighty, ceaseless, complicated (and quite perfect already, tremendous as they are) systems of transportation everywhere of passengers and intelligence. No works, no painting, can too strongly depict the fullness and grandeur of these—the smallest minutiæ attended to, and in their totality incomparably magnificent.

IT IS quite amusing, in the vortex of literature and the drama in America, to see the supplies of imported plays, novels, &c., where the characters, compared with our earthly democracy, are all up in the clouds—kings and queens, and nobles, and ladies and gentlemen of the feudal estate—none with an income of less than ten thousand a year—the dress, incidents, love-making, grammar, dialogue, and all the fixings to match. There is, too, the other extreme,—the scene often laid in the West, especially in California, where ruffians, rum-drinkers, and trulls only are depicted. Both are insulting to the genius of These States.

DO WE not, indeed, amid general malaria of Fogs and Vapors, our day, unmistakably see two Pillars of Promise, with grandest, indestructible indications:—One, that the morbid facts of American politics and society everywhere are but passing incidents and flanges of our unbounded impetus of growth—weeds, annuals of the rank, rich soil,—not central, enduring, perennial things?—The Other, that all the hitherto experience of The States, their first century, has been but preparation, adolescence—and that This Union is only now and henceforth (*i.e.*, since the Secession war) to enter on its true Democratic career?

VII *Memoranda During the War, 1875–76.*

[Reprinted without change in *TR*, with the same pagination.]

1

[A passage from the footnote, pp. 22–23, consisting of all the second paragraph and the last part of the last sentence of the first paragraph; previously printed in *NYWG*, "Ten Years," First Paper, and resembling lines 62–95 of "Death of Abraham Lincoln," *q.v.* Quoted above in Appendix, V, 1.]

VIII *Two Rivulets, 1876.*

[Including *MDW* and *DV* with the same pagination.]

1

[For a passage reprinted from *MDW*, see VII, 1 above; for passages reprinted from *DV* 1871, see IV, 2–7 above.]

2

[A passage from the "Preface, 1876," after line 23 in the main text.]

One will be found in the prose part of Two Rivulets, in *Democratic Vistas*, in the Preface to *As a Strong Bird*, and in the concluding Notes to *Memoranda* of the Hospitals. The other, wherein the all-engrossing thought and fact of Death is admitted, (not for itself so much as a powerful factor in the adjustments of Life,) in the realistic pictures of *Memoranda*, and the free speculations and ideal escapades of *Passage to India*.

Has not the time come, indeed, in the development of the New World, when its Politics should ascend into atmospheres and regions hitherto unknown—(far, far different from the miserable business that of late and current years passes under that name)—and take rank with Science, Philosophy and Art? . . . .

3

[Three paragraphs omitted after line 62 of the main text.]

The varieties and phases, (doubtless often paradoxical, contradictory,) of the two Volumes, of LEAVES, and of these RIVULETS, are ultimately to be considered as One in structure, and as mutually explanatory of each other—as the multiplex results, like a tree, of series of successive growths, (yet from one central or seed-purport)—there having been five or six such cumulative issues, editions, commencing back in 1855, and thence progressing through twenty years down to date, (1875–76)—some things added or re-shaped from time to time, as they were found wanted, and other things represt. Of the former Book, more vehement, and perhaps pursuing a central idea with greater closeness—join'd with the present One, extremely varied in theme—I can only briefly reiterate here, that all my pieces, alternated through Both, are only of use and value, if any, as such an interpenetrating, composite, inseparable Unity.

Two of the pieces in this Volume were originally Public Recitations—the College Commencement Poem, *As a Strong Bird*—and then the *Song of the Exposition*, to identify these great Industrial gatherings, the majestic outgrowths of the Modern Spirit and Practice—and now fix'd upon, the grandest of them, for the Material event around which shall be concentrated and celebrated, (as far as any one event can combine them,) the associations and practical proofs of the Hundred Years' life of the Republic. The glory of Labor, and the bringing together not only representatives of all the trades and products, but, fraternally, of all the Workmen of all the Nations of the World, (for this is the Idea behind the Centennial at Philadelphia,) is, to me, so welcome and inspiring a theme, that I only wish I were a younger and a fresher man, to attempt the enduring Book, of poetic character, that ought to be written about it.

The arrangement in print of Two RIVULETS—the indirectness of the name itself, (suggesting meanings, the start of other meanings, for the whole Volume)—are but parts of the Venture which my poems entirely are. For really they have all been Experiments, under the urge of powerful, quite irresistible, perhaps wilful influences, (even escapades,) to see how such things will eventually turn out—and have been recited, as it were, by my Soul, to the special audience of Myself, far more than to the world's audience. [See, further on, Preface of *As a Strong Bird, &c.*, 1872.] Till now, by far the best part of the whole business is, that these days, in leisure, in sickness and old age, my Spirit, by which they were written or permitted erewhile, does not go back on them, but still and in calmest hours, fully, deliberately allows them.

4

[A passage omitted after "expression." and before "Besides" in line 163*n*, in the footnote.]

. . . . Poetic literature has long been the formal and conventional tender of art and beauty merely, and of a narrow, constipated, special amativeness. I say, the subtlest, sweetest, surest tie between me and Him or Her, who, in the pages of *Calamus* and other pieces realizes me—though we never see each other, or though ages and ages hence—must, in this way, be personal affection. And those—be they few, or be they many—are at any rate *my readers*, in a sense that belongs not, and can never belong, to better, prouder poems.

5

[The first part of the first paragraph of "Thoughts for the Centennial," *TR*, p. 15, omitted in *SDC* from the section "Little or Nothing New."]

THOUGHTS FOR THE CENTENNIAL.—Thoughts even for America's first Centennial, (as for others, certainly waiting folded in hidden train, to duly round and complete their circles, mightier and mightier in the future,) do not need to be, and probably cannot be, literally originated, (for all thoughts are old,) so much as they need to escape from too vehement temporary coloring, and from all narrow and merely local influences—and also from the coloring and shaping through European feudalism—and still need to be averaged by the scale of the Centuries, from their point of view entire, and presented thence, conformably to the freedom and vastness of modern science. . . . . . And even out of a Hundred Years, and on their scale, [the next word in the sentence is "how." *SDC* makes it the beginning of the first sentence of the section.—ED.]

6

[Omitted first paragraph, introductory to the two paragraphs from *TR*, p. 16, clipped to form "Lacks and Wants Yet."]

IN THOUGHTS for the Centennial, I need not add to the multiform and swelling pæans, the self-laudation, the congratulatory voices, and the bringing to the front, and domination to-day, of Material Wealth, Products, Goods, Inventive Smartness, &c., (all very well, may-be.) But, just for a change, I feel like presenting these two reflections:

7

[Paragraphs 11 and 12, the last of the series "Thoughts for the Centennial," *TR*, p. 22, omitted in *SDC*. See notes to "Little or Nothing New, After All."]

THOUGH These States are to have their own Individuality, and show it forth with courage in all their expressions, it is to be a large, tolerant, and all-inclusive Individuality. Ours is to be the Nation of the Kosmos: we want nothing small—nothing unfriendly or crabbed here—But rather to become the friend and well wisher of all—as we derive our sources from all, and are in continual communication with all.

OF A grand and universal Nation, when one appears, perhaps it ought to have morally what Nature has physically, the power to take in and assimilate all the human strata, all kinds of experience, and all theories, and whatever happens or occurs, or offers itself, or fortune, or what is call'd misfortune.

8

[Passage in *TR*, p. 28, omitted in *SDC* after the title "NEW POETRY—*California, Mississippi, Texas.*—", lines 28–62 of "Ventures, on an Old Theme."]

Without deprecating at all the magnificent accomplishment, and boundless promise still, of the Paternal States, flanking the Atlantic shore, where I was born and grew, I see of course that the really maturing and Mature America is at least just as much to loom up, expand, and take definite shape, with immensely added population, products and originality, from the States drain'd by the Mississippi, and from those flanking the Pacific, or bordering the Gulf of Mexico.

For the most cogent purposes of those great Inland States, and for Texas, and California and Oregon, (and also for universal reasons and purposes, which I will not now stop to particularize,)

[In *TR* the sentence continues "in my opinion" which, in *SDC*, begins the first sentence of the paragraph.—ED.]

9

[Three paragraphs from *TR*, p. 31, not reprinted. The first and third had not previously been published.]

'FINE MANNERS.'—In certain moods I have question'd whether far too much is not made of Manners. To an artist entirely great—and especially to that far-advanced stage of judgment beyond mortality which Kant is fond of suggesting as a standard and test—we can conceive that all of what is popularly call'd 'fine manners' would be of little or no account—and only positive qualities, power, interior meanings, sanities, morals, emotions, would be noticed. . . . . . The Exquisite-Manners School, if not foreign to Democracy, is surely no help to it; but moral and manly Personalism is the help. Why not, like Nature, permit no glamour to affect us? . . . . . . (But are not really fine manners the natural perfume, as it were, of all healthy, inward, even Democratic qualities?)

TRANSPORTATION, EXPRESSES, &C.

[This paragraph had been previously printed in "A Christmas Garland," *NYDG*, Christmas Number, 1874, with the sidehead "Transportation, the Mails, &c." See Appendix VI, *4*.]

WOMEN, AND CONSCIENCE.—In my judgment it is strictly true that on the present supplies of imaginative literature—the current novels, tales, romances, and what is call'd 'poetry'—enormous in quantity, and utterly tainted and unwholesome in quality, lies the responsibility, (a great part of it, anyhow,) of the absence in modern society of a noble, stalwart, and healthy and maternal race of Women, and of a strong and dominant moral Conscience.

10

[Part of the footnote, *MDW*, p. 23. See Appendix VII, *1*.]

IX "*Emerson's Books, (the Shadows of Them).*"

BLW, May 22, 1880.

[Portions of this article were reprinted in "A Democratic Criticism," New York *Tribune*, May 15, 1882.]

1

[The last part of the paragraph after line 104 and the two following paragraphs in *BLW*, omitted in *SDC*, with variations in *NYTR* inserted in brackets.]

Democracy (like Christianity) is not served best by its own most brawling advocates, but often far, far better, finally, by those who are outside its ranks. I should say that such men as Carlyle and Emerson and Tennyson—to say nothing of Shakspere or Walter Scott—have [*NYTR:* Tennyson, to say nothing of Shakespeare or Walter Scott, have] done more for popular political and social progress and liberalization, and for individuality and freedom, than all the pronounced democrats one could name.

The foregoing assumptions on Emerson and his books may seem —perhaps are—paradoxical; but, as before intimated, is not every first-class artist, himself, and are not all real works of art, themselves, paradoxical? and is not the world itself so? As also intimated in the beginning, I have written my criticism in the unflinching spirit of the man's own inner teachings. As I understand him, the truest honor you can pay him is to try his own rules, his own heroic treatment, on the greatest themes, even his own works.

[The preceding paragraph is omitted in *NYTR*, the omission indicated by marks of ellipsis.]

It remains to be distinctly avowed by me that Emerson's books form the tallest and finest growth yet of the literature of the New World. They bring, with miraculous opportuneness, exactly what America needs, to begin at the head, to radically sever her (not too apparently at first) from the fossilism and feudalism of Europe.

Walt Whitman.

[*NYTR* has "By Walt Whitman" under the title "A Democratic Criticism" and omits the name at the end.]

X "*A Democratic Criticism.*"

NYTR, May 15, 1882.

[This is a single paragraph including lines 12–30 of "Emerson's Books, (the Shadows of Them.)" in *SDC*. The rest of the article is drawn from portions of the *BLW* article omitted in *SDC*. Marks of ellipsis indicate omissions. See Appendix IX, 1.]

XI "*A Backward Glance on My Own Road.*"

CR, January 5, 1884.

[This essay has 17 paragraphs, of which 11 (1–2, 5–10, 13–14, and 16) were preserved in the *DVOP* version of the essay. Six paragraphs were omitted for the following reasons: 3–4 were used in *HMB-DVOP* paragraphs 9–10, 12 appeared in *HMB-DVOP* 8, 15 in *HMB-DVOP* 23, 17 in *HMB-DVOP* 25, and 11 (except the first sentence) in *MBI-DVOP* 14. Paragraphs 3–4, 6, 11–15, and 17 were reprinted in whole or in part in *BG-NB;* in the present edition, they appear as follows: 3–4 in lines 349–363, 6 in lines 232–238, 11 in lines 93–97 and 175–201, 12 in lines 340–342 and textual notes, 13 in lines 22–43 and textual notes, 14 in lines 152–158 and textual notes, 15 in lines 489–492 and textual notes, and 17 in line 510 and textual notes. Paragraphs 1–2, 5, 7–10, and 16 were not reprinted in *BG-NB;* they are printed below, with the *BG-DVOP* variants in brackets.]

1 (Paragraphs 1–2)

It is probably best at once to give warning, (even more specific than in the head-line,) that the following paragraphs have my 'Leaves of Grass,' and some of its reasons and aims, for their radiating centre. Altogether, they form a backward glimpse along my own road and journey the last thirty years.

Many consider the expression of poetry and art to come under certain inflexible standards, set patterns, fixed and immovable, like iron castings. To the highest sense, nothing [*BG-DVOP:* castings. Really, nothing] of the sort. As, in the theatre of to-day, 'each new actor of real merit (for Hamlet or any eminent rôle) recreates the persons of the older drama, sending traditions to the winds, and producing a new character on the stage,' the adaptation, development, incarnation, of his own traits, idiosyncrasy, and environment—'there being not merely one good way of representing a great part, but as many ways as there are great actors'—so in constructing poems. Another illustration would be that for delineating purposes, the melange of existence is but an eternal font of type, and may be set up to any text, however different—with room and welcome, at whatever time, for new compositors.

2

[Paragraph 5—3 in *DVOP*—omitted in *BG-NB*, immediately precedes in *BG-CR* and *BG-DVOP* the paragraph incorporated in lines 232–238 in *BG-NB*.]

I should say real American poetry—nay, within any high sense, American literature—is something yet to be. So far, the aims and stress of the book-making business here—the miscellaneous and fashionable parts of it, the majority—seem entirely adjusted (like American society life,) to certain fine-drawn, surface, imported ways and examples, having no deep root or hold in our soil. I hardly know a volume emanating American nativity, manliness, from its centre. It is true, the numberless issues of our day and land (the leading monthlies are the best,) as they continue feeding the insatiable public appetite, convey the kind of provender temporarily wanted—and with certain magnificently copious mass results. But as surely as childhood and youth pass to maturity, all that now exists, after going on for a while will meet with a grand revulsion—nay, its very self works steadily toward that revulsion.

3

[Paragraphs 7–10—5–8 in *DVOP*—omitted in *BG-NB*, immediately precede in *BG-CR* and *BG-DVOP* the paragraph incorporated in lines 22–43 in *BG-NB*.]

The intellect of to-day is stupendous and keen, backed by stores of accumulated erudition—but in a most important phase the antique seems to have had the advantage of us. Unconsciously, it possessed and exploited that something there was and is in Nature immeasurably beyond, and even altogether ignoring, what we call the artistic, the beautiful, the literary, and even the moral, the good. Not easy to put one's finger on, or name in a word, this something, invisibly permeating the old poems, religion-sources and art. If I were asked to suggest it in such single word, I should write (at the risk of being quite misunderstood at first, at any rate) the word physiological.

I have never wondered why so many men and women balk at 'Leaves of Grass.' None should try it till ready to accept (unfortunately for me, not one in a hundred, or in several hundred, is ready) that utterance from full-grown human personality, as of a tree growing in itself, or any other objective result of the universe, from its own laws, oblivious of conformity—an expression, faithful exclusively to its own ideal and receptivity, however egotistical or enormous ('All is mine, for I have it in me,' sings the old Chant of Jupiter)—not mainly indeed with any of the usual purposes of poems, or of literature, but just as much (indeed far more) with other aims and purposes. These will only be learned by the study of the book itself—will be arrived at, if at all, by indirections—and even at best, the task no easy one. The physiological point of view will almost always have to dominate in the reader as it does in the book—only now and then the psychological or intellectual, and very seldom indeed the merely aesthetic.

Then I wished above all things to arrest the actual moment, our years, the existing, and dwell on the present—to view all else through the present. What the past has sent forth in its incalculable volume and variety, is of course on record. What the next generation, or the next, may furnish, I know not. But for indications of the individuality and physiognomy, of the present, in America, my two books are candidates. And though it may not appear at first look, I am more and more fond of thinking, and indeed am quite decided for myself, that they have for their nerve-centre the Secession War of 1860–65.

Then the volumes (for reasons well conned over before I took the first step) were intended to be most decided, serious *bona fide* expressions of an identical individual personality—*egotism*, if you choose, for I shall not quarrel about a word. They proceed out of, and revolve around, one's-self, myself, an identity, [*BG-DVOP:* around, express myself, an identity,] and declaredly make that self the nucleus of the whole utterance. After all is said, it is only a concrete special personality that can finally satisfy and vitalize the student of verse, heroism, or religion—abstractions will do neither. (Carlyle said, 'There is no grand poem in the world but is at bottom a biography—the life of a man.')

[From Carlyle's review of Lockhart's *Memoirs of the Life of Scott*, *London and Westminster Review* (1838), reprinted in *Critical and Miscellaneous Essays* (Boston, 1839), IV, 279–280. Carlyle actually said: "For there is no heroic poem in the world but is at bottom a biography, the life of a man . . ."]

4

[Paragraph 16—11 in *DVOP*—omitted in *BG-NB*, is the last in *BG-DVOP*, and follows the paragraph reprinted in *BG-NB*, lines 152–158.]

That America necessitates for her poetry entirely new standards of measurement is such a point with me, that I never tire of dwelling on it. Think of the absence and ignorance, in all cases hitherto, of the vast ensemble, multitudinousness, vitality, and the unprecedented stimulants of to-day and here. It almost seems as if a poetry with anything like cosmic features were never possible before. It is certain that a poetry of democracy and absolute faith, for the use of the modern, never was.

XII "*How Leaves of Grass Was Made.*"

LPM, June, 1892.

[Presumably reprinted from the New York *Star*, 1885, as a footnote states, or some other newspaper. In an autobiographical MS quoted by Traubel in *With Walt Whitman in Camden*, IV, 511, Whitman says in recounting the year May 31, 1885, to May 31, 1886: "He wrote the two column piece, How I Made a Book or Tried To last June." He also says he sold it to "the New York newspaper syndicate for $80 last June." (This should have been June, 1885, though it might possibly have been 1886. It is possible that this was the same article published as "How I Made a Book" in *PP*, July 11, 1886; yet *HMB-PP* does not correspond closely to *HLGM-LPM*.—ED.) All of *HLGM-LPM* was reprinted in *BG-NB* except the passages quoted below and the shorter passages included in the textual notes.]

1

[A passage omitted after "rolling in." in line 298.]

I absorbed very leisurely, following the mood. May I not say that in me, there, those old works certainly had *one* fully appreciative and exultant modern peruser? . . . Returning to New York, I alternated with the attendances mentioned by Dr. Bucke, especially the singing of the contralto Alboni and the Italian opera generally. All this and these, saturating and imbuing everything before I touched pen to paper on my own account.

2

[A passage omitted after "be any other." in line 316.]

Then the two conflicting forces of a character fitted to our New World—not only the free and independent "sovereignty of one's self," but the acknowledgment of that self as result of the past and part of its whole variform social literary and political product, with the many dominating ties and involvements thereof (from the past, from our mothers and fathers, and theirs before them) imperatively to be considered and allowed for—assumed a settled part in my scheme.

3

[A passage omitted after "hitherto." in line 347.]

I have thought to sing a song in which America should courteously salute all the other continents and nations of the globe. I have dreamed that the brotherhood of the earth may be knitted more closely together by an internationality of poems (indeed, one might ask, Has it not been so already?) than by commerce or all the treaties of the diplomats.

4

[A passage omitted after "unchanged." in line 395.]

The military and caste institutes of the Old World furnished them in choice and selected specimens from a few narrow nurseries, at the expense of the vast majority and of almost continual war. The New and the West are to grow them on the spacious areas of a hemisphere in peace, with ample chances for each and all, and without infringement on others.

5

[A passage omitted after "of the poems." in line 458.]

In my plan, the shows and objects of Nature, and the endlessly shifting play of events and politics, with all the effusions of literature, are merely mentionable as they serve toward that growth. Accordingly, any one man, or any one woman—perhaps laboring every day with his or her own hands—is at the head of all of them, and in himself or herself alone is more than all of them. I only chant even the United States themselves, so far as they bear on such result, though they have the very greatest bearing.

XIII *"New Orleans in 1848."*

New Orleans *Picayune*, January 25, 1887.
[Reprinted in *NB* (galley proofs in Feinberg Collection).]

1

[Paragraphs 13–15 after line 128, omitted in *NB* though printed in the galleys. Galley readings, when different from *NOP*, are inserted in brackets.]

On Friday night we passed through Mackinaw Straits, north; weather cold, and wind stiff. Saturday we had rather a pleasant passage, although the fog was dense. We steamed along, however, without interruption, and in the evening it cleared off beautifully. We ran down the St. Clair River and anchored there. Starting at daylight, we soon ran on the St. Clair flats, where we stuck for some four hours or more. The passengers, and much of the freight, were transferred to a steam-lighter, and we got off at length.

From the captain of the lighter we learned that Gen. Taylor had been nominated by the Whig National Convention, at Philadelphia. [In the galley proof the preceding sentence is the last sentence of the paragraph beginning "On Friday night", and the remaining four sentences of this paragraph are omitted altogether in the galley proof.—ED.] From present appearances, there is every likelihood of his election. Cass is too unpopular with a large number of the Democratic party. Taylor will most likely carry New York. (I am curious to see what course my Radical friends will adopt in New York.)

It doesn't seem much like Sunday today, on board the boat. The passengers are amusing themselves in various ways; or rather trying to amuse themselves, for it seems rather dull work with most of them. We have a pretty [Galley proof: have as before a pretty] full complement.

XIV *"Old Brooklyn Days."*

NYMJ, August 3, 1890.

1

[Two paragraphs after line 28, concluding the article in *NYMJ*, omitted in *GBF*. A passage similar to them, clipped from an unidentified newspaper, had appeared in *SDC* as a footnote to "Printing Office.—Old Brooklyn," *q.v.* in *Prose 1892*, I. Variations in the *SDC* clipping are inserted in brackets.]

But of the Brooklyn itself of those sixty-five years ago, how little now visibly remains! [Clipping: Of the Brooklyn of that time (1830–40) hardly anything remains, except the lines of the old streets.] The population was then between 10,000 and 12,000. [Clipping: ten and twelve thousand.] The character of the place was thoroughly rural.

Who remembers the old places as they were? Who remembers the old citizens of that time [Clipping: of the time] with their well-known faces? Among the former were Smith and Wood's, Coe Downing's and other public houses at the old ferry; [Clipping: ferry itself,] Love Lane, the Heights, the [Clipping: Heights as then, the] Wallabout with the wooden bridge, and the road out beyond Fulton street to the old toll-gate. Among the persons of those old times was the majestic [Clipping: Among the latter were the majestic] and genial General Jeremiah Johnson, with others, all passed away—Gabriel [Clipping: others mentioned at random, mostly passed away before now, but a few, yet among us, Gabriel] Furman, Rev. E. M. Johnson, Alden Spooner, Mr. Pierrepont, Mr. Joralemon, Samuel Willoughby, Jonathan Trotter, George Hall, Cyrus P. Smith, N. B. Morse, John Dikeman, Adrian Hegeman, William Udall and the old Frenchman, M. Duflon [Clipping: and old Mr. Duflon] with his Military Garden.

XV *"Some Personal and Old-Age Memoranda."*

LIP, March, 1891.

[The article was used in *GBF* in the section titled "Some Personal and Old-Age Jottings."]

1

[Two paragraphs, following Emerson's letter to Whitman, in the footnote relating to the first three lines; omitted in *GBF*.]

I met Chas. A. Dana (he was always friendly to me—he was then managing editor of the *Tribune*) in the street in New York, where we had a confab, and he requested the letter to print, but I refused. Some time after, at a second request of Dana, and knowing he was a friend of Mr. Emerson, I consented. The following from a newspaper of Aug. 1890 [the *Camden Post*, August 12, 1890.—ED.], contains an authentic and further explanation of the general matter:

"A person named Woodbury says in a just published book that R. W.

Emerson told him how Walt Whitman appeared at a dinner party, in New York, coatless, in his shirt sleeves. Of course and certainly Walt Whitman did *not* so appear, and quite as certainly, of course, Emerson never said anything of the sort. The extreme friendliness of a few critics toward Walt Whitman is met by the *extremer* malignance and made-up falsehoods of other critics. One of the latter printed in a New York weekly that Whitman always wore an open red flannel shirt. Another story was that the Washington, D. C., police 'run him out' from that town for shamelessly living with an improper female. In a book of Edward Emerson's, a foul account of his father's opinion of Walt Whitman is sneaked in by a foot note. The true fact is, R. W. Emerson had a firm and deep attachment to Whitman from first to last, as person and poet, which Emerson's family and several of his conventional literary friends tried their best in vain to dislodge. As Frank Sanborn relates, Emerson was fond of looking at matters from different sides, but he early put on record, that to his mind, 'Leaves of Grass' was 'the greatest show of wit and poetry that America had yet contributed,' and to this mind he steadily adhered throughout.' "

[Emerson's letter, the clipping, and the note about the publication of the letter were also printed, as in *LIP*, as a broadside for personal distribution.—ED.]

2

[A footnote in *LIP*, line 158, is omitted in *GBF*.]

From an English letter, summer of 1890, to J. C. T., jr., Philadelphia:

"Speaking of Browning, do you know that Walt Whitman is enthusiastically admired in England? Mr. Harrison, for instance, is quite devoted to him and says that Tennyson says that W. W. is one of the greatest, if not the greatest, of living poets, or words to that effect. Mr. Gordon, you know, surprised me by manifesting the greatest interest in him. Verily, a prophet is not without honor, save in his own country. In this, too, I must want training. There are fine things in W. W.'s writings, but I cannot help wishing he had put them into prose, instead of into such rocky verse."

3

[A passage after "publication." in line 168, omitted in *GBF*, with variations in brackets in the typescript before revision.]

Though paralyzed and sick I am probably [Typescript: sick W. W. is among old men living probably] one of the resultants of [Typescript:

the most marked results of] a sound natural constitution, good genesis and (may I say?) of [Typescript: and of] temperate and warm (not ascetic) habits. That I have come out from many [Typescript: that he has come out from his many] close calls of war and peace, and live and write [Typescript: lives and writes] yet after all, is attributable to that physical solidity, born and grown. As to my [Typescript: his] books they are less received and read in America, and more on the continent of Europe, in translations everywhere, and especially in their own text in the British Islands. They certainly obtain there a curious personal regard, and fulfil something of what is looked for from the New World.

Today, "old, poor, and paralyzed," I keep generally buoyant [Typescript: W. W. keeps buoyant]...

Appendix B

CHRONOLOGY OF WALT WHITMAN'S LIFE AND WORK

1819	Born May 31 at West Hills, near Huntington, Long Island.
1823	May 27, Whitman family moves to Brooklyn.
1825–30	Attends public school in Brooklyn.
1830	Office boy for doctor, lawyer.
1830–34	Learns printing trade.
1835	Printer in New York City until great fire August 12.
1836–38	Summer of 1836, begins teaching at East Norwich, Long Island; by winter 1837-38 has taught at Hempstead, Babylon, Long Swamp, and Smithtown.
1838–39	Edits weekly newspaper, the *Long Islander*, at Huntington.
1840–41	Autumn, 1840, campaigns for Van Buren; then teaches school at Trimming Square, Woodbury, Dix Hills, and Whitestone.
1841	May, goes to New York City to work as printer in *New World* office; begins writing for the *Democratic Review*.
1842	Spring, edits a daily newspaper in New York City, the *Aurora;* edits *Evening Tattler* for short time.
1845–46	August, returns to Brooklyn, writes for *Long Island Star* from September until March.
1846–48	From March, 1846, until January, 1848, edits Brooklyn *Daily Eagle;* February, 1848, goes to New Orleans to work on the *Crescent;* leaves May 27 and returns *via* Mississippi and Great Lakes.
1848–49	September 9, 1848, to September 11, 1849, edits a "free soil" newspaper, the Brooklyn *Freeman*.
1850–54	Operates printing office and stationery store; does free-lance journalism; builds and speculates in houses.
1855	Early July, *Leaves of Grass* is printed by Rome Brothers in Brooklyn; father dies July 11; Emerson writes to poet on July 21.
1856	Writes for *Life Illustrated;* publishes second edition of *Leaves of Grass* in summer and writes "The Eighteenth Presidency!"
1857–59	From spring of 1857 until about summer of 1859 edits the Brooklyn *Times;* unemployed winter of 1859-60; frequents Pfaff's bohemian restaurant.
1860	March, goes to Boston to see third edition of *Leaves of Grass* through the press.
1861	April 12, Civil War begins; George Whitman enlists.

1862 December, goes to Fredericksburg, Virginia, scene of recent battle in which George was wounded, stays in camp two weeks.

1863 Remains in Washington, D. C., working part-time in Army Paymaster's office; visits soldiers in hospitals.

1864 June 22, returns to Brooklyn because of illness.

1865 January 24, appointed clerk in Department of Interior, returns to Washington; meets Peter Doyle; witnesses Lincoln's second inauguration; Lincoln assassinated, April 14; May, *Drum-Taps* is printed; June 30, is discharged from position by Secretary James Harlan but re-employed next day in Attorney General's office; autumn, prints *Drum-Taps and Sequel*, containing "When Lilacs Last in the Dooryard Bloom'd."

1866 William D. O'Connor publishes *The Good Gray Poet.*

1867 John Burroughs publishes *Notes on Walt Whitman as Poet and Person;* July 6, William Michael Rossetti publishes article on Whitman's poetry in London *Chronicle;* "Democracy" (part of *Democratic Vistas*) published in December *Galaxy.*

1868 Rossetti's *Poems of Walt Whitman* (selected and expurgated) published in England; "Personalism" (second part of *Democratic Vistas*) in May *Galaxy;* second issue of fourth edition of *Leaves of Grass*, with *Drum-Taps and Sequel* added.

1869 Mrs. Anne Gilchrist reads Rossetti edition and falls in love with the poet.

1870 July, is very depressed for unknown reasons; prints fifth edition of *Leaves of Grass*, and *Democratic Vistas* and *Passage to India*, all dated 1871.

1871 September 3, Mrs. Gilchrist's first love letter; September 7, reads "After All Not to Create Only" at opening of American Institute Exhibition in New York.

1872 June 26, reads "As a Strong Bird on Pinions Free" at Dartmouth College commencement.

1873 January 23, suffers paralytic stroke; mother dies May 23; unable to work, stays with brother George in Camden, New Jersey.

1874 "Song of the Redwood-Tree" and "Prayer of Columbus."

1875 Prepares Centennial Edition of *Leaves of Grass* and *Two Rivulets* (dated 1876).

1876 Controversy in British and American press over America's neglect of Whitman; spring, meets Harry Stafford, and begins recuperation at Stafford farm, at Timber Creek; September, Mrs. Gilchrist arrives and rents house in Philadelphia.

1877 January 28, gives lecture on Tom Paine in Philadelphia; goes to New York in March and is painted by George W. Waters; during summer gains strength by sun-bathing at Timber Creek.

1878 Spring, too weak to give projected Lincoln lecture, but in June visits J. H. Johnston and John Burroughs in New York.

1879 April to June, in New York, where he gives first Lincoln lecture, and says farewell to Mrs. Gilchrist, who returns to England; September, goes to the West for the first time and visits Colorado; because of illness remains in St. Louis with his brother Jeff from October to January.

1880 Gives Lincoln lecture in Philadelphia; summer, visits Dr. R. M. Bucke in London, Ontario.

1881 April 15, gives Lincoln lecture in Boston; returns to Boston in August to read proof of *Leaves of Grass*, being published by James R. Osgood; poems receive final arrangement in this edition.

1882 Meets Oscar Wilde; Osgood ceases to distribute *Leaves of Grass* because District Attorney threatens prosecution unless the book is expurgated; publication is resumed in June by Rees Welsh in Philadelphia, who also publishes *Specimen Days and Collect;* both books transferred to David McKay, Philadelphia.

1883 Dr. Bucke publishes *Walt Whitman*, a critical study closely "edited" by the poet.

1884 Buys house on Mickle Street, Camden, New Jersey.

1885 In poor health; friends buy a horse and phaeton so that the poet will not be "house-tied"; November 29, Mrs. Gilchrist dies.

1886 Gives Lincoln lecture four times in Elkton, Maryland, Camden, Philadelphia, and Haddonfield, New Jersey; is painted by John White Alexander.

1887 Gives Lincoln lecture in New York; is painted by Thomas Eakins.

1888 Horace Traubel raises funds for doctors and nurses; *November Boughs* printed; money sent from England.

1889 Last birthday dinner, proceedings published in *Camden's Compliments.*

1890 Writes angry letter to J. A. Symonds, dated August 19, denouncing Symonds's interpretation of "Calamus" poems, claims six illegitimate children.

1891 *Good-Bye My Fancy* is printed, and the "death-bed edition" of *Leaves of Grass* (dated 1891 - 2).

1892 Dies March 26, buried in Harleigh Cemetery, Camden, New Jersey.

Index

Index to Volumes I and II

Erratum

This page is inserted to correct an editorial note to "Paumanok, and My Life on It as Child and Young Man" (*Prose Works 1892*, I, 11–12) which states that the clipping from which Whitman drew his footnote on "Paumanok" appears to be from a newspaper. Professor DeWolfe Miller has kindly called attention to a very similar passage in an advertisement-review of the 1872 edition of *Leaves of Grass* in a section of advertisements bound in with *As a Strong Bird on Pinions Free*. The Editor can now state positively that the clipping, which Whitman made a part of the MS of *SDC*, was not from a newspaper but was cut from this advertisement, where it also appears as a footnote, without ascription or quotation marks. Professor Miller thinks this advertisement-review was written by Whitman. It may have been. On the other hand, it may have been written by Burroughs, or by Burroughs with Whitman's collaboration. Since, in the opinion of the Editor, it is not indubitably Whitman's work, it is not included in the present edition of *Prose Works 1892*.

www.ingramcontent.com/pod-product-compliance
Lightning Source LLC
Chambersburg PA
CBHW082057090726
47909CB00011B/3064